Race in Translation

Race in Translation

Culture Wars around the Postcolonial Atlantic

Robert Stam | Ella Shohat

NEW YORK UNIVERSITY PRESS
New York and London

NEW YORK UNIVERSITY PRESS
New York and London
www.nyupress.org

References to Internet Websites (URLs) were accurate at the time of writing.
Neither the author nor New York University Press is responsible for URLs
that may have expired or changed since the manuscript was prepared.

Library of Congress Cataloging-in-Publication Data
Stam, Robert, 1941-
Race in translation : culture wars around the postcolonial Atlantic / Robert Stam and
Ella Shohat.
p. cm.
Includes bibliographical references and index.
ISBN 978-0-8147-9837-9 (cl : alk. paper)
ISBN 978-0-8147-9838-6 (pb : alk. paper)
ISBN 978-0-8147-2392-0 (ebook)
ISBN 978-0-8147-2525-2 (ebook)
1. Race. 2. Culture. 3. Postcolonialism — Atlantic Ocean Region.
4. Multiculturalism — Atlantic Ocean Region.
5. Ethnicity — Atlantic Ocean Region. I. Shohat, Ella, 1959- II. Title.
CB195.S73   2012
305.8009163 — dc23   2011050487

New York University Press books are printed on acid-free paper,
and their binding materials are chosen for strength and durability.
We strive to use environmentally responsible suppliers and materials
to the greatest extent possible in publishing our books.

Manufactured in the United States of America

c   10 9 8 7 6 5 4 3 2 1
p   10 9 8 7 6 5 4 3 2 1

To Jacob

Contents

Acknowledgments

IN THE LONG process of gestation of this book—going back to its first conceptualization realized in an essay ("Travelling Multiculturalism: French Intellectuals and the U.S. Culture Wars") published in *Black Renaissance Noire* in 2001—we have received the support of many friends, colleagues, and institutions. We would like to thank the following for offering insightful commentary on earlier drafts or sections or on oral presentations of the project: Christopher Dunn, Patrick Erouart, Ismail Xavier, Jim Cohen, Manthia Diawara, Ziad Elmarsafy, Sérgio Costa, James Stam, Anne Donadey, Marcelo Fiorini, Randal Johnson, George Yúdice, Diana Taylor, Neil Smith, Michael Hanchard, Yaël Bitton, Randy Martin, Robert Young, and Rajeswari Sunder. Various readers for NYU Press—notably Arturo Escobar, Minoo Moallem, and Dilip Gaonkar—made useful suggestions. We are also grateful for the indispensible assistance we have received at various stages from Benjamin Minh Ha, Cecilia Sayad, Paulina Suarez-Hesketh, Karen Wang, Sandra Ruiz, Leili Kashani, Karim Tartoussieh, and Leo Goldsmith, and especially from Jennifer Kelly, who has been wonderfully helpful during the diverse stages of the project, including up through the demanding work of indexing. We are also grateful to NYU Press editor in chief Eric Zinner for his support and patience and to managing editor Despina Papazoglou Gimbel and copyeditor Andrew Katz for their meticulous work.

The intellectual conversations promoted by various centers at NYU have been an endless source of stimulation and inspiration. Here we would like to cite La Maison Française, the Institute of French Studies, the Center for Latin American and Caribbean Studies, the Hemispheric Institute of Performance and Politics, the Juan Carlos of Spain Center, the Center for Media, Culture and History, and the Center for Art and Public Policy in Tisch School of the Arts, along with various seminars and discussion groups such as the Postcolonial Studies Seminar and the Comparative Race Studies Group. Our warm appreciation also goes to the following: Evelyn Alsultany, Awam Amkpa, Vincent Carelli, Ernesto Ignacio de Carvalho, Moncef Cheikrouhou, Luiz Antonio Coelho, Marc Cohen, Amalia Cordova, Karel Depollo, Ayse Franko, Eti and Selim Franko, Faye Ginsburg, Inderpal Grewal, Maurice Hazan, Caren Kaplan, Kate Lyra, Ivone Margulies, Anne McClintock, Rob Nixon, Yigal Nizri, Marcelle Pithon, Mary Louise Pratt, Yvette Raby, Jolene Ricard, Ilda Santos, Eyal Sivan, Shouleh Vatanabadi, João Luiz Vieira, and Anne Wax.

We would like to thank the following colleagues and institutions for facilitating the presentation of our work (alone or together): Inderpal Grewal and the "Culture and Theory" Lecture Series at the University of California, Irvine; Caroline Cappucin and L'Institut d'Amérique Latine in Paris; Yasuko Takezawa and the Institute for Research in Humanities at Kyoto University, Japan; Patrick Wolfe and the University of Melbourne, Australia; Deane Williams and Monash University, Australia; Manuela Ribeiro Sanchez and the "Europe in Black & White" conference at the Centro de Estudos Comparatistas at the University of Lisbon, Portugal; Arnold H. Itwaru and the University of Toronto; Armida de la Garza and Nottingham University in Ningpo, China; Manuela Boatcă and the "Critical Thought/Transformative Practice Seminar" at the Instituto Universitário de Pesquisas in Rio de Janeiro, Brazil; Diana Accaria and the "Seminar on Postcolonial Theory" and the Departments of English, History, and Comparative Literature at the University of Puerto Rico at Río Piedras; Suvir Kaul and Ania Loomba and the "Postcolonial Studies and Beyond" conference, the University of Illinois at Urbana-Champaign; Vermonja Alston and York University, Toronto; the Borcher's Lecture Series, University of Wisconsin, Madison; Timothy Powell, Eve Troute Powell, and the "Multicultural Studies" conference at the University of Georgia; Frederic Viguier and Francine Goldenhar at the Maison Française at New York University; Diana Taylor and NYU's Hemispheric Institute of Performance and Politics and its *encuentros* in Monterrey, Mexico, and Lima, Peru; Edward Said, Joseph Massad, and Gil Anidjar and the Comparative Cultures University Seminar, Columbia University; Dora Baras and the Subversive Film Festival in Zaghreb, Croatia; the "Area Studies in the Era of Globalization" seminar at the Social Science Research Council, New York; Lucia Nagib and the World Cinema program at Leeds University, England; Leslie Bethell and the Center for Brazilian Studies at Oxford University; Sérgio Costa and the Conference on Brazil at the Free University in Berlin; Armida de la Garza and the Conference on Co-Productions in Puebla, Mexico; Zé Gatti, SOCINE, and the Federal University of Santa Catarina, Brazil; Omar Gonzales and ICAIC, Havana, Cuba; Brazilian Association of Comparative Literature (ABRALIC), Federal University of Salvador Bahia; the Alliance Française in New York City; Casa do Saber, Rio de Janeiro, Brazil; Faye Ginsburg and the Center for Media, Culture and History, NYU; and Tim Mitchell and ICAS, NYU.

We have also benefited from the opportunities to conduct seminars related to the issues of the book at the University of São Paulo, Brazil (Shohat, Spring 2010); the Federal University of Rio de Janeiro (Stam, Spring 2010); the Federal University of Cuiaba, Brazil (Stam, Spring 2010); the Institute of Postcolonial Transcultural Studies and at the University of Bremen, Germany, the Inaugural Lectures/Seminar Series hosted by Sabine Broeck (Shohat and Stam, June–July

2009); the NYU in Paris Program and Caroline Montel and Katherine Fleming at the NYU Center for European Studies, as well as Université Sorbonne Nouvelle, Paris III, hosted by Jacques Aumont and Philippe Dubois (Shohat and Stam, Fall 2008); the School of Criticism & Theory, and Dominick LaCapra, Cornell University, 30th Summer Session (Shohat and Stam 2006), and the Seminar in Experimental Critical Theory: Present Tense Empires, Race, Bio-Politics, and David Goldberg and Lisa Lowe, at the UC Humanities Research Institute, University of California, Irvine (Shohat 2005).

Several awards and fellowships have advanced our work on this project: a Fulbright Lectureship/Research Award in Brazil (Shohat, Spring 2010); the Shelby Cullom Davis Center for Historical Studies Fellowship at Princeton University (Stam, 2009); the International Center of Advanced Studies Fellowship at New York University on the theme of "The Authority of Knowledge in a Global Age" (Shohat, 2006–2007); and the fellowship at the Center for Place, Culture and Politics, CUNY Graduate Center (Shohat, 2000–2001). We also would like to thank Asya Berger and Jane Tylus and the Humanities Initiative at NYU for the Grants-in-Aid to support this project,(Shohat and Stam); to FAS Dean for the Humanities Lauren Benton for the supplemental fund in conjunction with the Fulbright award (2010, Shohat); and to dean of the Tisch School of the Arts Mary Schmidt Campbell for the TSOA Senior Faculty Development Grant (Shohat, 2003–2004).

Some earlier versions of sections of the book have been published in the following journals or books: Stam/Shohat, "Postcolonial Studies and France," *Interventions* (forthcoming, Spring 2012); Stam/Shohat, "Transnationalizing Comparison: The Uses and Abuses of Cross-Cultural Analogy," *New Literary History* 40, no. 3 (Summer 2009); Shohat/Stam, "What Is Eurocentrism?," in Arnold H. Itwaru, ed., *The White Supremacist State: Eurocentrism, Imperialism, Colonialism, Racism* (Toronto: Other Eye, 2009); Shohat, "On the Margins of Middle Eastern Studies: Situating Said's *Orientalism*," in "On *Orientalism* at Thirty," special section of *Review of Middle Eastern Studies* (published plenary session lecture, MESA 2008) 43, no. 1 (Summer 2009); Shohat/Stam, "Cultural Debates in Translation," in Revathi Krishnaswamy and John Hawley, eds., *The Postcolonial and the Global* (Minneapolis: University of Minnesota Press, 2008); Shohat/Stam, "Imperialism and the Fantasies of Democracy," *Rethinking Marxism* 19, no. 3 (July 2007); Shohat, "Post-Fanon and the Colonial: A Situational Diagnosis," in *Taboo Memories, Diasporic Voices* (Durham: Duke University Press, 2006); Shohat, "Black, Jew, Arab: Postscript to *The Wretched of the Earth*" (first published in the Hebrew translation of Fanon's book in 2006), in Christopher Wise and Paul James, eds., *Being Arab: Arabism and the Politics of Recognition* (Melbourne, Australia: Arena, 2010); Shohat/Stam, "Traveling Multiculturalism: A Debate in

Translation," in Ania Loomba, Suvir Kaul, Matti Bunzel, Antoinette Burton, and Jed Esty, eds., *Postcolonial Studies and Beyond* (Durham: Duke University Press, 2005); Shohat/Stam, "De-Eurocentrizing Cultural Studies: Some Proposals," in Ackbar Abbas and John Nguyet Erni, eds., *Internationalizing Cultural Studies: An Anthology* (Malden, MA: Blackwell, 2005); Stam, "Fanon, Algeria, and the Cinema: The Politics of Identification," in Shohat/Stam, eds., *Multiculturalism, Postcoloniality and Transnational Media* (New Brunswick: Rutgers University Press, 2003); Shohat/Stam, "Travelling Multiculturalism: French Intellectuals and the U.S. Culture Wars," *Black Renaissance Noir* (Fall 2001); Stam, "Multiculturalism and the Neo-Conservatives," in Anne McClintock, Aamir Mufti and Ella Shohat, eds., *Dangerous Liaisons: Gender, Nation, and Postcolonial Perspectives* (Minneapolis: University of Minnesota Press, 1997); Shohat/Stam, "From the Imperial Family to the Transnational Imaginary: Media Spectatorship in the Age of Globalization," in Rob Wilson and Wimal Dissanayake, eds., *Global/Local: Cultural Production and the Transnational Imaginary* (Durham: Duke University Press, 1996).

Finally, we would like to thank Matthew Cusick for generously allowing us to use his artwork "Fiona's Wave, 2005" for the book cover of *Race in Translation*. What drew us to the image was its collage conjugation of displaced fragments of maps and its powerful evocation of oceanic movement. The suggestion of breaking surf, conjuring up tempests and shipwrecks, resonates in the context of the book with the Middle Passages of the Black (Afro-diasporic) Atlantic, as well as with the travails of the Red (indigenous) Atlantic. Learning that *Fiona* in Gaelic means "white" or "fair," meanwhile, rhymes with our theme of the White Atlantic and critical Whiteness studies. Our book traces, in a sense, an epic encounter of perspectives—between the view-from-the-ship and the view-from-the-shore, or between the caravels and the canoes—generating the turbulent crossings of epistemologies. The cover image opens up to the various aquatic metaphors that run through the book and to the oceanic intellectual space charted here. The disorienting dispersal of the maps, meanwhile, reverberates with our emphasis on the diasporas, passages, dislocations, and interconnections that have shaped the multidirectional flow of ideas around the post/colonial Atlantic.

Robert Stam/Ella Shohat
New York University

Preface

RACE IN TRANSLATION: *Culture Wars around the Postcolonial Atlantic* is at once a report from various fronts in the race/colonial debates, a mapping of the germane literature in several languages, and an argument about the politics of the cross-border flow of ideas. Against the backdrop of an Atlantic space shaped by the conquest of indigenous people, the enslavement of Africans, and massive colonial and postcolonial dislocations, our book visits key ports along an oceanic continuum. We follow the transatlantic traffic of "race" within and between three national zones: the United States (and more broadly the Anglophone zone), France (and the Francophone zone), and Brazil (and the Lusophone zone). Our study goes beyond the three zones, however, in that it continually asserts the cultural presence of multiple geographies, while inscribing the race/coloniality problematic in the Atlantic generally. The various itineraries of the race debates, we argue, intersect in some surprising and illuminating ways.

Each chapter of *Race in Translation* treats a different dimension of the issues while highlighting the interlinked similitudes among the various manifestations of what we are calling the "Atlantic Enlightenment." Most of the chapters chart the career of a series of ideas—Eurocentrism, the decolonization of knowledge, identity politics, multiculturalism, Affirmative Action, postcolonial theory, and so on—as they unfold in and across the public spheres of distinct spaces. The early chapters provide the broad historical framework by tracing the overall genealogy of the debates to the Renaissance "encounter" with indigenous societies, to the Enlightenment's negotiation of the freedom/slavery dialectic, and to modernity's fraught relation to the objects of its imperial "civilizing mission."

The later chapters, meanwhile, examine the reeditions of these debates as encapsulated in the present-day culture wars. While the term "culture wars" is usually taken to designate the heated polemics in the English-speaking world whirling around identity politics, Affirmative Action, the canon, feminism, multiculturalism, gay rights, anti-imperialism, and antiglobalization, the verbal skirmishes triggered by these wars form but the surface ripples of a deeper oceanic struggle to decolonize power structures and epistemologies. If in one sense the culture wars emerged in the post–World War II period, in a much longer view they participate in the five-century process by which the European powers reached positions of economic, military, political, and cultural hegemony in much of Asia, Africa, and the Americas. Some of the major corollaries of this colonial process were the massive expropriation of territory; the large-scale destruction of indigenous peoples and cultures; the enslavement of indigenous Americans and Africans; and racism within the colonized world and within the West itself. Although resistance to colonialism has existed since the very beginnings of colonization, we focus on the resistance that reached critical mass in the post–World War II period, generating what we see as the "seismic shift" in scholarship that contested established racial hierarchies, Eurocentric narrativizations of history, and canonical modes of knowledge production.

Against the grain of nation-state-centered analysis, we set the debates within what we term an "intercolonial" frame that addresses the tensions between colonizing nation-states that are at once collaborators and rivals. All nations are, in the end, transnations, indelibly marked by the presence of the other nations for and against which they have diacritically defined themselves. The cultural borders between national zones are therefore porous, often confounding "inside" and "outside." Cultural phenomena imagined to be unique to one "nation" may in fact be shared. Intellectual debates deemed irrelevant and untranslatable in one historical conjuncture turn out to be relevant, even urgent, in another. As the debates move across national borders, we ask, how are they translated both literally and figuratively? Under what rubrics, keywords, and evaluative repertoires are they conducted? How do the terms themselves shift their valence as they move from one cultural geography and political semantics into another? How are ideas displaced, reinvoiced, and recontextualized as they move back and forth between national fields? What are the grids, prisms, tropes, and even fun-house mirrors through which the debates are seen? What are the national doxa, the cultural institutions, and the global economic alignments that block, or facilitate, the transit of ideas about race/coloniality? What is the impact of exceptionalisms, narcissisms, and disavowals in what one might call, fusing Freud with Bourdieu, a "narcissism of national distinction"?

Our concern is with the ways intellectuals have textualized, mediated, and mobilized ideas. What anxieties and hopes, what utopias and dystopias, are provoked by words such as "race," "multiculturalism," and "identity politics" in the diverse sites? Why is the concept of *la République* central to the debates in France but not in the United States or Brazil, even though all three nation-states are republics? Why is miscegenation a dominant theme in Brazil but not in France or the United States, even though all three countries are, each in its own way, miscegenated? Why does "communitarianism" carry such a potent negative charge in France yet rarely figure in Brazil and the United States? What is the mediating role of language? In this sense, we not only engage the politics of translation but also cite and literally translate texts from French, Portuguese, Spanish, and other languages in order to convey the thrust of the arguments, as well as the tone, the grain, and the cultural accents of the voices through which the arguments are presented.

The various chapters explore the multiple dimensions of these transnational/translational intersections. The first three chapters set out the larger conceptual and historical framework. Chapter 1, "The Atlantic Enlightenment," outlines the intertextual backdrop of the "culture wars" in the foundational contradictions of the Enlightenment. How was Enlightenment republicanism, with its professed values of freedom and equality, to be reconciled with the actual practices of colonialism, slavery, and imperialism? Did colonialism represent a rupture with the Enlightenment, or its clearest expression? Was the Enlightenment an alternative to racism, or its very source? In what ways do contemporary polemics recapitulate while reconfiguring Enlightenment debates about the universal and the particular?

It is in this context that we advance, in conjunction with the well-known work on the "Black Atlantic," the idea of the "Red Atlantic" and, on a different register, the "White Atlantic."[1] Although the expression "Red Atlantic" has been deployed to refer strictly to the indigenous peoples of the Americas, we conceptualize it in a broader sense to suggest that the entire Atlantic world is "Red" and indigenized, in that it has been impacted not only by the Conquest that enriched Europe materially but also by indigenous modes of thought and sociability that triggered a salutary epistemological crisis by provoking European thinkers—from Montaigne and Diderot to Pierre Clastres—to question the dominant social norms. What we call "the discourse of indigenous radicalism" has been invoked to support such varied progressive causes as Jacobin and socialist revolutions, communal property, class, gender, and sexual equality, ecology, collective jouissance, antiproductivism, and alter-globalization. The concept of a "White Atlantic," meanwhile, conjures up the hegemonic ethnicity and "critical whiteness studies" as an integral part of the broader anticolonial project.

Subsequent chapters zoom in to specific currents within the Atlantic continuum. Chapter 2, "A Tale of Three Republics," examines Atlantic republicanism and the transatlantic looking relations or intellectual polylogue between France, Brazil, and the United States. Transoceanic in their genealogies and repercussions, the colonialism, slavery, and race debates have been profoundly constitutive of the Brazilian, American, and French social formations. Here we highlight the longstanding role of France as cultural mentor of Brazil; the cornucopia of comparative race scholarship concerning Brazil and the United States; and the Afrodiasporic search for nonracist utopias, especially in France and Brazil. We also question the Anglo-Saxon/Latin culturalist dichotomy as an ideological construct that still haunts the race/coloniality debates. We thus shift the focus from Latins and Anglo-Saxons as putative panethnic groups to what we call Latinism and Anglo-Saxon*ism* as discourses. Both "North" and "South," we argue, have reproduced Eurocentric Hegelian-Weberian theories that naturalize the subordination of the African and indigenous elements in the "New World." We call, finally, for a translational analysis of intellectual exchange as a way of avoiding petrified conceptualizations of national culture.

Chapter 3, "The Seismic Shift and the Decolonization of Knowledge," delineates the protocols of Eurocentrism as the discursive precipitate of colonialism and sketches out the post–World War attempts to decolonize scholarship within diverse fields of inquiry. Here we discuss Frantz Fanon's work as a metonym for the broader decolonizing move that led not only to national independence in the "Third World" but also to the radicalization of academic disciplines and ultimately to novel transdisciplinary formations such as ethnic studies, critical race studies, and postcolonial studies. This seismic shift, we argue, forms the indispensable backdrop for the post-1960s debates about such fraught issues as race, identity, and multiculturalism. The critique of Euro-diffusionist narratives of knowledge dissemination and the discussion of the radicalization of the disciplines here lay the groundwork for our critique of some otherwise progressive thinkers later in the book.

The remaining chapters explore the debates as they have evolved from the 1990s to the present. Chapter 4, "Identity Politics and the Right/Left Convergence," examines a certain left's hostility, shared with the right, toward identity politics, as voiced by such writers as Walter Benn Michaels, Pierre Bourdieu/ Loïc Wacquant, and Slavoj Žižek. What explains this bizarre secret sharing between political adversaries? The leftist arguments against "critical race" and "multicultural identity politics" bear an uncanny resemblance to those advanced by the right, even if they are articulated in the name of opposed visions. The dismissal sometimes derives, as we shall see, from a fool's choice between class and race, or between economy and culture. The blithe dismissal of an easily criticized "liberal multiculturalism," we argue, distracts attention from the less easily dismissible work on race and coloniality. The problem, we argue, lies not so much in the arguments themselves as in the uninformed and Eurocentric assumptions undergirding them.

Chapter 5, "France, the United States, and the Culture Wars," traces the shift in French intellectual life that takes us from the ardent Third Worldism of the 1960s to the backlash against it in the 1970s, on to a certain left-right United Front against multicultural identity politics in the 1990s. Here we dissect the attacks on critical race/multicultural thought by prominent French intellectuals such as Pascal Bruckner, Tzvetan Todorov, and Alain Finkielkraut. What anxieties underlie this defensive stance toward what some have called the "specter" of multiculturalism? How can we explain the immense gap between the multicultural France of hip-hop and the antimulticultural stance of French intellectuals? Here we also examine the rightward turn—summed up in the catch-phrase "from Mao to Moses"—taken by the self-defined "pro-American" and "Zionist" *nouveaux philosophes*. Against those who see Jews and Muslims, and Jews and blacks, as necessarily antagonistic, we stress their historical, discursive, and allegorical affinities, from the catalytic moment of 1492 up to the present. In the end, we argue, issues of colonialism, anti-Semitism, Indian-hating, Orientalism, Eurocentrism, Islamophobia, and antiblack racism are all intimately connected, sharing intersecting impulses and logics. Finally, the chapter evokes what could be called the "multicultural turn" in French scholarship since the turn of the 20th century.

Chapter 6, "Brazil, the United States, and the Culture Wars," explores the South Atlantic version of the seismic shift as expressed in anti-imperialism, dependency theory, and the black consciousness movement in postwar Brazil. What explains a certain Brazilian skepticism, at once similar to and distinct from that found among French intellectuals, toward multicultural identity politics, at least in the 1990s? We frame these issues against the backdrop of the prolific comparative scholarship concerning Brazil and the United States. What are the advantages and disadvantages of the comparative method? In this chapter, we also foreground the brilliant ways that Brazilian popular musicians such as Gilberto Gil and Caetano Veloso have staged debates about race and indigeneity through lyrics, music, and performance. Deploying multicultural dissonance as a creative resource, we argue, these musicians give aesthetic form to social desire. At the same time, we show that Brazilian academics, in tandem with the artists, have been exploring the race/colonial debates with great depth and precision, often challenging the "racial democracy" myth.

Chapter 7, "From Affirmative Action to Interrogating Whiteness," explores the debates about Affirmative Action and reparations as new editions of Enlightenment debates about freedom and slavery and the universal and the particular. Here we anatomize the ricocheting conversations about the long-term consequences of colonialism and slavery in the three zones, especially emphasizing the cross-referential and transnational character of the conversation. Why do both the supporters and critics of Affirmative Action constantly bring up comparisons to the United States? At the same time, we note the emergence of "whiteness studies"—or its functional equivalents—in all three sites, with an eye to potential zones of reciprocity.

Chapter 8, "French Intellectuals and the Postcolonial," further probes the gap between France as a multiracial postcolonial society and a French academic field that has only recently begun to wrestle with race and postcoloniality, despite the historically seminal role of French and Francophone anticolonial thinkers. What explains the initial aversion to postcolonial theory and the subsequent partial fading of that aversion? Here we probe some of the ironies of this hesitation-waltz about postcoloniality, while also pointing to the recent writing, especially since the 2005 rebellions, that traces the continuities between colonial practices and postcolonial France. The various genres of postcolonial writing, we suggest, now form part of what has become a lively intervention close to the pulsating center of French public life.

Chapter 9, "The Translational Traffic of Ideas," theorizes the axioms operative in multilateral polemics in which scholars from one country (France) engage scholars from another country (the United States) who write about a third country (Brazil). We focus especially on the polemic between Bourdieu/Wacquant and political scientist Michael Hanchard concerning the Brazilian black consciousness movement. In an infinite regress of readings, Brazilian intellectuals themselves "read back" against the Bourdieu/Wacquant reading of an African American reading of Brazil. We contextualize the polemic against the intertextual setting of the work of the French and American "Brazilianists." At the same time, we explore the impact of the dissemination of poststructuralist French theory in Brazil and the United States. Examining the transregional circulation of ideas, we criticize narratives of intellectual exchange that posit dichotomous axes of foreign/native, export/import, and original/copy, proposing instead a more fluid transnational and translational methodology appropriate to cross-border intellectual interlocution.

Hovering around and in the interstices of our text is the metaquestion of theories and methodologies that address questions of transnational intellectual exchange. How do cultural practices such as hip-hop and Tropicália, in tandem with academic scholarship, bring their "excess seeing" (Bakhtin) to the table? What advantages accompany the "view from afar?" (Lévi-Strauss), especially when the "view from afar" and the "view from within" become intermingled when intellectuals such as Claude Lévi-Strauss and Roger Bastide are transformed by their Brazilian *séjour*? What is the cognitive function of comparison? What does it illuminate or fail to illuminate? How can comparison take on board the constitutive unevenness that structures the world in dominance? Are national comparisons always tendentious, narcissistic, prescriptive, hiding what R. Radhkrishnan calls the "aggression of a thesis"?[22] Does comparison assume, or construct, an illusory coherence on both sides of the comparison? How does comparison change when we move from the comparison of two entities (with the danger of reified binaries) to comparing three or more entities (with the danger of a chaotic proliferation)?

Cross-national comparisons are imbued with affect, fears, vanities, desires, and projections. Comparatists can idealize or denigrate the "home" country, just as they can idealize or denigrate the "away" country. They can also deconstruct nation-state thinking by discerning commonalities. Comparison is both problematic and inescapable. (Even when one rejects comparison as a method, after all, one is still comparing comparison to other supposedly superior methodologies.) The epistemological impasse occurs when reified dichotomies based on nation-state units ontologize a putative national character, now locked into what might be called an "ontologi-nation." The Venn diagrams of comparison focus on the shared comparable territory, leaving outside the anomalies not susceptible to comparison, that which is incomparable. We attempt to avoid this bind through formulations that conjoin identity and difference, emphasizing shared contradictions, differentiated commonalities, and family resemblances—differences that connect and similarities that separate. We will thus highlight a multidirectional polylogue within which intellectuals are constantly hybridizing, indigenizing, translating, and transforming "ideas from elsewhere," while still being shaped by their national contexts and by uneven relations to power.

Comparison often entails generalization, yet any sentence that connects an entire nationality or ethnicity to the verb "to be" ("The French are . . .") is inevitably problematic, as suggested by the ancient conundrum "All generalizations are false." But even more circumscribed generalizations concerning "all white French sociologists" are equally likely to be false. Comparisons that result in static overdrawn dichotomies make one wish for a comparative analysis of exceptions, focusing on Brazilians who hate soccer and samba, Americans who despise hot dogs and baseball, and French people who abhor Beaujolais and Camembert. Such analyses would at least have the virtue of unpredictability, of not leaving complex cultures incarcerated in the prisons of national stereotype.

This book's title, *Race in Translation*, signals the dominant thread that runs through the volume. In a relational frame, we recount how Brazil, France, and the United States have been historically implicated in the dynamics of race and coloniality, and how those dynamics still reverberate in the present in the form of palpably unjust social formations. While the specific demographic ratios and power hierarchies might vary, the historical interplay between race and coloniality is constitutive in each national case. The evasion, the refusal, and the sheer denial of this constitutiveness is what triggers and propels the "debates." The evasion/denial draws on different rhetorics in each case: "racial democracy" in Brazil, "republicanism" in France, and "equal opportunity" in the United States. The crux of the debate, in our view, is between those who acknowledge the shaping presence of race and coloniality as against those who deny it.

Race in Translation evokes a multicolored Atlantic seascape. In this sense, our work forms part of a movement within scholarship toward postcolonial and transnational frames, a trend manifested linguistically in the proliferation of such prefixes as "trans-" "cross-," and "inter-" and in words such as "intercultural," "transnational," "transcultural," "diasporic," "exilic," "global," and so forth. A stream of aquatic and oceanic metaphors—"Black Atlantic Civilization" (Robert Farris Thompson), "the Black Atlantic" (Paul Gilroy), "flux and reflux" (Pierre Verger), "circum-Atlantic performance" (Joe Roach), and "tidalectics" (Edward Kamau Brathwaite)—gives expression to a poetics of flows and eddies mingling myriad currents, reflecting a search for a more fluid language of analysis. At the same time, fluidity is no panacea. Slavery too was transnational, and Atlantic waters harbor the corpses of the enslaved thrown overboard. Moreover, not all flows are progressive; Wall Street bankers also speak of "liquid assets" and "capital flows." Our Atlanticist title, in this sense, clearly echoes the triangular traffic by which Europe, in a lucrative loop of commercial appropriation, sent manufactures to Africa, African slaves to the colonies, and raw materials back to the metropole.

The metaphor of "currents" is especially suggestive here in that the Atlantic Ocean is literally swept by vast circular "rivers" and "streams"—a northern circle running in a clockwise direction from its southern beginnings and a southern circle flowing in a counterclockwise direction, in a swirling movement in some ways evocative of the trade of ideas and goods back and forth between Africa, Europe, and the Americas.[3] Given these liquid transfers and "trade winds"—an expression redolent of the slave trade—the goal becomes one of discerning the common currents running through the various zones, the ways that histories, texts, and discourses mingle and interact within asymmetrical power situations. We are interested, in this sense, in what Édouard Glissant calls "transversalities," or the hierarchical and lateral syncretisms and dialogisms taking place across national spaces. We hope to shed light on the linked analogies between three colonial/national zones too often viewed in isolation, in order to provoke a salutary confrontation of perspectives concerning shared and discrepantly lived histories.

1 The Atlantic Enlightenment

THE ENTIRE ATLANTIC world was shaped by 1492 and what is euphemistically called the "encounter," which engendered not only a catastrophe for indigenous peoples but also a crisis in European thinking. The clash of Europe and indigene provoked a multifaceted reflection on utopia (Thomas More) and dystopia (Bartolomé de las Casas). The intertextual backdrop of the contemporary "culture wars" lies in the contradictions of an Enlightenment that was not exclusively European. The phrase "Atlantic Enlightenment" refers both to a geography and a concept. Enlightenment thought was a hybrid intellectual production; it was generated not only in Europe but also in the Americas, by the Founding Fathers in the United States, by Haitian revolutionaries, and by representatives of indigenous people. The Enlightenment was a debate, conducted in many sites, about the relation between Europe and its Others, with a left and a right wing, with proslavery and antislavery, colonialist and anticolonialist factions.

The Atlantic world has been shaped by the intellectual heritage of Enlightenment republicanism, as expressed politically in the American Revolution in 1776, the French Revolution in 1789, and the Haitian Revolution in 1791, as well as in the Brazilian independence movements of the 18th century and in the Brazilian Republic in 1889. A clear historical thread thus leads out from the Enlightenment debates within the American and French Revolutions to the contemporary "culture wars," as actualized, recombinant versions of earlier debates. The "culture wars," in this sense, inherit centuries of discursive struggles going back to the Renaissance and the Enlightenment and their antecedents, going back to the Conquest of the Americas and even to the Crusades. Versions of the debates were present, in germ and under different names, in the intense exchanges about Conquest, colonialism, and slavery. They were argued in religious/political language in the 16th century when Juan Ginés de Sepúlveda and Bartolomé de las Casas asked whether Indians had souls and as a consequence enjoyed "*derechos humanos*" (human rights). They were present when indigenous people rebelled against European conquest or resisted Christian proselytization. They were present when enslaved Africans fought and argued against enslavement, or when the U.S. Founding Fathers took positions for and against the inscription of slavery into the Constitution. They were present when French Enlightenment philosophers spoke about "freedom" and "natural goodness," and when "free men of color" opposed slavery in the French colonies.

Contemporary critiques thus lend new names to old quarrels, now rearticulated within altered idioms and paradigms. Throughout its history, colonialism has always generated its own critique, whether by the dominant culture's own renegades or by its colonized victims. When Montaigne in the late 16th century argued in "Des Cannibales" that civilized Europeans were ultimately more barbarous than cannibals, since cannibals ate the flesh of the dead only in order to appropriate the strength of their enemies, while Europeans tortured and murdered in the name of a religion of love, he might be described as a radical anticolonialist *avant la lettre*. When Diderot in the 18th century called for African insurrection against European colonialists, he too might be seen as part of this same anti-Eurocentric lineage. And when Frantz Fanon in the 20th century spoke of accepting "the reciprocal relativism of different cultures, once colonialism is excluded," he gave us a working definition of radical forms of postcolonial critique.[1]

When we say that the contemporary culture wars go back to colonialism and the Enlightenment, we do not mean this claim in a vague "everything goes back to history" way. The contemporary debates are quite literally rooted in Enlightenment quarrels. In contemporary France, for example, both right and left invoke the French Revolution and "Enlightenment values" to articulate their views of "identity politics," whether seen as a praiseworthy expansion of Enlightenment equality or as a particularist departure from Enlightenment "universality." In the United States, both left and right invoke the Founding Fathers and the Declaration of Independence, but in opposite ways; Obama appeals to the "more perfect union" of the Preamble, while Tea Party Republicans interpret the Constitution to defend right-wing libertarianism. The left channels the radical Enlightenment of Diderot and Toussaint Louverture, while Newt Gingrich channels Adam Smith. The quarrels about indigenous land rights and intellectual property rights go back to the Conquest and to John Locke. The various discursive positions for and against conquest, slavery, racism, and imperialism, in sum, have been "available" for a long time; contemporary debates thus form reformatted versions of those earlier debates. Past and present reverberate together; old debates anticipate and haunt the present.

The Red Atlantic

Our invocation of a "Red," "Black," and "White" Atlantic is not meant to detract from the work performed under the rubric of the "Black Atlantic," but rather to place that blackness within a relational spectrum that also embraces the metaphorical "redness" of indigenous America and, in a very different way, the metaphorical "whiteness" of Europe and Euro-America. Colonialism and slavery completely transformed racial, national, and cultural identities in what might be called the "Rainbow Atlantic." Colonial conquest turned an extremely heteroge- neous group of indigenous peoples—formerly defined as Tupi, Carib, Arawak, Mohawk, Peguot, and so forth—into generic "Reds" and turned an equally het- erogeneous group of Africans—formerly named Kong, Hausa, Yoruba—into generic "blacks," all under the domination of a motley crew of Europeans—Span- ish, English, Dutch, French—now turned into generic Whites, thus forging the constitutive Red/White/Black demographic triad typical of the Americas. The cultures of the Atlantic are thus not only Black and White; they are also figura- tively Red. Even slavery was "Red" in that in the Americas the indigenous peoples were kidnapped and enslaved before the Africans. In Brazil, both Red and Black groups were called "negros": enslaved natives were "Negros da Terra" (Blacks from the Land) as opposed to "Negros da Guinee" (Blacks from Guinea, Africa). At times, one enslaved group was used to replace another, as when bandeirantes from São Paulo enslaved one hundred thousand "indios" to compensate for the loss of enslaved Africans during the suspension of the slave trade between 1625 and 1650. Colonialism, conquest, slavery, and multiculturality are thus inextricably linked. The Atlantic world became syncretic and hybrid precisely because of these vio- lent transcontinental processes.

As tropes of color, the concepts of a "Red," "Black," and "White" Atlantic cast a prismatic light on a shared history. While "Black Atlantic" evokes the Middle Passage and the African diaspora, the notion of a "Red Atlantic" registers not only the dispossession of indigenous peoples by Europeans but also the impact of indigenous ideas on European thinking. The settler colonialism that dispossessed the "Red" and the racial slavery that exploited the "Black" were the twin machines of racial supremacy. Yet the relations between Red and Black and White were always unstable. Red and Black could ally against White or collaborate with White against the Black or the Red. White supremacy, as David Roediger puts it, "situated itself at some times in opposition to a 'red' other and at others to a 'black' one."[2] Stances on imperialism were also conjunctural. A French observer such as Alexis de Tocqueville could urge French imperialists in Africa to look not to the U.S. treatment of the Black but rather to U.S. treatment of the Red as a model. During the Conquest of Mexico, American racists would argue about whether Mexicans were Black or Red; what was important to the racists was that they not be White.

We have not forgotten the other "colors" in the Atlantic rainbow, for exam- ple, the metaphorical yellowness and brownness of diasporic Asians, mestizos, Latinos, and Arabs. At this point in history, conquest, slavery, immigration, and globalization have thoroughly scrambled, in the manner of an action painting, an already mixed color palette, in an intermingled spectrum. Switching from a chromatic to a linguistic register, Eugene Jolas speaks of an "Atlantic, Crucible Language" as the verbal precipitate of transracial synthesis.[3] Gilles Deleuze's description of contemporary U.S. English as "worked upon by a Black English, and also a Yellow English, a Red English, a broken English, each of which is like a language shot through with a spray-gun of colors,"[4] could be extended to the Atlantic world generally. By the same token, one might suggestively attach various modifiers to the noun "Atlantic" to speak of a Moorish Atlantic, a Jewish Atlantic, a Yoruba Atlantic, and so forth.

Here we will focus not on the full rainbow spectrum but rather on the Red, the Black, and the White. The rainbow metaphor, in any case, risks implying the facile "postracial" harmony and transcendence of race. While race has no scientific substance, "race" still effectively evokes the persistence of deep inequalities affecting visible minorities. The spectrum is also spectral, haunted and shadowed by the ghosts of various oppressions. Some colors crowd out or absorb or hide and "spook" others. Our goal, then, is to complexify a multileveled chromatic relationality shot through with power-laden inequalities. And as the metaphor of a spectrum implies, the colors fade and blur into one another; despite hierarchical regimes, they defy segregated boundaries. The indigenous Red and the diasporic Black, in both the United States and Brazil, for example, are densely interwoven: demographically through mixture, politically through coalition, academically through research, and culturally through a miscegenated popular culture. Our assumption throughout is that "colors" are situated, overlapping, and relational utterances that slip and slide in their reference; they take on meaning only as part of larger systems striated by power and inequity.

The legal foundation for conquest was the "Discovery Doctrine" that granted Europeans sovereign claim over "Red" lands and peoples. That doctrine encoded ethnocentric assumptions of European superiority over other cultures, religions, and peoples, so that Europeans, in the words of Robert Miller, "immediately and automatically acquired property rights in native lands and gained governmental, political, and commercial rights over the inhabitants without . . . the consent of the indigenous peoples."[5] Initially developed by the Roman Catholic Church as part of the Crusades to recover the Holy Lands, the Discovery Doctrine was first applied to Muslim-dominated "infidel lands," declared by various popes to lack "lawful dominion." A 1455 papal bull by Pope Nicholas authorized Portugal to "invade, search out, capture, vanquish, and subdue all Saracens and pagans" and to enslave them in perpetuity, all part of bringing all humankind into the fold of the one true religion. Subsequent papal bulls extended the right of conquest to the Americas. England, France, Holland, Sweden, and the United States later cited these precedents as legitimating their own conquests. Various popes asserted a worldwide papal jurisdiction—an early incarnation of the "universal"—rooted in the papacy's divine mandate to care for the entire world. The Conquest and Discovery Doctrine officially became part of U.S. law with the seminal Supreme Court case *Johnson v. M'Intosh* in 1823, which provides the legal foundations for the U.S. takeover of Indian lands.

Church and State were mobilized to legitimate the new racial/colonial order. A key instrument of the Conquest was the *Requerimiento* (requisition), which Spanish conquerors read to the natives as a form of legitimation. This document communicated the idea of a chain of command extending from God to the pope to the king to the conquistadores themselves, all of whom agreed that the native territories and peoples belonged to the pope and the Spanish monarch. Some Hollywood films devoted to the Conquest (for example the 1949 film starring Fredric March) show Columbus reading from the *Requerimiento*, but they fail to include the document's warning of massive retaliation for any refusal to collaborate, promising that the Spanish "with God's help will make war against you by every means available to us, and will submit you to the yoke of obedience of the Church and His Majesty, will take your women and children and enslave them, . . . will take all your goods and do all kinds of ill to you and cause all the damage which a sovereign can commit against disobedient vassals." The document then blames the victim by declaring that "all the death and damage inflicted . . . will be your fault and not that of His Majesty, nor of ourselves."[6] (The provocative 2010 film *Even the Rain*, about a Spanish director in Bolivia making a film about Columbus, does include the final warnings.)

The *Requerimiento* was supposed to be read in Spanish to "Indians" unfamiliar with that language. It is as if the Spanish wanted to believe—or pretended to believe—that the Indians were willingly giving up their land, abandoning their beliefs, renouncing their leaders, and adopting Spanish rule. Less a contractual agreement than a fable that the Spanish told themselves, the document absurdly promises that the natives will *not* be forced to convert—as long as they spontaneously convert on their own. The indigenous people were portrayed as devoid of any political, legal, or religious system of belief. Spanish and Portuguese ideologists claimed, incorrectly, that the indigenous languages lacked three letters—the r for *rei*, or "king"; the l for *lei*, or "law"; and the f for *fe*, or "faith." While European kingdoms proclaimed, "One King, One Faith, One Law," the "natives," through a logic of deficit, were depicted as a tabula rasa awaiting European inscription. The Conquest also had a linguistic dimension. All over the Americas, first peoples had named, mapped, and described the continent through language. As a result, states in Brazil and the United States bear native names (Ceara and Piaui in Brazil; Idaho and Ohio in the United States). In the present day, indigenous peoples have proposed an alternative to the word "America" itself: *Abya-Yala*, Kuna for "place of life," extrapolated for the continent as a whole.[7] Yet historically, many indigenous groups were denied the right even to name themselves. Thus, the "Navajos" in the United States were self-named the "Dineh," and the "Kayapo" of Brazil are self-named "Mebengokre" (or "people of the eye of the water").

In both Brazil and the United States, early religious figures learned indigenous languages in order to proselytize: John Eliot translated the Bible into native tongues; Father José de Anchieta devised a Tupi grammar. The American Founding Fathers learned Native American languages, and indigenous words came to enrich English vocabulary. In Brazil, the Tupi-Guarani language, first used as a language of communication between the Portuguese and the Tupi coastal peoples, even became the lingua franca, or *língua geral*, called Nheengatu, up until the 18th century, including among non-Tupi natives. Indeed, Portuguese became dominant only in the 18th century.[8] (A 2005 *New York Times* article reported that the *língua geral* was making a comeback in the interior of Brazil.)[9] Presently indigenous Brazilians speak some 180 languages, with the number of speakers ranging from more than twenty thousand (Guarani, Tikuna, Macuxi) to a mere handful. In the United States, meanwhile, Native Americans are "resurrecting" native languages, such as Wampanoag, barely spoken for over a century.

The European response to the indigenous civilizations of the Americas reveals a general pattern of denial of indigenous cultural agency. Although native agricultural practice had sustained indigenous people for millennia, it was not recognized by Europeans as authentic agriculture but only as a kind of animal-like foraging. The fact that a densely populated and culturally remolded land was seen as "virgin" reflects a kind of mental "ethnic cleansing," a discourse of imaginary removal. The idea of the "vanishing Indian" had its own colonial productivity, shaping a widespread impression that Indians had already disappeared or were about to disappear with the next hot breath of conquest. Yet the enduring presence of indigenous America looms behind many cultural debates, posing questions about the very legitimacy of colonial-settler states.

To think deeply about the Red Atlantic is necessarily to think in ways that transcend the nation-state: first, because many indigenous communities came into existence before the emergence of modern nation-states; second, because the national identity of colonial-settler states in the Americas was always constituted in relation to the "Indian," whether as the enemy or as a symbol of the national socius; third, the dispossession of indigenous communities was partially the product of the colonial expansionism of nation-states; fourth, many native communities have actively rejected the very concept of the nation-state, not because they could not achieve it but because they did not want it; fifth, because the present-day boundaries of many indigenous communities actually exceed the borders of nation-states (as with the Yanomami in Brazil and Venezuela, the Mohawks in the United States and Canada); and sixth, because many indigenous peoples, due to multiple dislocations, no longer live only on their ancestral land base but are dispersed regionally and transnationally. The Quechua, for example, not only inhabit Peru, Ecuador, and Bolivia; they are also dispersed into North America and Europe.

The Indigene and the Epistemological Crisis

Questions about the status and social systems of the misnamed "Indian" were disputed all around the Atlantic countries by Spanish jurists (Sepúlveda, Francisco de Vitoria), French humanists (Montaigne), British empiricists (Locke), American statesmen (Jefferson, Franklin), German philosophers (Hegel), and Brazilian writers (from Pêro Vaz de Caminha to Darcy Ribeiro), as well as by the indigenous themselves. The figure of the Indian got caught up in controversies about religion, property, sovereignty, and culture. Indeed, no in-depth analysis of modernity can bypass the indigenous peoples of the Americas, whether negatively, as the "victims of progress," or positively, as the catalysts for Western thinking and artistic production, discernible in the work of Jean de Lery, Shakespeare, Hobbes, Rousseau, Diderot, Voltaire, Melville, Marx and Engels, Oswald de Andrade, Gilberto Freyre, Claude Lévi-Strauss, Pierre Clastres, and countless others.

The European part of the Atlantic world, in this sense, is also "Red" in something like the sense that it is "Black"—that is, it is impacted both by the conquest and enslavement of indigenous America and by the transforming ferment of native modes of thought and sociality. Inspired by sensationalist travel literature, some philosophers projected the native peoples as barbaric savages, while others saw the small-scale consensus indigenous societies as offering an alternative social model. The philosopher Michel de Montaigne recalled meeting three Brazilian Tupinamba in 1562, at the court of King Charles IX, where the Tupinamba asked provocative questions about French society; they wondered why tall adults could bow down to a small boy (the regent) and why some people ate well and others ate barely at all and why those who barely ate did not strangle those who were eating well. Montaigne's unnamed Tupi interlocutors shifted his own thinking by posing corrosive questions based on their assumptions about what constituted a good society—in this case their own. In "Des Cannibales," Montaigne subsequently practiced a rhetoric of civilizational reversals by arguing that the violence of Tupinamba cannibalism paled in comparison to that triggered by religious wars in Europe. With a few irreverent queries, the Tupinamba demolished the prestige of the hereditary monarchy and the class system. In a sense, the indigenous Brazilians were theorizing prerevolutionary France as much as Montaigne was theorizing pre- and post-Conquest America. Although the three

Tupinamba arguably form part of European theory, we do not know their names but only that of Montaigne. Yet their refusal to be impressed by European social systems constituted a mode of implicit critique that catalyzed Montaigne's own societal self-criticism.

On innumerable occasions, European and Euro-American thinkers deployed "the Indian" as an inspiration for social critique and utopian desire. The emergence into European consciousness of the indigene triggered an epistemological excitement that generated both the dystopian imagery of the nasty and brutish savage and the utopian imagery of an egalitarian social system markedly different from that of a rigidly hierarchical Europe. The concept of the free Indian living in a society without coercion helped spark revolutionary ideas in Europe. Jean-Jacques Rousseau deployed the notion of the "natural goodness of human beings" and "societies without coercion" as a means of undermining European authoritarianism. Rousseau lent Montaigne's ideas political efficacy, thus helping foment the French (and indirectly the American) Revolution. In the Constitutional Assembly of 1789, the representatives of the left were avid readers of Montesquieu, Voltaire, Rousseau, and Diderot, all of whom spoke of the natives of the Americas.

A more complex narrative of the Renaissance and the Enlightenment thus would have to take on board the literal and figurative encounter of Europe and indigene, both in terms of direct influence and of more diffuse transtextual relations, tropologies, and allegories. The motif of the Indian as "exemplar of liberty" pervades the discursive atmosphere not only of the French Enlightenment but also of the American Revolution and of Brazilian anticolonial nationalism. In the United States, the Founding Fathers were avid readers of the philo-indigenous French philosophers, but they also "read," as it were, the Native Americans themselves. The philosophically inclined Founding Fathers, while entirely capable of Indianist exoticism and even exterminationism, had a more direct experience of Native Americans than did the French philosophers. They had diplomatic exchanges with them, traded with them, learned their languages, and were influenced by their political thought, even if—and this point is crucial—they ultimately dispossessed them. American revolutionaries brandished the Indian as an icon of national difference vis-à-vis England, whence the Iroquois (Haudenosaunee) symbolism of the eagle's quiver of arrows (representing the thirteen states) on the dollar bill, and the Indian statue gracing the Capitol building. Native American tropes such as the "Great Tree" and "chain of friendship" were absorbed into revolutionary discourse. The revolutionary hero Paul Revere cast a Native American woman as America's first national symbol.[10]

A recurrent leitmotif in the writings of the Enlightenment philosophers and in those of the Founding Fathers such as Jefferson was the idea that Indian societies never submitted themselves to any laws or coercive power. Marx and Engels later picked up on native themes in their readings of Lewis Henry Morgan's *Ancient Society*, in which Morgan lauded the profoundly democratic organization of the Iroquois League. For Marx and Engels, the Iroquois meshed a communal economic system with a democratic political organization, thus offering a model of economic equality achieved without state domination, in a society devoid of nobles, kings, governors, soldiers, and police and where all, including the women, were free and equal. Although the Marxist term "primitive communism" evokes a long-vanished communitas, this "utopia" was an actually existing 19th-century society with an actual location in what is now Canada and the United States.

Contemporary Native American scholars have highlighted the indigenous influence on American political institutions. Donald A. Grinde, Jr., argued in his 1977 book *The Iroquois and the Founding of the American Nation* that the authors of the U.S. Constitution partially borrowed the concept of a federal government from the example of the Six Nations Iroquois Confederation. In 1982, Bruce Johansen published *Forgotten Founders: Benjamin Franklin, the Iroquois, and the Rationale for the American Revolution*. Within a few years, both authors became caught up in the culture wars. The gatekeepers of the right derided the thesis of such books as ridiculous on its face, apparently unaware that even President John F. Kennedy had supported the Iroquois-influence thesis, writing in 1960 that "the League of the Iroquois inspired Benjamin Franklin to copy it in planning the federation of States."[11] A decade earlier, legal scholar Felix Cohen had argued that universal suffrage for men, federalism, and the view of chiefs as servants rather than masters of the people were part of the American way of life before Columbus landed."[12]

The colonizing powers, after "enclosing" communal land within Europe itself, enclosed and appropriated communally held indigenous land under the pretext that the native peoples had no "deed" or "title" to the land. Just as rights were distributed according to a racialized schema in the past, today the question of "copyrights" is linked to the corporate appropriation of resources formerly held by indigenous peoples. Today the very idea of "title" is wed to conceptions of contracts between individual actors or corporations, an individualist conception of intellectual property rights completely alien to many indigenous peoples. Unlike pirates and conquistadores, transnational corporations no longer seize only gold and silver and diamonds; rather, they declare themselves "entitled" or "empatented" to exploit traditional communal forms of knowledge such as rainforest herbal remedies, for example, which they then market at high cost to the world at large, including even to the descendants of the people who originally developed the remedies.

The question of intellectual property rights provides a vivid example of the historical "morphing" that takes us from Columbus to the CEOs of contemporary transnational corporations. The word "patents" referred in 16th-century Europe to the official royal letters (*litterae patents*) by which sovereigns conferred privileges, rights, and land titles on various members of the nobility, for example, the *capitanias* in Brazil granted by the Portuguese king. In the "Age of Discovery," these "letters" became associated with the literal conquest of territory; five hundred years later, they are associated with transnational corporations' updated version of the conquest of economic rights in the Global South, whose biodiversity is very much linked to the cultural knowledges of indigenous peoples. As Djelal Kadir points out, the letter authorizing Columbus's conquests, conceded on April 17, 1492, by Fernando and Isabel and ratified by Juan de Colona, was "the literal prototype, the paradigm, the *locus classicus* of its genre." Columbus possessed, as it were, the "patent of patents and the license to appropriate the land and material wealth of the New World."13

Five centuries after the Conquest, the World Trade Organization rules concerning copyrights constitute reformatted versions of the papal bulls and regal edicts that legalized the Conquest. For Vandana Shiva, "The freedom of action which transnational corporations demand today is the same freedom of action that European colonies demanded, after 1492, as a natural right over the territory and riches of non-European people."14 The earlier religious language has been replaced by the secular language of market fundamentalism. Rather than control territory, the new regime controls markets, intellectual property rights, and the legal parameters of profiting from biodiversity. Under the pressure of transnational corporations, all aspects of life are becoming "patentable." Since "the soil, the forests, the rivers, and the oceans were all colonized and polluted," as Shiva puts it, "capital has to find new colonies to invade and exploit in order to continue the process of accumulation. These new colonies . . . are the interior spaces of women, plants, and animals."15 Just as European colonizers saw indigenous land as "empty" because it had not been made "productive" of commodities—even though it had successfully nourished native peoples for millennia—transnational corporations do not recognize indigenous peoples' title to biodiversity unless it has been turned into a marketable product.

The Amazon, in this sense, forms the epicenter of the conflicts emerging from the crisis of five centuries of productivism and the instrumental domination of nature. The process initiated in 1492 is reaching a finale as globalizing capitalism strains against the limits of planetary ecology while coming into naked conflict with the indigenous peoples occupying the land. The Amazon has become the last frontier, at the point where frontiers are at once everywhere and nowhere. As the planet reaps the bitter fruits of instrumental reason, in an age of the end of all utopias (including the neoliberal utopia of the "end of history"), the way of life of those who were always there, of those who never went away, opens up a new horizon of the politically possible. Biodiversity and sociodiversity, hegemonic biopower and indigenous sovereignty, the local and the global, all become interlinked, unstable, and interactive.

"First contact" is still occurring, but this time some of the "Indians" have computers, digital cameras, and websites. Already in the 1980s, the documentary *Kayapo: Out of the Forest* (1989) showed Brazilian "Indians," armed with camcorders, protesting a hydroelectric dam that would have flooded their communities. Within the globalized contact zone, indigenous leaders and the corporate representatives of the firm Eletronorte conduct a lively debate about the nature of progress, energy, knowledge, and ownership. Corporate rationality, at the height of its arrogance but also at the end of its rope, meets articulate indigeneity. Appealing to a common humanity, one Kayapo woman tells the Eletronorte representative, "Since you also love your children, you should understand us." Another Kayapo shows samples of the herbal remedies threatened by the construction of the dam. A woman presses a machete against the company spokesman's face as she scolds him in Kayapo. In a reversal of colonial *écriture*, she tells the spokesman to write down her name, since she is one of those who will die if the dam is built. Kayapo Chief Raoni appears with the rock star Sting in a successful attempt to attract international media attention. It is as if the Tainos had videotaped their encounters with Columbus and disseminated the images on YouTube.[16]

The unending current of indigenous critique continues unabated. Yanomami leader Davi Kopenawa Yanomami, whose group was devastated by an induced epidemic and who subsequently became a community spokesperson, claims that "white people design their words in visible form because their thinking is full of forgetfulness." In an essay whose title—"Discovering White People"—inverts the usual Euro-oriented trope of discovery, Yanomami offers his own version of the "dialectic of Enlightenment." In early times, he writes,

> whites lived like us in the forest, ... but once they created tools, machines, cars and planes, they became euphoric and said: "We are the only people to be so ingenious, only we know how to produce machines and merchandise." That is when they lost all wisdom. First they damaged their own land, before going off to work in other lands in order to endlessly create their merchandise. And they never stopped to ask: "If we destroy the earth, will we be able to create another one?"[17]

Another activist from a threatened group, Ailton Krenak, during the discussions in 1987 about the new Brazilian constitution, painted himself black with jenipapo paste for a speech before the National Congress as a token of mourning for the legal blockage of indigenous rights. Krenak insists on the intellectual/historiographic agency of indigenous peoples, who also "wrote" their history not in the form of books but rather in the form of sayings, rituals, and narratives. The conflicts initiated by the Conquest continue up to the present and take place every day. Confirming the views of anthropologist Pierre Clastres, who lived with the Nhandeva and M'bia, about the active refusal of the nation-state, Krenak adds, "There is no ideology here, we are naturally against the state, we do it the way the wind follows its path, or the river follows its path, we naturally follow a path which does not affirm state institutions as necessary for our health, education, or happiness."[18]

Indigenous critique incarnates a temporal paradox: it is very traditional and ancient and, at the same time, very radical and new. Not only does it challenge the logics of colonialism, Eurocentrism, and the nation-state; it also questions the productivism of Marxism, the nomadism of postmodernism, and the constructivism of poststructuralism. We see this paradox of maximum radicality and maximum traditionality in the dialogue between the thinkers of indigeneity and the multicultural left. In *Red Pedagogy*, Sandy Grande, a Quechua professor at Connecticut College, dialogues with the radical leftist advocates of "critical pedagogy." While giving them immense credit, she finds them wanting from an indigenous perspective. The left (and at times the right) speaks of "democracy," but forgets that from an indigenous perspective, democracy has often been a weapon of mass disempowerment. The Marxist left speaks of "revolution," but Latin American revolutions have dispossessed Miskitus, Sumus, Ramas, and Quechua. For Grande, critical pedagogy critiques the colonialist project yet remains informed by individualism, anthropocentrism, and stagist progressivism, epistemic biases that worsen the ecological crisis. Students are encouraged to be "independent" (implying an individualist suspicion of collaboration), successful (i.e., competitive), and antitraditional. Thus, far-left thought does not go far enough; Marx is anticapitalist (yet secretly shares many of capitalism's deep cultural assumptions), and critical pedagogy is transformational (but ignores the value of intergenerational knowledge). Yet Grande seeks to engage with all these currents, while literally "indigenizing" them.[19]

The interchange between European and indigenous thought has been both uneven and unending, lending support to such varied progressive causes as Jacobin and socialist revolutions, confederation and the separation of powers, class, gender, and sexual equality, communal property, ecology, jouissance, antiproductivism, and alter-globalization. As a situated utterance, the conversation changes with historically shaped challenges and ideological needs, as different features of the discourse of Indian radicalism come to the fore in different epochs: the critique of monarchy during the Renaissance (Montaigne), the idea of "Indian freedom" during the Enlightenment (Rousseau, Tom Paine), the critique of capitalism and bourgeois property relations in the 19th century (Marx and Engels), the valorization of societies without coercion in the 20th century (Pierre Clastres, Marshall Sahlins), and the protest against ecological devastation and transnational exploitation of biodiversity in the 21st century. In this sense, the two "red"—red as radical and red as Indian—merge.

Although indigenous people have always reflected on their collective life and their relation to other peoples, now Native intellectuals are becoming visible in the public sphere. Contemporary indigenous thinkers such as Davi Kopenawa Yanomami, Luiz Gomes Lana, and Ailton Krenak, for example, maintain an intense dialogue with nonindigenous scholar-activists such as Arturo Escobar, Eduardo Viveiros de Castro, and Giuseppe Cocco. While Eurocentric commentators see Indians as vanished and "behind the times," others see them as "ahead of the curve." Viveiros de Castro reminds us of the intellectual debts of anthropologists to the peoples they study. The "most interesting concepts, problems, entities and agents introduced by anthropological theory," he suggests, "find their source in the imaginative power of the societies (or peoples, or collectives) that the anthropologists propose to explain."[20] As theory becomes a hybrid coauthored practice, the anthropologist is inspired by the theoretical imaginary of the indigene, who in turn responds to the anthropologist. Indigenous activists are more and more articulating their own political positions, thus relieving nonnatives of the burden of speaking for them. Indigenous people and their nonindigenous interlocutors, in sum, have never stopped posing profound questions about culture, nature, property, energy, wealth, and equality. Indigenous thought, in its theoretical and practical manifestations, has thrown up challenges to the nostrums of Marxist, modernist, and postmodernist thought.

The Black Atlantic and the Aporias of the Universal

Just as the partly real, partly imaginary figure of the Indian generated both a critique of European social hierarchies and the utopia of an alternative social order, so Afro-diasporic resistance to slavery revealed the limitations of white bourgeois revolutions while implicitly proposing a utopia of egalitarian freedom. The violent diasporization of Africans had the paradoxical consequence of enabling "blacks" to play an indispensable economic, political, military, and intellectual role in the Americas. Apart from their crucial participation in economic production, and apart from their military service in American, Brazilian, and French wars, diasporic Africans have also formulated powerful indictments of the dominant system.

The critical agency of enslaved Africans in the Americas is all the more remarkable given that slavery as an institution tried to crush all knowledge, and even the desire for knowledge, on the part of the enslaved. Charles W. Ephraim describes the process as follows:

Africans were effectively deprogrammed as persons; they were depersonalized, robbed of their identity, with the intention of making them completely subservient to the white captors.... They were forbidden to form meaningful group relationships, for fear of the very real possibility of insurgency.... They were forbidden to speak their native languages and were allowed to learn only so much of the rudiments of a perverted version of English as would render them serviceable in bondage. Strict laws were enacted forbidding anyone to teach black people to read and write—effectively prohibiting communication and access to any information that might arouse their curiosity about their peculiar and insupportable condition as bondsmen in a strange land amidst utterly freakish and cruel men....

The white obsession with self-aggrandizement necessitated a full-scale program of dehumanization of the Africans, the wiping away of all traces of their past, an obliteration of their sense of ever having been somebody.[21]

Thus, massive amounts of energy were expended to block not only all black political resistance but even the material and cognitive conditions that might make possible the public articulation of critical thinking.

Not unlike the indigenous peoples, diasporic Africans were well aware of the vacuity of official U.S. proclamations about "freedom" and "equality," of Brazilian ideas about "order and progress" and "racial democracy," and of French boasts about the *"mission civilisatrice."* The innumerable rebellions against slavery (beginning already in Africa), meanwhile, put into practice a political vision. The 17th-century maroon republic of Palmares in Brazil set up an alternative social order while fending off military attack by the Dutch and the Portuguese. Recent archeological research has confirmed earlier speculations that Palmares included, along with the African majority, Indians, mestizos, renegade whites, Jews, and Muslims, ultimately becoming a refuge for the persecuted of Brazilian society.[22] Covering an area roughly a third the size of Portugal, Palmares lasted almost a century in the face of repeated assaults, withstanding on the average one military expedition every fifteen months.[23] Palmares bears witness not only to the Afro-Brazilian resistance against slavery but also to the capacity to mobilize an alternative life.[24] Indeed, Brazilian anthropologist José Jorge de Carvalho calls for a present-day "political actualization of Palmares" as a place where black leaders created a shelter for the integrated conviviality of Indians, enslaved Africans, and poor whites, thus shaping a model for a coalition of blacks, Indians, and progressive whites in contemporary Brazil.[25]

Uruguayan writer Germán Arciniegas points out in his *America in Europe* that Reds and Blacks in the Americas were in the vanguard of republican revolution, even if they did not use the word "republic": "The blacks of Cartagena became strong in Palenque in 1602, proclaimed a free republic and kept it so for a hundred years. . . . The Indians of Tupac Amaru in their insurrection against

Spain were forty years ahead of the whites."[26] Indigenous rebels and maroon leaders, in a sense, "acted out" republican ideas of self-rule and autonomy, sometimes even before Enlightenment philosophers had articulated them in essayistic form. Afro-diasporic intellectuals, in this sense, have called attention to the aporias of the Enlightenment's universalistic claims. Exotopically positioned to call the bluff of official ideologies and idealizations, Afro-diasporic people can be seen as proleptic deconstructionists.[27] While black Americans exposed the internal contradictions of the "master-race democracy" (Pierre van den Berghe) installed by the American Revolution, black critics in the French colonies such as Haiti and Guadeloupe, and their allies in France itself, exposed the contradictions of "colonial republicanism."

Enlightenment thinkers wrestled with dilemmas that resonate with those of today, and any deeply historicized reflection on coloniality and race requires dealing with this contradictory heritage. The white-dominated "racial contract" (Charles Mills) was contested from the outset. Free blacks in the United States expressed their antislavery views publicly in the early days of the republic. A good deal of black thought, as Charles Mills put it, "has simply revolved around the insistent demand that whites live up to their own (ostensibly universalist) principles."[28] In 1779, Connecticut slaves petitioned their state's general assembly to assert basic principles of equality, protesting, "We are the Creatures of that God who made of one Blood, and Kindred all the Nations of the Earth; we perceive by our own Reflection that we are endowed with the same Faculties as our masters, and there is nothing that leads us to a Belief, or Suspicion, that we are obliged to serve them, than they us."[29] The overture editorial in *Freedom's Journal*, founded in 1827 as the nation's first black newspaper, pleaded for a basic right of self-representation: "We wish to plead our own cause. Too long others have spoken for us."[30]

While some white Enlightenment thinkers tried to calibrate the hierarchical gradations of black and white intelligence, some black thinkers denounced such theories as cruel and frivolous. Black Americans rebutted Jefferson's claims in *Notes on Virginia* concerning the intellectual inferiority of blacks. The free black Benjamin Banneker, a mathematician and astronomer, sent Jefferson a copy of his own about-to-be published *Almanac* in 1792, along with a letter rebuking Jefferson for underestimating blacks' intelligence. Banneker hoped that Jefferson would "embrace every opportunity, to eradicate that train of absurd and false ideas and opinions, which so generally prevails with respect to us." Your sentiments, he wrote, "are concurrent with mine; which are that one uniform father hath given being to us all; and that he hath not only made us all of one flesh, but that he hath also, without partiality, afforded us all the same sensations and endowed us all with the same faculties."[31] Jefferson responded cordially but rejected Banneker's argument. In a private letter to Joel Barlow, Jefferson claimed that Banneker's *Almanac* "proved nothing."[32] In 1827, the free black David Walker published his *Walker's Appeal . . . to the Colored Citizens of the World*, in which he pointed out the contradiction between the "all men are created equal" clause in the Declaration of Independence and the antiegalitarian racism of Jefferson's *Notes on Virginia.* Confronting Jefferson with the aporias of his own discourse, Walker exhorted Jefferson, "Compare your own language, extracted from your Declaration of Independence, with your cruelties and murders inflicted by your cruel and unmerciful fathers on ourselves and on our fathers, . . . men who have never given your fathers or you the least provocation."[33]

Although slavery stood in glaring contradiction to professed Enlightenment principles, the dominant historiography has traditionally emphasized the ideals and downplayed the contradictions. Many U.S. school textbooks treat slavery as a minor glitch within an overarching narrative of inexorable progress. Presented as the exception to the "rule" of democracy, slavery and segregation have in fact been more the rule, while freedom and equal rights have been more the exception. Although some of the delegates to the Constitutional Convention in 1787 called for the abolition of slavery, they ultimately accepted it as part of a compromise with the South. The Constitution was thus based on a Faustian bargain between southern slaveholding interests and northern economic interests. The founders essentially agreed to disagree about slavery, indirectly legalizing it while also planting Enlightenment-derived language that would gesture toward (and concretely enable) its ultimate demise. In so doing, they merely postponed the Civil War that came seventy years later.[34] In the long term, the privileging of the South led to the southern domination of U.S. politics and to "states' rights" as a euphemism for racial segregation. The dilemmas of the American Revolution have long been breathing hot down American necks, from the shamefaced compromises of the founders, through the racist abolitionism of Abraham Lincoln, up to Nixon's "southern strategy" in the 1960s and 1970s, the Republican "wedge-issues" of the 1980s, and the Bush Jr. sham diversity in the 1990s, presently culminating in the anti-Obama "birther" hysteria in the 21st century.[35]

Over the course of history, Afro-diasporic intellectual resistance consisted in pleading for what should have been taken for granted: black humanity and subjecthood. As Charles Mills puts it, "The most salient feature of the experience of those classified subpersons in [the dominant racial system] will be the need, for their own self-respect, to contest the racial disrespect that they routinely receive. For if they accept it without protest, they are accepting the official definition of themselves as less than human, not really persons."[36] Positionality at the bottom of the social hierarchy sometimes allowed for a dearly bought epistemological advantage, one that enabled African Americans to demystify self-flattering nationalistic narratives. Displaying what we have called, amending Raymond Williams, an "*analogical* structure of feeling," a product of the intersubjective flow of affect among the marginalized, a number of the black protestations of intellectual and moral equality paraphrase Shylock's "Hath not a Jew eyes" speech from *Merchant of Venice*.[37] In 1789 one free black pointed to the limits of Enlightenment universalism by asking, "Has not a negro eyes? Has not a negro hands, organs, dimensions, senses, affections, passions?"[38]

All of U.S. history can be seen as a struggle over the political hermeneutics of the founding documents, rooted in the tensions between the "all men are created equal" of the Declaration of Independence and the slaves-as-property clauses of the Constitution. The abolitionist William Lloyd Garrison, at an Anti-Slavery Society meeting, burned a copy of the Constitution, calling it "a covenant with death and an agreement with hell."[39] It is as if the United States were haunted from the beginning by two competing political models, each concretized in a symbolic edifice, one democratic—embodied in the town hall—and the other tyrannical—embodied in the Big House. The crucial question was which model would exercise greater power.

Antinomies of the Enlightenment

Many of the central historical conflicts and debates in the three countries discussed in this book revolve around this highly ambiguous legacy. How were Enlightenment values such as freedom and equality before the law to be squared with the actual practices of colonialism, genocide, slavery, and imperialism? Did colonialism represent a rupture with Enlightenment ideas, or its clearest expression? Was the Enlightenment the disease or the cure or both at the same time? Is it the Enlightenment or is it decolonization that is unfinished, or are both unfinished in mutually correlated ways? Shying away both from idealization and demonization, we would reject both the view of the Enlightenment as an unsullied fount of reason, science, freedom, and progress along with the contrary view that reduces the Enlightenment to the barbarity of instrumental reason and the annihilation of difference. ("We must free ourselves," Foucault wrote, "from the intellectual blackmail of 'being for or against the Enlightenment.'")[40] As a master code, to use Jamesonian terms, in which competing ideologies fight it out, the Enlightenment is a contradictory project, both in terms of the gap between ideals and practices and in terms of its own discursive aporias. Janus-faced, it forms above all a matrix of dilemmas and conundrums. Rather than provide a single cohesive view of race and difference, the Enlightenment implied the necessity of a debate that continues to this day. It is therefore not a question of a blanket rejection—of throwing out the baby of civil liberties with the bathwater of colonialist racism—but rather of probing the positive as well as the negative dialectics of Enlightenment.

One aspect of radical critique involves an archeological reading of the racist stratum of some Enlightenment thinking. Intellectual historian Louis Sala-Molins, in his 1987 book *The Black Code, or The Calvary of Canaan,* examines the "Code Noir," the French legal code that regulated treatment of the enslaved in the colonies.[41] Drawn up in 1685 under the monarchy, and only definitively eradicated in 1848, the Code legalized slavery in general and authorized torture, mutilation, and even the killing of slaves. The Code provides a template for many of the laws and practices of exception that have characterized life in racial states: the harassment of blacks, a racially rigged justice system, the exclusion of black witnesses in trials (thus prevented from recounting their own experience and history before the law), and the rejection of black economic autonomy. The Code's articles can also be read in an against-the-grain manner as exposing the inherent difficulties in imposing slavery on a recalcitrant population. Article 33, for example, acknowledges slave resistance by calling for the punishment by death of the slave who slaps his master, mistress, or the husband of his mistress or their children.[42] The article that makes any theft, whether by a slave or even by a freed black, punishable by death similarly reveals the frequency of theft as a subversive gesture.

Sala-Molins distinguishes between three distinct ideological positions among the Enlightenment philosophers: (1) the racist advocacy of slavery, (2) the non-racist advocacy of slavery, and (3) racist antislavery. (Denis Diderot—antiracist, antislavery, and anticolonialist—offers a fourth position.) Voltaire (not unlike Abraham Lincoln) was a racist who opposed slavery. Montesquieu, a major influence on French and U.S. political institutions, can be quoted to look either like a staunch abolitionist or like an advocate for slavery. His abstractly grand and rhetorical condemnations of slavery in France were undercut by his defense of slavery "in certain climes" where slavery is "less offensive to reason."[43] Many Enlightenment thinkers deployed "slavery" metaphorically, to apply to the domination of whites by other whites: the "slavery" of common people by the ancien régime or the slavery imposed by the British on colonized Americans. For the revolutionaries, Sala-Molins concludes, they themselves were the slaves.[44]

Rather than speak only of a single European Enlightenment, we should speak of multiple transatlantic Enlightenments. It was in Haiti, for example, that the Enlightenment's contradictions became most explosive and intellectually provocative. Thanks to the densest slave population in the New World, 18th-century Haiti, as supplier of half the world's sugar and coffee, provided one of the keys to French prosperity and power. Colonized Haiti, as historian Laurent Dubois puts it, "was the ground zero of European colonialism in the Americas."[45] For Aimé Césaire, it was there that the "knot" of colonialism was first tied, and then untied.[46] And as "the first independent modern state of the so-called Third World," Michel-Rolph Trouillot points out, "Haiti experienced early all the trials of postcolonial nation-building."[47] Yet the historical and philosophical importance of the Haitian Revolution has been silenced. The textbooks and popular writings that treat the various world revolutions usually bypass the most radical of them all, a revolution at once national, social, and racial. Since the idea of a black-led revolution more thoroughgoingly radical than the American and French Revolutions was more or less unthinkable, the Haitian Revolution was slowly turned into a nonevent.

It was writers of fiction, more than historians, who registered the impact of the Haitian Revolution, as when Herman Melville in *Benito Cereno* named the slave ship, subject to a rebellion, the *St. Dominic*, the contemporaneous term for Haiti. Historians neglected Haiti, even though the United States gained a large part of its territory thanks to the rippling shock effects of the Haitian Revolution, which triggered French fears and thus the Louisiana Purchase. Eric Hobsbawm's Marxist classic *The Age of Revolutions, 1789–1843*, virtually ignores Haiti, even though both France and England lost more soldiers in Haiti than at Waterloo. In France, neither the centennial celebrations of emancipation in 1948 nor the French translation of C. L. R. James's *The Black Jacobins* catalyzed a substantive debate. In the United States, only the reedition of James's book in 1962, the Civil Rights Movement, and the "New Social History" began to reignite a discussion of the monumental legacy of the Haitian Revolution.[48]

The Haitian Revolution demonstrates how the cultural politics of the Enlightenment have to be mapped across a broad Black Atlantic spectrum. Although some Enlightenment philosophers condemned slavery in abstract terms, they seldom engaged its actual brutality. In Haiti, as in much of the Black Atlantic, whippings and even castrations were performed as a disciplinary spectacle. In Haiti, hot peppers were rubbed into open wounds as a form of punishment, and gunpowder was placed in the anus of slaves and then exploded. "Master Race Rule" became intertwined with what might be called "Master Race War." General Leclerc called for a "war of extermination" that would "spare only children under twelve years of age."[49] Germaine de Staël describes what she calls a "horrible" episode: the French, fearful that Haitians might support the rebels, "threw 1800 of them into the sea without any trial."[50] When burning, drowning, and asphyxiation proved counterproductive, General Rochambeau purchased fifteen hundred attack dogs, specialized in devouring blacks, making sure that they were famished and therefore more violent.[51] Yet the sadistic practices of a republican government abroad, and what they suggested about the nonfreedom of the republic's noncitizens, were not necessarily the subject of philosophical treatises in the metropole. In order to synchronize theory with practice, some conservative thinkers devised classificatory rankings that constructed the victimized as representing a different order of human being, unworthy of the rights accorded white Europeans. Although cruelty was common in all forms of colonialism, it became more glaringly anomalous in a situation where French philosophers had articulated principles of equality with uncommon power and scope, thus heightening the contrast between the ideas in all their glory and the abuses in all their horror.

The negative dialectics of Enlightenment republicanism must be conceptualized on the colonial ground outside of Hexagonal France. "Liberté, Égalité, Fraternité" were not to be unloaded off the boats. As one planter put it in 1792, "We did not fetch half a million savage slaves off the coast of Africa to bring them to the colony as French citizens!"[52] The debate about the intellectual and political consequences of the Haitian Revolution rippled all around the Atlantic world. The Creole slaveholding elites of the Americas, for example, were haunted by the specter of the Haitian precedent. In Brazil, the 18th-century Minas revolutionaries who planned a revolt against Portuguese colonialism contemplated abolishing slavery but also worried that independence might bring a "Haitianization" of the situation. (The multiracial "Tailors' Rebellion" in Bahia in 1798, in contrast, consciously emulated the Haitian revolutionary model). While blacks and some whites exulted in the success of the Haitian Revolution, white slave owners and their allies were alarmed by the prospect of similar rebellions in the United States. The arrival of thousands of white French planters seeking refuge in cities such as Philadelphia and Charleston also dramatized the Haitian specter. Jefferson, branding Haiti's leaders "Cannibals of the Terrible Republic," sided with his French partners in crime, the white plantation owners, even though Haitian Revolution leader Jean-Jacques Dessalines had modeled his draft of the Declaration of Haitian Independence on the U.S. declaration penned by Jefferson. The fears of the Haitian contagion were confirmed in January 1811 when a small army of Louisiana's enslaved faced up to a much larger army of slaveholders. Those who worked to build a new Saint Domingue along the Mississippi, as Daniel Rasmussen put its, "did not realize the extent to which they were also creating the conditions that [created] the Haitian revolution."[53]

Supremacist thinking kept dominant white America from seeing the Haitian Revolution as a "sister revolution" like the French one. If a familial metaphor imaged the French and American Revolutions as sisters, the Haitian Revolution was seen at best as a bastard child and at worst as not part of the revolutionary family at all. The refusal of Haiti's entry into the revolutionary Enlightenment metanarrative was especially ironic in light of the fact that Haitians fought with the French troops supporting the Americans at the Battle of Savannah. It was also ironic in light of another debt owed the Haitians. It was their freedom struggle that had exposed France to losses and perils that necessitated the sale of French Louisiana. Historian Henry Adams wrote in 1889 that "prejudice of race alone blinded the American people to the debt they owed to the desperate courage of 500,000 Haytian negroes who would not be enslaved."[54] The refusal of diplomatic relations with Haiti was to last until 1862, when the Union victory made it possible for the abolitionist senator Charles Sumner to open up relations again. The Haitian Revolution brought not only the first black republic/former colony but also the first war of colonial reconquest in the Americas. And just as we can trace out the lines that connect the Faustian bargains of the U.S. Constitution to latter-day segregation and discrimination, so we can trace out the lines that lead from the suppression of Haitian revolutionaries to the neocolonial violence exercised by France and the United States against Haiti in later periods.

Haiti provided stunning exemplars of revolutionary vision for the black diaspora. In Richmond, Virginia, in 1800, the Haitian example inspired a slave named Gabriel to plan an insurrection that involved whites as well as blacks.[55] In Rio de Janeiro in 1805, soldiers of African descent wore medallions honoring Haitian Emperor Desssalines.[56] The transformation of a humiliated slave such as Dessalines into a brilliant general whom C. L. R. James called "one of the towering figures in the political history of the Atlantic world" certainly spoke volumes about the human potential of the enslaved.[57] In response to Napoleon Bonaparte's promise of only a qualified and merely local freedom for blacks, Toussaint Louverture reportedly responded, "It is not a circumstantial liberty conceded only to us that we want. . . . It is the absolute acceptance of the principle that no man, whether born red, black, or white, can be the property of another."[58] Ultimately, the Haitian Revolution sought to dismantle the idea of a racialized republicanism, including within the metropole itself.

If for many Enlightenment thinkers the Haitian Revolution failed to register as an "event," many diasporic Africans recognized its world-historical importance. C. L. R. James's coinage "Black Jacobins" fuses Caribbean blackness with the most radical avatars of the French Revolution. Some insurgents "explicitly phrased their demands in the language of Republican rights."[59] William Wells Brown dreamed that "a Toussaint, a Christophe, a Rigaud, a Clervaux, and a Dessalines may some day appear in the Southern States of this Union, when the revolution of St. Domingo will be reenacted in Southern Carolina or Louisiana."[60] In 1893, Frederick Douglass, the U.S. ambassador to Haiti, declared that the "black sons of Haiti" had "struck for the freedom of every black man in the world."[61] The writing of the period even foreshadowed a kind of "Third Worldism" usually assumed to have emerged only a century and a half later. Anticipating Alfred Sauvy's "Third World" coinage centuries later, the Haitian free colored leader Vincent Ogé compared the demands of the free people of color to those of the Third Estate within the French Revolution. The African American writer Martin Delany, long before the Civil War, similarly called for an alliance of all people of color. In Haiti, Henri Christophe's secretary, the Baron de Vastey, conjured up the vision of "five million black, yellow, and dark-skinned men, spread across the surface of the globe, [laying] claim to the rights and privileges that have been bestowed on them by natural right." J. Michael Dash rightfully calls the statement a "remarkably early appeal to the power of the 'wretched of the earth.'"[62] The Haitian Revolution, in sum, reverberated around the Black Atlantic, becoming a nodal point in the genealogy of what would later be the struggles around colonialism.

White Voices against Imperial Reason

Some white voices were also raised in favor of Haitian revolutionaries and, more generally, in favor of the intellectual agency of people of color. English writers such as Wordsworth, French writers such as Lamartine, and American writers such as the abolitionist John Whittier all wrote tributes to the Haitian Revolution. In France, the Abbé Grégoire defended the full intellectual equality of black people in his *De la Littérature des Nègres, ou Recherches sur Leurs Facultés Intellectuelles* (1808), for which he was congratulated by none other than King Christophe of Haiti—the prototype for Eugene O'Neill's *The Emperor Jones*—who bought fifty copies in London and invited the Abbé to visit the country he ruled. Indeed, the case of the Abbé Grégoire reminds us that a radically antiracist position was "available" among whites at the time of the French and Haitian Revolutions.

For North American revolutionaries, meanwhile, Haiti posed a challenge. What were to be the relations between the first white-dominant republic and the first black republic in the Americas? It is in this historical context that a white North American statesman, Timothy Pickering, deserves mention. A leader of the Salem militia during the Revolutionary War, a general in Washington's army, third secretary of state, and a senator, Pickering denounced slavery in the streets of slave-trading ports as well as in the halls of Congress. In 1783, Pickering drew up a state constitution that called for the "total exclusion of slavery." As a senator from Massachusetts, Pickering protested the double standard that supported the French Revolution but condemned the Haitian Revolution, since the same principles that led to support the French Revolution applied "with tenfold priority and force to the rude blacks of Santo Domingo."[63]

The egalitarian thrust of one wing of the Enlightenment is exemplified not only by the Black Jacobins but also by some white French philosophers. Denis Diderot serves as an eminent example of our point that radically egalitarian thinkers could take clear antiracist and anticolonialist positions and even support the performative enactment of radicalism in slave revolts and revolutions. Scholars in France have been unearthing the anti-imperialist side of Diderot ever since the publication in 1970 of Yves Bénot's *Diderot: From Atheism to Anti-colonialism*.[64] Bénot disinterred Diderot's contribution to anticolonial discourse, often buried because written anonymously or attached to another name in such works as Abbé Raynal's *L'Histoire Philosophique et Politique des Établissements et du Commerce des Européens dans les Deux Indes*. Drawing on Diderot's contributions to Raynal's *Histoire*, along with Diderot's own *Supplément au Voyage de Bougainville*, one is struck by the extremely radical nature of Diderot's ideas. Although Diderot's highly protean and polyvocal texts stage a plurality of voices and discourses, a persistently anticolonial theme clearly emerges from the body of his work.

Here we point to some of the salient features of Diderot's radicalism that make him a forerunner of anticolonial theory, critical race theory, and even critical whiteness studies. First, Diderot sees imperialism as a pan-European phenomenon, refusing to endorse national exceptionalism of any kind, including French. Second, he focuses on the intrinsic violence of imperialism. Third, he stresses the ways that imperialism corrupts Europeans themselves. Fourth, he refuses the Euro-diffusionist notion that holds up Europe as a model to be emulated. Fifth, he critiques the narcissistic epistemologies that misperceive non-Western societies through an ethnocentric grid. Sixth, he refuses the temptation of ranking societies in a hierarchy. Seventh, he sees imperialism as a "mask" that drops away with distance from the metropole and even falls off at the frontier. Finally, and this is perhaps the most subversive feature of his thought, Diderot believes less in colonial or humanitarian reforms conducted by the colonizers than in the right of the colonized to resist by taking arms.

Diderot also engaged colonized subjectivity; in contemporary parlance, he "imagined the other." In passages he contributed to the *Supplément au Voyage de Bougainville*, Diderot warned Tahitians against Europeans armed "with crucifix in one hand and the dagger in the other," who would "force you to accept their customs and opinions."[65] Diderot mocked the "just show up" discovery doctrine by having a wise old Tahitian address the white colonizer as follows: "This country belongs to you! Why? Just because you landed here?" As Sankar Muthu points out in his *Enlightenment against Empire*, Diderot does not base his defense of the "natives" on exotic "noble savage" ontologies but rather on a taken-for-granted cognitive equality between reasoning human beings.[66] What is good for the colonizing goose is good for the colonized gander.

Boomeranging the colonialist metonym of "beast and savage," Diderot advised the African "Hottentots" that the ferocious beasts living in their forests were "less frightening than the monsters of the empire under which you are about to fall." Diderot also scored the hypocrisy of Europe's sentimental moralism in refusing sympathy to the peoples to whom Europe owed its own material advantages:

Europe has been reverberating for a century with the most sublime moral maxims. The fraternity of all men is established in immortal writings.... Even imaginary sufferings provoke tears in the silence of our rooms and more especially at the theatre. It is only the fatal destiny of unfortunate blacks that fails to touch us. They are tyrannized, mutilated, burned, stabbed, and we hear about it coldly and without emotion. The torments of a people to whom we owe our delights never reach our heart.[67]

This passage is rich in anticipations of subsequent anticolonial thinking. In Diderot's "a people to whom we owe our delights," we find the germ of Fanon's idea that "Europe is literally the creation of the Third World." Diderot's denunciation of the hypocrisies inherent in white humanist sentimentality, meanwhile, provide the seeds of "critical whiteness studies." Diderot's critique of the blind spots of Western bourgeois spectatorship not only "imagines the other" but also imagines how Europeans might themselves be imagined through colonized eyes. Diderot thus exemplifies the European intellectual who identifies with the colonized against European colonialism, anticipating later renegades such as the Jean-Paul Sartre of the 1961 preface to Fanon's *The Wretched of the Earth*.[68] In a geopolitics of relationality, Diderot offers what Bénot calls "a utopian vision of a united and fraternal future planet, where violent and unequal relations will give way to pacific relations between all peoples."[69]

Diderot's critique of the imperialisms of his time, according to Muthu, resonates with contemporary critiques of globalization.[70] In book IV (chapter 33) of *L'Histoire des Deux Indes*, Diderot depicts European imperialism or "global commerce" as spreading material and ecological ruin everywhere: "It seems as if from one region to another prosperity has been pursued by an evil genius that speaks our several languages, and which diffuses the same disasters in all parts."[71] Diderot denounces the ravages of imperial-fostered monopolies through a transposition of voice. Transvocalizing, Diderot gives ironic voice to the planetary predators of global commerce and the homogenized world they strive to create in the name of their own greed: "Let my country perish, let the region I command also perish; perish the citizen and the foreigner; perish my associates, provided that I can enrich myself with his spoils. All parts of the universe are alike to me. When I have laid waste, exhausted, and impoverished one country, I shall always find another, to which I can carry my gold."[72] Diderot's words, which could describe the operations of Union Carbide in India or of Chevron in Peru or of Haliburton and Blackwater in Iraq, sound today like anticipatory rumors of later critiques of globalization, whether made by the victim-outsiders or by disenchanted insiders such as Joseph Stiglitz. Despite euphoric promises of a universal prosperity, globalization has produced instead a viral inequality. Trickle-down colonialism morphs into trickle-down imperialism, which morphs into trickle-down globalization, all feeding into a flood of contemporary crisis and pain.

Foreshadowing what Chalmers Johnson later called the "Sorrows of Empire," Diderot also utters a still timely warning for the people of North America:

> [Let] the example of all the nations which have preceded you, and especially that of the mother-country, serve as a lesson to you. Dread the influence of gold, which with luxury, introduces corruption of manners and contempt of the laws. Dread too an unequal distribution of wealth, which yields a small number of rich citizens, and a multitude of citizens plunged in misery. . . . Keep yourselves free from the spirit of conquest. The tranquility of an empire diminishes in proportion to its extent.[73]

These words, in a situation where conservatives such as Niall Ferguson have implored the United States to proudly take on the British imperial mantle, and where "unequal distribution of wealth" is at its zenith, are terribly resonant.

2 A Tale of Three Republics

HAVING SKETCHED OUT the larger Atlantic seascape as the backdrop to our discussion, we now examine the long-term strands of historical connection between the United States, Brazil, and France as three national zones positioned both similarly and differently toward the race/colonial question. Our trilateral focus is on (1) a "paradigmatic" European nation-state—France—an erstwhile imperial power with a defined territory and a common language, a country historically linked to foundational theorizations of nations and nationalism; and (2) a continent-sized colonial-settler "nation of nations"—the United States—the superpower headquarters of an empire of bases classified with the "First World" and the imperial West; and (3) a continent-sized emerging colonial-settler "nation of nations"—Brazil—associated with the "Third World" and the Global South.

How one aligns the nation-states conceptually depends on the principle of pertinence selected. In geopolitical terms, the United States shares with France its status as a Western or First World or Global North country, while Brazil represents an emerging "second-tier" power from the Global South. The double status of Brazil as at once a colonial-settler state and a Third World country is conveyed by the Brazilian coinage *Belindia*, which posits Brazil as a North-South amalgam of Belgium and India. In another sense, however, the diverse geopolitical positionings mask a historical substratum shared by all three nation-states, that is, their colonizing relation to the indigenous peoples as part of the Red Atlantic; their common shaping by the triangular slave trade as part of the Black Atlantic; and their shared pattern of racial hegemony in the "White Atlantic."[1] Thus, the three nation-states represent distinct conjunctural formations within intercolonial oceanic configurations.[2]

All three nation-states partake of a multiculturality forged in the cauldron of the colonial process. The United States and Brazil, the Americas' two largest "multi-nation-states" (Will Kymlicka), orchestrate at least three major constellations of groups, all internally differentiated: (1) those who were *already here* in the Americas (indigenous peoples in all their variety and heterogeneity), (2) those who were *forced to come* (largely enslaved Africans but also indentured Europeans and Asians), and (3) those who *chose to come* (conquistadores, colonizers, immigrants).[3] France, meanwhile, is also multicultural, first, in terms of internal differentiations based on region, ethnicity, or religion (Celts, Franks, Gauls, Basques, Bretons, Huguenots, Jews, Roma); and, second, through its long colonial entanglements in Asia, Africa, and the Americas. In this sense, we would distinguish between "colonial multiculturality," a formulation in which the noun calls attention to the de facto multicultural demographic character of contemporary nation-states, and its converse phrase "multicultural coloniality," which calls attention to the colonial formations that generated this very diversity. A certain oscillation between these emphases lies in the background of some of the debates about the political valence of multiculturalism, which has, at times, been instrumentalized for Eurocentric or national-exceptionalist ends.

Deeply intermeshed from their very beginnings, the United States, France, and Brazil have been shaped by asymmetrical interactions not simply with one another but also with indigenous America, with Africa, and with the Afro-diaspora. Within a veritable daisy chain of cultural intercourse, the United States is "in" Brazil, which is "in" France, which is "in" the United States. Indeed, the interconnections begin with the speculative "might have beens" of history, including the fact that both Brazil and the United States might have been French. If the Portuguese had not expelled "France Antartique" in the 16th century, Brazilians might be speaking French today. And if France had not ceded land to the United States in the 1803 Louisiana Purchase, French might have become the official language of the American Southwest. Although American Francophobes harp on French "ingratitude" for the U.S. liberation of France, the French might remind Americans of the gratitude owed them for having saved the American Revolution itself, when French help prevented George Washington and his men from losing the War of Independence. If France saved the United States in its symbolic infancy, the United States saved France in its adulthood.

While the historical affinities between France and the United States are widely accepted, the parallels between the United States and Brazil are generally known only to specialists. As the two most populous settler states in the Americas, the two histories run on parallel tracks. Both "began" their official histories as European colonies: São Vicente, the first Portuguese settlement, was founded in 1532, and Jamestown was founded almost a century later in 1607. In both countries, the colonizers—called pioneers in the United States and *bandeirantes* in Brazil—initiated a process that reduced an indigenous population of many millions to hundreds of thousands. Massive extermination, theft of land, and the destruction of communal societies took place in both sites, but the modalities of domination, and their discursive filtration, differed dramatically. The U.S. legal system treated indigenous people as "aliens" and "domestic dependent nations" within a regime of very limited sovereignty, while the Brazilian legal system refused to recognize any indigenous sovereignty and instead adopted the "Indians" as legal "orphans." Although the discursive, ideological, and political constructions were distinct in the two countries, the result—indigenous dispossessions—was similar.

The United States and Brazil came to form the two largest slave societies of modern times, until slavery was abolished in the United States with the 1863 Emancipation Proclamation and in Brazil in 1888 with the "Golden Law." Both countries received similar waves of immigration from all over the world, ultimately forming multiracial-colonial societies with substantial indigenous, African, Italian, German, Japanese, Slavic, Syro-Lebanese, and Jewish (Ashkenazi and Sephardi) populations and cultures. Despite widely trumpeted cultural contrasts, the two nations constitute "cousins" with similar historical and ethnic formations, but where a hierarchically structured kinship has been obscured by nationalist and imperialist assumptions. All three zones form part of a continuum of Atlantic republicanism. The French and U.S. republics were called "*soeurs*" (sisters), while the Brazilian Republican Constitution was inspired by both the French and the American models. At this point in history, all three countries are constitutional republics. Unlike the United States, which has retained the same Constitution since 1787, France has lived through five republics and five constitutions. While the American Revolution was a national revolt against one colonial empire and the founding of another, the French Revolution was a social overturning of the ancien régime and the continuation of an empire.

Whereas both France and the United States are products of violent revolutions, Brazil achieved independence without bloodshed, when the son of the Portuguese monarch decided to stay in Brazil. France was not a neutral bystander in these events, however, since it was the Napoleonic invasion of Iberia that triggered the removal of the Portuguese court to Brazil. Brazil's 1824 Imperial Constitution borrowed and even translated parts of the 1789 French Declaration of the Rights of Man and the Citizen.[4] Brazil followed the republican course relatively late, since it was first a colony, then a monarchy and an empire, and finally a republic, founded in 1889 and lasting until 1930. Highly conscious of U.S. and French precedents, the framers of the Brazilian constitution drew on elements of U.S.-style federalism, presidentialism, bicameral legislature, and separation of church and state, while avoiding the express principles of universal equality elaborated in both the French and the American constitutions.

Many of the central conflicts in the histories of all three nation-states revolve around the ambiguous heritage of Enlightenment republicanism. All three stressed the sanctity of the Lockean triad of life, liberty, and property. But the innocent-sounding word "property" had terrible implications for Blacks—for whom it meant their reduction to the status of chattel—and for Reds—for whom it invalidated the notion of communal property. Nothing is more revelatory of these contradictions than the way the three nation-states dealt with slavery. In the United States, some of the delegates to the 1787 Constitutional Convention called for abolition but ultimately accepted slavery as part of a compromise favoring a stronger federal government. Brazil abolished slavery in 1888 but did little to compensate or employ the newly freed blacks, preferring to invite European immigrants as the ethnically approved labor force. France, meanwhile, abolished slavery during the Revolution but reestablished it in the colonies, ending it only in 1848.

At the core of our tale of three republics is the contradiction between liberal Enlightenment principles of political democracy and social equality and the illiberal legacies of discrepant citizenship. James Holston usefully schematizes the three-way variations in citizenship: Brazil has been "inclusively inegalitarian" (i.e., everyone belongs to the nation but in an unequal way), the United States has been "restrictively egalitarian" (i.e., the principles are egalitarian, but entire groups were excluded from the benefits of these principles), and France has been "inclusively egalitarian" (i.e., every citizen belongs to the nation, and the principles are egalitarian).[5] There were, we would add, exceptions to France's "inclusive egalitarianism": Jews were granted citizenship but discriminated against in a "restrictively egalitarian" practice. Meanwhile, people of color in the French colonies, given their status as colonial subjects, belonged to the "inclusively inegalitarian" category.

For Brazil and the United States, colonization, slavery, and racialization were constitutive and "internal" to the newly invented nation; for Hexagonal France, in contrast, they were seen as "external," not requiring a shift in the conception of the nation. The externalization of "race" delinked Enlightened France from its "overseas" extensions. Yet French history has hardly been free of institutional and ideological racism. Philosopher/political scientist Achille Mbembe speaks of four eras of French racism: (1) the long ancien régime period that includes the slave trade, the Code Noir, and anti-Semitism; (2) the colonial period of the Native Codes and assimilationist "selective inclusion"; (3) the postwar state racism of the laws of exception for African immigrants in France; and (4) the globalized era of the "alien" as phantom enemy and trigger for the *ressentiment* of the supposedly silent majorities representing *la France profonde*.[6]

While contemporary U.S. conservatives dismiss slavery as existing only way "back then," French conservatives have classically downplayed colonialism and slavery as not only "back then" but also "far away" and "over there." Yet the 20th-century colonial war in Algeria was not distant in time or space; it was recent and felt intimately in France because Algeria, as an aggregation of three administrative departments, formed an integral part of France. Yet Algerian Muslims were disenfranchised by the "Code Indigene" and, in France itself, were subject to curfews and police brutality and a segregated existence in *bidonvilles*. In a sense, Algeria formed a French counterpart to the American South. Azouz Begag, France's first cabinet minister of North African origin, claims that France in

Algeria "practiced forms of institutional racism similar in spirit to segregation in the American South."[7]

The supposedly race-blind *République*, despite its professed universalism, did inscribe a normative (white) identity. The French constitution declares itself the product of a specific people: "The French people has adopted . . . , The French people solemnly proclaims . . . ," and so forth. French constitutional citizenship implies entry into a primordially unified community, as if "the French people" were a homogeneous ethnic group that collectively decided to adhere to democratic principles.[8] The United States, in contrast, despite the overriding reality of colonial/racial hierarchy, did not officially define itself in linguistically or even ethnically specific terms. Thus, a certain theoretical flexibility, along with a high potential for antistate libertarian individualism, was built into the conceptualization of the republic. One result is a different relation to the very concept of the nation-state. In France, the already existing nation—the French people—created the new state, while in the United States, the new state created the nation, as one very heterogeneous people (the Americans) dissolved their formal-legal links to another people (the British).

At the same time, unlike the French constitution, the U.S. Constitution did encode race through specific laws tacitly premised on the enslavement of blacks and the dispossession of Native Americans. The very names of the United States and Brazil, moreover, indirectly betoken ethnicity. "America" gives a European imprimatur to an indigenous continent by paying homage to the Italian explorer Amerigo Vespucci, while "Brazil" replicates the name, by some accounts, of a mythical island (near Ireland) that subsequently became associated with the "Brazil wood" sought after by European colonists. Like the Ivory Coast, Brazil was named after an export product, a prefiguration of its long-term role as provider of raw materials within the racialized/gendered division of labor typical of the world economic system.

All three countries have a special relation to the "universal." As what Bourdieu calls "the two imperialisms of the Universal," the French and American republics have historically proposed themselves as models for all peoples. Brazil, meanwhile, has also been seen as a universal model, but in two very different senses of the word "universal." In the late 1940s and 1950s, in the wake of Nazism and the Shoah, Brazil was seen as a positively universal model of racial tolerance, an alternative to fascist racism and to South African and U.S. apartheid. In subsequent decades, however, Brazil began to be interpreted as a negative universal model, crystallized in the term "Brazilianization" as summoning up associations with economic inequality, social segregation, drug-related violence, and precarious work relations. If in the 1950s Brazil was seen as universal panacea, in the 1990s it began to be seen as the harbinger of a universal threat, the fearsome telos toward which the entire world might be heading. Figures as diverse as the Americans Michael Lind and Mike Davis, the Frenchman Alain Lipietz, the German Ulrich Beck, and the Indian Ravi Sundaram have all spoken of Brazilianization as the imminent condition of the entire world as a "planet of slums" (Davis).[9] This quasi-Orientalist singling out of Brazil carried the unfortunate implication that there were no slums in the Global North and that the Global North was not implicated in the immiseration of the Global South. The word "Brazilianization," in Paulo Arantes's words, suggests a "contamination" of the organic nucleus of the Global North by the "new barbarians of its own internal peripheries, [so that] who spread the fracture comes to be seen as the separation between those who are capable, or incapable, of controlling their own impulses."[10] In this sense, the Brazilianization trope constitutes an updated deterritorialized version of the colonialist demonization of "tropical climes." Its negative connotations are especially inappropriate at a time when Brazil is becoming more equal and democratic, while the United States and France are arguably becoming less equal.

Franco-Brazilian Liaisons

Our discussion of the race/coloniality debates takes place against the backdrop of the longstanding intellectual conversations among the three zones. French writers, for example, not only have influenced both the United States and Brazil but also became major theorists of their national character and identity. French intellectuals have found both countries, to coin a phrase, "good to think with." The French "thinking" of the United States goes back to Crèvecoeur in the 18th century, through to Tocqueville's *Democracy in America* in the 19th century, on to Jean Baudrillard and Emmanuel Todd in the 20th century. The French "thinking" of Brazil, and especially of indigenous Brazil, meanwhile, goes back even further, to Jean de Léry in the 16th century, and continues through to Lévi-Strauss and Pierre Clastres in the 20th century and Jean-Christophe Rufin in the 21st century, resulting in an extraordinarily rich vein of dialogue between French philosophers and the Brazilian indigene.

It was the early French attempts to colonize Brazil, interestingly, that first catalyzed Brazilian nationalism. Through much of the 16th and 17th centuries, French warships tried to dominate the littoral from Guiana down to the northern side of the Amazon but eventually retreated in the face of what one might call the proto-Brazilian resistance. Yet the French military failure indirectly opened the way for a strong French cultural influence. The relationship was freed of the *ressentiment* that characterized Brazil's relationship with Portugal. The fact that Brazil was not a colony of France facilitated a view of France as the revolutionary homeland of liberty rather than as an imperial power. As a voluntary colony, Brazil was not commandeered by the menacing metal of French arms or by economic blackmail; rather, the Euro-Brazilian elite was persuaded by the seductive *rayonnement* of French culture and ideas.

The strong political/intellectual French influence on the Brazilian elite became evident already in the 18th century and continues to this day. The "Inconfidência Mineira," the abortive 1789 revolt in Minas Gerais against Portuguese colonialism, was led by Brazilians who had absorbed French Enlightenment ideas in Europe, whether indirectly, through studies in Coimbra, Portugal, or directly, in Montpellier, France. The Brazilian revolutionaries compartmentalized the *douce France* of literate culture and *égalité* from French participation in the slave trade, colonialism, and imperialism. It was thus no accident that it was not white Brazilian intellectuals but rather the direct objects of French imperialism—Haitian revolutionaries in the 18th and 19th centuries and black Francophone intellectuals in the 20th century—who demystified French hypocrisies.

In the realm of literature, virtually every French literary trend—realism, naturalism, symbolism, Parnassianism, surrealism—had its Brazilian "translation." The romantic Indianist movement in Brazil, for example, was partially inspired by Chateaubriand and Ferdinand Denis. Some Brazilian intellectuals even wrote in French. The abolitionist Joaquim Nabuco wrote poems in French ("Amour et Dieu," 1874) and a play (*L'Option*) about Alsace-Lorraine. Indianist José de Alencar's own death was mourned in French verses in Brazilian newspapers: "Avant l'heure frappé par l'aveugle barbare."[11] Even in the modernist period, Manuel Bandeira wrote his first poems in French, and Brazilian elites tended to be fluent in French up through the late 1950s.

Other key moments of French influence in Brazil include (1) the architectural, urbanistic, and painterly impact of the 19th-century French artistic "missions"; (2) the political/philosophical influence of the "positivism" of Auguste Comte; (3) the artistic influence of French avant-garde movements such as surrealism on 1920s Brazilian modernism; (4) the academic impact of the French mission to the University of São Paulo in the 1930s; and (5) the postwar impact of French intellectual trends, from existentialism to poststructuralism. It was precisely the lack of a strong political/economic relationship, and the lack of a major French demographic presence in Brazil, that opened the way for phantasmatic projections on both sides. The Brazilian elite's fascination with French culture served many purposes. Since the Westernizing elite had traditionally seen itself as a civilizing force enlightening the dark-skinned masses, its relationship to France facilitated a connection to a prestigious (non-Iberian) European cultural tradition. At the same time, the elite adopted a symbolically indigenous identity, within what Pierre Rivas calls "a phantasmagoric . . . family romance in which the figure of the real father is denied and expanded into a generic concept, more cultural than genetic, which indirectly reveals the figure of the French Father/Mother."[12]

Some French writers reciprocated Brazilian Francophilia with Brazilophile exoticism. Victor Hugo exalted Brazil as a Europe in the making: "You are the spring / While I am winter. . . . / You will be Europe, the day after next."[13] Comte Arthur de Gobineau in his travel accounts described the 19th-century educated Brazilian as "a man who dreams of living in Paris."[14] (A century later, Paulo Emílio Salles Gomes evoked this Hamlet-like alienation of Brazilian intellectuals by speaking of the "painful construction of ourselves within the rarefied dialectic of not being and being other.")[15] French commentary on Brazil has been very diverse and in many ways contradictory. In ideological terms, French intellectuals have both advanced and contested racist currents of thought. Gobineau, author of the influential racist tract *Essai sur L'inégalité des Races*, called for the Europeanizing and whitening of Brazil as an antidote to what he called "the disagreeable elements within [Brazil's] ethnic constitution."[16] In his personal correspondence, Gobineau expressed aesthetic repulsion toward that racially mixed Brazilian family that made it "very disagreeable to look at."[17] Yet for every racist ideologue such as Gobineau or Gustave le Bon, scholars can cite an antiracist such as Montaigne (in an early period) and Roger Bastide and Pierre Clastres (in a later period).

Much of the doctrinaire racism in Brazilian intellectual history is concentrated in the period of the First Republic, and its sources were not only French but also British, North American, and, derivatively, Brazilian. U.S. Brazilianist Thomas Skidmore discerns three sources of racialist thought in Brazil: (1) the American "polygenic" school, which saw the races as distinct "species"; (2) the historical school of Gobineau, which saw race mixing as a source of "degeneracy"; and (3) Social Darwinism, the survival-of-the-fittest doctrine popularized by such writers as Gustave Le Bon and Lapouge. Part of a much wider and international eugenicist current strongly developed in Great Britain, the United States, and Germany, some French thinkers, like some Brazilian thinkers, condemned the African element in Brazil as the source of the country's "backwardness."[18]

If some French visitors to Brazil never transcended a racially tinted elitism, others transformed their Brazilian experience into a trampoline for a cognitive leap. In the time of France Antartique, as we saw earlier, Montaigne rethought European social hierarchies through a Tupinamba prism, resulting in a profound critique of dominant views of religion, power, and social hierarchy. Centuries later, anthropologists such as Lévi-Strauss and Clastres respectfully absorbed and illuminated indigenous knowledge and disseminated it throughout the world. Brazilians, for their part, returned the compliment of French fascination by endlessly indigenizing, as it were, French ideas. The 1920s "anthropophagic" modernists, for example, devoured French avant-gardism but went beyond it, with Oswald de Andrade whimsically referring to surrealism as the best "pre-anthropophagic" movement.[19]

In the 1930s, the founders of the University of São Paulo decided to strengthen that institution's intellectual quality by inviting prestigious French intellectuals to occupy key positions. The result was a series (in 1934, 1935, and 1938) of French "missions"—the word itself recalls the quasi-religious *mission civilisatrice* aspect of such projects—aimed at shaping modern education in Brazil. France would thus consolidate its cultural influence, and Brazil would modernize its university. Some of the invited scholars, such as Lévi-Strauss in anthropology and Fernand Braudel in history, were then on the cusp of becoming world renowned. In *Tristes Tropiques*, Lévi-Strauss offered an affectionate picture of the Nambiquara and the Bororos and an ironic portrait of the Europeanized São Paulo elite. A standard *boutade* among São Paulo academics had it that Lévi-Strauss saw them, and not the Indians, as the real "savages." As an anti-Eurocentric European, Lévi-Strauss mocked the elite's passion for the latest Parisian intellectual fashions.[20] Despite the long tradition of quasi-official Indianist sentimentality, the French ethnographer was surprised by the *aversion* of the Brazilian elites toward "*os indios.*" The Brazilian ambassador in Paris "reassured" Lévi-Strauss that Indians no longer existed, this only a decade or two after a time (1918) when maps of the state of São Paulo indicated that two-thirds of the territory was inhabited only by Indians.

Lévi-Strauss constitutes a clear case of circum-Atlantic connectivities among France, the United States, Brazil, and indigenous America. In the wake of his work in Brazil in the 1930s, Lévi-Strauss spent the World War II years in New York, researching the indigenous cultures of the Americas at the New York Public Library. There he was strongly influenced by the German-Jewish American anthropologist Franz Boas, whom Lévi-Strauss considered a "master builder" of modern anthropology and the originator of the modern critique of racism.[21] As a methodological maverick, Lévi-Strauss synthesized French ethnology with American sociology and anthropology, while also learning from Brazilian natives as experts, so to speak, on themselves. At the same time, he brought the outsider perspective of a Jew forced into exile, for whom the gregarious ways of the indigenous Americans offered a humane alternative to what John Murray Cuddihy calls the "ordeals of [European] civility."[22]

The anthropologist/sociologist Roger Bastide (1898–1974) constitutes a stellar example of a French intellectual transformed by his Brazilian *séjour*. As professor of sociology at the University of São Paulo, Bastide ultimately created an impressive corpus of some thirty books on an astonishingly wide variety of topics, including psychoanalysis (*A Psicanálise do Cafuné*, 1941), literature (*A Poesia Afro-Brasileira*, 1943), mysticism (*Imagems do Nordeste Místico em Branco e Preto*, 1945), racial relations (*Relações entre Negros e Brancos em São Paulo*, 1955), folklore (*Sociologia do Folclore Brasileiro*, 1959), and Afro-Brazilian religions (*As Religiões*

Africanas no Brasil, 1971). As a liminal figure working on the borders between anthropology, sociology, psychology, literature, and history, Bastide transgressed the frontiers not only between disciplines but also between the "high" and "low" arts, between the sacred and the profane, and between the sciences and the humanities. A comparatist, Bastide pointed to the paradoxes of Brazil's relative tolerance; the very rigidity of the racial/social structure in the United States, he argued, fostered the creation of a black poetry reflective of the "genius of the race," while the sinuosity of the Brazilian social system encouraged black intellectuals and artists to identify with the white elite, thus undermining specifically black cultural creativity.

Bastide broke with the dominant views of African-derived religions as pathological and irrational. Stressing the intellectual, political, and cultural agency of Afro-diasporic blacks, Bastide saw religious syncretism, for example, not as a naive confusion of incongruous entities but rather as an exercise in spiritual/ intellectual agency based on the comparative translation of mystical equivalencies.[23] The dominant monotheistic as well as the Euro-secular view, in contrast, had seen such spirit religions as superstitions rather than as legitimate belief systems. A patronizing vocabulary—"animism," "fetishism," "ancestor worship," "cult," and so forth—embedded a superimposed set of hierarchies—written over oral, monotheistic over polytheistic, science over magic, mind over body—that undermined the legitimacy of African religions. Seen as overly corporeal and ludic (danced) rather than abstractly and austerely theological, African spirit religions were symbolized as wildly gregarious, drowning the bounded individual personality in the collective and transpersonal fusions of trance.[24]

Bastide's affirmation of Afro-Brazilian spiritual values formed a clear break with the antecedent views of those French and American visitors inclined to reject West African religions. Writing in the 1950s, French novelist Henri Troyat mingled a whole series of racist tropes in his nauseated description of a Candomblé priestess as a "prehistoric creature, a veritable mountain of black flesh [who] despite her corpulence . . . glided, jumped, and pirouetted with the lightness of a rubber balloon . . . [whose] wet skin made me want to vomit."[25] Bastide's recuperative project, in contrast, was to show that these religions "embraced a cosmology, a psychology, and a theodicy" reflective of an "erudite and deeply cultivated African thought."[26] Candomblé helped Bastide see the limitations of Enlightenment rationalism. Three centuries of Cartesianism, he acknowledged, had blinded him to the complex and subtle philosophy of African religion:

> I learned then, when I entered the Candomblé terreiro, that I had to let myself
> be penetrated by a culture that was not mine. Scientific research required that
> I myself go through the ritual of initiation. I will be grateful till the day I die to
> those Candomblé priestesses like Joana de Ogum and Joana de Iemanja who

regarded me as their own little white child, who understood my desire for new cultural "food,"—and who sensed, with that superior gift of intuition so typical of them—that my Cartesian thought could not handle these new elements, not in terms of purely scientific relations, which remain at the surface of things, but that they had to metamorphose into vital experiences, the only source of real understanding. . . . After this, the knowledge of Africa has always had for me a taste of maternal love, the scent of these kneading black hands, this infinite patience in giving the gift of one's knowledge. . . . The question is: Have I been faithful to them?[27]

Bastide's sense of identification plunged him deep into the Candomblé ethos, to the point of becoming himself initiated as a son of Xango.

Had Bastide not published primarily in Portuguese, he might have become a key figure in the "seismic shift" in scholarship. Long before the advocates of "reflexive anthropology," Bastide developed an "anti-ethnocentric method" based on "transforming ourselves into that which we are studying. . . . As in the act of love, we transcend our own personality in order to join ourselves to the soul linked to what is being studied."[28] Here ethnography becomes the trigger for a psychic transformation, a kind of methodological trance, that recalls the exchange of identities literally "at play" in Candomblé, where male can become female, the adult a child, and so forth. In a form of ecstatic cognition, Bastide practiced cultural "immersion," even while maintaining a certain reflexivity about his own methods and limitations. He believed, as it were, in both identification and exotopy, both in the trance itself and in the distanced analysis performed subsequently.

Every religion arguably opens up a specific aesthetic field favoring some arts and senses over others. The iconoclastic suspicion toward the representational image typical of Judaism, Islam, Protestant Christianity, and neo-Platonism, for example, favors the scriptural and the auditory over sensuous visual representation. "Religions of the book" tend to be theological at their core; the arts come later as illustrations or adumbrations of the sacred word. In the case of an Afro-Brazilian religion such as Candomblé, in contrast, the arts form the energetic matrix of the religion. As a multiart practice, Candomblé engages music, dance, poetry, narrative, costume, and cuisine not as decorative extras but as an integral part of the religion as a synaesthetic system of belief. In a faith in which "soul claps its hands and sings," the faithful are also performers, the mediums and the priests and priestesses above all but also the community as the addressee for whose benefit the ritual is performed. Since there is little abstract doctrine per se, the religion exercises its power through artistic expression and performance. Without the drums (or at least percussion), the spirits cannot "descend," and without dance, the orixas cannot be incarnated.

It would be fascinating, in this sense, to juxtapose Bastide's anthropological study of trance with three contemporaneous artists who combined anticolonial left politics with a deep affection for West African trance religions: first, Maya Deren, the American avant-garde filmmaker who participated in and filmed the rituals of Haitian Vodoun and wrote a classic book (*The Divine Horseman*) on the subject; second, the French ethnographic surrealist Jean Rouch, who not only filmed African trance religions but also coined the term "cine-trance"; and third, Brazilian filmmaker Glauber Rocha, who filmed Candomblé trance in *Barravento*—the title refers to the stormy vertigo just prior to the onset of possession—but also referenced trance in the very title of his *Terra em Transe*.[29] For Rouch, the trance phenomenon was an essential engine both of spirituality and of artistic creation. Theatrical directors such as Julian Beck, Peter Brook, and Jerzy Grotowski, he pointed out, all used ethnographic information about possession in their training of actors.[30] In *Les Maîtres Fous*, Rouch filmed trance rituals that functioned metaphorically as a coded mockery of the British colonial authorities. At the same time, Rouch's metaphor of "cine-trance" evoked a sense of danced and kinetic alignment between the camera-carrying filmmaker and the possessed subject of religious ecstasy.[31]

Like these artists and like James Clifford's "ethnographic surrealists," Bastide was extraordinarily sensitive to the aesthetic ramifications of African religion, to its dynamic mise-en-scène and its synesthetic embrace of the various senses, whereby the religion "penetrates through hearing, through the nose and the mouth, touches the stomach, imposing its rhythm on body and mind."[32] Here Bastide was clearly influenced by the Franco-Africanism of ethnographic surrealists Michel Leiris and Marcel Griaule. In his *O Candomblé da Bahia: Rito Nagô* (1958), Bastide found echoes of what Griaule found with the Dogon: "the duality of the primordial deity, the disorder introduced into the world due to the loss of this duality and the distinction of the sexes, the importance of numbers."[33] At the same time, again like the ethnographic surrealists, Bastide was linked to artistic modernism, in that the Brazilian modernists were his friends and in that he analyzed their work sympathetically in his texts.

Bastide exemplifies a polyperspectival, parallax view that illuminates both French and Brazilian culture. Rather than see himself as a disseminator of French culture in Brazil, Bastide saw himself as a student/scholar learning about and from Brazil. Returning to France in the 1950s, Bastide became a kind of cultural ambassador. In his "Lettres Brésiliennes" column for *Mercure de France*, Bastide reversed the currents of neocolonial intellectual exchange by keeping French readers abreast of Brazilian literary events. Bastide shows that a "First World" intellectual could identify with Brazil's subalternized populations, in an "excess seeing" that mingles distance with intimacy, exotopy with empathy. And while Bastide certainly impacted Brazilian intellectual life, that Brazilian life transformed his thinking as well through a reciprocal process of interfecundation.

Since France was never a key political or economic interlocutor of Brazil, its relationship with Brazil has always been less material and more symbolic than Brazil's relationship with the United States. French influence in Brazil cannot be reduced to an epiphenomenon of cultural neocolonialism, however, first because Brazil was never a colony or even a neocolony of France and second because France became a cultural mentor for much of the world. At the same time, the Brazil-France relationship has also been asymmetrical in its way. "In this love story," as Leyla Perrone-Moisés puts it, "Brazil was always the more passionately in love of the two partners, often standing in amazed admiration before the undeniable superiority of the beloved object."[34] Along with its rapturous interludes, the Franco-Brazilian love affair also had its moments of coldness and even rejection, within a double movement of attraction and repulsion linked to Brazil's anxieties about its own identity and the possibilities of alternative alliances and coalitions.

Within a regime of complementary needs and desires, France played the role of the refined intellectual superego for Brazil, while Brazil offered the raw material of the carnivalesque id, a view summed up in de Gaulle's (perhaps apocryphal) dismissal of Brazil as not a "*pays sérieux.*" Brazilian intellectual historian Mario Carelli sums up the relationship as follows: "For the French, Brazil retains a bit of dream and Dionysianism; for Brazilians, France remains linked to the principal stages of its own construction as a modern state."[35] While the French image of Brazil was relatively exoticized, the Brazilian view of French influence was that it was seminal and substantive. The Franco-Brazilian relationship defies generalization, however. If writers such as Bastide and Clastres analyzed Brazil in terms that Brazilians themselves found stimulating, other French writers saw Brazil through a paternalistic lens. The relation has often been one of mutual, affectionate consumption, but where the *rapports de force* have historically favored the more empowered European country. Now that France exercises less global influence, while Brazil is an emerging BRIC power with an international voice, the earlier asymmetries have diminished considerably. (These mutating geopolitical and intellectual dynamics form the background, as we shall see, of many contemporary polemics.)

Brazilo-American *Encontros*

If the Franco-Brazilian intellectual dialogue dates back to the 16th century, the Brazilian-American connection begins a century later in New Amsterdam, then a multifaith, multiracial, and polyglot island speaking diverse indigenous, African, and European languages. New Amsterdam received Jews, Muslims, and some enslaved Mdumbu and Kongo people who came to North America via Africa and Brazil. The word "Negro" comes to English via Portuguese, as does "pickaninny" (for black child, from Portuguese *pequininho*). Some of the Africans in New Amsterdam arrived with the Dutch expelled from Recife. The first "Afro-Brazilians," to adopt an anachronistic term, arrived in the city in chains. Their names—Paulo d'Angola, Simon Congo, Antonio Portugues—indexed their conjoined African and Portuguese origins. Pressed by a food shortage, Governor Willem Kieft liberated the slaves and granted them farmland, situated in an area that would now include Washington Square, Soho, and our own New York University. The site of S.O.B.'s (Sounds of Brazil), where Afro-Brazilian musicians such as Gilberto Gil and Jorge Ben Jor have played, was then the farmland of Simon Congo, suggesting well over four centuries of Afro-Brazilian presence in the city.

A century later, the leaders of the Inconfidência Mineira revolt against Portuguese rule in 1788–1789 were inspired both by the French and American Revolutions. According to historian Kenneth Maxwell, Jefferson sympathized with the Brazilian rebels, and the Monroe Doctrine (1823) was first formulated in conversations between Jefferson and Brazilian representatives in Washington. The doctrine initiated, in principle if clearly not in fact, a hemispheric system in which the two great nations of the Americas would act in concert. In 1817, Henry M. Brackenridge was perhaps the first U.S. writer to suggest the need for a systematic comparison. While recognizing that he was comparing a "young giant" to a "mature dwarf"—Brazil was a colony at the time—Brackenridge emphasized that it was necessary also to imagine what the two countries would become in the future:

> The only empires that one can compare to Brazil, in terms of size, are those of China, Russia, and the United States, and even though Brazil is today the smallest in terms of population, the day will come when it will be the largest.... Although it might seem premature at this time to compare Brazil and the United States, the moment will come when such a comparison will seem natural, even inevitable.[36]

Contrasting the stormy disunity of the Spanish-speaking nations in Latin America with "the unified and indivisible" Brazilian nation, Brackenridge concludes that, "given the vast capacities and resources of Brazil, it is not to be a visionary to foresee that this [Brazilian] empire is destined to rival our own."[37]

As a kind of palimpsestic "postcolony," Brazil has been shaped by diverse national forces, including Portugal as the (ever-declining) colonial progenitor, France as the preeminent intellectual mentor, and Great Britain and later the United States as imperious trading partners. Despite political tensions, deep historical affinities prodded Brazil to perceive itself as parallel, if only in a distant, mediated, and often resentful way, to the United States. Apart from their shared status as breakaway slaveholding settler states, the two countries were positioned, as Thomas Skidmore points out, in similar ways in relation to other powers.

First, both countries butted up, on their frontiers, against a common rival: the Spanish. Second, Brazil needed a strong ally to assure its geopolitical advantage in South America, especially against Argentina. Third, despite cultural differences, Brazilians sensed an affinity with the United States in terms of certain shared traits: continental size, abundant resources, and polyethnic and immigrant populations.[38] Both countries see themselves as *abençoado por Deus* (blessed by God) with a unique historical role to play, with their own versions of national exceptionalism, the "armed and dangerous" U.S. variety and the "exceptionalism-lite" God-is-Brazilian variety in Brazil.

The question posed in both Brazil and the United States, in the 19th century at least, was how to create a national culture in "adverse" conditions, with and against an often haughty Europe that scorned its own offspring as illegitimate spawn. The question of whether the Americas could produce serious art was itself a symptom of a cultural colonization that saw the Americas as constituted by lacunae: in the United States, the lack of an aristocracy, and in Brazil, the concrete absence of viable cultural institutions and of a literate public. The literary histories of both countries were marked by parallel struggles for cultural independence from Europe. Emerson's "American Scholar" address in 1836, which Oliver Wendell Holmes called "our intellectual Declaration of Independence," came just one year after a similar declaration by Brazilian poet Gonçalves de Magalhães.

Relations between the two countries soured with the Monroe Doctrine, the U.S. conquest of Mexico, U.S. meddling in the Amazon, and later Teddy Roosevelt's "Gunboat Diplomacy," all part of an imperialist policy that saw Latin America as a despised "backyard" and "sphere of influence." The Good Neighbor policy in the 1930s and early 1940s tried to undo some of the damage created by this arrogance, preparing the way for what was to become a veritable explosion of cultural exchange between Brazil and the United States in the postwar period. Brazilians generally became more familiar with the United States due to the spread of American popular culture, a process that had begun already in the 19th century. A gradual shift away from the Parisian orientation led some elite Brazilian cultural institutions to model themselves on U.S. institutions. Brazil's Museum of Modern Art, for example, was modeled on the Museum of Modern Art in New York.

It was in the postwar period that many prestigious Brazilian writers/scholars—novelists (Erico Verissimo and Clarice Lispector), anthropologists (Gilberto Freyre), historians (Sérgio Buarque de Holanda), dramatist-activists (Abdias do Nascimento), sociologists (Fernando Henrique Cardoso), film scholars (Ismail Xavier, João Luiz Vieira), and literary intellectuals (Antônio Cândido, Silviano Santiago, Haroldo de Campos, Augusto de Campos, Massaud Moisés, Milton Hatoum, Márcio Souza, Walnice Nogueira Galvão, Roberto

Schwarz, and countless others)—came to teach in prestigious American universities. In this same period, U.S. historians began to write about slavery and race in Brazil within a comparative perspective sympathetic to Brazil. Drawing on Gilberto Freyre, Frank Tannenbaum argued in *Slave and Citizen* (1947) that Latin American slavery, unlike the North American model, recognized the moral and spiritual personality of the slave, regarded as temporarily degraded rather than as essentially and eternally dehumanized. More than a decade later, Stanley Elkins claimed in *Slavery: A Problem in American Institutional Life* (1959) that Latin American slavery was tempered by religious institutions that prevented the reduction of blacks to mere commodities. Other scholars disputed such theories. Eugene Genovese noted that the supposedly benevolent Catholic model of slavery did not prevent violent revolutions, as in Haiti, or slave insurrections, as in Brazil, while Marvin Harris, in *Patterns of Race in the Americas* (1964), mocked the "myth of the friendly master." The Brazilian slaveholding class, he argued, created an intermediate group of mixed-race soldiers and slave drivers only because whites were not available for such services.[39]

U.S. scholars such as Franklin Frazier, Lorenzo Turner, Ruth Landes, Donald Pierson, Charles Wagley, and Carl Degler researched Brazilian race relations, often finding much to admire in Brazilian culture. In an indirect critique of the homophobic and sexophobic attitudes in the North, Landes lauded the sexual freedom of interracial love in Brazil and the lack of phobia about same-sex relations within Afro-Brazilian religions. Sometimes, the scholars seemed more naively enthusiastic (a mental state Brazilians call *deslumbrado*, or overwhelmingly charmed) about Brazilian social relations than Brazilians themselves were. Although institutional exchanges were largely from North to South, there were occasional gestures toward a more equal exchange, especially in the arts. First of all, as cultural historian Isabel Lustosa points out, the dominant U.S. culture, despite its ethnocentrism, shares with Brazilian culture a porosity that makes it "permeable to what comes from outside . . . but always changing what comes from outside into something which is theirs, with an American face."[40] The fantastic success in Hollywood of Carmen Miranda, marketed as a caricatural icon of *Latinidad*, offers a preeminent example of this highly ambiguous process of appropriation. In the early 1960s, meanwhile, bossa nova, itself a mélange of samba and cool jazz, offered an acoustic image of sophistication, ultimately entering the very bloodstream of jazz (Sarah Vaughan, Stan Getz, McCoy Tyner, Pat Metheney) and of American popular music generally (Burt Bacharach). Here we find the North American equivalent of Brazil's anthropophagic indigenization of alien culture, but now in the form of superaltern anthropophagy, or cannibalization from above, yet where both popular cultures were energized by a common Afro-diasporic current.

Diasporic Longings

All three national spaces have been projected as utopian geographies within the Afro-diasporic imaginary. Within these crisscrossing transatlantic gazes, various sites became the object of longing. Within this play of desire, many diasporic intellectuals participated in a search for an *ailleurs*: Frantz Fanon saw revolutionary Algeria as an alternative to an accommodationist Martinique; African Americans looked to both France and Brazil as spaces of conviviality; and, very occasionally, black Brazilians looked to African Americans as models of pride and activism. According to Patricia Pinho, U.S. abolitionists cited Brazil's relatively peaceful racial relations as early as the mid-1800s.[41] Yet in 1918, the black journal *O Alfinete* exhorted fellow blacks to "see whether or not we can imitate the North American blacks."[42] In 1933, another black Brazilian writer praised the "confident and self-possessed" African American who "lifts up his head," arguing that the Brazilian model is more devastating for blacks even than the brutal U.S. model: "The Americans lynch fifty Negroes a year. We kill the entire Brazilian Negro race."[43]

African Americans, meanwhile, looked to Brazil as an escape, if only in fantasy, from the horrors of U.S. segregationism. Their reflections are anthologized in David J. Hellwig's comprehensive collection *African-American Reflections on Brazil's Racial Paradise*.[44] Hellwig charts a trajectory that moves from hope to disenchantment, schematically registered in the titles of the book's three major sections: "The Myth of the Racial Paradise (1900–1940)," "The Myth Debated (1940–1965)," and "The Myth Rejected (1965–)." In the first stage, Brazil is largely seen as a color-blind utopia. Prejudice, E. R. James reported in 1920, "is not there. It is not there socially, it is not there economically, it is not there politically. It is not there at all."[45] In Hellwig's second historical phase, U.S. blacks became more skeptical. Refused entrance in eleven Brazilian hotels, Ollie Stewart, in 1940, concluded that he has traded "U.S. jim crow for the Brazilian run-around." Meeting a young black Brazilian who longed to study at Tuskegee Institute, Stewart comments, "If it hadn't been so tragic, I could have laughed."[46] In a kind of specular fantasy, at least one Brazilian black man imagines a racial paradise in an idealized United States. Stewart underlines the irony: "Here he is in Brazil, dying to get to Alabama to escape the awful hell of a color bar, . . . and nothing would satisfy me [when I was at Tuskegee] but to get to South America where I could be a free man."[47] In Hellwig's third phase, in the era of "Black Power," U.S. black observers became somewhat disenchanted. American anthropologist Angela Gilliam, who spent many years in Brazil, where she was often mistaken for a Brazilian *mulata*, suggested that U.S. blacks are better treated in Brazil because they are seen as Americans.[48] Diasporic blackness, in other words, also gets caught up in Global North/South power relations.

In the wake of earlier African American scholars (e.g., Franklin Frazier and much later Michael Turner), a number of African American scholars have addressed race in Brazil, sometimes thematizing their own identity as part of the question of methodology. Sociologist France Winddance Twine offers an African American look at Brazil in her *Racism in Racial Democracy: The Maintenance of White Supremacy in Brazil*. Based on extensive field research and many life-history interviews with black and white Brazilians, Twine was surprised by the hostility she encountered as a "black feminist researcher in Brazil" not only from Brazilian whites but also from many blacks: "In a context in which I was subjected to a high degree of racism every day, my adopted family constantly told me that I had 'misinterpreted' someone's statements or actions. . . . I was also told on numerous occasions that it was inappropriate for me to raise this issue, particularly in the presence of children."[49] The same people so eager to claim that "we are all racially mixed," Twine notes, rarely claimed actual African ancestry. Twine's research sheds light on (1) the degree to which some black Brazilians practice a kind of social self-segregation ("I don't insist on going where I don't belong") and (2) the degree to which Brazilian blacks sometimes exercise self-censorship with regard to their own experience of discrimination.[50]

Kia Lilly Caldwell, meanwhile, focuses in *Negras in Brazil* not on false consciousness but rather on the resistant subjectivity of black women activists, going back to the early black feminist trailblazers such as Lelia Gonzalez, Sueli Carneiro, and Thereza Santos and culminating in the swelling wave of recent activists. Taking issue with the Bourdieu/Wacquant disqualification of Michael Hanchard on the basis of his African American identity, Caldwell thematizes the role of her own identity within her diasporic research. Where "the impact of local and global racial practices [becomes] further compounded by racialized constructions of gender,"[51] the body itself becomes an instrument of knowledge. Since field research involves cultural immersion, the diasporic anthropologist is "subjected to many of the same racialized and gendered discourses and practices that we set out to examine."[52] In Caldwell's case, immersion meant being interpellated as a prostitute in Copacabana and as a maid in upscale apartment buildings and occasionally being sent to use the service elevator. Thus, she gained "firsthand knowledge of the social indignities experienced by many Afro-Brazilian women on a daily basis."[53] Rather than define Brazil, or the United States, as better or worse, Caldwell argues for the existence of "multiple culturally and historically specific racisms."[54] Her goal, like ours, is to "place the cultural and historical particularities of Brazilian racism in dialogue with global practices of racial domination."[55]

Patricia de Santana Pinho, a Brazilian professor at SUNY–Albany, meanwhile, argues that some African American commentators such as Twine confuse black Brazilians' attempt to realize the inherent promise of "racial democracy" with a failure to confront it.[56] In her *Mama Africa: Reinventing Blackness in Bahia*, Pinho highlights the role of Salvador Bahia—celebrated as the "Black Rome" and the "Mecca of Negritude"—as a magnet for African Americans in search of African roots and the culture of Candomblé.[57] In an intense cultural exchange mediated by publications, tourist agencies, Candomblé centers, universities, *Afro-blocos*, and blogs, African American trips to Brazil form part of a broader itinerary that includes not only Africa itself but also the Afro-Caribbean, charting a "map of Africanness" wherein Egypt represents the site of monumental pride, West Africa the place of cultural origin, and Brazil still another point on the Atlantic spectrum, all places where African Americans "might have been born." Pinho cites rapper M1 of Dead Prez as conveying a common perception among African Americans that "black Brazilians have remained more connected to Africa, [which constitutes] a step in resisting colonial domination, a strategy against the kind of brainwashing which took place in the United States."[58] In a complex analysis, Pinho charts the crossing of looks between Afro-Brazilians and Afro-Americans, with each projecting their desires and utopias and, at times, an ethnocentric U.S.-centered cultural frame.

African Americans have also looked to France as a beacon of hope in a time of despair. Unlike the love of Brazil, the love of France formed part of a widespread Francophilia in the United States, encapsulated in the memory of the two "sister republics" and Jefferson's maxim that "every man has two countries, his own and France." Indeed, the France–United States relationship began as a passionate romance. In a reciprocal movement of ideas, French Enlightenment thinkers inspired the American revolutionaries, just as the American Revolution inspired French thinkers. The love affair was consummated, as it were, by the public embrace of Jefferson and Voltaire in a Paris square. Subsequently, Thomas Paine, Henry Wadsworth Longfellow, Ralph Waldo Emerson, Nathaniel Hawthorne, Frederick Douglass, Henry Adams, and Edith Wharton all penned affectionate travel memoirs about France. For the United States as for Brazil, France provided an alternative cultural model to the more obvious metropolitan father figures— Great Britain and Portugal, respectively.

Despite France's historical involvement in slavery and imperialism, its relatively good reputation in terms of race is based on certain historical moments: the frequent alliances between the French and native peoples in the Americas, the readiness to mate with Native American women (in contrast with the Puritans' repugnance for miscegenation), the warm reception for black American soldiers and artists in France, and France's reputation as a *terre d'asile*. In France, religious prejudice—against Jews and Protestants—had historically been more virulent than racial prejudice. The first African Americans known to have arrived in France were probably Thomas Jefferson's slaves, one of whom, Sally Hemmings, became the mother of at least one of his children. While African Americans participated in a general American attraction to France, they also had a distinct perspective based on a perceived lack of racism. Frederick Douglass expressed his surprise during an 1887 visit: "I have everywhere been received in this country . . . with civility, courtesy, and kindness."[59]

It was only decades later that there occurred a substantial movement of African Americans to France. Beginning in 1917, some 160,000 African Americans served in the armed forces in France, generally receiving a warm welcome. Many black musicians went to Paris; Sidney Bechet arrived in 1919, and Josephine Baker and *La Revue Nègre* opened in 1925 to the enraptured applause of the surrealists. African American adoration of Paris, as Tyler Stovall points out, constituted an indirect commentary on the sorry state of "race relations" in the United States: "African Americans shared the surprising realization that French whites could treat them with affection and respect, that a color-blind society just might be possible after all."[60] Euphoric in Paris, James Weldon Johnson felt suddenly free from danger and intolerance:

> From the day I set foot in France, I became aware of the working of a miracle within me. . . . I was suddenly free; free from a sense of impending discomfort, insecurity, danger; free from the conflict within the Man-Negro dualism and the innumerable maneuvers in thought and behavior that it compels; free from special scorn, special tolerance, special condescension, special commiseration; free to be merely a man.[61]

That African Americans could feel such dramatic relief from the "burden of race" simply by landing in France constitutes a burning indictment of the ambient racism of the United States at that time.

In the wake of 1920s *negrophilie*, the Paris of the 1950s and 1960s became what Stovall calls the "literary capital of black America,"[62] animated by such figures as Richard Wright, Chester Himes, James Baldwin, and Melvin Van Peebles. By the 1950s, the exoticist primitivism of the 1920s had faded from fashion, and African Americans were playing a major role in French erudite and popular cultures. While white French audiences in the 1920s and 1930s sometimes saw African Americans through a primitivist grid as surrogate Africans—incarnated by Josephine Baker playing the "jungle" African on stage or the Maghrebian Bedouin in *Princesse Tam Tam*—in the 1950s they were more likely to see them as dark-skinned Americans, or as white America's preeminent victims, or simply as talented artists. Eartha Kitt played Helen of Troy in a 1950s version of *Faust* directed by Orson Welles, and jazz musicians such as Dizzy Gillespie, Miles Davis, and Thelonious Monk performed in "*les caves*" of the Latin Quarter, while composing soundtracks for New Wave films such as *Les Liaisons Dangereuses* and *Ascenseur pour L'échafaud*. Melvin Van Peebles wrote novels in French in the early 1960s and directed the New Wave–ish film *Story of a Three-Day Pass*, about an African American soldier who encounters American racism (and occasional French paternalism) in France.

For African American intellectuals and artists, it was especially gratifying to be honored in Paris. As Bourdieu-influenced literary scholar Pascale Casanova points out, Paris constituted "the capital of that Republic without frontiers, the universal homeland without any narrow patriotism, . . . a transnational site whose only imperatives are those of art and literature—the Universal Republic of Letters."[63] In France, African American artists could do an end-run around systemic U.S. racism, garnering praise in a capital of artistic prestige that was respected by white intellectuals as well. African Americans came to mediate the complex relation between black-inflected U.S. popular culture and the Parisian intelligentsia. If in Paris French people could discover black Americans, black Americans in Paris could discover not only France but also French Africa and the West Indies.

The very different reactions of the diverse Afro-diasporic intellectuals to postwar France present a striking anomaly, however, forming a kind of diasporic conundrum. Why would Francophone Caribbean intellectuals such as Aimé Césaire and Frantz Fanon find France terribly racist, while African Americans, in the very same period, could find it deliciously *nonracist*? In the same period that African Americans were experiencing newfound feelings of freedom, Fanon discovered blackness in France, made aware of his "ethnic characteristics . . . battered down by tom toms, cannibalism, intellectual deficiency, fetishism, racial defects, slave ships."[64] In France, Fanon felt his sense of identity shattered: "dissected under white eyes, the only real eyes. I am *fixed*. . . . I am laid bare."[65] Why, then, did African Americans experience an almost opposite sensation of freedom? To begin, the difference was real; the sensation of freedom was not just another word for a collective hallucination, as shown by the many incidents in which everyday French people reprimanded white Americans for bringing racist attitudes into France itself.[66] Memoirs and travel accounts by black Americans in France suggest that they experienced France as indeed less racist. Despite widespread ideological racism, everyday encounters did not necessarily involve acts of racism or violent behavior toward black Americans. (The colonies were another story.) Since French-style racism, where it existed, was more likely to take the form of exoticist paternalism and role stereotyping than of virulent hatred, African Americans in Paris, especially in the postwar period, did indeed breathe in relative freedom, liberated from the pernicious folkways of U.S.-style apartheid.

A number of other factors help explain the difference between the African American and the black West Indian reaction. First, it is a testament to the horrors of U.S. segregation in the postwar period, which made almost any other situation seem an improvement. Second, Afro-Caribbean intellectuals such as

Césaire and Fanon were moving from a semicolonized yet black-majority country (Martinique), where blackness was the normal condition, to France, where blacks were a minority and blackness a "problem." Many West Indian blacks, in this sense, "discovered" their blackness only in France or in colonial armies. (For Fanon, according to David Macey, the Free French army was "structured around an ethnic hierarchy, with white Europeans at the top.")[67] African Americans, meanwhile, were moving from one black-minority country (the United States) to another black-minority country (France), one less marked by chattel slavery and white supremacy, where blacks were less scarred by the memory of segregation, and where whites were less guilty and phobic toward black people. African Americans did not have to "discover" their blackness in France; their American experience had already made them painfully aware of it. Third, from the French side, black Americans were often seen first as Americans and only secondly as blacks. As Stovall writes in relation to a later period, "if the best defense against police brutality in Los Angeles is a video camera, in Paris it is an American passport."[68] Fourth, African Americans, like most Americans not necessarily fluent in French, missed some of the nuances of social intercourse. Much of Fanon's rhetorical fire in Black Skin, White Masks is directed at the subtly paternalistic discourses and intonations of whites claiming "there is no racism here." Fifth, black artists and intellectuals benefited from the prestige habitually accorded artists and intellectuals in France. Sixth, French problack affirmation was more than a little ambiguous and "overdetermined." While the warm welcome for African Americans was undoubtedly sincere, the good treatment of American blacks also afforded a narcissistic payoff for French whites, who could simultaneously demonstrate their relative lack of racism while also using blacks as a vehicle for expressing resentment against U.S. power in Europe.

Contemporary scholars Robert Stepto, Michel Fabre, Melvon Dixon, Benetta Jules-Rosette, Petrine Archer-Straw, and Brent Hayes Edwards have all stressed the profoundly transnational character of diasporic black movements in relation to France. Edwards examines the various Afro-diasporic journals in the United States (Negro World, Messenger, Crisis, Voice of the Negro) and in France and Africa (La Voix des Nègres, La Race Nègre, L'Étudiant Noir, La Revue du Monde Noir, Le Périscope Africain, La Voix du Dahomey) to highlight the diverse crosscurrents (the Harlem Renaissance, Négritude) moving between France, Africa, Afro-America, and the Caribbean. Black internationalism, as Edwards notes, is not a "supplement" to nation-based black thinking; rather, it exists at the very kernel of a struggle for emancipation against racism, colonialism, and imperialism.[69]

Afro-diasporic encounters also impacted the concepts developed by the Négritude writers. If for Anglophone blacks Paris was a key site, for Francophone writers New York at times became an extension of Africa. Léopold Senghor's visit to New York City, according to Emmanuel Chukwudi Eze, helped trigger his "Europe is Reason, Africa is Emotion" polarity. Senghor saw New York City as polarized into the white downtown European culture and the uptown black culture of Harlem. As he puts it in "To New York," white Manhattan knew "no mother's breast, . . . no tender word, and no lips, only artificial hearts paid in cold cash," while Harlem presented "life immemorial, . . . hips rippling like silk and spearhead breasts, ballets of water lilies and fabulous masks, and mangoes and love rolling from the low houses." For Senghor, the white mind is detached, analytical, and nonparticipatory, while the black mind is integrative, sympathetic, and participatory. Yet a marriage between the two was possible, if only "black blood" could enter "[American] steel joints" and make flow the "oil of life."[70] Within this essentialist, quasi-metaphysical vision, articulated in transit, Senghor inverted the culture/nature hierarchy, this time to the advantage of Harlem and Africa.

As a key site for exchanges about race, metropolitan France was the place where African Americans encountered white French citizens but also other Afro-diasporic people, some of them soldiers in the service of the French empire. The role of Paris, as Stovall puts it,

> was both fascinating and deeply ironic. After all, the city was the seat of one of the world's great colonial empires, a place where anonymous French officials supervised the subjugation of millions of Black Africans, . . . [yet] more so than in the United States, even New York, African-Americans found that in Paris the abstract ideal of worldwide black unity and culture became a tangible reality. . . . French colonialism and primitivism thus paradoxically combined to foster a vision of pan-African unity.[71]

Paris had been at the epicenter of political discussion for black American exiles ever since 1919 and W. E. B. Du Bois's first Pan-African Congress. Almost four decades later, in 1956, Richard Wright, along with Césaire and Senghor, organized the Congress of Negro Artists and Writers. The various race-related movements thus all had their local variations while sharing a cross-border dialogical gaze. In a multidirectional movement of identification, African Americans identified with liberation struggles in Africa or looked to Brazil and France as models of nonracist societies, just as Africans identified with freedom struggles in the "internal colonies" of the diaspora.

While not as central as in the United States or Brazil, Afro-diasporic culture has nevertheless often been a catalytic source of artistic vitality and social critique within French popular and erudite culture. A more in-depth analysis, in this sense, might address the black influence in French artistic culture in terms of: the presence of mixed-race French authors such as Alexandre Dumas; black characters in French literature; the denunciations of slavery by poets such as Victor Hugo; the impact of African aesthetics on painters such as Picasso and

Braque; negrophile novels such as Philippe Soupault's *Le Nègre*; the role of jazz in novels such as Sartre's *La Nausée* and in the music of Erik Satie ("Ragtime du Pacquebot") and Francis Poulenc ("Rapsodie Nègre"); the dialogue with Africa and Africans in the films of Jean Rouch (*Les Maîtres Fous*); the role of blacks in Genet's plays (*Les Nègres*) and films (*Un Chant d'Amour*); and the intellectual polylogue involving Frantz Fanon, Richard Wright, Simone de Beauvoir, and Jean-Paul Sartre.[72]

From *Black Orpheus* to Barack Obama

A recently published book by Brazilian Fernando Jorge, with a title that translates as *If It Were Not for Brazil, Barack Obama Would Not Have Been Born*, offers an insight into the crossed gazes typical of what might be called "transatlantic looking relations." The book's thesis is based on Obama's account (registered in *Dreams from My Father*) of going to see the 1959 film *Black Orpheus* with his mother: "The film, a groundbreaker of sorts due to its mostly black, Brazilian cast [treated] the myth of the ill-fated lovers Orpheus and Eurydice set in the favelas of Rio during Carnival. In Technicolor splendor, set against scenic green hills, the black and brown Brazilians sang and danced and strummed guitars like carefree birds in colorful plumage."[73] According to Fernando Jorge, it was Ann Dunham's experience of *Black Orpheus*, which she called "the most beautiful thing she ever saw," and the resemblance between the film's black male star (Breno Mello) and Dunham's later Kenyan husband that led to her marriage and thus to Obama's birth.[74] The book's thesis is terribly simplistic; surely a more complex constellation of factors (the Civil Rights Movement, Boas's antiracist anthropology, the brilliance of Obama's future father, Dunham's culturally open personality) could help explain Dunham's choice of marriage partner. Nevertheless, the book's claim and *Black Orpheus* itself serve to open up the question of the relay of racialized gazes that forms the subject of this book.

First, within this transatlantic layering of gazes, *Black Orpheus* conveys a certain French view of Brazilian Carnival and culture. The film's French title, *Orphée Noir*, foregrounds blackness (and echoes Sartre's preface to Léopold Senghor's collection of poetry),[75] while the Brazilian title of the play on which the film is based, *Orfeu da Conceição*, emphasizes the film's location in an imaginary Rio favela. The French director, Marcel Camus, saw Brazil through a preexisting French and Franco-American intertext that included (1) French and American updates of classical texts (O'Neill's *Mourning Becomes Electra*, Sartre's *Les Mouches*); (2) "Orphic" poetry from France and elsewhere; (3) American all-black-performed versions of the classics, such as Orson Welles's "Voodoo Macbeth" in 1936; (4) the negrophilia of the French avant-garde, triggered by *La Revue*

Nègre and Josephine Baker, the African American who became a French star and heroine; and (5) the Hollywood tradition of all-black musicals such as *Hallelujah* and *Cabin in the Sky*, all of which was relayed through the vibrant performativity of Rio's Carnival.

The Brazilian source play, for its part, conveyed a specifically white elite look of Vinicius de Moraes, poet, diplomat, and later popular singer-composer who referred to himself as the "blackest white man in Brazil," and who subsequently authored "Afro-sambas" with guitarist Baden Powell, a black musician named after the British founder of the Boy Scouts. A multilingual cosmopolitan, Moraes lived for long periods in Paris and in Los Angeles, where he socialized with Orson Welles and met Louis Armstrong and Billie Holiday. At the same time, not all black Brazilians endorsed Moraes's vision of the favelas, nor did Brazilians necessarily adore the French film; many called it an exoticist "macumba for tourists." Abdias do Nascimento, founder of the Black Theatre group that provided many of the actors for *Black Orpheus*, was acerbic about the film and similar products:

> White actors in blackface, black Christ, Black Orpheus: in the final analysis, all
> of these conspired in the historic rape of our people. African religious culture is
> rich and very much alive in our communities spread around Brazil. We do not
> have to invoke ancient Greece or the Bible to elevate the status of our mythology.
> Greece and Europe, meanwhile, owe much of what they call "western civilization"
> to Africa.[76]

Interestingly, the conception of the play was also shaped by two of Moraes's American friends who happened to be in Rio when the play was first conceived: first, the pro–Latin American Jewish American literary critic Waldo Frank, who told Moraes that the black Brazilian women "looked like Greeks," and who according to Moraes himself introduced him to "another Brazilian reality" by asking to be shown the favelas; and second, the equally pro–Latin American Orson Welles, then in Rio making the pan-American and antiracist documentary *It's All True*, a fervent celebration of samba, the favelas, and Afro-Brazilian culture. Thus, the perspectives of two Latin Americanized North Americans intersected with the point of view of an Americanized white Brazilian then in the process of immersing himself in Afro-Brazilian culture.[77]

Black Orpheus, which launched the worldwide popularity of both samba and bossa nova—the triangulated musical genre that itself fuses Afro-Brazilian samba with the cool jazz of Miles Davis and Chet Baker, along with the subtle harmonies of Ravel and Debussy—intermingles these various transnational looks, recapitulated again in Jorge's recent Brazilian book about Obama. At the same time, the filmic gaze is differentiated: there is no single American or French or Brazilian perspective. In fact, Obama himself contrasts his mother's look at *Black Orpheus* with his own. While the mother is transfixed "in a wistful gaze," the son is ready to leave halfway through the film. While the film transports her to a dreamy elsewhere, it leaves him skeptical about the film's idealized portrayal, triggering melancholy reflections about the burdens of race: "The emotions between the races could never be pure; even love was tarnished by the desire to find in the other some element that was missing in ourselves. . . . The other race would always remain just that: menacing, alien, and apart."[78] Differences of race, gender, age, and generation, then, separate Ann Dunham's gaze on *Black Orpheus* from Obama's. The mother's enchanted gaze at "the most beautiful thing that [she] ever saw," formed during the Civil Rights era, differs dramatically from Obama's much more distanced reaction in the post–Black Power era. In any case, the Jorge book conjures up a number of our themes: the artistic intercourse of French, Brazilian, and American culture; the play of social desire across the Black Atlantic; the multiplicity of differentiated gazes within single national formations; and one Brazilian author's wish to see Brazil, thanks to *Black Orpheus*, as saving the United States from its own racism.[79]

Between Anglo-Saxonism and Latinism

Such an investment in the idea of Brazil's redemptive role betokens the extent to which the race/coloniality debates in the three zones are always-already haunted by the culturalist divide between the "Latins" and the "Anglo-Saxons," a binarism every bit as mythic as Lévi-Strauss's "the raw and the cooked." As a discursive palimpsest, the Anglo/Latin dichotomy bears the traces of many historical conflicts, from the perennial rivalry between "perfidious Albion" and its "sweet enemy" France, military battles such as the Norman Invasion, the Hundred Years' War (1328–1453), and the Second Hundred Years' War (1689–1815), all the way to contemporary tensions over the place of Britain in the European Union, over Anglophone and Francophone spheres of influence in Africa, and recently over the Anglo-American invasion of Iraq. As part of a larger intercolonial rivalry, the Anglo/Latin dichotomy has impacted the ways that the histories of colonial conquest have been written. Citing Bartolomé de las Casas, English writers spoke of the "black legend" of Spanish massacres against the native peoples. The Spanish, meanwhile, disputed the legend while accusing the English of even greater violence. Yet this early interimperial squabble obscured a shared past of violent practices. In fact, the racialized violence of both groups predated the Conquest of the Americas. The English historian Henry Hallam (1777–1859), for example, drew parallels between the Spanish *Reconquista* and the English conquest of Ireland, between the massacres of the Moors and the brutalization of the Irish.[80]

French and Latin American discussions of intellectual exchange often deploy the epithet "Anglo-Saxon" in implied opposition to "French" or "Latin." In a reified polarity, the factitious solidity of "Anglo-Saxon culture" is "answered" by the equally factitious solidity of "*Latinidad.*" Yet both terms are misnomers. North America (and Great Britain) are not exclusively Anglo-Saxon, and France and Latin America are not exclusively Latin, especially when imagined "from below." At a time when "cultural studies" and "postcolonial" studies are transcending narrow ethno-national paradigms, the twinned terms "Latin" and "Anglo-Saxon" resuscitate them. As specular projections of pan-ethno-nationalism, the Anglo/Latin dichotomy blocks a more open and transnational understanding of the intercourse of ideas. The two terms must therefore be thought (and unthought) in relation to each other. As a form of ethno-cultural exceptionalism, "Anglo-Sax-on*ism*" is associated with northern Europe and its expansion into the Americas and around the world. Figures such as Hegel, Max Weber, and Samuel Huntington give expression to this exceptionalism. "Latin*ism,*" meanwhile, is associated with France and southern Europe and their expansion into the Americas, serving as a means of lateral differentiation from the "Anglo-Saxons" and vertical differentiation from non-Europeans in the Americas.[81] While "Anglo-Saxon" goes back to the 4th century, "Latin" goes even further back to Latin as the language of the Holy Roman Empire (as opposed to the various vernaculars). Only later did "Latin" become a geopolitical and cultural category (Latin America) and an ethnic classification (Latinos) in the U.S. culture wars.

The concept of *Latinité* was originally conceived, within Europe itself, as a response to other panethnic movements such as pan-Germanism and pan-Slavism. In the Americas, it was a response to the swelling ambitions of the "Anglo-Saxons." French Latinist figures such as Prosper Vallerange and Paul Adam, in this sense, echo the Hegelian and Weberian discourse of European superiority, but in its warm-water Mediterranean variant. The ideal portrait of Latin "idealism," "culture," and "spirituality," as incarnated in the diaphanous figure of Ariel in José Enrique Rodó's version of *The Tempest*, was foiled by Anglo-Saxon "mercantilism," "expansionism," and "vulgarity."[82] From another perspective, however, both "Latinism" and "Anglo-Saxonism" form variants of that transregional self-love called Eurocentrism. We propose, therefore, to speak not of "Anglo-Saxons" and "Latins" as cohesive ethno-cultural groups but rather of Anglo-Saxon*ism* and Latin*ism* as historically situated discourses.

As an elastic term, "Latinity" has been stretched to fit changing geopolitical conditions. For Prosper Vallerange, the term *included* the English. For Hegel, France, England, and Germany together formed the "heart of Europe." The various European empires all narrated themselves within a Roman genealogy, seeing themselves as latter-day versions of the *Pax Romana*—whence such symptomatic terms as *Pax Hispanica, Pax Britannica,* and *Pax Americana.* The ideologists of the nation-states of the Americas, meanwhile, elaborated the conceit of founding

"New Romes," an idea concretized architecturally in the geometrical monumen-
tality of many capitals in the Americas, including of course Washington, D.C.
Even Brazilian anthropologist Darcy Ribeiro, a passionate advocate for indigenous peoples, resorts to this Euro-tropism, or turning toward Europe for legitimacy, when he calls Brazil (in O Povo Brasileiro) a "New Rome."[83] The French,
meanwhile, claimed a Roman lineage for French colonial domination in North
Africa. Since the Roman presence predated that of the Arabs and Muslims,
French colonialism could be narrated not as an invasion but as a "return."[84]

Anglo-Saxonism has always been deeply entangled in imperialist xenophobia,
making "Anglo-Saxon" a virtual synonym for national chauvinism and imperial
racism. In the 19th-century United States, imperialists saw a superior "Anglo-
Saxon race" as divinely authorized to take land first from the Native Americans
and then from the Mexicans and later to intervene wherever it wished. Echoing Hegel's words about the vanishing of the native "at the breath of European
activity," Josiah Strong in 1885 lauded "the extinction of inferior races before the
advancing Anglo-Saxon," proudly noting that Anglo-Saxons represented only
"one-fifteenth part of mankind" but ruled "more than one-third of its people."[85]

The Anglo-Saxonists prefer to forget that most of North America was Spanish before it was Anglo, and it was indigenous before it was Spanish. For the
Spanish, the east coast of the continent was called Florida; for the English, it
was called Virginia. The conquest of the American West first took place on a
South-North axis, as the conquistadores moved northward from the Caribbean
into Florida and from Mexico into Texas. Los Angeles began as a multilingual
pueblo with a mestizo majority. New Spain was almost a century old when Jamestown, the oldest English settlement in North America, was founded. But what
had begun as North American admiration for the superior wealth and power of
Spanish America gradually turned into a racialized sense of superiority. A highly
gendered sense of muscular potency became linked to a putative special Anglo-
Saxon capacity for self-government and, by extension, for the domination of
"lesser breeds without the law." In 1899, the year after the misnamed "Spanish-
American War," journalist William Allen White argued that "only Anglo-Saxons
knew how to govern themselves" and that it was their "manifest destiny" to go
forth as "world conqueror."[86] (The prestigious journal Foreign Affairs traces its
origins to a turn-of-the-century Anglo-Saxonist publication called the Journal of
Race Development.)

While the Anglo-Saxonists prattled about their "inevitable" march to the
west, the Latinists also marched west while lamenting their victimization by the
Yankees. As part of this intra-European family feud, the term "Latin America"
was first introduced by the French in the 19th century. Associated with Emperor
Napoleon III's campaign to promote the unity of all Latin peoples, French intel-

lectuals and state officers brandished *Latinité* as an antidote to the rising power of the "Anglo-Saxons."[87] With the United States distracted by the Civil War, Napoleon III ordered the invasion of Mexico in 1861 as part of a strategic plan to counter U.S. influence. France installed a monarchical regime under Maximilian but was defeated in 1867, an event commemorated annually in the Cinco de Mayo celebration. For centuries, the Spanish, the Portuguese, the French, the British, the Dutch, and the Americans all vied for domination, with all parties convinced that their particular form of colonialism was well intentioned and beneficial. As byproducts of intercolonial rivalry, the current debates often revisit the petty enmities rooted in these interimperial wars and debates. As an instance of Freud's "narcissism of minor differences," national chauvinists laud one form of imperialism over another, while attributing the differences to a putatively fixed cultural character.[88] These rivalries over race and empire must be seen, then, within the larger frame of a racialized intercoloniality that flatters one set of colonialists over another without seeing the deeper links between them. At the same time, the later "northern" imperialisms have clearly superseded, subalternized, and overtaken the earlier "Latin" colonialisms.

The haughty "Anglo-Saxonists" and the proud "Latinists," despite their apparent disagreements, do share fundamental axioms: first, that the Anglo/Latin polarity points to a *real* substantive contrast between peoples; second, that North America is essentially Anglo-Saxon and that Latin America is essentially Latin. The discordance is only in the valence. The two dominant groups also agree, if only tacitly, on a European right to dispossess the indigenous peoples of the Americas. Walter Mignolo has underscored the Janus-faced character of a concept of "Latin America" that served to restore European, Meridional, Catholic, and Latin "civilization" in South America and simultaneously to produce absences (indigenous and Afro-diasporics). "Creole consciousness," as Mignolo puts it, "was indeed a singular case of double consciousness: the consciousness of not being who they were supposed to be (Europeans)." The critical consciousness of Afro-Creoles and indigenous people, meanwhile, emerged not from not being considered Europeans but from not being considered human.[89]

The intellectuals who have embraced the Anglo/Latin dichotomy have not necessarily supported their own side, however; they are not like soccer fans who always root for the national team. Many Latin American intellectuals have endorsed Anglo-Saxonism, just as many Anglo-American intellectuals have supported Latinism. A signal example of the latter case was the American historian Richard Morse, whose book *Prospero's Mirror* (published in Mexico in 1982) contrasted the warm and gregarious collectivity of Iberian and Latin American culture with the cold and individualistic competiveness of his own Anglo culture.[90] More pro-Latin than the Latins themselves, Morse was criticized by some Brazilian intellectuals for glorifying an Iberian influence that in their view had left a sad legacy of authoritarianism.

The Anglo-Saxon/Latin dichotomy becomes especially pernicious, in our view, when used to ethnicize questions that are fundamentally political. Although often used *en toute innocence* as a synonym for *Anglo-American*, as when French bookstore rubrics alert us to "La Littérature Anglo-Saxonne" as a signal for Shakespeare's plays and Toni Morrison's novels, in most cases the term is no longer appropriate. It should logically be used only to refer to (1) the two Germanic tribes that moved to England in the 4th century, (2) the written literature (*Beowulf, The Seafarer*) later produced by the 8th-century descendants of that tribe, and (3) the 19th-century white-supremacist ideology called "Anglo-Saxonism." Just as one would not call contemporary French people the "Gauls," or Italians the "Etruscans," or Portuguese the "Lusitanians," no present-day people should be called "Anglo-Saxons." Indeed, there is something paradoxical about denunciations of "Anglo-Saxon communitarianism" in that the charge performs exactly what it denounces. The term itself, that is, "communitarizes" a complex society while blaming it for that which the accusation has itself just performed: reducing a complex and differentiated society to a single ethnos.

At this point in history, "Anglo-Saxon" is sometimes extended to refer to political and economic systems and ideologies. Building on the classical contrast between an economically liberal Britain and a statist "social" France, some French analysts speak of "Anglo-Saxon neoliberalism," as though an economic policy with broad European/global roots could be tethered to a single ethnos. As should become clear through the remainder of the book, we are skeptical about ethnic/religious/culturalist explanations for social systems. The imperialistic policies of the United States do not derive from the "Anglo-Saxon" nature of the American populace—in fact there are more people of African descent in the United States than of English descent, and even more predominantly Anglo countries such as Canada are not necessarily imperialist—but from the ways power has been historically constituted in the United States to favor the white and the wealthy.

Today "Anglo-Saxon" and "Latin" are deployed asymmetrically. First, Latin American intellectuals are more likely to claim "Latin" than Americans or British intellectuals are likely to claim "Anglo-Saxon." Second, those deploying "Anglo-Saxon" with pride almost always occupy the extreme right end of the political spectrum, while those wielding the same term as an accusation are usually on the left, as when Latin Americans denounce "Anglo-Saxon imperialism." Given this political asymmetry, the word "Latin" is more likely to designate progressive projects, such as the political/economic solidarity of Latin America as a counterweight to imperialism or the empowerment of Latinos in the United States, for whom the Anglo/Latino distinction names a hegemony premised both on color and language. Anglo-Saxonness, in contrast, would never today be associated with any progressive project, which is why qualifying any political project as "Anglo-Saxon" is to disqualify it in the eyes of the left. The term itself, whether used positively or negatively, is inextricably linked to racial essentialism and national exceptionalism.

Today Anglo-Saxonism has mutated into new forms, such as the genteel Anglo-Protestantism of an Arthur Schlesinger, Jr., or the clash-of-cultures essentialism of a Samuel Huntington, the world-renowned "expert" on world civilizations whose Americo-Eurocentrism has been variously articulated on both an East/West and a North/South axis. Anglo-Saxonist xenophobia is currently expressed in the "English Only" movement, in the militarization of the U.S.-Mexico border, and in the harassment of "illegal aliens," that is, undocumented workers. Anglo-Saxonism has reared its head again in the form of the Tea Party's expert on the Constitution, W. Cleon Skousen. In his 1981 book *The Five Thousand Year Leap*, Skousen argued that the Founding Fathers rejected European "collectivism" in favor of the limited government typical of 5th-century Anglo-Saxon chieftains. For Skousen, the enshrinement of Christian free-market principles in the Constitution enabled the leap that placed the Anglo-Saxons at the head of humanity. Thus, a slightly sublimated form of white-supremacist Anglo-Saxonism grounds the historical vision of at least some in the Tea Party.[91]

While the old Anglo-Saxonists proudly proclaimed their white supremacism, the new Anglo-Saxonists claim that they are *not* racist. They even claim, ludicrously, to be the victims of (black and Latino) racism. Currently, a nativist right wing in the United States has been demonizing Latinos, Chicanos, Mexicans, and Latin American immigrants as a threat to the body politic, exploiting the minoritized body as a distraction from the failures of a corrupt system dominated by finance capital. A demagogic campaign cultivates the fears of engulfment on the part of the empowered majority. A sense of a precarious legitimacy haunts the nativists, however, in that their xenophobic hysteria reflects a political unconscious haunted by their own tenuous claim on the land. From an indigenous perspective, after all, the first illegal aliens were the conquistadores (coming from the South) and the pioneers (coming from the East).

Yet at the same time, the Latinization of the United States through "magical urbanism" (Mike Davis) also proceeds apace, as more and more American cities are becoming nonwhite-majority cities with large Latino populations, thus undercutting the Anglo-Saxon/Latin divide itself.[92] Major populational transfers, meanwhile, drain Latin America of its human substance: 11 percent of the Mexican population, 18 percent of the Ecuadorean population, and 25 percent of the Salvadorean population now reside in the United States, scrambling the Anglo/Latin divide.[93] Yet even while border artists such as Guillermo Gómez-

Peña and border theorists such as Gloria Anzaldúa and Cherríe Moraga have torn down symbolic walls, the U.S. state has constructed a grotesque wall between the United States and Mexico, a monument to hatred for *nuestra America* and the Global South. The United States is not alone in this exclusion, however. Just as thousands of Central Americans die trying to cross the border where, in Anzaldúa's words, the "Third World grates against the first and bleeds,"[94] so thousands of African would-be immigrants drown in the currents of the "moat" that separates Africa from "Latin" Spain and from "fortress Europe."

The challenge for critical intellectuals, we would argue, is to support *Latinidad* against anti-immigrant hysteria, while also favoring the political/economic unity of "Latin America" as a counterweight to the neoimperial unilateralism of the United States, but to do so without falling into the obfuscations typical of some forms of *Latinidad*. Our project, in this sense, hopes to dismantle the ethno-nationalist binarisms that have obscured the interconnectedness of race and coloniality in the colonial-settler states of the Americas. In this sense, the dichotomy itself has become too intertwined with national and panethnic exceptionalisms and has stood in the way of transregional and transnational analysis of the intercourse of ideas.

Racing Translation

The movement of ideas across borders inevitably brings up the question of language, whether marshaled for culturalist purposes or to articulate the in-between fluidities of culture. In the case of traveling debates, translation is not merely a trope; it is entangled in the concrete arena of language conflict and dissonance. The French language, for example, has been crucial both to national pride and to the civilizing mission. "What is not clear," in Rivarol's famous formulation, "is not French." Official Jacobin ideology has generally favored a unitary conception of language and an educational system hostile to linguistic diversity. Within the Hexagon, Bretons and Corsicans were expected to assimilate into standard French, just as the colonized were expected to abandon their indigenous languages and creolized patois. At home and abroad, only the normative version of French could carry the Cartesian light of "clear and distinct ideas."

At the same time, French too is a creolized language, marked not only by English and German but also by Brazilian indigenous words such as Tupi-Guarani *toucan* (parrot, from *tucano*) and by Arabic words such as *bled* (village) and *tbib* (doctor). English, meanwhile, is already half French in vocabulary. Some French expressions in English are barely recognizable *as* French: the "dozy-dooh" of Cajun-influenced American square dance, from French *dos-à-dos* (back-to-back), like "promenade" and "aleman" (*à la main*). Here one could also mention patois such as *petit nègre*, a legacy of World War I, defined as a "simplified, deformed version of French that the military codified and deliberately *taught* to African soldiers . . . as a means both to infantilize them and to control their modes of interaction with their mainly white French commanding officers."[95]

Language crosses borders and refracts the traffic of ideas; terminological clashes lurk in the background of the culture wars. National languages in postcolonial spaces are especially syncretic and polyvocal. The same words, due to different histories, carry very different connotations and intonations. One foundational clash has to do with the naming of the indigenous peoples of the Americas. The very word "America," as a synonym for the United States, for example, has provoked objections from indigenous people, since it gives a European name (Amerigo Vespucci) to an aboriginal continent, and from non-indigenous Latin Americans, for whom "America" designates the entire hemisphere. The designation of indigenous peoples as "Indians," meanwhile, relays Columbus's bedazzled belief that he had arrived in Asia. The question is whether indigenous peoples should be called "first peoples," "fourth-world peoples," or "native peoples" or be named according to their specific self-designations such as "Dineh" or "Ikpeng." Should we speak of the "Indians *of* Brazil"—using a genitive of nation-state belonging—or the "Indians *in* Brazil," signifying only location and not affiliation? In *Manifest Manners*, "postindian warrior" Gerald Vizenor objects to the word "Indian" as hopelessly tainted. Yet many indigenous activists have boomeranged the term as an empowering vehicle for pan-Indigenous movements.[96]

Racial perception is also filtered through language. The French language features varied terms for blacks, ranging from the pseudo-descriptive *noir* to the more frankly pejorative *nègre* (a term of abuse recoded as praise by the *Négritude* movement), the borrowed-from-English "black," and the more inclusive *personnes de couleur* (persons of color). Poet-statesman Léopold Senghor pointed out that technically everyone in the world is a "person of color."[97] In Brazil, *preto* (black) originally referred to African blacks, while *crioulo* referred to blacks born in Brazil. But now *negro* has become a term of pride. In the United States, in contrast, "Negro" evokes the putative Uncle Tom–style passivity of the pre–Civil Rights era, while "black" and "African American" connote racial pride. The Brazilian term *Afrodescendente* (Afro-descended) emphasizes both African ancestry and a shared diasporic experience. Many Brazilians use *nego* (slang for black man) and *nega* (black woman) as terms of affection for people of any race. Although Brazilians often claim that "we are all mestizo," the meaning of the sentence varies with the speaker and the circumstances of interlocution, sometimes communicating the idea that "we are mestizo, not black," and sometimes that "we are all part black." Given hegemonic grids of understanding, similar ethnic groups define themselves differently in North and South America: descendants of Sicilian immigrants in Brazil might call themselves "mestizo"; it is hard to imagine Sicilian Americans describing themselves in the same way.

Brazil has a vast catalogue of racially descriptive terms that highlight a miscegenated heterogeneity in which color forms part of a nuanced spectrum, whence such terms as *mameluco* (white and red), *caboclo* (black and red), and *pardo* (dark). Cognate words bring distinct tones and evaluations. "Miscegenation" has historically carried a negative odor in the United States, redolent of anti-race-mixing laws, while *métissage* in French and *miscigenação* in Portuguese, as the products of assimilationist societies, have gained positive connotations. The same racial hybridity once demonized by many 19th-century Brazilian philosophers is now lauded as a source of national pride. (Antonio Risério distinguishes between Portuguese *miscigenação* as simple biological mixture and *mestiçagem* as a mix of biology and culture, a discursivization of mixture.)[98] One might also contrast the "top-down miscegenation" carried out by the *bandeirantes* and *mamelucos* as part of a demographic imperative of territorial domination with the lateral miscegenation between enslaved Africans, Indians, and poor whites as practiced in Palmares in the 17th century and that continues in new forms to the present day. The dominant discourse of Brazilian miscegenation often conflates these very different phenomena.

The word "immigration" also resonates differently in the various sites. In the United States, it conjures up Ellis Island and the "American dream" as part of an official discourse of a self-defined "immigrant society." A frequent Brazilian formulation describes Brazil as a nation that "receives immigrants well," which presupposes a preexisting mixed core prior to immigration. The U.S. nation was defined from the beginning as an amalgam of different migratory waves of European settlers, from which would emerge "America" as a space of pan-European fusion. The critique of this discourse, meanwhile, casts a critical light on the exclusionary practices on which the "immigrant nation" is premised. While contemporary France too is shaped by immigration, its official discourse has minimized this history, partly because French foundational myths were already well established before mass immigration began.[99] Whereas official U.S. discourse has always seen immigration as "of the essence" of the nation (while relegating people of color to the polity's outer limits), France has seen immigration as a latter-day graft on a preexisting white-European core. At the same time, American and French conservatives like to distinguish between authentic nationals ("real Americans," "Français de souche") and the ersatz newcomers.

The transformations generated by the linguistic encounter of European and indigene in the "contact zone" (Mary Louise Pratt) of conquest are also at the kernel of historical tensions that pass through language. During the "rosy dawn" of colonialism, both sides were fumbling, as it were, in linguistic darkness. Since translation was often transcosmological, there were zones of "opacity" (Édouard Glissant) and "untranslatability" (Emily Apter).[100] Colonialism generated intercultural equivocation, or what we have called "a collision of partly incommensurable vocabularies."[101] Catholic priests in Brazil diabolized indigenous religion by translating the deity Tupa (or the Yoruban orixá Exu) as "devil." Colonial hermeneutics thus interpreted cultural phenomena through a fundamentally Christian matrix. The power dynamics of coloniality thus inevitably inflected translation, with each side invested in certain understandings. European conquerors and settlers sometimes "heard" only what they wanted to hear: that the natives were eager to convert, that gold was to be found on the other side of the nearest hill, that Europeans were regarded as gods, and so forth.

Yet we have only begun to scratch the surface of the complexities of "racing" translation. The discussion is not simply one of matching vocabularies and concepts between Portuguese, English, and French. Postcolonial and diasporic writers have troubled established linguistic hierarchies. Glissant has lauded "creolity" and "Antillanite" as creatively decentering official, Hexagonal French. Glissant defines "creolization" as "the meeting, interference, shock, harmonies and disharmonies between the cultures of the world. . . . [It] has the following characteristics: the lightning speed of interaction among its elements; the 'awareness of awareness' thus provoked in us; the reevaluation of the various elements brought into contact . . . with unforeseeable results."[102] Building on Deleuze/Guattari, Glissant imagines a poetics of relation in which Third Worldism is replaced by the "All Worldism" of a dialogical and reciprocal planetary consciousness.[103] As a site of cultural (mis)encounter, translation, both within and between languages, in sum, is key to our discussion. To focus on the ramifying differences of language exchange as opposed to furthering petrified conceptions of national character is one way to avoid the fetishizing of the ethno-cultural essences of what might be called "ontologi-nations."

3 The Seismic Shift and the Decolonization of Knowledge

CENTRAL 20TH-CENTURY EVENTS—WORLD War II, the Jewish Holocaust, and Third World independence struggles—all simultaneously delegitimized the West as axiomatic center of reference and affirmed the rights of non-European peoples emerging from the yoke of colonialism. Although resistance to colonialism has existed since the very beginnings of colonization, this resistance reached critical mass in the postwar period. In the wake of centuries of struggles, decolonization achieved climactic expression with Indian independence in 1947, the Chinese revolution in 1949, Algerian independence in 1962, up through the independence of Mozambique and Angola in the mid-1970s. Thus, if Nazism, fascism, and the Holocaust revealed in all their horror the "internal" sickness of Europe as a site of racism and totalitarianism, the Third World liberation struggles revealed the "external" revolt against Western domination, provoking a crisis in the taken-for-granted narrative of European-led Progress. What we call the "seismic shift" refers to the intellectual/discursive fallout of these events, seen as catalytic for a broad decolonization of knowledge and academic culture. But in order to prepare the ground for our critique in later chapters, we must first outline what this shift was reacting *against*.

The Protocols of Eurocentrism

Embedded in our attempt to posit a genealogy for the culture wars is a concept foundational to our critique: Eurocentrism. As we argued in *Unthinking Eurocentrism*, Eurocentrism is the discursive-ideological precipitate of colonial domination. Eurocentrism enshrines and naturalizes the hierarchical stratifications inherited from colonialism, rendering them as inevitable and even "progressive." Although forged as part of the colonizing process, Eurocentrism's links to that process are obscured through a buried epistemology. Eurocentrism does not refer to Europe in its literal sense as a continent or a geopolitical unit but rather to the perception of Europe (and its extensions around the world) as normative. In this sense, it might better be called "Euro-hegemonism" or the "occidental world view" or "coloniality" (Anibal Quijano) or "European planetary consciousness" (Mary Louise Pratt).[1] Eurocentrism has little to do with positive feelings about Europe; it has to do, rather, with assumptions about the relationship between the West and the non-West. It is not Eurocentric to love Shakespeare or Proust, but it is Eurocentric to wield these cultural figures as "proof" of an innate European superiority.

Our coinage "Eurotropism," meanwhile, calls attention to an orientation, a tendency to turn toward the West as an ideal Platonic Sun, much as phototropic plants turn toward the literal Sun for their sustenance. Indeed, Hegel develops precisely this solar metaphor in *The Philosophy of History*: "It is in the West that the inner Sun of self-consciousness rises, shedding a higher brilliance."[2] Tropes of light (enlightenment, *rayonnement*) envision democracy, science, and progress as emanating outward from a luminously radiating European source. Rather than a systematic philosophy, Eurocentrism consists in an interlocking network of buried premises, embedded narratives, and submerged tropes that constitute a broadly shared epistemology. Eurocentrism is not usually a conscious political stance but rather an implicit positioning and a dominant "common sense" or "monoculture of the mind" (Vandana Shiva).[3] Far from being a European monopoly, Eurocentrism is often shared with non-Europeans. Even the creators of the first black republic in Haiti, as Michael Dash points out, idealized Europe and denigrated an Africa they had been taught to despise.[4]

Some of the basic principles of Euro-hegemonism can be found in remarkably explicit form in the writings of some of the most celebrated Enlightenment thinkers. Hegel, often regarded as the progressive John the Baptist who prepared the way for Marx, offers a striking example. On the one hand, the Hegel of the *Phenomenology of Spirit* engendered the progressive lineage that leads out to Marx, Kojève, Sartre, Jameson, and Butler. On the other hand, the Hegel of *The Philosophy of History* leads out to Francis Fukuyama and Samuel Huntington. For that Hegel, world history "travels from East to West, for Europe is absolutely the end of History." Asia for Hegel represents the "childhood of humanity," while Jews, Africans, and indigenous Americas are "outside of history." At times, Hegel's rendering of human suffering becomes chillingly matter-of-fact. Native America, Hegel tells us, "has always shown itself physically and psychically powerless, and still shows itself so. For the aborigines, after the landing of the Europeans in America, gradually vanished at the breath of European activity."[5] In this naturalization of ethnocide, the indigenous peoples simply disappear, not because of colonial guns, massacres, and microbes but only because of a preternaturally powerful European "breath" or "spirit."

Hegel baldly states in his *Encyclopedia* that "against the absolute right of that people who actually are the carriers of the world Spirit [i.e., Europeans], the spirit of other peoples has no other right."[6] In a formulation that recalls the *Dred Scott* decision's claim that "the Negro has no rights that the white man need respect," Hegel argues in *Philosophy of Right* that Europe knew that "the rights of barbarians [were] unequal to its own and treats their autonomy as only a formality."[7] Declaring blacks "incapable of development or culture," Hegel in *The Philosophy of History* seems to deny even the existence of black subjectivity:

> In Negro life the characteristic point is the fact that consciousness has not yet attained to the realization of any substantial objective existence—as for example God or Law—in which the interest of man's volition is involved and in which he realizes his own being. . . . The Negro . . . exhibits the natural man in his completely wild and untamed state. . . . There is nothing harmonious with humanity to be found in this type of character.[8]

Unlike those who discerned black critical capacity, Hegel sees a generic intellectual and moral handicap:

> Among the Negroes moral sentiments are quite weak, or more strictly, nonexistent. Parents sell their children, and conversely children their parents, as either has the opportunity. Through the pervading influence of slavery all these bonds of moral regard disappear, and it does not occur to the Negro mind to expect from others what we are enabled to claim.[9]

In a particularly egregious case of what Foucault called the "indignity of speaking for others," Hegel portrays the enslaved, but not the enslavers, as lacking in moral feeling. Unacquainted with Africans and untraveled on the continent, presumably basing his judgments on secondary sources such as travel literature, Hegel grants himself the sovereign right to generalize about the intimate feelings of millions of Africans. We are not suggesting, of course, that Hegel was "nothing but a racist" or that there were no progressive aspects of his work as a theorist of freedom. The problem is that the freedom he theorized was usually meant only for Europeans. Hegel's provincial prejudices have migrated and "settled" in diverse regions of thought. We hear explicit somewhat euphoric echoes of Hegelianism in Fukuyama's *End of History*, with the idea of the inevitably planetary victory of neoliberal democracy.[10] And even though George W. Bush has clearly never read Hegel, his declaration that "freedom is God's gift to the world" reveals him to be an unwitting (and inarticulate) vulgar Hegelian.

Hegel's philosophy of history can be understood through philosopher Charles Mills's concept of the "racial contract," defined as

> that set of formal or informal agreements or meta-agreements (higher level contracts about contracts, which set the limits of the contracts' validity) between the members of one subset of humans, henceforth designated by (shifting) "racial" (phenotypical/genealogical/cultural) criteria . . . as "white," and coextensive (making due allowance for gender differentiation) with the class of full persons, to categorize the remaining subset of humans as "nonwhite" and of a different and inferior moral status, subpersons, so that they have a subordinate civil standing in the white or white-ruled polities the whites either already inhabit or establish.[11]

White supremacy, for Mills, is the "unnamed political system that has made the modern world what it is today."[12] Although no longer explicitly racial, the "color line" still runs through all these forms of domination. Paul Gilroy speaks of a "hemispheric order of racial domination," while Mills speaks of "the metaphysical infrastructure of global white supremacy."[13] African and African American philosophers such as Mills have thus called attention not only to the Eurocentric blind spots inherent in Hegel's views on Africa but also to his ethnocentric conception of freedom.

Marxism, meanwhile, although progressive in many respects, mingles Eurocentrism with its critique. While egalitarian in economics and politics, Marxism still privileges the historical agency of Europe and Europeans. For many Marxists, an intrinsically European capitalism, despite the cruelty so lucidly noted by Marx himself, opened the way for the global liberation of productive forces. The subalternization of Asia, Africa, and the Americas ultimately served to advance human progress. At the same time, Kevin B. Anderson makes a strong case, partly on the basis of previously untranslated texts, that Marx posited a strong connection between capitalism and slavery. In articles written in French, Marx argued that slavery was "an economic category of paramount importance," since slavery "in Surinam, in Brazil, in the southern regions of North America [are] the pivot on which our present-day industrialism turns. . . . Without slavery there would be no cotton, without cotton there would be no modern industry. It is slavery that has given value to the colonies, it is the colonies which have created world trade."[14] The "veiled slavery of the wage-laborers in Europe," for Marx, formed the "pedestal" for "the unqualified slave labor of the New World."[15] Marx threw himself into the antislavery struggle and saw the fight against racism as crucial in the creation of a strong labor movement in the United States. W. E. B. Du Bois, C. L. R. James, Eric Williams, Angela Davis, Cedric Robinson, and Robin Kelley. are among the black Marxists who furthered this trend within Marxist thought.

Although Eurocentric historiography invokes classical Athenian democracy as the unique and originary fount of European democracy, Jack Goody speaks of parallel forms of democratic representation in Phoenicia and in Carthage, which voted annually for its magistrates. The desire for some form of representation, he suggests, is "intrinsic to the human situation."[16] Amartya Sen, similarly, has spoken of the "global" as opposed to exclusively European roots of democracy. Rather than seeing democracy as synonymous with formal elections and representative government, Sen focuses on cultural pluralism, minority rights, and the variegated forms of "public reason." He quotes Nelson Mandela's *Long Walk to Freedom* on the subject of indigenous African forms of public reason and deliberative consensus. Mandela describes the local meetings held in the regent's house in Mqhekesini as "democracy in its purest form. Despite a hierarchy of importance among the speakers, everyone was heard, chief and subject, warrior and medicine man, shopkeeper and farmer, landowner and laborer. . . . All men were free to voice their opinions and equal in their value as citizens."[17] Venerable traditions of public reason and pluralism, Sen argues, can be found in India, China, Japan, Korea, Iran, Turkey, the Arab world, and many parts of Africa.[18]

In the 20th century, we find Eurocentric formulations even in the writings of a philosopher such as Edmund Husserl. Here is a passage from his *Phenomenology and the Crisis of Philosophy*: "[In Europe we find] something unique, which all other human groups, too, feel with regard to us, something that, apart from all considerations of expediency, becomes a motivation for them . . . constantly to Europeanize themselves, whereas we, if we understand ourselves properly, will never, for example, Indianize ourselves."[19] Husserl here articulates what is often assumed: that Europeans display a unique mental vitality and purpose, that Europe is the fundamental source of new ideas, and that both Europeans and non-Europeans agree that this is the normal and proper order of things. What Husserl has done, as Emmanuel Eze points out, is to naturalize within the terms of transcendental philosophy the power effects of colonialism, rendered as a racial superiority.[20] It is precisely the universalization of one provincial set of cultural values that provokes the need to "decenter" Europe.

Eurocentrism does not designate the consistently expressed beliefs of individuals or of a group of people, however. Nor do all elements in the system appear at the same time. Rather, Eurocentrism is an analytical construct pointing to a structured set of protocols or discursive tendencies disseminated around the globe. "The current dimensions of both time and space," as Jack Goody puts it, "were laid down by the west . . . because expansion around the world required time-keeping and maps which provided the frame of history as well as geography."[21] At this point in history, with the United States in precipitous decline and Asia and Latin America in the ascendant, Eurocentrism has a vestigial, out-of-sync quality, yet it still exercises immense discursive and mediatic power. Although Eurocentrism is complex, contradictory, and historically specific, its composite portrayal as a mode of thought might point to a number of mutually reinforcing operations.

Expanding on our very brief analysis in *Unthinking Eurocentrism*, an "ideal portrait" might posit the following patterns: (1) Eurocentrism's narrative is diffusionist; it assumes that Europe generates ideas that then spread around the world thanks to their inherent power of persuasion. Eurocentrism roots Europe's putative superiority in intrinsic traits such as rationality and curiosity, engendering a fictitious sense of superiority and entitlement. Within the Kantian conception, the enlightened nations give out the laws that eventually reach "the others." (2) Eurocentric temporal discourse develops an evolutionary narrative within which the West is figured as "ahead" and its others as "behind." In this metanarrative of progress, a linear ("Plato-to-NATO") teleology sees progress as an express train moving inexorably north-by-northwest from classical Greece to imperial Rome on to the metropolitan capitals of Europe and the United States. A "presentist" historiography writes history backward so that Europe is seen as always tending toward the progressive and innovative, while the periphery is always in danger of reverting to the backward and static. (3) Eurocentrism operates through a figurative substratum of embedded metaphors and allegorical motifs that encode Western superiority through interlocking binarisms such as center/periphery, order/chaos, depth/surface, light/darkness, maturity/immaturity, activity/passivity, and self-reflexivity/blindness. (4) Eurocentric discourse denies the political, religious, juridical, and cultural agency of colonized peoples, treating the indigenous peoples of the Americas, for example, as characterized by a primordial lack through a production of nothingness that decrees native land *terra nullius* and native culture *cultura nullius*. (5) Eurocentric political discourse attributes to the West an inherent drive toward democratic institutions. The Inquisition, King Leopold II, Mussolini, Hitler, Pétain, Franco, Salazar, and other European despots, within this narrative, are mere "aberrations" to be edited out within an amnesiac logic of selective legitimation. The West's antidemocratic practices—colonialism, slave trading, imperialism—are seen as contingent "accidents" rather than as evidence of oppressive historical patterns. (6) As a corollary to the Europe-equals-democracy formula, Eurocentric discourse elides the democratic traditions of non-Western peoples, while obscuring both the manipulative limits of Western formal democracy and the West's not infrequent role in subverting democracies (often in collaboration with local kleptocrats) in the Global South. Non-Western social systems are seen as in excess (Oriental despotism) or in deficit (societies without states). (7) Eurocentric ethics, meanwhile, is nonreciprocal. It demands of others what it does not itself perform. It places the West as moral arbiter, preaching nuclear nonproliferation, ecological stewardship, corruption-free elections, and other values that the West has practiced only intermittently.

Eurocentric literary discourse (8) emplots literary history as emerging out of biblical Hebraism and classical Hellenism, all retroactively projected as "Western," even though the Bible was rooted in Mesopotamia, Canaan, and Egypt, and ancient Greece was impacted by Semitic, Phoenician, Egyptian, and Ethiopian cultures. A provincial narrative has the novel beginning in Europe—with *Don Quixote* and *Robinson Crusoe* often posited as origins—although one could just as easily see the novel, defined as fiction in prose, as emerging from outside of Europe and then spreading *to* Europe. (9) The Eurocentric narrativization of artistic modernism, similarly, has the West generating artistic forms such as Cubism and collage, which then spread to the "rest of the world." The non-West provides unsigned raw materials to be refined by named Western artists, while Western museums retain the power not only to own non-Western artifacts but also to define what qualifies as "art." (10) A white-supremacist "aesthetic corollary" grants whites a monopoly on beauty, while associating people of color with darkness and moral ugliness. (11) Eurocentric philosophical discourse traces philosophical thinking to the "Greek miracle," with the history of philosophy as working out the problematics formulated from the pre-Socratics up to the present. It cultivates the myth of self-critical reflexivity as a Western monopoly, whence the self-aggrandizing claim that only the West has had the reflexive capacity to criticize its own practices. Eurocentric philosophical discourse inscribes Western thought as Universal and non-Western thought as Particular. Western thinkers address universal subjects; non-Western thinkers address only their "particular" concerns. (12) Eurocentric religious discourse determines that the entire world lives by the Christian periodization (BC/AD) and the Christian calendar. The Enlightenment enshrines a secularism that remains subliminally Christian, recoding divine Providence as Progress and Sin as Unreason. While placing Christianity at the apex, Eurocentrism also hyphenizes Christianity with Judaism (Judeo-Christian) while deleting the Judeo-Muslim hyphen, and marginalizing the third Abrahamic "religion of the book" (Islam). (13) Eurocentric narrations of nationalism contrast the older, mature, civic, and inclusive forms of Western nationalism with the young, irresponsible, and exclusivist forms of non-Western nationalism. Forgetting the nation-state's definitional tendency to monopolize legitimate violence (Weber) both toward otherized indigenous peoples and toward internal minorities, Eurocentrism projects the "new" nationalisms as unprecedentedly violent.[22] (14) Eurocentric discursive and mediatic practices devalue non-Western and nonwhite life in a media-saturated world where white, Western lives are taken as more precious than the lives of people of color. Within the algorithms of human devalorization, people of color have to die en masse for the Western media to take notice.

(15) Eurocentric economics attributes Europe's spectacular success to its enterprising spirit, forgetting that European advantages derived largely from the immense wealth that flowed to Europe from the Americas and other colonized regions. Eurocentric political economy in its various mutations (free-trade imperialism, modernization take-off theory, and neoliberal globalization discourse) develops a diffusionist "trickle-down" economics on a global scale. Just as wealth supposedly trickles down from rich to poor within Western nation-states, so the wealth of the Global North trickles down to the Global South. Eurocentrism does not acknowledge that this one-way narrative can be reversed, that the West became developed thanks to precious metals, fertile land, and enslaved and indentured labor from the non-West. European prog-

ress is seen as self-generated, autonomous, unrelated to the appropriation of wealth or ideas from colonized regions. The "Northern" nations, after pursuing protectionist policies in their own interest, discourage such policies in the Global South. Economic crises in the South are seen as serious only when they impact the North. In the 2008 financial crisis, Wall Street exported not prosperity but rather what were oxymoronically called "toxic assets."

In sum, a Eurocentric perspective systematically upgrades one side of the civilizational ledger and systematically downgrades the other. As a form of hubris, it rigs the historical balance sheet by sanitizing Western history while patronizing and even demonizing the non-West and the nonwhite. It thinks of the non-West in terms of its deficiencies, real or imagined, but thinks of itself in terms of its noblest achievements—science, progress, humanism—while forgetting to add that "science" was often racist science, that "progress" could be genocidal, and that humanism could be a mask for barbarism. All of which is not to say that Eurocentrism is the only "-ism" plaguing the world or that generic social ills cannot be found in other cultural locations or that some other "-centrism" is not lurking around the corner. We do not believe in the inverted narcissism that posits Europe as the source of all evil in the world and exempts non-Western patriarchal elites from all responsibility. Our narrativization of the debates does not emphasize the "virtue" of non-European peoples but rather their cultural and intellectual agency in relation to historically configured relations of power. The point is not to demonize Europe but to relativize and relationalize Europe (*lato sensu*) as a (multi)culture alongside and interacting with other (multi)cultures. The point is not to disqualify Western perspectives per se but rather to multiply looks and to analyze the power relations that inform them. (These issues lie in the background of our later critique of figures such as Bourdieu/Wacquant, Slavoj Žižek, and Walter Benn Michaels).

The Postwar Rupture

What we are calling the postwar seismic shift shook to their foundations many of the Eurocentric axioms just outlined, yet they persist, on the right and sometimes, as we shall see, on the left. While anticolonial movements began to transform relations *between* nations, minority liberation movements began to transform relations *within* nations. Just as newly independent Third World nations tried to free themselves from colonial subordination, so First World minorities challenged the white-supremacist protocols of their own societies.

The seismic shift brought to the surface the tensions inherent in centuries of literal and discursive struggle. Hundreds if not thousands of writers and activists in the early postwar period participated in this shift. Indeed, philosopher Simone

Weil anticipated the shift even during World War II. Writing in 1943, shortly before she died, she foresaw the coming storm, warning with a terrible prescience that France would "have to choose between attachment to its empire and the need once more to have a soul. . . . If it chooses badly, . . . it will have neither one nor the other, but simply the most terrible affliction, . . . and all those capable of speaking or wielding a pen will be eternally responsible for a crime."[23] Another early warning of the shift came in 1948 with Sartre's "Orphée Noir" incendiary preface to Senghor's *Anthologie de la Nouvelle Poesie Nègre et Malgache de Langue Française*: "What would you expect to find, when the muzzle that has silenced the voices of black men is removed? That they would thunder your praise? . . . Do you expect to read adoration in their eyes?"[24] Here the collective self-image of Europeans was being challenged by the changing self-image of the colonized, leaving both a severe narcissistic wound and, at times, new openness to the non-European other. Jean-François Lyotard, in his account of the effects of decolonization, in tandem with Sartre's account of the return of the colonial gaze, speaks of the psychic fallout of decolonization: "One cannot understand the European's anguish in the face of Algerian resistance without placing it within the context of a self-placating paternalism in which colonials tried to live. . . . Can you imagine the stupefaction of well-heeled Frenchmen! It was not even any longer their world in question, it was—exactly—their world reversed."[25]

According to Elisabeth Young-Bruehl, three antiracist public discourses predominated in the immediate postwar period: (1) the critical analysis of anti-Semitism; (2) the discussions of the oppression of colonized peoples and racism against African Americans; and (3) the critique of sexism.[26] The latter critique goes back to Simone de Beauvoir's *The Second Sex* (1949) and to the Women's Liberation movement. At times, a discursive crossover transpired, as when Beauvoir spoke of the:

> deep similarities between the situation of woman and that of the Negro. Both are being emancipated today from a like paternalism, and the former master class wishes to "keep them in their place." . . . The former masters lavish more or less sincere eulogies, either on the virtues of the "good Negro" with his dormant, childish, merry soul—the submissive Negro—or on the merits of the woman who is "truly feminine"—that is, frivolous, infantile, irresponsible—the submissive woman. In both cases the dominant class bases its argument on a state of affairs that it has itself created.[27]

These polemics inevitably revisit the Enlightenment debates. Were human rights universal or reserved for a privileged few? Was slavery, or its latter-day correlatives such as discrimination, legitimate in "certain climes" or to be everywhere condemned? Were women truly the equal of men? Did sorority coexist with fraternity? Was the Social Contract also racial and sexual?

While building on the progressive wing of the Enlightenment, and on the anticolonial thinkers and activists who preceded them, figures such as Ho Chi Minh, Che Guevara, Julius Nyerere, Kwame Nkrumah, Sékou Touré, Amílcar Cabral, Malcolm X, Patrice Lumumba, Martin Luther King, Jr., and Aimé Césaire began to dismantle taken-for-granted racial hierarchies and the colonial architecture of the world. Césaire's *Discourse on Colonialism*, first published in 1950, for example, challenged the racist currents within dominant discourse in France, drawing examples from a wide spectrum of politicians, geographers, theologians, psychologists, and novelists.[28]

In the background of the U.S. culture wars, meanwhile, were the first Civil Rights marches and massive antiwar demonstrations. After having helped defeat Nazism in Europe, African American veterans confronted apartheid-style racism in the United States itself. In 1954, the Supreme Court struck down the law dictating "separate but equal" schools on the grounds that "separate" could never be "equal." Rosa Parks refused to sit in the back of the bus, "freedom riders" turned Greyhound buses into vehicles for protest, and many blacks (and a few white supporters) were murdered by white racists. In Birmingham, Alabama, in 1963, thousands of protesters faced police clubs, dogs, and high-powered water hoses. Martin Luther King, Jr., in his struggle against segregation, drew on the taproot of two foundational American rhetorics—first the biblical language of justice, exodus, and the "promised land" and second the Enlightenment language of the Bill of Rights and the Declaration of Independence—in order to move the larger public toward the Preamble's "more perfect union."

As the postwar years witnessed the waning of a French empire second only to Britain's, France too became a key site in the postwar shift in thinking about race and colonialism. At first, the French government maintained an intransigent colonial posture in the immediate postwar period, first in Southeast Asia, where the French suppressed Vietnamese independence until the 1954 French army defeat at Dien Bien Phu—when it was replaced by U.S. "advisers"—and then in Algeria, where colonialism ended in 1962 after bitter political battles in France itself. Much of the French contribution to the intellectual shift formed part of these battles, as anticolonial writers such as the Martinicans Césaire and Fanon, Algerians such as Gisèle Halimi, and the Tunisian Albert Memmi, alongside African American expatriates such as Richard Wright, found white French allies in figures such as Henri Alleg, Jean-Paul Sartre, Simone de Beauvoir, Edgar Morin, Francis Jeanson, and François Maspero. At the same time, the postwar economic expansion of France itself led to the recruiting of colonial subjects as workers. First seen as temporary guests by the majority population, the immigrants were expected to return home after a brief stint of factory work. But the attraction of the postwar prosperity of *Les Trente Glorieuses*, combined with postindependence instability in Algeria, resulted in massive dislocations. At the end of the 1960s there were 600,000 Algerians, 140,000 Moroccans, and 90,000 Tunisians in France, along with thousands of West Indian French people and French West Africans.

France, Brazil, and the United States all had their anti-imperialist, anticapitalist, antiracist, antisexist, antihomophobic, and antiauthoritarian movements. Such projects were not only allied metaphorically but also concretely linked in transnational networks of activism. The movements varied in their emphases, however, depending on whether they took place in the formerly imperial and now authoritarian France of de Gaulle or in a neocolonized Brazil oppressed by a U.S.-supported dictatorship or in what José Martí called the "Belly of the Beast" (the United States). In France, the vociferously Third Worldist May '68 movement offered its support to revolutions (in China, Vietnam, Cuba, Algeria, Cuba) and minority U.S. "internal colony" movements (the Black Panthers, the American Indian Movement, the Young Lords), seeing them as partial models for First World revolutionaries. A "tricontinental" united front combined a left-tinged revolutionism with an ardent anticolonialism.

The postwar shift in Brazil, meanwhile, took forms both similar to and different from those in France and the United States. Since Brazil, unlike the United States and France, was not an imperialist power, there was no need for a movement against "Brazilian imperialism," only one against U.S. imperialism. And since Brazil was not a legally segregated country, there was no need for massive Civil Rights marches against de jure segregation. In Brazil, unlike in France, issues of racial difference had always been part of the debate about national identity, whether in the form of romantic "Indianist" discourses or of racist theories of "degeneracy" or of "racial democracy" discourses. In political terms, the post–World War II period was a time of relative democratization after the demise of Getúlio Vargas's authoritarian New State. Right-wing "Integralism" was on the defensive, and democratic movements were on the upswing. Many left Brazilian intellectuals sympathized with anticolonial movements, including in the Portuguese colonies (Angola, Mozambique, Guinea-Bissau, and São Tomé). It was also in this postwar period that Brazilian intellectuals, influenced by dependency theory, began to speak of Brazil's status as a "dependent," "peripheral," and "neocolonized" nation.

Here we briefly focus on Frantz Fanon as an exemplary figure who embodies the seismic shift and who deeply impacted intellectual life and activism in all three zones. Fanon serves here as both metonym and metaphor for a paradigmatic shift generated by many thinkers. Fanon, whose work built on Césaire's call for "Copernican revolution" in thought, became best known as an eloquent critic of colonial oppression and as an astute diagnostician of the twinned pathologies of whiteness and blackness. Forging a link between colonialism and racism, Fanon called attention to metropolitan racial tensions, in *Black Skin, White Masks*, and to Third World revolutions, in *The Wretched of the Earth*. Fanon inspired black liberation thinking around the diaspora, even while he himself was inspired by the Algerian revolution.

A kind of posthumous wrestling over Fanon's legacy has triggered a resurgent interest in his work, with lively debates about the gendered politics of the veil, about Fanon's "therapeutic" theory of violence, and about the relative merits of the psychoanalytically oriented *Black Skin, White Masks* versus the revolutionary socialism of *The Wretched of the Earth*.[29] Contemporary scholars have been disentangling what now seems archaic and retrograde in Fanon's work from what seems anticipatory and prescient. A "postnationalist" era has become more aware of Fanon's limitations: his occasional romanticization of violence, his idealization of the peasantry, his slender knowledge of Arab/Muslim culture, his blind spots concerning forms of oppression rooted in gender and sexuality. At the same time, an anti-Fanon backlash has sometimes caricatured him (1) as an advocate of violence for its own sake, (2) as a crypto-totalitarian accomplice of the "Third World gulag," and (3) as the Manichean partisan of simplistic colonizer/colonized dichotomies. Fanon's denunciation of the binarist character of the colonial situation—for example, of an Algeria ripped in two by checkpoints and ghettoization—has occasionally been exploited to charge Fanon himself with binarism. Still another trend turns Fanon into a proto-poststructuralist analyst of sinuous postcolonial hybridities.

Yet a contemporary rereading of Fanon also reveals his extraordinary farsightedness as a precursor for a number of intellectual movements. In his lapidary phrases, we find the germ of many radical theoretical developments in various fields of relevance. Fanon's anticolonialist decentering of Europe in *The Wretched of the Earth* (1961) can now be seen to have both provoked and foreshadowed Derrida's claim (in "Structure, Sign, and Play in the Discourse of the Human Sciences," 1966) that European culture has been "dislocated," forced to stop casting itself as the exclusive "culture of reference."[30] What Fanon called "socialtherapy," similarly, clearly anticipated the "antipsychiatry" of such figures as David Cooper, R. D. Laing, and Felix Guattari. With his questions, Fanon pushed the Eurocentric envelope of psychoanalysis. How can Freud's "talking cure" facilitate a transition to "ordinary unhappiness," he asked, in a situation where social oppression itself generates "extraordinary unhappiness"? How can psychoanalysis help the patient "adjust" when colonialism provokes unending maladjustment? How can patients feel "at home" in their environment when colonialism turns the colonized into strangers in their own land?[31]

It was in this same spirit that Fanon criticized psychoanalyst Octave Mannoni, who argued in his *Prospero and Caliban: The Psychology of Colonization* that colonized peoples suffered from a "dependency complex" that induced them to identify with the father-like colonizer. But for Fanon, the colonized did not identify with Shakespeare's colonizing Prospero but rather with the angry and rebellious Caliban. Indeed, Fanon's fellow Martinican and mentor Césaire pursued this same identificatory logic in his revisionist version of *The Tempest*, in which Caliban becomes Caliban X, the black militant who denounces Prospero for teaching him to jabber his language well enough to follow orders but not enough to study science. A profound complementarity, in this sense, links the antiracist psychology of *Black Skin, White Masks* and the revolutionary sociology of *The Wretched of the Earth*. Although Fanon occasionally cited Lacan, as David Macey points out, he was not a Lacanian. While Lacan opposed "ego-psychology," Fanon stressed the need to strengthen the ego of the colonized.[32] At the same time, Fanon himself did help shape a discourse very much inflected by psychoanalysis, to wit, the academic field of "postcolonial discourse," both through his analysis of metropolitan racism and in his trenchant critique of nationalism in the "Pitfalls of National Consciousness" chapter in *The Wretched of the Earth*.[33]

Although Fanon never spoke of "Orientalist discourse," his critiques of colonialist imagery provided proleptic examples of what would later be called "anti-Orientalist critique" à la Edward Said. When Fanon argued that the colonizer could not speak of the colonized without invoking the bestiary, he was calling attention to the animalizing trope by which the colonizing imaginary rendered the colonized as beast-like and animalic. Fanon's foiling of the dynamic settler who makes history against the background of torpid creatures mired in tradition anticipated Johannes Fabian's critique of classical anthropology's projection of the colonized as "allochronically" mired in a putatively inert "tradition" seen as modernity's antithesis.[34] For Fanon, as for Fabian, the colonizer and the colonized are contemporaneous and coeval. Rejecting the "progressive," Eurocentric two-speed paradigm of progress, Fanon insists that the colonized do not want to "catch up" with anyone.

Fanon can also be seen as a precursor of "cultural studies," "critical race studies," and even "whiteness studies." Although cultural studies had not yet been formulated as a project, Fanon certainly practiced a version of what later went by that name. Already in the 1950s, he took all aspects of cultural life—the veil, dance, language, trance, radio, and film—as legitimate objects of study and overdetermined sites of social and cultural contestation. Although Fanon has often been caricatured as a racial hardliner, he in fact anticipated the antiessentialist critique of race. "Lumping all Negroes together under the designation of 'Negro people,'" Fanon writes in *Toward the African Revolution*, "is to deprive them of any possibility of individual expression."[35] In Fanon's relational view *in Black Skin, White Masks*, the black man not only is obliged to be black, but "he must be black in relation to the white man."[36] The black man, as Fanon puts it, is "comparison."[37] Nor was race a preeminent category; colonialism, he argues, "was only accidentally white."[38] Race was an imposed artifact, not a matter of intrinsic traits. Perceptions of race and of color were inflected even by language; "the black," he wrote in *Black Skin, White Masks*, "will be the proportionately whiter . . . in direct relation to his mastery of the French language."[39] Like the later poststructuralists, Fanon saw identity as languaged, situated, constructed, projected. "When the West Indian goes to France," he writes, "his phenotype undergoes a mutation."[40] (Jean Genet evoked this instability in *The Blacks* when he asks, "What then is a black, and first of all, what is the black's color?")[41] As someone who became acutely aware of his own blackness only in France and who was regarded by some Algerians as culturally European, Fanon inevitably had an acute sense of the conjunctural, malleable character both of racial categorizations and of communitarian self-definition.

Fanon's work also foreshadowed what is variously called "dependency theory," "systems theory," and "center/periphery theory." His claim in *The Wretched of the Earth* that "Europe is literally the creation of the Third World,[42]—that is, that the wealth and prosperity of an overstuffed Europe were extracted from the misery and impoverishment of the Third World—anticipated in stereographic form the arguments of later theorists such as Andre Gunder Frank and James Petras (for Latin America), Walter Rodney (for Africa), Manning Marable (for Afro-America), and Samir Amin and Immanuel Wallerstein (for the world in general). Fanon's remark that "for the colonized subject, objectivity is always directed against him,"[43] similarly, provides a historically precocious example of the anti-imperialist and anticapitalist media critique that became so pervasive during the 1960s and 1970s and beyond.

Fanon's work was subsequently disseminated not only in France and the Francophone world but also in the Arab and Muslim world and throughout much of the Americas, Africa, and Asia. In Brazil, Fanon became a key reference for the black movement, as represented by such figures as Abdias do Nascimento, Clóvis Moura, Lelia Gonzalez, Amauri Mendes Pereira, and Yedo Ferreira.[44] Fanon's work helped inspire the "pedagogy of the oppressed" developed by Paulo Freire, the "theatre of the oppressed" staged and theorized by Augusto Boal, and anticolonialist artistic manifestoes such as filmmaker Glauber Rocha's "Aesthetics of Hunger." In the United States, Fanon's work became exceedingly well known both among black activists and among academics, who regularly assigned his work in a wide array of fields. Speaking more generally, Fanon provided a formative text for Latin American intellectuals articulating the neocolonial dimension of their histories. In intellectual-academic terms, Fanon's key anticolonial concepts radiated outward, impacting feminism (which "gendered" Fanon's three-stage theory of disalienation), situationism (which denounced the metaphorical "colonization" of everyday life), and sociological radicalism (which saw French peasants as "the wretched of the earth").

The Radicalization of the Disciplines

Continuing the legacy of the anticolonial thinkers, countless intellectuals in all three sites have worked to decolonize knowledge production. The earlier Third Worldist and the later critical race, multicultural, ethnic studies, and postcolonial projects can be seen as forming the scholarly wing of the seismic shift, serving both to support and to theorize social movements. In the U.S. academy, a number of institutional and demographic changes favored this decolonizing move. The end of de jure segregation and the rise of a black middle class led to greater black access to education. Changes in immigration laws (especially the 1965 Hart-Cellar Immigration Act), meanwhile, facilitated the granting of citizenship to Asians, Africans, and Latin Americans, resulting in community pressures on the academy to include these populations both as students and as professors. Native American, black, Chicano/a, Asian American, and Euro-American radicals assumed roles as teachers, leading to new programs and courses incorporating the histories, theories, and perspectives of people who had been traditionally marginalized by patriarchal Eurocentric elites. Professors began to integrate issues of race, class, gender, nation, sexuality, and empire into their pedagogy and scholarship, leading to an ideological battle royal both on and off campuses.

Many scholars also began to rethink their disciplines in terms of the global changes triggered by decolonization and by minority struggles. Disciplines in which the West was assumed to be both the speaking subject and the object of study were subjected to critique. The challenges to the protocols of Eurocentrism clearly impacted most of the academic disciplines, but at different times and in diverse ways. Critical and even insurgent proposals were expressed in recombinatory coinages such as "revisionist history," "critical law," "radical philosophy," "reflexive anthropology," and "critical pedagogy"—where the qualifiers suggested a reconceptualization of a canonical discipline from the periphery and from below. The thrust was doubly critical, first of the *presence* of Eurocentric perspectives and second of the *absence* of non-European and nonwhite faculty, students, and cultural topics. Decolonizing projects called for more inclusionary educational systems, more culturally diverse political representation, more racially equitable justice systems, and greater indigenous, immigrant, gay, and women's rights. The goal was to create egalitarian social formations, where the state was not dominated by a single ethnicity but rather represented the totality of its citizens, all with an equal claim to both recognition and redistribution. This meant, inevitably, taking into account the historical practices that had generated the structural inequalities in the first place.

Here we sketch out a few examples of direct challenges to the protocols of Eurocentric knowledge production, as they emerge both from within disciplines and through the formation of interdisciplines. A decolonizing economics discipline, for example, moved away from the standard modernization and free-market-based development theories that saw Western financial investments as fueling prosperity in the Third World. Dependency theory rejected the "development" discourse that conceived a Promethean West as catalyzing an economic "takeoff" that would recapitulate the historical sequencing of Western development. Such a view, for dependency theorists, falsely assumed that the world's resources were available to the Third World as they had been "available" to the colonizing powers during what Marx called the "rosy dawn of the era of capitalist production."[45] An amalgam of the radical ideas of an international group of thinkers such as Raúl Prebisch, Fernando Henrique Cardoso, Celso Furtado, Andre Gunder Frank, James Petras, and Paulo Singer, dependency theory saw world poverty and wealth as dialectically intertwined. The same hierarchical world system controlled by metropolitan capitalist countries and corporations simultaneously generated both the wealth of the First World and the poverty of the Third World, as opposite faces of the same coin. Wealth implies poverty, just as a North implies a South.

Dependency theory both critiqued and extended Marxism by transposing the analysis of class within nations to the economic relationships between classes of nations, ranked as subordinate and superordinate. Thus, it moved beyond class struggle as exclusive focus to envision subordinated nations as protagonists of world-historical progressive change. Initially associated with Latin America, dependency theory was extrapolated for Africa in Walter Rodney's *How Africa Underdeveloped Africa* and for Afro-America in Manning Marable's *How Capitalism Underdeveloped Black America*. The theory was also popularized in a widely disseminated book by Uruguayan journalist Eduardo Galeano, whose title—*The Open Veins of Latin America*—metaphorically sums up the drift of dependency theory as a narrative of vampiric exploitation and Christ-like suffering, within which Center and Periphery are locked in mortal struggle.

Dependency theory was subsequently criticized for its "metrocentrism," for its incapacity to conceptualize the interplay of the local and the global, and for its blindness to the modernizing power even of reactionary regimes. Although the drift of the movement was clearly anti-imperialist, dependency theory sometimes purveyed an unconscious Prometheanism that still saw the Third World as the passive victim of an all-powerful First World. Future Brazilian President Fernando Henrique Cardoso therefore called for a more nuanced theory allowing for the very varied "situations" of dependency.[46] In any case, any thoroughgoing analysis of North-South relations requires at least partial recourse to an updated dependency theory, refashioned as "world systems theory" (Wallerstein) and "delinking" and "center/periphery theory" (Samir Amin). While rendering the dependency thesis more subtle and flexible, the new incarnations of the theory still saw colonialism and neocolonialism as constitutive factors in present-day economic inequalities.[47]

The decolonizing project also challenged the protocols of historiography. Instead of one-track, single-rhythm narratives of modernization, revisionist historians began to see parallel yet differentiated narratives of multiple modernities. In the United States, revisionist historians focused on the "underside" of American history by calling attention to the foundational dispossession on which the U.S. nation-state was built. Scholars such as Richard Slotkin, Richard Drinnon, and Francis Jennings rewrote the "Conquest of the West" as an exemplum of colonial expansionism. Rejecting cheerleading versions of U.S. history, the practitioners of "social history," "radical history," and "bottom-up history" called attention to genocide, antiblack racism, and imperialism as well as to black and indigenous rebellions. African American scholars such as John Hope Franklin, Darlene Clark Hine, Cedric Robinson, Manning Marable, Thelma Wills Foote, Angela Davis, and Robin D. G. Kelley, meanwhile, foregrounded the central role of racism in American history and the black struggle for freedom and justice. At the same time, scholars adopted new research methods for rendering audible the subaltern voices of history, for example, by reading court records "against the grain" to unearth the secret histories of resistance. (Some of this radical work took the form of best-seller popular histories such as Howard Zinn's *People's History of the United States* and James Loewen's *Lies My Teacher Told Me*).

Revisionist history questioned U.S. exceptionalist ideologies concerning the "frontier," a euphemism for the indigenous land being occupied by European intruders. Richard Drinnon traced the process by which white hostility toward "savages" has been recycled throughout American history. The process began with the "proto-victims," the Pequots massacred in 1637, when the Puritans made some four hundred of them "as a fiery oven" in their village near the Mystic River and later finished off three hundred more in the mud of Fairfield Swamp, in an early example of the "righteous massacres" that have constituted one very violent strain within American history.[48] This aggressivity subsequently expanded through "Manifest Destiny" to the "Conquest of the West." With the Monroe Doctrine, the U.S. power elite established Latin America as its "sphere of influence," a concept later extended during the "imperialist binge" at the turn of the century to the Philippines, where many of the commanding generals had previously fought in the Plains and Apache Wars.[49] Indeed, the model of frontier conquest provided a paradigm for the relations between the United States and much of the world. With the neoconservative "Project for a New American Century," the frontier became the world itself, bringing to an exhausted climax a territorial and capitalist expansionism whose origins trace back to the formative years of the U.S. nation-state.

Within the legal field, meanwhile, "critical law," "critical race," and feminist legal scholarship questioned the universality of the dominant masculinist forms of Western legal theory and practice. As represented by scholars such as Derrick Bell, Patricia Williams, Richard Delgado, Regina Austin, Roberto Unger Mangabeira, Paulette Caldwell, Randall Kennedy, and Kimberlé Crenshaw, among others, the fields of Critical Law and especially critical race theory disinterred the class, gender, and racial protocols underlying a U.S. legal system rigged against the poor, the black, and the female, while assuming capitalist regimes of ownership as normative. Writing with passionate precision and literary power, critical race theorists demonstrated that racism in U.S. law and society was not aberrant but rather normal and hegemonic.

Philosophy, long one of the whitest, most masculinist, and most Eurocentric of disciplines, also did not escape critique. Rather than assume that Europe always generates ideas, critical philosophers such as Lewis Gordon, Anibal Quijano, Enrique Dussel, Adrian Piper, Lucas Outlaw, Charles Mills, and Emmanuel Eze discerned reverse currents in the non-European critiques of Western philosophy. Rather than accept the myth of the uniqueness of Western self-reflexivity, critical philosophers suggested that the West itself should be more reflexive, as it were, about its own reflexivity. Rather than inscribe the West as universal and the non-West as particular, critical philosophers suggested that the universal can be thought and addressed from any location. Afro-diasporic philosophers called attention to the racist and colonialist dimension of Enlightenment thought. The clearly racist ethnological writings of a Kant or a Hegel, they argued, could no longer be neatly cordoned off from their philosophy. Critical philosophers began to speak of "counter-Enlightenments" and "para-Enlightenments." Black and Chicana feminists, meanwhile, stressed a politics of location, while feminist-inflected standpoint theory suggested that race and gender inescapably impacted the supposedly neutral philosophical and scientific gaze.

In the field of education, the proponents of radical pedagogy, some influenced by Brazilian philosopher-pedagogue Paulo Freire's theories of *conscientização* (consciousness raising), challenged the ideological conservatism of the educational systems of the Americas. In the hands of such figures as Ivan Illich, Chandra T. Mohanty, Peter Maclaren, and Henry Giroux, pedagogy became a subversive project. In many fields, scholars began to question the positivist, objectivist, and scientistic assumptions regnant in their fields, for example the notion of an objective and dispassionate history, supposedly unperturbed by the identity and experience of the historian or by the political and ideological currents of the moment. The field of anthropology, similarly, once a locus of the colonial nexus of power and knowledge, meanwhile, was critiqued by figures such as Talal Assad, Johannes Fabian, Renato Rosaldo, Angela Gilliam, Mick Taussig, Ann

Laura Stoler, Terence Turner, and Faye Ginsburg. Going against the grain of the colonialist tradition, anthropologists in all three zones came to speak of "shared anthropology," "reflexive anthropology," "symmetrical anthropology," "reverse anthropology," and "dialogical anthropology." Brazilian anthropologist Eduardo Viveiros de Castro, within this spirit, redefined the mission of anthropology as the "permanent and unending decolonization of thought." In tandem with similar moves elsewhere (e.g., "provincializing Europe" and "Third Worldizing at home"), Viveiros de Castro speaks of "anthropologizing the Center," in a situation where the anthropologist merely "relationalizes interpretations" and where the goal is not objectification but subjectification.[50]

Apart from engendering a salutary crisis within traditional disciplines, the seismic shift also generated new "interdisciplines" and "transdisciplines." In North America, these transdisciplinary trends took institutionalized form in "ethnic studies," an umbrella term that came to embrace programs and departments in Native American studies, African American studies, Asian American studies, Latino Studies, e.g. Chicano studies (in the Southwest), and Puerto Rican studies (in the East). According to Manning Marable, by 1996 there were nearly one hundred ethnic studies departments in the United States, with roughly forty-five black studies departments, seventeen Chicano/Puerto Rican studies departments, and eight Asian studies departments.[51] Ethnic studies created new institutional spaces for decolonized forms of knowledge, opening the way for new courses, texts, and canons.

The political/academic transformations linked to the various social identities were products of bottom-up and top-down forces, with varying coefficients of hegemony and resistance. Ethnic studies programs/departments emerged as responses to community activism, yet they were helped along by philanthropic foundations. Partly as a response to the 1960s urban rebellions, the Ford Foundation, beginning in 1968, funneled money into African American studies programs/departments. Between the founding of the Student Non-Violent Coordinating Committee (SNCC) and the strident demands for black studies, as Noliwe Rooks puts it, "the country lurched reluctantly toward a semblance of racial equality in an atmosphere of assassinations, lynchings, war, urban rebellions, campus upheavals, and police riots."[52] Black studies became a site of contestation between radical community activism and those who would "manage" that activism. While Black Power advocates saw black studies as "a revolutionary groundswell capable of overturning the existing order," liberals usually saw it "as a means of racial integration and access to increased opportunity."[53] Those who speak derisively of self-indulgent "campus quarrels" often forget the politically consequential clashes at the origin of these debates. The institutional challenge for ethnic studies has been that it become a synergistic coalition rather than a competitive cockfight in which hyphenated Americans fight for the leftovers from the master's table. The intellectual challenge has been to produce a lateral conversation between the marginalized, rather than a pageant of subalterns of color revolving around a white center within the boundaries of the United States.

While ethnic studies was formed institutionally as part of the 1960s and 1970s battles, in the 1980s and 1990s the more established disciplines came under multicultural and Affirmative Action pressures. The canon debate in literature departments, on one level, continued and extended the ethnic studies effort to embrace minoritarian perspectives, but now within the canonical disciplines themselves. In parallel moves, academic umbrella organizations such as the MLA (Modern Language Association) and SCS (Society for Cinema Studies) began to multiculturalize the canon and diversify their membership, leading to significant quarrels not only between the multicultural left and the monocultural right but also within the left concerning the relative importance of class, race, gender, and sexuality and the shifting relations between the various theoretical grids such as Marxism, feminism, and poststructuralism.

Impacted by ethnic studies, American studies took a multicultural turn in the late 1980s. Scholars questioned the American exceptionalist Anglo-normativity that had informed the field, calling attention to U.S.-based literature written in languages other than English and exposing the imperialist undercurrents in canonical literature. At the same time, the multicultural turn highlighted the anti-imperial thrust of writing by figures such as Melville, Thoreau, Twain, and Du Bois. In a subsequent transnational turn, impacted by the transnational feminist studies represented by scholars such as Caren Kaplan, Inderpal Grewal, Chandra Mohanty, Minoo Moallem, and Jacqui Alexander, the field has emphasized cross-border flows of people and cultural information across all the Americas, while still acknowledging the hierarchical "channels" of these flows. As scholars in other fields began to cite and incorporate the insights of ethnic studies scholars, issues of race, colonialism, and multiculturality came to be seen as relevant to all fields of inquiry and to all communities, even if the issues were experienced in uneven ways.

Another set of interdisciplinary formations, based on geographical regions, was designated "area studies," composed of Latin American/Caribbean studies, Asian/Pacific studies, African studies, and Middle East studies. (Western Europe and the United States, symptomatically, did not constitute an area; rather, they formed the quietly normative headquarters from which all the other areas were strategically mapped.) Although the origins of area studies trace back to 19th-century imperial mappings of the disciplines, the field took off with the advent of the Cold War. A clear thematic complementarity operated between ethnic studies and area studies. U.S. minorities "back here" were clearly linked to majorities "over there": African Americans to Africa, Latinos to Latin America, and so forth. But if the themes of the two fields were complementary, their genealogies and political drift were clearly divergent. While "ethnic studies" emerged out of the activism of racialized communities, "area studies" was decreed from above by the U.S. government, reflecting a hunger for expertise in the various regions where U.S. hegemony was being challenged by nationalist and communist insurgencies.

Various ironic turnabouts in this process, however, led to a partial convergence between progressive scholars from the two interdisciplines. If Latin American studies began as a government-supported effort, many of the academic beneficiaries of government grants, especially in the 1960s and 1970s, were not at all inclined to get with the program; many became outspoken critics of U.S. government policy. Historian Warren Dean noted that the U.S. government reduced its grants to Latin Americanists because "95% of the recipients of the grants were against the dictatorships."[54] Brazilianist Robert Levine describes the situation in the 1970s as follows:

> The younger academics [in the United States], many of whom had struggled in the Civil Rights Movement or served in the Peace Corps or demonstrated against the Vietnam War, were sympathetic to the aims of the Cuban revolution and critical of the foreign policy of the United States. . . . With the increased repression in Brazil after 1968, most of the young foreign scholars in Brazil showed solidarity with the opponents of the regime.[55]

Historian James Green traces this process in telling detail in his *We Cannot Remain Silent: Opposition to the Brazilian Military Dictatorship in the United States*.[56] In a 2001 talk, historian Barbara Weinstein recalled the feelings of the period:

> At that time, I fervently believed that a worldwide socialist transformation was a historical possibility. And I felt that Latin America would be in the vanguard of this global revolutionary process. I regarded as elitist or hidebound my peers who opted to study US political history or European intellectual history. In contrast, my choice of Latin America highlighted my political identification with the Third World over the First.[57]

Weinstein's recollections foreground a built-in asymmetry between North and South in the political roles of left intellectuals pressured by nation-state governmentality. The very meaning of "left" changes its valence and affect. For Latin Americans, coming from the Global South, to be "left" is to be nationalist and anti-imperialist, a participant in a struggle to affirm one's nation's rightful place in the concert of nations. Adversary scholarship becomes part of a "national allegory" (Jameson, Xavier), in which the scholar writes the nation within a narrative of resistance. For North Americans, coming from an imperializing country, in contrast, to be "left" is to be a dissident, to be in a sense *anti*-U.S. nationalist and anti-imperialist, a participant in the struggle to *combat* Americano-centrism and restrain American power abroad.[58]

Multiculturalism and the Decolonizing Corpus

What often gets lost in the culture war polemics is the actual scholarly work—what might be awkwardly called the "decolonizing corpus"—generated by the seismic shift. The broader corpus includes work practiced under diverse names and rubrics and performed by hundreds of scholars in many countries. At this point, the corpus includes such diverse currents of thought as Third Worldism, the modernity/coloniality project, anti-imperialist media studies, critical race theory, critical whiteness studies, Latin American subaltern studies, (multi)cultural studies, transnational feminism, "minor" and feminist Francophone studies, Latino studies, Asian studies, visual culture, social-movement analysis, cross-racial and cross-national literary history, race-conscious queer theory, critical science theory, radical pedagogy, reflexive and experimental anthropology, postmodern urbanism and geography, counter-Enlightenment philosophy, border theory, alter-globalization theory, and postcolonial studies, to name just a few of the many adversarial currents and formations. Indeed, each of these categories opens up onto others, and we could easily swell the list with more subfields.[59] Although our rubrics are schematic, and although there are tensions between and even within the diverse modes of critique, what all these heterogeneous fields have in common is a critical engagement with the historical legacies of colonial and racial oppression.

In the 1980s and the 1990s, two keywords—"multiculturalism" and "identity politics"—came to crystallize these trends. Just as the American right had opposed Third Worldism and Civil Rights in the 1960s, it opposed multiculturalism and identity politics in the 1980s. What provoked the right's howls of execration in this period was not the indisputable fact of the dappled variety of the world's cultures—what we call multiculturality—but rather the larger decolonizing project. As one academic face of the late 20th-century decolonizing project, "multiculturalism" became a kind of shorthand to designate a vast array of initiatives. For those leftists who invested the term with hope, what one might call "the desire called multiculturalism" aimed to restructure the ways knowledge was produced and cultural resources were distributed. Emerging out of the eclipse of the somewhat euphoric Third Worldist discourse that imagined an imminent tricontinental revolution lying in wait around the next bend of the dialectic, radical versions of the multicultural project challenged power relations in a less direct way. The germ of radicalism in some versions of multiculturalism, in the United States at least, trace back to the long tradition of anticolonial, antiracist, and anticapitalist movements among leftists of color and their white allies, jointly forming a coalition that Cynthia A. Young calls the "U.S. Third World Left."[60]

Although multiculturality defines any situation where various ethnic cultures interact within the same nation-state, multicultural*ism* celebrated precisely those cultures and perspectives that had been suppressed and stigmatized by the dominant culture. In this sense, it provided an umbrella for diverse projects and constituencies, translating the seismic shift into a language deemed more appropriate during the ebb tide of Third Worldism. Multicultural discourse was above all protean, plural, conjunctural, existing in shifting relation to various institutions, discourses, disciplines, communities, and nation-states. Despite rejection by the right as well as by some on the left, it is useful to recall the term's advantages at the time: (1) its very inclusiveness favored a broad progressive coalition, something lacking in terms such as "Latino liberation" that applied to only one band on the radical spectrum; (2) its strategic vagueness equipped it to prod cultural institutions such as museums and universities into hiring more minorities and diversifying programming and curricula; (3) the polysemy of its constituent terms embraced the "multi-" that evoked a fundamental heterogeneity based on multiple axes of identification, and a "culture" that addressed a silent rebuke to reductionist Marxists blind to the centrality of culture and race alongside class, as well as to feminists blind to the importance of race alongside gender. The term contained within itself the move from an undeniable demographic reality to a break with the institutional status quo.

The "culture" in multiculturalism opened the way to the celebration of the many vibrant cultural expressions emerging from the interstices of oppression, a dimension often missing from economistic accounts that saw culture as merely superstructural. Orchestrating critique and celebration, words such as "colonialism" and "race" evoke a dystopia of oppression, while words such as "multiculturalism," "interculturalism" "alter-globalization," "multitude," and "the commons" evoke utopias of justice and conviviality. While history, as "that which hurts" (Jameson) is undeniably painful, art and popular culture sometimes manage to transfigure historical pain through the incomparable creativity of, for example, Afro-diasporic music.[61] Furthermore, the term "multiculturalism" embedded the memory of two historically interrelated source movements: the decolonizing independence movements in the "Third World" and the minority struggles in the "First World." The linguistic performative of putting "multi-" and "cultural" together, meanwhile, verbally enacted a coalitionary strategy transcending the binarism of "race relations" discourse.

Over time, the concept of "multiculturalism" became a dissensual matrix or code, to use Jamesonian language, within which different discourses competed for hegemony. Since the word "culture," as Raymond Williams had long before pointed out in *Keywords*, already embraced a multitude of significations—ranging from the elite Arnoldian sense of the "best that has been thought and written" to the anthropological sense of shared ways of life—the "multi-" could only further amplify that initial polysemy into a veritable cacophony of meanings.[62] As a term designating a social and intellectual project produced at the intersection of critical knowledges, "multiculturalism" was open to various interpretations and subject to various political force fields; it became a slippery term onto which diverse groups projected their hopes and fears. Intrinsically polysemic, the word simply pointed to a debate. Its very open-endedness made it susceptible, as we shall see, to both idealization and demonization by both the left and the right.

As a transnationally situated utterance, "multiculturalism" altered its drift and valence in diverse situations.[63] In the United States, it emerged against the backdrop of minority struggles, Civil Rights, and U.S. neoimperialism; in Canada, against the backdrop of Anglo-French biculturalism and native Canadian rights; in Australia, against the backdrop of aboriginal dispossession and immigration from Asia and the Mediterranean; in Mexico, against the ideological backdrop of *la raza cósmica* and *mestizaje* and the demographic reality of quasi-autonomous indigenous groups such as the Maya and the Zapotec. In Brazil, it entered a discursive field where the keywords had been "miscegenation," "racial democracy," and "social exclusion." The English word "multiculturalism," meanwhile, migrated to Holland and Germany, where *Multi-Kulti* struggled against *Leitkultur* normativity. Unlike France, where tensions revolved around postcolonial immigration, German tensions had to do with a *Gastarbeiter* Turkish/Kurdish minority unconnected to any prior German colonization yet marginalized by blood-and-soil definitions of national identity. In the international arena, meanwhile, a 2003 UN report on "cultural liberty in today's diverse world" posited "multicultural democracy" as an alternative to two mistaken options: (1) ethnic separatism and (2) assimilation.[64] The UN formulation was striking because critics had often rejected multiculturalism in contradictory ways as either separatist or assimilationist, while the UN report defined it as rejecting both, suggesting that there was no consensus even about the core meaning of the term itself.[65]

If multiculturalism became quasi-official policy in Australia and Canada, in the United States it was part of a coalitionary opposition politics. Nonetheless, some African Americans saw it as drowning black specificity in a bland minestrone rather than serving up a spicy Afro-diasporic gumbo. Some Native Americans, meanwhile, were reluctant to be seen as just one more oppressed "minority" rather than as the heirs of sovereign nations belonging to a preexisting panindigenous continental majority. In this sense, Native American and African American intellectuals have formulated slightly different critiques. For African Americans, the fear was of a loss of specificity of oppression that would undermine the rationale for compensatory measures for slavery and discrimination. Native Americans, meanwhile, feared the loss of the specificity grounded in being the only aboriginal (but displaced) sovereigns of the land.

The more radical versions of these projects provoked rightist ire because they called for seeing world history and contemporary social life from a decolonizing perspective. But these projects also provoked anxiety on the left, as more co-optive versions, or "multiculturalism light," came to evoke corporate-managed (united colors of Benetton) pluralism whereby established power marketed difference for commercial purposes. A submerged ethnocentrism sometimes resulted in what we have called "star-striped multiculturalism," or "nationalism with a tan." Educational institutions sometimes envisioned the issues through an exceptionalist lens that celebrated difference without deconstructing either class hierarchies or nationalist paradigms. The celebration of multicultural diversity became meaningless when not articulated together with a critique of the political economy of racism and imperialism and when not conjoined with political projects of justice, empowerment, and redistribution. Without such articulations, multiculturalism risked becoming the feel-good diversity pabulum derided by some leftists.

Situating Postcolonial Studies

Over the past two decades, much of the decolonizing work has been performed under the rubric of "postcolonial studies," defined as an interdisciplinary domain of inquiry—embracing and synthesizing such disciplines as literature, geography, history, and media studies, among others—which explores the colonial archive and postcolonial identity, often in work inflected by poststructuralism. The postcolonial field, in Brett Christophers's succinct summary, offers a "wide-ranging critique of the political-economic conditions and the ways of thinking, seeing and representing that empire instilled, and which ... continue to persist to one degree or another after the formal dismantling of empire."[66] If the key axes of discussion during decolonization had been empire and nation, postcolonialism multiplied the axes to include race, gender, class, region, religion, sexuality, and ethnicity, without nation and empire ever disappearing from view. The rise of "postcolonialism" coincided with the partial eclipse of the "Third World" revolutionary paradigm. The genealogy of the field traces back to the anticolonial struggles themselves and to the accompanying debates about postindependence policies and theories. The postcolonial existed in germ in the anticolonial. The "Pitfalls of National Consciousness" chapter in Fanon's *The Wretched of the Earth* (1961), written during the twilight of French colonialism in Algeria, was an anticipatory gesture toward the postcolonial field. And while Fanon mobilized the theoretical idioms available in his day—phenomenology, psychoanalysis, Marxism, and so forth—postcolonialism mobilizes the theoretical (largely poststructuralist) idioms available in its period. Within the academy, the founding text of postcolonial studies is usually thought to be Edward Said's *Orientalism* (1978), with its deployment of Gramsci's idea of hegemony and Foucauldian notions of discourse and the power-knowledge nexus to examine the ways that Western imperial power, in affiliation with colonizing institutions, constructed a stereotypical "Orient."[67] Although anticipated by Fanon and Anouar Abdul Malek, Said's method highlighted questions of representation in a poststructuralist manner. Postcolonialism thus brings on board a new idiom in which "discourse," the "knowledge-power nexus," and "hegemony" figure prominently.

While "multiculturalism" and "critical race" can conceivably (but not ideally) apply to single nation-states, postcoloniality is necessarily inscribed in a relationality between at least two national geographies: the colonizing metropolis and the colonized nation. At the same time, the race/coloniality debates are linked to larger global patterns and thus exceed even binational analytical categories. Indeed, postcolonial studies often addresses much larger relationalities that go beyond a single metropole and colony, to wit, those broadly obtaining between the diverse metropolitan countries in general (the Global North) vis-à-vis the colonized or formerly colonized or peripheralized countries in general (the Global South). While critical race studies and (multi)cultural studies have a mediated relation to anticolonial struggles, postcolonialism references them directly, even when urging a move beyond anticolonial politics and discourse.

Postcolonial theoretical discourse often practices a rhetoric of destabilization. Within this discursive mutation, tropes of "roots" mutate into metaphors of "routes" and "passages" and "rhizomes." A rhetoric of unsullied purity gives way to tropes of mixing, whether religious (syncretism), genetic (miscegenation), linguistic (creolization), botanical (hybridity), or culinary (masala, bouillabaisse, gumbo, feijoada). The visible checkpoints of *The Battle of Algiers* become the invisible barriers between banlieue and city center in the France of *La Haine*. Rather than the presumably binary oppositions of anticolonialism, postcolonial theory focuses on continuous spectra. Notions of ontologically referential identity metamorphose into a multifaceted play of identifications. Rigid paradigms collapse into sliding metonymies. Erect, militant postures give way to a supple play of mutually invaginated positionalities. Revolution with a capital *R* transmutes into a lower-case resistance. Teleological narratives of linear progress are replaced by zigzagging interrogations of change. Notions of progressive, stagist development give way to tropes of simultaneity and counterpoint. The nation, losing its unitary form, is now seen as palimpsestic, as embodying multiple times, rhythms, and perspectives. The idea of the originary nation—expressed in biological metaphors of growth and evolution—is replaced by the nation as imagined, narrated, figured, constructed, troped.

The flowering of postcolonial studies in the late 1980s partly derives from the entry of intellectuals from the formerly colonized countries into the Anglophone academy as well as from the increased visibility of immigrant-descended populations in the United States and Europe. Although Francophone thinkers such as Césaire and Fanon were seminal thinkers for postcolonial thought, many French intellectuals, for reasons that we explore in a later chapter, have until recently been reticent about the project. Latin American intellectuals, meanwhile, have been somewhat ambivalent, saying in effect that postcolonialism is "old news." If Latin America was in some ways "behind" Europe—for example, in technology or industrialization—in other ways it was culturally "ahead" of European thinking, having the "advantages of their disadvantages," that is, the double, parallax vision that comes with knowing both center and periphery. The Anglo-American–Indian orientation of much of postcolonial studies, meanwhile, too often relegated Latin American intellectuals to the theoretical sidelines. At the same time, Latin American and Latino scholars (Enrique Dussel, Fernando Coronil, Walter Mignolo, Arturo Escobar, Anibal Quijano, Nelson Maldonado-Torres, and Ramón Grosfoguel, among others) have been formulating the "colonial/modernity project," which takes the critiques developed by indigenous peoples, and by Latin American anti-imperialists, as fundamental to any thoroughgoing postcolonial project.[68]

Postcolonial theory has been critiqued for (1) an elision of class (sometimes linked ad hominem to the elite status of some of the key theorists themselves); (2) a tendency to subjectivize large-scale political struggles by reducing them to intrapsychic tensions; (3) an avoidance of political economy in a globalized age when neoliberal economics drives many of the cultural changes registered by the theory; (4) an obsessive antibinarism that ignores the intractable binarism of the colonial situation itself; (5) a supercilious attitude toward "ethnic studies," projected as lacking the aura of theory but which often constituted a more direct challenge to established power through its links to potentially insurgent communities; (6) a tendency to focus on faded European empires and to forget actually existing American neoimperialism; (7) a kind of Commonwealth centrism that privileges the British-Indian relation as paradigm for colonialism in general; (8) an insufficient theorization of postcolonial theory's own conditions of emergence; (9) the adoption of a highly theoretical idiom that projects the reader into a rarefied atmosphere of vertiginous slippage, allowing little sense of precise time or place except when the theoretical helicopter "lands" on a random historical example or literary citation; and (10) the overprivileging of themes of hybridity, diaspora, and cosmopolitanism, to the detriment of the power dynamics inherent in colonial and neocolonial violence. Some theorists linked to Latin America prefer a "decolonial" and "colonial difference" approach that stresses manifold colonial and postcolonial contexts in an attempt to foreground an "epistemic diversality of world decolonial interventions."[69] Needless to say, many of the criticisms of postcolonial theory do not apply to all versions of postcolonial studies, and the criticisms themselves arguably form an integral part of the larger field. Indeed, the postcolonial field is the site of incessant self-questioning and ramifying autocritique, where every new book or essay seems to correct some sin of omission or commission by earlier scholars. The point now, as formulated in the call for papers for a 2010 conference at York University titled "What Postcolonial Theory Doesn't Say," is not to denounce postcolonialism for its inevitable oversights but rather to dynamize the field's enormous cultural and institutional capital for progressive ends.

The postcolonial privileging of "hybridity" has particular implications for indigenous communities. Indeed, the indigenous issue throws into question some of the favored topoi of postcolonial discourse and cultural studies. First, indigenous thinkers often see their situation as colonial rather than postcolonial, or as both at the same time. While a certain postcolonial theory celebrates cosmopolitanism, indigenous discourse often valorizes a *rooted* existence rather than a cosmopolitan one. While postcolonial and cultural studies revels in the "blurring of borders," indigenous communities often seek to *affirm* borders by demarcating land against encroaching squatters, miners, corporations, and nation-states. While the poststructuralism that helped shaped postcolonialism emphasizes the inventedness of nations and "denaturalizes the natural," within an idiom that surrounds "nature" with protective scare quotes, indigenous thinkers have insisted on love of a land regarded as "sacred," another word hardly valued in the post- discourses. What Eduardo Viveiros de Castro calls indigenous "multinaturalism"[70] challenges not only the rhetorical antinaturalism of the "posts" but also what might be called the primordial Orientalism that separated nature from culture, animals from human beings.

"Hybridity" is also often associated with the peregrinations of diasporic elites, with little space for the more hazardous itineraries of desperate refugees, including those exiled on their own land in trails of tears. For indigenous peoples, "hybridity" is especially double-edged. On the one hand, indigenous nations were borrowing from one another long before Columbus, as objects, ideas, and populations traveled around the Americas, a process only intensified by the Conquest. The post-Columbian indigenous appropriation of European technique began as early as 1503, when the French captain Paulmier de Gonneville brought the young Carijó Indian Essmoricq from Brazil to France to study munitions technology to help his tribe in their struggles back home.[71] On the other hand, "hybridity" has just as often been used as a weapon against indigenous peoples of mixed heritage, sometimes dismissed, in both Brazil and the United States, as not "real" Indians deserving of rights.

The British Empire/Commonwealth focus of postcolonial theory, meanwhile, has resulted in the overlooking of the long-term antecedents of hybridity discourse in the work of Latin America and Caribbean intellectuals. A 1971 essay by Brazilian novelist/literary critic Silviano Santiago calling attention to the "in-between of Latin American culture," for example, clearly anticipated Homi Bhabha's formulations concerning the "interstitial," the "in-between" and the "third space of negotiation."[72] While the wide circulation of race/postcolonial work is partly due to the global reach of the English language and the power of the Anglo-American academy, it would be misleading to chart a linear trajectory whereby these movements "originated" in Anglo-America and then "traveled elsewhere." Conquest, colonialism, slavery, U.S. imperialist policies, military interventions, expulsions, immigration, and the "brain drain" brought a translocated and hybridized mix of peoples and ideas, helping to shape the various progressive projects. In discursive terms, these projects were impacted by anticolonialist discourse, by the poststructural theory associated with France but also with the North African Jacques Derrida, by the black British cultural studies associated with the United Kingdom, by the subaltern studies associated not only with India but also with postcolonial diasporas, by the hegemony theory associated with Gramsci and Italy, by the dependency theory associated with Latin America, and by the center/periphery and world systems theory associated with many different sites.

Walter Mignolo and others have usefully summarized the underlying philosophical/historical drift of postcolonial projects as the critical thinking together of coloniality and modernity, seen as inseparable and mutually shaping concepts. Insisting, as we do, on the intellectual agency of the victims of colonialism, Mignolo borrows Valentin Mudimbe's coinage "border gnosis" to refer to "knowledge from a subaltern perspective, . . . conceived from the exterior borders of the modern/colonial world system," and uses "border gnoseology" to refer to discourse about colonialism "conceived at the conflictive intersection of the knowledge produced from the perspective of modern colonialisms."[73] These forms of knowledge are often not recognized by academic institutions, whether out of sheer ignorance or because they are associated with stigmatized peoples assumed to be "disappeared" or as lacking in cultural agency.

Parallel to work performed under other rubrics, the modernity/coloniality group, largely formed by Latin American and Latino scholars, highlights the interconnectedness of modernity and coloniality, postmodernity and postcoloniality. Arturo Escobar highlights the following axioms that guide the modernity/

coloniality research project: (1) there is no modernity without coloniality; coloniality is constitutive of modernity; (2) the modern/colonial world and the colonial matrix of power originates in the 16th century and has two almost opposite "faces": on the one hand, the dispossession of native peoples and the enslavement of Africans and, on the other, the Renaissance and the Enlightenment; (3) the Enlightenment and the Industrial Revolution are derivative movements that further transform this colonial matrix; (4) coloniality, as the dark side of modernity, is simply another name for Europe's "progress" toward world hegemony; (5) capitalism is essential to both progress and coloniality; and (6) coloniality/modernity underwent a further transformation when the United States took over the leadership of global imperial processes.[74]

As a mutation in global capitalism, globalization both shuts down and opens up political possibilities. The World Social Forum, the activist congress on alternatives to globalization, was at first a Franco-Brazilian project, conceived by the Parisian editors of Le Monde Diplomatique but first carried out in Porto Alegre, Brazil. Designed to counter Davos as the conference of the financial elites, the Social Forum became the discursive mediator for the massive antiglobalization "movement of movements" that generated huge protests in Seattle, Genoa, Davos, New York, Cancun, Miami, and elsewhere. Although radical scholarship is not a specific focus in the Forum documents, the Forum offers many parallels to the scholarly work. The Charter of Principles (quoted by Cassen) declares that the Forum is "open to the plurality of genders, ethnicities, cultures, [and] generations [and] seeks a "truly democratic and participatory practice, characterized by egalitarian and pacific relations of solidarity between persons, races, sexes, and peoples." Race, colonialism, and slavery are also concerns. In the "Appeal for Future Mobilizations" (January 2001), the authors denounce the role of neoliberalism in worsening racism, "in continuity with the genocide caused by centuries of slavery and colonialism, which have destroyed the foundations of the black civilizations and societies of Africa." Indigeneity as well makes its mark, as the document calls for solidarity with "indigenous peoples in their historic combat against genocide and ethnicide, in defense of their rights, their natural resources, their culture, their autonomy, their land and their territory."[75]

With an alert eye to the possibilities of dialectical jiujitsu within a situation of globalized domination, Portuguese scholar Boaventura de Sousa Santos, an intellectual deeply familiar with the Portuguese, French, Brazilian, and Anglo-American academic scenes, points to five "fields" in which counterhegemonic globalization creates viable opportunities: (1) participatory democracy, (2) alternative systems of production, (3) multicultural justice and citizenship, (4) biodiversity and communitarian knowledge versus corporatized intellectual property rights, and (5) new working-class transnationalism. While provoking new forms of transnational racism, globalization can also create new conditions for the emergence of transnational resistance. Globalization can therefore be oppressive or resistant, conservative or emancipatory. To our minds, all of these issues are imbricated in race/multicultural/coloniality issues: "participatory democracy" is an answer to "master race democracy," biodiversity is linked to the cultural diversity and intellectual agency of indigenous peoples, a transnational working-class solidarity depends on transcending racism and xenophobia, and so forth.[76]

A good deal of energy has been expended in the search for terminological panaceas, as if finding the right label would in itself provide a solution. Concepts such as "multiculturalism" and "postcoloniality," in our view, cannot stand alone; they must be articulated together with companion concepts such as "Eurocentrism," "white supremacy," "colonialism," "capitalism," "master race democracy," "border gnosis," and "modernity/coloniality." Each term highlights a different aspect of the issues: "colonialism" refers to the actual historical practices of domination; "modernity/ coloniality" refers to the mutually imbricated processes of Western hegemony and non-Western otherization; "white supremacy" highlights the color-line aspects of this domination; "capitalism" refers to the system first spread around the world by colonialism and later by neocolonialism and globalization; "border gnosis" and the Nahuatl word *neplanta* refer to "the liminal state in between worlds, in between realities, in between systems of knowledge";[77] "master race democracy" emphasizes the racialized oppression that plagues sometimes even apparently democratic political and social institutions and practices; and "Eurocentrism" highlights the unstated, taken-for-granted doxa of occidental entitlement. Other terms—"polycentrism," "para-Enlightenment," "alter-globalization"—point to alternative discourses and utopias.

No single term can simultaneously evoke such diverse fields as "revisionist history," "critical race studies," "whiteness studies," "postcolonial discourse theory," "subaltern studies," "border theory," "transnational feminism," and the "coloniality/modernity project." Most terms bring both advantages and disadvantages. In the 1990s, some scholars constructed a kind of adjectival *cordon sanitaire* around multiculturalism and identity politics through prophylactic qualifiers such as "critical," "radical," "counterhegemonic," and "polycentric" as antidotes to potential co-optation. (Prophylaxis also works in reverse when critics predefine multiculturalism a priori as "neoliberal.") Manuela Boatcă and Sérgio Costa propose "interculturality" as an option, especially as defined and implemented by indigenous movements in Latin America, seen as entailing a deeper questioning and transformation of hegemonic models of power.[78]

Contrarian words such as "antiracist" and "anticolonialist," meanwhile, sum up the drift of much of the work but remain too reactively locked into the paradigms being contested. "Postcolonial studies" designates an important field of research but remains too exclusively academic, with all the problems of a "post-" that is not really yet "post-." "Critical race theory" references an extremely innovative and consequential field but one very much tied up with the legal discipline in a single national context. "Transnational studies" is useful and suggestive but politically tainted through its association with "transnational" corporations, and it risks eliding national and infranational forms of oppression. A kind of "battle of the prefixes" also forms part of this discussion—the conventional sequencing being from "multi-" and "inter-" and "post-" to "trans-"—and of the suffixes, with the programmatic ideological thrust of "-ism" giving way to a more distanced and abstract "-ity." The "-ism" in "multiculturalism," meanwhile, claims too much by inserting itself in the same paradigm as other "-isms" referring to systematic explanatory grids (Marxism), historical epochs (postmodernism), systems of production (capitalism), and ideologies (socialism).

All these proliferating revisionist (inter)disciplines, whatever their precise character, share a strong anticolonial and egalitarian thrust. They unpack hegemonic discourses of racism, colonialism, Orientalism, and Eurocentrism while simultaneously engaging the mantra of race, nation, gender, class, and sexuality. What matters, in the end, is not the specific label but rather the decolonizing thrust of the work itself, not the exact rubric but the depth of the engagement with questions of coloniality. In any case, no term is pure or unproblematic; each gets buffeted about by the winds of history, which is why analysts distinguish between co-optive "top-down" and radical "bottom-up" versions of the multicultural, the postcolonial, or the transnational. All the terms, while problematic, cast some light on a very complex subject. It is crucial to examine their relationality, their syntagmatic deployment, and their social/historical positionality, deploying them in a differential, contingent, and relational manner. It is not that one term is "wrong" and the other "right" but, rather, that each term only partially illuminates the issues. Rather than simply correct or incorrect, the terms can be seen as productive or unproductive, as generating or not generating liberatory energies and concepts in specific historical conjunctures. In the end, no single term can possibly represent such variegated work, and it is misleading to use single terms such as "multiculturalism" or "identity politics"—as critics such as Bourdieu/ Wacquant and Žižek do—to designate a wide array of fields. We can use all the terms, but under partial erasure, as part of a more mobile set of grids, a more flexible set of disciplinary and cross-cultural lenses adequate to the complex politics of contemporary location, while maintaining openings for agency and resistance.

4 Identity Politics and the Right/Left Convergence

PREDICTABLY, CONSERVATIVES IN many countries were not enthusiastic about the "seismic shift" manifested in these decolonizing projects. In the United States, the right accused multicultural "identity politics" of causing racial "balkanization" and "ethnic separatism." In a faux populist attack stage-managed by elite circles in the Republican Party, the right ridiculed these projects as a new politically correct version of the communist menace. Right-wing polemicists mocked what they saw as oversensitive do-gooders stifling free speech in the name of touchy-feely sympathy for minorities. In an analogy that aligned the tumultuous 1960s with the French Revolution and the politically correct 1990s with the Reign of Terror, journalist Richard Bernstein accused multicultural leftists of wanting to install a "dictatorship of virtue."[1] Recycling Cold War rhetoric, conservative figures such as Allan Bloom, William Bennett, Dinesh D'Souza, and Lynne Cheney, in tandem with liberals such as historian Arthur M. Schlesinger, Jr., denounced any identity-based critique of inequality as un-American. Thus, George H. W. Bush in May 1991 publicly denounced the "political extremists . . . setting citizens against one another on the basis of their class or race." In a sense, the right was retrofitting its old "class warfare" rhetoric—that is, the notion that to call attention to class inequality was to wage "class warfare"—to the issue of race. To speak of racial inequality, by analogy, was to wage "race warfare," just as to speak of gender inequality was to wage "gender warfare."

The virulence of these attacks manifested a fear not only of greater racial, economic, and political equality but also of nonexceptionalist narrativizations of history. Thus, Schlesinger ridiculed "underdog," "compensatory," and "there's-always-a-black-man-at-the-bottom-of-it" approaches to historiography, whose sole function was to provide "social and psychological therapy" and "raise the self-esteem of children from minority groups."[2] But if minorities have indeed been traumatized by their experience in dominant educational institutions, "therapy" is clearly preferable to "trauma." Why should only the dominant Euro-American group have its narcissism massaged by official histories, while others suffer the body blows of stereotype and marginalization? In any case, the call to decolonize historical pedagogy was not ultimately a question of self-esteem. Nor was it a question of a bland "I'm OK, you're OK" history or of "telling both sides." Apart from the fact that historical debates have innumerable "sides," a polycentric anticolonial history by definition would benefit the dissenting voices that have been excluded from official history. Nor is it a question of randomly "adding" voices but rather of taking on board voices that challenge the dominant, top-down version of history. Nor was it a matter of "lowering standards" but rather of raising them by requiring knowledge of more cultures, more languages, more perspectives.

In a literary corollary, the partisans of multicultural politics were portrayed by the right as wanting to eject all the great writers—the notorious "dead white males"—from the literary canon. For William Phillips, "politically correct" teachers were "denouncing the traditions and values of the West . . . [and substituting] African and Asian traditions and values."[3] The race-conscious left was depicted as eager to replace the great writers, in a literary/pedagogic coup d'état, with mediocre authors whose only qualification was their gender or their color. Alice Walker was replacing Shakespeare! But the goal was never to eliminate Shakespeare but rather to expand the canon, and even to explore the multiculturality of Shakespeare's capacious Globe, which embraces not only European culture in all its exuberant diversity but also the ethnic relationality of Moor and Venetian in *Othello*, of Egyptian and Roman in *Antony and Cleopatra*, of European and African/indigenous American in *The Tempest*, and of Jew and gentile in *The Merchant of Venice*. Indeed, *The Tempest*'s confrontation between Prospero and Caliban has generated a vast anticolonial posttext. It is this multiculturality that makes it possible to reread *The Tempest*, as Aimé Césaire, Roberto Fernández Retamar, and Jean Franco have done, as anticolonialist or to see *The Merchant of Venice* as sympathetic to Shylock or to relocate *Romeo and Juliet* in the barrios of New York (*West Side Story*) or in the favelas of Rio de Janeiro (*Maré*).

But the most frequently reiterated charge was that of "separatism," as evidenced in the constant recourse to metaphors of "balkanization," "Lebanonization," and "tribalism." For Charles Krauthammer, multicultural identity politics "poses a threat that no outside agent in this post-Soviet world can match—the setting of one ethnic group against another, the fracturing not just of American society but of the American idea."[4] The most extreme accusation was to speak of ethnic cleansing as a logical end product of multiculturalism, as when P. J. O'Rourke defined multiculturalism as "that which is practiced today in the former Yugoslavia."[5] Thus, the right gave the impression that the Serbs, the Bosnians, and the Croatians, fresh from reading Cornel West and bell hooks, were rushing into fratricidal slaughter brandishing the banner of "identity politics." Arthur Schlesinger was the most vocal proponent of the "disuniting" perspective and, not by coincidence, a vociferous opponent of the "rainbow curriculum" designed for New York schools. Formulations such as Schlesinger's that portray a "common culture" threatened by ethnic difference come close to blaming the victim by implying that cultural difference itself causes social strife, when in fact it has always been the inequitable distribution of power that generates divisiveness and tension. The critics were generally unable to cite any actual multicultural writers or activists calling for separatism, for the simple reason that the "separatists" did not exist; rather, they were imaginary creatures, ideological ogres invented to frighten the uninformed. In fact, many of the multiculturalists were shaped directly or indirectly by the struggle against segregation. Yet the separatist charge has been repeated so often that it has become part of the received wisdom, even, as we shall see, for some on the left.

The right also portrayed left identity politics, in an oxymoronic characterization, as at once puritanical and hedonistic. One of the right's public relations coups was to associate the left with negative personal attributes such as self-righteousness, as a diversion from what was really an argument about social change and political power. Thus, the label of "political correctness" was affixed only to those who were calling for more egalitarian relations between races, genders, ethnicities, and sexualities. In a new twist on Cold War imagery, the multicultural left was portrayed as lugubrious, dour, and drab, in short, as neo-Stalinist. In a historical inversion of letters, the CP (Communist Party) became PC (political correctness). Amplifying the preexisting association of communism with austere rigidity, the right portrayed all politicized critique as the neurotic effluvium of an uptight subculture of morbid guilt-tripping.[6] At the same time, paradoxically, the right depicted the cultural left as the heirs of the permissive 1960s. An incoherent portrait presented the same people as at once uptight puritans and as self-indulgent do-your-own-thingers. The contradiction arose from the melding of the negative portrayals of two very different historical lefts: (1) the Stalinist Communist Party left of the 1930s through the 1950s and (2) the more ludic "New Left" of the 1960s and 1970s.

In any case, the "PC" rubric generated its own ontology, ultimately taking on a life of its own and spreading, due to the reach of U.S. media to other regions such as Europe and Latin America. The various decolonizing projects unleashed fierce polemics not because they were separatist but because they called for a decisive transformation in the ways history would be written, literature would be taught, art would be curated, films programmed, cultural resources distributed, and political representation shaped. They challenged the regnant doxa prevalent in education and the media up until the 1960s. While the left wanted to wrest control of the political from elites, the right wanted to place the political back in elite hands. What was left unsaid by the right was the assumed desirability of the status quo ante. At least by implication, the right was calling for a return to the pre-1960s default position of white male heteronormative hegemony, a time when there were virtually no students of color and relatively few women on campuses, when history texts were blandly noncommittal about slavery and segregation, and when Native Americans, African Americans, Latinos, and other minorities, along with women, gays, lesbians, and transsexuals, had very little voice. What was for the right an object of nostalgia was for minorities a searing memory of trauma.

The Politics of Scapegoating

If the right was hostile to identity politics, liberals and some on the left were critical as well. Some feminists, such as Susan Moller Okin, called multicultural-ism "bad for women."[7] Some liberals lamented the assault on the Western canon. Some Marxists, meanwhile, saw identity politics as "dividing the left" through a cultural detour that distracted from "real" struggles over class and power. Those who would press critical race issues were caught between the "dividing-America" arguments from the right, the "dividing the left" arguments from the left, and the "dividing the feminist movement" from (usually white) liberal feminists. While some leftists rejected multicultural identity politics as mere liberalism, rightists conflated it with Afrocentrism, ethnic separatism, Marxism, and Islamo-fascism. We find a recent illustration of the partial convergence of left and right on these issues in two February 2011 denunciations of "multiculturalism," one by the con-servative British Prime Minister David Cameron, the other by radical leftist Slavoj Žižek. The former asserted in a speech that multiculturalism had failed, that tolerance had led to Islamic radicalism, and that what was needed was a "robust liberalism" and a return to Western values and pride in British identity. For Cameron (and other conservative leaders such as Sarkozy and Merkel), it is multiculturalism—and not discrimination—that creates separate communi-ties; thus, they blame the proponents of a solution to a problem for the problem itself. Žižek, meanwhile, in an interview on Al Jazeera (February 1, 2011) about the democratic movement in Egypt, also denounced the multiculturalists who supposedly believed that "Egypt has a separate culture and does not need democ-racy." While Cameron sees liberalism as the answer to radicalism, Žižek has long argued that multiculturalism is not the opposite of neoliberalism but rather its ideal form. Both Cameron and Žižek were speaking up for Western Enlighten-ment values, although Cameron was channeling Adam Smith, while Žižek was channeling Hegel and Marx.[8] In the interview, Žižek mixed valid political cri-tiques—in this case of U.S. and Israeli policies in the Middle East—with a rant against an imaginary bogeyman, that is, multiculturalists rejecting freedom and democracy in the name of culturalist separatism. (We have no idea where Žižek finds "multiculturalists" who claim that "Egypt does not need freedom because it has a separate culture." There are of course people who say such things; we call them "colonialists," "racists," "Orientalists," and "Samuel Huntington.")

At this point in history, some of the keywords have become exhausted. "Mul-ticulturalism," for example, has suffered a fate reminiscent of that suffered earlier by "socialism," whereby a call to fuse political democracy with economic equality was dismissed by some on the left as too soft and co-optive and denounced by the right as merely another form of "totalitarian communism." In the next three chapters, we frequently refer to "multiculturalism" and "identity politics" not because they form our ideal rubrics for the variegated critical work already referenced but rather because those keywords came to encapsulate favored targets for right and for some left critics, becoming synecdoches for a whole set of complexly affiliated fields. The deeper race/coloniality issues got lost in superficial polemics. Through much of the 1990s, figures representing antipodal points in the political spectrum heaped opprobrium on something they called "multiculturalism." Lynne Cheney and Slavoj Žižek, Samuel Huntington and Pierre Bourdieu, Dinesh D'Souza and Tzvetan Todorov, strangely, have all been hostile to multiculturalism. This chapter explores what might lie behind this partial convergence between ideological adversaries.

What is surprising, then, is not the right's hostility to identity politics but rather that of some on the left. After mapping the general direction of the left arguments, we will address specific interventions by Walter Benn Michaels, Pierre Bourdieu/Loïc Wacquant, and Slavoj Žižek. Some left critics expressed apprehension about what they saw as the supervalorization of culture over political economy. This critique was less about the "multi-" than about the "culture," seen as an inconsequential distraction from the economy as the determinative instance shaping all other spheres. Yet while political economy is absolutely essential to any substantive left critique, it is also important to articulate culture and economy together, to conceive of them as existing in and through each other. In the post-Fordist era of globalization, culture has become a privileged site for the articulation (and sometimes the disarticulation) of the reproduction of capitalist social relations. For Lisa Lowe and David Lloyd, culture gains political efficacy when it enters into contradiction with political or economic logics of exploitation and domination.[9] The point is not to look for a utopia of pure resistance outside of capitalism but rather to discern what elements emerge historically in difference with and in relation to capitalism. Here many people have questioned forms of Marxism that exalt class struggle while belittling struggles revolving around other modalities of social inequality. Feminist theory, postcolonial theory, subaltern studies, queer theory, coloniality/modernity theory, critical whiteness studies, and indigeneity theory all offer conceptual instruments relevant to multiple, historically sedimented forms of inequality. Rather than replace class struggle, these projects complicate it, seeing multiaxial forms of oppression as engendering similarly multiaxial forms of resistance and struggle, shaping new social actors, new vocabularies, and new strategies.

Another leftist critique claims that multicultural identity politics itself is ethnocentric, custom designed only for a prosperous and liberal Global North that imposes its concepts on a reluctant South. According to this view, "Northern" or "First World" multicultural ideas end up providing a new, apparently progressive, veneer for Western cultural domination. Yet we would argue that multicultural left politics partly emerged from the Global South and from racialized communities in the Global North with links to the Global South, forging a critique relevant to *all* the settler-colonial states in the Americas and to the Black and Red Atlantic.[10] As we shall see in the case of Brazil, most of the Americas configure similar racialized stratifications forged by colonial history, including not only indigenous genocide (true of the Americas), slavery (likewise), and discrimination but also immigration (from Europe and beyond), along with cultural syncretisms of all kinds. Historical dynamics generate differentiated yet in some ways analogous configurations in the various settler states, resulting in social patterns that are not so much identical as eminently comparable and relationalizable. The demographics might vary, yet issues of indigenous sovereignty, multicultural pedagogy, Affirmative Action, and reparations are pertinent to the entire hemisphere. The Global South and the Global North, Center and Periphery, are co-implicated, linked in multifarious but uneven ways. The 2001 Durban Conference on Racism and Xenophobia brought representatives not only from the Black and Red Atlantic world—Africans, indigenous peoples, African Americans, and black Brazilians—but also from the world at large (for example, Dalit from India) to accuse the dominant powers (including some nation-states in the South) of complicity with colonialist racism, making them the object of demands for compensatory measures. These issues, in sum, are not relevant only to the prosperous North.

The notion of a unilateral "Northern" imposition on the South, furthermore, assumes that the South exercises no intellectual agency, when in fact such projects partially come "from there." North and South are intellectually commingled in a transnational discursive space. Many of the source theories—anticolonialism, dependency theory, the critique of Enlightenment humanism—have been associated as much with the South as with the North. The objection about Northern imposition often has less to do with the work itself than with the institutional location of the production and dissemination of some work that seems to privilege certain national sites (the United States and the United Kingdom), certain languages (especially English), certain Anglo-American institutions, and a largely European and Euro-American corpus of writing and theory. But the North/South divide, while heuristically and politically useful as pointing to deeply entrenched power differentials, is premised on overly stark lines of separation; the lines in fact are much more porous.

Todd Gitlin, in his 1995 book *The Twilight of Common Dreams*, blames the decline of the American left on "identity politics" as expressed by "groups overly concerned with protecting and purifying what they imagine to be their identities." The left, in Gitlin's view, abandoned what he sees as the real struggle in favor of a narcissistic quest for a chimerical identity.[11] Neglected in his account are the diverse causes of left decline: the right-wing attack on the '60s legacy, the murderous repression of the Black Panthers, the conservative agitprop of well-funded think tanks, a rigged two-party system, winner-take-all politics, laissez-faire economics, a Constitution favoring conservative rural states, the corporate corruption of Congress, the wedge-issue tactics of the Republican Party, and the ideological vacillations of an ever more corporate-dominated Democratic Party. An analysis that scapegoats multicultural identity-politics for left decline offers a flattened version of a complex historical narrative, forgetting the global and local factors that have undermined the left generally as an overarching progressive project: globally, the end of actually existing socialism, the *embourgeoisement* of Third World liberation movements, and the weakening of unions and the workers' movement.

The scapegoating analysis forgets that (1) the left has historically often been fragmented for reasons having little to do with "identity politics"—one need only recall the left's self-cannibalizing due to the Stalinist/Trotskyist/Marxist/Leninist/Anarchist/Socialist/Spartakist schisms that plagued the left during much of the 20th century; (2) the Old Left versus New Left debate had more to do with ideological vision, generational tensions, and political tactics than with identity politics; (3) the Marxist left has declined in much of the world due to the collapse of actually existing socialism, often in situations where identity politics played little role; (4) anxieties around race, class, gender, and sexuality were present in U.S. left politics long before the advent of "identity politics" (evident, for example, in black intellectual disenchantment with the CP in the 1930s); (5) participation in race-inflected left politics in no way precludes participation in other forms of left politics; and (6) the major exceptions to left decline in the world—Latin America and now the Arab Spring—have often embraced cultural identity and social movements as an integral part of coalitionary politics. If it is true that the multicultural left has been more effective in defending the right to difference than in guaranteeing political-economic equality, that does not mean that the left has not achieved political-economic equality *because* of the multicultural achievements.

Quite apart from identity politics, divisions based on race, class, and gender have shaped American history from the very beginning. Propertied, slave-holding white men have classically used race to hide class by "conferring" the cultural capital of whiteness on nonpropertied whites. The color line also subtly marked even left organizations, from the Communist Party to labor unions, which privileged whites over working-class people of color despite ideologies of equality. Blaming identity politics for left division is thus a form of sideways scapegoating. Gitlin's derisive reference to "groups overly concerned with protecting and purifying what they imagine to be their identities" is an especially low blow. It betokens a privileged, pseudo-objective standpoint that deems itself in a position to judge which identities are authentic and which imaginary, as if Gitlin knows the "real" identities of people of color better than people of color themselves do. Social identities are neither a luxury nor imaginary; they are historically shaped and have consequences for who gets jobs, who owns homes, who gets racially profiled, and so forth. Rather than an investment in a phantasmatic affiliation, identities have to do with a differential relation to power as lived in the world, with discrepant experiences of the judicial system, the medical system, the economy, and everyday social interchange. Social identities are not pre-fixed essences; they emerge from a fluid set of diverse experiences, within overlapping circles of belonging. It is these overlapping circles of identity and identification that make possible transcommunal coalitions based on historically shaped affinities. Anxieties about identity are asymmetrical. While the disempowered seek to affirm a precariously established right, the traditionally empowered feel relativized by having to compete with previously unheard voices. What is missed in the dividing-the-left argument is that each "division" can also be an "addition" within a coalitionary space. Disaggregation and rearticulation can go hand in hand.

The debates over identity have featured a complex range of positions, ranging from essentialism to social constructivism. If the right's attack on "identity politics" was framed in nationalist terms, the left's critique was framed either in political terms or in philosophical poststructuralist or skeptical postmodernist terms. For many scholars, the goal was therefore to avoid both essentialist and anti-essentialist traps, whence "strategic essentialism" (Spivak).[12] That identities are socially constructed does not mean that they do not exist and have real-life consequences. In this vein, the postpositivist "realist" approach advanced by such scholars as Linda Martin Alcoff, Satya P. Mohanty, and Chandra Mohanty offers an alternative conceptualization to the postmodern skeptical view of identities as merely fictional constructs.[13] For advocates of this approach, identities are markers of history, social location, and positionality, lenses through which to view the world. Rather than ethno-characterological essences, identities are chronotopic positionings within social space and historical time, the place from which one speaks and experiences the world. The class-based argument against identity politics ignores the difference that race makes and the ways that the refusal of cross-racial coalitions have hurt the left itself. One axis of analysis (class) is applauded, while others (race, gender, sexuality) are derided. Opposition to the "special" claims of racial minorities, as George Lipsitz has suggested, often masks the hidden "identity politics" of the dominant group's possessive investment in white Europeanness.[14] Although a certain kind of salami-slicing identity politics can turn identity into a form of cultural capital in a competitive fight for status, the denunciation of "identity politics" itself can also subtly normativize the dominant identity.

Troubling Diversity

The various left critiques of multicultural identity politics share certain motifs but also touch on distinct notes. A class-over-race hierarchy dominates Walter Benn Michaels's *The Trouble with Diversity*.[15] His argument, in its simplest form, is that "we love race and identity because we don't love class."[16] Most of the book consists of formulaic permutations of the same basic structural grammar of mutually exclusive paradigms, along the manner of "We love to talk about A (race, diversity) because we refuse to talk about B (class, economics, capitalism)." In a zero-sum approach, each and every invocation of race implies a denial of class. Within a grammar familiar with only two conjunctions—"either/or"—we are exhorted to choose between "a vision of our society as divided into races" or as divided "into economic classes."[17] Sentence after sentence is premised on a rhetoric of stark dichotomy—"We would much rather get rid of racism than get rid of poverty"[18]—or of invidious comparison: "We like the idea of cultural equality better than we like the idea of economic equality."[19]

We cannot emphasize enough that we applaud Michaels's critique of the erasure of class, especially in the United States. Unfortunately, he merely replaces one erasure (of class) with other erasures (of race, culture, identity). Although Michaels's vaguely socialist politics differ sharply from those of a Dinesh D'Souza, he shares with D'Souza the fantasy that racism was basically outlawed and eliminated in the 1960s. Deploying a tacitly white liberal "we," Michaels writes that "we like programs such as affirmative action because they tell us that racism is the problem we need to solve and that solving it requires us to give up our prejudices."[20] The formulation is unfortunate, however, since (1) Affirmative Action today is under constant attack, including by the Supreme Court, (2) even its supporters are not defending it very vigorously (Obama seems to prefer a William Julius Wilson–style class-over-race approach), and (3) Affirmative Action was about concrete legal/practical issues such as hiring minorities and correcting past injustice, not about a mushy and unrealizable "giving up prejudices."

Michaels's sunny portrait of an America "in love with diversity," moreover, ignores many ominous clouds. Although university brochures prominently feature the word "diversity" and proudly display photographs of chromatically diverse students and faculty, that is hardly the same as achieving substantive social equality. There seems to be a race-informed difference of perception here. While Michaels describes campuses as "in love with diversity," many black, Latino, and Middle Eastern students call American campuses, including even diversity-friendly campuses such as UC Berkeley, "hostile environments." A 2004 survey at the University of Virginia, for example, found that 40 percent of the black students had been the target of a direct racial slur, while 91 percent had either experienced or witnessed an act of racial discrimination or intolerance.[21] Meanwhile, black students are vanishing from U.S. campuses as the race and class divides worsen under the onslaught of the financial crisis, trickle-up economics, high-priced education, and the assault on Affirmative Action.

As evidence of the American "love of diversity," Michaels cites the absence of "pro-hate rallies."[22] But this sets a terribly low bar. The KKK and the white militias do not call their demonstrations "hate rallies," but that is what they are. Even Hitler, after all, did not call the Nuremberg rallies "hate rallies," but one suspects that Jews and Bolsheviks, gays and gypsies got the drift. Building on a long tradition of paranoid, nativist political speech, venomous celebrities such as Ann Coulter and Glenn Beck stage the mediatic equivalents of hate rallies, with TV audiences larger than those of any Nuremberg spectacle. The galling experience of watching TV shows such as *Lou Dobbs Tonight* and *The O'Reilly Factor* or of listening to the hate radio of Michael Savage or Rush Limbaugh reveals at the very least a deep ambivalence about "diversity." And while the election of Obama offered evidence of another America that does indeed love diversity, right-wing voices that do not love diversity have become even more strident since his election. Rather than demonstrate that Americans have become "postracial," the irrational hostility to Obama has shown just how many Americans still adhere to the "racial contract." The doubt cast on Obama's Americanness is allegorically addressed, and received, as an insult to all Americans of color.

Race as an analytical category is crucial because racism structures social advantage. Every economic crisis that afflicts whites—for example, the subprime lending crisis—impacts racialized communities even more dramatically. When white America sneezes, black America gets influenza. The Great Depression, as a bitter black joke has it, was a time when white Americans got to live the way blacks had always been living. The wealth divide, meanwhile, is even larger than the income divide. "For every dollar owned by the average white family in the U.S., the average family of color has less than one dime."[23] For blacks, as Mel King puts it, "white men of means" often coincide with "mean white men."[24] Thus race and class must be seen as interarticulated, since they are so completely "imbricated in the consciousness of working-class Americans," as David Roediger puts it, "that we do not 'get' class if we do not 'get' race." Indeed the refusal to engage the complexities of race can result in the "retreat from class" just as surely as can "a reductive obsession with race as an ahistorical essentialist category."[25] A certain left wants to move "beyond race," but in fact a retreat from race, as Roediger points out, will not solve the problem of the denial of class and will ultimately "get us closer to addressing neither."[26] Although Michaels thinks "we" are overly "eager" to centralize race, in fact race and class (and gender and sexuality) are at the burning core of American politics. Underscoring the symbiotic interconnection of race and class, Marx saw chattel slavery as the pedestal on which wage slavery was based. Du Bois spoke of "the wages of whiteness."[27] Later, Martin Luther King, Jr., asked, "What does it profit a man to be able to eat at an integrated lunch counter if he doesn't earn enough money to buy a hamburger and a cup of coffee?"[28] Henry Louis Taylor, Jr., noted that "the black job ceiling has been the floor of white opportunity."[29] Black Marxism told us that race and class were interarticulated, while black feminism reminded us that race, class, and gender all intersect.

Throughout most of the 20th century, the black liberation movement has been engaged in a complex debate about the strengths and weaknesses of Marxism in terms of explaining and remedying black oppression. Critical race theory, for example, points to the political limitations of both liberalism and Marxism. While liberalism reduces racism to attitudinal bigotry, Marxism reduces racism to an epiphenomenon of class. Although Marxism has provided a powerful theory of the dialectic of social oppression, the historical forces that produced Marxism as a theory, as Charles Mills points out, "have now thrown up other perspectives, other visions, illuminating aspects of the structured darknesses of society that Marx failed to see."[30] Although Michaels claims to shift our attention from individual prejudice to the social system, he sets up a false dichotomy between individual and society when he asserts that even when "we" as individuals "are racist, the society to which we are committed is not."[31] Bypassing all the critical race scholarship on institutional, systemic, and even epistemic racism, this claim of societal innocence is ultimately rooted in a U.S.-American exceptionalist discourse.

An emerging left consensus assumes that (1) race is not a biological reality—human beings share 99.9 percent identical DNA, and all humanity shares a common ancestor in Africa; (2) the issue is not race but racism and racialization; and (3) race as a social construct and racism as a social practice shape the contemporary world by skewing the distribution of power and resources. Rather than move from race to discrimination, it is in some ways more useful to move in the opposite direction, from the discrimination revealed by statistics (e.g., the disproportionate incarceration of black people) to the categories that explain the discrimination, whether having to do with race, color, national origin, religion, accent, or some other visible or audible difference. The very concept of "race," moreover, has been historically transfigured. Nowadays, Du Bois's "color line" has been retraced and blurred. Some prominent American blacks such as Colin Powell and Condoleezza Rice can be "deracialized" to join the white side. Islamophobia and the War on Terror, meanwhile, have racialized a religion (Islam) embracing people of many colors, rendering its followers subject to suspicion and profiling.[32] Today the color line involves not only what is visible—color—but also less visible social demarcations involving religion, clothing, body language, speech, etiquette, cultural capital, and Europeanness. Yet "race" and "racism" still serve to designate the persistence of strong inequalities linked to race, despite the lack of scientific substance to the notion of race itself.

Michaels mocks the politics that "consists of disapproving of bad things that happened a long time ago." Here he forgets (1) that such radically reconstructive historiography is aimed at countering a dominant historiography that ignores those "bad things" or even paints them as "good things" and (2) that those "bad things" still shape and help explain the present. Michaels echoes the conservative caricature of identity politics as invested in preserving "the differences between blacks and whites and Native Americans and Jews and whoever."[33] But the issue is not one of preserving difference for difference's sake—a notion redolent of salvage anthropology rescuing "tribes on the verge of extinction"—but rather of recognizing discrepancies in historical experience. Like French intellectuals such as Alain Finkielkraut, Michaels belittles accounts of the victimization of racialized communities as a form of narrative envy in relation to Jews, an accusation already mounted against Said's articulation of a Palestinian counternarrative in the late 1980s. Citing Leslie Marmon Silko's mention of the sixty million Native Americans eliminated by Europeans, Michaels responds, "They aren't just engaging in a kind of victimization one-upsmanship. They aren't trying to replace the Jews; they're trying to join them."[34] In this account of competition over ethical and narratological capital, it is as if Native Americans, who have been lamenting (and fighting) genocide since 1492, were trying to hitchhike on the prestige of the Holocaust.

The ethnocentric limits of Michaels's dichotomization of class-versus-race and culture-versus-economy become manifest in his analysis of Latin American activism. "There's a big difference," he writes, "between dealing with indigenous peoples who want to protect their culture and socialists who want to nationalize their industry. . . . When Evo Morales talks about 'nationalizing industry,' he is speaking as a socialist; when he talks about fulfilling the dreams 'of our ancestors,' he is speaking as an Indian."[35] In his embrace of the socialist Morales as against the Indian Morales, Michaels overlooks not only Morales's self-characterization as both socialist and Indian (and specifically Aymara) but also the mutual imbrication of culture and political economy in present-day Bolivia. By lauding Morales *only* as a socialist, Michaels ignores the public perception of Morales as "*indio,*" as well as the cultural politics that got him elected. The victory of Morales and MAS (Movement for Socialism), confirmed again in the elections of December 2008, forms a historic landmark for a country shaped by the oligarchy's racism toward the Quechua and Aymara majority. The new constitution recognizes the "multinational" character of the nation. For much of Bolivia's history, as Morales himself has frequently pointed out, "Indians" were not allowed to share the sidewalks with the *criollos*. Morales's enemies, for their part, are defined not only as capitalists but also as Bolivian "whites." Thus, it was in great part by "speaking as Indians" that the indigenous movement managed to coalesce into a powerful force able to challenge transnational corporations and the Bolivian oligarchy.

Any analysis like Michaels's that is based on the stigmatization of an abstract "identity" per se is likely to create a number of theoretical problems. First, the stigmatization of identity is usually asymmetrical; it rejects certain identities but not usually the identity of the analyst, which is assumed but silenced. Second, the very abstraction of the term makes it easy to practice guilt by association between the various "identitarians." Michaels, for example, compares the Aymara in Bolivia to Samuel Huntington, on the basis that both Huntington and the Aymara want to preserve identities. Such a formulation completely overlooks the question of power, rather like equating the politics of David Duke and Cornel West since both want to preserve their (respectively, Aryan and Black) identities. Michaels amalgamates the situations of a well-connected geopolitical strategist (Huntington) speaking a dominant language, with an Aymara people victimized by a five-century siege. Renewing the linguistic spirit of the Conquest, Michaels calls the disappearance of languages such as Aymara a "victimless crime."[36] As anyone knows who has lived situations without having a language available for communication, language is a form of power; to lose one's language is to be disempowered. It is passing strange to hear someone whose identity and livelihood derive from mastery of a hegemonic language be so cavalier about language, but that is perhaps why Michaels can be so cavalier; he knows *his* language is not about to disappear.

There is increasing recognition on the left that the social movements in Latin America, from Zapatismo to the indigenous movements in Bolivia, Peru, and Ecuador, are now at the cutting edge of social change. In the wake of indigenous activism and the UN declaration of indigenous rights, Ecuador and Bolivia have begun to inscribe indigenous rights and even the "right of Nature not to be harmed" into their constitutions, and Bolivia now has a "Ministry of Decolonization." The era of neoliberalism and the weakened nation-state has brought more and more direct confrontations pitting transnational corporations against indigenous groups defending their rights, in a new "contact zone" (Pratt) where land, biodiversity, and intellectual copyright are all at stake.

While classical Marxism is anticapitalist yet ultimately productivist, the Andean movements are often more radically anticapitalist in their assertion that "mother earth" should not be commodified. This culturally instilled refusal of commodification was one force-idea that helped energize the Bolivian movement and enabled it to prevent the corporated privatization of water and "even the rain."

Activists speak of communal forms of politics and of what Arturo Escobar calls "the political activation of relational ontologies." In Escobar's account, the activists call for (1) substantive rather than merely formal democracy, (2) "biocentric" sustainable development, and (3) interculturality in polyethnic societies. The goal is to move beyond capitalism, liberalism, statism, monoculturalism, productivism, Puritanism, and the ideology of "growth."[37]

For many indigenous people and societies, "culture" implies a norm of egalitarian economic arrangements, ecological balance, and consensus governance. Thus, indigenous culture and economic globalization confront each other in the form of very real battles fought in the name of "biodiversity," communal "intellectual property rights," and the noncommodification of nature.[38] Culture and economics, in sum, are deeply enmeshed in the Andes, with some ancestral traditions of communal property and collective decision-making combined with a rejection of instrumental/productivist attitudes toward nature. Indigenous resistance thus passes through culture. The Bolivian left won victories against the transnational corporations by mobilizing the cultural memory of the *ayllus*, or the chronotopic space-time of indigenous sovereignty. They won by *not choosing* between socialism and culture and instead constructing a socialist culture and a culturally inflected socialism.

The Bourdieu/Wacquant Polemic

Two of the most widely disseminated left attacks on multicultural identity politics took the form of two essays coauthored by Pierre Bourdieu and Loïc Wacquant, the first on neoliberalism and what they call "American multiculturalism," and the second on globalization, race, and Brazil. The essays suit our purposes here because, first, they exhibit the political passions, even in the early 21st century, invested in the "culture wars" and, second, as a French commentary on these issues, they reveal the transnational/translational dimension of the debates. In this chapter, we focus on the first essay, reserving the second for a later chapter.

Hailed in some quarters as a landmark refutation, Bourdieu/Wacquant's first essay commingles a completely legitimate critique of the mystifying doxa of neoliberal globalization with a misfired attack on multicultural identity politics. To our minds, their very brief commentary forms a remarkable condensation of how *not* to articulate issues of race, nation, multiculture, and transnational intellectual exchange. Their static and monolithic theoretical model will hopefully serve here as a productive foil for the more dynamic, polycentric, and multidirectional approach that we are proposing. In fact, the arguments in both essays seemed to conflict even with Bourdieu's method in general, as if his usually subtle argumentation becomes shrill when misinformation and a submerged national agenda inflect the analysis. While hardly major interventions in the "culture war" debates, the two essays achieved high visibility and thus serve as samples of an unproductive approach undergirded by nation-state-based and class-over-race assumptions.

Although some readers might wonder why we bother to refute an ill-informed diatribe by intellectuals with whom we would normally be politically aligned, a response strikes us as important for a number of reasons. First, the strong and contradictory responses to the first essay are a sure sign that something major was at stake. Broadcast by a prestigious name from a powerful platform (*Le Monde Diplomatique*), widely translated and disseminated, the essay was taken as authoritative by many readers around the world. At the same time, a "critique of the critique" can help us clarify other larger theoretical, methodological, and political problems inherent in their approach, bringing to the surface larger anxieties that go far beyond this specific polemic.

Our goal is not to criticize Bourdieu's work in general, which has had the salutary effect of repoliticizing the social sciences and even the humanities. We applaud Bourdieu's critique of neoliberalism and his highlighting of the role of symbolic domination in hiding and reinforcing social inequality. Nor do we have any sympathy for the positivistic American sociology rejected by Bourdieu. As Robert Blauner puts it in *Racial Oppression in America*, "virtually all the new insights about racism and the experience of the oppressed have been provided by writers whose lives and minds were uncluttered by [American] sociological theory."[39] Furthermore, we are vastly more sympathetic to leftists such as Bourdieu/Wacquant than we are to "pro-American" French intellectuals such as Jean-Claude Milner, Alain Finkielkraut, and Pascal Bruckner. Not only do we favorably cite and deploy Bourdieu's concepts and those of many Bourdieu-influenced scholars such as François Cusset and Pascale Casanova, but we also support many aspects of his life and work: his early solidarity with the Algerian independence struggle; his critique of colonialism in his collaborations with Abdelmalek Sayad; his dissection, in *Reproduction* and *The Inheritors* (with Jean-Claude Passeron), of the structures of privilege in the French educational system; his analysis of the social stratifications of taste in *Distinction*; and his activism on behalf of marginalized social groups in France (the homeless, the unemployed, striking workers, illegal immigrants, gays and lesbians), as well as his 1995 intervention in support of striking students and workers. Bourdieu's critique of neoliberal globalization and of the incursion of market values into the intellectual field, as well as his "new internationalist" campaign against the catastrophic effects of neoliberal economic policies, have been indispensible contributions to progressive politics.

Furthermore, we concur with the authors' critiques of the U.S. social, political, judicial, and prison systems and of U.S. policy abroad. Bourdieu's concepts of "habitus," "field," and "cultural capital," moreover, can illuminate processes of cultural domination. Bourdieu's conceptual categories, to put it paradoxically, can be productive even in deconstructing some of Bourdieu's (and Wacquant's) own assessments. Indeed, a number of scholars have extended Bourdieu's concepts by "racing" them through such ideas as "racial capital," "racial habitus," and "racial doxa." Wacquant, for his part, has done valuable work on prisons in the United States and France and has popularized Bourdieu's work. In sum, our argument is not with their work as a whole but rather with their narrow views of a complex intellectual field.

Although Bourdieu/Wacquant devoted only a few short paragraphs in the first essay to multicultural identity politics, those paragraphs managed to distill a remarkably dense concentration of historical elisions and methodological blind spots. To avoid caricature, we present most of what Bourdieu/Wacquant say about these issues in this essay:

> In all the advanced countries, international c.e.o.s and administrators, media intellectuals and high-flying journalists are beginning to speak a strange new language: . . . "globalization," "flexibility," "governance," "employability," "underclass" and "exclusion," "new economy" and "zero tolerance," "communitarianism," "multiculturalism," and their cousins "postmodernity," "ethnicity," "minority," "identity." . . . American "multiculturalism" is not a concept, nor a theory, nor a social or political movement, while pretending to be all those things at the same time. It is a screen-discourse whose intellectual status results from a gigantic effort of national and international allodoxia [the act of confusing one thing with another] which deludes those who are part of it as it deludes those who are not part of it. It is an American discourse, even though it presents itself as universal, in that it expresses the specific contradictions of academics who, cut off from all access to the public sphere and submitted to a strong compartmentalization in their professional milieu, have no other place to invest their political libido than in campus quarrels disguised as conceptual epics.[40]

Here Bourdieu/Wacquant extrapolate a few valid insights into a broad-brush caricature. The insights have to do with, first, with the disastrous impact of capitalist globalization and the dissemination of neoliberal doxa around the world, second with the fact that American exceptionalist discourses do falsely present themselves as universal, and third with the fact that many U.S. academics are indeed cut off from the public sphere—although usually not of their own choosing—and are subjected to careerist pressures and a "strong compartmentalization." Thus, there is a disconnect between campus radicalism and the steady drift toward the right of the American polity as a whole. In this sense, the American *homo academicus* shares some of the traits of homo *academicus universalis* generally, along with some local peculiarities.[41]

The arguments made by Walter Benn Michaels and those made by Bourdieu/Wacquant are only partially congruent. While they all share class-over-race assumptions, Bourdieu/Wacquant are more concerned with American imperialism and global capitalism. Yet like the Michaels book, the Bourdieu/Wacquant essay is riddled with false dichotomies: academics must either do real politics or do multiculturalism, the oppression of blacks in the United States is either about access or about recognition, and so forth. Although the essay portrays multicultural identity politics as completely detached from the public sphere, the American right's hostile reaction bespoke precisely the opposite fear: that such projects were having *too* much impact on the public sphere. Where Bourdieu/Wacquant discern a wall between academe and public sphere, moreover, we see a permeable membrane. Ironically, the U.S. right, especially in the Bush-Cheney era, did not see academic multiculturalism as apolitical but rather as "politicizing the university." Right-wing foundations such as the John M. Olin Foundation, the Heritage Foundation, the Cato Institute, the American Enterprise Institute, and the Scaife Foundation all spent millions of dollars to combat such projects. Lynne Cheney, wife of the former vice president, during her tenure as head of the National Endowment for the Humanities systematically blocked all projects having to do with revisionist history, racism, multiculturalism, imperialism, and genocide. Was it the hallucinatory force of multiculturalism, with "its power to delude those who are part of it and those who are not part of it" that made Lynne Cheney misrecognize as anti-American and subversive what the two sociologists see as neoliberal and pro-American?

Bourdieu/Wacquant conflate a partial insight—the relative isolation of "campus quarrels"—with a false conclusion that these quarrels are inconsequential. Bourdieu-influenced intellectual historian François Cusset offers a more complex account in his *French Theory: How Foucault, Derrida, Deleuze, & Co. Transformed the Intellectual Life of the United States:*

> Despite [its] isolation . . . the university is a focus of national concern in the
> United States, and is often the sounding box, or the dramatic relay point, for some
> of the most pressing questions of American society. To use Gramsci's distinction,
> one could even say that, although it is separated from *civil society,* the university
> nonetheless maintains a close link with American *political society,* because of its
> role as an ideological crossroads and in the formation of elites. Hence the far-
> reaching echoes, resounding well beyond the bucolic campuses, of the polemics set
> off there.[42]

Critical projects in the United States, furthermore, have often focused attention on the socially crucial areas of pedagogy and the teaching of history. The sulfurous mid-1990s debate about "National History Standards," for example, pitted the advocates of a critical, multivocal "history from below" against the advocates of the American exceptionalist account.[43] Since the educational arena, as Bourdieu's own work demonstrates, is crucial in both reproducing and demystifying dominant ideologies, the teaching of history has immense social significance in forming citizens and shaping debates. The more radical versions of the multicultural project have questioned American myths of innocence. Radical pedagogy, for example, disputes the dominant racist and imperialist narratives. It seems spurious to lament American provinciality and at the same time to oppose the challenges from within to American exceptionalist discourse.

Like Bourdieu/Wacquant, we too would prefer that critical intellectuals enjoy more access to the so-called public sphere, but where does the "public sphere" begin and end? Do the contours of all public spheres necessarily resemble one another? Since the Enlightenment, and more specifically since the Dreyfus affair, French intellectuals have enjoyed a special status. When asked to arrest Sartre in the 1960s, de Gaulle famously objected that "one does not arrest Voltaire." Figures such as Sartre, Beauvoir, Foucault, and later Bourdieu have been regarded in France (and elsewhere) as designated spokespersons for the universal, even when they themselves call for more modest "specific intellectuals." Bourdieu was widely seen as having occupied the space left empty by Foucault's death. But whose interests are served by a hierarchical *maître à penser* model with a single magisterial figure at its apex, even when the scholar in question is politically progressive? Bourdieu/Wacquant measure the efficacy of intellectuals according to a French standard, despite the fact that the French model of the universal intellectual brings with it the problems highlighted by Foucault concerning "speaking for others." The Bourdieu/Wacquant formulations also risk reproducing a gendered splitting between "hard" masculine public politics and "soft" feminine private culture, when in fact both spheres are intimately linked and reciprocally inflect each other in a complex interchange.

In an unwittingly paradoxical account, Bourdieu/Wacquant describe multiculturalists as powerless domestically yet all-powerful globally. Restricted to "campus quarrels" and thus impotent in national terms, they become omnipotent in international terms due to their shadowy alliance with corporate globalizers. Isolated from the public sphere, multiculturalists yet form part of the overpowering hegemony that cunningly dominates the globe. Like U.S. right-wingers, Bourdieu/Wacquant see multiculturalism as allied with powerful forces. But the U.S. right attributes this power to a cunning communism, while Bourdieu/Wacquant attribute it to a cunning imperialism. For U.S. right-wingers such as Paul Weyrich, multiculturalism has a "death grip" on the body politic, on the Church, the academic community, and the entertainment industry, threatening to control every aspect of our lives.[44] (Weyrich made this claim, ironically, in a historical conjuncture in which the right dominated all three branches of government, much of the media, and even parts of the Democratic Party).[45] While Bourdieu/ Wacquant mock derisory "campus quarrels," Weyrich sees multiculturalism as a powerful form of "Cultural Marxism" dominated by an "alien ideology . . . bitterly hostile to Western culture."[46] Both accounts, we would suggest, are partial and even paranoid, although the paranoia springs from opposite political sources.

The paranoid anticommunism of the U.S. right has a long historical pedigree, going back to the Red Scare persecution of anarcho-syndicalist immigrants in the 1920s, the repression of the black-leftist alliance in the 1930s, and the FBI targeting of communist "outside agitators" supposedly stirring up Civil Rights protests in the 1950s and 1960s. In a belated version of the old right's misrecognition of the Civil Rights Movement as "communist," Frank Ellis sees "today's 'political correctness'" as the direct descendant of communist "brainwashing." And if "the war of attrition" against multiculturalism fails, he warns ominously, "the insanity of multiculturalism is something white Americans will have to live with."[47] What is missed in the Bourdieu/Wacquant account is the fact that both France and the United States have seen similarly orchestrated assaults on the radical heritage of 1968, whether led by politicians such as George W. Bush and Sarkozy or by intellectuals such as David Horowitz and Alain Finkielkraut. Ellis's arguments, in this sense, recall the French *nouveaux philosophes'* equations of Third Worldism with totalitarianism.

For Bourdieu/Wacquant, "multiculturalism" hides social crisis by depoliticizing a struggle "that is not really ethnic or racial but has to do with access to the instruments of production and reproduction." This formulation creates a false dichotomy, since race partially determines who has "access to the instruments of production and reproduction." If the struggle is on one level about access, it is not only about access. Rather than have a fixed preordained status, moreover, class is an arena of negotiation mediated and reshaped through race, gender, and sexuality, which is precisely what necessitates discourses of "relationality" and "intersectionality." In the Bourdieu/Wacquant analysis, one cannot think race and chew class gum at the same time, while gender and sexuality are not there to "chew" at all. In the United States, for historical reasons, the struggle for justice—the fight for entitlements, the broadening of the left into the various antiwar, green, proimmigrant, and antiglobalization movements—all invariably pass "through" both race and class. Nor can we separate culture and economy in an age when the two are becoming more and more confounded. Jack Lang's famous slogan "Economics and culture—the same struggle" is not relevant only to France.

Only a dichotomous form of thinking, in any case, would ask us to choose between analyzing "structures and the mechanisms of domination" and "celebrating the culture of the dominated and their point of view." It is precisely the structures of domination, after all, that make it necessary to celebrate the culture of the dominated, since one of the mechanisms of domination is to devalue the culture of the dominated while normativizing the culture of the dominant. Only those whose "point of view" is customarily empowered could be so dismissive of the "culture of the dominated" and so scornful about struggles to crack open spaces for the dominated "point of view." This myopically solipsistic, "objective" view fails to see its own vantage point as interested and affiliated, as merely one perspective among others. For those working on critical race and coloniality, moreover, a "point of view" is not a merely subjective issue of psychology; it is a social/epistemological vantage point within social space and historical time.

Interestingly, Bourdieu himself has offered keen and very personal insights into the social dimension of point of view. In *Sketch for a Self-Analysis*, Bourdieu explains how he was shaped intellectually by the social hierarchies of his rural milieu of origin, in ways that allowed him to "see" the classed nature of prestige in the Parisian "center."[48] He evokes, in other words, the epistemological advantage facilitated by a subordinated social positionality, in this case one inflected by class and region. Gendered and racialized people, in this sense, potentially exercise a similar epistemological advantage due to a multifocal perspective linked to an intimate acquaintance with the quotidian workings of oppressive systems and the concrete need to "code-switch" to survive. Gloria Anzaldúa, the Chicana exponent of "border theory," speaks of "*la facultad*," or the coping capacities developed by people confronting various forms of oppression in the neoimperial borderlands.[49] Structures of oppression and point of view are thus completely imbricated. For Fanon. the psychoanalysis of the colonized point of view in *Black Skin, White Masks* was intimately linked to the socio-analysis of the structures of colonial domination in *The Wretched of the Earth*. Bourdieu/Wacquant thus fail to engage with a major intervention performed by critical race and postcolonial studies: the historicized articulations of subaltern subjectivity.

Bourdieu/Wacquant eloquently denounce the doxa of neoliberalism, rejecting a model of "modernization" and "globalization" that would undo the social welfare state in the name of the "market." They make a metonymic (allodoxic?) slide, however, from the legitimate critique of neoliberalism into an uninformed critique of multicultural identity politics. They do not separate out specific co-optable forms from more progressive forms; rather, they condemn the entire set of projects en bloc. The authors manage this conflation of globalization and multiculturalism not only by ignoring the kaleidoscopic variety of the actual work but also through a series of abstractly rhetorical links between the efficacy of the market and the recognition of identities. The new planetary doxa, for the two authors, include terms such as "globalization," "racial minorities," and "multiculturalism," which impose on all societies specifically American concerns and viewpoints, "naturalizing" one particular historical experience as a model for humanity in general. An update of Borges's "Chinese Encyclopedia," this lexicon of the new vulgate forces into the same discursive sack very contradictory terms, with very distinct genealogies and histories of deployment, presenting them as forming part of a coherent and unified reactionary discourse. "Globalization," "markets," and "flexibility" clearly emerge from the ideological world of the "Washington Consensus"; "multiculturalism," "identity," and "minority" just as clearly do not emerge from that world.

An "American" Discourse?

While Bourdieu/Wacquant see multicultural identity politics as quintessentially American, the U.S. right sees the very same project as anti-American and sometimes, ironically, as too "French." In this sense, the Bourdieu/Wacquant essay exhibits the pitfalls of nation-state framing. Since the authors see "American multiculturalism" as a politically compromised tool of global capitalism from the outset, they do not use the word "co-optability" or engage even the possibility of a more complex narrative that would see a generally progressive project subsequently "co-opted." Yet even co-optive multiculturalism was co-opting something, in this case what began as the political/cultural mobilization of racialized communities within the United States in tandem with decolonizing movements in the "Third World." Only later, in the 1990s, was the multicultural theme (but not the project) appropriated through the merely epidermic diversity of corporate advertising. Transnational corporations have sometimes "multiethnicized" their image to sell products through a skin-deep display of chromatic exoticism, while simultaneously abusing the marginalized laborers (largely women of color) who helped generate their profit margins. But corporations have never invoked "multiculturalism" as a sociopolitical project, preferring blander terms such as "diversity" and "cultural sensitivity," terms more easily instrumentalizable for doing business in a global market. Bourdieu/Wacquant do not distinguish between bottom-up movements and discourses and the top-down instrumentalization of those discourses. And if the dangers of nationalism are very real, nationalism can also be encoded in the *rejection* of multiculturalism as well.

To define multiculturalism as always-already complicitous with corporate neoliberalism places all the burden of left purity on just one project within a broad spectrum of progressive movements. Blaming that project for the collapse of left unity is simplistic. In the United States, the multicultural left projects entered into a world already shaped by the fait accompli of the violent FBI crushing of the radical Black Power, Young Lords, and American Indian movements, in tandem with the harassment of the white radical left. Moreover, the charge of a general depoliticization could easily be extended to academic life in the many countries that have witnessed massive retreats from historical material-ism, Third Worldist revolution, and radical politics. This worldwide retreat from radicalism—and here indigenous, Latin American, Middle-Eastern, and alter-globalization activism form luminous exceptions to the rule—has variously been named postmodernism, the eclipse of utopias, and the end of metanarratives. From a neoliberal point of view, it was a return to capitalist normalcy, a state of homeostatic complacency revealed to be factitious with the bursting of the vari-ous financial bubbles in 2008. The capitalist euphoria that followed the fall of the Berlin Wall gave way to the anxieties about cracks in another wall: Wall Street. Even if the hegemonic United States has been the leading reactionary Western power ever since the dissolution of the European empires, and even if the domi-nant political debates in the United States are in many ways pitched far to the right of cognate debates in Europe and in Latin America, one cannot attribute a general depoliticization to a single national site or to a single project.

Bourdieu/Wacquant, subtle analysts of their own "national fields," commit an act of symbolic violence by denying any conceptual or theoretical validity to what they mislabel "American multiculturalism." For them, multiculturalism is a particular American discourse that "presents itself as universal." The right-wing polemicists in the United States, paradoxically, usually score multiculturalism for a "cultural relativist" refusal to invoke universal values. And in what sense do mul-ticultural writings claim universality? Here the two sociologists miss the radical situatedness of such work. Surely Bourdieu/Wacquant are not suggesting that revisionist American historians believe that their site-specific critique of excep-tionalist U.S.-American historiography can be borrowed wholesale to apply to Poland and Thailand or that critical race theorists' deconstructive reading of the U.S. Constitution is meant to apply literally to the legal documents of France, Senegal, and China?[50] Since radical versions of the multicultural project cri-tiqued the "false universalism" of Enlightenment modernity, it is not clear why the authors would not see that critique as allied with their own.

We can only applaud Bourdieu's denunciation, in *Acts of Resistance*, of the "false universalism of the West [and] . . . the imperialism of the universal."[51] Indeed, many multicultural, feminist, and postcolonial scholars have questioned the "false universalism" of both the American and the French Revolutions, whose liberatory discourse did not prevent them from enslaving blacks or disempow-ering women. The critique of false universalizations does not go far enough, however, for the question is not one of critiquing only one national form of false universalism but rather of interrogating the very premises by which the West in general has constructed and been constructed by the "universal." Who gets to speak on behalf of the universal? Who are its caretakers and regulators? Who gets relegated to the merely "particular"? What are the articulations between the particular and the universal, the local and the global? It was colonialism as a global enterprise, after all, that projected onto a world scale the very notion of the "universal." To detach U.S.-style false universalisms from this broader colonial genealogy is myopic, ethnocentric, and covertly nationalist.

It is questionable, furthermore, whether multiculturalism can be reduced to an "American" discourse. Self-declared "liberal multiculturalist" Canadian scholar Will Kymlicka argues that "the specific models of multiculturalism and minority rights being advanced by IOs [international organizations] . . . are not drawn primarily from the American experience. . . . Similarly, international debates about the rights of 'indigenous peoples' are not dominated by American models or scholars."[52] At a historical moment when critical scholars have troubled homogeneous conceptions of national belonging, Bourdieu/Wacquant never clarify the meaning of the term "American." Within their essay, it carries a strong odor of negativity. While the United States richly deserves its unsavory reputation as a criminal violator of human rights and international law, in Bourdieu/Wacquant's prose, "American" becomes part of a fixed, essentialist mode of dismissal. Resistant scholarship is tainted, as it were, by virtue of its provenance. Even an imperialistic nation, after all, can serve as a scapegoat or a decoy. The scapegoating function does not depend on the *innocence* of the scapegoat but rather on the phantasmatic uses to which the scapegoat is put.

The meaning of "American," then, slides from nation-state location to inferences about intellectual substance. Some of the critical work produced in North America—much generated by scholars who are not Americans by birth or ancestry—might better be called "adversary" or "counterhegemonic" scholarship that questions the reigning nationalist doxa embedded in the myth of "America" itself. This scholarship at times questions the very legal/moral foundations of the United States as a settler-colonial state rooted in genocide and slavery. When a revisionist historian such as Francis Jennings dismantles American founding fictions such as the "right of discovery" and "manifest destiny," his work is deeply demystificatory of American exceptionalism. When Native American critics such as Oren Lyons, John Mohawk, Jack Forbes, Annette Jaimes Guerrero, Ward Churchill, and Andrea Smith deconstruct the shared antiecological and productivist substratum of both capitalist and Marxist philosophies, or when critical race theorists preform between-the-lines critical readings of the U.S. Constitution to expose the class/racial/gender ghosts lurking in the interstices of the law, their discourse is not reducible to a nation-state qualifier.

Bourdieu/Wacquant share with many left critics a basic lack of familiarity with the decolonizing corpus. The bibliography of their later "imperial cunning" essay references only two neoconservative *critics* of multiculturalism (Allan Bloom and Dinesh D'Souza). One looks in vain for any reference to the many left intellectuals who address race and class, economy and culture.[53] In the French context, sociologist Michel Wieviorka speaks of the "rigged" aspect of a certain leftist anti-Americanism: "The U.S. is criticized for its racism, for example, but also for its attempts to combat racism." Rather than a complex society character-ized by competing modes of thinking, the United States is imaged as a mono-lith that must be kept at a safe distance, lest "France run the danger of losing its identity, its soul, its cultural personality." Anti-Americanism becomes an ide-ology, Wieviorka argues, "when it is the premise and not the conclusion of an argument."[54]

The Bourdieu/Wacquant argument seems to be founded on an unarticulated syllogism: The United States is imperialist; American discourse is imperialist; multiculturalism is an American discourse; ergo, multiculturalism is imperialist. But a strictly national framing provides only a very blunt instrument for reflecting on transnational intellectual flows. The multicultural project emerged, within a number of nation-states, due to concrete historical conditions, notably the forma-tion and dissolution of colonial empire and the overlays of multiply diasporized cultures existing in relations of subordination and domination within nation-states, all combined with the copresence of academics knowledgeable about those cultures operating in institutional spaces where it became possible to articulate those issues. For complex historical reasons, including the Civil Rights Move-ment, "minority" activism, changes in immigration laws, the South-North "brain drain" and other migratory cross-currents, and the Thatcherization of the United Kingdom, the U.S. academy has played host to a mélange of diasporic postcolo-nial intellectuals, becoming a magnet for what George Yúdice calls "centripetal and centrifugal academic desires," resulting in the "deterritorialization and denational-ization of academic debates."[55] Postcolonial theory, for example, partially gained strength in the U.S. academy because a number of diasporic intellectuals moved to the United States, but it would not have succeeded had not ethnic studies, area studies, and Third World studies already created a hospitable space for such the-ory. At the same time, U.S. geopolitical interventions and neoliberal globalization provoked the movement of political refugees and economic immigrants toward the United States—a process summed up in the postcolonial maxim "We are here, because you were there." An in some ways racist, imperialist, and often xenophobic nation, paradoxically, became a refuge for antiracist and anti-imperialist thought, much as France in the 1930s—to evoke a partial parallel—was simultaneously the seat of a racist empire and a shelter for anticolonial thought.

In describing multicultural identity politics as symptomatic of three "vices" of "American national thinking"—notably "groupism," "populism," and "moralism"—Bourdieu/Wacquant resort to a Volkish vocabulary alien to both Marxism and to French republicanism. A discourse of "national traits" is distinctly unhelpful in the realm of transnational intellectual exchange. Redolent of 19th-century pseudosciences such as phrenology and mesmerism, talk of "national vices" seems incongruous in the writing of leftist social scientists. In line with postnationalist theories of "imagined communities" (Anderson) and "invented traditions" (Hobsbawm), we would question analyses premised on cultural-essentialist systems of explanation.[56] Although nation-states have characteristic interests and policies, and peoples might have a dominant cultural style, there is no single national spirit or ethos regulating the "national thought" of any nation, much less the variegated "multinations" of the Black Atlantic. Virtually any nation, furthermore, will have its "groupists," its "populists," and its "moralists." The word "vices" itself, ironically, exemplifies the very moralism being attributed to others.

The label "American" monoculturalizes a complex set of projects by seeing them through a homogenizing grid that stabilizes what the more radical work had tried to destabilize. Who, then, are the real "identitarians": the very varied participants in a transnational project, or those who reduce that movement, in a kind of *repli identitaire*, to a kernel of alien nationality? Identitarian thinking, after all, does not operate only in relation to one's own group; it also operates in relation to the projected identities of other groups. Moreover, Bourdieu/Wacquant overlook the French and Francophone dimensions of this supposedly "American" discourse. When a text written by a non-French scholar bears the traces of French or Francophone discourses, that text, in its *écriture* at least, becomes hybrid, transnational, in-between. Far from depoliticizing French theory, it could be argued that U.S.-based race/coloniality scholars pushed French theory into a more politically engaged direction by bringing Derridean ideals onto what François Cusset calls "the battleground of identitarian discourses," thus becoming "champions of subversion."[57]

The dismissal of multiculturalism as "not a theory," finally, is a red herring. Rather than a grand Theory with a capital T, it is one of many umbrella terms sheltering a constellation of critical discourses. Yet on another level, multicultural discourse at its most radical did inherit, and transform, a specific set of theoretical frameworks, to wit, the diverse theories, methods, and perspectives forming part of the "decolonization of knowledge," including Marxism, feminism, dependency theory, poststructuralism, standpoint theory, the coloniality/modernity project, and so forth. To claim that multiculturalism is not a social movement, similarly, is a genre mistake, since it is not an organized political movement per se but rather a discursive formation potentially allied to a number of social movements as part of a loose coalition for justice and equality. That coalition, moreover, has had real-world effects in changing the demographic makeup of institutions, in diversifying faculty and students in higher education, and in de-Eurocentrizing the canon. Like any complex critical formation, such projects do not deploy a single discourse but rather constitute a heteroglossic arena of competing and sometimes contradictory currents, which cannot be reduced simply to any one national banner. The United States is just one terminal in a transnational network of ideas, not a point of origin or final destination.

Žižek and the Universal Imaginary

Another vigorous voice raised against multicultural identity politics has been that of theorist Slavoj Žižek. Here again, we would distinguish between the op-ed Žižek of political pronouncements, with whom we are usually in agreement, and the Eurocentric Žižek analyzing race and coloniality, with whom we are not. Žižek is a tremendously agile and engaging writer and in many ways a progressive theorist. We applaud not only his provocative film criticism but also his critiques of global capitalism, of right-wing populism, and of nationalistic ideologies. His critiques of liberalism, published in *Le Monde Diplomatique*, are incisive and on point. His ideas are compelling in part, as his exegete Jodi Dean puts it, because "they open up and enliven what has become fixed and stale."[58] The problem occurs when Žižek pontificates on issues about which he is ill-informed.

In "Multiculturalism, or, The Cultural Logic of Multinational Capitalism," Žižek calls multiculturalism "the ideal ideological form of global capitalism." Transferring the Marxist critique of the merely formal democracy of interest-group liberalism as a mask for bourgeois domination, Žižek usefully questions the liberal view of the American state as a "simple formal framework for the coexistence of ethnic, religious, or life-style communities."[59] But two slippages operate in Žižek's writing. One moves from the "United States as a multicultural society" to multiculturalism as a project. Another moves from multiculturality to global capitalism, a conflation that elides those numerous multicultural voices that decry the role of global capitalism as rooted in colonialism and imperialism. Contemporary transnational corporations inherit the unequal structures and tendentious ideologies bequeathed by centuries of colonial/imperial domination. While some liberal forms of multiculturalism might be compatible with certain forms of global capitalism, it is not clear why multiculturalism would be its "ideal ideological form," given that the neoliberal ideology of market fundamentalism—which hardly references race or multiculturalism at all—was serving quite well, at least until the world economic meltdown, as "the ideal form of global capitalist ideology."

We of course applaud Žižek's critique of global capitalism. Matt Taibbi's description of the Wall Street investment company Goldman Sachs as "a great vampire squid wrapped around the face of humanity, relentlessly jamming its blood funnel into anything that smells like money" could easily be extended to global capitalism generally.[60] To say that the real struggle is against global capitalism has an immediate appeal. Most of what is wrong with the contemporary world can be traced to global capitalism's privatization of virtually everything—land, natural resources, public utilities, health care, and even war. There is scarcely any American social problem—militarism, gun control, health care—that does not have corporate greed as its trademark. If we could defeat global capitalism, one might argue, it would seem that we would not even have to worry about trivialities such as race. If the United States were truly socialist, would not race be irrelevant? Perhaps so, but the case of Cuba suggests that even socialist societies still struggle with racism. A perspective more attentive to race, gender, and coloniality, moreover, would offer a fuller account of the genealogy of global capitalism itself as rooted in racialized conquest, slavery, and the oppression of women. The "vampire squid," in this sense, has been largely white and male and spawned in the Global North, while the "face of humanity" has been largely brown and female and located in the Global South. And while capitalism still reigns, what antidote do we offer against existing racism, discrimination, and Islamophobia? Brandishing "universality" and Saint Paul will simply not do.

At times, Žižek equates multiculturalism with "tolerance" as an apolitical category that leaves power relations untouched. But the concept of "tolerance," which goes back at least as far as the Jewish *ve-ahavata le-re'kha kamokha* (Love Your Friend/Neighbor as yourself) or to Jesus's "cast not the first stone" or to *Ahel al-Kitab* (People of the Book) in the Islamic world, is in no way central to many multicultural projects. Indeed, the more radical wings of those projects have rejected the paternalism inherent in "tolerance" and, more generally, have criticized psychologistic and moralistic approaches to racism. "Tolerance" is premised on a prior normativity, an assumption of major and minor elements in a society. Even the tolerance within the Abrahamic "religions of the book" marginalizes those who adhere to other nonmonotheistic religions or to nonscriptural religions or to those who prefer no religion at all. Tolerance also encodes class superiority by forgetting that the powerless can also practice "tolerance" without learning it from their "betters."

Žižek's critique of multiculturalism mingles the class-over-race rhetoric of Walter Benn Michaels with the multiculturalism-equals-globalization arguments of Bourdieu/Wacquant. His portrayal of multiculturalism as "ideal ideological form" implies that economic neoliberalism has no problem accommodating race, gender, sexuality, and multiculturalism and that only a socioeconomic analysis poses a meaningful challenge to global capitalism. It is indeed true that transnational capitalism and its ideological forms inevitably pressure and work over all contemporary political projects. Global capitalism has been highly creative in its capacity to absorb and contain opposition movements and discourses. However, the struggle against neoliberal globalization, like that against colonialism and neocolonialism earlier, inevitably also involves struggles against the racialized and gendered international division of labor, if only because global capitalism especially exploits women of color.

Left critics such as Žižek fail to distinguish between co-optive forms of multiculturalism and more counterhegemonic formations such as the coloniality/modernity project, black radicalism, indigenous activism, transnational feminism, and so forth. Such critics deploy a caricature version of "multiculturalism" as a metonym for the *entire* range of race-related anticolonial adversary projects, which are then subsumed under the category of the hegemonic forces evoked by phrases such as "global capital" that give a Marxist veneer to a superficial critique. In his frequent denunciations of multiculturalism, Žižek gathers his examples randomly from a show seen on television, a joke heard in a bar, a comment at a party, ignoring the intellectual labor that went into the projects that he caricatures. Symptomatically, Žižek rarely refers to work performed under the postcolonial banner, where many of the theoretical coordinates are much closer to his own. For Žižek, "multiculturalist" becomes an adjective to be randomly attached to words such as "late capitalism," "tolerance," and "postmodernism," in a discursive conjuncture where the adjective discredits the noun or, conversely, the noun the adjective. The very levity with which Žižek treats such issues signals the lack of a deep engagement.

Žižek deploys colonialism not as a fundamental category of analysis but only as a rhetorical stick to beat multiculturalism with, as in his claim that multiculturalism treats "local cultures in the way the colonizer treated colonized people," as "natives whose customs should be studied and respected."[61] But it is precisely this colonial paternalism that has been the object of critique in much of the decolonizing corpus, including in its multicultural variant. Žižek's critique thus involves a series of low blows. In a case of poaching masquerading as critique, Žižek echoes multicultural and critical race arguments, as if they were his own, only to discredit such projects. Indeed, his critique seems persuasive only to the extent that such projects have prepared the ground for its acceptance. In other words, the very field that Žižek rejects has shaped the discursive environment that makes his argument seem compelling.

For Žižek, multiculturalism operates from an invisible vantage point presumed to be universal from which it can appreciate or depreciate other cultures: "The multiculturalist respect for the Other's specificity is the very form of asserting one's own superiority."[62] Here again Žižek draws virtually every term and argument from the decolonizing corpus itself. It is as if someone were to borrow Marxist concepts to accuse Marx himself of "commodity fetishism," without acknowledging Marx as the originator of the concept. The critique of the arrogant yet unmarked Western vantage point has long been a part of the larger race/colonial field. The analysis of normative whiteness as "unmarked," for example, can be found in the work of Toni Morrison, David Roediger, Vron Ware, Ruth Frankenberg, Caren Kaplan, George Lipsitz, and other scholars. Mary Louise Pratt speaks in *Imperial Eyes* of the "monarch-of-all-I-survey" topos within colonialist travel literature,[63] and we have analyzed in *Unthinking Eurocentrism* the ways that network news sutures spectatorial identification with imperial militarism.[64] Indeed, such notions as "writing back," the "imperial gaze," and "returning the gaze" are by now taken-for-granted concepts within multicultural and postcolonial critique.[65] Nor is such work a cute endorsement of folkloric customs, as Žižek suggests; rather, it deconstructs the binarism that produces "folklore" as an allochronic residue of the past rather than as a form of cultural productivity in the present.

In a strategy of simultaneous externalization and incorporation, Žižek attributes to the multicultural project the very terms and procedures that radical versions of that project have rejected. Žižek's spatialized social schema positions multiculturalism as instantiating a panoptical vantage point from the observing tower of privilege. The entire project is assumed to come from the heights of power, when in fact multicultural identity politics emerged from very different contexts in different locations, usually in collaboration with minoritized communities. This coalitionary project won for the socially marginalized an institutional "looking space" from which to view the hegemonic social order. Thus, Žižek's text performs a double legerdemain: it does not acknowledge that the multicultural left has advanced many of the same ideas that he himself is advancing, while it attributes to multiculturalists ideas that they do not claim.

In a rather clumsy class analysis, Žižek assumes throughout that multiculturalism, or what he, like the right, calls "the politically correct," represents a "narrow elitist upper-middle-class circle clearly opposing itself to the majority of common people."[66] It is hard to know on what statistical information or sociological analyses he has based this judgment, but he has clearly missed the crisscrossing bottom-up and top-down currents operative in multicultural activism as the product of a coalition of diverse communities of color, and progressive whites. In what sense were intellectual multicultural heroines such as Audre Lorde and Gloria Anzaldúa "upper middle class"? Are the working-class black activists in Brazil calling for "multicultural pedagogy" or indigenist anticorporate activists calling for a "multicultural Bolivia" all upper middle class? Only a class-reductionist view, furthermore, would deny that people on the "top" can work together with people at the "bottom" to undermine social/racial hierarchies. Those at the social "bottom," furthermore, produce theoretical and practical knowledge that feeds into pedagogical projects.

The fact that multicultural identity politics tended to be strong on U.S. campuses did not mean that the movement was "only academic" or, for that matter, "only American." That Native Americans, African Americans, Asian Americans, and Latinos now have even a limited voice in the academy was the result of struggles that took place in the streets, neighborhoods, and campuses. Although Žižek paints multiculturalists as elitist, in fact it was the radical movements of the 1960s that made the university *less* elitist by facilitating the entry of marginalized groups. Žižek's antielitism here risks aligning itself with the right-wing populism that focuses its hostility not on the corporate-military-political elite but only on the "tenured radicals" of the campus left. The performative act of academics trashing other academics for being academics—as in Woody Allen's joke that intellectuals, like mafiosi, only kill their own—would suggest a need for a greater measure of critical self-reflexivity. The actual connections between progressives in the universities and resistant communities require a more complex articulation. The parallel struggles to decolonize knowledge production and to transform the demographics of the university cannot be narrated as beginning with conversations only at the high tables of elite universities. Žižek papers over the struggle to reconstitute the university, thus denying intellectual agency to people of color who have formed a quintessential part of a larger coalition.

This same class-over-race prism becomes manifest in Žižek's casual dismissal elsewhere of black demands for reparations. Gleaning his information not from reparations advocates but rather from the media—in this case from a press report on an August 17, 2002, "Rally for Slave Reparations"—Žižek sarcastically asks "if the working class should get compensation for the surplus value appropriated by capitalists over the course of history." Here Žižek misses the "nuances" that (1) the white working class was not violently kidnapped from another continent and (2) working-class labor, unlike slave labor, is in principle voluntary and paid! For Marx, a metaphoric "wage slavery" was built on the pedestal of literal chattel slavery. Žižek then moves to a reductio ad absurdum comparison meant to discredit the whole reparations project, wondering if we should not "demand from God himself a payment for botching up the job of creation."[67] Žižek's tone and argument are reminiscent of the conservatives who lament the "culture of complaint" in the United States or the "cult of repentance" in France.

Behind Žižek's derisive attitude lies a failure of the historical imagination, an inability even to imagine why oppressed communities might feel the urgency and justice of reparations. While the "true task" is indeed "not to get compensation from those responsible, but to deprive them of the position which makes them responsible,"[68] it strikes us that massive transfers of wealth from exploiters to their victims might actually help restructure power relations and thus deprive "those responsible . . . of the position which makes them responsible." Here "the best"—the goal of overturning global capitalism—has become the enemy of "the good." At one point, Žižek claims that he is "not opposed to multiculturalism as such" but only to the idea that "it constitutes the fundamental struggle of today."[69] But this is a straw-man argument, since most multiculturalists make no such claim. We would argue, more cautiously, that anticolonial and radical race critiques form a legitimate and even indispensable part of the larger struggle for equality and justice in a globalized world.

Žižek recycles the diffusionist cliché that European ideas alone inspired the revolt against colonialism. The Congress Party in India, he reminds us, was founded by Indians educated at Eton, Cambridge, and Oxford; their collective endeavor to end English colonialism was therefore in fact "strictly a product of English colonialism."[70] Here we find a demonstration of William David Hart's point that in Žižek's writing, the West is "dynamic, historical, revolutionary and universal while the East is not."[71] Behind such denials of the intellectual agency of non-Western people lies all the dead weight of a certain Enlightenment: Hobbes's view of savages living in a nasty and brutal "state of nature," Hume's and Kant's dismissal of the possibility of black intelligence, Hegel's view of the primitive world as a décor for the unfolding of the *Weltgeist*. In this sense, Žižek offers the leftist version of the conservative historiography of a figure like Hugh Trevor-Roper, who in 1965 (!) reduced non-European history to the "unrewarding gyrations of barbarous tribes in picturesque irrelevant corners of the world." Žižek's view of decolonization bears a familiar resemblence to Trevor-Roper's claim that "it is European techniques, European examples, European ideas which have shaken the non-European world out of its past—out of barbarism in Africa, out of a far older, slower, more majestic civilization in Asia; and the history of the world, for the last five centuries, in so far as it has significance, has been European history. I do not think that we need to make any apology if our study of history is European-centric."[72]

While it is true that many anticolonial intellectuals were indeed partially educated in the West and conversant with Western political idioms, they were not "mimic men" (Bhabha) aping metropolitan trends.[73] Rather than simply learn about democracy, Third World revolutionaries in the metropole came to discern the hypocrisy of Europe's democratic claims. Like Caliban, they learned Prospero's language in order to curse. It is absurd to suggest that the colonized learned their anticolonialism in Europe, if only because anticolonialism was such a weak and dominated current in Europe. The Colonial Exposition of 1931, for example, was seen by some thirty million people; the surrealists were virtually alone in condemning it. Critics such as Žižek speak as if anticolonialists always came into radical consciousness in Europe, when in fact they were often anticolonialist prior to their arrival. The anticolonialists needed the dominant European languages and discourses, as Chinua Achebe puts it, "to transact our business, including the business of overthrowing colonialism itself."[74] In Europe, the Third Worlders came to see the racially defined *limits* of European humanism. Conversely, the behavior of French abroad sometimes discredited metropolitan ideals. France, as Ho Chi Minh put it, "hosts admirable ideas but, when the French travel, they do not bring those ideas with them."[75] When the French state offered scholarships in order to assimilate colonial intellectuals, their invitation backfired, as African scholars formed anticolonial organizations and journals such as *Légitime Défense*.

Fanon's disillusionment, in *The Wretched of the Earth*, with the false humanism of the European left and his call for a "truly universal humanism" must be seen in this same context. Anticolonialist thinkers did not simply absorb European ideas; they changed those ideas. Thus, Fanon adopts, and criticizes, a whole series of intellectual trends: Sartrean phenomenology, Lacanian psychoanalysis, and Western Marxism. Moreover, a Jarryesque element of "without Poland there would be no Poles" tautology characterizes this familiar argument. It amounts to saying that "without British colonialism there would have been no anticolonialism," a claim not so different from neocon David Horowitz's claim that without slavery there would have been no abolitionism. One must admire the retrospective Panglossian optimism that finds a silver lining in every oppressive cloud: colonialism generates anticolonialism, slavery generates abolitionism, and so forth—all is for the best in the best of all possible worlds.

We are not suggesting that anticolonialists learned nothing from the West but only that the movement of ideas was ambivalent and multidirectional. As we argued earlier, European thinkers themselves partially learned of freedom and egalitarianism from the indigenous Americans or from the writers, such as Montaigne, Diderot, Tom Paine, and Engels and Marx, influenced by native political thought. The indigenous peoples of the Americas, furthermore, resisted European invasion from the very beginning, without the benefit of a European education. Indigenous leaders in the Spanish Americas did not have to study in Salamanca to oppose Spanish conquest, just as natives in North America did not have to study at Oxford or the Sorbonne to oppose the French or the British. The 16th-century Tupinamba leader Cunhambebe, head of the Confederation of the Tamoios in what is now Brazil, similarly, did not learn how to fight the Portuguese in Lisbon. Enslaved Africans did not have to read Hegel on the Master-Slave Dialectic before striking their masters or planning flight. The best "school" for the indigene was the Conquest itself, just as the best school for Ho Chi Minh, Lumumba, and Mongo Beti was the firsthand experience of colonial oppression. Žižek's diffusionist narrative has liberatory ideas always-already originating in the West, when in fact the sources of egalitarian social philosophies are not exclusively Western, while the West itself has been impacted by non-Western forms of social practice and theory.

Žižek has been explicit about his turn toward what he himself calls "radical Eurocentrism." His work reelaborates many well-worn Eurocentric leitmotifs: the German romantic and Heideggerian idea of the "Greek breakthrough," the dismissal of the valorization of indigenous culture as a form of romanticism, and a preference for a paradoxically atheist form of Christianity. Invoking Saint Paul's claim that within Christianity "there are no men or women, no Jews or Greeks," Žižek condemns identity politics as the site of disharmonious differences. Yet Saint Paul's injunction did not prevent the subordination within Christendom of women to men, of Jews to Christians, and of blacks to whites. Most Christian societies advanced anti-Semitic ideas, whether in the crude Catholic form of the "Christ killer" charge or in the more sublimated form of Old/New Testament Protestant supersessionism. In Žižek's prose, Saint Paul is canonized alongside secular saints such as Hegel, Marx, and Lacan. (In fact most of Žižek's saints are either explicitly Christian, like Hegel, or covertly so, as with Lacan's doctrine of psychic "fall" into the Symbolic.) In *The Fragile Absolute, or, Why Is the Christian Legacy Worth Fighting For?* (2000), Žižek places Marxism, as a product of the Judeo-Christian tradition, on the same side as Christianity against the "neo-pagan" multicultural multitude.[76] In reintroducing "pagan" as a put-down, Žižek resurrects the very Christian-versus-pagan dichotomy that was mobilized by Christian Europe to dispossess indigenous and African peoples.

We need not linger on Žižek's "leftist plea for Eurocentrism" (in *Critical Inquiry*, 1998), except to point out a fundamental misapprehension that becomes obvious already in the first paragraph: "When one says Eurocentrism, every self-respecting postmodern leftist intellectual has as violent a reaction as Joseph Goebbels had to culture—to reach for a gun, hurling accusations of protofascist Eurocentrist cultural imperialism. However, it is possible to imagine a leftist appropriation of the European political legacy."[77] Apart from the whimsical equation of anti-Eurocentrists with a genocidal Nazi propagandist, the passage displays a twofold confusion. First, the term "Eurocentric" does not refer to Europe as a geographical location, identity, or culture but rather to a hegemonic epistemology that universalizes the West as paradigm. The critique is not directed at the people and cultures originating in Europe but rather at the economic/political/discursive power of Euro-hegemony. Within this perspective, "Europe" is a geographical trope and "turning toward," hence our coinage "Eurotropism." In this sense, nothing could be more logical than what Žižek calls "a leftist appropriation of the European political legacy." It is not even a question of imagining such an appropriation, since that appropriation has been unending, which is why critical race, multicultural, and postcolonial scholars such as ourselves constantly invoke European and Euro-American thinkers and critics. That Žižek thinks it is even a question of whether we can take advantage of the "European political legacy" reveals a fundamental misconstrual of what is at stake.

Although Žižek finds anti-Eurocentrism to be a taken-for-granted concept among "postmodern leftist intellectuals," publications by writers of color unfold a different story of a frustrating encounter between critical race scholars and their diverse progressive colleagues who react as if all of Western civilization and Marxism with it were being cast overboard. Anti-Eurocentric critique sometimes triggers a kind of rushing-to-defend-the-ramparts syndrome, manifested in such questions as "By attacking Eurocentrism, aren't you still being Eurocentric?"—a question as fatuous as asking "By attacking fascism, aren't you being fascistic?" This syndrome is also manifested in the frequent charges of "romanticization," "idealization," and "utopianism" as all-purpose put-downs to challenge any claim that democratic or egalitarian ideas might also have emerged from non-European sources. Any positive mention of indigenous societies, for example, instantaneously elicits the "romanticization" charge, usually wielded by those who are utterly clueless about indigenous thinking and its impact on European thought. "Perhaps it is you," one is tempted to respond, "who romanticizes Europe, modernity, progress, and the Enlightenment."

The Ghosting of the Particular

Many of the critics of identity politics get hung up on one horn of the Enlightenment antinomy of the "universal" and the "particular," by choosing to opt only for the universal rather than seeing the mutual imbrication of the two categories. In our view, a philosopher such as Diderot defended a rational universality but also saw that many peoples—he mentions Tahitians, Hottentots, and Indians—were oppressed *as groups*. For Žižek, true politics is predicated on "universality, in its eminently political dimension," as opposed to "identifying the specific problems of each group and subgroup, not only homosexuals but African American lesbians, African American lesbian mothers, African American single unemployed lesbian mothers, and so on."[78] But what makes certain struggles particular and others universal? Referring to political movements in the former Yugoslavia, Žižek applauds their appeal to specific demands that at the same time invoked a notion of universality. Yet other activist "specificities," which happen to be those of people of color, get immediately beaten down with the police truncheon of the universal. An isomorphism operates between the hierarchy of real-world social domination and the hierarchy of the universal/particular asserted in Žižek's writing. Unemployed black lesbian single mothers, one of the most abused segments of any population, also happen to be the most abused in Žižek's prose. Their travails simply do not register within Žižek's view of political/emotional economy—they are the butt of his joke.

In this sense, Žižek incarnates what Adrienne Rich called "white solipsism," that is, the "tunnel vision which simply does not see nonwhite experience or existence as precious or significant."[79] His blindness resembles that of the Republican U.S. senators who applauded future Supreme Court Justice Samuel Alito's claim that his Italian-immigrant background had a positive impact on his role as an appellate judge but who quickly condemned as racist Justice Sonia Sotomayor's parallel claim that being Latina would make her a better judge. One expects the mockery of socially induced human pain from the Social Darwinist right but not from a leftist such as Žižek. Indeed, the situation of unemployed black lesbian single mothers can be seen as condensing a series of socioeconomic disadvantages: those of African Americans, those of women, those of the unemployed, of lesbians, and of single mothers lacking the financial security provided by an employed (male) partner. Subjects dwelling on multiple margins, as victims of multiple prejudices—of sexism, racism, and homophobia—one would think, might possess the epistemological advantage of being aware of the oppressive aspects of many borders. Multiple subalternizations in terms of class (as being unemployed), race (as blacks), sexuality (as lesbians), and marital status (as single), one might think, would grant this social category more, rather than less, claim on the universal, once the universal is conceived not as an abstract neo-Platonic ideal but rather as a mottled profusion of intersecting particularities. And it is not merely an issue of superimposed oppressions; it is also a matter of the social creativity of resistant knowledges and code-switching survival strategies.

Žižek revisits the Enlightenment debates by echoing Hegel—for whom Africa lacked the dimension of universality—by accusing multicultural identity politics of exactly the same thing. He advances a more sophisticated version of the accusation advanced by the liberal Schlesinger in *Disuniting America*. Although Schlesinger and Žižek have almost nothing in common, they do share (1) a failure to acknowledge the decolonizing corpus; (2) a false certainty that multiculturalism, as implied by Žižek's comic-surrealist enumeration of proliferating social identity differences, is divisive and separatist; and (3) a Eurocentric epistemology that allots universality to a blessed few. For Žižek, the idea that unemployed black lesbian single mothers might make intellectual claims or political demands with a universal dimension is simply ridiculous on its face. Union activists, meanwhile, are something else entirely. But why assume that such women are not also activists in unions or critics of global capitalism? Thus, Žižek reproduces not only the classic Marxist class-over-race paradigm but also the class-over-gender/sexuality paradigm, along with the hierarchies of white over black, heterosexual males over lesbian females, and the West over the non-West.

Žižek echoes the right-wing charge that identity politics calls for "separate" identities, but he adds a leftist touch. "The postmodern identity politics of particular (ethnic, sexual, and so forth) lifestyles," he writes, "fits perfectly the depoliticized notion of society," one "in which every particular group is accounted for and has its specific status (of victimhood) acknowledged through affirmative action or other measures."[80] As arbiter of political legitimacy, Žižek depoliticizes movements based on gender and ethnicity by calling them mere "lifestyles" and then blames the movements themselves for depoliticization. Žižek dismisses feminism, multiculturalism, and Affirmative Action as mere diversions from real politics into the dead end of identity, yet all these projects could be seen as an integral part of a progressive left coalitionary politics. Perhaps lurking behind this dismissal are the vestiges of a base/superstructure model, combined with reminiscences of a gendered tropology that favors real, hard politics over soft cultural matters, where a post-Marxist cultural politics does not enter the picture. Nor does Žižek see that gender and sexuality also have an economic dimension in terms of glass ceilings, unequal pay, and tax code discrimination against gay couples. Extrapolating the same dismissive logic to working-class activism, one might just as easily condemn workers for practicing the "politics of the particular" by complaining about their loss of pensions and health benefits.

Žižek productively defines the political struggle proper as "the struggle for one's voice to be heard and recognized as a legitimate partner." When those who are excluded protest against the ruling elite, he points out, "the true stakes [are] not only their explicit demands but their very right to be heard and recognized as an equal participant in the debate."[81] Žižek's formulations echo myriad similar formulations from advocates of the various projects that he so breezily dismisses. His insight that universal claims can be inferentially embedded within concrete local demands, furthermore, can easily be extended to all those groups concerned with social and cultural justice and equity. Alert to the overtones of the universal in some protests, Žižek becomes deaf to the universal in the cries of "unemployed black lesbian single mothers," relegated to an amusing particularity. Some identities remain locked up in the solitary cells of their specificity, while others "open up" toward the bright skies of the universal. Indirectly relaying the venerable Hegelian binarism of historical and nonhistorical peoples, of European "universal" and non-European "local," Žižek's universalizing formulation is paradoxically nonuniversal, in that it refuses to extend its circle of reference.

Žižek frankly privileges class over all other axes of social domination: "I disagree with the postmodern mantra: gender, ethnic struggle, whatever, and then class. Class is not just one of the series." (The adolescent shrug of "whatever" here downgrades gender and ethnic struggle.) In a move reminiscent of Althusser's "the economy in the last instance," Žižek accords the economy a "prototranscendental status."[82] And while political economy is absolutely essential, that does not mean that we can simply "return" to exclusively class-based analyses. An understanding of capitalism, moreover, must pass "through" colonialism, empire, slavery, and race. In an intersectional perspective, all of the axes of stratification work in concert and mutually inflect one another. It is not clear why Angela Davis's work on class, race, gender, and sexuality, within an overall Marxist and feminist grid, should be any less universal than Žižek's own work. One could easily argue precisely the opposite, that her multiply intersectional prisms engender a more inclusive universal, one rich in conflictual particularities, a universal in the Shakespearean concrete universal sense, rather than an abstract Racinian universal, cleansed of the vulgar materialities of existence.[83]

Žižek's 2009 book *First as Tragedy, Then as Farce*, meanwhile, explores the aftermath of two 21st-century calamities: 9/11 and the 2008 financial meltdown. We agree with Žižek's argument, a partial echo of Thomas Frank, that the "culture war is a class war in a displaced mode."[84] For Žižek, populism screams, "I don't know what's going on, but I'm mad as hell and I've had enough!" But even here Žižek neglects the key role of racism as an integral part of class war and populist outrage. A clear expression of the right-wing deployment of race to obscure and displace class is found in the right-wing mantra that equates any redistribution of wealth with reparations for blacks. The strategy is to confuse whites, the major victims of trickle-up economics, by nurturing their hostility to blacks, Latinos, and people of color generally. Slogans such as "health reform is reparations on steroids" are designed to catalyze white hostility toward universal health care—or more accurately toward its pathetically inadequate simulacrum—by suggesting that universal health care is actually a favor to blacks. In other words, racial resentment is used to trump class interest in affordable health care. In the context of Europe, Žižek rightly calls attention to the material force of ideology. But his analysis elides the fact that the scapegoating of minorities, an expression of what Appadurai calls the "fear of small numbers," has been the key to many rightist victories in Europe, in that at least some of the vote was motivated by white *petits blancs ressentiment* against "aliens" arriving from the Global South.[85] (To his credit, Žižek does condemn the European social-democratic left's endorsement of a "reasonable" racism toward immigrants.)

The new Žižek of *First as Tragedy* does link a critique of global capitalism to a critique of "postcolonial dependence." His Eurocentric perspective, however, blocks a materialist conceptualization of colonial history in relation to contemporary globalization. Žižek delineates four major points of antagonism in the present: (1) the threat of an ecological catastrophe, (2) the inappropriate transfer of the notion of private property so as to apply to "intellectual property," (3) the ethical implications of biogenetics, and (4) the creation of new forms of apartheid. What is missed, however, is that race, colonialism, multiculturality, and indigeneity intersect with all these points of antagonism, because (1) the peoples of the Global South are the major victims of the kinds of environmental catastrophes generated by Union Carbide in India or Chevron in Peru, (2) indigenous people are the primary victims of "intellectual copyright" when transnational corporations patent indigenous knowledge and turn communal biodiversity into a commodity, (3) it is indigenous people who have gone the furthest in rejecting privatization in favor of communal ownership of land and water and so forth, (4) indigenous peoples are in the forefront of the struggle against transnational corporations, and (5) people of color, whether Latinos in the United States, Algerians in France, or Moroccans in Spain, are the primary objects of the new forms of apartheid.

Žižek belatedly discovers the political virtues of indigenous movements in the Global South. The new Žižek acknowledges that the politics of the Evo Morales government in Bolivia "is on the very cutting edge of contemporary progressive struggle."[86] He hails radical populist Hugo Chávez for following a policy not of "including the excluded" but rather of taking the excluded slum dwellers "as his base and then reorganizing political space and political forms of organization so that the latter will fit" the excluded, thus moving from "bourgeois democracy" to the "dictatorship of the proletariat."[87] While we do not endorse Žižek's phraseology as describing either Chávez's policies or the slum dwellers of Caracas, we do appreciate his invocation of the "commons," a term increasingly used on the left to evoke shared noncommodified access to nature, open-source collaboration, and practices such as copyleft and creative commons. Defined as "the theory that vests all property in the community and organizes labor for the common benefit of all"[88]—the idea of "the commons" animates the work of such diverse figures as Peter Linebaugh, Naomi Klein, Arundhati Roy, Giuseppe Cocco, Vandana Shiva, Arturo Escobar, David Graeber, and Michael Hardt and Antonio Negri. Coming full circle, we would assert a further connection between the commons as conceived by the indigenous cultures of the Red Atlantic (including Evo Morales) and the theory and praxis of the commons within the West itself (going back to the "Charter of the Forest" section of the Magna Carta), all part of a multipronged struggle against all forms of "enclosure," including that of the "intellectual commons."

While the new Žižek also discovers the Haitian Revolution, that revolution "scans" for him, symptomatically, not thanks to C. R. L. James or Trouillot but rather through Susan Buck-Morss's essay "Hegel and Haiti," which calls attention to the Haitian Revolution as the "silent—and for that reason all the more effective—point of reference (or the absent Cause) of Hegel's dialectic of Master and Slave."[89] In this rather generous recuperation of Hegel's work—one wonders why Hegel had to keep the reference "silent" and why that would be more "effective" and for whom—the Haitian Slaves' actually overturning the Masters' power seems to pale in significance next to the fact that their actions inspired a sly between-the-lines reference in the great philosopher's work.[90] While giving credit to the Haitian revolutionaries, Žižek portrays them as more French than the French, implementing revolutionary ideology better than the French themselves did. This account prolongs Žižek's earlier portrayal of Third World revolutionaries as conceptual mimic men.[91] The unasked question is why it was black Haitians in particular who were able (1) to discern the limits of the *mise en pratique* of the revolutionary ideologies and (2) to act decisively on that discernment. The intellectual agency, again, remains with Europe. "The West," Žižek reminds us, "supplied the very standards by which it (and its critics) measures its own criminal past."[92] Yet from another perspective one wonders exactly why we need Hegel, the philosopher who thought that blacks had neither moral sentiments nor intellectual reflexivity, to appreciate Haitian revolutionaries? Were not such revolutionaries implicitly rejecting the racial hierarchies constructed in *The Philosophy of History*, in which blacks lacked all critical consciousness and were placed, along with the indigenous peoples of the Americas (who gave Haiti its very name), in the bottom ranks of the civilizational hierarchies? Must all revolutions pass through the West?

First as Tragedy also bears telltale traces of the old Žižek as the enemy of "identity politics." In the paragraph immediately following his praise of Haitian revolutionaries, Žižek endorses Pascal Bruckner's mockery—which we ourselves mock in the next chapter—of European "self-flagellation" over colonialism and slavery. Žižek then resurrects the old Eurocentric axiom of critical reflexivity as European monopoly: "The true reason some in the Third World hate and reject the West lies not with the colonizing past and its continuing effects but with the self-critical spirit which the West has displayed in renouncing this past, with its implicit calls to others to practice the same self-critical approach."[93] Žižek's claim here is virtually identical to conservative Allan Bloom's claim in *The Closing of the American Mind* that "only in the Western nations, i.e., those influenced by Greek philosophy, is there some willingness to doubt the identification of the good with one's own way."[94] This provincial claim of nonprovinciality and this uncritical claim of a unique self-critical capacity substitutes for the right's "They hate us for our freedom" the Hegelian-Žižekian "They hate us for our reflexivity."

The contradictory critiques of race/coloniality discourse from left and right bring us back to the domain of the blind men and the elephant. The very same project is described variously as falsely universalist (the Žižek and Bourdieu/Wacquant charge) or as particularist and anti–French republican (as we shall see with Alain Finkielkraut) or as simultaneously dogmatic and relativist (the U.S. right wing's contradictory charge) or as relativist and patriarchal (a white feminist charge) or as dogmatically revolutionary (the right-wing charge) or as neoliberal (Žižek again) or as divisive of the left (the Todd Gitlin charge) or as divisive of the nation (the Schlesinger charge) or as pro-American (as many French intellectuals assume) or anti-American (the U.S. right-wing charge, echoed by French allies such as Finkielkraut). In the next chapter, we examine how these debates get reinvoiced in the travel back and forth between the French and the American intellectual zones.

5 France, the United States, and the Culture Wars

AS WE NOTED in chapter 3, France and the Francophone zones
formed key sites in the postwar paradigm shift in thinking about race and colonialism, with May 1968 forming the high-water mark of Third Worldism. While
de Gaulle pursued his independent path between the United States and the
Soviet Union, the left mounted massive demonstrations, along with an immense
intellectual production in support of Third World revolutions and resistance
movements in the United States. The postwar period also witnessed the emergence of an embryonic black movement ensuant to the arrival in France of a new
generation of African and West Indian students, thanks to a system of scholarships, leading to a substantial intellectual community. This group reached critical
mass in the formation in 1950 of FESNF (Federation of Students from Black
Africa in France), along with its official journal, *L'Étudiant d'Afrique Noire*, bringing continuity to the decolonization struggles theorized by writers such as Césaire, Memmi, and Fanon.

France, and especially Paris, served as a key node in the network of Third
Worldist thought, contributing to the postwar critique of dominant trends in the
human and social sciences as reflecting the economic and cultural imperialism
of the European colonial powers. In the 1970s, the Laboratory for Third World
and African Studies, at University of Paris VII, for example, combined African,
Asian, and Latin American studies. That postcolonial studies at first found little
purchase on the French intellectual scene was thus partly due to the fact that the
postcolonial field was seen as *already* occupied by anticolonial and anti-imperialist writing and therefore seemed, despite the new theoretical wrinkles, a case of
"déjà vu all over again." Present-day postcolonial studies in France, in this sense,
cannot be seen as merely as an epigonic or belated copy of work performed outside of France; rather, it must be situated intertextually, in relation to the anticolonial corpus fashioned by these earlier writers.

What could be called "proto-postcolonial" work was also performed by Arab
intellectuals in France, in what might seem like a surprising place: French Oriental studies. French-speaking Arab intellectuals formed part of a linguistic,
cultural, and scholarly continuum. As insiders/outsiders, they resembled the
British-educated "white but not quite" colonial elites or the English-speaking
Arab scholars in Middle Eastern studies in the United States. Beginning in the
1950s, Oriental academic institutions in France began to recognize the indepen-

dence struggles in the Arab world, while also absorbing a few Arab intellectu-als into their ranks.[1] In 1963, a decade and a half before Edward Said, Anouar Abdel-Malek published "Orientalism in Crisis" in the journal *Diogenes* (vol. 44, Winter 1963). For Abdel-Malek, Third World independence struggles inevitably impacted Oriental studies by turning those who had been "objects of study" into sovereign subjects. "The hegemonism of possessing minorities, unveiled by Marx and Engels, and the anthropocentrism dismantled by Freud [had been] accompa-nied by Europocentrism in the area of human and social sciences, and more par-ticularly in those in direct relationship with non-European peoples."[2] A decade later, Abdallah Laroui's *La Crise des Intellectuels Arabes* (1974) denounced the Orientalist penchant for "speaking for [Arab] others" and attacked the Oriental-ists as a bureaucratic caste.[3]

French leftists saw themselves as allied with minority and leftist movements in the United States, just as American (and Brazilian) leftists were inspired by May '68. The situationists saw the 1964 Berkeley protests as inspiration for their own campus movements. Jean-Luc Godard's *Vladimir et Rosa* fictionalized the Chi-cago 8 trial, while Agnès Varda lauded the black liberation movement in her film *The Black Panthers*. The Black Power movement was especially influential for the Prison Information Group formed in 1971 by Michel Foucault and Daniel Defert. Foucault had read the Black Panther political writings in the late 1960s, and they perhaps influenced his subsequent theories of the "racial state." Writer Jean Genet toured the United States in 1970 in support of the Panthers as advocates for a "red ideology in a Black skin."[4] According to Richard Wolin, it was Genet's sup-port for the Panthers that led Huey Newton to support gay liberation.[5]

After the left's defeat in 1968, the 1970s in France formed a period of conflict between the Third Worldist revolutionary paradigm and the more conservative position that was emerging. Defeatism set in on the left, and Third Worldism gave way to the anticommunism of the *nouveaux philosophes*. In the post-'68 hangover period, in the wake of Solzhenitsyn's denunciations of the Soviet Gulag, anticommunism came to the center of the discussion, while Camus replaced Sar-tre as intellectual model. The simultaneous discrediting of Marxism and Third Worldism left the field open, later, for neoliberalism and ethno-national chauvin-ism. Anti–Third Worldism crystallized with a 1978 polemic in the pages of *Le Nouvel Observateur*, published later as *Le Tiers Monde et la Gauche*. In Kristin Ross's account, some former '68 leftists rewrote history, including their own, as that of leftists deluded into seeing the enemy as colonialism when the real enemy was communism.[6] Third World socialism, some ex-*gauchistes* argued, could only lead to the "gulagization" of Africa, Asia, and Latin America. "Disappeared" in this account were the horrors of Vietnam (conducted first by French and then by U.S. armed forces), the French massacres and torture in Algeria (and even in

France itself), the U.S. military/economic domination of Latin America, and the general hegemony of the North. The new anti–Third Worldism bore an uncanny resemblance to that of the colonialists who lauded the "civilizing mission" of the West while deriding all possibility of democratic rule after independence. In both the United States and France, anticommunism became articulated together with anti–Third Worldism (and later antimulticulturalism).[7]

Sobbing for the White Man

An important text in this anti–Third Worldist backlash was Pascal Bruckner's 1983 book *Le Sanglot de l'Homme Blanc* (The White Man's Sobs).[8] A contemporary reading of Bruckner's text in the light of the "culture wars" reveals the extent to which Bruckner anticipated the lachrymose tone of hysterical victimization of the right in both the United States and France a decade later. Bruckner does, to be sure, score some valid points. He rightly calls attention to a certain religious (largely Christian) substratum in some leftist thought. (Unfortunately for his argument, the point is equally true, if not more so, of right-wing thought.) He scores the tendency of some Western leftists to project themselves into idealized Third World revolutionaries, romanticizing regimes about which they knew virtually nothing. This charge is certainly accurate in relation to French and American Maoists who turned China into a site of romantic projection, a revolutionary *ailleurs*, forgetting Mao's megalomania and the depredations of the Cultural Revolution. But Bruckner places an unnecessarily insidious interpretation on the left's overly generous assessment of revolutionary movements abroad, reading it as a sign of a totalitarian project, when in fact these sometimes naive projections were often premised on disillusionment, within the binaristic logic that "if the West is so imperialist and racist, the East must be the opposite." Yet in other cases, First World support for anti-imperialist struggles, for example in Vietnam, was more informed. Although Bruckner also rightly scores the hypocrisies of European Third Worldists who reject U.S. imperialism yet fail to account for the common origins of European colonialisms and U.S. imperialism.

As a kind of camera obscura Fanon, Bruckner offers the white man's inverted version of Fanon's *Black Skin, White Masks*. While Fanon speaks of the colonialist and racist mechanisms that generated self-hatred on the part of the colonized, Bruckner speaks of the ways that Third Worldism itself has imbued white Europeans with irrational guilt and insecurity. Rejecting what he calls Fanon's "ridiculous" plea to "go beyond Europe," Bruckner warns that for the peoples of the Third World to become themselves, "they must become more western," since it "is impossible to 'go beyond' democracy."[9] The equation of Europe and democracy is, of course, a staple of Eurocentric discourse. Bruckner makes this equation just four decades after the advent, in the very heart of Europe, of the fascist regimes of Mussolini, Franco, Hitler, and Pétain and just three decades after a period when Muslim Algerians under French colonialism were living rules of exception that deprived them of their rightful vote. Fanon had called for going "beyond Europe" precisely because Europe had not been truly democratic itself and had not advanced democracy abroad.

The role of Maurice Papon in events that transpired just two decades before the publication of Bruckner's book vividly illustrates the limits of Bruckner's depiction of a democratic postwar Europe. Papon, who had organized deportations of Jews to the concentration camps during his tenure as police chief of Bordeaux during Vichy, served in the 1950s in the French colonial administration.[10] On October 17, 1961, Papon, in his function as Paris's chief of police, presided over a horrific massacre. After a peaceful protest march by thousands of Algerians, police fired machine guns into the crowd and literally clubbed demonstrators into the Seine to drown. Six thousand Algerians were herded into a sports stadium, where many died in police custody. Over two hundred people were known to have died, hundreds were reported missing, and corpses bobbed up all along the Seine.[11] The official police-led cover-up relayed by the press claimed that the Algerians opened fire and that the police were obliged to restore "law and order." Despite Papon's murderous past toward both Jews and Muslims, he reached the highest ranks of the French government before he was tried and jailed in 1998 for his role in deporting Jews. Long repressed, the memory of the massacre has been recently resurrected in books (Einaudi's *La Bataille de Paris*), television dramas (*La Nuit Noire*), and feature films (Haneke's symptomatically titled film *Caché* and Bouchareb's *Hors-la-Loi*).

Despite such crimes, Bruckner uses the language of anticolonialism in an upside-down manner to portray the West as the real victim. Here is Bruckner:

> Indeed, there weighs on every westerner an a priori presumption of crime. We Europeans have been brought up to hate ourselves, in the certitude that there was at the heart of our world an essential evil which required a vengeance without any hope of forgiveness. . . . We have been led to regard our own civilization as the worst, after our parents thought it the best. To be born after the Second World War was to be sure that one belonged to the very dregs of humanity, to an execrable milieu which, for centuries, in the name of a supposed spiritual adventure, had suffocated the totality of the globe.[12]

Poor Europeans! Poor whites! Powerless, persecuted, and penniless all over the globe, oppressed everywhere by the color line, subject to racist taunts, disproportionately imprisoned, harassed by police, their languages forbidden, their land stolen, stereotyped as lazy and criminal, their culture repressed, living in poverty because of their race, "'buked and scorned" because of nothing more than the white color of their skin! It turns out that Bruckner really does not mind "the white man's sobs," as long as those sobs are for himself. Anticipating the beleaguered tone of the U.S. right, presumably defending the ramparts of a threatened Western civilization, Bruckner conveniently forgets that the West has been overwhelmingly empowered in military, economic, cultural, political, and mediatic terms. It is as if Bruckner has lived the seismic shift and decolonization of culture as a trauma of personal and collective relativization, a mourning for a lost moral grandeur. But rather than offer a self-reflexive analysis of such feelings of loss, Bruckner recrowns the West and demeans the Rest, in what amounts to a return to the Eurocentric status quo ante.

Like U.S. rightists, Bruckner resuscitates colonialist nostrums as if they were courageous forays in truth telling. He resurrects the hoary canard that the West alone is capable of self-criticism and of "seeing itself through others' eyes."[13] Bruckner proclaims Europe's willingness to criticize itself, ironically, at the same time that he displays his own hypersensitivity to criticisms against the West. Bruckner makes this argument, curiously, shortly after demonstrating his own incapacity to see Europe through the eyes of its others, thus undermining his own claims about a unique European capacity for self-critique. The subtitle of Bruckner's book—"The Third World, Culpability, and Self-Hatred"—reflects a psychologistic emphasis on the "imbecilic masochism" and needless feelings of guilt supposedly forced on white Westerners. The issue, ultimately, is not so much one of guilt over the West's past and present actions—although guilt is on one level a perfectly normal reaction to the conjugated histories of anti-Semitism, slavery, and colonialism—but rather of lucidity and responsibility to make sure that such ills do not occur again and that their memory be preserved.

The dominant emotion among Third Worldists in the 1960s, whether in Paris or Rio or Berkeley, as Kristin Ross points out, was not guilt but anger:

> Third-worldist discourse, far from being masochistic or self-hating in its attention
> to the unevenness and disequilibrium between rich and poor nations, was an
> aggressive new way of accusing the capitalist system—multinational firms, aid
> programs from the United States or Western Europe—the whole neo-imperialist
> apparatus, culminating in Vietnam. Third-worldists did not feel "personally"
> responsible for third-world misery, as Bruckner asserts; rather, they were actively
> pointing a finger at those—the military, state leaders, big business—who they
> thought indeed were responsible.[14]

Is Bruckner suggesting, Ross asks, that the United States did well to drop more bombs on Vietnam than were dropped by the Allies during all of World War II or that the French empire in Vietnam and Algeria should have been maintained at all cost? Bruckner develops a hysterical discourse of victimization in defense of a West presumably on the verge of extermination yet in fact as dominant as ever, whether in its U.S. "bad cop" form (Iraq, Guantánamo, etc.) or its European "good cop" form.[15]

Minorities and the Specter of Identitarianism

Metropolitan France in the postwar period underwent huge demographic changes as it absorbed former colonial subjects seeking jobs, education, or political asylum. The attractive "pull" of the postwar French prosperity, combined with the "push" of postindependence travails in North Africa itself, subsequently reinforced by new French laws facilitating family reunification, led to a situation in which hundreds of thousands of Algerians, Moroccans, and Tunisians in France, along with thousands of West Indian French people and sub-Saharan West Africans, came to form the country's "visible minorities." For a period in the 1970s and early 1980s, members of these minorities—and especially the second-generation children of the largely North African migrant workers displaced to the colonial metropole in the 1950s and 1960s—rose up in protest movements in favor of minority and immigrant rights. The high point was the 1983 March for Equality against Racism, dubbed by the media "Marche des Beurs," modeled on the demonstration, two decades earlier, led by Martin Luther King, Jr., in Washington. D.C. The activists of SOS Racisme and other antiracist organizations couched questions of identity in the assimilationist terms favored by the Socialist Party.

While Mitterrand in the early 1980s had endorsed a multiculturalism-light known as le droit à la différence (the right to difference), the left subsequently retreated from that project when confronted by the Lepenisation des esprits. The celebration of a difference-friendly France was cut short when the Socialists, practicing a nonstrategy of avoidance, took refuge in an abstract rhetoric of human rights and republicanism. The result was what some called a "neoracist consensus" shared by the far right and the center left. Azouz Begag is unsparing in his evaluation of this historical error: "The Left carries a heavy historical responsibility for this [neoracist consensus]. . . . It instrumentalized the question of the banlieues in its political struggle with the Right, stifling the Beurs' desire for political emancipation by backing SOS Racisme, which, in 1985, snatched out of the hands of the young activists . . . the political momentum."[16] The return of the right wing to power in 1986 brought the harsh Pasqua laws and the televised debacle of the forced embarkation of 101 Malians onto a charter plane at Orly Airport. The socialist left became cautious, aware that while only a minority might actually vote for Jean-Marie Le Pen, a much larger group sympathized with his xenophobic stance. In 1993, the code of nationality was changed so as to require a declaration on the part of children of immigrants, at eighteen years of age, of a desire to be French. The targets of the law denounced it as a way of stigmatizing the descendants of the earlier postcolonial migrants. A decade later, the 2002 election revealed a shockingly strong showing by the extreme right, with Le Pen in second place and the final victory going to the center-rightist Jacques Chirac. (Le Pen was scapegoated, as Žižek correctly points out, for taking the mask off a more general consensus racism.)[17]

The developing minority movement ran up against what David Blatt calls a "resurgent popular and political xenophobia" rooted in the struggles over decolonization, now reinforced by contemporary social and political developments.[18] Postcolonial immigrants and their descendants became "a lightning rod for fears about worsening socio-economic conditions, the breakdown of public order in urban areas, and the erosion of national identity and culture."[19] Nativists such as Le Pen went so far as to call for forced repatriation of Maghrebians to North Africa. As the anti-immigration agenda of the National Front gained ground, a new generation of the immigrants' children underwent what Begag identifies as a "three-phased disintegration, moving from indifference, to frustration, to la haine (hatred, rage)."[20] It was in this context that a politically diverse spectrum of intellectuals, such as Julia Kristeva, Tzvetan Todorov, Pierre-André Taguieff, Régis Debray, and Alain Finkielkraut, while criticizing the racism of the far right, also expressed reservations about what they saw as the American "differentialist" approach to race.

In many cases, the left's intention was to protect social solidarity and avoid what many in France saw as a fragmentation characteristic of U.S.-style pluralism. The left's overreaction was in some ways the result of a consensus forged between mainstream political forces of the right and the left with the aim of marginalizing the National Front. As Jim Cohen explains,

> According to the prevailing argument at the time, racism and xenophobia could only be combated in the name of a universal notion of citizenship, not in the name of any particular group interests, such as the interests of "minorities" (the very term became a no-no). Otherwise, it was said, two dire consequences would ensue: (1) the minority groups themselves . . . would be tempted to organize along "community" lines and thus contribute to the rise of "communautarisme," another definite no-no; and (2) as a result of this (supposed) danger of particularistic expression by ethnic groups stigmatized by racists, the racists themselves would have a good pretext for accusing the dominant order of "favoring" the immigrants, while neglecting the "true" French people—and this would presumably result in a ballooning of the National Front's share of the electoral vote. By occupying the terrain of national citizenship and by defining it as a non-racialist, non-particularist, universal form of collective belonging, the republican model was conceived as an arm of struggle against the far right.[21]

The attempt to marginalize Le Pen by appealing to republican ideals ultimately backfired. The National Front kidnapped the idea of "right to difference" to mean "yes, they are different, and let them preserve their difference back in their countries of origin." As Herman Lebovics points out, Le Pen "cleverly transformed an appeal for a new democratic vision of pluralism into a formula for cultural and racial exclusion."[22]

It was in this larger context that multicultural identity politics came to be seen as a pernicious American import. For much of the 1990s, a large swath of the French political spectrum denounced multiculturalism as a symptom of hysterical American identitarianism. Journalists spoke of *"une Amérique qui fait peur"* (a frightening America). The words "identity politics" and "multiculturalism" were mobilized to evoke all the problems associated with U.S. "race relations" that France presumably did not have and did not want. This united front led to bizarre alignments and strange bedfellows. Appealing to the same tropes of imminent "Balkanization" and "Lebanonization" deployed by the U.S. right, the French left, as incarnated in *Les Temps Modernes*, *Esprit*, and *Libération*, portrayed multiculturalism as inherently divisive. Some even linked the "cult of difference" to fascism, much as Rush Limbaugh spoke of "femiNazis" and totalitarian "thought-control." Politically diverse figures converged in their rejection; Touraine, Bourdieu, Todorov, Jospin, Le Pen, Chirac, and Finkielkraut were not closely aligned politically, yet they all shared a common hostility to multiculturalism. For very complex reasons, the dominant French line was not so far from that of a Schlesinger in the United States, even though its historical sources and political drift were quite distinct, and even though the French critics sometimes had little else in common.

The language of the French left came to overlap, on a discursive/rhetorical level, with the U.S. right's view of race and identity-based movements. The same left French intellectuals who would normally have denounced George H. W. Bush adopted a Bush-like stance toward "political correctness." It was Bush Sr., after all, who weaponized the PC phrase—initially a self-mocking coinage of the left—against leftist campus movements. The right's goal was to "bury the Vietnam Syndrome" and place all 1960s-derived egalitarian, Third Worldist, and antiracist forms of activism on the defensive. But this context was often missed by the French left, even though France itself was undergoing its own parallel wave of conservative demonization of the '68 legacy. Just as the U.S. campus left was absorbing (and transforming) the poststructuralist ideas of Foucault, Derrida, and Deleuze, the French left portrayed the U.S. movements as rooted in essentialist notions of "identity." Indeed, the paroxysm of this transatlantic short circuit came when the originally "leftist" (later centrist) newspaper *Libération* turned for an account of identity politics to none other than Dinesh D'Souza, the neoconservative whose book *The End of Racism* argues, to put it crudely, that slavery was not so bad (and anyway Africans did it too), that segregation was well intended, and that racial discrimination could be "rational."[23]

The 1990s, then, brought a spate of French attacks on "American multiculturalism." A special 1995 issue of *Esprit* was devoted to what was tellingly called the *"spectre"* of multiculturalism. The hostility at times became codified even in French dictionaries and encyclopedias. The entry on "multiculturalism" in the *Dictionnaire des Politiques Culturelles* contrasts U.S.-style multiculturalism, alleged to favor the mere "coexistence" of "separate cultures," with French "interculturalism," which stresses the process of exchange. (In fact, both terms have been used to emphasize exchange and interaction.) The *Dictionnaire* mentions blacks and women as constituent members of the coalition but elides such key groups as Native Americans, Latinos, and Asian Americans. It nonetheless adds to the list, in a tone of ridicule, the "handicapped, gays, criminals, non-smokers, and bicyclists." This derisive kind of surreal enumeration has become a topos in both left (Žižek) and right (D'Souza) attacks on identity politics. In the wake of U.S. right-wing discourse, the entry emphasizes the putative penchant for euphemistic language ("vertically challenged" for "tall") and repeats the (largely apocryphal) right-wing anecdotes about the supposed purging of bibliographies, the firing of "incorrect" professors, and hysterical sexual harassment suits.[24] This caricatural portrait of a censorious multicultural left coincided, ironically, with a historical moment when it was the U.S. right that was censoring the left while busily reshaping governmental institutions in a procorporate and militaristic direction.

An essay by Tzvetan Todorov, "The Cult of Difference and the Sacralization of the Victim," offers a similar caricature. A moderately progressive humanist thinker, Todorov too derided multiculturalism in terms redolent of those of the U.S. right, seeing it as symptomatic of a competition for victim status, as giving "special rights" to blacks, and so forth. Intoning some of the favorite tunes from the neoconservative songbook, Todorov asks readers if "they would like to be operated on by a doctor who got his diploma through Affirmative Action," as if Affirmative Action had been designed to grant diplomas to the incompetent. Ignoring the centuries of corporeal abuse and aesthetic brainwashing that made whiteness normative and blackness undesirable, Todorov declares the slogan "black is beautiful" to be racist, since its political equivalent ("black is just") would never be accepted. Approvingly citing black conservatives such as Shelby Steele, Todorov adopts a "reverse racism" argument that sees blacks as asking for special rights, since "the former victim is now supposed to be treated, not just like all the others, but better than all the others."[25] (A decade later, at a Columbia University conference, Todorov blamed the 2005 banlieue riots on the "dysfunctional sexuality of Muslim youths.")[26]

In the 1990s in France, as in the United States and Brazil, animosity toward multicultural identity politics sometimes became linked to an animus toward the "excesses" of feminism. Sliding into the standard litany about the harassment of male professors due to trumped-up sexual harassment charges, Todorov complains that whereas "men and whites used to be privileged, now it is women and blacks."[27] What is it about male intellectuals (of diverse national origins), one wonders, that makes them hypersensitive to something as statistically rare as "trumped-up charges" of harassment even when sexual harassment is not the theme under discussion? What is seen as a paranoid obsession with sexual harassment sometimes gets linked in French antimulticultural discourse—at times even by declared feminists—to the stereotype of "puritanical" and "hysterical" Anglo-Saxon women,[28] as when journalist Françoise Giroud repeatedly ridiculed American feminism as an antimale movement with castrating tendencies. Unlike American women, Giroud often declared, "French women love men."[29]

A common deep-structural impulse fueled the hostility to both feminism and multicultural identity politics. Since they could not be denounced as "egalitarian"—given that "equality" forms part of the French creed—they were denounced as "identitarian," "separatist," and "communitarian." Whereas American (and French) feminists saw patriarchy as appropriating the universal for the male gender, writers such as Mona Ozouf censured any appeal to gender as "identitaire." Yet in the political sphere, France did adopt one identity-based policy, to wit, gender "parity" for female political candidates. The critics of parity, as Joan Wallach Scott suggests in her nuanced account, deployed cross-national comparison to denounce the new policy: "Parité was likened to American affirmative action—by definition a failed attempt to reverse discrimination. . . . The complex facts of the American experience were beside the point in these arguments: it was the image of America, riven by conflicting ethnic, religious, and racial communities, that served as the antithesis of the desired unity of France."[30] French sociologist Michel Wieviorka sums up the general attitude behind these arguments:

> In France [the multicultural debate] is almost impossible, and it serves to reveal
> a deeply rooted political culture which brooks no opposition or discussion. The
> debate touches on a postulate which is seen as self-evident: [multiculturalism]
> supposedly constitutes a danger for democracy and for the national collectivity
> because it would consider recognizing cultural particularisms within institu-
> tions and within political life, where it could only have disastrous effects. These
> particularisms should not flourish outside of the public sphere, and any identitary
> or communitarian pressure within the public realm should be rejected, repressed,
> condemned. . . . The Republic is the best rampart against inter-community
> tensions, against violence, against political and cultural fragmentation and the
> destruction of democratic public space.[31]

Multiculturalism, in sum, became a "repoussoir," an obscure object of projective hostility. The blanket rejection of multiculturalism conjugated an idealization of the homegrown republican model, on the one hand, and a caricature of an "alien" project on the other. The incantatory appeals to republicanism ended up having an intellectually repressive function. The caricature of an alien movement yielded narcissistic benefits by flattering French readers that they had avoided the absurd fanaticism of the United States. At the same time, the caricatures served to ward off fears of similar movements emerging in France. What Clarisse Fabre and Éric Fassin call (in their *Liberté, Égalité, Sexualités*) the "American scarecrow" was wielded as part of a demagogic rhetoric that contrasted a sensible universalist French republicanism with the out-of-control particularism of "political correctness."[32]

The Anxieties behind an Antagonism

But what cultural intertext, what historical unconscious, and what categories of perception molded this antagonism? What explains the specific forms of these anxieties about race, identity, and multiculturality? A number of factors were at work. First, there was the issue of language, arising from the relationship between two similar yet distinct political cultures, resulting in a problem of translation due to a partial mismatch of vocabularies. Many of the terms common to both French and U.S. discourse have similar connotations, but others are ideological *faux amis*. Whereas in the United States "Republicans" and "Democrats" refer to the two political parties, in France *républicain* refers to the *République* and its ideas of citizenship, while *démocrate* often refers to a society made up of "communities." Indeed, the concept of *multiculturalisme* is sometimes translated as *communautarisme* (ethnic separatism or communitarianism), seen as a regrettable descent from the lofty abstraction of republican citizenship into basely embodied identities and communities. For many French intellectuals, *communitarianisme* is reminiscent externally of a fetishized German *Volk* and internally of those regional monarchist movements that threatened the early republic. Thus, French critics of multiculturalism warn against *l'engrenage communautaire*, roughly translatable as a dangerous downward spiral into communitarianism. Often linked to Islam, "*communautarisme*" in French suggests a threat to secular *laïcité* and thus tends to trigger a reflexive antipathy.

Even the same word can alter its meaning in a novel ideological environment. Whereas in the United States, "identity" and "difference" emerged as critical terms to evoke oppressed "minorities," in French left discourse, "identity" and "identitarian" are just as likely to evoke anti-immigrant right-wingers and Islamic fundamentalists, seen as specular reflections of the same impulse. Some French hostility therefore focuses on terms such as "identity politics," "affirmative action," and even "race," seen as inappropriate foreign impositions. "Affirmative action" is often translated, in France, as *discrimination positive*, a translation that encodes hostility by framing the concept as a subset of the larger category "discrimination" and thus feeding into "reverse discrimination" arguments. "Race," especially, is seen as injection of U.S. race obsessions into a presumably race-blind France. (And, indeed, "race relations" discourse does carry the unfortunate implication that objectively distinguishable "races" exist and interrelate, effectively eliding asymmetrical commonalities.)

Second, the anxiety is embedded in the long intertext of French commentary on the United States. Not unlike American commentators on France, French commentators on the United States often generalize about "America" without the benefit of any substantive knowledge. As Jean-Philippe Mathy explains, the French "rhetoric of America" serves local political purposes; judgments passed on the United States from France must be read as discourses about France.[33] And while multiculturalism in the United States was seen both by its advocates and by its opponents as a challenge to Anglo-hegemony, in France, paradoxically, it was seen as incarnating that very same Anglo-hegemony. Socialist president Lionel Jospin, for example, publicly rejected what he called "the Anglo-Saxon model of the communities." That "model," it must be said, is very much a French-Latinist theoretical construct, since it has never been articulated as a model by intellectuals in the nations in question. In any case, the critics on both sides of the Atlantic seemed to share the Eurocentric and white-normative assumption that U.S. society has an inevitable Anglo-Saxon coloration.

Third, the hostility to "Anglo-Saxon differentialism" correlates with a common view of French society itself as at least in principle unified. Privileging national unity and uniformity over diversity, the constitutions of the First, Fourth, and Fifth Republics all portray France as a "Republic, one and indivisible," with one legislative body, one centralized administration, and, implicitly, one (Jacobin) ideology. Any questioning of this foundational unity was traditionally seen as a form of complicity with the *ancien régime* or with external foes. Decentralizing federalizers were viewed, often correctly, as being in league with counterrevolutionary forces. The very precariousness of unity generated panic in the face of multiplicity, symptomatic of a need to overcome centrifugal dispersal through a vast central organization. The threat was of a loss of cohesion triggered by supposedly "inassimilable" differences. French national discourse, as Mathy points out, often lumps together those against whom the French had traditionally defined themselves: the Germans, the English, and, later, the Americans, in sum, the "Anglo-Saxons."[34] French antidifferentialism can thus be located within a specific history embracing both the internal Jacobin and the external assimilationist model by which non-French-speaking provincials, formerly colonized peoples, and noncolonized immigrants were all supposed to repress traces of their dialectal identities and assimilate to the *langue* of an elusive "Frenchness." Any sense of hyphenated, conflictual, or polyphonic identity was excluded.

Fourth, the anxiety has had to do with the assumption that nations embody single political models. Herman Lebovics traces the exclusivist idea of one "true France" to a shared French universalism derived from a mélange of "Gallic Catholicism, absolutism, the Enlightenment and Jacobinism."[35] In France, as a result, right and left often argue over what should be *the* model for French identity and society, in contrast with an imagined single U.S. model, at once suspectly individualist—a brewing Hobbesian war of "each against each"—and as overly communitarian, premised on separate, ethnically defined groups rather than on the universal rights of *citoyens*. At the same time, French republicanism brings some undeniable social advantages. France has largely avoided, at least in the Hexagon itself, many of the problems characteristic of the U.S. polity. French constitutions, unlike the U.S. Constitution, have never even implicitly endorsed slavery or racism. There is no French equivalent to the "federal ratio" or to the *Dred Scott* decision nationalizing slavery or to the claim that blacks "had no rights which the white man was bound to respect." The anti-Semitic Vichy regime, revealingly, felt obliged to repudiate the republican triad of "Liberté, Égalité, Fraternité," substituting instead "Work, Family, and Tradition." Rather than a rigid orthodoxy, republicanism offers a broad matrix of debate. For some analysts, the real debate in France takes place *within* the republican model, between left-leaning and neoliberal versions of the model or between difference-friendly and difference-erasing models. There is nothing in the republican model itself that requires the prohibition of religious insignia in schools or that prohibits an effective multiculturality. The real problem, for Jim Cohen, occurs when a "dogmatic version" of normative republican discourse and the ideal of the universal equality is "hypostasized into a 'truly-existing' equality of opportunity."[36]

Fifth, the anxiety has to do with the Jacobin view of the *citoyen* as blankly universal, somehow "beyond" and "above" race and gender. If the U.S. system is individualistic, the French system is both collective and atomistic, in that it sees the citizen as a substitutable monad interpellated only by the state and not by intermediaries such as "communities." In the French republican equivalent of "color-blind" ideology, to speak of race is to besmirch republican ideals. A commonplace attitude contrasts the race-obsessed Germanic Volkish idea of the nation with the traditional French idea of the nation as a free association of consenting individuals adhering to a common political project reaffirmed by the "daily plebiscite" of national belonging. Le Penist racism and "separatist" multiculturalism, in this view, form twin subversions of republican unity. The precepts of the republican model as executed by a socially narrow elite, as Blatt puts it, serve to "legitimize and hide the exclusion of identity-based groups and complicate the tasks of minorities attempting to gain a role, either collectively or individually, in the political process."[37]

Sixth, the anxiety has to do with a widespread rejection of "race" as shadowed by the memory of scientific racism and Vichyiste anti-Semitism. Acutely aware of the catastrophic results of Nazi race theory, progressive intellectuals hoped that eliminating the pernicious vocabulary of race might also eliminate the evils of racism. Any recognition of ethnic particularity is presumed to dilute the force of the transcendental principle of "equality before the law."[38] Yet denying the existence of race hardly diminishes the reality of racism. And French intellectual history is hardly raceless, since French thinkers played a role in three of the principal forms of racism to emerge in Europe: anti-Semitism, Islamophobia, and prejudice against people of color.[39]

Seventh, the anxiety has to do with the projection of cultural movements as separatist. In some French accounts (which mirror and sometimes draw on U.S. right-wing accounts), multicultural identity politics calls for a world in which societies should be divided up into autonomous communities. This caricature acts in tandem with a view of U.S. society itself as ethnically ghettoized. Although the United States is in some ways segregated (especially in residential terms), this pattern has not been actively designed by multiculturalists seeking racial ghettos but rather by longstanding discriminatory policies. While inaccurate, the charge of separatism helps us name the fear lurking behind the virtually consensus rejection of multiculturalism by established French intellectuals in the 1990s.

Eighth, another anxiety, among the literarily inclined, has to do with the critical interrogation of the "canon," which goes against the grain of the traditional French investment (in all senses of that word) in high literary culture and the arts as "the canonical expressions of what the *mission civilisatrice* was all about."[40] Like the republic, the canon too was seen as threatened by particularism. What was missed was that the rethinking of the canon in the English-speaking world has also opened it up to Francophone and French writers of color, leading to a new wave of translations and the reshaping of French departments to include North African, West African, and French-Caribbean writers.

Finally, the anxieties are rooted in contemporary anxieties about a double sense of engulfment in the era of globalization. French nationhood, for some people, now seems challenged by *infra*national forces (Le Pen and the right wing), *trans*national forces (the European Union, a reconfigured NATO, U.S.-led globalization), and *post*national forces (immigration from former colonies). The attack on the multicultural projects comes to allegorize vulnerable self-assertion and *l'exception française*, a way of saying that we French will deal with these challenges on our own terms. But alongside this legitimate aspiration to sovereignty lurks a *malentendu* that sees multiculturalism and globalization, as Mathy puts it, "as related manifestations of transnational capitalism, combined to undermine the national idea, the one from within and the other from without."[41]

The project being denounced was in many cases not even the same object. For Bourdieu/Wacquant, multiculturalism was simply neoliberalism and imperialism by another name; for Alain Finkielkraut, in contrast, it was a new edition of May '68 revolutionism. As a result of these superimposed anxieties, the transatlantic discussion, in the 1990s at least, came to have the air of a *dialogue des sourds*. The "static" of different grids, vocabularies, and prisms meant that much was "lost in translation" due to nonsynchronous repertoires of understanding. Many French intellectuals were conditioned by the "national cultural field" to hear "multiculturalism" as meaning "American," "Anglo-Saxon," "separatism," "globalization," and "threat to the republic," while "identity" conjured up the image of French Le Penists or Muslim fundamentalists.

Hip-Hop and the Racialization of the Everyday

Culture and politics are not always "in sync." Just as the antagonism to multicultural identity politics was at its height, France was also undergoing a thoroughgoing and irreversible process of multiculturalization, manifest especially in the arts and popular culture. In the ironically titled *Paris Est Propre* (Paris Is Clean), the Zairian painter Chéri Samba, in pop faux-naïf images, portrays the Third World workers who sweep the streets and pick up canine feces in front of the Trocadéro. In the late 1980s and 1990s, Paris was becoming a capital of African fashion, animated by figures such as the Malian Lamine Badian Kouyaté, the designer who created Xuly Bët with boutiques in Paris and New York, and Alphadi, creator of the Festival of African Fashion. The City of Light had also become the main global center for the diffusion of African and Arab "world" music, a major disseminator of raï music, Salif Keita, Cheb Khaled, Papa Wemba, Youssou N'Dour, Cesária Évora, and Nusrat Fateh Ali Khan. The names of popular bands such as Les Négresses Vertes, Mano Negra, and Raffik were redolent of Third World and Afro-diasporic culture. In 1998, the Académie Française gave its Grande Médaille de la Chanson to the rapper MC Solaar. The "beur" or "banlieue" films such as *Bye-Bye* and *L'Hexagone*, meanwhile, offered a triangular bouillabaisse of North African, French, and African American culture. Syncretism also took linguistic form in the *verlan* of the banlieue, which drew on Arabic, African languages, black American slang, and French gangster argot.

As a global phenomenon, hip-hop illustrates the transoceanic crossings of diasporic cultures. As an international lingua franca, rap is performed not only in French and Portuguese but also in Hindi, Chinese, Arabic, Aymara, and Yoruba. The U.S. movement that began in the Bronx in the 1970s was energized by figures such as Afrika Bambaataa and Zulu Nation who mingled pop culture, high art, Caribbean, and Brazilian influences (capoeira). The French version too was simultaneously musical (rap), graphic (graffiti), and choreographic (break dance). Emerging into the public sphere in the early 1980s, hip-hop became the privileged mode of expression of what was variously called *"la banlieue," "la cité,"* or *"les quartiers sensibles."* Disseminated by DJs such as Sydney and Dee Nasty, hip-hop attracted thousands of fans from the immigrant neighborhoods, providing a cultural alternative to young people for whom neither official French culture nor the Maghrebian/sub-Saharan home culture of origin provided a comfortable fit.[42]

In France as elsewhere, rap turned social stigmata into a badge of honor. And like rappers in the United States and Brazil, French rap groups such as Assassin and La Rumeur have all denounced the police harassment of young men of color. The group Nique Ta Mère (literally, "Fuck Your Mother"—*niquer* being a loan word from Arabic), partially modeled on the gangster-rap group NWA, lambasted police brutality and racial profiling. Nique Ta Mere was denounced for cop-killing fantasies such as the 1993 "J'appuie sur la gâchette" (roughly "My Finger on the Trigger"). In July 2002, Sarkozy, then interior minister, pressed charges against the rapper Mohamed Bourokba (a.k.a. Hamé) from La Rumeur for slandering the national police. Both a commercial product and a vehicle of social desire, hip-hop also resonated in France because it offered an open, protean medium for treating social issues common to the Black Atlantic. For Mehdi Belhaj Kacem, rap culture flourishes especially in France and the United States, because both societies "are essentially founded on the idea of the universal combined with a culture of immigration and miscegenation."[43]

French rappers do not merely "imitate" African American rappers, however; rather, they address partially analogous situations through distinct artistic forms, within the constantly mutating Afro-diasporic transtextuality of sampling and cut 'n' mix. Rappers forged their own layered constellation of styles, combining U.S.-style hip-hop with African dance, Islamic *majdoub*, Japanese *butoh*, and French avant-garde elements. Styles have ranged from the gross provocations of Nique Ta Mère to the alexandrines of MC Solaar, an Afro-French admirer of Ronsard and Baudelaire. Signifying on Godard's "children of Marx and Coca Cola," Elsa Vigoureux calls rappers the "children of hip-hop and Derrida," since they draw not only on Derrida but also on Deleuze, Said, Fanon, and Bourdieu.[44] Just as Brazilian rappers constantly shout out to James Brown, French rappers often cite black American music, as when IAM samples Stevie Wonder's "Past Time Paradise" to speak of slavery and the Middle Passage. While Brazil offers the soulful Phat Family, France gives us Fonky

Family. While African American rappers point to a monumental Egypt as a locus of symbolic pride, and while Brazilian rappers affectionately invoke the homegrown spiritual Africana of Candomblé and Xango, French rappers carry a genetic link to Africa in that many are themselves of direct African descent— MC Solaar is from Chad, Hamed Daye from Mali, El Tunisiano (as his name implies) from Tunisia, and so forth. As practitioners of "polyglossia" (Bakhtin), some rappers shift from French to Wolof and Arabic and back.[45]

At times, French rappers perform a percussive version of what in an academic context would be called postcolonial critique. Perhaps inspired by Louis Sala-Molins, the rapper Fabe titled one of his songs "Code Noir." MC Solaar, in the same vein, connects past colonial and present-day exploitation in "Les Colonies," while Liste Noire (Blacklist) called their first album "Les Damnés de la Terre" (Wretched of the Earth) in honor of Fanon. La Brigade's "Partir Ailleurs" reminds its audience of the role of Africans in French colonial armies. French rappers, like their counterparts in the United States and Brazil, also denounce racial profiling, corrupt politicians, and the lack of political representation, sometimes in a gendered and masculinist language.[46] A rap by Monsieur R., provocatively entitled "FranSSe," begins with a description of a state of institutional violence and moves to a call for violent opposition:

> France is wearing us down
> To the point that we don't trust our neighbor
> The laws are conceived to kill us off
> With brothers behind bars and now
> Our mission is to exterminate the ministers and the fascists
> For today it's useless to yell, it's like talking to the wall
> The only way to be heard
> Is by burning cars . . .
> France is a bitch and we got betrayed
> It's the system that makes us hate
> And anger that makes us speak in a vulgar way
> So we fuck France with our music
> We mock their repression
> And don't care about the Republic
> and its freedom of expression.

But the song ends with a call for political representation:

> We have to change the laws so we can see
> Arabs and blacks in the Elysées.

French hip-hoppers (like their Brazilian peers), in sum, identify not only with the percussive kineticism of black American music but also with the social drift of lyrics denouncing police brutality, racial profiling, media stereotypes, and political exclusion.[47]

Despite (the often legitimate) antagonism to the concept of race in France, everyday life in France is very much racialized. Despite different historical trajectories and despite a well-oiled welfare state that takes some of the edge off the pain of discrimination, French social problems partially resemble those of Brazil and the United States. In Brazil, the victims might be the poor mixed-race people from the favelas of *City of God*; in the United States, blacks and Latinos from the inner city of *Do the Right Thing*; and in France, the children of Maghrebian and sub-Saharan Africans from the banlieue of *La Haine*. Yet despite clear differences, the social situations bear a family resemblance. Accounts of certain aspects of everyday life in the inner cities, in the banlieues, and in the favelas, often seem more or less interchangeable. Here is Azouz Begag's account of the daily lives of the marginalized children of immigrants in the banlieue:

> The social damage arising from the confusion of personal success with financial gain goes far wider than the banlieues and youths of immigrant origin. The question of value at stake here could be summarized in the following terms: "If we take young people living in poverty who have seen their fathers exploited as cheap labor, then thrown onto the scrap heap of unemployment, who have no culture [*sic*], are completely depoliticized, are subjected to constant racism and are able to express themselves only through violence, how can we expect them to accept a temporary job for a thousand euros a month when they can earn that much in a day or two in the parallel economy?[48]

A social version of what linguists call a "commutation test" would show that with minor alterations—the substitution of "dollars" or "reais" for "euros" and "favela" or "inner city" for "banlieue"—this text could be describing the life of a clocker in a U.S. inner city or a *falcão* in a Brazilian favela. But in other ways, the dynamics and histories are distinct and partly untranslatable. Islamophobia and North African immigration, filtered through the bitter memory of the Algerian War, for example, play a greater role in French postwar history. Addressing anti-Muslim discrimination in France, critics speak of the "racialization of religion" and "the religionization of race." Marine Le Pen of the Front National has compared Muslims praying in the French streets to the Nazi occupation of Paris. Practicing other-demonization as electoral strategy, Sarkozy has maintained a steady drumbeat of anti-Muslim rhetoric, declaring Islamic veils "unwelcome in France" and calling for debates about "national identity" and about "Islam in France." His focus on the burqa neatly conjoins fears of the "Islamicization of France" with post-9/11 evocations of the Taliban, terrorism, and the oppression of women. It is often noted that in France it is worse to be North African than to be black. At the same time, the current wave of Islamophobia in the United States, and the hysteria about mosques, suggests that the United States is far from immune to the contagion.

The Atlantic world is not only Red, Black, and White; it is also Brown, in the sense of being Arab, Muslim, and even Moorish/Sephardic in terms of the Iberian roots of much of the Americas. Since 9/11 and the "War on Terror," however, mingled strains of anti-Arab racism and Islamophobia have become virulent in both France and the United States. Historically, Orientalism and Islamophobia are embedded in a long intertextual chain: crusading anti-Islamic tales, Orientalist narratives, anti-Semitic protocols, imperial adventure novels and films. The historical conjunctures and discursive genealogies, of course, display national nuances. Whereas France has defined itself against the Islamic world since the Battle of Poitiers in 732, the U.S. hostility to Arabs and Muslims begins a millennium later, with U.S. interventions against the Barbary pirates. U.S. Arab-hating also "borrows" from antecedent racisms exercised against Jews, Native Americans, African Americans, and Latinos. In the 20th century, preexisting prejudices became superimposed on geopolitical tensions in the Middle East.

Whatever its genealogies, Islamophobia is currently raging in France and the United States. In both countries, politicians exploit racialized divisions—"wedge issues" in the United States; "politique de clivage" in France—as a lever to gain power. A wide range of phenomena—acts of desecration, expulsion, violence, and even murder, alongside racist discourses and tropes—express and foster the resentment of the majority population. Azouz Begag inventories the discursive mechanisms of prejudice (many of which find counterparts in the United States): the rhetorical demonization of "multiculturalism" and "communitarianism" as code for hostility toward Muslims; a discourse of false victimization on the part of the majority population that sees itself as "invaded" or even "occupied" by an alien force; the definition of Islam (like Judaism earlier) as a "problem"; the journalistic association of young men of color with crime and illegality; the monologization of "national identity" as a ploy to reassert a normative Frenchness; and the constant otherization of French citizens of North African background, born in France and distanced from North Africa yet told to "go back where you came from."[49] The attack on the veil, we would add, recycles the colonial doxa that positions white European men (and sometimes women) as protecting brown Muslim women from their brown overlords. Thus, French editorialists express hostility to Islamic dress such as the veil or the burqa, seen paradoxically as ostentatoire (showing off) and self-denying; Muslim women are condemned for calling attention to themselves by hiding, in a kind of visible invisibility. A culturally connoted choice of clothing engenders moral panics and irrational hatreds.

The American right, meanwhile, exhorts "real Americans" to "take back" the country, presumably from blacks, Latinos, and Arabs. As in France, politicians fan the flames of xenophobia for electoral purposes. Surges of hysteria about mosques and minarets are carefully orchestrated to coincide with electoral campaigns. Protestant pastors burn the Quran, while rightist politicians warn absurdly of the imminent imposition of Sharia law in the American heartland. Congressional committees, meanwhile, investigate the "radicalization" of Arab neighborhoods, regarded as breeding grounds for terrorism. A panoply of marginalizing rhetorics—exclusionary definitions of Americanness, racist taunts such as "cameljockey," and the characterization of Islam as an "evil religion"—serve to otherize Arabs/Muslims. The crudeness of right-wing Islamophobia is encapsulated in Ann Coulter's atavistic call for a new crusade—"We should invade their countries, kill their leaders and convert them to Christianity"—hardly an empty threat in the age of the Iraq and Afghan wars.[50] Far from marginal, anti-Arabism and Islamophobia have moved to the center of the neoconservative movement and the Republican Party. An important difference separates the French and American versions of xenophobia, however. Unlike the American right, the French right does not hate the welfare state; it simply prefers not to share its benefits with immigrants of color.

Despite differentiated social systems, the complaints of people of color in France resemble those of their diasporic peers in the United States. They concern everyday humiliation, job discrimination, suspicious salespersons, racial profiling, and harassment by the "physiognomists" of the discothèques. According to a Sofres/Cran poll of 581 French blacks, 67 percent said that they had been victims of discrimination, 37 percent had experienced scornful or disrespectful behavior, 64 percent had suffered in public spaces and transport.[51] Three quarters of those interviewed recognized the existence of discrimination in housing, and 65 percent recognized discrimination in employment.[52] As in the United States, researchers use "testing" (the English word is used) by having blacks and whites apply for the same positions. The tests reveal a multistage discrimination: (1) initial lies to the applicant about the availability of the position, (2) extra demands made on people of color but not of whites, and (3) the stipulation of inferior conditions when the job is offered.[53] (The television series *Living in a Black Skin* staged and illustrated these forms of discrimination.) The refusal to compile race-based statistics has the practical effect of making it difficult to assess the social well-being or material disadvantage of discriminated populations.

The media, meanwhile, are only beginning to offer a sociologically proportionate representation of people of color on television screens. As François Durpaire points out, it took one of the worst air disasters in history—the August 16, 2005, crash that led to the death of 152 Martinicans—for that demographic group to finally appear on French television.[54] News anchors in France are rarely black or Maghrebian, and the dominant perspective relayed by the news reports is usually "Franco-Français." (The situation on French cable television is significantly better.) Black faces on French television were more likely to be from U.S. television programs. The mediatic image of France, in short, does not resemble the France of the streets. Television fictions feature a few stars of color—Mouss Diouf, the policeman in *Julie Lescaut*, Jacques Martial in *Navarro*, Sonia Rolland in *Léa Parker*—but they are the exception. Actors of color in France, like their homologues in Brazil and the United States, point out that roles have to be designated "black" for them to be considered; white casting is the assumed default position. French people of color, again like their peers elsewhere, have formed organizations such as Collectif Égalité to protest discrimination and to organize boycotts and have created black magazines such as *Amina* (for African women), *Cité Black, Miss Ébène*, and *Couleur Métisse* (addressing hip-hop), and *Pilibo* (for West Indians), clear counterparts to *Essence, Jet*, and *Ebony* in the United States and to *Raça* in Brazil.[55]

Despite the inveterate racism of U.S. media, some French visitors have been struck by the visibility of minorities in the U.S media. According to Yazid and Yacine Sabeg, members of French ethnic minorities visiting the United States are often astounded "at the spectacle of the American street and the American media: one sees black journalists, lawyers, bankers, prime-time black and Asian anchors and reporters, members of the government, business leaders, high-grade military people, black and Asian Secretaries of State."[56] Azouz Begag offers a similar account of his late-1980s sojourn at Cornell as a visiting professor: "I was struck the most by what I saw on television. Journalists of every color under the sun held front-rank positions in prime-time slots. . . . And the more they were mixed by ethnicity and gender, the less attention you paid to their origins, and the more you listened to what they had to say and why they were there—the news!"[57] This by now taken-for-granted multicolored representativeness constitutes in itself a form of empowerment in a mass-mediated age in which cultural power is certified by media visibility. At the same time, all that "color" does not make the dominant coverage more progressive or less procorporate. In fact, television political talk shows often privilege that social anomaly called the black conservative—some (such as Armstrong Williams) literally in the pay of the right and others serving as tokens for the Republican Party.

One social feature common to the United States, France, and Brazil is the constant police harassment of young men of color. In the United States, police (usually white) have killed hundreds of defenseless blacks and Latinos, often motivated by phantasmatic hallucinations of imaginary weapons, whereby a cell phone or a wallet, especially when in black hands, is perceived as a weapon.[58] In

Brazil, police and death squads (sometimes composed of off-duty police) have killed thousands of "marginals," the vast majority black or of mixed race. In France, young children of immigrants are subject to the *délit de faciès*—the crime of having a certain kind of face. In other respects, of course, the situations are distinct. Stricter gun control in France, for example, makes the situation much less lethal than in Brazil and the United States. The long-term historical contexts are also different. In colonial-settler states such as Brazil and the United States, present-day discrimination emerges out of centuries of conquest and slavery, while in France, it morphs, at least in part, out of a colonialism that was "external." At the same time, it reflects the historic residues of earlier discriminations both in the colonized Maghreb itself and in the dilapidated *bidonvilles* of France.

French philosopher Alain Badiou's eloquent account of an incident involving his sixteen-year-old adopted son testifies to the kinds of harassment all too typical of the multiracial metropolises of the Black Atlantic. In an essay entitled "Daily Humiliation," Badiou explains that his son had been arrested six times in eighteen months, for doing nothing at all except existing while black, and as a result was interrogated, insulted, and left handcuffed to a bench for hours on end, sometimes for a day or two. Badiou explains in detail one incident in which his son's Turkish friend buys a bicycle only to discover that it had been stolen. Honorably, they decide to return the bicycle to its rightful owners, even though they would lose the money spent. Badiou describes what happened next:

> It is at this point that a police car, brakes screeching, pulls up to the curb. Two of its occupants jump out and pounce on Gerard and Kemal, pinning them to the ground; they then cuff their hands behind their backs, and line them up against the wall. Insults and threats: "Idiots! Arseholes!" Our two heroes ask what they've done. "You know damn well. Turn around." Still handcuffed, they are made to face the passersby in the street: "Everyone should see who you are and what you did." A revival of the medieval pillory (they are exposed like this for half an hour) but with a novelty: it's done prior to any judgment, prior to any accusation. . . . Handcuffed to a bench, kicked in the shins every time a policeman passes, insults, especially for Gerard: "Fat pig." "Filth." This goes on for an hour and a half without their knowing what they're accused of. . . . At home, I await my son. Two and a half hours later the telephone rings: "Your son is being held in detention on probability of gang assault."[59]

It turns out that Badiou's son was misidentified by a school supervisor and that the police requested, and received, photos and school files of all the black students at his son's school. Badiou concludes acerbically, "We get the riots we deserve. A state in which what is called public order is only a coupling of the protection of private wealth and dogs unleashed on children of working people and people of foreign origin is purely and simply despicable."[60]

Allegorical Crossings: Blacks, Jews, Muslims

Since the postwar seismic shift, racial identifications have taken many twists and turns, as some minority communities have gradually come to be viewed as white, although never quite.[61] While Jews have been racialized by anti-Semitic discourse, the U.S. Census has never offered a nonwhite slot for "Jews" or, for that matter, for "Arabs" or "Middle Easterners." Jewish status in the United States has been ambiguous and floating in relation to normative notions of whiteness. The black-Jewish relationship, meanwhile, has mingled solidarity and tension. In the late 1960s, James Baldwin claimed that blacks identified with Jews because both groups shared a common history of oppression rooted in Christianity: "The crisis taking place in the word, and in the minds and hearts of black men everywhere, is not produced by the Star of David but by the old, rugged cross on which Christendom's most celebrated Jew was murdered. And not by Jews."[62] At the same time, Baldwin attributed anti-Semitism among blacks to mingled anger and envy toward Jews who had assimilated into the white mainstream. From the Jewish side, meanwhile, countless Jewish intellectuals declared their problack sympathies. Hannah Arendt, for example, declared, "As a Jew I take my sympathy for the cause of the Negroes, as for all oppressed or underprivileged peoples, for granted."[63]

Many authors trace a certain solidarity between the two minorities back to Jewish and black participation in the U.S. Communist Party and in the labor movement in the 1930s and subsequently to Jewish support for Civil Rights in the 1960s, culminating, perhaps, in the moment when Martin Luther King, Jr., about to address the Rabbinical Assembly of the Conservative Movement, was greeted by one thousand rabbis singing "We Shall Overcome" in Hebrew. In one narrative of the intercommunal relationship, this initial camaraderie was undercut beginning in the late 1960s by divergent attitudes toward community control of schools, Affirmative Action, Israel/Palestine, and so forth. During the 1980s, public controversies sometimes degenerated at their worst into black accusations of a supposed Jewish domination of the slave trade (e.g., by Leonard Jeffries) and Jewish allegations of black genetic inferiority (by Michael Levin). Overstated claims of unity and alliance in the past have sometimes given way to equally overstated claims of unalloyed hostility in the present. The Israeli-Palestinian conflict, meanwhile, was falsely portrayed as rooted in age-old enmities of two peoples entangled in a civilizational clash entailing an unbridgeable divide between Arab and Jew, or Muslim and Jew.

In our view, black-Jewish and Jewish-Muslim relations, as well as the interlinked issues of anti-Semitism, Islamophobia, and antiblack racism, must be framed within a longer perspective that stresses overlapping but also distinct histories over the *longue durée*. Often forgotten in the discussion is that some Jews are black and some blacks are Jewish and that while Jews are definitionally not Muslim, they can be Arabs.[64] But even apart from these hybrid forms, the destinies of Jews, Arabs, Muslims, and blacks have been interwoven for centuries. These linked trajectories and submerged analogies can be traced, as we have argued elsewhere, back to the events associated with the cataclysmic moment summed up in what might be called "the two 1492s," when the conquest of the "new" world converged with the expulsion of Muslim and Jews from Spain. At that time, the ground for colonialist racism was prepared by the Inquisition's *limpieza de sangre*, by the expulsion edicts against Jews and Muslims, by the Portuguese expansion into the west coast of Africa, and by the transatlantic slave trade. Spain in the 15th century provided a template for ethno-religious cleansing and the creation of other racial states. The crusades against Muslim "infidels" abroad coincided with anti-Semitic pogroms in Europe itself. Although the *limpieza de sangre* was formulated in religious terms—Jewishness and Muslimness could be "remedied" by conversion—the metaphor of purity of "blood" prepared the way for biological and scientific racism in subsequent centuries.

Christian demonology about Muslims and Jews thus set the tone for racialized colonialism, equipping the conquistadores with a ready-made conceptual apparatus to be extended to the Americas. Amerigo Vespucci's travel accounts drew on the stock of anti-Jewish and anti-Muslim imagery to characterize the indigenous peoples as infidels and devil worshipers.[65] The conquest of the Indians in the West, for 16th-century Spanish historian Francisco López de Gómara, prolonged the struggle against the Muslim infidels in the East.[66] The Hieronymite friars, for their part, referred to the inhabitants of Hispaniola as "Moors."[67] Shakespeare's Caliban in *The Tempest*, meanwhile, mingled the traits of African Moors and indigenous Americans. Within a transoceanic drifting of tropes, the frightening figure of the cannibal, first elaborated in relation to the Caribs and Tupi of the Americas, was transferred to Africans. A partial congruency ties the phantasmatic imagery projected onto both the internal non-Christian "enemy" and the external indigenous American and African "savage," all portrayed as "blood drinkers," "cannibals," and "sorcerers." West African orixas (such as Exu) and indigenous deities (for example, the Tupi deity Tupan), meanwhile, were diabolized to fit into a normatively Manichean Christian schema.

The Iberian wrestling with its legacy of "the Orient," associated with Africa and the South, and "the Occident," associated with Europe and the North, persisted in the Americas. In this version, the concept of "Orientalism" functioned as synonym for the negative view of the Moorish Muslim and Sephardic Jewish "Orientalization" of Iberia and consequently of its new territories in the Americas.[68] In this expanding Atlantic space, the ritual legacy of the struggle between

Christians and infidels, such as the equestrian combats between Spaniards and Moors, continued to be reenacted, for example, in Brazil in the form of Easter Sunday street festivals. "The Christians," in the words of Gilberto Freyre, "were always victorious and the Moors routed and punished. And Easter Saturday ended or began with the effigy of Judas being carried through the streets and burned by the urchins in what was evidently a popular expression of religious hatred of the Catholic for the Jew."[69] Jews were viewed, in the words of Freyre, as the "secret agent of Orientalism."[70] Thus, before the contemporary Eurocentric erasure, as it were, of the hyphen in the "Judeo-Islamic" and the insertion of the hyphen in the "Judeo-Christian," the "Jew" and "the Muslim," or "the Sephardi" and "the Moor," or "the Morisco" and "the converso" were articulated within the same conceptual space, as one allegorical unit. As a form of Iberian anxiety about its Arabization/Judaization, "Orientalism" was thus carried over to the Americas, where it participated in the shaping of emerging regional and national identities.

Yet, if Iberia witnessed centuries of an ideology that justified the cleansing of the "Orientalized" Moorish/Sephardic past, Latin America, as a complex site of global cultural encounters and of ambivalence toward the colonial metropole, has also witnessed a certain nostalgia for that "Oriental" past. The tropical imaginary has been partly shaped by what could be called "the Moorish unconscious" of Latin America, where denial and desire of that forgotten origin have coexisted simultaneously. The mundane pride of some families in their Moorish Morisco or Sephardi *converso* lineage has been expressed in popular tales and registered in the work of various writers. From José Martí's exhortation "Seamos Moros!" to Carlos Fuentes's celebration of Mexico's "buried mirror," the question of the Moor never stopped haunting the Latin American imaginary, even if only on the margins.[71] In Freyre's theorization of Brazilian identity, he gives great weight to the Moorish/Sephardic cultural history of Portugal as actively shaping Brazilian customs and practices. In the early colonial era, Brazilian people maintained Moorish/Sephardic traditions such as the covering of women attending church, the preference for sitting on rugs with legs crossed, and the use of Moorish architectural structures and artistic designs, including the glazed tiling, checkered window panes, and so forth.[72] But the programmatic adoption of Occidental-European customs, institutionalized with Brazil's independence in 1822, catalyzed a detachment from the Moorish/Sephardic heritage.[73]

Part of a shared cultural landscape, both Muslims and Jews were seen by Iberian and Ibero-American authorities as alien excrescences to be extirpated from a putatively pure body politic. Although one can argue about the degree or the depth of the religious *convivencia* of Al-Andalus, clearly Muslims and Jews lived in a densely textured cultural intimacy, in which the more potent divide was not between Muslim and Jew but between Christians, on the one hand, and Muslims and Jews on the other.[74] A swelling corpus has documented the long history of a cultural continuity and political alliance between Muslim and Jew.[75] Key philosophical, literary, grammatical, and medical texts within Judaism were written in Arabic and in dialogue with Islamic writings, while Sephardi (and even some Ashkenazi) synagogues were built in the Moorish style. The Star of David hexagram (also known as the Seal of Solomon) adorned the façades of some mosques such as the Testour mosque in Tunisia, as well as Moroccan coins and the Moroccan flag. Muslims and Jews also revered some shared holy figures, such as Sidi Abu-Hasira, whose graves became sites of pilgrimages for both faiths.

Similar zones of Muslim-Jewish affinity, embedded within a larger Judeo-Islamic cultural geography, mark even the modern period. Although "Arab" and "Jew" have come to be seen as antonyms in the wake of the Israeli-Palestinian conflict, this dichotomy is of recent vintage. In Orientalist discourse, Arabs and Jews were seen not only as speaking similar Semitic languages but also as actively allied or as sharing similar origins. "The Jewish question," as Gil Anidjar puts it, "has never been anything but the Arab question. . . . Islamophobia and Judeo-phobia have always been the two faces of the same and only question."[76] With the emancipation of the European Jew, the Orientalist figure of the single Jew-ish/Muslim Semite was split into two, in the form of the assimilated European Jew and the backward Muslim Arab, with the Arab-Jew occupying an ambivalent position between the two.[77] Approaching the same question with regard to a later point in history, Domenico Losurdo points to the continuities between Judeo-phobia and Islamophobia. The same charges once advanced against Jews—tribal-ism, antimodernity, dual loyalty, the refusal to integrate—are now pressed against Arabs/Muslims. The diabolical figure of the Islamo-fascist terrorist has replaced the old Jewish-anarchist.[78]

Foundational to our approach is an engagement with the inherent relational-ity of the intra-European and the extra-European, thus rendering problematic the internal/external distinction itself. If Nazi exterminationism in one sense grew out of the millennial "internal" traditions of anti-Semitism, in another sense it grew out of "external" colonialism. The Shoah and colonialism were linked both metaphorically and metonymically, metaphorically comparable in their demoni-zations of internal and external "others" but also metonymically connected in historical and discursive terms. Hitler, as he began to frame the Final Solution, appealed to the precedent of colonial genocides. Already in a 1932 speech, Hitler hailed the Spanish Conquest of Central America and the British colonization of India as based on the absolute superiority of the white race. The large-scale mur-der of indigenous Americans, Tazmanians, and Armenians, for Hitler in *Mein Kampf*, showed that entire peoples could be exterminated with impunity, pro-vided that the people in question were powerless and defined as beyond the pale of the human. Hitler himself cited the North American extermination of "red savages" as an example to be emulated. Around the turn of the century, German colonists themselves had virtually annihilated two southwest African peoples (the Herrero and the Nama) in what retroactively looks like a rehearsal for the later attempt to annihilate the Jews, along with the Gypsies, homosexuals, and other "pathological" bodies.

In this sense, both anti-Semitic pogroms in Europe and colonial annihilations outside of Europe could be seen as training sessions for Nazi genocide of the Jews. While the Holocaust, as the paradigm for exterminationist racism, has its own horrific specificity, it also exists on a historical continuum with other forms of colonial racism. Even Nazi experiments on Jews can be viewed on a continuum with the scientific racism that made the bodies of Africans and indigenous Americans available for experimentation and dissection. To see the Shoah and colonial slavery as completely unrelated, or as involved in a grotesque rivalry over the ethical capital of victimhood, or even worse to lapse into anti-Semitism or antiblack racism by dismissing the historical centrality of either, is not only to miss their inherent connectedness but also to downplay the significance of such affiliations as perceived by racialized intellectuals themselves. To place in relation different histories of victimization is not to rank them in an obscene hierarchy but rather to mutually illuminate them as partially analogous yet also distinct forms of racialized degradation. For Césaire in *Discourse on Colonialism*, the Holocaust constituted the "crowning barbarism" of a long history of massacres in Africa, Asia, and Latin America.[79] Césaire conceptualized the Holocaust as a blowback or *choc en retour* of colonialist racism. Hannah Arendt, similarly, in *The Origins of Totalitarianism*, saw the formation of racist societies within imperialism as a key step toward racial exterminationism in Europe itself.[80] Delinking the Shoah and colonial genocides downplays zones of historical affiliation and potential coalition and identification.

In the aftermath of the war and the Shoah, Jewish intellectuals played a boldly progressive role in both the United States and France, often becoming key contributors to the seismic shift. Jewish historians such as Herbert Aptheker, Lawrence Levine, Howard Zinn, and Stanley Elkins disinterred the buried histories of black resistance through sympathetic histories of slave revolts. Formed both by the Civil Rights struggle and the vibrant tradition of Jewish radicalism, many Jews became catalytic figures in the 1960s radical movements. Herbert Marcuse, I. F. Stone, George Mosse, Studs Terkel, Jerry Rubin, Abby Hoffman, Mark Rudd, Paul Wellstone, Bettina Aptheker, Michael Lerner, and Todd Gitlin became highly visible figures on the radical left. Indeed, Jewish intellectuals such as Noam Chomsky, Bernie Sanders, Zillah Eisenstein, Seymour Hirsch, Joel Kovel, Amy Goodman, Melanie Kaye/Kantrowitz, Alissa Solomon, Tony Kushner, Naomi Klein, and so many others have formed an indispensible part of left and antiracist movements. (To even begin to list such figures risks implying an impossible comprehensiveness.)

In France, similarly, Jewish writers such as Claude Lévi-Strauss, Henri Alleg, Léon Poliakov, Maxime Rodinson, Pierre Vidal-Naquet, and Benny Lévy were in the forefront of the struggle against racism, anti-Semitism, and colonialism. The communist Alleg, a supporter of the Algerian anticolonial struggle, was imprisoned and tortured (including electroshock, waterboarding, and "truth drug" injections) by the French in Algeria. His 1958 book about the experience (*La Question*) provoked a firestorm of controversy. Another supporter of Algerian independence, the Tunisian Jew Albert Memmi, in *Portrait du Colonisé, Précédé de Portrait du Colonisateur* (1957) and *L'Homme Dominé* (1968), stressed the affinities among oppressed people, including Jews. In France, the mutually respectful structure of feeling between Jews and Muslims became evident in the reaction of prominent Jews to the police massacre of Algerians, on October 17, 1961. Representatives of the Jewish community expressed solidarity with the Algerian Muslim community on the basis of a common memory of oppression. A text largely written by Claude Lanzmann but signed by such figures as Laurent Schwartz and Pierre Vidal-Naquet denounced what might be called an anti-Arab pogrom:

> If we do not react, we French will become the accomplices of the racist fury for which Paris has been the theatre and which bring us back to the darkest days of the Nazi occupation. We refuse to distinguish between the Algerians piled up in the Palais des Sports waiting to be "refoules," and the Jews parked in Drancy before being deported.... The undersigned demand that all parties, unions and democratic organizations, not only demand the end of these terrible measures, but also manifest their solidarity with the Algerian workers by inviting their members to resist any renewal of such violence.[81]

French Jews and Maghrebian Arabs, in this case, were comrades in arms. But this was hardly the only case of such solidarities. In the post–World War II period, considerable testimony points to alliances within France between Jews and other stigmatized groups such as blacks and Arab/Muslims. Many of the Jewish participants in the May 1968 movement—notably Daniel Cohn-Bendit, Alain Geismar, Alain Krivine, Benny Lévy, Henri Weber, Serge July, Edgar Morin, Benjamin Stora, Ilan Halevi, and Sophie Bessis, to name just a few—developed a rhetoric of solidarity and alliance among the victims of racism, xenophobia, and anti-Semitism. (Conversely, during Vichy, the Paris mosque protected Jews.)

At the same times, many black anticolonialist thinkers expressed an identification with Jews as peers in suffering. In a contemporary context where Jews and Arabs, and Jews and blacks, are often discussed as separate and even antonymical, it is useful to reread Fanon, writing in an earlier historical conjuncture when progressive thinkers often linked Jewish and black oppression. Fanon cites his West Indian philosophy professor as warning him, "Whenever you hear anyone abuse the Jews, pay attention, because he is talking about you. . . . An anti-Semite is inevitably anti-Negro."[82] Fanon's recollection of his professor's words reverberates with the broader tradition of diasporic cross-cultural identifications found, for example, in the black allegorization of Jewish biblical stories of slavery, Exodus, and the Promised Land. It is this long historical *durée* that provides context for the following Fanon statement: "Since I was not satisfied to be racialized, by a lucky turn of fate I was humanized. I joined the Jew, my brother in misery."[83] Drawing parallels between the anti-Semite and the racist, Fanon recalls Sartre's argument that the Jew is a creation of the anti-Semite's fixating gaze. For Sartre, "it is the anti-Semite who makes the Jew," just as, for Fanon, it is the white who makes the black.[84] The emotional life of both is "split in two" as they pursue "a dream of universal brotherhood in a world that rejects [them]."[85] The attempts by the Jew, for Sartre, or by the black, for Fanon, to assimilate into an oppressive society lead only to the pathologies of self-hatred and inferiority.

Along with identification, "the Jew" and "the black" served as sites of comparative analysis of racism. Expanding Sartre's dialectics of identity in *Anti-Semite and Jew*, Fanon delineates the distinct psychic mechanisms that emplot the Jew and the black within the racist imaginary. The assimilated black, unlike the assimilated (European) Jew, remains overdetermined by the visibility of the black body. The Jew is also "a white man. . . . He can sometimes pass unnoticed, . . . [while] I am not the slave of the idea others have of me, but of my appearance."[86] Significant distinctions separate anti-Semitic and antiblack imageries, then, precisely in terms of corporeality. "The Negro," Fanon writes, symbolizes the biological danger; the Jew, the intellectual danger.[87] While Jews are feared in their presumed "control over everything," blacks are feared in their mythically "tremendous sexual powers."[88] Seen as possessing self-control and the power to control others in subtle, even invisible ways, the Jew functions as superego, while the black is projected as id, lacking in self-control, signaling immanent chaos. It is in this context that Fanon began to explore the differential overlappings, the Venn diagrams of racism.[89] Comparing the violence toward Jews and blacks, Fanon writes,

> No anti-Semite would conceive of . . . castrating the Jew. He is killed or sterilized. . . . The Jew is attacked in his religious identity, in his history, in his race, in his relations with his ancestors and with his posterity; when one sterilizes a Jew, one cuts off the source; every time that a Jew is persecuted, it is the whole race that is persecuted in his person. But it is in his corporeality that the Negro is attacked. It is as a concrete personality that he is lynched. It is as an actual being that he is a threat. The Jewish menace is replaced by the fear of the sexual potency of the Negro.[90]

Fanon's comparative framework does not conflate the experiences of Jews and blacks, then, but places them in productive relationality.

Affinities in victimization, however, do not guarantee cross-communal identification and may even result in a rolling series of resentful transferences among the oppressed. While different forms of victimization should ideally illuminate each other mutually, they have too often come to overshadow each other.[91] Fanon, in this sense, touched on the question of the black in the eyes of the Jew. He writes of Michel Salomon, "He is a Jew, he has a 'millennial experience of anti-Semitism,' and yet he is racist."[92] Fanon's attention to a "racist Jew" in a period immediately following the Jewish Holocaust serves as a harbinger of the later fissures in the black-Jewish alliance. Fanon invites us to reflect on the parallel and distinct forms of interminority racism in comparison with that of "normal" white Christian racism. Fanon's text anticipates the gradual entry—however tenuous and contradictory—of the Jew into the terrain of whiteness in the post–World War II era, especially in the United States. In Fanon's text, one finds the seeds of whiteness studies—discussed in chapter 7—and specifically the study of the whitening of the Jew within the general imaginary and even within the social psyche of some Jews.

Although Fanon carved out spaces of black identity in relation to Jewishness and Arabness, and although he saw both anti-Semitism and anti-Arabism as an integral part of French colonial ideology, the question of Palestine and Israel is not present in his work. Yet Fanon's life and text did not fully escape it. While Fanon was experimenting with new social-therapeutic methods in Tunisia, rival colleagues tried to have him dismissed by accusing him of being a Zionist undercover agent maltreating Arab patients on orders from Israel, an accusation dismissed outright by Ben Salah, then Tunisian minister of health.[93] In the wake of the 1967 war, Fanon's French widow, Josie, then living in Algeria, insisted that the publisher omit Sartre's preface from the French reprint of *The Wretched of the Earth* because of his pro-Zionist position.[94] Sartre and Beauvoir had been among the most vocal French leftists in support of Algerian self-determination. Their journal *Les Temps Modernes* offered a crucial platform for denouncing the rampant torture of Algerians and the daily violence generated by the colonial system. Those who supported an independent Algeria suffered retaliation in the form of blacklisting and terror; Sartre was declared "public enemy number one," and on July 19, 1961, a bomb exploded at the entrance hall to his apartment.[95] Yet, in the post-1967 era, many Arab critics found that Sartre had crossed over to the other side by signing a petition describing Israel as threatened by its Arab neighbors.[96] The French writer Jean Genet, in contrast, supported the Palestinian cause, just as he supported the Black Panthers in the United States. Retrospectively, one might locate in this post-1967 moment the beginnings of a gradual shift away from the enthusiastic embrace of Israel by some French leftist intellectuals. It was also the moment when a number of Jewish intellectuals in the West, disturbed by Third World support for Palestine, began to move to the right.

"From Mao to Moses": Neocons and the *Nouveaux Philosophes*

It was largely in the wake of the 1967 war and the ongoing occupation of the West Bank and Gaza that the Jewish-black and Jewish–Third World alliance began to fray. Initially associated with the left, a number of Jewish-French figures—notably Claude Lanzmann, Bernard-Henri Lévy, André Glucksmann, and Alain Finkielkraut—and Jewish American figures—notably Norman Podhoretz, Irving Kristol, and David Horowitz—slowly moved away from solidarity with blacks, Arabs, and Third World causes. In France, some of these figures became associated with the *nouveaux philosophes*, while in the United States, those associated with the neocons moved even further to the right. An impassioned defense of the state of Israel slowly became knitted together with an anti–Third World "structure of feeling" (Williams). A kind of zero-sum rivalry surfaced within the public sphere, whereby attention paid to racism came to be seen not only as detracting from the fight against anti-Semitism but also, worse, as propagating anti-Semitism. Although simplistic equations between Zionism and Judaism at times stem from anti-Semitism, the response of these intellectuals was not to deconstruct the equation or to engage the dilemmas that Zionism poses to leftist Jews and even to certain Enlightenment principles but rather to forge a new (old) vanguard in defense of "the West."

In a shift in qualifier and noun, a number of leftists evolved from being "Jewish radicals" to being "radical Jews." The itinerary of Benny Lévy, the Egyptian-born leader of the radical "Proletarian Left" movement, condenses the rightward turn of some Jewish 1968 leftists in France. An intimate of Sartre, Lévy abandoned his revolutionary nom de guerre Pierre Victor in the mid-1970s as part of an odyssey from "Mao to Moses."[97] Lévy replaced the 1968 slogan "Under the paving stones, the beach" with the more Judaic "Under the cobblestones of politics, the beach of theology." In 2000, he moved to Jerusalem, where he founded, together with Bernard-Henri Lévy and Alain Finkielkraut, an institute dedicated to the work of the French-Jewish philosopher Emmanuel Levinas. The trajectory of Albert Memmi also personifies a (more mild) turn to the right. The radical anticolonialist of *The Colonizer and the Colonized* (1957) has become progressively more critical of the Arab/Muslim world. In *Decolonization and the Decolonized*, Memmi also voices anxiety about what he calls the "Trojan Horse" of Islamic immigration in Europe itself. He stigmatizes the banlieue youth as resentful "zombies" who adopt the insignia of the hip-hop subculture as a sign of revolt. Although Memmi remains resolutely secular, he also pathologizes and essentializes an "Arab mind" constructed as coherent and without contradiction.[98]

In retrospect, we can detect an anticipatory sign of the post-1968 turn to the right in Pascal Bruckner's already discussed 1983 polemic *The White Man's Sobs*, which intermittently links Jewish concerns with antagonism to Third Worldism. At times, and especially in the footnotes, one senses that for Bruckner, in the period following the "Zionism is racism" proposition in the United Nations, Israel and Jews are at the very kernel of the West; for him, a threat to one is a threat to the other, as we see in the hyperbolic language of the following very revealing sentence: "No one has the right to declare the West guilty for the sole reason that it exists, as if the West were an insult to creation, a cosmic catastrophe, a monstrosity to be wiped off the map of the world (and that is why the question of Israel is capital: through the non-recognition of Israel, it is the illegitimacy of the West which is really at stake)."[99] Here Israel (and by implication Palestine) comes to allegorize the West/East relation generally. Bruckner thus relays a foundational Zionist trope, dating back to Herzl's notion of "the state of the Jews" as an outpost of Western civilization, a Switzerland in the Middle East. But unlike a Herzl traumatized by the Dreyfus Affair, Bruckner, a century later, rhetorically transfers to the imperializing and often anti-Semitic West the moral authority bestowed by the historical legacy of Jewish pain in Europe. And here we find a contradiction between one of the central premises of Zionism—that is, that Jews need Israel as unique refuge from Western anti-Semitism—and the paradoxically pro-Western bias of Zionism itself, even though the movement's founding assumption was that the experiment with Jewish safety and equality in Europe had *failed*, not that it had succeeded.

In hyperbolic language, Bruckner claims that the West's enemies regard it as a "cosmic catastrophe" and a "monstrosity" to be "wiped off the map." He thus associates Third Worldist intellectuals with the idiom of exterminationist anti-Semitism. Bruckner asserts a homology between the two issues: just as Israel's enemy, the Arabs, are presented as wanting to wipe Israel off the Middle Eastern map, so Europe's enemies are presented as wanting to erase the West off the world map. Bruckner here displays an astonishingly short historical memory. Writing only forty years after the Jewish Holocaust took place in Europe and only in Europe, and after the Vichy government sent thousands of Jews to the death camps, Bruckner portrays the West as innocent. Whereas Fanon mobilized the figure of the Jew to draw analogies and affinities between the various groups oppressed by Western racism, Buckner deploys the same figure to portray the West itself as oppressed. Israel, meanwhile, is for Bruckner the incarnation of Western modernity, while Arabs/Muslims reincarnate traditional anti-Semitism. While assuming the perspective that Zionism was a national liberation project for Jews, the representatives of the rightward turn do not engage the possibility that it was at the same time, within the fraught dialectics of "independence" and "*nakba*," a national destruction project for Palestinians.

Bruckner transfers what in Israel has been termed the "siege syndrome" to the West as a whole, imaged as besieged by Third World barbarians yelping at the gates of Europe. Bruckner anticipates the rhetoric of North American neoconservatives David Frum and Richard Perle, who warn, in *An End to Evil*, of a new Holocaust, this time directed not at Jews but rather at the United States: "There is no middle way for Americans: It is victory or Holocaust."[100] The United States is viewed as the potential victim of an imminent Final Solution project—this time conducted by fanatical Arabs/Muslims—analogous to that which victimized Jews during the Shoah. The equation of Arabs/Muslims with Nazis has often served in Zionist discourse to justify the policies of the Israeli state, an equation updated and reconfigured by the post-9/11 neoconservative coinage "Islamo-fascism," a term that tars a vast and variegated cultural-religious sphere with a totalitarian brush. In a period of anti-immigrant racism and ongoing battles over *le voile* in France, the *nouveaux philosophes* have been asserting the metanarrative of "the West." The U.S. neoconservatives, meanwhile, have been forging a strong "Judeo-Christian" alliance, including with American Christian fundamentalists. (Here the "Judeo-Christian" hyphen not only asserts a strong Jewish-Christian alliance but also embeds a supersessionist Christian teleology implying a progression from the "Old Testament," i.e., the Jewish Bible, to the "New Testament.") Although anti-Semitism remains a serious and persistent problem, including among fundamentalist Christians and fundamentalist Muslims, an isomorphism here connects the right-wing Israeli and right-wing American self-portrait; a rhetoric of siege and encirclement depicts vastly militarily and geopolitically powerful nation-states as weak and vulnerable.

Bruckner continues this line of thought in his 1995 book *The Temptation of Innocence*.[101] For Bruckner, the nearly universal condemnation (including by some Israelis) of concrete Israeli actions—settlements, "targeted assassinations," and so forth—derives not from the actions themselves but rather from resentment against Jews for not conforming to the stereotype of the Jewish victim. What is missed in this pop-psychological diagnosis is that often the same kind of sensitivity to injustice that made some non-Jews sympathetic to Jews as a minority and to Israel as a project also motivates contemporary sympathy for the Palestinian victims of Israeli policies. In our view, anti-Israelism coincides with anti-Semitism only when the critic's anticolonial passion applies uniquely to Israel or when the criticism becomes entangled with anti-Jewish pathologies and essentialist characterizations of Jews or Israelis in general, or equates Jews everywhere with Zionism and Israeli policies, or forgets that Israeli policies resemble those of settler-colonial states generally (with the difference that Jews, unlike the French in Algeria, had no metropole to which to return and did have an abiding cultural-religious-historical attachment to the Holy Land). Bruckner typifies the ideological mutation by which some Jewish thinkers—and we insist again on this "some"—moved from the antiracist left to the center right of the political spectrum, and to the far right in terms of Israel.[102] The New Right thus came to participate in a discourse that frames the Israeli-Palestinian conflict as about anti-Semitism, thus placing all the weight of European anti-Semitism on the backs of Palestinians, who had no role in the Shoah, while ignoring issues of land, dispossession, ethnic cleansing, and autonomy.

Like the neoconservatives in the United States, the *nouveaux philosophes* are former leftists who now despise everything evoked in the phrase "the 1960s." In the discursive encounter between some pro-American French and Francophobic neocon American commentators, the analogy between anti-Americanism and anti-Semitism has been pervasive, as if Americans had become, in symbolic terms at least, the new Jews. This conflation pervaded American right-wing commentary about France, seen as both anti-Semitic and anti-American in the wake of French resistance to the Iraq War. One has to "look to France," wrote Charles Krauthammer in "Europe and Those People" in the *Washington Post* (April 26, 2002), to find "perennial anti-Semitism." Although it is true that France, like Europe generally, had indeed been the site of a long history of anti-Semitic prejudice and violence, it is also true that France was also the first European country to emancipate the Jews, and many French Jews reached high positions of literary prestige (Marcel Proust), economic influence (the Rothschilds), and political power (Léon Blum, Pierre Mendès France, Simone Weil, Bernard Kouchner). Setting aside the barefaced anti-Semitism of Le Pen and the Holocaust negationism of Faurisson, most of the denunciations of French anti-Semitism centered on anti-Jewish attacks in France (some perpetrated by right-wing anti-Semites and others by resentful Maghrebian youth scapegoating French Jews for events in the Middle East). Violence against French Jews has usually been followed by strong denunciation by the authorities and often by massive popular protests, for example, in the case of the brutal torture and murder of a Ilan Halimi, a French Jew of Maghrebian origin. The anti-French stance of the neoconservatives also had do with the fact that France did not support the Iraq War and was critical of the Israeli occupation, an attitude taken as emblematic of anti-Semitism by American neoconservatives and by some from the French New Right.

The name Alain Finkielkraut has been a constant reference in the French discussions of multiculturalism, "identity politics," and Zionism. A charismatic mediatic presence, praised by Sarkozy as a key public intellectual, Finkielkraut combats left antiracist identity politics in the name of a very French Enlightenment that emancipated the Jews and favored the universal over the particular. Over the years, he has become increasingly hostile to people of color and to antiracist movements. Like his counterparts in the United States, Finkielkraut sets up a series of Jewish-over-black hierarchies, claiming that Jewish immigrants, unlike others, made it "on their own," without the help of special remedial measures. Ignoring the very different circumstances of Jews emigrating from eastern Europe and of immigration from spaces colonized by France, Finkielkraut adopts a resentful discourse reminiscent of that of some "white ethnics" in the United States by proclaiming his *own* Jewish group a "model minority." At the same time, in a French variation of the "Asian Americans as model minority" discourse—a way to subtly marginalize blacks as the "non-model minority"—he contrasts the peaceful hardworking Vietnamese immigrants with the rebellious North Africans. Unlike the others, blacks and Arabs are after "personal gain."[103]

In Finkielkraut's discourse, ethno-national narcissism goes hand in hand with the otherization of Arabs/Muslims and the endorsement of the *mission civilisatrice.* Finkielkraut expresses a Mandarin disgust for the way "they" speak French, "a French whose throat has been cut." Finkielkraut has even complained that contemporary school curricula "no longer teach that the colonial project also sought to educate, to bring culture to the savages."[104] In a postrebellion (November 15, 2005) interview with the Israeli newspaper *Haaretz,* later translated in *Le Monde,* Finkielkraut resorted to an anti-immigrant version of "love it or leave it!": "They have a French ID card, so they are French. And if not, they have a right to leave. . . . No one's keeping them here."[105] Forgetting that banlieue youth were deeply imbued with the civic values of French republicanism but excluded from its social benefits, Finkielkraut saw the 2005 banlieue rebellions as triggered not by police brutality, unemployment, or institutional racism but rather by the Muslim *identity* of young blacks and Arabs. The critics of "identity politics," we see, can also deploy identity as an explanatory principle when it serves a culturalist argument against their adversaries.

Whereas Fanon discerned affinities between the victims of racism and the victims of anti-Semitism, Finkielkraut has increasingly come to equate antiracism both with racism and with anti-Semitism, usually in conjunction with a blinkered adoration of the United States as a supposedly victimized nation-state. Finkielkraut's most dangerous idea, repeated ad nauseam in his books, is the absurd notion that antiracism is the new totalitarianism. Seduced by the elegance of his own paradoxes, Finkielkraut sees opposition to racism as the opposite of what it is and what it appears to be. Finkielkraut also sees the very idea of a "black people" as racist and anti-Semitic. Those who speak of a black nation, or of a "black people," as he put it in an October 16, 2005, interview with Radio de la Communauté Juive (RCJ), "are creating a black Ku Klux Klan. And who is their principal enemy? It's not the white, no, it's the Jew who is both rival and model. It is the model of the exterminated Jewish people that constitutes the image of enslaved and colonized black people. A model which it tries to combat, discredit, to place out of the competition, in order to supplant it, to occupy its throne."[106] Where others might see historical affinities and affective solidarities, Finkielkraut sees a malicious plagiarism or mimetic usurpation of the Jewish narrative. Just as some Zionists accused Palestinian intellectuals of Jewish "narrative envy," Finkielkraut laments that the Shoah now belongs to everyone: "La Shoah pour tous!" Refusing to put the "Shoah and slavery on the same level," Finkielkraut goes so far as to deny that slavery was a crime against humanity. Rather than envision black history and activism in terms of cross-community dialogue, Finkielkraut sees it as encroaching on Jewish terrain in an ethnic turf war.

Parallel to Finkielkraut's denial of the existence of a black people comes his denial of the existence of a Palestinian people. Melding Sartre's "the anti-Semite creates the Jew" with Golda Meir's "there is no Palestinian people," Finkielkraut regards the Palestinians as merely an epiphenomenon of Israel. "Is there anything in Palestinian identity," he asks in his book of dialogues with Peter Sloterdijk, "besides the refusal of Israel?"[107] Finkielkraut has even claimed that blacks detest Israel because it is not a "pays métissé" (miscegenated country). Here Finkielkraut paints himself into a corner by denying something recognized, now even celebrated, by official Israeli discourse—that is, the multiculturality of Israel itself, with its people "gathered from the four corners of the earth," a country whose phenotypical spectrum ranges from Russian blonds to Ethiopian blacks and which features a linguistic polyglossia embracing scores of languages both European and non-European (Arabic, Amharic, Farsi, Kurdish, and Turkish, among others). For millennia, Jews have been miscegenated and hyphenated almost by definition, with new Zelig-like mixings even in "the Jewish state."

And what is the substantive content of Israel "Westernness," and why would "Westernness" necessarily be positive (or negative)? Here we see that the idea of "the West," a complex, contradictory, and partly imaginary concept like "the East," can become a screen onto which very diverse desires are projected. In this sense, Finkielkraut occidentalizes Judaism. But can Judaism, rooted in the geography of the East, be defined simply as a Western religion? Are Aramaic, Hebrew, Arabic, Farsi, Kurdish, and Turkish—all spoken by Jews—"Western" languages? How did Jews become part and parcel of a West seen as synonymous with tolerance, given the West's well-documented history of the oppression of its perennial Jewish other? In demographic terms, is Israel's majority population of Palestinian Arabs and Sephardi/Mizrahi/Arab Jews "Western"?[108] Even Israel's Ashkenazi Jews (the Ostjuden) came largely from the "East" of Europe. Israeli Westernism, then, is less a demographic/cultural fact than an ideological tropology. Arab Jews, that is, those from the Arab/Islamic world who are Jewish in religion and Arab in culture, complicate neat divisions between East and West. What is their relation, in the dominant imaginary, to the neo-Orientalist splitting of "bad Semite" (the Muslim Arab) and "good Semite" (the Westernized Jew)? A certain Ashkenazi-centrism surfaces in Finkielkraut's derisive comments about the contemporary exaltation of hybridity and syncretism: "In fact, I have never heard anyone openly proclaim the hybridization of Jews and Arabs, even though that would be a logical consequence of the grammar of absolute mélange."[109] Finkielkraut's evocation of what he sees as the purely hypothetical possibility of Arab-Jewish hybridization—presented as a "witty" reductio ad absurdum—gives voice to his Arab-versus-Jew Manicheanism. His formulation ignores a millennial history of hybridization between Jews and Arabs, whence the hyphenated existence of Arab-Jews, the long-term product of Judeo-Islamic syncretism. While naturalizing one "Judeo-Christian" hyphen, he declares the other "Judeo-Muslim" hyphen beyond the pale.

Finkielkraut's defense of French universalism is directed against a specific political target: the anti-imperialist and antiracist left as potential allies of the Palestinians, North African immigrants, and the Global South. The enemy is not always named, however; it is sometimes evoked in villainized abstractions such as "differentialism," "postmodernism," "relativism," and "communitarianism," representing tendencies that in Finkielkraut's eyes abandon the very category of "the universal." (Here we see a partial convergence with the views of leftists such as Žižek, but without Žižek's Marxism or his capricious embrace of Pauline Christianity.) Despite the ponderous elegance of Finkielkraut's style and the weight of his cultural baggage, his arguments bear a family resemblance to those of the much cruder David Horowitz in the United States, although a different political spectrum positions Finkielkraut farther to the left than his U.S. peers.

A number of progressive French Jewish intellectuals have lamented the "neoconservatization" of some French Jews. French Jewish intellectuals are extremely diverse in ideological terms, and the debates are much too rich and complex to survey here; but we can provide a rough schema of the issues at stake. An obsessive defense of the state of Israel, in the view of these progressives, has led to a defensive, almost paranoid posture on the part of some French Jews. Jean Daniel, founder of the left-of-center *Nouvel Observateur*, argues in his *La Prison Juive* that French Jews have committed a kind of self-incarceration whereby they live in a ghetto of their own construction.[110] Many draw parallels with neoconservatives in the United States, with the difference that neoconservatism is now filtered not through the American exceptionalism of "the New American Century" but rather through French republicanism.

Jean Birnbaum, in *Les Maoccidents*, writes that the French neoconservative "is not a Trotskyist who joins the elite but rather a Maoist who has lost his people, passing from the cult of the Red East to the defense of the West."[111] Birnbaum points to Gérard Bobillier, André Glucksmann, Guy Lardreau, and Jean-Claude Milner as political figures who moved from the extreme left of *La Cause du Peuple* and Mao's Cultural Revolution to Mosaic Judaism and Zionism. The alliance with French conservatism was sealed when former Maoist André Glucksmann was granted the Legion of Honor by Sarkozy. Ivan Segré develops a similar thesis in *La Réaction Philosémite*, criticizing a number of intellectuals (Jewish and non-Jewish) for whom Islamophobia, Zionism, and a turn to the right go hand in hand.[112] The total embrace of Zionism has led to the veritable excommunication of any Jews who dare to criticize the state of Israel: Edgar Morin (known for a half century of principled leftism) is accused of negationism, that is, Holocaust denial; Eyal Sivan, Israeli filmmaker, is accused of the same thing on the basis of his film (made with Michel Khleifi) *Route 181*; Stéphane Hessel, diplomat son of the Jewish German writer Franz Hessel (prototype for the "Jules" of *Jules and Jim*, model of the flâneur for Walter Benjamin, and a victim of Vichyiste anti-Semitism), is prosecuted by the tribunals of BNVAC (National Bureau for Vigilance against Anti-Semitism) for having supported economic sanctions against Israel.

Guillaume Weill-Raynal, meanwhile, has denounced in a series of books, the ways that Zionist pressure and propaganda have made it virtually impossible to discuss the Israel/Palestine conflict in a rational manner. He speaks of a "climate of McCarthyism" surrounding any criticism of Israel. Emphasizing disinformation, he criticizes public intellectuals such as Alain Finkielkraut and Pierre-André Taguieff, who have created the phantasm of a "new anti-Semitism" in France. The idea of a Judeophobic France and Europe has spread around France, the United States, and Israel. In *Une Haine Imaginaire: Contre-Enquête sur le Nouvel Antisémitisme*, Weill-Raynal argues that figures such as Taguieff, Finkielkraut, and Jacques Tarnero, allied with media elites, have constructed an "imaginary hatred," whereby the struggle against anti-Semitism has been "instrumentalized" as an arm of intimidation and disqualification.[113] Those diasporic "more Israeli than the Israelis" Jews find anti-Semitism everywhere. In *Les Nouveaux Désinformateurs*, Weill-Raynal speaks of "an ensemble of procedures and precise mechanisms through which opinion is manipulated," in this case through the "marketing" of Israel and the demonization of the Arabs, Muslims, and the pro-Palestinian left.[114] The point of this manipulation is to cast in an anti-Semitic light even the most mild and indirect criticism of Israel. Within the "new anti-Semitism," it is argued, Israel is being vilified, demonized, Nazified. For Weill-Raynal, these attitudes have led to the worst forms of racism and Islamophobia, resulting in a double standard: the mildest statements are taken to be anti-Jewish, a comment about Jews and commerce, a remark in the "some of my best friends" genre, if pronounced by a critic of Israel, is taken to be Hitlerian, while the pro-Israeli side can say the most outrageous things. Weill-Raynal cites numerous examples from the website of the UPJF, the Union of the Jewish Managers and Professionals of France: claims that there are "too many mosques in France," that there is no "economic migration" from the Islamic countries but only a fourteen-hundred-year Caliphate conspiracy to take over Europe. The same kind of "verminization" of the other practiced against Jews in anti-Semitic Vichy newsreels is now recycled in the idea that Arabs/Muslims "breed like mice." Instead of the conspiracy of the "Protocols of the Elders of Zion," we have an emplotment of the "Elders of the Caliphate."

The figure of the Jew has been mobilized in remarkably diverse ways by intellectuals in France. For Finkielkraut, the Jew is virtually consubstantial with the West, much as Israel was preimagined by Zionism as a Jewish Switzerland. Jews in this discourse become a metonym for Europe, the threatened part representing the Western whole. For the Tunisian French writer Mehdi Belhaj Kacem, meanwhile, the figure of the Jew is the paradigmatic example of historical victimization. Some people might object that this equation positions Jewish people, à la Sartre, as lacking any history or identity apart from anti-Semitism, but that is not really Kacem's point. The Jew, for Kacem, has become the emblematic figure of alterity through which to think all oppressions. Those who protest racism constantly invoke the Jewish analogy as a kind of "gold standard" for prejudice : "Would you say that about a Jew?" The question itself recognizes that anti-Semitism bears a historical-existential kernel that makes it analogous to other racisms. Historical conditions, Kacem argues, have laid down a "just and salutary taboo against anti-Semitism," since the Shoah represented the only time that the West came close to fulfilling "its morbid fantasy of exterminating the other." At the same time, Kacem warns against the "instrumentalization of anti-anti-Semitism" as part of the constitution of new "second-zone" racisms. For Kacem, Auschwitz concerns all of humanity; it is not an ethical capital to be exploited in a victimological competition. "Never again," for Kacem, cannot mean "never again" only for Jews; it must mean "never again" for everyone.[115]

If for Kacem the Jew forms the very paradigm of irreducible alterity, for the Moroccan American Anouar Majid, in We Are All Moors, it is the Moor who becomes emblematic of exclusion, but a Moor who is very connected to the Jew, a Moor who might actually be a Jew. If for the 1968 supporters of Daniel Cohn-Bendit, "nous sommes tous des Juifs allemands," for Majid, "nous sommes tous des Maures." Writing in the wake of Victor Frankel, Primo Levi, Giorgio Agamben, and Gil Anidjar, Majid sees the Nazi nomination of the most helpless and abject Jews as Muselmänner (Muslims) as historically overdetermined by the intertwined status of the two groups as the expellable others of European purity. Through a process of crisscrossing analogy, Jews and Muslims have sometimes occupied the place of the other, and at times identified with one another. The dichotomous discourse generated by the Israel/Palestine conflict, unfortunately, has too often conspired to drown out the voices of analogy, identification, and affiliation. In *Derrida, Africa, and the Middle East*, Christopher Wise suggests that Jacques Derrida at times envisions the Messianic Jew as the appropriate figure for all non-European people, including African Muslims. Wise points out both the major limitation of Derrida's thinking on these issues—his failure ever to challenge Zionism—and the advantages offered by a deconstruction that could be amplified and opened up to be more inclusive than its articulation in Derrida's own writing.[116]

Like progressive Jewish intellectuals in the United States, many French Jewish intellectuals have taken nuanced positions combining condemnation of racism and anti-Semitism, criticism of Zionism and of Israeli policies, and solidarity with racialized minorities in France. While deploring the anti-Semitism both of Le Pen and of some Muslim/Arab militants, Joëlle Marelli writes that "Jews have shared with non-European peoples and particularly with colonized peoples, the fate of being considered as belonging to a specific 'race' seen as inferior to the white European race."[117] Although anti-Semitism has a specific history, those specificities exist on a continuum with other forms of racism. Figures such as Bruckner, in Marelli's view, isolate anti-Semitism from other racisms, resulting in a hierarchy that delegitimizes other antiracist struggles. In contrast to the rightward turn of the *nouveaux philosophes*, French Jewish intellectuals such as Henri Alleg, Alice Cherki, Maxime Rodinson, Benjamin Stora, Edgar Morin, Eric Hazan, Joëlle Marelli, Ilan Halevi, Emmanuelle Saada, Simone Bitton, Eyal Sivan, and Sophie Bessis do not see Jews as consubstantial with the West but rather as allied on some levels with the West's internal and external others. The identification, to put it in "figural" terms, is with Jews as the slaves in Egypt and not, as with the neoconservative Pentagonites, with the modern "Pharaohs." Since the 1980s, Jewish-black and Jewish-Muslim collaboration has persisted through such groups as Perspectives Judeo-Arabes, the Black Jewish Friendship Committee, and Les Indigènes de la République, which have given concrete political expression to this coalitionary impulse.[118]

Jews have been an integral part of the leftist coalition and indispensible contributors to the left antiracist intellectual corpus. A long tradition of Jewish activism has supported revolutionary causes, and countless radical thinkers have fought for justice and equality, although they have not necessarily spoken *as* Jews. The American group Jews for Racial and Economic Justice (JFREJ), for its part, has offered robust solidarity with people of color, while working on the grassroots level against discrimination, racial profiling, police harassment, and so forth. Such activists, acknowledging both Jewish advantages via whiteness and the Ashkenazi dimension of their Jewishness, also resuscitate the progressive history associated with the New York Yiddishkeit that faded with postwar embourgeoisement and the post-1967 turn to Zionism. As signified by the slogan "Not in Our Name," these leftists refuse the idea that the dominant Zionist organizations speak for all Jews. JFREJ calls attention to the hybrid spaces of Jewishness of those of mixed backgrounds, as well as to the sexual diversity of the Jewish community. The San Francisco Jewish Film Festival, founded by Deborah Kaufman and Janis Plotkin, meanwhile has shown what can be done on the cultural front; the festival began in the 1980s to encourage a filmic dialogue not only between Jews and non-Jews but also between Jews and Muslims/Arabs and between Israelis and Palestinians.

Many Jewish intellectuals are finding new ways to formulate diasporic Jewishness, delinking it from Zionism. In *Destins Marranes*, Daniel Lindenberg argues that the Marranism provoked by the Spanish Inquisition, resulting in the philosophy of heroes of reason such as Baruch Spinoza, furnished the matrix not only for Jewish emancipation but for European emancipation generally.[119] In *Figures d'Israël: L'identité Juive entre Marranisme et Sionisme (1648–1998)*, Lindenberg speaks of the "Marranism" of Menasse Ben Israel, Sabbatai Tsvi, and Spinoza as alternatives to nationalist mythologies.[120] In *The Jew and the Other*, Esther Benbassa and Jean-Christophe Attias explore the long tradition of openness to the other in many of the earliest strands of Jewish thought.[121] Melanie Kaye/Kantrowitz, for her part, speaks of "radical Diasporism" as an answer to Zionism: "Where Zionism says go home, Diasporism says we make home where we are. The word *Zionism* refers uniquely to Jews; Diasporism deliberately includes the variety of diasporic experience. . . . Diasporism is committed to an endless paradoxical dance between cultural integrity and multicultural complexities."[122] This social and cultural activism has challenged hegemonic definitions of Jewishness, opening Jewishness up to gay and lesbian Jews and to Arab Jews, all in collaboration with multicultural, critical race, and whiteness scholars. Kaye/Kantrowitz's book *The Colors of the Jews: Racial Politics and Radical Diasporism* and anthologies such as Tony Kushner and Alisa Solomon's *Wrestling with Zion* and Adam Shatz's *Prophets Outcast: A Century of Dissident Jewish Writing about Zionism and Israel* have charted alternative paths for Jewish leftists.[123]

France's Multicultural Turn

Although we have been critical of the positions of some French intellectuals on issues of race and coloniality, it is worth recalling the achievements of French and Francophone intellectuals, as well as the many features of French social system—universal health care, virtually free education, worker benefits—that meliorate the situation of all citizens, regardless of color. Despite political corruption and Enarchist elitism, a relatively well-lubricated welfare state does make life less anxious and more egalitarian than in the United States. Unlike George W. Bush's "ownership society" that left the largely black victims of Hurricane Katrina "on their own," the French social system offers a much more secure safety net for the entire population. The collective life, as a result, is less Social Darwinist and in some ways more equal, although this rough equality has not yet reached the virtually all-white political class in France (including the Socialist Party). Nonetheless, the 2005 banlieue rebellions demonstrate that the welfare state is simply not sufficient. Although French police do not kill people of color at anything like the rate that applies in the United States or, even more, in Brazil, scores of young men of color have been killed by French police. Playing with the resonances of the word *banlieue*, Mehdi Belhaj Kacem calls the banlieue the "place of the banned of the republic," recalling Agamben's notion of *homo sacer*, the dead man outside of the law yet caught up in the mechanism that bans him, perpetually in relation with the power that bans. Kacem links the word "banned" to "ban-dits," the half-human, half-animal "scum" (*racaille*) denounced by Sarkozy. For the first time since the war in Algeria, Kacem points out, we find "states of exception," ethnically defined curfews, and the "Palestinization" of the banlieue, generating a kind of "Euro-intifada." Kacem expects little from a French Parliament that is male, white, bourgeois, and heterosexual and "has not represented anyone for a long time."[124]

The Bourdieu/Wacquant screed against multiculturalism was published, ironically, just as French public debate was on the cusp of a massive discursive shift. In the first decade of the 21st century, many people on the left moved from a broad rejection of race-conscious critique and postcolonialism toward a partial embrace of both projects. Clarisse Fabre and Éric Fassin, in their book *Liberté, Égalité, Sexualités*, point to an ironic trajectory, in France, from a position that "the culture wars in the United States have absolutely nothing to do with us" to a position that "they have everything to do with us." A 2000 book by Fred Constant, titled simply *Le Multiculturalisme*, offers evidence of this shift. The French model, Constant asserts, privileges unity *against* diversity, while the Anglo-American model constructs unity *through* diversity. But Constant rejects a reified dichotomy between pluralism and assimilationism that would make the models seem more opposed than they really are: "In France, not only has the State always been the agent for the definition and structuration of identities, but also the republican model has accommodated identitary groups and communities much more than is generally admitted."[125] In a generally unacknowledged convergence, "pragmatism tends to triumph over the rigidity of abstract models and the purity of ideal types."[126]

Given the new respectability of diversity arguments, some on the French right are now less preoccupied with *American* multiculturalism than with *French* multiculturalism. The January–March 2005 issue of the conservative French journal *Géopolitique* on the theme of *"le politiquement correct"* offers a striking exemplum of this trend. In an idiom redolent of the U.S. right, the issue associates PC with censorship, feminism, totalitarianism, anti-Christianity, and, paradoxically, both moral relativism and moral rigidity. But now, as French conservative Paul Thibaut asserts in his essay "Exception Française!," these feared trends have reached French shores. In the 1990s, he recalls, French intellectuals had seen multiculturalism and political correctness as typically bizarre products of American idiosyncrasies. Thus, "American Puritanism" could explain "the aggressivity of feminism," the absence of an aristocratic tradition could explain the populist critique of the canon, and so forth.[127]

This falsely reassuring discourse, for Thibaut, implied that "none of this nonsense would ever come to France." Yet it is now France, he laments, that has introduced gender parity in politics, has flirted with quotas and "positive discrimination," and has framed laws against Holocaust denial and racism. While the United States has "survived" political correctness—thanks to what Thibaut sees as the "far-seeing policies of George W. Bush" and the brilliant analyses of Allan Bloom—France has revealed itself to be even more vulnerable to "the multicultural epidemic" than the United States itself. Like Ronald Reagan speaking of a paradisal time "back when we didn't have a race problem," Thibaut conjures up an idyllically unified prelapsarian France subsequently fractured by identity politics. The situation has become so extreme, he complains, that people now feel free to denounce Christianity while regarding Islam as sacrosanct. While political correctness was "marginal in the U.S.," he notes, "it is not at all marginal in France."[128] In a remarkable turnabout, multiculturalism, once derided as an "American thing," has now become, at least in the mind of this French rightist, a thoroughly "French thing."

6   Brazil, the United States, and the Culture Wars

THE POST–WORLD WAR II period in Brazil was a time of relative democratization after the demise in 1945 of Vargas's authoritarian New State first installed in 1937. Internationally, the defeat of Nazism led to the global discrediting of fascist racism. After 1945, the chauvinistic right-wing movement called "Integralism" was on the defensive, and democratic, union, and black movements were on the upswing. At the same time, Brazilian left intellectuals expressed support for the decolonization of much of Asia and Africa, including in the region that most directly concerned Brazil: the Portuguese colonies of Angola, Mozambique, Guinea-Bissau and São Tomé, which ultimately achieved independence relatively late, in the 1970s. Many left Brazilian intellectuals sympathized with Indian independence in 1947, the Cuban Revolution in 1959, and Algerian independence in 1962. At the same time, left intellectuals began to analyze Brazil's status as a geopolitically "neocolonized," "dependent," and "peripheral" country.

The Brazilian left's strongly nationalist political project was also marked by "the rejection of European and U.S. economic liberalism and cultural imperialism . . . and the construction of state-regulated capitalism and an indigenous national culture with a popular foundation."[1] In this conjuncture, Brazilian intellectuals focused on colonial aspects of the Brazilian situation. Dependency theory, to which Brazilian intellectuals were major contributors, was a product of this colonial awareness, which went in hand in hand with a critique of U.S. political and economic hegemony. While left sociologists in the United States attacked the dominant "sociology of celebration," Marxist social scientists such as Florestan Fernandes and Octávio Ianni dismantled its rough equivalent in Brazil, what might be called the Freyrean "*anthropology* of celebration." The challenge for Brazilian intellectuals of all colors was to move away not only from academic dependency on the dominant codes and lexicon of U.S. and European social sciences but also from the conservative Freyrean tradition.

"Racial Democracy" and Black Consciousness

At the same time, postwar Brazil witnessed a growing black consciousness movement. Building on earlier black journals such as *Menelik* and *A Voz Negra* in the 1920s, Afro-Brazilian actor/poet/dramatist/plastic artist/activist Abdias do Nascimento founded *Quilombo*, which published from December 1948 through

July 1950. The journal came in the wake of Nascimento's founding of the Black Experimental Theatre (BET; 1944–1968), an institution whose goal was to train black actors and fight against discrimination. Outraged by a Lima, Peru, performance of O'Neill's *Emperor Jones* starring a white actor in blackface, Nascimento resolved to valorize actors of color. In a summary of the group's goals, he wrote,

> Both on a social and artistic level, the Black Experimental Theatre strives to restore, valorize, and exalt the contribution of Africans to the Brazilian formation, unmasking the ideology of whiteness which created a situation such that, as Sartre puts it, "As soon as he opens his mouth, the negro accuses himself, unless he tries to overthrow the hierarchy represented by the European colonizer and his civilizing process."[2]

The goals of the BET were (1) to integrate blacks into Brazilian society, (2) to criticize the ideology of whitening promoted by the dominant social sciences, (3) to valorize the African contribution to Brazilian culture, and (4) to promote the theater as a privileged medium for these ideas. The BET also organized the National Black Conference (1949) and the First Congress for Black Brazilians (1950). The BET highlighted the theatrical aspects of African and Afro-diasporic culture, exemplified by the continent's religious feasts, its danced liturgies, and the primordial role of performance. No more "folkloric" than Christianity, African religions deployed song and dance to "capture the divine and configure the gods, humanizing them and dialoguing with them in mystic trance."[3]

Quilombo from its first issue took an uncompromising stance on racism: "Only someone characterized by a perfectly obtuse naivete or by cynical bad faith," Nascimento wrote in the inaugural editorial, "could deny the existence of racial prejudice in Brazil."[4] The leading figures in *Quilombo*—Guerreiro Ramos and Nascimento—fused class-conscious Marxism with pan-Africanism. But as Abdias do Nascimento and Elisa Larkin Nascimento note in their preface to the facsimile version of the journal, *Quilombo* was riven by tensions between the more radical black-activist insiders and the largely white guest-essayist outsiders (including Gilberto Freyre), some of whom clung to the nostrums of "racial democracy." In the overture editorial, Nascimento anatomized the recombinant varieties of racism in the Black Atlantic. Racism can take the form, Nascimento wrote, of "depriving indigenous blacks of political and economic power over their own territory, as in South Africa, or of violently depriving them of their rights in a land which they helped build, as in the United States, or of cleverly depriving them of the psychological and mental means for acquiring the consciousness of their real condition despite formal equality, as in Brazil."[5]

Quilombo published some of the most incisive black Brazilian thinkers on race (Guerreiro Ramos, Solano Trindade, and Nascimento himself), alongside progressive (white) French writers such as Roger Bastide and Jean-Paul Sartre, as well as African Americans such as Ralph Bunche and George Schuyler, while also maintaining regular contact with *Présence Africaine*, the house organ of *Négritude* in France. *Quilombo's* range of themes reflected this Afro-cosmopolitanism, with essays on such subjects as the relations between black Brazilian intellectuals and *Présence Africaine* and the achievements of African Americans such as Nobel Prize winner Ralph Bunche, opera singer Marian Anderson, and choreographer Katherine Dunham. *Quilombo* also published translations from French (Sartre's "Orphée Noir" preface) and English (George Schuyler's *Pittsburgh Courier* article comparing racism in the United States and Brazil).[6]

Abdias do Nascimento personifies the pan-Atlantic dimension of Afro-diasporic cosmopolitanism, evidenced by his in-the-flesh dialogue with such figures as Aimé Césaire, Leroi Jones (Amiri Baraka), Bobby Seale, Keorapetse Kgositsile, and C. L. R. James. Exiled by the dictatorship, Nascimento taught at SUNY–Buffalo before returning to Brazil to create the United Black Movement against Racism and Racial Discrimination (in 1978) and the Institute for Afro-Brazilian Research and the Memorial Zumbi (in 1980). For Nascimento, "the construction of a true democracy necessarily passes through multiculturalism and the effective implantation of compensatory measures in order to make possible full citizenship for all the discriminated groups."[7] In 1992, year of the anti-Columbus quincentennial protests, Abdias and Elisa Larkin Nascimento contested the concept of a "Latin" America, which in their eyes "spreads only the domination of a white elite minority over the majority indigenous and African population, . . . resulting in a grotesque distortion of the demographic and sociocultural reality of the region."[8] As Nascimento's career suggests, Afro-Brazilian intellectuals form an essential part of the larger "practice of diaspora" deftly anatomized by Brent Hayes Edwards. Indeed, Nascimento's writings thread together a palimpsestic multiplicity of currents: Third World Marxism, pan-Africanism, problack Brazilian nationalism, West Indian *Négritude*, and the U.S. Civil Rights Movement.

The 1950s UNESCO studies of race constituted another key vector in the postwar shift as it took place in Brazil. UNESCO deputized an international team of scholars: Florestan Fernandes, Roger Bastide, and Oracy Nogueira were assigned to research racial relations in São Paulo; Thales de Azevedo and Charles Wagley were assigned to Bahia; and Darcy Ribeiro was to study the assimilation of indigenous people. In most cases, the research uncovered a subtle web of structural disadvantage and prejudice entrapping blacks and indigenous people. According to Peter Fry's summary of the work of Marcos Chor Maio, the UNESCO studies produced three ideas that subsequently became academic "common sense": (1) that understanding racial relations in Brazil also requires understanding class; (2) that racial taxonomies in Brazil are extremely complex; and (3) that, despite "racial democracy," the strong correlation between poverty and color reflects a prejudice against those who are "darker."[9]

Building on the pan-Africanist work of Nascimento and *Quilombo*, and on the Marxist-inflected work of the UNESCO-sponsored scholars, a black consciousness movement gained strength in the postwar period. Although the movement was partially derailed by the hostility of the dictatorship (1964–1984) to any manifestations of "subversive" Afro-Brazilian activism, the 1970s were nonetheless a time of increasing militancy. Inspired by a wide array of movements, from the U.S. Civil Rights and Black Power movements to the independence movements in the Portuguese colonies in Africa and to the "Third Worldism" and "tricontinentalism" sweeping much of the world, Brazilian black activists created innumerable cultural organizations, culminating in 1978 in the founding of the MNU (Unified Negro Movement), itself a coalition of diverse groups such as São Paulo's CECAN (Center for Black Art and Culture), Rio de Janeiro's Institute for Research on Black Culture, and various Bahian Afro-cultural groups.[10]

In Bahia, the *Afro-blocos* Ilê Aiyê (founded in 1974) and Olodum (founded in 1979) organized blacks culturally and politically.[11] Also in the 1970s, a wave of black pride began to spread through Rio and other cities. Sambista Candeia founded the Quilombo Samba School in 1975. Urban youth, especially in Rio, adopted African American symbols of black pride, such as coded handshakes and soul music, in a style dubbed *bleque pau* (a Portuguese pronunciation of "black power"). Shaping black Brazilian identity, soul and reggae inspired "black Rio" in Rio, "black samba" in São Paulo, and "black mineiro" in Minas Gerais. The ever more conservative Gilberto Freyre, who supported Portuguese colonial rule in Africa, denounced such movements as North American exports that would replace "happy and fraternal" sambas with a melancholy revolt.[12]

Many of these issues came up on the occasion of the one hundredth anniversary of the abolition of slavery in 1988. For the first time, "the manifold forms of racial inequality against Afro-Brazilians became a principal theme in national debate."[13] A persistent leitmotif was the idea that "slavery has not really ended," with Rio's samba pageant protesting the "farce of abolition."[14] The champion samba school Vila Isabel, with its "Kizombo: Feast of the Race," lauded Zumbi as the force behind abolition: "Zumbi's the one / The strong shout of Palmares / Crossing land, and air and sea / Shaping abolition." For many Brazilians, the *quilombos* symbolized the power of black resistance. May 13, the traditional commemoration date for abolition as granted by Princess Isabel, was replaced by November 20, celebrating the memory of Zumbi, as the "National Day of Black Consciousness."

As suggested earlier, the seismic shift took a different form in Brazil than in France and the United States. Since Brazil was not an imperialist power, the struggle was not against Brazilian imperialism but against U.S. imperialism and the U.S.-supported dictatorship that lasted from 1964 to 1984. Although black activism existed, it did not take the form of massive marches to end segregation. Nonetheless, throughout this period, Brazilian scholars were producing progressive work on Portuguese colonialism, on U.S. imperialism, on Brazilian racism, and on Afro-Brazilian and indigenous culture. This work is much too vast to survey here, but a small sampling only of the work on race from the 1980s would include such texts as Nascimento's *Quilombismo* in 1980; Lana Lage da Gama Lima's *Black Rebellion and Abolitionism* in 1981; Lelia Gonzalez and Carlos Hasenbalg's *The Place of Blacks* in 1982; Clovis Moura's *Brazil: The Roots of Black Protest* and Solange Martins Couceiro de Lima's *Blacks on Television in São Paulo*, both in 1983; Zila Bernd's *The Question of Negritude* and Décio Freitas's *Palmares: The War of the Slaves*, both in 1984; Oracy Nogueira's *Neither Black nor White* in 1985; João José Reis's *Slave Rebellions in Brazil* in 1986; Clovis Moura's *Quilombos, Resistance to Slavery* in 1987; João José Reis's edited volume *Slavery and the Invention of Freedom* and Clovis Moura's *Sociology of the Black Brazilian* in 1988; Manoel de Almeida Cruz's *Alternatives for Combating Racism* and Lilia Schwarcz's *Portrait in Black and White: Slaves and Citizens in São Paulo in the 19th Century*, both in 1989.

The Anatomy of Skepticism

It was against this longer backdrop of redemocratization, U.S. hegemony, the emergence of the black movement, and substantial scholarship on race that we find a partial backlash against multicultural identity politics in the 1990s. While many Brazilian intellectuals had pursued cognate race/colonial research (largely under others rubrics), some media journalists, rather than see the affinities linking such work to similar work in Brazil, rejected multiculturalism in terms largely borrowed from the U.S. right. Some in the Brazilian media depicted multiculturalism as flawed in its own terms and irrelevant, even dangerous, for Brazil. The hostility came especially from the dominant media and publishing establishments, which sometimes bought into, and literally translated, the U.S. conservative portrayal of multiculturalism as separatist, puritanical, and "politically correct." Major newspapers and periodicals such as *Folha de São Paulo*, *Veja*, and *Isto É* were more likely to feature translations of essays by critics such as Harold Bloom, Camille Paglia, and Tom Wolfe rather than the work of the multicultural writers themselves.

Contemporaneous with similar articles in France, a February 1, 1995, article in the Brazilian weekly news magazine *Isto É* (roughly the Brazilian *Newsweek*), titled "The World Upside Down," illustrates the terms and drift of the rejection. The article's subheading reads, "In the U.S., politically correct schools, in the name of minorities, are creating new prejudices." Signed by former leftist Osmar Freitas, Jr., the article mocks the notion that Columbus did not "discover" America and that ancient Greece was not the birthplace of universal culture, statements that the author, without engaging the actual scholarship, regards as outrageous on their face. Conflating Afrocentrism with multiculturalism—when in fact the two projects are quite distinct and at times mutually wary—Freitas defines multiculturalism, rather tendentiously, "as a pompous name for politically correct behavior when applied to teaching and learning, especially University teaching and learning." According to Freitas, minorities in the United States were calling for a "new segregationism." The article cites Arthur Schlesinger's usual equation of multiculturalism with ethnic separatism, without citing a single writer who actually calls for separatism. But by the mid-1990s, the charges of "ethnic separation" and "Balkanization" had been repeated so often that they acquired, despite the lack of evidence, a discursive density that contaminated left and right discussions of the subject.

Two entries in *The Critical Dictionary of Cultural Politics*, edited by Teixeira Coelho, meanwhile, reflect almost opposite takes on multiculturalism.[15] The first, by Solange Martins Couceiro de Lima, sees multiculturalism in the United States as the legitimate heir of the 1960s radical and Civil Rights movements. For Lima, multiculturalism critiques melting-pot assimilationism, which the author compares to Brazilian-style "racial democracy," as an ideology that sees minorities as progressing toward a single white-dominant national identity. For Lima, it is the strength of the assimilationist racial democracy ideology that makes multiculturalism seem alien in Brazil. The second entry, by Teixeira Coelho himself, in contrast, basically translates into Portuguese the U.S. conservative view of multiculturalism as "discriminatory," "politically correct," and even "totalitarian." The "obsession" with race makes the movement itself racist and emblematic, for Coelho, of a "culture of victimization." As occurred with some French critics, the argument gets linked to anxious projections about Anglo-feminism. Like Todorov in France, Coelho symptomatically slides from "multiculturalism" to "sexual harassment," recycling the right's anecdotal claims about "tragic" situations in which perfectly innocent (male) professors lose their jobs due to unfair accusations by hysterical females. All of Coelho's terms of abuse, hurled at the "demagogues of diversity," are drawn from the U.S. far-right lexicon. The bibliography features no actual multiculturalists at all but only two of the project's critics: Richard Bernstein's *Dictatorship of Virtue* (1995) and Harold Bloom's *The Western Canon* (1995).

In Brazil, multiculturalism was sometimes portrayed as an unwelcome U.S. export, at times for the same reasons as for the French but usually for reasons specific to Brazilian cultural politics. In Brazil, unlike France, the topic of race was not taboo. The concept of a multicultural society—encapsulated in the oft-repeated story of Brazil as a mélange of three races—had long been the normative view. The question was not whether Brazil was de facto multicultural but rather what kind of race-related project was appropriate. Was multiculturalism pertinent or just one more "out-of-place idea"? For some people, it was the North American ideological correlative to the "racial democracy" that emerged in Brazil in the 1930s. For Italo Moriconi, "multiculturalism has been the state ideology since Vargas, but the problem is the gap between the official discourse and the quotidian reality of racist violence."[16] Yet "racial democracy" is not an exact equivalent to multiculturalism. While "racial democracy" was a top-down concept forged by the Brazilian state in alliance with establishment intellectuals, multiculturalism was never an official ideology embraced by the U.S. political establishment. The equivalent to "racial democracy," in this sense, would be the mythology of the American "melting pot" or of "equal opportunity."

Some Brazilian scholars have examined the crisscrossing movement of ideas about multicultural identity politics between France, the United States, and Brazil. In *Atlas Literaturas* (1998), Leyla Perrone-Moisés, whose indispensable work on Franco-Brazilian cultural relations we have already cited, offers the high-literary version of the antimulticultural backlash. Based on Fulbright-supported research undertaken at Yale, her book denounces identity politics in an idiom largely drawn from the U.S. conservative lexicon. The "politically correct" tendency to analyze texts in terms of "race, gender, and class," she laments, threatens the study of literature as an autonomous discipline. In tones reminiscent of Yale's own Harold Bloom, she regrets that "Western ideology" has been disqualified as "sexist, imperialist, and bourgeois." The PC squads, she reports, have thrown Twain and Melville out of the curriculum, Twain because of his writings on slavery and Melville because he was "anti-ecological."[17] She cites no one who actually censors Twain or Melville, and in fact both writers are often seen as multicultural heroes, Twain (by Susan Fishkin, for example) for his questioning of slavery in *Huckleberry Finn* and for his opposition to U.S. imperialism (for example, in the Philippines) and Melville (by Eric Sundquist) for his multiracial *Pequod* and his incisive chronicling of slave revolts in "Benito Cereno."[18]

Perrone-Moisés's Franco-diffusionist approach figures good ideas as emanating from Europe and then degenerating during their transatlantic passage. Along the classical Latin/Anglo divide, she sees good French ideas as "out of place" in the United States, but not in Brazil. She credits the French poststructuralists with generating the "good ideas" that transformed the U.S. academy, while she elides (1) the contribution of Third World Francophone thinkers such as Césaire and Fanon to "French" poststructuralism itself; (2) the role of Native American, African American, Latino, and progressive white intellectuals in transforming the U.S. academy; and (3) the role of North American scholars in reenvisioning and indigenizing French theory itself. Misidentifying the Parsi-Indian-English now

U.S.-based Homi Bhabha as "a Turk" and the "founder" of postcolonial studies, a status usually attributed to Said, Perrone-Moisés declares postcolonial theory symptomatic of a puritanical and Manichean American culture.[19] In fact, of course, the postcolonial intellectuals in question are highly cosmopolitan figures, whose work reveals a deep abhorrence for Manichean notions and an affection for a fluid tropology of "slippage," "hybridity," and the "in-between." By transforming three diasporic postcolonial intellectuals, of Palestinian and Indian background, into stereotypical Anglo-Saxon puritans, merely on the basis of their U.S. *location*, Perrone-Moisés denies the transnational complexity of the circuitries of ideas. (We return to Perrone-Moisés in chapter 9.)

Given the fundamental asymmetries of knowledge and power shaped by neocolonial hegemony, some Brazilians understandably resisted multiculturalism precisely because it was seen as "American." At a time when IMF and World Bank–style globalization, for many Brazilians synonymous with "Americanization," was exacerbating inequality both within and between nations, resentment inevitably spilled over against anything associated with the United States. Although both Brazilian and French responses to multicultural identity politics can be seen as defensive of the national terrain, the context and trajectories were quite distinct. Two major differences distinguish the Brazilian reaction from the French. First, while many French intellectuals in the 1990s saw multiculturalism as a dangerous antirepublican import, Brazilian intellectuals did not speak in the name of the Brazilian republic. They were more likely to see multiculturalism as a constitutive feature of Brazil, as something Brazil already had and did not need North Americans to name for them. If for the French, the question was "How can we import something so alien and contrary to the values of the republic?" for Brazilians the question was "Why import something we already have?" In the academy, as Italo Moriconi points out, the critique of multiculturalism in Brazil "usually comes wrapped as resistance to 'American imperialism.' The idea is that if anyone is going to offer lessons to Brazilians, it will certainly not be Americans."[20]

Despite some overlap with French attitudes, the Brazilian anxieties had their own sources. For Marxists, it was the *culture* in "multiculturalism" that was disconcerting, signaling for them a "superstructural" distraction from more consequential "infrastructural" matters of class and political economy. The anti-imperialist left worried about new modes of hegemony on the part of the Colossus to the North, now transmitted through its academic/artistic projects. For many Brazilians, endorsing multiculturalism (perceived as American) would mean throwing the baby of Brazilian cordiality out with the bathwater of racism. Brazil, they feared, would become a more harsh, rigid, judgmental, and puritanical place, rather than the fluid, flexible, gregarious, sensual, and caressing place that Brazilians (and others) know and love.

The occasional Brazilian left rejection of multiculturalism and cognate projects carried with it a number of ironies, however. First, in opposing race/multicultural projects, some on the Brazilian left took up arguments associated in the United States with the far right. Second, while the U.S. right wing saw such projects as a challenge to Anglo-hegemony, some Brazilian (like French) intellectuals saw them as themselves Anglo, as in that oxymoronic phrase "Anglo-Saxon multiculturalism." (If a movement is essentially Anglo-Saxon, it is by definition *not* multicultural.) Third, left Brazilians were rejecting a project that constituted a "Latinization" or "Brazilianization" of North American self-conceptualization, in that it opted out of the binary "race relations" model to highlight a rainbow spectrum of ethnicities as constitutive of the nation. What could be more Brazilian in style than to conceive of the United States as a fundamentally mixed nation? Caetano Veloso's description of the United States as "inevitably mestizo," in this sense, corresponds to Albert Murray's description (in his 1970 book *The Omni-Americans*) of the American culture as "incontestably mulatto."[21] Fourth, such intellectuals were rejecting a project that aimed to open up space in the American media and in schools for Latin American curricula, faculty, and scholarship, part of an attempt to reverse the asymmetrical flows of cultural knowledge between North and South.

The Uses and Abuses of Comparison

The intertext of these debates partly lies in the vast cross-national corpus of comparative writing that focuses on Brazil and the United States. The sheer volume of this corpus, which swells with every passing year, is remarkable. These comparisons are asymmetrical and power laden, of course, since Brazilians have historically made the comparisons from a position of relative geopolitical weakness, while Americans have made them from a privileged position of taken-for-granted power. Brazil-U.S. comparisons take place against the larger ideological frame of the widely disseminated Hegelian and Weberian comparisons of South America and North America. In *The Philosophy of History*, Hegel, for example, contrasted a prosperous, orderly, and unified Protestant North America with a militarized, disorderly, and disunited Catholic South America.[22]

In the case of Brazilian thinkers—from Gilberto Freyre and Sérgio Buarque de Holanda to Vianna Moog and Roberto DaMatta—contrasts between Brazil and the United States have sometimes come close to the very heart of debates about *Brazilian* identity, at times forming an integral part of a specular process of national self-definition. Sociologist Jessé Souza discerns a stubborn pride behind the obsessive comparisons: "Explicit or implicit comparison with the United States is the central thread in practically all of the 20th-century interpretations of

Brazilian singularity—because we perceive that only the United States is as great and influential as we are in the Americas."[23] For many Brazilian intellectuals (and for many American Brazilianists), then, the inevitable historical comparison has not been with the mother country Portugal or with a European country such as France or even with a Spanish-speaking neighbor such as Argentina but rather with the United States. Because of this predominance, some have called either for South-South comparisons or have questioned the Eurocentric premises of the comparative paradigm itself.[24]

Although cross-cultural comparisons are often narcissistic, in the case of Brazil they have sometimes entailed ambivalence and even self-rejection, whether about Brazil's supposedly derivative culture or about its inadequate political institutions. Indeed, playwright Nelson Rodrigues famously called Brazilians "upside-down Narcissists" who spit on their own mirror image. In the wake of the Hegelian (and later Weberian) dichotomies of dynamic North and indolent South, many Brazilian intellectuals searched for culturalist explanations for Brazil's putative "failure," in comparison, usually, with the United States or Europe. In an animal fable of inferiority, Brazilian historian João Capistrano de Abreu claimed that Brazil's most appropriate national symbol would be the sad-eyed and lazy jaburu bird.[25] In contrast to later stereotypes of Brazil as the site of paradisal jouissance, Paulo Prado, in *Retrato do Brasil* (1928), portrayed Brazil as a melancholy mélange of "three sad races." Contrasting what he saw as Brazil's libidinous languor with the United States' hygienic dynamism, Prado blamed Portuguese colonialism for creating an ethos in which manual labor was scorned, culture was ornamental and derivative, and *malandragem* (roughly, quick-witted street-smart improvisations) was the cultural norm. Portugal, in this discourse, became a kind of bad father in a postcolonial family romance, with some Brazilians suggesting, only partly in jest, that Brazilians would have been better off with a more worthy European progenitor such as Holland.

Eduardo Freire answered Prado in a book whose title says it all: *The Brazilian Is Not Sad* (published in 1931). Although Brazil does not exercise power in the larger world, Freire argued, its culture is vibrant, capacious, and harmonious. In the same period, Brazilian modernists such as Mário de Andrade and Oswald de Andrade also highlighted Brazil's positive cultural features. And decades later, José Guilherme Merquior recast what had been seen as tropical deficiencies into cultural strengths by arguing that Brazilian "carnivalism" inoculated the country from the deadening rationalization, puritanism, and disenchantment typical of the relentlessly productivist Occident.[26]

Over the span of history, comparisons have served diverse, even contradictory, purposes, sometimes working to denigrate Brazil as lawless, corrupt, and inefficient and sometimes to exalt it as tolerant, sensuous, and pacific. Even the phrase "racial democracy" was comparative in origin, intended as a contrast with the non-racially-democratic United States. It is not always easy, in these comparative discourses, to separate actual cultural differences from clichés about a presumably unified national character. What matters is the very centrality of cross-national comparison and how it has impacted the reception of the race/colonial debates. Within the fraught dialectics of attraction/repulsion, even strong statements of difference—"We are not at all like you!"—are nonetheless addressed to a privileged interlocutor, whether defined as imperial nemesis or as ideal ego. While comparison can illuminate national self-understanding by drawing distinctions, it can also obscure transnational relationalities between those such as indigenous or Afro-diasporic peoples who have historically had a more ambivalent relation to the nation-states of the Americas and who are therefore less invested in certain nationalist exceptionalisms.

Despite the limitations of a methodology that too often lapses into overdrawn national contrasts, comparative race studies have nonetheless made a signal contribution to the understanding of variant modalities of slavery and discrepant conceptualizations of race.[27] These studies have highlighted many commonalities between Brazil and the United States. In both, the historical inertia of colonialism and slavery, and an abolition negotiated on white ruling-class terms, shaped racialized hierarchies even under a free-labor regime. In both, the ruling elite favored European immigrants over blacks, a fact perhaps more obvious in Brazil only because European immigrants arrived en masse in the immediate aftermath of emancipation, rather than decades later, as in the United States. And in both countries, self-exculpatory myths "covered" the reality of racialized oppression: in the United States, myths of the "American dream" and "equal opportunity"; in Brazil, the myth of "social harmony" and "racial democracy." Comparatists have also underlined points of contrast: (1) racism in Brazil has been less virulent, explicit, and phobic than in the United States; (2) Brazilian history has not been marked by lynchings, race riots, and so forth; (3) Brazil has generally rejected legal segregation, although an informal segregation, premised on blacks' "knowing their place," did sometimes exist; (4) the Brazilian situation encouraged a paternalistic dependency on white elites (*padrinhos*), in contrast to the North American racial segregation that ironically favored the development of parallel institutions—black colleges, the black church, an independent black press, sports organizations.

At the same time, not all the historical comparisons work to Brazil's advantage. Brazilian slavery began earlier than U.S. slavery and lasted longer; it was national rather than regional; and Brazilian society has been structured in depth by the relations between the Big House and the Slave Quarters, in ways that still leave traces in the everyday social dynamics of Brazilian life. In a kind of shifting of figure and ground, just as a barely concealed class subtext lurks behind racialized injustice in the United States, so a barely concealed racial subtext lurks behind the everyday social inequities of Brazilian life. The cliché that blacks are discriminated against only because they are poor, meanwhile, forgets that the nonblack poor do not carry the stigma generated by racialized slavery and white-supremacist ideology and that the perception of blackness as an index of poverty (and thus powerlessness) is itself an oppressive burden in a stratified society. In this sense, racism can be seen both as a kind of salt rubbed into the wounds of class and as a wound in itself.

Another leitmotif in comparative discussions is the contrast between the Brazilian racial spectrum and the U.S. bicolor system based on the "one-drop rule." This strange "rule," which rarely enunciates itself *as* a rule, has played a deeply pernicious role in American life. Originally, it gave expression to "the virulent racist sentiment that pervaded white society in the early twentieth century, [which] reinforced the low regard in which European Americans held African Americans and the stigma they attached to African ancestry."[28] Rendered official only at the end of the 19th century, the one-drop rule codified into law what had become—at least for whites—the racial common sense. The idea that all Americans fall on one side or the other of an imaginary racial line leads to situations of labyrinthine incoherence, which is why a tremendous effort was required to make it stick. There was nothing natural or inevitable about its (always partial) triumph.

Indeed, the United States, like Brazil, began as somewhat miscegenated, although hardly to the same degree. During the 17th century, the distinction between white indentured servants and black slaves, for example, was often blurred. The two groups shared similar working conditions and sometimes jointly resisted bondage by escaping together. Even in the 18th century, the shortage of women in both communities led to indentured or free whites marrying African slaves, sometimes the only women they knew, and white female servants accepting offers of marriage from black men, both slave and free.[29] In the U.S. "Lower South," also known as "Latin North America," the situation was closer to the Brazilian model, including in terms of liaisons between white men and native women. The earliest laws did not forbid interracial unions, and when such laws were enacted, it was precisely because interracial unions were so common.[30]

In the long term, the United States became much more miscegenated than is commonly recognized. The country's largest minority, Latinos, are mixed almost by definition. The majority of Native Americans intermarry with other ethnic groups. DNA testing has shown that one-third of African Americans have partial white ancestry. Black public intellectual Henry Louis Gates, Jr., in his research discovered that more than 50 percent of his genetic material is European.[31] But such statistics are not something about which to be either "proud" or "ashamed."

In the case of African Americans, the miscegenation could often be traced back to a rape by an empowered white. Although racial mixedness clearly existed in both countries, however, it was more harshly stigmatized, both legally and culturally, in the United States. The difference, then, did not have to do with the sheer fact of mixing but rather with (1) its extent and (2) its ideological drift and judicial definition. The African Americans who "passed over" to the white side, for example, did so by denying their mixedness. At the same time, Brazilian-style mixing began earlier, on a more massive scale, with the intermarriage of Portuguese and indigenous people. In Brazil, the mixing accrued to the nation itself, while in the United States, the mixing was separated off, officially quarantined, at least until the advent of the multiracial movements of the last decades. What we find, then, is two complementary forms of denial: a segregationist U.S.-American model that downplays interracial mixing and intimacy and an assimilationist Brazilian model that downplays the hierarchies that structure intimacy.

An analysis of the question of political and economic power results in a paradox. In the United States, which is clearly more segregated in terms of the one-drop rule and informally segregated residential neighborhoods, blacks have nonetheless exercised considerable power as political figures, business executives, military leaders, artists, and entertainers. While not racially segregated in the U.S. or South African manner, Brazil, meanwhile, has its own subtle forms of social segregation, in the perverse urban dialectics of the ghettoized and the gated and in the self-segregation of the rich, who retreat behind "walled islands of wealth that become girdled by new favela settlements."[32] Many blacks feel imprisoned in what samba composer/historian Nei Lopes calls "invisible bantustans," from which they can escape only thanks to a very special kind of passport: that by which one abandons one's black identity.[33] The social separation takes place not only within the urban geography of the divided city but also within the shared space of apartment buildings, with their two entrances, two elevators, and two independent circulation systems, where "the organizing principle is controlled separation to ensure minimal informal contact between the servant and master classes."[34] Brazil is also segregated in terms of power, in the sense that the higher echelons of the military, the diplomatic corps, the legislature, the judiciary, corporate boardrooms, and the university are all very white. Even in Salvador, Bahia, where blacks and people of mixed race compose the overwhelming majority, and where Afro-Brazilian popular culture is vibrant, the political and media elite remains white dominated. On the other hand, the ruling PT party has nourished black advances and a cautious Affirmative Action, and the 2010 presidential election featured, with remarkably little fanfare in the media, the first self-declared black woman presidential candidate, the Green Party's Marina Silva, who won 19 percent of the vote.

Another historical difference is that in Brazil, those who oppress people of color, going back to "mulatto slave-catchers," might also be themselves people of color. Some major historical instances of state repression—of the maroon republic of Palmares in the 17th century, of the millenarian rebellion in Canudos in the 19th century, and of the Carandiru prisoners in the 20th century—have not simply pitted black against white; rather, people of color have fought on both sides, even if an overarching chromatic hierarchy still structures the whole. This difference becomes evident when one compares two 1990s secret video recordings of police brutality: the Rodney King beating in the United States and the recorded beatings in two Brazilian favelas (Diadema in São Paulo and City of God in Rio). While most of the police officers beating Rodney King were white, in Brazil both the police and their victims were mixed, yet in both cases race was a factor in the brutality. In Brazil, some of the police officers were black or of mixed race, but the leader-killer (nicknamed "Rambo") was white. The victims, meanwhile, were largely black or mestizo, defining the confrontation as, if not directly racial, at least highly racialized. Yet the beatings in both instances were entirely gratuitous, and the Brazilian case became a cold-blooded murder of a completely innocent man. The body language of the favela residents conveys a sense of resignation, as if such abuse were a taken-for-granted quotidian routine.

The same social problems that plague the United States—police brutality, a cruel prison system, class inequality, and so forth—also plague Brazil. The Brazilian police murder literally thousands of "marginals" every year, most black or of mixed race. A *Globo* editorial on April 4, 2006, pointed out that the police (municipal and federal) in Rio de Janeiro alone "kill more people than are killed by the police in all of the United States." A December 2009 Human Rights Watch Report titled "Lethal Force" revealed that police in Rio de Janeiro and São Paulo killed more than eleven thousand people between 2003 and 2009, often disguising summary execution as "resistance to arrest."[35] Thus, we find a commonality of racialized domination, expressed in distinct ways, in which the coefficient of class versus race and gender might vary but each modality has minor echoes in the other country.

At the same time, it would be inaccurate to see Brazil as a mirror image of the United States, where exactly the same racism exists but in veiled form. Many comparatists emphasize the relatively less stressful manner of living race in Brazil, evoked in such affect-laden words as "cordiality" and "gregariousness." The cold statistics of racial advantage, in this sense, do not convey imponderables such as affection, solidarity, and emotional comfort zones. Atmospherics lubricate social relations and shape the daily texture of existence, even if they are not amenable to statistical proof. The fact of greater miscegenation also makes black Brazilians less easily otherizable, more an assumed part of the social totality. As long as one speaks of epidermic appearances ("We are all mixed") or of atmospherics, the

Brazilian situation seems much more "livable" than the American. It is when one poses the crucial question of economic, political, and cultural power that the situation seems less than ideal.[36]

Desire, Denial, and Linked Analogies

Over the past half century, the myth of racial democracy has severely frayed. Recently, Brazilian scholars have highlighted the ways that various ethnic groups in Brazil have, as Antonio Guimarães puts it, "carefully distanced themselves from the racial democracy model ... [whereby] middle-class whites looked for a second nationality in Europe, the United States, or created a regional xenophobia in the Europeanized south; the black in search of roots constructed an imaginary Africa, or saw the United States as an Afro-American mecca, while the misnamed 'Indians' identified with their group of origin or with Indians in general."[37] The rearticulation of the black movement, the emergence of the feminist and gay movements, the growth of non-Catholic religions, the flourishing of indigenous movements, and the celebration of immigrant hybridity have all pointed to the centrifugal fracturing of cohesive myths of a unified Brazil.

A recent polemical book, Antonio Risério's *The Brazilian Utopia and the Black Movements*, is framed, revealingly, by the author's discomfort with the black movement in Brazil. Writing from a position of a man besieged by "politically correct" critics, Risério argues,

> Today we have a serious problem here in Brazil. The discussion and the debate are constantly becoming more suspect and cursed. There is no room for criticism, only for adhesion or denunciation. Almost all of the people who speak of dialogue do not really believe in it. If I criticize feminists, I'm macho. If I don't like some form of popular culture, I'm elitist. ... If I have objections to the black movement, I'm a racist. And so forth.[38]

The discourses of "minorities," Risério continues,

> have been incorporated literally. And thus they stayed, undiscussed and unquestioned. A religious attitude emerged. Women, gays, Indians, blacks, lesbians, etc. were all in the right. They were the humiliated and offended ones, the victims of oppression and prejudice, the ones who spoke of their pain and resentment, their anxieties, projects, and demands. The role of the others, the "majority," was to listen to them and support their struggles. As if the majority was guilty and were there to expiate a racist and macho past ... since only women could speak for women in a macho world, since only blacks knew what it meant to be black in a racist society, since only minority people could speak for minorities, etc.[39]

A brilliant advocate and analyst of Afro-Brazilian culture and coauthor (with Gilberto Gil) of a major book on slavery and negotiation, Risério shares with some Brazilian, French, and American critics of identity politics a feeling of displacement and a *ressentiment* about the putative impugning and silencing of white men. Black Brazilian activists, for Risério, have overinvested in the idea that the camouflaged form of Brazilian racism is worse than overt U.S. racism because it is harder to fight. Those whom Risério derisively calls the "neo-negros" have adopted the binary black/white U.S. model in a miscegenated Brazil where that model simply does not fit. The identification that some black Brazilians feel with blacks in the United States irritates Risério, which is hardly surprising since diasporic minority movements challenge nationalist framings. Risério dismisses these identifications, typical of the Black Atlantic, as merely a byproduct of the dissemination of the U.S. racial model, now spread by American foundations and by Brazilian black elites influenced by the American academy. His position is close to that adopted by Bourdieu/Wacquant in their critique of Hanchard's *Orpheus and Power*—discussed in chapter 9—even though Risério is infinitely more knowledgeable about the debates and about Afro-Brazilian culture than are Bourdieu/Wacquant.

Risério's text betrays an acute anxiety about the status of individuals who are socially positioned as white, who identify with Afro-Brazilian culture and with black people, yet who feel a certain malaise when a black movement names the power structure *as* white. Terms such as "whites" and "white power structure," by naming the color of power, position even sympathetic and knowledgeable whites ambivalently vis-à-vis black subjects. Both in the United States and Brazil, the black movements dared to go beyond the question of prejudice to pose the question of racially coded power. As a consequence, whites became "raced," no longer universal floating human beings but rather a group with a precise relation to a power structure. For a North American reader, Risério's lament has a familiar ring. It recalls the complaints of liberal-leftist veterans of the Civil Rights struggles who felt eclipsed by the rise of the Black Power movement and later by identity movements. If Risério at times sounds like the disenchanted white American leftist, at other times, his resentment makes him sound like an American right-winger, as when he tries to discredit the reparations movement by reminding his readers, as Dinesh D'Souza might, that some freed slaves acquired slaves themselves, a point that, while not completely false, is marshaled tendentiously.

If Risério loves Afro-diasporic culture, he loves it mainly in its Afro-Bahian "Nago" form. Thus, "African" for Risério means *acarajé*, capoeira, and the orixas. If we follow out the logic of this approach, the vast majority of Africans themselves, and the thousands of contemporary Africans who have emigrated to the United States, would not qualify as truly "African." In line with his regionalist, nationalist, and Yoruba-centric delineations, Risério disparages African Americans as alienated and de-Africanized.[40] Blind to their endless activism, Risério contrasts black American "passivity" with the rebelliousness of black Brazilian maroons. And here we come to his most provocative claim: "For the simple, strong, and profound reason that Negro-African cultures came to impregnate and nurture, progressively and in a seductive way, the whites of Brazil, thus coming to constitute their codes and symbolic repertoires . . . to the point that we feel free to say that Brazilian whites are, for the most part, more 'black,' or more precisely, more 'African' than black Americans."[41] Risério here gathers into himself the various credit lines of "cultural capital" (Bourdieu) and, we would add, "racial capital."[42] On the one hand, he enjoys the cultural/racial capital of whiteness—he grants that he has never suffered racial ostracism "in his skin"—while also claiming the cultural capital associated with intimate knowledge of African cultural codes. That insider knowledge, in his view, makes him "more African" than African Americans, whom he assumes to be ignorant of the orixas and mired in soul-deadening Protestant pietism.

Risério's claim is premised on a separation between culture and history. Without making primordial claims about any "essential black subject" (Stuart Hall), certain incommensurabilities of experience, rooted not in blood but in the memory of slavery and the experience of discrimination, inevitably create a certain gap in perspectives and sensibilities. It is one thing for those who are socially identified as white to appreciate the cultural practices of Afro-diasporic people, and even to live them virtually as their own, and to identify with the victims of slavery and discrimination; it is quite another to be the literal heirs of that history and to have been discriminated in one's flesh due to one's visible, epidermal difference. Even a deep knowledge of African culture does not completely fill that gap.

Although Risério argues for a kind of Brazilian exceptionalism, what has struck us repeatedly while researching this book is how a claim about one country can easily be extended to another country, even when the authors claim to be stressing some national uniqueness. Risério, for example, offers extremely evocative descriptions of Brazilian cultural diversity, as in the following passage:

> Brazil is an anthropological mosaic. A world made of many worlds, each with its own physiognomy, its distinctive traces. That is what allows us to speak of a Brazilian reality, but also of Brazilian realities, in the singular and in the plural. Because what we constructed, in our segment of the planet, was a country of foci, or cultural poles or spaces for special matrices of a differentiated population, as a consequence of—and as a response to—diverse social historical processes and dissimilar ecological circumstances. . . . Our singularity is made up of many singularities, visible in the internal variations of our culture. But this rich internal diversity, unlike what one might think, given the huge territorial dimensions of the country, did not result in a chaotic mess or a bizarre collage of mutually alienated and separate elements.[43]

Risério's richly textured portrait eloquently describes the fantastic cultural cornucopia that is Brazil. Yet many of his formulations—"anthropological mosaic," "worlds made up of many worlds," "multiple foci," "internal variations"—are conceptually apt descriptions of many national cultures. Most nation-states in the Americas, as invented collectivities, have tried to forge a fragile coherence out of "bizarre collages" of native, European, African, and Asian peoples, partly through the enforcing power of the state. The U.S. "E Pluribus Unum," the Mexican "Raza Cósmica," and the Brazilian "fable of three races" were all attempts to muster a semblance of order out of a "chaotic mess." But these *bricoleur* identities are not merely celebratory; they also mask real conflicts. In all of the Americas, indigenous concepts of land ownership, for example, still collide with Euro-dominant conceptions. Stressing the uniqueness of single nation-states edits out the analogies linking all of the colonial-settler states of the Americas.

Some of the most perceptive commentaries on comparative racial politics come, not surprisingly, from intellectuals familiar with both national contexts. Hermano Vianna, author of illuminating books on samba and popular culture, speaks of his encounter with multicultural identity politics during his doctoral research in the very segregated city of Chicago. Feeling at first like "an anthropologist doing field-research in a remote village of New Guinea," Vianna soon realized that the discussion was very serious and profound. On his return, "full of respect for [his] American colleagues," he reports that he "could not bear to see such a serious and emotionally charged debate treated as a kind of joke in Brazil." For Vianna, the United States "was performing a service for humanity with this anthropological experiment," one that "deserves our respect, collaboration, and constructive critique." Whereas other Brazilian analysts regarded multiculturalism as a ready-made product packaged for export, Vianna regarded it as an audacious experiment:

> Seeing all the suffering provoked by that movement (certainly much less serious than that caused by centuries of discrimination and racism, but still suffering) I confess that I felt relieved to not be from the U.S. . . . and for having the opportunity to leave, since I was feeling suffocated (including because I was classified as "Hispanic," something I never imagined, despite my love for the culture of the Chicanos and Puerto-Ricans of Chicago). But I was thankful to North Americans for going through all that pain, in such a demanding and in my view, such a radical manner. Who knows if important lessons would emerge for other peoples, lessons which could be adopted world-wide, since we would know what worked and what did not. Since it is obvious, even for the most politically correct Americans, that aspects of this experiment—like any other experiment—will not work out.[44]

Vianna's account shows respect for the multicultural project as a brave social experiment (along with an awareness of its limitations) as well as an appreciation of the Brazilian difference (and awareness of its limitations).

At the same time, Vianna's terms are perhaps exaggeratedly Christological, as if Chicago academics were taking on the racial sins of the world. While Vianna recognizes the "unbearable heaviness" of these discussions, he perhaps misses another element, to wit, a certain exhilaration and sense of joyful discovery not only in liberatory ideas but also in new forms of coalitionary conviviality. The selective emphasis on pain reflects a reaction of a Brazilian accustomed to a "lighter" approach, where the "lightness" is at once an unselfconscious social code and, at times, a way of artfully dodging confrontation through practices and discourses of flexible accommodation. It is in this context that Vianna emphasizes the social functionality of Brazilian humor and its deriding of some American movements. Although Vianna does not mention it, feminism too was initially disqualified on the basis of jokes, going back to the naming of a seasonal flu after Betty Friedan because her arrival in Salvador, Bahia, happened to coincide with the flu's onset. While carnivalizing North America power, such humor can also serve to marginalize egalitarian ideas.

In the end, Vianna calls for a relational study of the ways that "different peoples experiment and try out things so that they can subsequently be compared, exchanged, and mixed by others."[45] He does not categorically defend Brazil as a "racial democracy," however. One can affirm Brazilian miscegenation, he points out, and yet still not believe that Brazil is a racial democracy. At the same time, he sees U.S.-style multiculturalism ultimately as "out of place" in Brazil because it risks costing Brazil its "trump card"—the "mixing of differences."[46] Yet one wonders if the mixing of differences remains such a "trump card" when it has become the norm in much of the Atlantic world. Nonetheless, Vianna's praise for Americans' courage offers an ironic twist on a theme from the period of the UNESCO studies. In the 1950s, Brazil's "racial democracy" was seen as a model for a world then emerging from the battle against Nazism. But now the terms of discussion have shifted dramatically. The present-day United States is not regarded, as Brazil was then, as a "racial paradise"; rather, it is the place where the "racial hell" is being openly confronted, in an atmosphere of pain and suffocation. While it was the Brazilian socius itself that served as model in the early 1950s, now it is not the United States itself but rather U.S. self-critique that provides the model.

Drawing on British cultural studies and postcolonial studies, Brazilian sociologist Sérgio Costa skillfully negotiates between the various positions in *The Two Atlantics: Social Theory, Anti-racism, Cosmopolitanism*. Most Brazilian intellectuals, Costa points out, no longer dispute the existence of racism but only the best methods for dealing with it. For him, the Brazilian academic debate has polarized into two antiracist camps: the "integrationist antiracist camp" and the "racially defined antiracist camp." The integrationist camp places excessive faith in culture, neglecting material inequalities, while the race-conscious camp is overly tied to a specific (African American) model. "The concrete historical form taken by the struggle to create a just social order in the United States, with its successes and failures," he reminds us, "constitutes only one possibility [with] no guarantees that it will produce good results everywhere." Both groups neglect the "postnational and transnational dimensions" of the debate, since national frontiers no longer demarcate an adequate analytical unit for sociological investigation in an era when social, cultural, and political processes exceed such borders.[47]

Popular Culture, Tropicália, and the Rainbow Atlantic

Nothing better illustrates the dysfunctionality of forcing cultures into sealed national compartments than Brazilian popular music. As a cosmopolitan orchestration of vernacular and erudite musical idioms, Brazilian musi reflects, and reflects on, Brazil's constitutive multiculturality. Part of an endlessly creative multidirectional movement of ideas flowing back and forth around the Atlantic, Brazilian music generates such hybrids as jazz-samba, samba-rap, samba-reggae, *reforengue* (a blend of rock, merengue, and *forró*), and belly-samba (a blend of samba and belly-dance). Incorporating a broad variety of musical styles—the melisma of African American singing, the deep-breath South African choral style, the whiny steel guitar of country music, the thump of funk, and the offbeat syncopation of reggae—into an overall Brazilian ensemble, it displays an anthropophagic capacity to devour a wide range of influences. It is this other-absorbing capacity, paradoxically, that defines Brazilian music *as* Brazilian.

U.S.-American and Brazilian music resemble one another to some extent, not only because of mutual influence but also because of common roots. Thus, we find clear parallels between *chorinho* and ragtime, between cool jazz and bossa nova, between funk and *axé* music. As syncretic products of the African-European encounter in the New World, the music of George Gershwin, Aaron Copeland, Duke Ellington, Heitor Villa-Lobos, and Antonio Carlos Jobim all mingle the popular and erudite, the European and the Afro-diasporic.[48] While U.S. jazz musicians have occasionally referenced Africa, Brazilian popular music demonstrates a much deeper familiarity with Afro-Brazilian religious culture, whether in the incorporation of Candomblé rhythms or in lyrical allusions to *iaô* (initiates in the West African religions), *terreiros* (the Candomblé temples), *acarajé* (religiously consecrated food), and the *orixás* (Oxum, Iemanjá). Even Carmen Miranda's fluid way of dancing and singing recalls the way that Oxum, the goddess of love and wealth, lifts her arms and proudly exhibits her adornments.[49] African references animated the "Afro-sambas" of Vinicius de Moraes and Baden-Powell in the 1960s, the sambas of Clara Nunes and Martinho da Vila in the 1970s, and the work of Caetano Veloso, Gilberto Gil, Carlinhos Brown, and Maria Bethânia throughout their careers.

But what is most germane for our purposes here is the extent to which Brazilian music directly thematizes multicultural, diasporic, and indigenous issues, not only through lyrics but also through percussion, melody, harmony, and performance. Prior to the 1960s, Brazilian popular music thematized race and multiculturality in a light and sometimes prejudicial mode, as in "Nega do Cabelo Duro" (Black Woman with the Bad Hair), or in a more serious patriotic mode, as with Ary Barroso's portrait of Brazilian culture as a multicultural stew in "Aquarela do Brasil" (known in the United States as "Brazil"). Many sambas directly thematize race. The 2009 Carnival, for example, brought samba tributes to Barack Obama. One song played on the sonorous links between Obama's name and the Yoruba expression *Oba* (a kind of *viva*): "African voices, sing your strength / Obama-la / Now, my love, the White House is black." Another Carnival song declared, "There's a black guy in the White House / Prejudice has gone to Baghdad [an expression meaning "went far away"] / Bye-bye, Bush." Some Brazilian songs stress themes of cross-racial identification and transformation, a theme also common in U.S. popular culture.[50] Thus, the phenotypically white singer Joyce sings, "I'm a mulata," and Caetano Veloso punningly sings "sou mulato nato" (I'm a born mulatto), while Moraes Moreira allegorizes Brazil, à la Freyre, as "the three graces of Brazil," that is, three feminine figures allegorizing the Amerindian, the African, and the European. (Scholars have rarely studied these cross-ethnic identifications in a transnational manner; one might compare, for example, the pro-Amerindian symbolism of the "Black Indians" of New Orleans Carnival and that of the largely black "Comanches" and "Apaches" of Carnival in Salvador, Bahia).

Rappers, for their part, foreground race and resistance through their very names. The young organizers of the "bailes funk" (funk dances) invoked "Black Power" and "Revolução da Mente," after James Brown's "Revolution of the Mind." Bahians called themselves "browns" in homage to Brown, and a number of Brazilian musicians—notably Carlinhos Brown, Mano Brown, and Berimbrown—named themselves after the Godfather of Soul. "Berimbrown" mingles an homage to Brown with the *berimbau*, the African gourd-and-bow instrument used in capoeira. One Berimbrown song performs a historical counterpoint by linking Jorge Velho, the Portuguese military leader who crushed the 17th-century maroon republic of Palmares, to the present-day racist police. What George Yúdice has called the "funkification" of Brazil has been proceeding apace for decades, with funk and rap and jazz entering the very bloodstream of Brazilian popular music, just as bossa nova entered into the bloodstream of U.S. popular music decades earlier. Popular musicians such as Ed Motta, Berimbrown, and Phat Family, for their part, have Brazilianized soul, funk, and rap. The rap groups, meanwhile, also interact with civil society, whether through "Rap in the Schools" projects or through the group Banda AfroReggae's concept of *batidania*—a neologism, roughly translatable as "percussive citizenship"—the rough equivalent of "one nation under a groove." The video *Batidania: Power in the Beat* (1998) shows, as Yúdice puts it, "that music and performance are acts of citizenship," a way of opening up "public spheres."[51]

Critical race analysis can take many generic forms: political speech, the religious jeremiad, academic research, and popular music. Rappers in the 1980s echoed the scholarly disenchantment with the ideology of racial democracy. The Urban Discipline song "High Tech Violence" informs us that the police "go up into the favelas / invade your home / without shame / and the treatment you receive / will depend on the color of your skin." Rappa makes contrapuntal links between past enslavement and present-day incarceration in "Every Police Wagon Is Reminiscent of a Slave Ship." "Journal of a Prisoner" by the rap group Racionais MC's, led by Mano Brown, memorialized the 1992 massacre of 111 prisoners in Carandiru prison. In "Pavillion Number 8," some of the prisoners themselves penned rap lyrics about the massacre. Rap has thus become a musical testimonial registering social oppression. At the same time, the sounds themselves—hard, machine-gun-like—signify on the good-natured sweetness both of middle-class bossa nova and of favela-based classical samba.

Brazilian artists have been fecund in innovative and subtly anticolonial aesthetic coinages, whether literary, painterly, cinematic, or musical, among them "anthropophagy" (Oswald de Andrade), the "aesthetics of hunger" (Glauber Rocha), the "aesthetics of garbage" (Rogério Sganzerla), and "Tropicália" (Gilberto Gil and Caetano Veloso). Most of these aesthetics revalorize by inversion what had formerly been seen as negative, especially within colonialist discourse. Thus, cannibalism, for centuries the very name of the abject savage "other," becomes with the Brazilian modernists an anticolonialist trope and a term of value. At the same time, these aesthetics share the jiujitsu trait of turning strategic weakness into tactical strength. Anticipating the postcolonial and postmodern stress on cut 'n' mix and sampling aesthetics, such movements have appropriated existing discourses for their own ends, deploying the force of the dominant against domination.

The Tropicália movement inaugurated in 1967, led musically by Caetano Veloso and Gilberto Gil, brought these trends into the mass-mediated arena. Updating the ideas of modernist Oswald de Andrade, the movement drew on the favored modernist trope of "anthropophagy," the Global South's version of "intertextuality" as seen from the standpoint of neocolonial power relations. Like the modernists, the Tropicalists eagerly cannibalized artistic movements. While the modernists devoured Dada and surrealism, the Tropicalists, as Caetano himself liked to put it, devoured Jimi Hendrix and the Beatles, all part of a "sampling" aesthetic later seen as a proleptic form of postmodernism. Cannibalizing foreign influences from a position of national pride, the Tropicalists easily absorbed rock, rap, reggae, country, and salsa into a very Brazilian synthesis.

A striking feature of Brazilian popular music is its naked intellectual ambition. "Pop star intellectuals" such as Gilberto Gil, Caetano Veloso, Chico Buarque, and Zé Miguel Wisnik write books and compose music that comment on the burning questions of the time. As a multiart movement, the Tropicália movement dynamized and reorganized the cultural field, while actively intervening in the debates about race and national identity. Whatever the vicissitudes of their sometimes problematic *prise de positions*, Gil and Caetano are major commentator-theoreticians on race in Brazil, both as incisive critics of racism and as celebrants of Brazilian conviviality. They perform those theories in very diverse genres and media, ranging from music, books, and interviews to happenings and public policies. Journalistic critics of the English translation of Caetano's memoir *Tropical Truth* were surprised to encounter a pop star who could write knowingly about European, American, and Brazilian culture, in a text in which names like Ray Charles and James Brown brush up easily against names like Stockhausen, Wittgenstein, and Deleuze. Both Caetano and Gil (onetime minister of culture in the Lula government) constitute Orphic intellectuals, or to coin a variation on Gramsci's "organic intellectual," "Orphoganic" intellectuals; they write books in one moment and lead dancing crowds in another. While performing popular culture, they also theorize it. In a multimedia intervention, they enact the cultural debates in visual, sensuous, written, lyrical, percussive, and even institutional-political form.[52]

The Tropicália movement was born, in a sense, in an audiovisual epiphany of Africanness. According to the Tropicalists themselves, one of the works of art that helped crystallize the movement was Glauber Rocha's 1967 film *Terra em Transe*, with its superimposition of the music of Candomblé with aerial views of the Atlantic coast. Caetano, who once described himself as a cross between Rocha and João Gilberto, delineated the film's impact on the movement. "That whole Tropicalist thing," as Caetano famously put it, "became clear to me the day I saw *Terra em Transe*. My heart exploded during the opening sequence, when, to the sound of a Candomblé chant, an aerial shot of the sea brings us to the coast of Brazil." Without that "traumatic moment," Caetano writes, "nothing of what came to be called tropicalism would have ever existed."[53] Tropicália was born, then, quite literally under the sign of the Black Atlantic.

As a musical "bard" of that same Black Atlantic, Gil has offered scintillating odes to Afro-Brazilian diasporic culture, whether to the orixas of Candomblé, as in "Iemanjá," or to Macumba, as in "Batmakumba" (a play on Batman and Macumba) or to Umbanda in "Umbanda Um." Gil's 1973 musical homage to the Bahian Afro-musical group Filhos de Gandhi helped reinvigorate that group. His "ChuckBerry

Fields Forever," meanwhile, links both the Beatles and Chuck Berry to the cane-fields of slavery, while "Quilombo, the Black Eldorado" memorializes the longest-lasting maroon republic in the Americas. A very cosmopolitan Gil composed "A Prayer for Freedom in South Africa" (1985) and created a theme song, "Touche Pas à Mon Pote," adopted by French antiracists. Although such music might not instigate a revolution, it can provide the sound track for social change.

Tropicália's contribution was both thematic and aesthetic. In its cultural pro-posals, it offered (1) a critique of the conservative cultural politics of the orthodox left; (2) an emphasis not on harmony and cordiality but rather on unharmoni-zable contradictions; (3) a simultaneous openness both to the "lowest" reaches of Brazilian popular culture and to the high reaches of the transnational avant-garde; (4) the parodic interrogation of Brazil's foundational myths and icons; (5) the audacious taking on of momentous historical questions such as slavery, syncretism, and transcultural relations; (6) a transtemporal and contrapuntal aes-thetic; and (7) a refusal of the norms of correctness in favor of the transformation of the very criteria of taste. Rather than aspire to technical correctness, the Trop-icalists preferred to make productive "mistakes" while forging a new revolutionary set of criteria rooted both in the avant-garde and in popular culture.

While Tropicália takes the entire world as its province, it does not create "world music," that bland concoction that channels music from the Global South into Northern markets, touching lightly on ethnicity while dodging painful issues of appropriation and racism. At its most radical, Tropicália nourishes a full-throated dissonance. In this sense, it echoes and instantiates some of the part serious, part tongue-in-cheek principles of the movement (led by Ned Sublette) called "Postmamboism" (from Kikongo *imbu*, as "word," "law," "song," or "impor-tant matter") as the "portable theory that places music at the center of under-standing and uses music to interrogate other fields of study." Although applicable to other musics, Postmamboism "begins with the study of African and African diaspora musics, given their historical centrality to the music of the world and their deep connection through slavery, neoslavery, and liberation struggles and expands to fundamental questions of colonialism, capitalism and civilization."[54]

Here we look closely at specific songs addressing diasporic flows around the Atlantic. The Caetano CD *Noites do Norte*, for example, constitutes a musical meditation on slavery and its sequels, moving from the Nigeria of "Two Naira Fifty Kobo" and the Angola of "Congo Benguela Monjolo Cabinda Mina" to the Brazil of "slave auctions" and "sugar cane fields forever," as well as to the call for revolt with "Zumbi" and later the ambivalent abolitionism of Joaquim Nabuco in "Noites do Norte," on to blacks celebrating abolition in "13 de Maio." The musi-cal genre chosen for each song—an animated *samba de roda* for "13 de Maio"; a melancholy-romantic *lied* style for the musicalization of Nabuco's reflections on slavery; and stylized dissonant-modernist rap music for "Haiti"—conveys a social intonation and perspective.[55] In short, the CD reaches back in time and outward in space to compose a veritable musical essay on the history of the Afro-diaspora.

The song "Haiti," in its treatment of the theme of police brutality, conveys in poetic form a sense of the intersectionalities of race and class in a country like Brazil, a sense of how race becomes "the modality in which class is lived" (Stuart Hall).[56] The lyrics recount an episode in which Caetano himself played a role. Just as he was being presented with a "Citizenship Award" on a stage overlooking Salvador's historic Pelourinho Square, Caetano saw mostly black police beating up a mostly black or mestizo or poor white crowd. The song begins,

> When you are invited to go up to the roof
> Of the Jorge Amado Foundation
> And see from above the line of soldiers, almost all of them black
> Hitting on the nape of the neck
> Black hustlers, mulatto thieves, and others almost white
> But treated like blacks
> Only in order to show to the others almost black
> (and they are almost all black)
> And to the almost white but poor as blacks
> How it is that blacks, poor people, and mulattos are treated

Caetano begins by acknowledging his own privileged position as honored citizen and middle-class observer—he is not the one being beaten. At the same time, his lyrics ventriloquize, in what Bakhtin would call "double-voiced discourse," a racist voice expressive of the doxa about how blacks are "supposed to be treated." The song treats race in a conjunctural and antiessentialist manner, since even poor and marginalized whites can be treated like blacks. Yet blackness remains the default position of oppressability, the "floor" of social deprivation.

Caetano's music generally orchestrates counterpoints of musical genres, each with their own social overtones. "Haiti," in this sense, encodes cultural tensions and syncretisms in the manner of "national allegory," not only through lyrics but also through melody, harmony, and percussion. The song stages the power relations between Europe and Africa, between the cello and the surdo, between melody and percussion, between the Big House and the Slave Quarters. The European-derived cello is used in an Africanized way, as a percussive instrument, and it yelps with anthropomorphic pain just as the lyrics mention the police blows on the nape of neck of the persons being beaten. The décor of the performance on the DVD, with a hint of a fencing in the black percussionists, evokes a mild Brazilian separationism.

The song continues:

> And it doesn't matter if the eyes of the entire world
> Are at that moment focused on that Square
> Where slaves were punished
> And today a drumming, a drumming
> With the purity of uniformed schoolchildren on parade day
> And the epic grandeur of a people in formation
> Attracts us, amazes us, and stimulates us
> All that has no importance
> Not the lens from the Fantastic Show
> Not the Paul Simon CD
> No one, no one is a citizen
> And if you go to the party in Pelourinho
> And if you don't go
> Think about Haiti, pray for Haiti
> Haiti is here, Haiti is not here

The song's refrain—"Haiti is here, Haiti is not here"—signifies on a famous phrase from Brazilian literary critic Sílvio Romero. Almost a century after the Haitian Revolution, on the eve of abolition, Romero, still frightened by what was for him the "spectre" of the Haitian Revolution, said that "Brazil is not, and should not become, a Haiti"—that is, there should be no revolution and no end of slavery. The song lyrics link Brazil to Haiti as a double site, both of a black revolutionary past and of a neocolonized present place where black police beat up black people. The lyrics also recall the legacy of slavery and the pillory as the site of disciplinary punishments—*Pelourinho*, after all, refers to the pillory used as part of a disciplinary spectacle during slavery. But now the whipping post has given way to mass incarceration and police murder, where "no one is a citizen." (Here Caetano plays with the double, even opposite meanings of *cidadão* [citizen] in Brazilian Portuguese, both as the bare-life unprotected rights-less individual and as the societally endowed rights-bearing person.) At the same time, the lyrics and the percussive style evoke the sounds of resistance in the drumming of *Afro-blocos* such as Olodum, whose "epic grandeur dazzles us." Yet such culturalist strength is ultimately insufficient when citizenship is so fragile and "no one is a citizen." And it does not matter that *Lente Fantástico* (a Globo network program) visits Salvador or that Paul Simon collaborates with Olodum to make *The Rhythm of the Saints*.

The music is interrupted by a dramatic announcement concerning the 1992 massacre of prisoners at Carandiru prison:

And when you hear the smiling silence of São Paulo
During the Massacre . . .
111 defenseless prisoners, but prisoners are almost all black
Or almost black, or almost white almost black because so poor
And poor people are like rotten people and everyone knows how blacks are treated
And when you take a trip around the Caribbean
And when you fuck without a condom
And offer your intelligent contribution to the embargo of Cuba
Think about Haiti, pray for Haiti
Haiti is here, Haiti is not here

The effect of the pause in the music is of an eruption of the real into a musical entertainment, as if to say, "We interrupt this performance to announce a catastrophe." The show must *not* go on. The song is declaimed, moreover, in a Brazilian variation on the rap style associated with black Americans but also linked to Brazilian traditions such as *embolada*, *repente*, and "talking sambas." In its principled incivility, the rap style "breaks" with the gentler harmonies of bossa nova and the suave discourses of "racial democracy." The aggressivity contrasts even with the sweetness of Caetano's song about surfers ("Menino do Rio"), whose refrain— "Hawaii, be here"—the song both echoes and transforms. Here relations are no longer cordial, and the music is no longer sweet; instead we find the politicization of avant-gardist dissonance.

The music video of the Gilberto Gil song "Mão de Limpeza" (Hand of Cleanliness) also deconstructs the racial doxa, this time by resignifying and carnivalizing what would usually be seen as a hopelessly compromised performance mode of blackface. As performed by Gil and Chico Buarque, the song's lyrics satirically upend a racist Brazilian proverb:

They say that when blacks don't make a mess at the entrance
They make it at the exit
Imagine!
But the slave mother spent her life
Cleaning up the mess that whites made
Imagine!
What a damned lie!
Even after slavery was abolished
Blacks continued cleaning clothes
And scrubbing floors
How the blacks worked and suffered!
Imagine!

Black is the hand of cleanliness
Of life consumed at the side of the stove
Black is the hand that puts food on the table
And cleans with soap and water
Black is the hand of immaculate purity
They say when blacks don't make a mess at the entrance
They make it at the exit
Imagine!
What a damned lie!
Look at the filthy white guy

Gil's song provokes a Brechtian *Verfremdungseffekt*; it estranges the racist common sense, asking us to imagine how anyone could ever have associated blackness with dirtiness. Within a Brechtian "separation of the elements," the gaiety of the music exists in tension with the gravity of the topic. The visuals, meanwhile, recuperate an "incorrect" stereotype within an anti-illusionistic chromatic schema that plays on and subverts the black/white dichotomy. The phenotypically white singer Chico Buarque appears in blackface and is dressed in black, while the black Gil appears in whiteface and is dressed in white. In cultural terms, the references are both to the *boneca de pixe* (tar doll) tradition in Brazil and to the racist North American tradition of minstrelsy. In the United States, the practice of blackface has been highly fraught, as evidenced by the confused reactions to the satirical use of blackface in Spike Lee's *Bamboozled*.[57] "Mão de Limpeza" reconfigures the old racist representational practice by counterpointing blackface with whiteface. Historically, blackface was unilateral—there was no whiteface—and white spectators often took the representation as "authentic." But here the choice of performance mode comes not from white media entrepreneurs but from the black artist himself. In a sly Brazilian rewrite of the costumed inversions of Genet's *Les Nègres*, the song overturns the racist binarism that equates blackness with dirtiness; blackness now connotes immaculate purity, while whiteness connotes the dirtiness of the *branco sujão* (filthy white guy). At the same time, the stylized performance itself implies the transcendence of the black/white binarism emphasized by the mise-en-scene: the two singers are obviously friends having a splendid time while playing at a kind of carnival. The racism of the proverb does not mean that whites and blacks cannot be friends or fight together against racism.

Already in the 1980s, Gil was commenting musically on the favored postcolonial theme of cultural hybridity. Gil's "From Bob Dylan to Bob Marley: Samba Provocation" poetically addresses the intercultural transit of ideas back and forth across the Black Atlantic, in this case between Brazil, Jamaica, North America, and Africa. The song's subtitle designates it as a "provocation samba," a play on the Vargas-era "exaltation sambas" that lauded Brazilian heroes. The "provocation" here is to exalt not the nation-state but rather Afro-diasporic hybridity. The lyrics go as follows:

> Soon after Bob Dylan converted to Christianity
> He made a reggae album as a form of compensation
> He abandoned the Jewish people
> But returned to them while heading in the wrong direction . . .
> When the peoples of Africa arrived in Brazil
> There was no freedom of religion . . .
> As a result, Africans in Brazil adopted Our Lord of Bomfim
> An act both of resistance and surrender

The refrain:

> Bob Marley died
> Because besides being black
> He was Jewish
> Michael Jackson, meanwhile
> Is still around
> But besides becoming white
> He's become very sad

The song explores the "roots" and "routes" of Afro-diasporic culture, ranging easily, in a musical version of magic realism, over five centuries and diverse continents, orchestrating a creative counterpoint between the early 16th century—"when Africans arrived in Brazil"—and the late 20th-century era of Bob Dylan, Bob Marley, and Michael Jackson. The allusion to a putative Dylan reggae album through which he returned to the Jewish people clearly references Rastafarianism as an Afro-diasporic religion imbued with Jewish symbologies (the "Lion of Judah," "Babylon," and so forth); Dylan, leaving Judaism, returned to it through the sacred music of Jamaica. "When the peoples of Africa arrived in Brazil," Gil goes on, "there was no freedom of religion." Significantly, Gil's lyrics speak not of "blacks" but of the "peoples of Africa," since the reifying totalization of "blacks" was itself the product of colonialism and slavery. The values of religious freedom and tolerance, the song reminds us, did not extend to African or indigenous religions in the Americas. Given this lack of freedom, "Africans in Brazil adopted Our Lord of Bomfim, an act both of resistance and surrender." The final refrain indexes two forms of syncretism, one in the form of the music of Bob Marley and the other in the more melancholy and compromised form of Michael Jackson: "Bob Marley died / Because besides being black / He was Jewish / Michael Jackson, meanwhile / Is still around / But besides becoming white / He's become very sad." In sum, the song allegorically contemplates one set of times and spaces through another set of times and spaces, in a suggestive contrapuntal haunting across national and epochal boundaries.

If Gil's "provocation samba" relationalizes blackness and Jewishness, Caetano's 1977 song "Um Índio" places in relation the indigenous past, present, and future. "An Indian" not only is written in the prophetic genre but also turned out to be literally prophetic of the indigenous resurgence that has been taking place since the 1970s throughout the Red Atlantic. Some of the lyrics go as follows:

> From a shining colored star will descend an Indian
> From a star that spins with dazzling velocity
> A star that will lodge in the heart of America in an instant of clarity
> An Indian preserved in his full physical presence
> In solid, in gas, in atoms, words, soul, color, in gesture, in smell, in shadow, in light, in magnificent sound
> As a spot equidistant between the Atlantic and the Pacific
> The Indian will descend from a resplendent object
> And the thing that I know he will say I do not know how to say explicitly
> And what is to be revealed at that moment to the people
> Will surprise everyone by not being exotic
> And by its power to have always remained hidden
> When in fact it was obvious

With uncanny prescience, "Um Índio" sets to music the theme of the transnational flow of ideas around the figure of the Indian. Encoding indigenous ideas about stars and astronomy, and specifically the idea that culture heroes become constellations, the Indian pictured arrives in the guise of a visitor from another planet, in a spaceship reminiscent of Spielberg's *Close Encounters of the Third Kind*. The song portrays a Columbus-like "discovery" in reverse, in terms that recall both native legends and blockbuster science fiction. But this time the "god who arrives from afar" is not European but indigenous, foreshadowing a passage in *Tropical Truth* in which Caetano speaks of "another discovery, this time mutual, in which the heart inclines more toward the Indian than toward Cabral."[58]

The song scrambles various genres (prophecy, science fiction, Indianist poetry), while at the same time resuscitating the Enlightenment topos, found in Raynal and Diderot, of the "New World Avenger," the Indian or black Spartacus who comes to redeem suffering peoples. The reference to the "most advanced of technologies," meanwhile, subverts any primitivist nostalgia by calling up not only Oswald de Andrade's *"indio tecnizado"* but also contemporary Indians who use technology to outwit the powerful, for example, the activist-politicians such as Juruna with his tape recorder registering political promises, since "politicians always lie to the Indians."

"Um Índio," in this sense, brings together many of our themes. The song's transnational references draw on the taproot of indigenous culture (the reading of the night's starry face for signs and omens), on 19th-century Indianism (Peri), as well as on 20th-century modernism. Ever the overturner of hierarchies, Caetano imagines the redemptive figure of the Red Avenger in pop-cultural terms, as a multiracial amalgam of postmodern culture heroes: first, Muhammad Ali, African American boxer and war resister who converted to Islam and whose transnational genealogy goes back to Africa, through an imposed European (slave) name—Cassius Clay—and finally to an Arabic/Islamic name; second, Peri, the pure romantic Indian from Alencar's Indianist novel *O Guarani*, valued here for his passion but not for his role as collaborator; third, Bruce Lee, an Asian master of a millennial martial art, with an Anglo-American name; and finally, the *axé* (Yoruba for "energy") of the *afoxé* (Africanized Carnival percussion group), composed mainly of black people from Bahia, which named itself "Sons of Gandhi" in 1948, a year after Indian independence, in an homage to a pacifist Indian leader (Mahatma Gandhi) by a Carnival *bloco* whose costumes were modeled on the imperial film *Gunga Din*.

These Tropicália songs offer a relational perspective on cultural crossings around the Black and Red Atlantic. They suggest the socially anticipatory power of music to provide metaphors and models for a more equal society. Tropicália shows how music can transfigure historical relationalities by staging multicultural conflicts and connections in ways that complement the methods of written history and the social sciences. Artists such as Caetano and Gil display a chameleonic ability to move easily between various cultural repertoires, to negotiate multiple worlds in a ludic dance of identities reminiscent of Carnival and Candomblé. They "perform" the cultural debates in visual, sensuous, and percussive form. Artistic practices here are not mere mirrors of identity; rather, they are communicative events that shape, critique, and fashion new forms of identity and identification. Music and art create new registers of feeling and new forms of social subjectivity. In the music of Tropicália, one hears not only the musical memory of pain and discrimination but also proleptic tones of a social utopia, communicating a visceral and kinetic sense of what freedom and equality might feel like in a society shorn of its oppressive features.

In this light, it is worth contemplating the political productivity of popular music as a source for mobilizing socially collaborative tropes such as polyphony, polyrhythms, call-and-response, and counterpoint. One could conceive of a transnational orchestration of a coalitionary "movement of movements," the political equivalent of a jazz-like ensemble—Wynton Marsalis's "jazz democracy"—a def-poetry jam of strong and diverse voices, or a Carnival of *blocos* and samba schools. The norm of a single nation or culture implies marginalization of other subnations or parallel nations within the "multination state." But in musical polyphony, the flute does not "win" over the guitar, nor the trumpet over the bass, nor melody over percussion. Tropicália, in this sense, shows music's capacity to give pleasurable, kinetic shape to social desire, to mobilize feeling in a mass-mediated form. In terms of our more immediate purposes in this book, it exemplifies an artistic form of thinking that goes beyond fixed and monolithic notions of culture to explore the linked analogies of the cultures of the Rainbow Atlantic.

Scholarship and the Persistence of Race

Race studies, (multi)cultural studies, and to an extent postcolonial studies have been a much more accepted part of Brazilian scholarship than they have been in France. Brazilian scholarship constantly engages, for example, the mantra of race, class, gender, sexuality, and empire. The Brazilian equivalent of the Modern Language Association, ABRALIC, at its 2000 conference in Salvador, Bahia, featured four frequently cited figures in race and postcolonial studies: Stuart Hall, Gayatri Spivak, Paul Gilroy, and Robert Young. Most young Brazilian academics in the humanities are comfortable—some critics would say too comfortable—with *estudos culturais* (cultural studies) while slightly more ambivalent about multiculturalism, both for the pretentiousness of the "-ism" and for its perceived North American provenance.

It would be inaccurate to see this efflorescence of scholarship as in any way an epiphenomenon of Anglo-American influence. First, (multi)cultural studies is a worldwide current with many points of origin, part of a broader democratization of culture that moves from Arnoldian elitist conceptions of culture as the "best that has been thought and written" to anthropological conceptions of culture as the way everyday people live and think. Second, Brazilian (multi)cultural studies build on Brazilian intellectual traditions: 1920s modernism with its appeal to popular culture as a source for art; the 1930s Freyrean exploration of such varied phenomena as cuisine, folklore, and sexuality; and Tropicália and Cinema Novo in the 1960s, with their rejection of the high-art/low-art hierarchy. Many of the artistic movements had in common an aesthetic based on the erudite reelaboration of popular materials, such as samba and *cordel* literature, and the indigenization of out-of-place ideas. The ground for "cultural studies," then, was richly prepared in Brazil; the phrase merely provided a rubric for energies and movements already well under way in the moving depths of the culture.

Recent years have also featured a remarkable surge of Brazilian scholarship on race and racism, generating such titles as *Racism in Brazil*; *Racisms and Anti-racisms in Brazil: Ethnic Pluralism and Multiculturalism*; *Removing the Mask: Essays on Racism in Brazil*; *Media and Racism*; *Media and Ethnicity in Brazil and the U.S.*; *Negritude, Cinema, and Education*; *Multiculturalism: The Thousand and One Faces of Education*; *The Social Psychology of Racism*; *Race as Rhetoric*; *The Persistence of Race*; and *Racism: Explained to My Children*. The collection *Removing the Mask: Essays on Racism in Brazil*, edited by Brazilian Antonio Sérgio Alfredo Guimarães and American Lynn Huntley privileges comparative, diasporic, and transnational perspectives. The trope of the "mask" in the title is itself Afro-diasporic, simultaneously evoking Du Bois, Fanon, and Paul Lawrence Dunbar, whose poem "we use the mask that laughs and lies" serves as epigraph to the volume. Part of the Comparative Human Relations Initiative, linked to various Brazilian institutions along with the Southern Education Foundation in Atlanta, Georgia, and the Institute for the Development of South Africa, the volume proposes a comparative study of race in the United States, Brazil, and South Africa. Despite nuances (more or less mixing, more or less tension), the three countries share salient points: historical legacies of colonialism and slavery, racially diversified populations, discrimination toward blacks, and rationalizations that explain away inequality.

Helio Santos speaks in his essay of various aspects of racial subordination in Brazil: the absence of blacks in advertising and television commercials; police abuse of "nonwhite subcitizens"; the denial of black historical agency in conventional pedagogy; and the left's dismissal of race as less urgent than class. He salutes the various manifestations of black activism in Brazil: the Palmares Cultural Foundation; the black movement within the Catholic Church; the non-governmental organization Geledes (Institute of the Black Woman); the *Afro-blocos* in Salvador, Bahia; the Black Culture Research Institute; and so forth. In "Reflections on the Black Movement in Brazil, 1938–1997," Abdias do Nascimento and Elisa Larkin Nascimento trace the history of black activism in the 20th century, going back to the 1910 "Revolt of the Whip" (the struggle against corporeal punishment in the navy led by the "Black Admiral" João Cândido). The authors cite various cases of discrimination against African American notables (anthropologist Irene Diggs, choreographer Katherine Dunham, singer Marian Anderson), along with an "International Seminar on African Culture," sponsored by UNESCO and the Brazilian government, to which no blacks were invited.

Another 2002 collection, titled *Race as Rhetoric: The Construction of Difference*, edited by Yvonne Maggie and Claudia Barcellos Rezende, features Brazilian, American, Belgian, South African, British, and Italian scholars. In the preface, Peter Fry argues that "racial democracy" is not a "mask" for racism but rather a "utopian projection."[59] Anthropologist Olívia Maria Gomes da Cunha, meanwhile, unpacks the racial politics of the putatively democratic space of Rio's famous beaches. She focalizes the media portrayal of the October 1992 *Arrastão* (dragnet), when hundreds of young *favelados* and *suburbanos* (residents of the poorer Northern Zone of Rio) frightened the usually dominant middle-class whites from Ipanema. "The arrival of summer," in Cunha's words, "foreshadowed chaos and violence through the explosive combination of young 'suburbanos,' theft, music, and confusion on the burning sands of a crowded Ipanema beach."[60] For Cunha, the media represented the incident as "a sample of the danger posed by the out-of-control horde uninhibitedly defying the subtle borders of Carioca sociability."[61] While a deracialized vocabulary described the participants as "vandals," "marginals," and "gangs," any telespectator could easily see that most of the participants were nonwhite. "The question of color was omnipresent, but in a mode of denegation."[62] In the next chapter, we will further explore the issue of denegation in relation to reparations, Affirmative Action, and whiteness studies.

7 From Affirmative Action to Interrogating Whiteness

THIS CHAPTER ADDRESSES, within a larger Atlantic context, two issues that might at first glance seem to be only vaguely related: Affirmative Action and whiteness studies. While the former represents concrete remedial measures, the latter forms part of an innovative academic trend. Yet the two issues are linked in that they address two forms of white privilege, one social and material, the other subjective and cognitive. Remedial measures have the effect of "outing" and "naming," as it were, a preexisting white advantage accumulated over centuries. While Affirmative Action centers on those who have been disadvantaged by a racialized system, whiteness studies performs a psychosocial analysis of the advantaged. Here whites are asked to relinquish not simply a material advantage but also a psychic advantage, that is, the luxury of imagining themselves as unimplicated in social/racial domination. If Affirmative Action is literally remedial, whiteness studies is metaphorically remedial in correcting the misconception that only blacks are "raced."

Our purpose here is not to offer a comprehensive institutional history or to detail concrete solutions but rather to examine the transnational dimension of the debates. Extending a discussion usually focused on the United States to France and Brazil highlights both the continuity and discontinuity of arguments across the borders. How have these discussions been conducted and translated across the three zones? While the debates have often mobilized a comparative method, either to endorse or to condemn remedial measures, they have sometimes remained premised on unitary conceptions of the nation. Our hope is to transnationalize the debates through a translational prism that accounts for the connectivities between diverse cultural geographies.

Remedial Measures and the Legacy of Affirmative Whiteness

The debates over reparations and Affirmative Action form new editions of Enlightenment debates about slavery and freedom and the universal and the particular. Is the "social contract" of Hobbes and Locke also racial and sexual? Are rights universal or limited on the basis of race, gender, and property? Such debates are not the product only of the 20th century. In the United States, David Walker's "Appeal," in 1829, already hinted at blacks' right to reparations. In 1868, just five years after the Emancipation Proclamation, hundreds of former slaves filed suit to compel former slave masters to pay wages earned during the prior season's work. (Whites responded by burning down the courthouse that held the eighteen hundred lawsuits filed by the freedmen.) Raymond A. Winbush delineates three distinct phases in the reparations discussion: (1) from 1865 to 1920, with U.S. government proposals such as "40 Acres and a Mule," to compensate the three million freed African Americans; (2) from 1920 to 1968, with the attempts by Marcus Garvey and other nationalists to educate blacks about the debt owed them; and (3) from 1968 to the present, with efforts by black nationalist groups such as "Republic of New Africa" and by leaders such as Randal Robinson to explore the possibility of congressionally mandated reparations.[1]

In Brazil, formal demands for reparations were submitted in 1987 to the country's Constituent Assembly. Over a century before, however, abolitionist Joaquim Nabuco, in 1883, had already called attention to the debt owed black Brazilians:

> Everything that has to do with Man's struggle against nature, with the conquest of the soil through habitation and culture, with roads and buildings, canefields and coffee plantation, the home of the master and the quarters of the slave, telegraphs and train tracks, schools and hospitals, everything, absolutely everything that exists in Brazil, as a result of manual labor and accumulation of wealth, is nothing more than a gift from the race that has done the work.[2]

The underlying premise of the reparations movement is that the transatlantic slave trade and slavery itself were crimes against humanity, among the most grave ever committed, and that these crimes had massive consequences that benefited the enslavers and their heirs and grievously harmed the enslaved and their descendants. Slavery constituted not a single crime but rather a constellation of crimes, including kidnapping, rape, and theft. The reparations movement thus calls attention to an in some ways unpayable debt. Indeed, one discursive advantage of emphasizing reparations rather than racism is that the proposal reminds whites of the cumulative benefits brought them as a result of slavery and its sequels, *even* if they arrived as immigrants who acquired some of the taken-for-granted "perks" of whiteness.

In both the United States and Brazil, reparations advocates cite significant historical precedents: U.S. payments to Native Americans (e.g., the Alaska Native Claims Settlement Act), U.S. payments to Japanese Americans for their internment during World War II, Florida legislature grants (in 1994) for the heirs of the black victims of white mob violence, Canadian land grants to first peoples, German and Austrian payments to Jews for the Holocaust, and so forth. Since individuals can be compensated for unfair individual incarceration, it is argued, groups too can logically also be compensated for their collective loss of personal freedom and the prerogatives of citizenship. But whether or not the reparations movement results in actual reparations, the discourse of the movement itself has a salutary effect. Short-circuiting the usual white defense mechanisms, the issue of reparations changes the subject from highly subjective and often narcissistic questions about prejudice to very concrete issues concerning unpaid labor, stolen land, and unkept official promises. Whites' standard reaction to accusations of racism has often been a flight from responsibility. But with the reparations debate, the energy wasted by whites' "proving" their lack of racism is channeled into more productive material questions: Precisely how much are indigenous people owed for genocide and the loss of land, or diasporic blacks for the physical, psychological, economic, and moral harm engendered by slavery? The legal system often compensates trauma; does not the historical trauma of segregation merit compensation as well?

A product of the Civil Rights Movement of the 1950s and 1960s, Affirmative Action in the United States proposed to rectify inequality through preferential treatment in the distribution of resources and jobs. Although often discussed by both detractors and proponents as if it were a uniquely American concept, Affirmative Action is not unique to the United States. Many nation-states have developed forms of Affirmative Action, although not necessarily under that rubric. In India, Bhimrao Ramji Ambedkar led the movement to include legislative mechanisms for remedial measures—called "reservations"—for the "untouchables" (Dalit) already in the 1948 Indian Constitution. Malaysia adopted a quota system for the *bumiputeras* in 1971, while Canada, Australia, and South Africa have all adopted similar measures for their respective minorities.

First appearing in the Civil Rights Act of 1964, Affirmative Action called for concrete action on the part of employers to promote equal opportunity and for developing concrete forms of assistance to minority ethnic groups officially recognized as having suffered a history of legal discrimination. (A 1965 executive order subsequently implemented the law in the field of employment.) Rather than being exclusively about race, Affirmative Action was also about color, religion, sex, and national origin. During the 1970s, a new positive argument—"diversity"—was added to the negative argument of prior discrimination. The problem with "diversity," however, is its vagueness: in a fission-like process, everyone, even white racists, can claim to be "diverse." More recently, we encounter a judicial fatigue with "group rights"—precisely because the groups demanding rights are potentially infinite—resulting in a defensive move from particular "group rights" to universal "equal rights." Thus, the argument shifts from the "rights of blacks" to "everyone's right not to be discriminated against" or from the "rights of the handicapped" to "everyone's right to have access to political institutions."

Lively debates about compensatory measures have emerged in all three countries, whether under the rubric of Affirmative Action in the United States or *la discrimination positive* in France, or *cotas* (quotas) in Brazil. In the United States, supporters have shied away from the word "quotas"—historically redolent of anti-Semitic decrees—while supporting mechanisms whereby race becomes one factor among others in opening up higher education and employment to historically disadvantaged communities. Some Brazilian activists argue the desirability of numerical quotas as asserting a general social goal—an equality of *results*—rather than an individualist competitive equality of *opportunity*. In all three zones, compensatory measures have provoked anxious discussions, sometimes exposing tensions about race and class within progressive movements. Given the concrete legal and practical consequences of Affirmative Action, it forms one place where the rubber of critical race theory meets the road of everyday social praxis. Kimberlé Crenshaw distinguishes between the "mere rejection of white supremacy as a normative vision" and a "societal commitment to the eradication of the substantive conditions of black subordination [through] the actual distribution of goods and resources, status, and prestige."[3] Affirmative Action, for perhaps the first time in history, calls for public policies that might actually entail the loss of some taken-for-granted privileges on the part of whites. No longer asked simply to condemn racism verbally, whites are asked actually to give up a modicum of power in the name of broader egalitarian goals.

As an attempt to undo injustices produced by centuries of inequality, Affirmative Action has embraced a wide range of initiatives having to do with public employment, access to education, hiring, community representation, and so forth. These initiatives are widely regarded as having diminished—but clearly not eliminated—racial and sexual discrimination in hiring, promotion, and wages. For more radical critics, Affirmative Action is but one small and inadequate gesture that risks becoming a fig leaf that hides the dirty secret of the systematic production of inequality. A deeper restructuring would feature a broader arsenal of redistributive techniques embracing class, race, gender, sexuality, and region. Race-sensitive measures such as Affirmative Action and reparations would ideally form part of a continuum of complementary strategies designed (1) to combat racial inequality and discrimination; (2) to penalize acts of discrimination against people of color, gays, lesbians, and transsexuals; (3) to heal injured minority self-esteem through cultural, educational, and media affirmation; and (4) to empower women and people of color in key media and educational institutions.

An alternative and in some ways complementary approach favors gender- and race-blind public policy initiatives to equalize wealth, prestige, and power generally.[4] Apparently race-neutral measures—free or affordable education, universal health care, day care for children, unemployment benefits, family leave, pensions—improve quality of life for the majority but also especially benefit the people of color usually placed at the bottom of the social ladder. (That the French welfare state already offers these advantages suggests both (1) how unequal the U.S. social system is and (2) that the welfare state in itself does not eliminate discrimination and marginalization.) To wax utopian, one could imagine a sharply progressive tax code calibrated in relation to intersecting factors of social exclusion including race, class, and gender, which might entail small sacrifices for the prosperous but could massively aid subalternized communities. A well-conducted form of a class-narrowed reparations might apportion financial help to those who are mired in transgenerational structural unemployment. A domestic "Marshall Plan," meanwhile, might reconstruct inner-city communities. Rather than grants for individuals, such remedial programs might transfer funds from corporations that demonstrably profited from slavery and discrimination toward institutions and communities that have just as demonstrably suffered from slavery and its sequels. The institutions directly or indirectly enriched by slavery—shipping companies, agribusiness, insurance firms, real estate companies—would be obliged to "give back" to the people and communities whose labor has enriched them. Such race-based remedial measures need not revolve around individual white guilt and resentment but rather around historical responsibility. Instead of a favor to people of color, such measures constitute a contribution to a more perfect union, one that potentially facilitates a reconciliation of the dominant group with the better angels of their own conscience. Remedial measures can constitute at once an expression of collective responsibility for historical injustice and an expression of gratitude for blood shed and labor spent, thus helping salve the racial wound for everyone.

While some conservatives acknowledge the successes of Affirmative Action, they argue that it is no longer needed and that it entails unfairness to white males, since gains by women and people of color, within a zero-sum game, necessarily entail white losses. Objections to remedial measures are often premised on individualist and moralistic assumptions that obscure the processes by which the racial system systematically allots advantages according to racial criteria that have little to do with merit. The meritocratic argument ignores the unacknowledged forms of preferential treatment that have historically operated in favor of white Europeans, going back to the Discovery Doctrine that authorized white Europeans to occupy sovereign indigenous territories. Transatlantic slavery, similarly, enriched Europe and its descendants in all of the Americas. In both the United States and Brazil, the white advantage persisted in the form of discriminatory land grants, discriminatory immigration policies, and property giveaways or simply through the disqualification, on the basis of race, of a large sector of the population from competition for jobs, benefits, and the vote.

In discursive-ideological terms, individualism, meritocratism, Social Darwinism, and antigovernment free-market ideology all play a role in the rejection of remedial measures. Some middle-class whites, convinced that their gains derive solely from individual merit rather than from inherited resources, reject not only Affirmative Action but also other democratizing measures such as universal health care, even though health care is to middle-class advantage. At the same time, longstanding prejudices project racialized minorities and immigrants of color as irresponsible parasites undeserving of "entitlements." A short-sighted narcissism seeks to deprive "others" of their fair slice of the pie yet ends up boomeranging against the prejudiced themselves, who lose their own slice.

One Orwellian claim by the opponents of remedial measures is that antiracist measures are actually racist. The claim equates the mere naming of racism with racism itself. As part of that equation, the opponents define racism in a constrictive and ultimately trivializing fashion. In *The End of Racism*, for example, Dinesh D'Souza calls racism "an opinion that recognizes real civilization differences and attributes them to biology."[5] This definition embeds a number of sleights of hand, beginning with the idea that racism is an "opinion." If racism is simply an "opinion," and if "we all have our opinions," then racism is just one more idea operating in the "free market of ideas," where the best idea wins in the most meritocratic of all possible worlds. But racism is above all a social relation—"systematized hierarchization implacably pursued," in Fanon's concise formula[6]—a structured ensemble of social discourses and institutional practices anchored in material structures and embedded in historical relations of power. Individuals do not have to actively express or practice racism to be its beneficiaries. If racism were merely an opinion, it would not be so dangerous.

Revisiting Enlightenment debates about race and civilizational hierarchies, D'Souza speaks of "real civilizational differences"—a polite way of saying civilizational hierarchies—thus siding with the ideologists who rank civilizations as superior or inferior. The very word "civilization" brings its own historical baggage of the line marking off civilized from savage. D'Souza's only concession to antiracist discourse is to reject the attribution of "civilizational differences" to biology, a move that opens the way for attributing these differences to "culture." On the one hand, D'Souza borrows from the critique of scientific racism, but his invocation of "civilizational differences" tips the scales toward hierarchical rankings and thus moves from biological to cultural racism. Confronted with the "affirmative" correction of historical injustices, the right, forgetting the history of white advantage, becomes the partisan of an abstract equality. The empty ideal of "color-blindness" posits progress as "transcending" race and therefore condemns both white racism and black liberationism as wrongfully "race conscious." But color-blindness itself can be a "particular discourse of power" used by the dominant group to rationalize its own privileged status.[7] Legalistic claims about equality and rights, in this sense, actually hide another unacknowledged set of social credentials (whiteness, maleness, propertiedness, Americanness), that off-the-books "racial contract" that constitutes the real basis of inclusion.[8]

In all three national zones, the backlash against Affirmative Action programs has been expressed in accusations of "reverse racism," "race-based quotas," "special rights for blacks," "rigid quotas," "preferential hiring," and so forth. But to those who reject compensatory measures in the name of "fairness" and "color-blindness," we pose the following questions: What explains this recently acquired passion for "fairness"? Why were there no protests about the discriminatory policies that historically favored your own group? And why not correct the horrendous legacy left by those prowhite measures? Also, the inertia of discrimination penalizes the nation as a whole, condemning a vital part of the citizenry to withered dreams and the waste of human resources. And how do we explain the selective outrage about cost? Why have so many white Americans willingly allowed their taxes to benefit the Pentagon yet reject measures to help people of color? (The Tea Party's hostility to "government," for example, is highly selective, aimed not at costly wars but only at programs benefiting the poor and people of color.) Why is it only when nonwhites benefit that whites develop a passion for cost cutting?

Critics of Affirmation Action call it divisive, impractical, and rooted in race thinking. But when asked for concrete alternatives, they usually offer only a motley of tired proposals such as improving education, in short, more of the same universalist proposals that fail to address the specifically racial dimension of the problem. Those who refuse all concrete proposals for moving the society toward substantive equality ultimately support the status quo of racial advantage. The real question is not who is racist but what can be done collectively to transform the systems of racialized inequality. Although the debates about remedial measures often devolve into passionately anecdotal quarrels about individual cases and comparative qualifications, the issues gain a different perspective when seen within the *longue durée* of colonial history and the Enlightenment debates. In our five-century perspective, the history of the Black Atlantic since 1492 becomes readable as a case of self-perpetuating affirmative whiteness, whereby some Europeans (obviously not all, since some were indentured servants) were granted the right to invade, dispossess, enslave, occupy, and dominate resource-rich land. Affirmative Action for whites operated even at the time of abolition, in that slaveholders were compensated for losing "their" slaves. "If blacks have the right to be free," as Alexis de Tocqueville put it, "the colonists [also] have the right not to be ruined by the freedom of the blacks."[9] The slave owners were compensated for their crime, while the enslaved were not compensated for their suffering and their loss of freedom.[10]

In the United States, postabolition official policies have almost always favored whites, including poor southern whites who were symbolically "compensated" for *not* allying with blacks. The U.S. government has blandished a cornucopia of benefits on whites, whether in the concessions of land taken from the Native Americans (e.g., the Homestead Act in 1862) or in laws that favored whites by segregating housing.[11] As William Julius Wilson points out, many government programs, such as the Federal Housing Administration inaugurated in 1934, were selectively administered to benefit whites.[12] Educational "set-aside programs," meanwhile, funnel the children of elite whites into prestigious universities. It was a "legacy" program that guaranteed George W. Bush—later an opponent of Affirmative Action—a place in Yale University despite his mediocre academic performance. In fact, Bush's entire career provides a striking exemplum of "Affirmative Action" for wealthy whites, even those with learning disabilities and a penchant for alcohol, cocaine, and destructive behavior.

The hostility to compensatory measures for blacks is undergirded by toxic prejudices about the history of Africa and slavery that go back to the right wing of the Enlightenment. First, the Eurocentric view of Africa as a dysfunctional continent lacking in legitimate culture implied that kidnapped Africans had lost nothing of value and were therefore undeserving of compensation. Second, the hostility is reinforced by the claim, traceable to conservative Enlightenment thinkers, now resuscitated by right-wing ideologists such as David Horowitz, that slavery served to "civilize" and "humanize" Africans. Third, the hostility is exacerbated by the outrageous notion that blacks owe whites compensation because whites such as Lincoln freed the slaves. Fourth, it is reinforced by the liberal mystification of a purely individual "freedom," supposedly violated by "group rights." The hostility is buttressed, finally, by a complacent gradualism, voiced by some abolitionists in the past and by some white liberals later, that blacks were not "ready" for freedom. This gradualism has a very old pedigree. Some 18th-century philosophers, some American Founding Fathers, and even some French and American abolitionists warned against a "precipitous" emancipation. Some 20th-century white liberals, meanwhile, warned black activists to "go slow." But only "master race" assumptions could normalize the idea that black people, after centuries of oppression, should patiently wait for full equality, especially when the promise of equality had been inscribed in official documents as the national creed from the very beginnings of the republic.

The Quotas Debate in Brazil

In Brazil, in the wake of redemocratization in the mid-1980s, and thanks to the efforts of activists of all colors, many remedial measures, based on both race and class, have been proposed or adopted. A first effort, Law 650, proposed by Senator Jose Sarney in 1998, mandated that blacks be granted 20 percent of the positions in public jobs and in higher education. In the state of Rio de Janeiro, state law mandated that 40 percent of the places in the state universities be granted to blacks. The Federal University of Bahia, the State University of Rio, the University of Brazilia, and the University of São Paulo have also developed projects to facilitate access for black students. Rosana Heringer, in her study of ten Brazilian cities between 1995 and 1999, identified 124 programs designed to combat racial discrimination, and such programs have increased exponentially since then.[13] The Lula government instituted a Ministry of Racial Equality. It also named Joaquim Benedito Barbosa Gomes, a black judicial scholar and an expert on comparative (United States–Brazil) Affirmative Action, to the Supreme Court. Barbosa Gomes argues in his writing that the Brazilian state, despite a rhetoric of impartiality, has indirectly supported the white elite through tax laws favoring private schools.

Along lines similar to those argued by proponents of critical law, critical race, and racial contract theory in the United States, Barbosa Gomes contrasts the merely formal and procedural equality of the oft-invoked "equality under the law" derived from classical contractarian theory with a more substantive equality that would rectify the inequities generated by a racialized system. Those nations that prattle the most about "equality before the law," Gomes points out, "often display the highest indices of social injustice, since the emphasis on process ignores all the factors that precede the entry of individuals within the competitive job market."[14] Anthropologist/activist José Jorge de Carvalho, similarly, argues that "Brazilian society has functioned . . . as a self-regulating system which constantly reproduces the same racial inequality."[15] He metaphorizes the unfairness as a race across a river in which whites cross by motorboat, while blacks have to swim.[16] (Deploying a different sports analogy, Kimberlé Crenshaw compares the U.S. situation to a racetrack where some socially privileged individuals are granted immediate access, while others are hampered by endless hurdles before even getting within sight of the track.)[17]

The 1988 Brazilian Constitution was remarkably progressive with regard to women's and indigenous rights, antiracist and antisexist laws, principles of tolerance and cultural pluralism, and the protection of individual dignity. The constitution rejected a merely formal "equality of opportunity" in favor of a material equality of results. The challenge has been to translate those golden proclamations into the leaden currency of everyday life, in a national context where the law is often more of a pious expression of "nice ideas" than of real-world practice. Affirmative Action, in this sense, gives flesh and vitality to the constitution's promises. Yet egalitarian provisions are not completely new: every Brazilian constitution has contained provisions for formal due process and fundamental rights—provisions inspired by the French and U.S. constitutions—but in practice the courts have only protected the rights of the powerful. Yet at the same time, the 1988 constitution has fueled what James Holston calls "insurgent citizenship," an unprecedented attempt to use the law to secure rights, but which has in turn exposed the incapacities of the law and amplified the problem of impunity.[18]

Some critics point to a technical flaw in the application of any quota system in Brazil, that is, the dependence on individuals' self-designation as "black," a procedure even more problematic in Brazil than elsewhere given the instability of racial definition. In one notorious case, one identical twin was declared "black," while the other was declared "white." Some phenotypically black students have refused, as a matter of principle, to take advantage of quotas, while some phenotypically white students have rushed to take advantage of them.[19] Thus, Affirmative Action raises fears of the opportunism spoofed in the Hollywood film *Soul Man*, in which a white student blackens his skin to qualify for financial aid. To the argument that "no one really knows who is black since we are all mixed," some black activists have responded that when the military police single out black people for arrest or a beating, or when doormen send black people to use the service elevator, they seem to know the code that determines essential blackness. When the military police raid a bus and arrest only black people, the police, in their assigned social role as impromptu "physiognomists," act according to a clear idea of who qualifies as black. "Black," in this sense, refers not only to phenotype and color but also to the oppressed positionality of those whom Brazilian philosopher Denise Ferreira da Silva calls the "affectables," those whom state disciplinary power treats as subcitizens.[20] Racial profiling in Brazil, denounced both in activist literature and in rap songs, in this sense, reveals the existential limitations of miscegenation as panacea, much as racial profiling of blacks and Maghrebians in France reveals the limitations of republican color-blindness, or as racial profiling of blacks for DWB (driving while black) or of Arabs for FWA (flying while Arab) in the United States reveals the limitations of "equal opportunity" and "all men are created equal."

Unlike in the United States, the Brazilian opposition to Affirmative Action does not necessarily come from those who are normally associated with right-wing or with laissez-faire market ideologies. Nor have Brazilian politicians exploited race as a wedge issue. The Brazilian left critics often endorse egalitarian goals while objecting to the means. A certain Marxizing left, meanwhile, argues that "it is not race but class," or "it will divide the working class." Yet the actual arguments, in another instance of the right-left convergence noted earlier, bear a *discursive* affinity with those of the U.S. right. On occasion, the Brazilian critics even explicitly cite U.S. conservatives. One of the most vocal opponents of Affirmative Action, journalist Ali Kamel, for example, cites as "obligatory reading" Thomas Sowell's attack on Affirmative Action, calling him "one of the most renowned American intellectuals," without explaining that Sowell, as an ally of the Bush administration and a Fellow of the right-wing think tank the Hoover Institution, forms part of that statistical *rara avis* called the "black Republican."[21]

The opposition to Affirmative Action in Brazil was expressed in the popular media and in protest petitions. The cover of the newsweekly *Veja* (June 6, 2007) declared that "race does not exist." An April 21, 2008, petition entitled "113 Anti-racist Citizens against Racial Laws," meanwhile, argued that educational laws (ADI 3.330 and ADI 3.197) favoring racial quotas violated the constitution by establishing distinctions between Brazilians. Signed by well-known academics (Alba Zaluar), poets (Ferreira Gullar), theater directors (Gerald Thomas), and novelists (João Ubaldo Ribeiro), the petition claimed that such laws risk "racializing" social life in Brazil by installing the U.S. black/white system of classification. Like U.S. conservatives, the petitioners quote Martin Luther King, Jr.'s "content of character" discourse, specifically citing Thomas Sowell's claim that Affirmative Action has aggravated the racial divide. The text even cites Bush-appointed Supreme Court Justice John G. Roberts, Jr., to the effect that Affirmative Action constitutes a form of racial discrimination. While acknowledging racial prejudice in Brazil, the petition reiterates the usual comparative commonplaces that Brazil, unlike the United States, is miscegenated, lacks racial hatred, and so forth, to claim that "Brazil is not a racist nation."

A former critic of the "myth of racial democracy," British-born anthropologist Peter Fry, meanwhile, argues for a kind of Brazilian exceptionalism that obviates the need for compensatory measures.[22] Due to the specific configurations of race and class in Brazil, Fry suggests, Affirmative Action risks sowing the seeds of racial division within the very group that is now the most socially integrated: the Brazilian lower middle class. While Fry would otherwise have little in common with Arthur Schlesinger or Dinesh D'Souza, he shares with them the idea that compensatory measures bring social division. Sambista/activist/intellectual Nei Lopes, in contrast, argues that Affirmative Action policies would help create a real "racial democracy" by forging full citizenship for black Brazilians.[23] While many activists reject the "myth of racial democracy," Fry argues that this myth has the virtue of giving voice to a progressive norm condemning racism and endorsing democratic tolerance as values shared by all Brazilians. "Racial democracy," for Fry, is not descriptive but prescriptive, an inspiring ideal or "good idea" with positive effects in the world.[24] (Here, one is tempted to invoke Gandhi's boutade about "Western Civilization" as a "good idea" that has also "never been tried.")

Although such myths can function as part of a consensus antiracism, however, they can also function as a form of denial. The rough functional correlative to "racial democracy" in the United States, in this sense, might be the "myth of equal opportunity" as a productive fiction or salutary belief shared by all Americans, even if, unlike "racial democracy," it does not explicitly invoke race. The "all men are created equal" clause of the Declaration of Independence, similarly, might also be seen as a "good idea" or promissory note that Civil Rights activists tried to "redeem." These value-laden slogans are invested with different significations by different groups; only concrete struggles give them flesh and meaning. In this sense, the fight for racial justice can take place within various discursive frameworks, whether within "racial democracy" in Brazil or the Bill of Rights and equal opportunity in the United States, or republican egalitarianism in France.

Fry roots his opposition within a larger comparative geographical/cultural schema that contrasts Anglo-segregationist societies such as the United States, the United Kingdom, and colonial Rhodesia/Zimbabwe (where Fry lived and worked), as places where cultural borders are rigid and strictly policed, with Luso-Tropical societies such as Brazil and Mozambique as sites of fusion, ambiguity, and flexibility. Fry thus reconfigures two traditional discourses: the perennial Anglo/Latin dichotomy and Luso-Tropicalism à la Freyre. But Fry's analysis departs from these antecedents in crucial ways: (1) Fry's choice of model is not a product of national or ethnic narcissism in terms of his own origins as an "Anglo," since he clearly favors the Latin/Luso-Tropical side of the dichotomy; and (2) unlike Freyre, whose visceral antipathy to black militancy was allied with a sentimental attachment to Portuguese colonialism, Fry has been a progressive antiracist and anticolonialist.

In "Affirmative Action in Brazil," João Feres, Jr., rebuts the anti–Affirmative Action arguments by pointing out (1) that roughly half the Brazilian population suffers from mechanisms of social exclusion despite the principles of formal equality expressed in the law; (2) that inequality is statistically evident in clear gaps in income, education, and employment; (3) that this chronic inequality has not been ameliorated by the modernization of the economic system or by the democratization of political and social institutions; (4) that the most prestigious positions in the country are occupied almost exclusively by whites; and (5) that education, rather than being a remedy for social exclusion, forms a key site in the reproduction of inequality. Since Affirmative Action seeks to counter precisely those forms of the reproduction of inequality that have escaped universal policies, Feres argues, it is nonsensical to assert that such universal policies must *precede* the adoption of Affirmative Action policies.[25]

The Brazilian Deleuzians associated with the thinking of Michael Hardt and Antonio Negri, meanwhile, contest "identity" while also scoring the "hypocrisy" of the opponents of Affirmative Action. Antonio Negri and Giuseppe Cocco object to the opportunistic use of miscegenation as a proof of lack of racism:

> The way in which the corporatist-nationalist oligarchy recognizes the rich processes of miscegenation only in order to negate them could not be more clear: they

deny the infinitely multiple dimension (in terms of colors, cultures, languages) produced by miscegenation (and not only in the past) while at the same time denying its element of resistance in contesting the most perverse forms of domination (of bipower, of power over life itself) that characterized the slaveholding state in Brazil. The necessarily multiple dynamics of miscegenation is opposed to the gray configuration of official discourses: "Here there are no blacks and whites; we are all dark; we are all gray." This is the argument used systematically, by both left and right, against Affirmative Action quotas. This double negation converges in a general consensus among the elites who claim that "the contemporary struggle in Brazil is social not racial." . . . By denying the general notion of "racism" the nationalist left closes its eyes to the evident modulation which connects class and color.[26]

The implicit contrast here is between miscegenation as a subversive bottom-up process and miscegenation as a stabilized reality of which a unitary nation, and especially its elite, is "proud." The alarmist warnings about an imminent chaos supposedly to be brought about by Affirmative Action, constitute what Negri/Cocco call "*chantagem*" (blackmail) aimed at distracting attention from the fact that it is the racialized inequality itself that is alarming.

Anthropologist José Jorge de Carvalho brings these arguments to bear on higher education. As the open sesame to opportunity, the Brazilian university forms the key to access to economic and cultural capital. Provocatively calling the Brazilian university one of the "most racist on the planet," for him even more discriminatory than the South African university during the twilight years of apartheid, Carvalho offers devastating statistics about white advantage. In a country generally considered to be 47 percent black or mestizo, the student population is roughly 2 percent black and 8 percent *pardo* (dark). The faculty, meanwhile, is 99 percent white. Black professors at the University of São Paulo represent less than half of 1 percent of the aggregate. At the current rate, Carvalho points out, it will take sixty years for the university to arrive even at a scandalously low 1 percent figure.[27] For black students and faculty, racial stress gets superimposed on socioeconomic and educational stress, to the ultimate advantage of whites: "The racial disadvantage suffered by blacks in economic terms provides an advantage to whites in the struggle to enter the best universities."[28] In a point also relevant to the United States, Carvalho links the racist immigration policies that favored European immigrants over blacks in the past to the fact that many of the present-day beneficiaries of the status quo, now opposed to Affirmative Action, are themselves descendants of these same European immigrants. Thus, a discrimination effectuated through immigration policy at the turn of the 20th century has mutated into another kind of discrimination at the turn of the 21st century, in the form of resistance to measures that would correct the social imbalance created by inherited advantages.

Affirmative Action for blacks (and Amerindians) in higher education, for Carvalho, could potentially bring many benefits: (1) reparations for three hundred years of slavery; (2) the substantive acquisition of the equal rights promised by the 1988 constitution; (3) the multiplier effect triggered by placing blacks in positions of power; (4) an intellectual life less hampered by the "blind Eurocentrism" of a university system rooted epistemically in an ethnocentric imaginary; and (5) the intensification of antiracist struggle in Brazil. To those who warn of increased tension, Carvalho argues that such tension is productive in that it forces intellectuals to abandon their pose of scientific objectivity in order to opt for or against concrete action. Finally, Carvalho calls for a black-white-indigenous alliance for justice and inclusion.[29] Lula's minister of racial equality, Matilde Ribeiro, answered the "increased tension" argument in an even more frontal way: "I'd rather have whites resentful, with blacks in the universities, than whites happy and blacks out of the universities."[30]

On June 17, 2010, the Brazilian Senate approved a "Racial Equality Law" aimed at reducing racial inequality. The law mandates the teaching of the history of Africa and of Afro-Brazil and recognizes the property rights of descendants of the rebel *quilombos*. To the chagrin of many activists, however, the law did not endorse quotas for blacks in Brazilian schools or fiscal incentives for enterprises hiring 20 percent black employees, or a proposal for a 10 percent quota of blacks in political party organizations. The law also rejected compensatory indemnization for blacks—that is, reparations—for the consequences of discrimination over the course of Brazilian history.

The American Foil

Many of the perennial Brazil-U.S. comparative topoi make their way into the current debates. Some defenses of the Brazilian racial status quo present themselves as resistance to the "American model," as if the refusal of measures to correct injustice against blacks were somehow a refusal of imperialism. (A similar sophism operates when Third World nationalists defend patriarchal practices by denouncing feminism as a "Western export.") The critics, at their most ideologically barren, use the United States as a foil, so that the angelization of Brazil goes hand in hand with a demonization of the United States. Some U.S.-based advocates of Affirmative Action, meanwhile, arrogantly assume that Brazilians, as colonial mimic men, need only copy the superior U.S.-American civil right model.

The U.S.-Brazil comparison is deployed by both advocates and detractors in the Affirmative Actions debates. Thus, the detractors invoke the very real horrors of U.S. segregation, lynching, and the one-drop rule to rebut Affirmative Action proposals. José Jorge de Carvalho speaks of a nationalist sophistry, whereby the question shifts from what measures would reduce social exclusion to the supposed national provenance of the measures. Carvalho therefore invokes comparisons not to the United States but rather to other countries such as Mexico, Cuba, Trinidad, Canada, the United Kingdom, and the Netherlands, countries whose universities, in his account, are all more racially integrated than the Brazilian university.[31]

One of the most brazen examples of the instrumentalization of comparison to narcissistic advantage is Ali Kamel's symptomatically titled *We Are Not Racists: A Reaction against Those Who Want to Transform Us into a Bicolor Nation*.[32] The title itself is perhaps more revealing than the author intends. First, the "We" and the "Us" are constructed as implicitly white, since it is to whites that accusations of racism are usually addressed. Second, the subtitle mistakenly assumes that Affirmative Action aims to promote a bicolor view of race, when in fact it indirectly *undermines* bipolarity by promoting greater equality for a transsectional series of discriminated groups, including Native Americans, Hispanics, Asian Americans, and, importantly, women. Even if seen as bureaucratically separable, the groups invoked actually form more of a spectrum. In fact, many analysts see women, of all colors, as having been the primary beneficiaries of these measures.

For Kamel, Affirmative Action signifies the danger of an Americanization whereby, as Kamel puts it, "we, who were so proud of our miscegenation, of our spectrum of colors, will be reduced to a nation of blacks and whites, and worse, a nation of whites and blacks where whites oppress blacks."[33] Kamel's use of the future tense to envision a Brazil that might someday become a nation where "whites oppress blacks" constitutes a remarkable piece of historical amnesia. The buried premise is that Brazilian whites have never oppressed blacks, while any future oppression will be due to outside influence! Three centuries of slavery and over a century of postabolition racial disadvantage are airbrushed away. This outrageous claim "passes" only thanks to the comparison to the United States, where, for Kamel, "racism is harder, more explicit, more direct, ... [where] there is a total repulsion toward everything that is associated with blacks; while here, almost everyone, including the racists, are in love with everything that is seen as coming from Africa."[34]

Despite the hyperbole—*total* repulsion, *everyone* in love with Africa—Kamel does point to some real differences. One can indeed find a broad enthusiasm in Brazil, at least in recent decades, for Afro-Brazilian culture, although one can also find hostility to it (from the Catholic Church in the past and from Pentecostalists in the present). Kamel's analysis elides the elite's historical hostility to African culture on the Brazilian side, or the millions of white Americans who treat blacks as equals, admire black celebrities, and vote for Barack Obama on the U.S. side.

A binaristic schema pits a very rosy portrait of Brazil against a very sinister portrait of the United States. The point is not that racism in the United States is not sinister, only that the standard contrasts require recalibration in the age of Oprah Winfrey and Barack Obama. They also require revision at a time when continental Africans—Nigerians, Ghanaians, Senegalese, Malians, Ethiopians—are immigrating to the United States in record numbers. In fact, the United States is experiencing the largest wave of African (and Caribbean) immigration since the importation of slaves was outlawed in 1808. Furthermore, these immigrants are the best-educated immigrants in the country—and the loss here is for Africa—better educated than immigrating Asians, Europeans, and Latin Americans. The point is not that the United States is "ahead" of Brazil—*au contraire!*—but rather that distinctions based on reified comparisons no longer enjoy the purchase that they once had.

Kamel's title, by giving voice to a falsely accused white "we," hints at the burning core of the "narcissistic wound." In Kamel's view, not only are white Brazilian individuals not racist, but also Brazil as a whole is not racist: "Here, and this cannot be denied, one finds fewer of those odious people—racists."[35] First, let us grant that there are more racists in the United States. The huge audience for racist demagogues such as Limbaugh, Savage, and Beck who envenom public discourse would suggest that Kamel is absolutely right. In our constant shuttle between Brazil and the United States, we are often horrified by the xenophobic meanness and race-baiting that permeates the U.S. media, where everything is seen through a black/white grid very much out of sync with the complex multiplicities of the actually existing country. Racism, xenophobia, and Islamophobia are close to the emotional center of the Tea Party, which is close to the center of the Republican Party, which is close to the center of power. Unlike the United States, Brazil has no vocal minority of white racists, no KKK, militias, Minute Men, no negrophobic politicians and pundits. In the wake of Obama's election, a boundlessly paranoid American right has questioned Obama's very legitimacy as an elected president by painting him as not really American or a Muslim or a communist or a fascist. No accusation is off-limits, and the corporate media amplify these absurd charges. It is as if hysterical white supremacists were busily confirming Charles Mills's idea that the "racial contract" exists for whites alone.

The racism of U.S. racists, moreover, is arguably more repulsive than that of Brazilian racists. Many horrendous practices—white riots against prosperous blacks, "sunset towns" where blacks were forbidden entry after sunset—find no equivalent in Brazilian history. In these struggles, Brazil also has important cultural advantages. Intermarriage and miscegenation do make minorities less "otherizable." Given the racial divisiveness that has marred many progressive movements in the United States, a class- and race-based interracial egalitarian politics now seems more likely in Brazil.[36] Brazil also has political advantages. Given a political spectrum pitched to the left, social-democratic, and green, Brazilian politicians, like French politicians but unlike U.S. politicians, can propose redistribution of wealth without being accused of "class warfare" and "communism." While millions of Brazilians have moved out of poverty, millions of Americans have moved *into* poverty.

Unlike the United States, where millions of people who want to vote are excluded, in Brazil virtually everyone who wants to vote can vote. And while Obama was demonized merely for being in the same room as a '60s radical (Bill Ayers), Brazil just elected a woman (Dilma Rousseff), who had actually participated in an outlawed guerrilla group (the National Liberation Command). Speaking more generally, one could argue for a kind of Brazilian exceptionalism in terms of a striking lack of xenophobic demonization. In both France and the United States, right-wing politicians develop discourses that contrast "real Americans" or "real French" with less legitimate others or that contrast those whose differences are "assimilable" with those whose differences are not. Such discourses are not part of mainstream political discourse in Brazil. Even the Brazilian dictatorship stigmatized ideological others—the enemy within—but not racial or alien others.

In some ways, the United States is struggling with problems—the legacies of racial segregation, the extremism of white-supremacist groups, and the anti-Latin and anti-Arab xenophobia of an out-of-control right wing—that do not exist in Brazil. Yet in other ways, Brazil confronts problems that do not currently exist in the United States to the same extent: massive poverty, favelafication, a dysfunctional judicial system, an almost exclusively white political and corporate class, and so forth. The real issue, in any case, is not either the relative severity of the racism or the exact proportion of racists but rather the structured (and structuring) system of cumulative racial advantage that characterizes both countries.[37] The dumb inertia of inequality in both countries can be said to have produced a situation of "racism without racists" or, more accurately, a system that no longer needs racists, a system that habitually allots privileges to one group and immiseration to the other. Within this social reproduction of inequality, class, caste, race, color, cultural capital, and the relative coefficient of behavioral "Europeanness" all play a role. The "Whose racism is worse?" and "Where are there more racists?" questions are the wrong questions. Critical race studies has long gone beyond them to explore the deeper institutional, legal, systemic, and epistemic undergirdings of racism. The more crucial question is what societies can do collectively to dismantle systems of racialized advantage.

The "we are not racist like the Americans" argument advanced by Kamel is ultimately a non sequitur. First, it implies that only North Americans are accusing

Brazilians of racism, when in fact it is largely Brazilians (black and some white) who make the claim. Second, Kamel seems to be making the absurd suggestion that the introduction of "American" measures in Brazil, even those designed to combat racism, can only bring . . . more racism! Kamel's argument is parasitic on the widely disseminated portrait of the odious American racist—and American racists are indeed odious—as a foil for the tolerant Brazilian. Transposing situations, it would be as if Americans, in the 1960s, were to oppose Civil Rights by pointing to the even harsher inequities of South African apartheid. The point, in our view, is not to establish "whose racism is worse" but rather to confront the specific modalities of racial domination in each zone, drawing on local cultural strengths along with global strategies of resistance.[38]

Although Kamel acknowledges that racism exists in Brazil, the acknowledgment comes accompanied by disqualifying asides such as "like everywhere else in the world" that downplay its significance. The admission is articulated in the manner of a recognition that "diseases exist," that is, problems exist, and of course we are trying to eradicate them. But racial hierarchy is rooted in the enslavement, subordination, and discrimination of African-descended peoples and is thus foundational to a Brazil that received some 40 percent of the Africans sent to the Americas. In what might be called the default mode of sentimental nationalism, Kamel offers an amnesiac history of a "Brazilian nation that always condemned racism," and where "after abolition, there were no institutional barriers to blacks."[39] Kamel's formulation leaves us with a question—"If there were no barriers, why did Brazilian blacks end up so poor and marginalized?"—and an implied answer—"They must have themselves to blame." Thus, a country whose structures were dominated by slavery during almost four centuries, that systematically favored European immigrants over the newly freed blacks, is supposed to have magically transformed itself into a nonracist country with the stroke of Princesa Isabel's abolitionist pen. In this sense, Kamel's narrative recalls the magical history proffered by American right-wingers, for whom U.S. racism ended with *Brown v. Board of Education* in 1954, leaving black Americans completely equal and ready for meritocratic normalcy, rendering superfluous any "racist" measures such as Affirmative Action.

Kamel's text demonstrates an implicit convergence with the arguments of U.S. conservatives. The difference is that for Kamel the problem to be addressed is the bicolor racial model itself. But while the bicolor model is indeed oppressive, discrimination can also occur without it. Like some "anti-antiracist" analysts in France and the United States, Kamel implies that calling attention to racial injustice is itself racist. But Brazil, like the United States, was already riven by social and racial disunity long before the Affirmative Action debates. Brazilian journalists have long spoken of "social apartheid" and an "undeclared civil war," which, while certainly not exclusively racial, clearly has a racial dimension, as becomes obvious in the sociological literature, in news reports of police massacres, and in the many feature films and documentaries about the favelas of Rio (*City of God, City of Man, Quase Irmãos, Falcão,* and others), all of which expose a situation of class *and* race oppression. Both class and race are inscribed in everyday language—in a society divided between the familiarly addressed *vocês* and the noble *senhores*—and in architecture, where even the Brazilia apartment buildings designed by the Communist Oscar Niemeyer are equipped with maids' quarters.

With a nod to "class-not-race" economism, the not-exactly-Marxist Kamel writes that "racism derives essentially from classism."[40] Ignoring the history of elite stigmatization of miscegenation as a cause of "degeneracy," Kamel also claims, "We Brazilians have always been proud of our miscegenation."[41] In any case, miscegenation is the ambiguous product of a painful power-laden process of contact and domination, not something to be praised for its own sake. (Serbian soldiers raping and impregnating Bosnian Muslim women engendered a kind of miscegenation, but few would call it progressive.) Miscegenation can even become a means of ethnocide. In Brazil, as Antonio Negri and Giuseppe Cocco point out, the native peoples were systematically annihilated through two mechanisms: "extermination pure and simple (through the sword or through contamination) as well as through a miscegenation calculated to make up for the demographic insufficiency of migrationary flow from the Iberian peninsula."[42] A society can be deeply miscegenated and structurally oppressive, like Brazil, or somewhat miscegenated and structurally oppressive, while in denial about its miscegenation, like the United States. Praising miscegenation per se runs the risk of sanctifying the fait accompli of the colonial violence that generated the mixing in the first place.[43]

Kamel's denial of racism is especially ironic in light of the fact that he is the news director at Brazil's powerful Globo network. Going back to protests over a blackface version of *Uncle Tom's Cabin* in 1968, Globo has been a prime target of black activists, who have accused both the entertainment and news divisions of discriminating against blacks. The star reporters are almost all white, as are the heroes and heroines of the vast majority of the telenovelas. As detailed in Joel Zito Araújo's book (and film) *Negation of Brazil*, telenovelas rarely include middle-class black characters, couples, or families. Under the pressure of boycotts and protests, Globo has made a few concessions, and the situation has improved in the wake of the commercial success of the film *City of God* and its television spinoff, *City of Men*. Some black actors, notably Taís Araújo and Lázaro Ramos, have broken out of the maid, servant, slave, and hustler syndrome to become leads, but in the news shows, only one black male reporter occasionally anchors weekend shows, and one black female reporter appears on Brazil's Sunday-night news show. Television networks and advertising agencies have lobbied vigorously against all bills that would require them to cast more blacks. Although Kamel speaks of a general Brazilian pride in "our miscegenation," the racial aesthetics of Globo telenovelas and commercials contradict this claim, seeming more appropriate to a Scandinavian country than to a black-mestizo-majority Brazil.

Kamel, in his desire to "protect" Brazilians from charges of racism, invents a Brazil that does not exist. "Bicolorism," after all, is hardly unknown in Brazil. "Black" and "white" are commonly used racial designations, not only by black activists and rappers but also on T-shirts, in popular music, in sociological literature, and in everyday discourse. When poet/composer Vinicius de Moraes called himself "the blackest white man in Brazil," when Florestan Fernandes and Roger Bastide wrote about "blacks and whites" in São Paulo, when Paulinho Camafeu wrote, "White guy, if you knew / the value of being black / you'd take a bath in pitch / and become black too," their words clearly assume that the black/white polarity has a recognized social meaning. A long line of black activists and artists have called attention to blackness in their very names: the theatrical Black Revue Company in the 1920s, the political Black Front Party in the 1930s, the Black Experimental Theatre in the 1940s, not to mention the chromatically tinged names of popular musicians such as Blecaute (Blackout), Chocolate, and Príncipe Pretinho (Little Black Prince). The lack of white parallels—there is no "White Experimental Theatre"—itself signals white normativity. The bicolor model, in sum, already coexists alongside the spectrum model, as it does, to a lesser degree, in the United States as well; the difference is one of degree.

An assimilationist spectrum model also brings its own problems. Given the hypervalorization of whiteness typical of such a model, whiteness as ego-ideal becomes an all-pervasive norm. Racism everywhere is a situated utterance; it depends on who addresses whom, with what intention, in what tone, and in relation to what power dynamic. Nothing better illustrates the Brazilian mix of camaraderie and paternalism than the situation in which white Brazilians, in order to spare the feelings of their black interlocutors, pay them the "compliment" of calling them *moreno* (brown-skinned) rather than preto (black). Such acts of interlocution conjugate sincere goodwill—the white person really is concerned with the black person's feelings—with a racist premise (that lighter is better than darker), along with a certain fluidity of racial definition. Within down-the-ladder racism, the white is constructed as superior to the *moreno*, who is constructed as superior to the mulatto, and so on; what is forgotten is the hegemonic whiteness that constructed the ladder in the first place.

Some Brazilian critics argue that remedial measures will bring all that is wrong with U.S. society into a tolerant Brazilian society. In the latter half of the 20th century, a putatively coherent and univocal "American Way of Life" came to be seen in Brazil, not without reason, as tense, stressful, hypercompetitive, and racially segregated, all contrary to a lived sense of "Brazilianness." The critics fear that such measures would undermine the hospitable, easygoing, live-and-let-live ways of Brazil, leading to censorious attitudes and increased racial tension, so that Brazilians would begin to look at each other across a chasm of suspicion all too common in the United States. But while this concern is completely understandable, Brazil would arguably be *even more* generous and cordial, and less hypocritical in its cordiality, were it shorn of the inequalities that rend the society. The issue, ultimately, is not one of Brazil's "borrowing" a movement from elsewhere but rather of seeing the potential zones of reciprocity, within parallel and interconnected struggles, as part of a transnational antiracist network.

In the 20th century, discourses of racial superiority have partially given way to discourses of fear, and here clear differences distinguish the various situations. In Brazil, some potential white fears are of a black-mestizo majority, whence resistance to melding *pardos* (dark-skinned people) and *pretos* (blacks) into one group of black-mestizos and the need to ward off a fear of that majority through ideologies of co-optive inclusiveness. Redefining Brazil as a black-mestizo country would change the social dynamics; the key question would no longer be about the relative degree of racial integration in comparison with other nation-states but rather about the historical process by which whites came to dominate a white-minority country. In the United States, meanwhile, the fear is of a relatively powerless *minority*, and in this sense the fear is an even more phobic and irrational attempt to ward off fear by otherizing the people supposedly "provoking" the fear. The Black Atlantic thus offers a variegated spectrum of white anxieties: the fear of a black minority (more typical of the United States), the fear of a black majority (more typical of Brazil), and the fear of what Public Enemy called "a black planet" (i.e., fears based on the minority status of whites in the larger world).

The Advent of Whiteness Studies

While a critique of whiteness was implicit in proposals for Affirmative Action, it was explicitly thematized in the academic project called "critical whiteness studies." The consolidation of positions for academics of color, and the increased institutional space for race-related fields of inquiry, helped open the way for this ancillary project. As an interdisciplinary formation, whiteness studies exposed whiteness as unmarked social norm, shedding light on the process by which whites have been authorized to fly above race in the bright skies of the wild blue yonder, while others remain mired, as it were, in the mud of their dark particularity.

Whiteness studies as a field would not have existed without its precursors: the black critics of white racism who suffered firsthand the consequences of white supremacy and were thus well equipped to discern and articulate the psychic disturbances of whiteness. As a matter of sheer survival, diasporic blacks have been obliged to become astute scrutinizers of the signs and evasions typical of the dominant group. David Roediger has written of the perceptive regard of the enslaved even in the depths of slavery, so that the stark realities of the auction block enforced "the urgent imperative for slaves to penetrate the psychologies of whites and the necessity to make distinctions even among white slave buyers."[44] Thus, what remained invisible to whites—not only the reality of white power but also the blindness of white perception—has historically been visible to most people of color. What Charles Mills calls the "antipodal" position of blacks enabled a critical grasp of the system in its entirety. A vantage point from the margins of the charmed circle of white privilege fostered a view not so much "from afar"—since the oppressed were often within breathing distance of the oppressors—as "from the bottom," a point from which, at least potentially, the marginalized could not but discern the crushing weight of the system pressing down on them.[45]

The first practitioners of "whiteness studies," in this sense, were the Afro-diasporic intellectuals who argued that racism was not a "black" but a "white" problem. Long before Francophone writers such as Césaire, Fanon, and Memmi unpacked colonial racism, and long before James Baldwin spoke of the "lie of whiteness," the forebears of critical whiteness studies emerged in all three zones. In 1910, in "The Souls of White Folk" essay, W. E. B. Du Bois asserted that the "world, in a sudden emotional conversion, has discovered it is white, and by that token, wonderful."[46] In oceanic metaphors, Du Bois declared, "Wave upon wave, each with increasing virulence, is dashing this new religion of whiteness on the shores of our time."[47] Du Bois, whiteness was a form of possessive individualism, a sense of "ownership of the earth, forever and ever, Amen."[48] In 1924, E. Franklin Frazier wrote a similarly seminal essay titled "The Pathology of White Prejudice." Racist whites, he argued, exhibited many of the defining symptoms of dementia. Frazier compared the white "negro complex" to the "somnambulism of the insane."[49] Stephen Steinberg rightly calls Frazier's groundbreaking essay "the seminal beginning of what much later came to be called 'whiteness studies'—a reversal of the lens whereby whites instead of blacks were made the object of inquiry."[50]

Another iconic figure, this time from the other side of the color line, was the white American abolitionist John Brown. Inspired by the Haitian Revolution, Brown led a cohort of black and white rebels in an armed attack at Harper's Ferry, Virginia, on October 16, 1859. His plan was to ignite a slave rebellion in Virginia, to establish a free state in the Appalachians, and to spread the rebellion throughout the South. American history textbooks, as James Loewen points out, tend to imply that Brown was insane,[51] failing to explain why Brown became a hero to many blacks and to abolitionist whites. After Brown's condemnation by a U.S. court, Victor Hugo wrote from France, "The gaze of Europe is fixed at this moment on America. [Hanging Brown] . . . may consolidate slavery in Virginia, but it will certainly shatter American Democracy. You preserve your shame but you will kill your glory."[52] Brown was inspired in his plans to found a multiracial maroon community not only by the Haitian Revolution but also by Native Americans rebellions, and especially by the black-Indian Seminole revolt in Florida.[53] Unlike many paternalistic abolitionists, Brown actually defended, and practiced, total and radical racial equality. Although "a white gentleman," said Frederick Douglass, he "is in sympathy a black man, and as deeply interested in our cause, as though his own soul had been pierced with the iron of slavery."[54] Brown illustrates our contention that radical positions in favor of full racial equality were historical options even for whites. Like Diderot, Brown believed not only in the black *right* to fight back but also in the black capacity to fight back. Blacks richly repaid Brown's love for them. For Du Bois, Brown was the equal of Toussaint Louverture and Nat Turner. "If you are for me," Malcolm X said, "you have to be willing to do as old John Brown did."[55] Many blacks regarded Brown as an honorary black because of his "complete identification with the oppressed. . . . [He] *was* a Negro, and it was in this aspect that he suffered."[56]

In the United States, "whiteness studies" responded to the call by scholars of color for an analysis of the role of racism in generating social injustice. Rejecting class-over-race arguments, scholars such as David Roediger have analyzed the "wages of whiteness" in dividing the working class, within texts that moved toward the goal of "the abolition of whiteness."[57] Whiteness scholars have questioned the quietly overpowering normativity of whiteness, the process by which "race" has been unilaterally attributed to racialized others, while whites themselves are silently enthroned as humanity in its pure, undeviant state. Within this critique, whites unknowingly dwell in a protected fortress of selfhood, which amounts to an unconsciously collective form of bourgeois (*un*)self-consciousness. (Feminists of color have made similar critiques about gender-over-race arguments that elided the advantages of white women.) While whites represented themselves in the cherished nuances of their individual complexity, blacks (and other people of color) carried the allegorical burden of representing a race, in relation to which they could be a "credit" (Martin Luther King, Jr.) or a "debit" (O. J. Simpson). Presumed to be nonimplicated spectators of the racial battles, whites could observe voyeuristically, without being seen. But with black critics of whiteness, as Sartre already pointed out in his "Orphée Noir" preface to Senghor's collection of poetry, the white Peeping Tom is caught in the act; the voyeur is *vu*.

A related scholarly trend calls attention to the complex identities within whiteness itself. It is often forgotten that many whites, especially in the early centuries of American history, had themselves been virtual slaves or, as they were then called, "indentured servants." In *White Cargo: The Forgotten History of Britain's White Slaves in America*, Don Jordan and Michael Walsh focalize the white "surplus people" who were "treated just as savagely as black slaves and, indeed, toiled, suffered and rebelled alongside them."[58] This group, composed of forced migrants, debtors, and vagrants submitted to enclosure or to British rule, were the ancestors of tens of millions of white Americans. The point is not that such whites were the equals in suffering with blacks—since white enslavement was relatively short-lived—but rather that the history of cross-racial victimization, and the possible solidarities implied by it, have been airbrushed out of official history. A "racial wedge" has separated out the two histories so as to abolish the memory of shared suffering and (potentially) mutual identification.

Other scholars, have explored the transmutational alchemy involved in the "becoming white" phenomenon. Historians Theodor Allen and Noel Ignatiev have shown how so-called white ethnics such as the Irish gradually came to define themselves as "white."[59] Caren Kaplan, meanwhile, has explored the fulcral in-between relationality of Jews, alternately colored "dark" in relation to "WASPs" but tinged with whiteness in relation to people of color.[60] While addressing the positionality of whiteness for British Jews, Ruth Frankenberg also shows that whites generally occupy a structural vantage point of assumed power, from which they see both themselves and others from within a comfort zone of the "geography of race."[61]

Opposition to the "special" claims of racial minorities, as George Lipsitz has suggested, often masks the hidden "identity politics" of the dominant group's possessive investment in white Europeanness.[62] Whiteness studies at its best denaturalizes whiteness as norm, exposing its unacknowledged privileges: easy access to institutions, the assumption of noncriminality, the luxury of being above police suspicion and of not being the object of media stereotyping. Critical whiteness studies, in its most radical form, has called for a "new abolitionism" or a radical opting out of white privilege and even for "race treason" in the John Brown tradition. Given actually existing social structures, such voluntaristic self-disenfranchisement is more easily said than done, since a racist system accords benefits even to those whites who do not demand them. Although whiteness, blackness, and redness are merely cultural fictions without any scientific basis, the socially constructed hierarchy between "races" is also a social fact with very real consequences for the distribution of wealth, prestige, opportunity, and psychic well-being.[63] The academic deconstruction of "race," furthermore, does not necessarily mean that race stops doing its pernicious work in the world. The same celebrated black professors who deconstruct race in their classrooms are liable to be harassed for "driving while black" in the streets or even for trying to enter their own homes in Cambridge, Massachusetts.

If "whiteness studies" at its best reveals the subtle operations of racial hegemony, at its worst it recenters whiteness, changing the subject—in a racial version of the show-business dictum that "all publicity is good publicity"—back to white subjectivity. This narcissistic turn amounts to saying, "So enough about you, let's get back to what really matters—us!" And at times, "whiteness," with its constant companion "blackness," remains locked into the old black/white dichotomy, slighting not only the rainbow of colors but also ignoring other factors in social oppression such as caste, religion, and cultural capital. Overall, however, whiteness studies has had the salutary effect of "outing" whiteness, revealing it to be a construct inseparable from its equally constructed black counterpart. Whiteness studies relativized whiteness by putting it in its place as just another ethnicity alongside the others—albeit one historically granted inordinate privilege. Whiteness studies thus signals the demise of what might be called, paraphrasing Stuart Hall, "the innocent *white* subject," putting an end to the unilateral ascription of race to minority "others," while whites remain "raceless" and above the fray.[64] This "outing" of whiteness has also come to pervade popular culture with best-sellers such as Michael Moore's *Stupid White Men* and Christian Lander's *A Whiter Shade of Pale.* Bill Maher, on his *Real Time* cable show (October 15, 2010), similarly mocked the pseudovictimized male crybabies of the Tea Party: "If penises could cry, and I believe they can," he said, "white penises are crying all over America."

Debating Blackness, Whiteness, and *Mestiçagem*

Whiteness studies per se began in Brazil in the 1990s, with a strong influence from the Anglo-American project, while also building on earlier Brazilian critiques of the "ideology of whitening," exemplified by such figures as Oliveira Vianna, who had argued for the "whitening" and "Aryanization" of Brazil, which would turn an "inchoate, pullulating mob of inferior mixed-bloods" into respectable Brazilians.[65] As in the United States, in Brazil too the first whiteness critics were the black writers who called attention to racism as a "white problem." Here a key figure was sociologist Alberto Guerreiro Ramos, who participated in the Experimental Black Theatre and its affiliate the National Black Institute in the 1940s. In the 1950s, Ramos organized group-therapy sessions aimed at healing the dilacerated psyches of black Brazilians. In 1957, Ramos published a seminal article whose title—"The Social Pathology of the Brazilian 'White'"—echoed that of Frazier's 1924 bombshell. Under slavery, Ramos writes, "the dominant minority, of European origin, not only resorted to force and violence, but also to a system of pseudo-justifications, stereotypes, and to processes of psychological domestication. The dogmatic affirmation of the excellence of whiteness and the aesthetic degradation of blackness formed the psychological supports for this exploitation."[66] Ramos socio-psychoanalyzed, as it were, the regnant white ideal ego as "a vestige or survival which hinders the process of psychological maturing of Brazilians."[67] As José Jorge de Carvalho points out, black radical thinkers such as Ramos, Edison Carneiro, and Clóvis Moura, despite their scholarly achievements, were never fully embraced by the Brazilian academy, sometimes dismissed as "militants" rather than scholars, as if social commitment were incompatible with scientific objectivity.[68]

Given the long discussion of race in Brazil, and the many links between the Brazilian and U.S. academies, it is hardly surprising that whiteness studies has emerged, resulting in, for example, the University of São Paulo's "Studies in Whiteness" project. Iray Carone and Maria Aparecida Silva Bento argue in their introduction to *The Social Psychology of Racism: Studies on Whiteness and Whitening in Brazil* (2003) that whiteness as lived in Brazil takes the form of not wanting to name oneself as white.[69] Whiteness, they argue, (1) is more apparent to blacks than to whites, (2) encodes difference as superiority, (3) entails discomfort with the subject of racial discrimination, (4) involves negative attitudes toward blacks who act as equal to whites and are seen as "uppity" exhibitionists. Edith Piza, in "White in Brazil? Nobody Knows, No One Saw," points out that white Brazilians might express pride in some safely distant indigenous ancestor—a Tupi great-grandmother, for example—but without relinquishing white status. For Piza, race is often euphemized, as when her Italo-Brazilian father would not explicitly forbid her befriending or dating blacks but only recommend that she socialize with "her peers." Understanding the implicit norm, she soon restricted her socializing to whites.[70] Rita Segato, meanwhile, stresses the insecurity of a Brazilian whiteness worried about a "contamination" rooted not in "ethnic distance and fear of aliens" as in more segregated societies but rather in "relatedness."[71]

If Ali Kamel proclaims, in effect, that "no white Brazilian is racist," Marco Frenette, in his *Black and White: The Importance of Skin Color*, proclaims exactly the opposite: "all white Brazilians are racist." Both accounts, to our mind, overemphasize the psychological question of racism while neglecting the question of systemic racism. Frenette describes his own childhood as an apprenticeship in white self-entitlement: "Already as a child, they taught me to praise the monotone of whites, and to confound dark skin with an absence of dignity and courage."[72] With whiteness as a "crutch for personhood," Frenette remembers that the black children who joined in games "were not our equals; they were black." Whites grew up with a "comforting sense of superiority," so that white skin was an "informal passport to the good things of life."[73] To be black, meanwhile, was to "live permanently in a hostile reality" veiled by a veneer of good manners.[74] For Frenette, racism can take a wide range of forms: irrational hatred, a desire to possess the (unusual) black body, a "zoological" curiosity about the black "specimen," or the self-congratulatory cultivation of camaraderie ("How extraordinarily generous I am to befriend blacks!").[75] For Frenette, the white Brazilian psyche, as the "involuntary repository of a shameful collective unconscious," is revealed in symptomatic expressions such as "pretty but black" and other "verbal gems" revelatory of an obsolete mentality.[76]

Frenette also questions the "quiet dictatorship of whiteness" that pervades the media. The occasional exceptions, such as black actresses in the telenovelas, merely confirm the rule, since their beauty largely fits into white aesthetic norms. Black children, meanwhile, internalize white ideals of beauty. At home, the mirror provokes quotidian torture, reinforced by harassment of the black body in the streets. "In the accumulation of countless humiliations, direct and veiled insults to one's blackness, the black child becomes conscious of her difference, . . . [obliging her] to develop psychological mechanisms of compensation in order to be emotionally integral, thus avoiding a dangerous fall into resentment or self-pity."[77] Frenette sums up his conclusions: (1) millions of white Brazilians are racist; (2) millions of black Brazilians suffer racism; (3) millions of mixed-race Brazilians oscillate between the attitudes of the dominant and the dominated; (4) the millions of nonracists in Brazil do little to concretely help black people; (5) the mediascape is dominated by a white aesthetic; and, the only positive point, (6) a black movement, the real "sleeping giant," educates children against racism. Like Kamel's book, but from the opposite standpoint, Frenette's book allows little space for contradiction and ambivalence within white attitudes.

Anthropologist José Jorge de Carvalho, meanwhile, offers a powerful indictment of white denial but places more stress on the structures of advantage: "All of us whites draw daily and illicit benefit from living in a racist society. Innumerable privileges . . . help us to maintain our advantages and garner resources. To the extent that Brazilian racism operates within the quotidian, we whites are favored with social, economic and cultural capital which has been distributed unfairly according to racial criteria."[78] In contrast to South African and American whites, Carvalho continues, Brazilian whites do not recognize their status as part of a white collectivity: "The white elite controls the general portrait of race in Brazil, but does not recognize itself as the author of this portrait, nor does it question the tendentiousness which results from its control of the portrait."[79]

Brazilianist John M. Novell, for his part, analyzes the "uncomfortable whiteness of the Brazilian middle class."[80] The clichés that "we Brazilians are a mixture of races" and that "there is no race in Brazil, only the Brazilian race," he argues, are highly ambiguous. If there are no races, he asks, how can there be a mixture of races? Novell traces the celebration of Brazilian miscegenation to three classic texts: Paulo Prado's *Portrait of Brazil* (1928), Freyre's *Masters and Slaves* (1933), and Sérgio Buarque de Holanda's *Roots of Brazil* (1936). In this period, something the white elite had earlier seen as a cause for degeneracy—racial mixture between black and white (as opposed to the red-white miscegenation celebrated by Indianism)—was transformed into a point of pride. But the typical formulation tendency has "we Brazilians mixing with blacks." Anthropologist Angela Gilliam calls this the Freyrean "Great-Sperm-Theory-of-National-Formation";[81] Novell, more discreetly, speaks of a "white indeterminate discursively privileged subject" choosing to mix with people of color.[82] Often this mixture becomes linked to a mythology of the bed, as when Brazilians joke that they have solved the racial problem through mixed sex.

Whiteness studies in Brazil might have been called "*moreno* studies," since some of Brazil's elite intellectuals figure Brazil as a basically *moreno* (brunette, dark white) country benefiting from injections of chromatic alterity. The *moreno* norm is implicit when blond Brazilians are told by other Brazilians that "they do not look Brazilian." Anthropologist Darcy Ribeiro gives voice to this *moreno* pride in *O Povo Brasileiro*: "We are better, because bathed in black and Indian blood, improved and tropical."[83] In this unidirectional formulation, the implicit "we" is Euro-Brazilian: "We [white] Brazilians mix with Indians and blacks" and not "We [black] Brazilians mix with Portuguese and Europeans." Given asymmetries of power, the first version implies top-down tolerance, while the second implies an opportunistic "improving the race." For Novell, the mixed Brazilian is a "genealogical paradox that, in a linguistic construction, is the mixed product of three different races, but as an active grammatical subject, mixes with different races, but not with Europeans, because the assumed underlying continuity and norm is European."[84]

In *Color Witchcraft: Identity, Race, and Gender in Brazil*, Elisa Larkin Nascimento examines the history of defensive reactions to black Brazilian radicalism. What happens to national identity, she asks, in a mestizo country where Eurocentric hegemonies infiltrate the general subjectivity? One result is the symbolic whitening of Brazil, whether through the concept of "Latin" America or through the calls for the "Aryanization" of Brazil or through the myth of a tanned Brazilian "metarace." The appeals to slippery categories such as *moreno* (brunette), *pardo* (dark), and *nordestino* (northeasterner), she points out, "hide" the blackness of the people being referenced. A relational approach to racism, she concludes, necessitates "naming whiteness as an identity and exposing the privileges and deficits generated by racism for different social actors."[85]

A major figure in Brazilian whiteness studies is cultural studies scholar Liv Sovik, a Norwegian American who has lived and taught in Brazil for decades. In *Here No One Is White*, Sovik points to the invisibility of Brazilian whiteness, in a situation where the supervalorization of whiteness goes hand in hand with the slighting of blackness.[86] Arguing against the mere extension of the U.S. movement to Brazil, she argues that whiteness studies is not a one-size-fits-all model that need only be applied; it must be theorized differently in different contexts. In Brazil, whiteness is a site of enunciation, a position at the apex of the social pyramid, one that does not necessarily preclude partial black ancestry but that orchestrates the valorization of color, style of hair, facial features, and literal and cultural capital. Race in Brazil is conjunctural; the person who is white in Bahia might not be white in Rio Grande do Sul.[87] The Brazilian approach to race, for Sovik, is in some ways more flexible and less moralistic and guilt ridden than in the United States. Unlike whiteness discourse in the United States, whiteness in Brazil develops an affective discourse that embraces unequals, while leaving social hierarchy intact.

Sovik points to the Janus-faced doubleness of *mestiçagem*, which deploys two discourses, one used by whites among themselves, the other reserved for racially mixed groups. The claim that all Brazilians are mixed, she argues, tends to be addressed either to foreigners or to those Brazilians who accuse other Brazilians of racism. (Kia Lilly Caldwell speaks usefully of "mestizo essentialism.")[88] The intent is to say, "How can we be racists if we're all mixed?" The implicit comparison, once again, is to North American whites, assumed not to be mixed and therefore more likely to be racist. At the same time, many Brazilians express an understandable irritation with some North American critical commentary on race. The irritation has to do with a smug and self-righteous tone, present in official pronouncements and in the American common sense regarding the peoples and nations of the Global South.[89] She quotes Caetano Veloso on the subject of this resentment of U.S. power:

> When you say "American," you are saying rapid, effective and immediate international protection for the American citizen, whether he is black, yellow, or white. To be an American citizen conveys a huge advantage, no matter the color of that citizen. The African American is immediately superior, because he is American, and this advantage is lived deeply and naturally by Americans, Brazilians, Peruvians and so forth.[90]

For Caetano, Brazilians are annoyed by the presumption that everything American is better, to the point that even American racism is better than Brazilian racism!

> Unlike those Brazilianists who wanted to show us that Brazil cultivated a racism which was hypocritical and therefore even more harmful than the open and declared racism once practiced in the United States, I—apart from preferring that a racist should be, at a minimum, constrained to pretend that he is not a racist—I think the Brazilian racial confusion reveals a profound miscegenation which inevitably also occurred despite the fact that they pretended—with racist laws and with its attempts at antiracist compensation—that in the United States the same thing did not take place.[91]

Some of those who resist Affirmation Action, according to Sovik, are motivated by a certain nostalgia "not for slavery or for black submissiveness, but for the sympathy of blacks and the memory of relations that were cordial despite the brutality of social hierarchy."[92] But this interracial harmony, she adds, usually takes place on the terrain of blacks welcoming whites into their space and not of whites welcoming blacks into the dominant space. The result is paradoxical. The harshness of U.S. racial relations led to more activism against segregation, while the relatively "suave" character of Brazilian racial relations made it easier to maintain slavery for decades after it had been extinguished elsewhere.

The Critique of Normative Frenchness

While the scholarly comparative literature on race in Brazil and the United States dates back centuries, now, for the first time, scholars are pursuing comparative analyses of race and racism in France and Brazil. In "Facing Racism in France and Brazil: From Moral Condemnation to Help for the Victims," Alexandra Poli compares the dominant racial mythologies of the two countries. The myth of "racial democracy" in Brazil, she points out, seems at first glance to be the polar opposite of the French myth of the *République*. While the orthodox Brazilian "line" makes the harmonious racial relations created by miscegenation the key to the practice of democracy, the French republican myth rejects cultural particularism in the name of the equality of all citizens. Yet for Poli, the two models share a denial of the lived experience of the victims of racism and discrimination, who are prodded to keep quiet about the aggressions they have suffered. "The expressions 'country of the rights of man' and 'the country of the mixture of races' both serve to reinforce the unity of the people and exclude from the outset any discussion of racism."[93] Yet in both France and Brazil, citizens have protested discrimination and asserted their "right to difference," in such a way as to bring the question of racism back to the table from which it had been banned.

The conventional contrasts drawn between France and the United States resemble those drawn between Brazil and the United States: racial segregation has never been legalized, racism is surrounded by a symbolic taboo, and so forth. Yet despite the discursive-ideological divides, many commentators have found unexpected similarities not only in patterns of inequality but also in the legal measures taken against discrimination. Azouz Begag speaks of a "convergence between French and American approaches to advancing equal opportunities."[94] Both countries share official definitions of discrimination as deliberate, individual actions such as refusing to hire someone because of his or her race.[95] The French state has passed some antiracist laws, going back to the first law against racism and anti-Semitism: the Anti-racism Law of 1972, subsequently completed by the

1990 Gaysott Law penalizing all "racist, anti-Semitic, and xenophobic actions." Given the legal difficulties in proving racism, the French Senate, in 2000, created the Fund for Social Action (FAS), which offers financial aid to "integrate" immigrant workers and their families, along with programs in French-language education and access to social institutions such as schools. French law also allows for the judicial condemnation of those who promote racial hatred, as in the February 2011 case in which prominent television and press commentator Éric Zemmour was fined $14,000 for justifying racial profiling and job discrimination against blacks and Arabs.

The "central aim of French law," as Erik Bleich points out, "has never been to foster numerical racial equality or to compensate a class of victims defined by race. Rather, French law is designed to punish racists committing bigoted acts motivated by racist intent."[96] At the same time, the French government "euphemizes" race-oriented policies through what Gwénaële Calvès calls "covert implementation," whether basing compensatory measures on geographical location, as with "urban revitalization zones," or on disparities in educational level ("priority educational areas"). Indeed, Calvès expresses surprise at the "remarkable speed with which Affirmative Action rhetoric and policies have been adopted in France," through the adoption of U.S. 1960s-style "outreach" and 1980s-style "diversity promotion," despite the widespread hostility expressed in the 1990s.[97]

Yazid and Yacine Sabeg's *Affirmative Action: Why France Cannot Escape It* (2004) traces contemporary discrimination to the colonial "Native Code," which imposed harsh measures such as forced labor and collective punishment.[98] This discrepant attribution of rights in the colonies morphed within France itself into discriminatory measures such as curfews, restrictions, and differential access to the welfare system. The subordination of visible minorities in France thus emerges from a complex set of institutional practices partially inherited from colonialism. After explaining the historical rationale for Affirmative Action, the authors rebut the objections: that it is reverse racist, violates meritocratic norms, is juridically impossible, and so forth, calling, finally, for an Affirmative Action à la Française, one that would avoid the legalism and litigiousness typical of the U.S. version.

While lively debates rage about Affirmative Action in France, whiteness studies has not scanned as a recognized field of knowledge. Indeed, at first glance, looking for "whiteness studies" in France might seem absurd. Common sense tells us that France is a "white," European, and Christian (Catholic and Protestant) country, hardly so deeply engaged with blackness (and redness) as are the settler-colonial states such as the United States and Brazil. Yet it is precisely this common sense that needs to be dismantled. For one thing, there have always been people of color in France, ranging from assimilated native people from Brazil to blacks working as slaves or servants, even under the ancien régime.[99] Yet the fact that 18th-century French naturalists and ethnologists felt obliged to explain the "anomaly" of black pigmentation (and for Cuvier, genitalia and buttocks), moreover, shows that they saw the black body as aberrant and the white body as normative. As Léon-François Hoffman puts it in *Le Nègre Romantique*, "Europeans never reflected on the problem of their own color; there is every reason to believe that they saw it as the norm."[100]

Two centuries later, on March 5, 1959, Charles de Gaulle gave voice to the power of white normativity:

> It's all very fine that there are yellow French people, black French people, brown French people—they show that France is open to all races and that she has a universal vocation. But on condition that such people remain a small minority, for if not France will no longer be France. We are in the end above all a European people, white in race, of Greek culture and Christian religion.[101]

The presence of some black Frenchmen, for de Gaulle in 1958, demonstrated the openness and "universal vocation" of France, but he put restrictions on that universality by warning that blacks should remain a "small minority" so that "France could remain France."[102] His native village, de Gaulle warned, would no longer be "Colombey-les-Deux-Eglises" but rather "Colombey-les-Deux-Mosquees."[103] Any serious injection of color, or of Islam, would compromise France's ethno-onto-logical essence *as* France. By implication, de Gaulle was naturalizing the French Christian presence in Algeria, while delegitimizing any substantive Muslim/black presence in France. In the 1950s, French blacks entered the public sphere largely in the terms delineated by Roland Barthes's famous analysis of the cover photo of *Paris Match*, showing a black soldier (actually a boy scout) saluting the French flag, in which every semiotic element sent a reassuring message of black adherence to the white imperial project. On June 19, 1991, Prime Minister Jacques Chirac outdid de Gaulle in a tirade about an "overdose" of immigrants, who were annoying hardworking French families with the horrendous odors emerging from their overcrowded polygamist apartments.[104]

Language too can quietly encode "normative whiteness" or in this case "normative Frenchness." Thus, the term *immigrants* in French evokes "people of color from the former colonies," while *étrangers* (foreigners) suggests light-skinned fellow Europeans. Even progressive 21st-century work on colonialism and discrimination tends not to engage whiteness. Whiteness, as Didier Gondola puts it,

> plays no part in the ways in which academics in France wrestle with notions that could gain clarity when paired with this critical issue. Most of the recent works by noted French academics [on slavery, colonization, immigration, and citizenship] make no explicit engagement with the concept of whiteness. In none of these works are blackness and whiteness seen as correlated and mutually constitutive. . . .

> This glaring omission mirrors the invisibility of whiteness in the French social
> landscape and, by contrast, magnifies the visibility of blackness and Arabness as
> inescapable conditions that account for the exclusion of Blacks and Beurs.[105]

This invisibility of whiteness continues decades after Fanon "outed" the normative whiteness that informed the French child's frightened "Look, a Negro!" For Fanon, even blacks show symptoms of what he calls a "lactification process,"[106] which in the French colonies existed both in relation to the most stigmatized group (those of dark black color) and in relation to mixed-race people seen as "assimilated" and "evolved" and therefore more compatible with French norms.

Scholars of color have long been contesting what Jean-Baptiste Onana calls (in his 2007 book *Be Black and Shut Up*) "the myth of white France."[107] Whiteness, as Pap Ndiaye points out, has been constitutive of French national identity, in ways that are not *essentially* different from the British and U.S.-American modalities of whiteness.[108] The privilege of belonging to the "dominant group," for Ndiaye, "is to be blind to one's color because it is thought to be universal."[109] While there is no scholarly wave of self-designated "whiteness studies" work in France, one finds a close equivalent in a book such as Pierre Tévanian's *La Mécanique Raciste*. The author begins by marking his own subject position as white: "I deal with the question 'What to do about racism?' from the only point of view available to me, that of a white man who occupies the place, within racial relations as socially constituted in our postcolonial Republic, of the dominant."[110] In a chapter ironically titled "The White Question," Tévanian asks what defines whiteness and answers with a paradox: "To be white is not to be obliged to answer the question what it means to be white."[111] To be white in France, for Tévanian, implies the privileges (1) of *not* being black, Arab, Asian, Turkish, or Muslim, in short, of *not* being made to bear the burden of a stigmatized identity; (2) of *not* suffering discrimination; (3) of assuming the double imposture of enjoying exorbitant privilege while denying its existence; and (4) of being seen, unlike racialized "others," as legitimate, credible, and serious. Tévanian ends with "An Ode to Treason"—reminiscent of U.S. "Race Traitor" manifestoes—concluding that whites must recognize white privilege while putting it in a troubled state of crisis.

French intellectual life does feature, if not critical whiteness studies per se, at least its functional correlative in the critiques of what might be called "normative Frenchness." Americanist François Durpaire, for example, speaks of a specifically French kind of denial: "If there is no specificity in French racism itself, there is a specificity in the manner of its negation."[112] In France, it is "always easy to say that one is not opposed to blacks or Arabs, but only to 'black communitarianism' and 'Arab communitarianism.'"[113] The key word used to stigmatize race-conscious activism and scholarship in France has been *communautarisme* (communitarianism), regarded as an ignoble descent into identitarian politics and a threat to republican color-blindness. Wielded as a kind of scarecrow, the word has the same repressive function as the "PC" and "separatist" charges in the United States. Instead of the warning, à la Schlesinger, that multiculturalism is dividing America, we find the admonition that "communitarianism is dividing France." The actual people identified as "minorities" disappear into the ether of stigmatized abstractions. The very definition of "communitarianism" in the 2004 edition of the *Petit Robert* dictionary stigmatizes it as divisive: "A system which develops the formation of communities (ethnic, religious, cultural, social) and thus divides the nation to the detriment of integration."[114] The logic undergirding the communitarianism-versus-republicanism binarism, in this sense, is ultimately not so distant from a Huntingtonian "clash of civilizations" discourse.

A racializing regard attributes an imagined unity of color to a disparate group—composed, for example, of a Maghrebian, a Martinican, a Senegalese— which it then projects as "communitarian." But for Durpaire, the real communitarianism resides in the racializing gaze itself, which (1) imagines a monolithic "black community" that does not exist and (2) denies the veiled communitarianism of the bearers of the racializing gaze. Ironically, the people condemned as "communitarian" are often precisely those who *leave* their communities of origin to join with others in activist coalitionary movements against racism. Durpaire offers a vivid example: "A 'noble' Soninke who marries a Soninke servant, thus ignoring the caste barrier, or a Senegalese woman who marries a man from Cameroun, or a Muslim African who marries a Christian African, or an African who marries a West Indian, can all be called 'communitarian' by a white majority that sees only the common black skin of the people in question."[115] Durpaire unveils the hidden whiteness of universalist discourse. Those who hurl the charge of communitarianism, he continues, "do not think of themselves as a particular group, but as the carriers of a universalist ideal. Only the difference of others is communitarian. In this selective denunciation, one finds an unconfessable reality, that of the communitarian character of anticommunitarian discourse."[116] Durpaire's strategic critique thus recalls what critical race whiteness theorists see as the unacknowledged white identity politics hidden in the attacks on the "identity politics" of people of color, attacks proffered by those who imagine themselves as universal subjects existing in a realm "beyond identity." Anticommunitarianism, in this sense, is a euphemistic form of racism.

Without using the actual phrase "normative whiteness," Durpaire, by speaking about the communitarian character of anticommunitarian discourse, makes an analogous point about normative white Frenchness.[117] The censure of "communitarian" discourse is intrinsically comparative and diacritical, in that communitarianism is very much associated in many French minds with a partly imagined Anglo-American type of society and thus encodes the Latin/Anglo-

Saxon dichotomy. The manifest evils of U.S. society—impoverished ghettoes, racial tension, a tattered social safety net—are often seen in France as inherent in an "Anglo-Saxon" approach that sees society as an agglomeration of ethnic lobbies. Yet one of the unfortunate byproducts of the rejection of the "Anglo-Saxon" model, for Durpaire, is that in France itself "ghettoization and anticommunitarianism work hand in hand: they marginalize certain populations, even while they take away the possibility of fighting against discrimination."[118]

Durpaire boomerangs "communitarianism" to make it designate not radical Muslims or neoliberal Anglo-Saxons but rather "normal" white French society. Postcolonial scholar Françoise Vergès, in the same vein, refers to the "colonial communitarianism" that cordoned off white French people into their own segregated clubs, churches, and balls. This typically colonial form of social organization, she argues, is now returning to France itself.[119] Fanon's sharply divided "two cities," at the time of the Algerian war, now morphs into the burning social divide separating prosperous city center from marginalized banlieue. We find a response to the charge that "differentialism" and "communitarianism" threaten republican unity in the subtitle of Frédérique Mouzer and Charles Onana's *Un Racisme Français*. Bringing to their paroxysm the contradictions addressed in this chapter, the book's jiujitsu subtitle reads, "White Communitarianism Threatens the Republic."[120]

8   French Intellectuals and the Postcolonial

IT IS IN FRANCE, one of the key sites of Enlightenment thinking, that the contemporary debates are most explicitly seen as continuous with early debates around *Les Lumières* and the Revolution. Both the popular media and high-profile public intellectuals portray the conflict as one between universal secular Enlightenment and religious and communitarian particularism. As we saw earlier, the dominant line in French intellectual life during much of the 1990s was antagonistic to discourses of critical race, identity politics, and multiculturalism. Until recently, postcolonial theory too formed a structuring absence in the dominant French discourse. This absence contrasted not only with the Anglo-American academic world but also with other parts of Europe (the Netherlands. Germany, Scandinavia) and with many parts of Asia and Africa, all sites where postcolonial studies have been a significant presence for decades. In France, the word "postcolonial" functioned largely as a chronological marker, a synonym for postindependence rather than as an index of a discourse or field of inquiry.[1] For complex reasons, many French intellectuals ignored at best, and maligned at worst, a constellation of interrelated projects such as postcolonial studies, cultural studies, and critical race studies. There was a manifest hostility to what were perceived as Anglo-American currents in general, whether in the form of multiculturalism (associated with the "Anglo-Saxons") or cultural studies (associated initially with the United Kingdom and later with the United States) or postcolonial theory (associated with the United States, the United Kingdom, India, and the Anglophone zone generally). Thus, the debates have taken on national-allegorical overtones, in terms of both how French intellectuals imagined their own role and how they imagined the role of intellectuals from other nations.

There was in France a postcolonial terrain, however, occupied not by postcolonial studies but rather by work within the traditional disciplines. Whereas postcolonial studies in the Anglophone world was initially the product of scholars in English and comparative literature and the humanities generally, what one might call "proto-postcolonialist" studies in France was dominated by anthropologists and historians. Already in 1971, anthropologist Georges Balandier, for example, anticipated Homi Bhabha's notions of "sly civility" as a coping mechanism within colonialism by speaking of "collective reactions that could be called clandestine or indirect" or of "calculated manifestations of passivity" as subtle ways of undermining colonial domination.[2]

This chapter charts a new situation where the old antagonisms persist but when new voices and discourses also emerge. In the late 1990s and in the first decade of the 21st century, we witness a major engagement with what has variously been called "postcolonial theory," "postcolonial critique," and "postcolonial studies." Numerous conferences and special issues of journals such as *Esprit*, *Labyrinthe*, *Rue Descartes*, and *Mouvements* treat "the colonial fracture," "the sequels of colonialism," and "the wars of colonial memory." Many of the recent publications thematize the historical delay itself through a quasi-ritualistic acknowledgment of the French hesitation in joining the postcolonial trend. To take just one of many examples, Dino Costantini's *The Civilizing Mission: The Role of Colonial History in the Construction of French Political Identity* begins by acknowledging a gap between France and the Anglophone countries. In the latter, "the fact that colonial history forms a constitutive part of a common Western identity has been recognized for decades," while France has only recently begun to "interrogate the theoretical and practical consequences of the centuries of colonial engagements and the way they have fashioned France's political identity up to the present."[3]

Ironies of an Aversion

A number of poignant ironies hover around the initial reluctance of French intellectuals to embrace postcolonial studies. The first and most obvious is that postcolonial studies itself has been very much shaped by Francophone anticolonial discourse. Many key problematics within postcolonial critique trace back to Francophone intellectuals such as Césaire, Senghor, Fanon, Memmi, and Anouar Abdel-Malek. The chapter titled "The Pitfalls of Nationalism" in Fanon's *Wretched of the Earth*, for example, anticipated the postnationalist aspect of postcolonial theory, while Abdel-Malek's critique of Oriental studies in the 1960s foreshadowed Said's classic *Orientalism*. The second irony is that "French Theory," as Robert Young pointed out in *White Mythologies*, was shaped by the colonial situation and by the fact that many of the leading theoreticians (Derrida, Althusser, Lyotard, Cixous) were linked to North Africa. The third irony is that French poststructuralism has had widely acknowledged impact on leading postcolonial thinkers—one thinks of Foucault's influence on Said, Derrida's on Spivak, Lacan's on Bhabha—and on the postcolonial field in general, manifested in myriad references not only to Derrida, Foucault, and Lacan but also to Deleuze, Guattari, Irigaray, Cixous, Lyotard, and Certeau. (This poststructuralist aspect of postcolonial theory is all the more striking given the fact that the leading poststructuralist thinkers themselves rarely engaged in any systematic way with anticolonialist texts.) It thus seems surprising that the "French Theory" aspect of postcolonial studies has had so little resonance in France.[4] In another sense, however, it is not surprising at all, since "French Theory" was often seen in France as a transatlantic invention.[5] Despite the French theoretical sources of the various "post-" movements, they generated little enthusiasm in France, partly because they came to be seen as themselves Anglo-American. Yet in another perspective, poststructuralism itself absorbed while reconfiguring some of the themes of anticolonial discourse, for example, its undermining of Europe's claim to being the "exclusive culture of reference."

A fourth irony about the aversion to postcolonial theory revolves around the fact that France in the 1960s and early 1970s had been the epicenter of "Third Worldism," precisely the tradition that postcolonialism was both embedding and superseding. With the postwar dismembering of the French empire, colonialism and decolonization were necessarily at the core of many polemics, even if only by implication. Indeed, much of the French contribution to the seismic shift stems from these early battles, as Third Worldist writers such as the Martinicans Césaire and Fanon, alongside African writers such as Amílcar Cabral, Cheikh Diop, and Mongo Beti and radical African American expatriates such as Richard Wright or Arab/Maghrebian/Francophone writers such as Albert Memmi, Gisèle Halimi, Anouar Abdel-Malek, Mohammed Harbi, and Assia Djebar found Hexagonal allies in figures such as Edgar Morin, Maxime Rodinson, Claude Lévi-Strauss, Jean-Paul Sartre, Simone de Beauvoir, Henri Alleg, Pierre Vidal-Naquet, François Maspero, Yves Bénot, and Francis Jeanson.

A fifth irony about the antagonism to postcolonial theory involves the slighting of a specifically French intertext, first the French tradition of thematic analyses of the colonial novel and of literary exoticism (for example Martine Astier-Loufti's *Littérature et Colonialisme* and Martine Mathieu's *Le Roman Colonial*) and second the highly politicized literary theories of Lukács, Goldmann, Althusser, Macheray, and Barthes and the work of journals such as *Tel Quel* (post-'68), *Cahiers du Cinéma*, and *Cinétique*. In the 1960s and early 1970s, French intellectuals were in the vanguard of "ideological" and "symptomatic" readings of literary, mediatic, and cultural "texts," a style of reading anticipatory of postcolonial-style analyses exploring the "fissures" and "structuring absences" both of the texts themselves (slavery in Jane Austen's *Mansfield Park*) and of the exegeses of such texts (the blindness to colonialism in New Critical analyses of *Heart of Darkness*).

A sixth irony about the antagonism to postcolonialism is that contemporary France, as a product of colonial karma, is itself a postcolonial nation in demographic, political, and cultural terms. This postcolonial legacy becomes evident in an endless chain of events with racial, colonial, or anti-Semitic overtones, events thoroughly mulled over by the press and the media: the national euphoria over the black-*blanc-beur* World Cup soccer victory in 1998 (contrasting with the scapegoating of the players of color after the 2010 defeat), the "scandal" of the children of Maghrebian immigrants booing the Marseillaise at soccer games, the diverse outbreaks of anti-Semitic or anti-Muslim violence (such as desecrations of Jewish or Muslim cemeteries), the accusations against Le Pen about torturing Algerians during the so-called Battle of Algiers, and the scandalous memoirs by key military figures such as Massu and Aussaresses. The tensions also manifested themselves in the ideological litigiousness of lawsuits accusing prominent pro-Palestinian intellectuals, whether French Jewish (Edgar Morin) or Israeli French (Eyal Sivan) of anti-Semitism and Holocaust negationism. On the other side, lawsuits were addressed to historians such as Olivier-Pétré Grenouilleau accused of slavery negationism. (The word *negationisme* represents a metonymic slide from the Shoah to slavery, symptomatic of the fraying of the black-Jewish postwar alliance and what some French intellectuals deride as "the competition of victims.")

Playing an active role in these debates, French president Nicolas Sarkozy demonstrated that colonialist/racist discourse was alive and well in his speech in Dakar on July 26, 2007. Sarkozy deployed the kind of rhetoric denounced over half a century earlier by Césaire in his *Discourse on Colonialism*:

> The tragedy of Africa is that the African has not sufficiently entered history. The African peasant who has lived with the seasons for millennia, whose life ideal is to be in harmony with nature, knows only the eternal recurrence of a time set to an endless rhythm of repetition of the same gestures and the same words. Within this imaginary where everything constantly begins again, there is no place for the human adventure or for the idea of progress. In this universe where nature controls everything, man escapes the anxiety of history which torments modern man, but man stays immobile in the middle of an unchanging order where everything seems decreed in advance. The African has not sufficiently entered History....
> The African peasant lives the rhythm of the seasons.[6]

Sarkozy's speech simply recycled a Eurocentric view of Africa as allochronically mired in a dead past, a perspective reminiscent of Hegel's interpretation of Africa as refractory to the dynamizing charm of the European *geist*. For writers formed in that tradition, "ahistorical" peoples lacked key human and social attributes: namely, writing, reason, and a state. Sarkozy described Africa, to the Africans themselves, as pretechnological, desperately in need of "science and modern technique," yet culturally rich in its capacity to "reawaken the simple and ephemeral pleasures ... and the need to believe rather than to understand, the need to feel rather than reason." The only hope was for Africans to give free expression to their "European part" calling for "freedom, emancipation, and justice." The real addressee of Sarkozy's speech, however, was the French public, and the goal was to bury once and for all what France's conservative humanist intellectuals saw as a masochistic "cult of repentance" concerning colonialism. In an exercise of national self-exoneration, Sarkozy declared that colonialism "was not responsible for all the present-day problems of

Africa, . . . not responsible for the bloody wars between Africans, . . . not responsible for the genocides, . . . not responsible for the dictators." Sarkozy reminded his Dakar audience that Africans themselves had often fought against and hated one another—as if such hatred were unimaginable in Europe—that no one should ask children to apologize for the faults of their parents, that while the colonizers had taken from Africa, they had also given to Africa. In this sense, Sarkozy transformed the "white man's sob" into a self-aggrandizing official metanarrative.

Implicitly, Sarkozy was denying what had been established by many critical scholars, to wit, that France had been enriched by colonialism and slavery. Francophone Africa—or what critics such as Jean-François Verschave punningly called "Françafrique" or "France-a-fric" (roughly, French money/Africa)—had been deeply corrupted by French support for African kleptocrats, whereby the corporate and political elite of France, together with African dictators, exploited Africa for their own purposes. At least two collections, *L'Afrique Répond à Sarkozy* and *Petit Précis de Remise à Niveau sur L'Histoire Africaine à l'Usage du Président Sarkozy*, feature African responses to Sarkozy's libel against Africa.)[7] On another occasion, Sarkozy addressed his own "love it or leave it" ultimatum to African immigrants in France itself: "We cannot change our laws and customs because a tiny minority doesn't like them. If certain people don't like France, they should feel free to take their leave."[8]

For Alain Badiou, Sarkozy's "new Pétainism" conjoins the fear of racialized minorities with the fear of a resurgent left (for Pétain, the Popular Front; for Sarkozy, May 1968).[9] Sarkozy's call for a discussion of "national identity," meanwhile, has placed minorities on the defensive by subtly reinforcing a normatively white French view of that identity. Like the U.S. right wing, the French right stokes fears of internal and external enemies: for Sarkozy, the banlieue "scum" at home and Islamicists abroad; and for the U.S. right, blacks, Latinos, and Muslims at home and "Islamic fascism" abroad. Just as American rightist politicians are proposing to repeal the Fourteenth Amendment in order to penalize undocumented Mexican workers (and indirectly American citizens of Mexican background), Sarkozy proposed stripping immigrants convicted of serious crimes of their citizenship. Just to clarify the anti-Muslim and anti-African drift, Sarkozy's interior minister added polygamy and female circumcision to the list of offenses bringing the loss of citizenship. Sarkozy also threatened to send one of Europe's paradigmatic "internal others"—the Roma—back to Romania and Bulgaria, for which he was duly chastised by the European Union.

Decolonizing *la République*

The reconceptualization of France as an oxymoronic "colonial republic" has challenged some of the key precepts of republicanism. As Seloua Luste Boulbina puts it, decolonization was experienced by some French as a *"morcellement"* (fragmentation), resulting in perverse effects: "It is as if the French postcolonial state was being raised on a field of ruins so that in order to exist it became necessary to rehabilitate the Republic (which ignores difference and "communities"), along with 'laïcité' (which rejects the veil), and national identity (which covers over cultural diversity)."[10] Recent French history, in this sense, has featured a veritable culture war between those who stress the negative legacies of colonialism and those who bemoan the "cult of repentance" concerning those very same legacies. The phrase "cult of repentance" served to downplay colonialism's crimes, while shifting attention to the whites who choose to repent or not to repent as the main actors, with the "rest" as spectators on an intrawhite quarrel. Thus, Daniel Lefeuvre, in *To Put an End to Colonial Repentance* (2008), mocks what he sees as an obsession with interpreting contemporary phenomena as aftereffects of colonialism: "The racism of police or administration? Colonial Legacy! The failure of schools? Colonial Legacy! The difficult insertion of Islam in national space? Colonial Legacy." Lambasting Marc Ferro's 2003 book *Le Livre Noir du Colonialisme*, Lefeuvre calls for a "white book of colonization" dedicated to the "glory of the French colonial enterprise, including works by indigenous authors themselves." To repent for colonialism, for Lefeuvre, is sheer "charlatanism and blindness."[11] In the same vein, Alain Finkielkraut, giving voice to his own colonial nostalgia, laments that French schools "no longer teach that the goal of the colonial enterprise was to educate and bring civilization to the savages."[12]

In these paradigm wars, the argument has not been about whether colonialism was violent but only about whether colonialism was essentially and irrevocably violent or only circumstantially and sometimes beneficially violent. The enemies of the "cult of repentance" rekindle the embers of the imperial-romanticist dream of the "colonial epic" and the "adventures of colonial pioneers." Academics like Lefeuvre and politicians like Sarkozy, in this sense, form part of an ideological coalition trying to reanimate the *mission civilisatrice* for the postindependence period. Presidential candidate Sarkozy even gave voice to his own neo-orientalist imaginary in a May 2007 Toulon speech lauding the dream that "sent the knights of Europe on the routes of the Orient, the dream of Napoleon Bonaparte in Egypt, of Napoleon III in Algeria, of Lyautey in Morocco, . . . a dream not of conquest but of civilization."[13] The consensus conservative line seems to be that despite some "abuses," colonialism was well intentioned and generally beneficial. These arguments produce political effects by undercutting any claims by formerly colonized peoples, or by the French people of color descended from them, that anything is owed them.

In the United States, similar cultural wars have opposed advocates of radical pedagogy against rightist superpatriots. The difference between the French and the U.S. culture wars derives, in part, from the differences between the practices of a grounded colonizing nation-state in Europe and those of a colonial-settler state in the Americas. In colonial-settler states, as the name implies, colonialism is at the very kernel of the social formation, yet that centrality is obscured by exceptionalist narratives such as "nation of immigrants" and the "Conquest of the West" or, in Brazil, "the March to the West" and "the fable of the three races." Colonialism is omnipresent yet rendered invisible, renarrated as a legitimate expansion into an empty space. In France, meanwhile, colonialism, even though it shaped the metropole economically, culturally, and politically, was seen as taking place "over there."

Our research has led us to a vast corpus of "intercolonial" texts that directly or indirectly assert the superiority of some colonialisms over others (British over French, American over both, and so forth). Many texts contrast the racially phobic and segregationist "Anglo-Saxon" colonialisms with the more open, assimilationist, and tolerant "Latin" colonialisms. This binarism haunts even books that engage postcolonial theory with sympathy. To cite just one example, Jacqueline Bardolph's *Études Postcoloniales et Littérature* calls for a study of "different colonial imaginaries, for a study of the way in which French history, marked by Catholicism and the spirit of the Enlightenment, might offer a less hierarchical vision of non-European peoples than the British imperial vision."[14] Thus, ancient Anglo-French tensions become reinvoiced in a new intercolonial rivalry, this time within postcolonial studies, about the relative humanity of variant forms of colonialism.

Such nationalist-exceptionalist narratives are absorbed through schools, history books, museums, colonial expositions, and the media. The official history, according to the classical protocols of "je sais, mais quand même" denegation, becomes a form of national apologetics. Nationalism, in this sense, entails obligatory amnesia. As Nietzsche put it, "Memory says 'I did that.' Pride replies, 'I could not have done that.' Eventually memory yields."[15] The various powers deeply entangled in slavery, for example, developed comparative discourses of relative innocence. This specular competition of preening national egos has historically generated claims that our conquest was more gentle, our slavery more humane, and our imperialism more cultivated. More productive, to our mind, would be a comparative study of the role of narcissism within intercolonial discourse. It would examine the various "vernaculars" of the larger language families of imperialism, such as U.S. militaristic exceptionalism ("We promote democracy and crave not one inch of Iraqi, Afghan, Vietnamese, Laotian, Korean . . . land"), British free-trade imperialism ("We only care about trade, which benefits everyone"), the French *mission civilisatrice* ("Vive la culture française"), Luso-Tropicalism ("We have Moorish blood and adore *mulatas*").

At the same time, certain asymmetries characterize theoretical exchanges in the various sites. The first asymmetry is between the power of the Anglophone academy, with its logistical capacity to project and disseminate ideas (reinforced by the hegemony of English), compared with the relative lack of projection (despite the celebrity of France's *maîtres à penser*) of the French academy. On the other hand, some asymmetries work in the opposite direction. First, the intellectual Anglophobia of many French intellectuals is not generally matched by Francophobia on the part of Anglo-American left intellectuals, who are just as likely to be Francophile. Anne Berger, professor of French and Francophone literature at Cornell and thus a *"passeur"* or *"truchement"* figure well placed to compare the two academic formations, points to a contrast between the two academies: "Unlike France, which hopes to export its knowledge and ideas and receive lessons from no one, America [*sic*] is an avid importer of ideas."[16] Rada Iveković makes a similar point about French intellectuals who might believe that they are resisting the "importation of ideas" but in so doing miss the "positive, enriching side of such importations." The polemic about postcolonial studies, Iveković elaborates, "begins in a somewhat vain and anxious way, since it revolves around Republican national pride and a desire for independence, whereby an unfortunate tendency leads to new ideas being received with simplistic 'fors' or 'againsts' which flatten out all structural complexity and historical depth."[17]

The problem on the Anglo-American side, we would add, is at times an insular, self-satisfied, monolingual provinciality, in tandem with a certain fashion-oriented superficiality that prefers ornamental citations of consecrated *maîtres à penser* to a deeper engagement with the substantive scholarship emanating from France and the French-speaking world. The point, then, is not that French intellectuals should simply join the postcolonial bandwagon but rather that all intellectuals should widen the circles of the debates, including by criticizing the provincialities of the local forms that the debate has taken. The question is not one of who is importing and who is exporting but rather of developing a more complex account of the circulation of ideas across boundaries, a point to which we shall return in the final chapter.

A colonial thread runs through many recent French polemics around such issues as the veil and religious insignia in French schools; laws prohibiting denials of the Armenian genocide and the Shoah; the commemoration of slavery and abolition and the Taubira law declaring slavery a "crime against humanity"; the colonial heritage of French museums; Sarkozy's proposal for a Ministry of Immigration, Integration, National Identity and Codevelopment; the film *Indigènes*, concerning pensions for the North African soldiers who liberated France at the end of World War II; the official recognition in 2005 by Chirac of the 1947 massacres in Madagascar; the "rediscovery" of the October 17, 1961, police massacre of hundreds of Algerians in Paris; the accusations, three decades later, of French complicity in the 1994 genocide in Rwanda; and the debates in Parliament about the "beneficial effects of colonialism." Occasionally, prestigious veterans of the anticolonial struggles have participated in these debates, as when Césaire refused to meet with Sarkozy, then minister of education, stating that "as the author of *Discourse on Colonialism*, I remain faithful to my credo as a resolute anticolonialist [who] cannot appear to be in agreement with either the spirit or the letter of the February 23, 2005, law [concerning the "positive effects of colonialism"]."[18]

Much of the postcolonial effervescence came to the fore in the year that might be called the winter of postcolonial discontent: 2005. The year began with the furor over the proposed parliamentary law calling for national recognition for the French repatriated from Algeria (i.e., the former *colons* or *pieds-noirs*) and the "positive accomplishments" of French colonization. (The proposed law was subsequently rescinded.) It ended with the banlieue rebellions of November, partially triggered by provocative comments by government officials, which turned into a paroxysm of anger against police violence, discrimination, racial profiling, and unemployment. More than ten thousand cars were burned, and over two hundred public buildings were torched all around France. The coalitionary optimism of the 1983 "Marche des Beurs," it appeared, had in two decades given way to the inchoate rage of the banlieue oppressed.

This was also the year of the formation of Indigènes de la République, the radical group whose very name fuses the memory of the colonial "indigenous code" with the Republic, thus asserting the persistence of the colonial in the presumably postcolonial era. In 2005, the organization issued a public appeal lamenting the situation of the new "natives":

> Discriminated against in hiring, housing, health, in school, and in leisure activities, the people of the ex-colonies or of the current ones, or whose presence in France is a result of post-colonial immigration, are the primary victims of social exclusion and privation. Independently of their actual origins, the populations of the "*quartiers*" are "indigenized," that is, relegated to the margins of society. . . . Identity checks, provocations, and persecutions of all sorts are multiplied; police brutality, sometimes extreme, is only rarely sanctioned by a system of justice that functions at two speeds.[19]

The text goes on to assert that "France remains a colonial state," whether in the form of territorial *départements* (Martinique, Guadeloupe, Guyane, La Réunion) or of overseas territories (Nouvelle-Calédonie, Tahiti), where the level of economic development is far below that of the metropole. "In France," the text states, "the children of these colonies are consigned to the status of immigrants—second-class French citizens without all their rights." The appeal boldly states that "the treatment of populations who are products of colonization prolongs colonial policy." At the same time, it underscores the economic dimension of oppression: "The figure of the '*indigène*' . . . has become interwoven with other logics of social oppression, discrimination, or exploitation. Thus, today, in the context of neo-liberalism, immigrant workers are made to play the role of deregulators of the labor market in order to facilitate the extension of the logics of precarious living and flexible production to the entire wage-earning population." The text ends by calling for (1) a radical questioning of the Enlightenment "chauvinism of the universal" and (2) radical measures to end discrimination in access to jobs, housing, culture, and citizenship, eliminating those "institutions which relegate formerly colonized populations to a subhuman status."

The Indigènes de la République describe present-day France, in sum, as a quasi-colonial state. The racial profiling and harassment of West Indians, sub-Saharan Africans, and North Africans, for *les indigènes*, merely transposed into the Hexagon the old racist attitudes and discriminatory practices that typified French colonialism. On January 16, 2005, the group disseminated an "Appeal for a Conference on Postcolonial Anti-colonialism." It also organized a rally on May 8—anniversary of the brutal French repression of an Algerian demonstration in Sétif in 1945—against the amnesia about past French massacres and a police brutality rarely punished by a "multiple-speed" judicial system. Among the other points made in the appeal,

> France is and remains a colonial state. . . . In its former colonies, it continues
> a policy of domination. . . . The treatment of the populations descended from
> colonialism prolongs, without being reducible to, colonial policy. . . . The figure
> of the "native" continues to haunt political, administrative, and judicial actions . . .
> imbricated with other logics of oppression, discrimination, and social exploitation.
> . . . We, descendants of slaves and of African deportees, daughters and sons of the
> colonized and of immigrants, we, French and non-French living in France, . . . we
> are the "natives" of the Republic.

The Indigènes de la République met with a hostile reception from much of the political spectrum, not only from the centrist *Nouvel Observateur*, which called their manifesto "a confused cocktail of poujado-leftism, shallow alter-mondialism, and post-Fanonian radicalism,"[20] but also from some on the left who found the movement "communitarian" and even "racist."[21] This partial convergence of right and left suggested that colonial attitudes rooted in a Eurocentric universalism persisted in the postcolonial era.

Also published in 2005 was the edited volume *The Colonial Fracture: French Society through the Prism of the Colonial Legacy*. As the editors write in the introduction,

> It is today difficult to ignore "postcoloniality," given the extraordinarily strong
> tensions that go with it: the extension of the comparison between the colonial
> situation and the situations of social, economic, cultural, educational, and religious
> marginalization in urban neighborhoods; . . . the demands concerning histori-

cal memory of the "children of colonization"; . . . the rise of a "sense of insecurity" regarding postcolonial immigration and the failure, on the part of republican elites, to understand "extranormal" identities (seen as *communautaristes*); the denunciations in the media of a so-called "antiwhite racism" at the same time as we witness a growing rigidity of the "French model of integration"; the rejection of France and policies of *francophonie* in Francophone Africa. . . . All these signs make the *colonial fracture* a multifaceted reality that can no longer be ignored.[22]

Absorbed in the struggle to change the way French history is presented in school textbooks and in the media, the volume features essays on the role of the dominant republican model in (1) suppressing critical thought about race (Achille Mbembe), (2) marginalizing postcolonial migrants and their descendants through the myth of "integration" (Ahmed Boubeker), and (3) stereotyping Arabs and Muslims (Thomas Deltombe and Mathieu Rigouste).

The reactions to the work of French postcolonial scholars reveal both similarities and differences vis-à-vis the Anglo-American situation. Referring to some 250 commentaries and critical references in the press, in the media, and on the Internet, Nicolas Bancel and Pascal Blanchard examine the responses to their influential *La Fracture Coloniale*. A first axis of critique consisted in denying any clear connection between colonialism and the contemporary situation. (The authors answer that the situation is both linked and distinct.) A second, more Marxist critique censured the privileging of race over class, and culture over economy. (For the authors, all are essential, intertwined, and complexly interarticulated.) A third critique accused the authors of subverting republican values, while a fourth lamented the "reopening of historical wounds." Such skittish reactions to postcolonial scholarship in both France and in the Anglophone world are symptomatic of a common "structure of feeling" (Williams) that resists any deeper engagement with the impact of colonialism on national history.

The fact is that contemporary France exhibits both continuities and discontinuities with the colonial past. As evidence for continuity, one might cite the facts that (1) the demographic majority in the overcrowded projects (banlieue) are literally a byproduct of the French colonization of parts of sub-Saharan Africa and the Maghreb; (2) the reinstatement of martial law on November 8, 2005, was based on a 1955 state-of-emergency decree originally used for repression in French Algeria; (3) repatriated *pieds-noirs* from Algeria form a major presence in the anti-immigrant National Front; and (4) many repatriated colonial civil servants from Algeria were placed in positions of control over postcolonial immigrants.[23] The residents of these areas, for urban sociologist Didier Lapeyronnie, "experience themselves as 'colonized people' in the sense that Frantz Fanon, Albert Memmi, or V. S. Naipaul give to this term: they are defined by external and dominant perceptions [*le regard*] and categories . . . like colonized people, the inhabitants of the 'sensitive zones' have the impression that they have no political existence, that they are not considered citizens."[24] Other analysts find the continuity thesis overstated: after all, the indigenous code itself is extinct, and even the Indigènes de la République are citizens. Taking a carefully calibrated position, Pap Ndiaye suggests that it would be "outrageously simplistic" to claim that contemporary racial discriminations are due to the old colonial slave order, while it would also be "quite dishonest" to claim that contemporary injustices have nothing to do with that order. The postcolonial project, for Ndiaye, invites us to reflect precisely on the "maintenance of structures of domination after decolonization." The reflection on this "non-indifferent difference [*différence non indifférente*] between past and present situations is precisely what is at stake in contemporary social sciences."[25]

The Hesitation-Waltz of French Postcolonial Studies

The past decade has generated a substantial body of postcolonial work in France, founded, according to Marie-Claude Smouts, on three propositions long accepted in the "Anglophone" academic world: (1) that the colonial fact forms an integral part of the history of the French present; (2) that colonialism has thoroughly transformed not only the former colonized societies but also the colonizing society itself; and (3) that France, in order to shape a more inclusive republic, has to recognize the legacy of its colonial past.[26]

Before examining the current postcolonial work, it is worth reflecting on the reasons for the defensiveness vis-à-vis postcolonial studies. What explains the specifically French hesitations about the postcolonial project? To reiterate our earlier questions about the reception of multicultural identity politics, in what ways do national interests, cultural institutions, and global socioeconomic alignments dictate the itineraries of "traveling theories" such as postcolonialism? What structure of feeling, what resistances and interferences, lie behind this initial antagonism? Here we first examine the reasons for the antagonism and then look at the remarkable recent flowering of writing on topics that directly bear on the postcolonial.

By way of preamble, it is important to draw some distinctions concerning the public reception of postcolonialism in the various zones. Despite the resistance to academic postcolonial theory, the political debates about colonialism became much more part of the public sphere in France than was the case in the United States and the United Kingdom. It would therefore be wrong to see the issue in a stagist and linear way, as if it were merely a question of French intellectuals getting up to speed with the Anglo-American academe. "The temporalities and historicities of different languages," as Rada Iveković puts it, " do not always coincide."[27] Some of the French hesitation about postcolonial studies derived, as we have seen, from a longstanding intellectual strength, that is, France's status as a privileged terrain for anticolonial, anti-neocolonial, and anti-imperialist writing by both French and Francophone writers within and beyond the Hexagon, going back to Césaire, Senghor, Édouard Glissant, Maryse Condé, Alioune Diop, Hamidou Kane, Amadou Hampaté Bâ, Abdelmalek Sayad, Alice Cherki, Yves Bénot, Francis Jeanson, and so many others. This anticolonial and anti-imperial work later morphed, it could be argued, not so much into the postcolonial academic field but rather into the activism associated with the antiglobalization and alter-globalization movements.[28] The World Social Forum, for example, began as a collaboration between progressive Brazilians and the anti-imperialist leftists of *Le Monde Diplomatique*. Thus, while there has been less postcolonial academic production in France, there has also perhaps been more political activism related to the latter-day sequels of colonialism and imperialism.[29]

At the same time, there was a marked difference in the role of the various disciplines. While postcolonial work in France was largely confined to specific disciplines, postcolonial studies in the Anglophone world has long been transdisciplinary. As a result of this difference in academic genealogies, what in the Anglophone world would have been called "postcolonial" in France might be simply called "history" or "anthropology" or "economics" or "literature." "Postcolonial literature," similarly, might be called in France "literature of development" or "emergent" literature.[30] Such work was often critical of colonialism in theory and practice, even if it did not sufficiently unpack such infantilizing terms as "emerging" and "developing." What was lacking in the French academy, perhaps, was the metatheoretical and transdisciplinary thrust of postcolonial studies, even though that thrust was partially inspired by French critical theory.

In the search for a more multidimensional analysis, some commentators have racialized and "postcolonialized," as it were, the categories of Foucault and Bourdieu. Rather than speak simply of "racism," sociologist Nacira Guénif-Souilamas foregrounds the normative biopolitics that shape citizenship and subcitizenship in postcolonial France, regulating the bodies and behavior of the children of immigrants of color. While the dominant discourse assumes a general freedom of self-invention for all people, the marginalized are made to feel incarcerated in their own bodies, held back by the invisible barrier that separates off those who lack "civilizational legitimacy."[31] In dense Foucauldian prose, Guénif-Souilamas critiques "biopolitics in the service of the reigning order":

> Our epoch, so solicitous of the freedom of everyone to invent themselves, has reserved for the most dominated a very particular kind of self-invention, a new form of captivity, a new privation of freedom which assaults those French people who are incarcerated in their own bodies. Thus, the barrier erected between those

who enjoy civilizational legitimacy and those who do not is no longer exterior. . . . This uncrossable border marries bodies themselves, enveloping them in a transparent film which resists all the corrosions of contact, . . . isolating those who are so circumscribed. . . . For those who have experienced or witnessed these virtual incarcerations prodded by racial profiling of bodies . . . it becomes clear that one can be imprisoned while apparently being free.[32]

Picking up on concepts developed by Bourdieu and by Norbert Elias, Guénif-Souilamas argues that customs and habitus play a crucial role in the economy of "distinction" and the maintaining of class barriers. "Presocial, literally natural, in other words, in our vernacular, profoundly cultural, racial traits are constructed to serve the purpose assigned to them: debase in order to separate, designate the evil in order to protect oneself from it."[33]

Guénif-Souilamas speaks of the "consubstantial link between colonialism and assimilationism [obscured by] integrationist rhetoric."[34] The most obvious link is the symbiotic connection between a racialized "civilizing process" that once took place abroad and that now takes place within French institutions. The body itself plays an allegorical role as the new "protagonists of alterity" incarnate the disquieting figure of the undomesticated "other." Just as the African American body has played an allegorical role as an ambulatory reminder of the repressed memory of white crimes against blacks, in France too "the very presence [of the protagonists of alterity] is a reminder of that which they are the involuntary recipients."[35] Even feminism is wielded against a generic Arab/Muslim other. For Islamophobes, only one (Islamic) faith is stigmatized as inherently sexist. Guénif-Souilamas mocks the "patriarchal feminism" of the white male French critics of Islam, who pose as chivalric defenders of Muslim women against Muslim men—inevitably reminding us of Spivak's evocative formula "white men rescuing brown women from brown men."[36] As in the United States, white feminists sometimes join in the condemnations, as when Elisabeth Badinter, in a kind of secular fundamentalism, pathologizes a religious tradition by calling veiled Muslim women "very, very sick." A religiously connoted choice of dress becomes the trigger for an undialogical analysis tinged with projections that completely deny the subjectivity of the wearer of the veil, which for Badinter, "symbolizes the categorical refusal to come into contact with the other, . . . a triple pleasure over the other: the pleasure of nonreciprocity, the pleasure of exhibitionism, and a voyeuristic pleasure."[37]

The field of the postcolonial in France was also "occupied" by another discursive formation, to wit, la Francophonie. Less a critical theory than an officially mandated postindependence reformatting of the *mission civilisatrice*, *la Francophonie* can be seen as a Gaullist cultural, diplomatic, and commercial project partially aimed at "Anglo-Saxon" rivals for influence in the Third World. This situation generated an ambiguous status, at once privileged and marginalized, for Francophone writers. Pascale Casanova pinpoints the awkward situation of Francophone writers: "Paris had never been interested in the writers from its colonial territories; in fact, it has for a long time scorned and mistreated them as provincials, too close for their differences to be recognized or celebrated yet too far to simply be perceived."[38] The Caribbean writers, for example, come to be seen as too Caribbean to be French and too French to be Caribbean. Much of the postcolonial "air" was thus sucked up, at least in literature departments, by *la Francophonie* and Francophone literature.[39] Yet the very concept of *Francophonie* is being more and more challenged both by the critics and by the writers themselves, who prefer such terms as "world literature in French."

A number of French-speaking scholars who transit easily between the Americas, Europe, and the Caribbean—notably Françoise Vergès, Anne Donadey, Françoise Lionnet, Winifred Woodhull, Brent Hayes Edwards, Tyler Stovall, Dominic Thomas, and Georges Van Den Abbeele, among others—speak of (and themselves instantiate) new hybrid transdisciplinary formations that subsume French and Francophone concerns into larger configurations such as "Francophone postcolonial studies." In the anthology *French Civilization and Its Discontents: Nationalism, Colonialism, Race*, Tyler Stovall and Georges Van Den Abbeele note the general lack of interest of the Hexagon in these currents. "The study of French literature and culture that has arisen outside of France and indeed throughout the French-speaking world," they note, "has emerged in spite of metropolitan French indifference and hostility." The "exhilarating expansion of the corpus of French studies," they continue, "finds few approving echoes in the metropolis, and this despite the sudden development of something like a global Francophone consciousness with an almost dizzying array of lateral contacts all around the periphery as Anglo-American scholars circumvent Paris to interact with their Caribbean, Canadian, African, and Pacific counterparts."[40] The increasing level of interchange between Francophone locations, the authors conclude, in what is perhaps an overstatement, "bypasses Paris entirely."[41] The notions of *tout-monde* and "creolization" drawn from Glissant's relational theories, now standard protocols of reading in the West Indies, black Africa, and the Maghreb, they point out, have been largely ignored in France itself.

France's "own" postcolonials, as a result, have been turning away from French tutelage and institutions in favor of other alternatives. Many French-speaking African and Caribbean intellectuals, including some who formerly lived in France, have immigrated to the United States. Despite the fact that Africans (and Afro-Caribbeans) in the United States are not exempt from the racism suffered by African Americans generally, prestigious French-speaking intellectuals and writers from the Caribbean and from Africa have taken up positions in American universities: Souleymane Bachir Diagne and Maryse Condé (emeritus) at

Columbia; Édouard Glissant at CUNY; Mamadou Diouf at the University of Michigan; Assia Djebar, Manthia Diawara, and Awam Amkpa at New York University; Jean-Godefroy Bidima at Tulane; Mbye Cham at Howard; and Valentin Mudimbe at Duke—without necessarily cutting off their links to France, Africa, and the Caribbean. During the 1998–1999 school year, for example, 165 African scholars came to the United States from Francophone countries.[42] Jean-Philippe Dedieu speaks of African appreciation for relatively open networks of scientific knowledge and professional recognition, in contrast with France, where "the circle of professional knowledges never widens." The African scholar in the United States, one historian reports, is showered with invitations for participation, creating a "familiarity and a continuity . . . never found on the French side."[43] American philosophy departments, meanwhile, are hiring in the field of African philosophy, even as academic job listings in French studies are increasingly specifying "Francophone and postcolonial literature."[44] African postcolonial thinkers in the United States also benefit, ironically, from the Francophilia of some branches of the U.S. academy. Francophonic scholarship in the United States, for Dedieu, has two advantages: (1) that it is African and (2) that it is French and philosophically oriented, thus benefiting from the aura of poststructuralism in the United States.

The causes of the French hesitation about postcolonial studies are at once linguistic (resentment against the hegemony of English), demographic (the relative lack of professors of color in French universities), and institutional (the lack of openings for such studies). Alec G. Hargreaves attributes French ambivalence toward postcolonial studies to (1) France's traumatic separation from its colonies, notably in Vietnam and in Algeria, leading to a desire for erasure; (2) the anti-Americanism of French intellectuals who resent the spread of (Anglo-)American influence both in France itself and in a larger world where French intellectuals once reigned supreme; (3) the unidisciplinary conservatism of French research institutions, in contrast with an Anglo-American academy in which literary scholars—in aspiration if not always in fact—became pluridisciplinary and transnational. While the terrain for such work was prepared in the Anglo-American world by various forms of interdisciplinary studies, in France transdisciplinary fields such as postcolonial studies fell into the limbo of the "unclassifiable."[45] This limbo status was caused less by a lack of transdisciplinary desire or vocation on the part of scholars themselves than by the centralized nature of the French state, since any transdisciplinary experiments would require the approval of the Ministry of Universities, which controls the creation of tenured faculty positions. Here the École des Hautes Études en Sciences Sociales (EHESS), with its encouragement of cross-disciplinary affinity groups, forms a partial exception to the rule.[46] The elitist and hierarchical character of French higher education allows little space for initiatives by graduate students to form associations, to publish essays and books, and so forth. All of these are mixed blessings, of course, and it would be absurd to idealize a U.S. academy plagued by billionaire trustees, outrageously high tuition, the intrusion of market values, an academic star system, and the publish-or-perish syndrome.

The ambivalence about projects such as postcolonial studies is also tied to the vexed question of how France sees its role in the world in the afterwash of empire, as at once the victim of U.S. imperialism and as the formerly colonialist but now benevolent patron of many of the countries not completely absorbed into the Anglo-American sphere of influence. De Gaulle presided over the end of the French empire and then almost immediately fabricated the image of France as the defender of the Third World against *"les Anglo-Saxons."* Although France could no longer pretend to be a superpower, it could speak for "the rest" as the sponsor of an alternative universality posed against the false universalism of the "hyperpower." Defensive and inferiorized in relation to the (now declining) hyperpower, France could be a spokesperson for the excluded by articulating the general resistance, for example, to the U.S.-led Iraq War. France, in this sense, has also come to play a special role in world cultural production. Already in 1984, Jean Guiart, from the Musée de l'Homme, had spoken of the new "mission" of French ethnology: "to valorize the cultural riches of each non-European people."[47] One finds this welcome valorization of non-European cultures in many manifestations of French cultural policies, whether in the area of the "World Republic of Letters," with the key French role, stressed by Pascale Casanova, as Gatekeeper or World Bank for Literature, or in World Music, of which France is a major producer, or in World Cinema, where France has helped finance emerging cinemas in Francophone Africa, Asia, and the Middle East, combating Hollywood hegemony while also walking a fine line between a generous pluralism and a subtle paternalism.

Other institutional factors impede the development of transdisciplinary fields such as "postcolonial studies" in France. Anne Berger criticizes certain features of the U.S. academy—the cult of success, celebrity intellectuals, the political impotence of many academics for whom "academic freedom" is merely academic—while also praising a flexible system that empowers students and teachers to create new objects of research. Contrasting the proliferation of spaces of encounter in the United States with the isolating *"morcellement"* typical of the French academy, she lauds the transdisciplinary research groupings or "studies" programs, defined by ethnicity, area, or subject. Such discursive formations, she argues, both shape new objects of study and inaugurate new reflections on ways of looking at those objects so as to encourage multiple and overlapping affiliations. Thus, a humanities professor can simultaneously participate in feminist studies, Francophone studies, cultural studies, critical race studies, transnational feminist studies, diaspora studies, and so forth. (Some grids, such as feminism, are potentially relevant to all fields.)[48]

Looking back at postwar intellectual history, what is perhaps most disappointing is the failure of the leading *maîtres à penser* to theorize race and coloniality, despite their usually progressive politics. Sartre wrote incendiary prefaces and opposed the Algerian War and American imperialism, but his literary and philosophical writings rarely addressed French imperial domination. The participants in "Socialisme ou Barbarie" defended the right of colonized people to self-determination, but they were largely ignored in France. Foucault briefly developed theories of the "racial state" but soon moved on to other issues. Here Étienne Balibar, who has for decades been theorizing "neoracism," "racism without race," and "universalism as racism" and who has seen racism as at the core of contemporary European politics, forms a major exception.[49] But apart from Balibar, the Foucault of the "racial state," and to a certain extent Derrida, Lyotard, Guattari, and Deleuze, most of the *maîtres*, left unexamined the racial/imperial architectonics of France itself.

Building on a Foucauldian metaphor, Ann Stoller speaks provocatively of "colonial aphasia," an impaired condition that interrupts connections through "disabled histories" and severed links in pathways of association.[50] Little of France's "high-powered theoretical energy across the disciplines (so incisive about political culture, totalitarianisms, state structures and class)," she writes, "was aimed at the racialized foundations of the French state."[51] A theory of "difference" animated theoretical movements from semiotics to poststructuralism, yet the idea of racialized and gendered difference was dismissed as "differentialist." Both Bourdieu and Derrida, Stoller writes, "divorced their sharp critiques of scholastic knowledge from the racial milieus of French empire that they knew intimately and on the ground."[52] Bourdieu, she points out, waited some thirty years before articulating the dilemma created by the separation between theoretical work and ethnographic practice. Bourdieu's theoretical constructs, according to Paul Silverstein and Jane Goodman, "entered the mainstream of social thought independently of the North Africa and French political and social contexts in which they were initially developed."[53] Phyllis Taoua sums up the situation as follows: "An accurate assessment of decolonization cannot have French theory of the 1960s as its ethical center of gravity, since that corpus of texts is antithetical to the basic necessities of what that struggle for freedom required. . . . Never in the history of France had theoretical inquiry resorted to such mystifying abstraction, even as its focus was allegedly the 'politics of difference.'"[54]

The Quarrel over Genealogy

One of the most massive critiques of postcolonial studies in France is Africanist Jean-François Bayart's "Postcolonial Studies: A Political Invention of Tradition?"[55] Words like "postcolonial" and "postcoloniality," Bayart notes, have become part of the intellectual debates in France, to the point that social scientists are no longer "sheltered"—the choice of adjective is symptomatic—from the polemics triggered by their usage. Bayart endorses many of the critiques of postcolonial theory already made in the Anglophone world by such Marxists as Arif Dirlik, for whom postcolonial theory began with the arrival of Third World intellectuals in the First World academy. Bayart also echoes what he himself calls Anthony Appiah's self-admittedly "mean" dismissal of postcolonial intellectuals as a "*comprador intelligentsia*" mediating cultural exchanges between world capitalism and its periphery. In Bayart's summary, this mediating group, now surrounded by white disciples, sees the "colonial situation" as shaping contemporary social relations both in the former colonies and in the metropolitan countries.

The "river" of postcolonial theory, for Bayart, has many currents, some pulling like the Bosphorus in opposite directions. While Gayatri Spivak stresses the epistemic violence of Western thought, others such as Depesh Chakravarty, Bayart points out, see Western thought as a gift to the world. What is new, according to Bayart, is that a proliferating postcolonial studies has generated as a corollary the image of a provincial, conservative France reluctant to confront its colonial past or, even worse, as tainted by a racist imaginary. The concern that motivates the essay, then, is a patriotic one—the image of France. Postcolonial studies, Bayart complains, essentializes France, obscuring its demographic, political, and ideological heterogeneity. Are French intellectuals being criticized, he asks, for refusing to speak a "new global pidgin" and avoiding the "civic rituals of affliction that now pass for political engagement"? Perhaps, he speculates, French researchers are right to reject a fashionable postcolonial trend "whose heuristic virtues have not yet been demonstrated."[56]

Bayart's essay, homogenizing postcolonial studies much as he claims that postcolonial studies homogenizes France, is dedicated to proving that writers in French (he mentions Césaire, Senghor, Memmi, and Sartre) were the founding fathers of postcolonialism. "Like Monsieur Jourdain, who spoke prose without knowing it, these French writers practiced postcolonial studies without knowing it."[57] In other words, postcolonialism is superfluous in France because the work has already been done. In what amounts to a Francocentric account of the genesis of the field, Bayart ardently scavenges intellectual history for any and all French-speaking writers who have performed scholarship in any way loosely analogous to what is elsewhere considered postcolonial. Francophone anticolonialists such as Césaire and Fanon become simply "French," even though Fanon, in the later period, insisted that he "had never been French" and that language and culture are "not enough to make you belong to a people."[58] Bayart's Francocentrism sometimes borders on the absurd, as when he claims that postcolonial studies was inspired to link the critique of colonialism to the critique of other forms of domination, notably in the area of gender, by borrowing from Bourdieu, Deleuze, and Foucault. Where one might have expected names like Simone de Beauvoir, Hélène Cixous, and Luce Irigaray, one finds instead, in a phallocentric narrative, the names of the latecomer male *maîtres*, with no recognition of the many feminist writers who analyzed gender in greater depth long before them.

Bayart seeks out a seminal French connection for almost every non-French thinker: Raymond Aron and Pierre Hassner influenced Hannah Arendt; Sartre was anti-Orientalist before Edward Said; Fernand Braudel influenced Immanuel Wallerstein; George Balandier examined "postcolonial situations" already in the early 1950s; and so forth. While informative, the discussion reminds one of jejune nationalist arguments about who invented the airplane. Bayart does provide a thorough inventory of all the colonial-related work by a wide array of French historians (Jean Suret-Canale, Charles André Julien, Charles Robert Ageron), political sociologists (Jean-Frédéric Schaub), creative writers (Jean Genet, Michel Leiris, Henri Michaux), Francophone novelists (Mongo Beti, Ahmadou Kourouma, Ousmane Sembène, Yambo Ouologuem, Sony Labou Tansi, Alain Mabanckou, Tierno Monénembo), and Maghrebian intellectuals (Mohammed Harbi, Mostefa Lacheraf, Abdallah Laroui, and Mohamed Tozy).

At the same time, Bayart is not uncritical of French institutions. The "mistreatment" of postcolonial studies in France, for Bayart, derives not from an "ideological allergy" but from institutional malaise, including the "misery" of the French university and of CNRS (the National Center of Scientific Research) that has hindered the recruitment of young African scholars subsequently welcomed by U.S. universities; an absurd visa policy that restricts intellectual exchanges with the Global South; the weakening of Présence Africaine; the absence of journals comparable to the *New York Review of Books* or the *Times Literary Supplement*; the archaic character of book distribution; the high cost of translation; and the institutional inertia of *la Francophonie*, which has distracted scholars from a deeper questioning of colonialism and its aftereffects.

Rather than a behind-the-curve France, Bayart sees only a different configuration of the academic field, one that French intellectuals should accept rather than risk becoming "new avatar[s] of academic Atlanticism."[59] Bayart discerns (or projects) a number of rather unsavory motivations for the postcolonial vogue: a strategy of niche self-promotion on the part of scholars covetous of their share of the academic "market"; a French coquettishness that mingles snobbism, Americanophilia, and Hexagonal masochism; the desire to resuscitate the figure of the Sartrean engaged intellectual; the migratory conformism of French academics paying homage to their Anglophone host institutions; the marketing strategies of French publishers profiting from an academic fashion; and a France-bashing typical of the neoliberal age.

Bayart accuses the French adepts of postcolonial studies of remaining within a national narrative even while inverting it by demystifying the French Revolution, the *République*, and the *mission civilisatrice*. In the end, he does not say that postcolonialism is wrong, only that it is unnecessary, since it is all déjà vu and déjà lu, all been done before and better by writers working in French. At the same time, he rejects postcolonial studies' embrace of the "identitarian proclivities" of the most extreme forms of the "cultural turn." For Bayart, postcolonialism ontologizes colonialism, according to a "tropical Calvinism" that "sees the colonies and slavery as predestined."[60] (Bayart's religious categorization embeds a sublimated version of the Anglo/Protestant/Latin Catholic dichotomy.) Finally, postcolonialism ethnicizes the social question of the banlieues through the "catastrophic" concept of identity, failing to see the internal differentiations and spatiotemporal variations within the colonizing process.

One leitmotif in some French critiques is the invocation of the ideal superego of sober scientificity, contrasted with the frivolous "grand academic carnival" of postcolonial studies. Bayart, like historians such as Frederick Cooper in the United States, whom he frequently cites, calls for more historical precision on the part of postcolonial scholars. While postcolonial studies, for Bayart, postulates a mechanical, univocal, overdetermined and Manichean reproduction of colonialism, colonialism is actually historically diverse, contingent, and ambivalent. "We can no longer maintain," he writes, "a static and binary vision of a reified tête-à-tête between colonizer and colonized." As an antidote to what he sees as the ahistoricity of postcolonial theory Bayart calls for the kind of comparative historical sociology exemplified by such figures as Fernand Braudel, Jean Aubin, Denys Lombard, and Serge Gruzinski. In the background of this argument against postcolonial studies lies the debris of the History-versus-Theory debate that took place during the heights of poststructuralism; the tension is not so much about political perspective as about different disciplinary methods of "reading" the past.

Some of Bayart's points are valid, even if most had already been made within the broader postcolonial field. We can appreciate his indispensable inventory of the French and Francophone contribution to scholarship, while regretting the resentful "we French did it first and better" tone and "vive la France" drift of the essay. Eagerly enlisting any and all critics of postcolonialism, even those of extremely diverse political stripes, Bayart mingles the Marxist-style critiques of an Arif Dirlik with the standard French "identitarian" charge. His metaphor of postcolonialism as a "global pidgin" carries an unfortunate colonialist aroma. His sarcastic account of "masochistic" exercises in "civic rituals of affliction," meanwhile, clearly echoes the French rightist lamentations about the "cult of repentance." Calling postcolonialism "politically dangerous" and a form of "cultural engineering,"[61] Bayart demonstrates a limited knowledge of the postcolonial field—he conflates Octave Mannoni with his archnemesis Fanon, for example—while manifesting an acute impatience with the more radical work. In the end, he illustrates the pitfalls of national narcissism in the realm of scholarly exchange. The point is not to claim a single origin for postcolonial studies but rather to insist on the multidirectional circuitries of intellectual flows.

Genres of Postcolonial *Écriture*

Despite such critiques, the past decades have seen a veritable explosion of post-colonial studies in France in the 21st century and especially after 2005. As Jim Cohen points out, the French debate over the postcolonial was not led by literary academics; rather, it was

> a crystallization of several different but converging *political* controversies over the heritage of colonialism and its possible effects in contemporary society. . . . It was a response to ongoing political debates over the "republican model of integration" in its various implications, including the question of how to treat ethnoracial discrimination and how to treat religious diversity—in particular as embodied by Islam; over the notion of "race" which many sociologists have begun to consider in spite of strong republican presumptions against the legitimacy of the notion; and, last but not least, over controversies concerning the memory of colonialism, slavery and abolition and the role of public authorities in recognizing and conserving such memory.[62]

Here we can delineate some of the major genres of such work, while acknowledging that the genres never come pure or unalloyed. While only some of the work is performed under the rubric of the "postcolonial," it is all directly or indirectly related to colonialism and its aftermath. Lacking the space here to thoroughly unpack the work, we will cite books whose very titles communicate the postcolonial thrust of the argument.

In terms of basic trends, first, a large body of current work focuses on the hidden history of French colonialism and the contradictions inherent in "republican colonialism": Bernard Mouralis's *Republic and Colony: Between History and Memory* (1999); Rosa Amelia Plumelle-Uribe's *White Ferocity* (2001); Yves Bénot's *Colonial Massacres* (2001); Marc Ferro's edited volume *The Black Book of Colonialism* (2003); Olivier Le Cour Grandmaison's *Colonize/Exterminate: On War and the Colonial State* (2005); Nicolas Bancel, Pascal Blanchard, and Françoise Vergès's *The Colonial Republic: Essay on a Utopia* (2003); and Jean Pierre Dozon's *Brothers and Subjects: France and Africa in Perspective* (2003). The Dozon book, for example, explores the central paradox of French-style colonialism in fashioning colonials who were simultaneously "citizens" within republican discourse and "subjects" and "indigenes" within colonial discourse.

Second, another body of work treats colonial/imperial popular culture as consumed by the French populace within the Hexagon: Nicolas Bancel, Pascal Blanchard, Gilles Boetsch, Eric Deroo, and Sandrine Lemaire's *Human Zoos* (2002); Pascal Blanchard and Sandrine Lemaire's *Colonial Culture: France Conquered by Its Empire, 1871–1931* (2003) and *Imperial Culture: The Colonies at the Heart of the Republic, 1931–1961* (2004); and Pascal Blanchard, Nicolas Bancel, and Sandrine Lemaire's *The Colonial Fracture: French Society Seen through the Prism of Its Colonial Heritage* (2005). These books address the ways in which ordinary French people could enjoy the spectacles provided by "imperial culture" as manifested in colonial expositions and "Human Zoos"—portrayed in Abdellatif Kechiche's film *Black Venus*—where colonials were displayed for the delectation of the European and American populace.

Third, other texts—Romain Bertrand's *Memories of Empire: The Controversy about the "Colonial Fact"* (2006), Benjamin Stora's *The War of Memories: France faces its Colonial Past* (2007), and the collective work *An Unfortunate Decolonization: France from the Empire to the Banlieue Riots* (2007)—critically explore the "war of memories" spiraling around colonialism.

Fourth, postcolonial texts treat the corollary theme of the history and memory of slavery: Françoise Vergès's *Chained Memory: Questions about Slavery* (2006) and Édouard Glissant's *Memories of Slaveries* (2007). The work on slavery presents an ambiguous relation to a postcolonial field that too often brackets slavery, as if it were not also at the very kernel of the colonial question. These texts seek to demonstrate a clear continuity between colonialism and slavery, including in the form of fervent abolitionists, such as Victor Schoelcher, who subsequently metamorphosed into equally fervent colonialists.

Fifth, some work probes the colonial dimension of French philosophical thought. Scholars such as Yves Bénot and later Louis Sala-Molins have examined the ways that the Enlightenment philosophers give voice to both colonialist and anticolonialist opinion. In Sala-Molins's study of the Code Noir, he notes the tendency of the *philosophes* to speak of slavery largely as a metaphor for white oppression, while eliding the financial benefits slavery brought to Hexagonal France. Books such as Odile Tobner's *On French Racism: Four Centuries of Negrophobia* and Alain Ruscio's *The White Man's Credo*, meanwhile, explore what might be called the *sottisier colonialiste* or the anatomy of colonial stupidities.

Sixth, there is work on postcolonial literary studies: Jean-Marc Moura's *Francophone Literatures and Postcolonial Theory* (1999) and Jacqueline Bardolph's *Postcolonial Studies and Literature* (2002). Pascale Casanova's massively informed *The World Republic of Letters* certainly engages postcolonial writers but generally avoids the idioms of postcolonial theory in favor of political and economic metaphors—the "stock market" of literary values, literary "currency exchanges" and "the

Republic of Letters"—drawn from Bourdieu's concepts of cultural capital and literary distinction.

Past years have witnessed an increasing engagement with race-conscious discourses, which Alec Hargreaves attributes to (1) the growing awareness on the part of political elites and civil servants of the reality of discrimination against immigrant minorities, (2) the greater visibility of violent protests (direct or indirect) against discrimination, and (3) political opportunities for antidiscrimination legislation.[63] The recent period has also seen the emergence of black studies à la Française in the form of Pap Ndiaye's 2008 book-manifesto: *The Black Condition: Essay on a French Minority*. French blacks, Ndiaye notes, are visible as individuals but not as a social group or as an object of academic study. In contrast with the profusion of French academic studies of Native Americans and African Americans, he points out, there are almost none of blacks in France itself.[64] The contemporary social, political, and mediatic presence of the "black question" had not been matched in the world of scholarship, with the result that race came to form a structuring absence in postwar French social theory.

Favoring a transdisciplinary approach that synthesizes the social sciences with the humanities, Ndiaye finds the conjunctural notion of a black "minority" more productive than the essentialist notion of a "community," a term seen as intrinsically antirepublican in France. The concept of "visible minority," meanwhile, has the advantage of embracing very varied groups, in disparate situations, who nevertheless confront common challenges and problems triggered by their visible (and sometimes audible or nominal) difference. Basing himself on extensive research, Ndiaye points out that his black interviewees insist on their Frenchness partly because it is constantly being placed in doubt, sometimes through "well-meant" questions such as "Where are you really from?" Even compliments—"Your French is so fluent" addressed to an *Antillais* who grew up speaking French—can become a dagger dipped in the poison of an ethnic insiderism that reminds black French citizens of their outsiderness.

Ndiaye discerns a supple, conjunctural deployment of racial identity on the part of French blacks. While some proudly affirm their blackness, others describe themselves as *métis* (mixed race) or affirm a national identity, such as Senegalese. Each option, as Ndiaye metaphorizes it, constitutes "one card in the identitarian wallet."[65] Code-switching within a complexly hierarchized classificatory repertoire, French blacks often place Frenchness in the primary position but add in other elements and affiliations—to a country, to a region, to an ethnic group—in an identity "bricolage." Although blacks in France live their blackness in ways that vary with class, gender, religion, language skills, national origin, and self-conception, they are still likely to be seen as "*noir*" by their white compatriots. Thus, there is a tension, to use the phenomenological language evoked by the titular concept of a black "condition," between the chosen *pour soi* identity and the prescribed *en soi* identity constituted by *le regard d'autrui*.

The real goal, for Ndiaye, is not to go "beyond race" but rather to eliminate race as a social marker of inferiority. Fighting antiblack racism has a universal dimension in that it will benefit not only black people but all of humanity, including some who suffer racism's consequences without even knowing it. Despite the obvious differences between the United States at the beginning of the 20th century and France at the beginning of the 21st, Du Bois's "double consciousness," for Ndiaye, retains contemporary relevance for French blacks:

> It means that we want to be French and black, without that seeming strange or
> suspect, or merely tolerated as a temporary problem while assimilation completes
> its work. We want to be invisible in terms of our social life, such that the abuses
> and discriminations that affect us as blacks are reduced. But we also want to
> be visible in terms of our black cultural identities, in terms of our precious and
> unique contribution to French society and culture.[66]

Within a nuanced, antiessentialist, intersectional, and coalitionary approach, Ndiaye recommends forms of black solidarity that ideally operate in tandem with other minority activisms. The real basis for solidarity is not identity per se but rather a common social experience and a common struggle. "Skin color," he argues, "designates an interest group, not a culture."[67]

In the 21st century, "race" has emerged as an analytical category within French academic work. This work takes various generic forms such as, first, work on immigration and the racial question in France, for example, Michel Wieviorka's *Racist France* (1992); Véronique de Rudder, Christian Poiret, and François Vourch's *Racist Inequality: Republican Universality Put to the Test* (2000); Eric Savarese's *Colonial History and Immigration: An Invention of the Foreigner* (2000); Dominique Vidal and Karim Bourtel's *The Arab Malaise: Children of Colonization* (2005); Jean-Michel Blier and Solenn de Royer's *Racial Discrimination: How to End It* (2001); and Nacira Guénif-Souilamas's edited volume *The Republic Exposed by Its Immigration* (2006). Second, this critical work takes the form of witness (*témoinage*) texts concerning everyday racial discrimination, for example, Frédérique Mouzer and Charles Onana's *A French Racism* (2007), Mongo Beti's *Africans, If You Could Speak* (2005), François Durpaire's *White France, Black Anger* (2006), and Jean-Baptiste Onana's *Be a Nigger and Shut Up* (2007).

In the anthology *From the Social Question to the Racial Question* (2006), Didier Fassin and Éric Fassin and their collaborators take up Balibar's challenge, in the *Actuel Marx* dossier, to "think racism after race," in a situation where race does not exist, where it is known to be constructed, yet where racism remains a tangible, brutal reality. Attempting to delineate new articulations of race and class, the contributors appeal to a cross-cultural comparative method. While the multicultural and critical race projects in the United States tend to be oriented around the idea of an equal recognition of formerly stigmatized identities, the struggle in France, according to some contributors, has less to do with identities per se than with the recognition of the reality of discrimination. As the Fassins sum up the situation, "one speaks *as* in order not to be treated *as*—Black, Arab, Jewish—but also Woman and Homosexual: that is the minoritarian paradox inscribed in the very condition of being a minority which means that one cannot get the critique of minorization heard without engaging the already constituted terms of the majoritarian discourse."[68] In the end, the Fassins conclude, "it matters little if one's discourse is universalist or particularist; what matters is that one reflect on the sense and performativity of one's discourse; what it really signifies, and, in the last analysis, what it does."[69]

In any case, probing questions about race and postcoloniality are now being asked in contemporary France, posed both along a spatial axis—concerning whether colonialism is internal or external to French history—and along a temporal axis, concerning whether colonialism still shapes contemporary French history. Subsequent to the mid-1990s demonizations of multiculturalism and to the initial antipathy to postcolonialism, the French academic scene has shifted substantially. As the editors of a special postcolonial issue of *Mouvements* put it, "So who is afraid of the postcolonial? There is no simple response to this question. There is no principal enemy to denounce, except for the colonial Unconscious that haunts French society and its social hierarchies, whose endurance it assures in a 'discontinuous continuity.' There is no republican plot to expose but only a specifically French difficulty in revisiting the fundamentals of republicanism and confronting them with the facts of its own historicity."[70]

9 The Transnational Traffic of Ideas

IN THIS CHAPTER, we theorize the multidirectional traffic of ideas concerning race/coloniality across the three zones through an analysis of a quadrille of readings whereby intellectuals from one country engage with intellectuals from a second country who make claims about a third country. We also sketch out the history of U.S. and French academic studies of Brazil, while intervening in the debates about the dissemination of French theory in the Americas. As part of our transnational and translational approach, we analyze Bourdieu/Wacquant's critique of Michael Hanchard's work on the black consciousness movement in Brazil, including a discussion of that critique's reception in Brazil, in order to explore the literal and metaphorical translation of ideas around the Atlantic.

France, the United States, and Brazil Studies

A thoroughgoing analysis of the triangular traffic of ideas requires contextualization regarding the history of academic writing on Brazil by both France-based and U.S.-based scholars. Whereas in the French case this writing traces its long-term origins to the 16th-century beginnings of the Franco-Brazilian relationship, in the U.S. case such writing is much more recent. In the postwar period, a number of factors—the surge of area studies in the United States, the Brazilian dictatorship's desire to improve higher education, and the Gaullist desire for alliances with the Third World—all led to a major expansion of scholarly exchange between the three countries. In Brazil, the military regime created scholarships for study abroad, with the United States being the most popular destination, followed by France.

Historian Edward A. Riedinger notes in his overview of Brazil-related research in France that from the time of the first doctoral dissertation on Brazil in 1823 up until 1999, 1,344 theses or dissertations about Brazil had been written in French universities, over 98 percent of them in the postwar period.[1] A cursory overview of the dissertations reveals certain patterns: First, the majority are by Brazilians working under French professors (such as Raymond Cantel and Guy Martinière) knowledgeable about Brazil or with Brazilian scholars based in France (such as Katia de Queirós Mattoso) or with celebrated scholars (such as Cornelius Castoriadis, Maurice Godelier, Pierre Bourdieu, and Alain Touraine) known more for their innovative social theories than for their knowledge of Brazil. Second, a prestigious gallery of Brazilian scholars on African, Afro-Brazilian, and indigenous culture and history—Luiz Felipe de Alencastro (the South Atlantic slave trade); Juana Elbein dos Santos (Afro-Brazilian religion); Renato Ortiz (Umbanda and popular culture), and anthropologist Eduardo Viveiros de Castro (indigenous philosophy)—did their graduate work in France. Third, the relatively rare comparative and cross-national dissertations tend to concern Brazil-Africa (Jean-Paul Coleyn on possession cults in Mali, Brazil, and Haiti) or France-Brazil (Gabriel Colo on French versus Brazilian images of the Brazilian; Claudia Andrade dos Santos on French travelers and the Brazilian slavery debates). Many dissertations treat Afro-Brazilian religion, and one treats black Brazilian activism (Luiz Alberto Oliveira Gonçalves's 1994 thesis "The Black Movement in Brazil"). While the theme of comparative race has been ubiquitous in scholarship by Brazilians and North Americans, little comparative race work has been done by French scholars, partly because the category of "race" is itself suspect.[2]

Riedinger notes in his comparison that (1) the French scholarship is largely in the sciences or the social sciences, while the U.S. work is in both the sciences and the humanities; (2) the French work is more inflected by Marxism; (3) the Annales School wields considerable influence, partially because of its focus on a Franco-Mediterranean sharing of certain cultural features with Brazil; (4) in geopolitical terms, French studies envision Brazil as a regional power in alliance with France and in opposition to the United States, while American studies see Brazil as complementary to the United States; and (5) in the United States, Brazilian studies research has been conducted largely by North Americans linked to Brazil, while Brazilian scholars in the United States tend to work with American experts for whom Brazil, or at least the "Third World," is an area of expertise.[3] (Some of this is changing as "Brazilian Brazilianists" enter the U.S. academy in greater numbers.)[4]

In any case, Brazilian studies has been a growing field in North America. BRASA (Brazilian Studies Association), founded in 1992, today has over a thousand members. At this point in history, we must speak of multiple generations of Brazilianists, going back to the founders, such as Ruth Landes, Donald Pierson, and Charles Wagley, on up to the hundreds of scholars working today. Some scholars express discomfort with the label "Brazilianist," feeling that the word distances scholars who in fact identify with a Brazilian perspective. While some prefer to call themselves *abrasileirados* (Brazilianized) rather than "Brazilianists," others emphasize a broad disciplinary affiliation, such as comparative literature, where the label "Brazilianist" seem overly restrictive. Others stress their special identity or their specific angle of approach, as when Ghanaian Anani Dzidzienyo calls himself an "Afro-Brazilianist."

A basic nonreciprocity has often marred the intellectual relationship between Brazil and its non-Brazilian interlocutors.[5] According to the regnant division of intellectual labor, the "periphery" is not supposed to study the "center"; rather, it is supposed to learn from the center how to study itself. While Brazilian students migrated to France and the United States in order to study Brazil or Brazil-related topics, French and American students did not flock to Brazil to study their own societies. Yet as a consequence of these asymmetries, the periphery also has less need to study the center; the periphery is already familiar with the center, which is why the center is called the center. At the same time, the center/periphery dichotomy can become an impediment in charting the more multidirectional exchanges that we address here. Despite the generally asymmetrical flows of information, Brazilian intellectual and artistic movements have often impacted cultural and political life in the United States and France, as occurred with dependency theory in economics (where future president of Brazil Fernando Henrique Cardoso played a major role), social geography (Josué de Castro's "geography of hunger"); education theory (Paulo Freire's "pedagogy of the oppressed"), radical theater (Augusto Boal's "theater of the oppressed"), cinema (Glauber Rocha's "aesthetics of hunger"), anthropology (Viveiros de Castro's indigenous "perspectivism"), and music (bossa nova, Tropicália).

French Theory In and Out of Place

In the background of the discussion of the trilateral exchange of ideas across France, Brazil, and the United States lie issues of center and periphery. In an essay titled "Post-structuralism and Deconstruction in the Americas," Leyla Perrone-Moisés laments the fact that the U.S. academy has popularized French poststructuralist thinkers to the point that Brazilian intellectuals now absorb French ideas "through" the United States. The main targets of her critique are "cultural studies," "multiculturalism," and the "politically correct," all seen as the deformed offspring of French philosophical parent trends. She correctly points to the strong French poststructuralist presence within cultural studies, which absorbed Althusser's antihumanist rereading of Marx, Lacan's rereading of Freud, Barthes's critique of "mythologies," Foucault's "genealogical critique of power," Deleuze's immersion in "difference and flux," Derrida's critique of "logocentrism," Lyotard's "end of metanarratives," Cixous's defense of *écriture féminine*, and so forth. (She leaves out Lefebvre, Certeau, and Bourdieu, but that is not germane here.)[6]

Perrone-Moisés contrasts what she calls the "unquestionably progressive" political causes defended by "cultural studies" with what she sees as its reductive method of reading. For her, French Theory has been dragooned into the service of the "politically correct," at great cost to literary and philosophical studies. In the barren soil of the U.S. academy, fertile French ideational seeds could only produce strange and grotesque hybrids. Our echo here of the language of 18th-century European "naturalists" is quite deliberate, for Perrone-Moisés inadvertently relays and updates the European naturalists' ideas about the Americas in general as a place of putrefaction and decay, where "dogs don't bark" and "plants don't grow." In her rejection of "American cultural studies," Perrone-Moisés draws on the same naturalist trope of infantilization that disqualified the Americas generally as culturally young and undeveloped. This perennial trope of New World youth underlies the following passage: "The most caricatural forms of cultural studies occur in countries of *recent* culture, lacking in a strong philosophical tradition and in the specific formation of diverse disciplines that such studies demand. In the Americas, there is a tendency to 'deconstruct' what has not yet been 'constructed.'"[7] Here Perrone-Moisés reproduces the venerable contrast of "old Europe" and the "young Americas," which have to "catch up" with a Europe that is both young in being at the cutting-edge of progressive thought and creativity yet also "old" in its philosophical maturity. That some of the nation-states of the Americas are technically "older" than some nation-states in Europe, and that Europe's progress culminated in World War II and the Holocaust, certainly casts doubt on any special claim to "maturity," just as the imperialistic practices of the United States cast doubt on exceptionalist claims of youthful innocence. In any case, the Americas generally are not "young" but palimpsestically "old," in that they inherit, by their very composition as nations, the millennial traditions of indigenous America, Europe, Africa, and Asia. What Melville wrote in *Redburn* applies to the Americas generally: "We are the heirs of all time, and with all nations we divide our inheritance. On this Western Hemisphere all tribes and people are forming into one federated whole; and there is a future that shall see all the estranged children of Adam restored as to the old hearth-stone in Eden. . . . The seed is sown, and the harvest must come."[8]

For Perrone-Moisés, North Americans impoverished Derrida's thought by turning "deconstruction" into a slogan. "Deconstruction became a prestigious label within American universities," she speculates, "because Americans were amazed at the vast philosophical and literate culture of Derrida, something not so frequent in the United States."[9] The observation mistakenly implies that Derrida's vast erudition is common in France—when it is his exceptional erudition that makes him a *maître*—and that such erudition is unknown in American (and Brazilian) universities. Derrida himself, ironically, saw the United States as an especially favorable terrain for the reception of his ideas, famously remarking that "America is deconstruction." In defending the "philosopher of difference" from his supposed vulgarizers, Perrone-Moisés denies the inevitability of "difference" when it comes to the transtextual extrapolations of Derrida's ideas into other idioms and locations, where they inevitably assume a local accent and coloration.

Behind Perrone-Moisés's polemical claims, one glimpses again the contours of the unproductive Latin/Anglo-Saxon binary:

> Some among us are faithfully adopting approaches which have to do with the Anglo-Saxon world, without taking into consideration the differences from our Latin American histories and cultures. . . . Multiculturalism, which has been criticized within the United States itself, favors the maintenance of separate ghettoes. . . . People speak of a Latin American postcolonialism. But Anglo-Saxon postcolonialism refers only to the use of English by recently decolonized writers, while our postcolonialism is already two centuries old, and our appropriation of metropolitan languages goes back a long way, as it does in the United States. Who would ever treat North American literature as postcolonial? [10]

On one level, Perrone-Moisés is right: some forms of postcolonial writing, as we ourselves have argued, *have* indeed been Anglocentric, downplaying the innovative Latin American discussions of hybridity, syncretism, and colony-metropole relations, along with the indigenous critique of coloniality/modernity. But the term "Anglo-Saxon" ethnicizes the political and essentializes the antiessentialist. The contradiction becomes flagrant in the last two sentences, where she notes that both the United States and Brazil appropriated metropolitan languages but then ridicules the idea that North American literature could also be called "postcolonial." But in fact all of the Americas are postcolonial in the sense of having achieved independence from European colonialism, even if Britain and the United States exercised hegemonic power in Latin America. But either all the colonial-settler states are postcolonial or none of them are. More precisely, they all form a palimpsestic mélange of temporalities and chronotopes, mingling the colonial (in relation to indigenous peoples), the postcolonial (in the sense of postindependence), the neocolonial (in the political economy of North-South domination), and the paracolonial (in that colonialism does not explain everything). The more crucial issue is the discrepant manner in which the diverse nations, and diverse groups within nations, live this same postcolonial moment.

Perrone-Moisés wraps her critique in the mantle of anticolonialism: "Brazil, in adopting North American proposals, celebrates the end of our cultural colonialism in relation to France, without noticing that at the origin of these proposals, are French theorists. The only difference, for us, is that in the past we sought theoretical inspiration within the French matrix, and now we do it through the United States."[11] This highly ambivalent critique seems almost to exhort Brazilians to imitate the French themselves, rather than "imitate the imitators," that is, the Americans. Perrone-Moisés views the "post-" movements as mere epiphenomena of "French Theory," when the more germane issue is not "fidelity" to a European "original" but rather the fascinating "infidelities," the translational twists and turns and transformations of the theories. The more productive question would have to do with the ways that Jameson politicizes Greimas or Spivak subalternizes Derrida or Stoller racializes Foucault or Bhabha postcolonializes Lacan and so forth. In the same vein, the issue is how Brazilian intellectuals and artists indigenize "out-of-place ideas," the ways that Roberto Schwarz indigenizes Adorno, that Glauber Rocha Africanizes Brecht, that Haroldo de Campos Brazilianizes Faust, that Ismail Xavier national-allegorizes Walter Benjamin, that Sérgio Costa samples Stuart Hall, and that Jessé Souza peripheralizes Bourdieu. Or, to move to another sphere, it is how rappers such as Racionais MC's Brazilianize the African American group Public Enemy or Carlinhos Brown Bahianizes James Brown or Gilberto Gil tropicalizes the Beatles.

Perrone-Moisés is hardly alone in pointing to the crucial U.S. role in disseminating French Theory. In *French Theory: How Foucault, Derrida, Deleuze, & Co. Transformed the Intellectual Life of the United States*, François Cusset offers a nuanced account of these disseminational processes. He describes the giddy heyday of French Theory, when French authors "reached a level of official notoriety and underground influence in the United States that they never achieved in their own country."[12] In what Cusset calls a "perfect chiasm" or "symmetrically reversed situation,"[13] the heights of French Theory in the United States coincided with its erasure in France itself. At the very same moment that Foucault, Lyotard, and Derrida were being eclipsed in France, they were becoming ubiquitous names in the American university. At that time, the French media were promoting the telegenic *nouveaux philosophes* eager to sweep away leftist, radical, multicultural, and postcolonial ideas. Yet the same "French Theory" demonized by the *nouveaux philosophes*, for Cusset, was becoming a powerful force not only in the U.S. academy but also even in "the most unexpected recesses" of the culture, "from pop art to the cyberpunk novel."[14]

The influence of French Theory abroad was mediated not only by French cultural institutions such as the Maison Française but also by a gallery of prestigious American universities, notably the "golden triangle" of Johns Hopkins, Cornell, and Yale, along with New York University, Columbia, and the University of California, in tandem with journals such as *Diacritics, Enclitic, Substance, Semiotexte*, and so forth. Using Bourdieu-style language, Cusset speaks of the "processes of selection, labeling and classification" through which American academics fashioned the intellectual trends of the 1980s.[15] Through a *dépaysement des idées*, French concepts were unmoored from their origins and made to drift into contact not only with concepts more common in the United States but also with concepts from other French thinkers. But for Cusset, this unmooring generated political use-value by reinventing French texts that in France had "become trapped in their editorial and publishing straitjackets."[16] Cusset sees a virtue, then, in what Bourdieu calls the "denationalization" of texts. As a result, French Theory, as what Cusset calls the "new transdisciplinary object fashioned by literary scholars from French poststructuralism," penetrated into the interstices of American intellectual life.[17]

One of the uses to which the "posts" were put, in the United States, was to theorize race, multiculturality, and the postcolonial. Postcolonial studies and cultural studies, in this sense, form transnational amalgams of diverse currents—French, certainly, but also British, African, Native American, Latin American, South Asian, Caribbean, Middle Eastern, and so forth. That U.S.-based academics, in contrast with the Francophobic U.S. right wing, have embraced these French thinkers might have been interpreted as an index of a salutary receptiveness to ideas from elsewhere or a sign that American and Brazilian intellectuals (like intellectuals around the world) all share a French-inflected intertext, even if absorbed, assimilated, and transmogrified in discrepant ways in the various locations. Perrone-Moisés censures only one of the "terminals" in a broadly global transtextual process. While invoking poststructuralism in a positive way, she conducts the argument within pre-poststructuralist paradigms. For Derrida, intellectual exchange involves an endless process of dissemination and intertextuality, entailing reaccentuations without "origins," where the "copy" can be as valid as the "original," indeed where it is the copy that produces the prestige and even the originality of the original. The defense of Derrida against betrayal implies an abandonment, paradoxically, of his critique of origins.

Allegories of Intrusion

Bourdieu/Wacquant's essay "On the Cunning of Imperialist Reason" also addresses the intellectual relations between France, the United States and Brazil. A polemic against African American political theorist Michael Hanchard's analysis of "black consciousness" movements in Brazil in his 1994 book *Orpheus and Power*,[18] the essay singles out Hanchard as an avatar of the "cunning" of imperial reason that now enlists people of color to promulgate the "Macdonaldization" of thought: "Cultural imperialism (American or otherwise) never imposes itself better than when it is served by progressive intellectuals (or by 'intellectuals of colour' in the case of racial inequality) who would appear to be above suspicion of promoting the hegemonic interests of a country against which they wield the weapons of social criticism."[19] In hyperbolic language, Bourdieu/Wacquant portray Hanchard as a pawn of imperialism who injects "ethnocentric poison" into the debate about race by imposing a binary North American grid on a Brazilian society substantially without racism.

Like many critics of "identity politics," the authors are not above using identity to their own ends. Hanchard's identity as an "Afro-American political scientist" forms a key piece in their argument; it cues the Hegelian "cunning" in the title that makes Hanchard part of an imperialist ruse. The identity that actually remains "above suspicion," meanwhile, is that of the authors' whiteness and Frenchness. Their identity is so far above suspicion that it is not even named *as* an identity. While it is true that the U.S. rightist power structure has "cunningly" used some rare black conservatives to support neoliberalism and imperialist interventions and even to attack Affirmative Action, Hanchard is hardly a black conservative. Indeed, few social theorists are less susceptible than Hanchard to the charge against U.S. social thought in general as depoliticized and blind to class and domination. Written from a densely theoretical/historical perspective, and informed by the conceptual categories of Marx, Gramsci, Fanon, and other left theorists, *Orpheus and Power* is defiantly political, class-conscious, and very much concerned with social domination. Yet for Bourdieu/Wacquant, Hanchard unilaterally exports the dichotomous American "folk concept of race" into a flexible and open Brazilian society.[20]

Bourdieu/Wacquant enter into contradiction by denouncing both multiculturalism and "American dichotomous thinking on race." The multicultural project, whatever its faults, generally eschewed racially dichotomous thinking in favor of discourses of cultural mixing and rainbow alliances. Indeed, many analysts discern a kind of "Brazilianization" of the United States, not only in terms of heightened class differences and disparities in wealth but also in terms of novel ways of thinking about the modes of intersection of class, race, and ethnicity, as some whites become impoverished (like many blacks), as some people of color claim a "multiracial" status, and as intermediate groups such as Latinos, Arab Americans, and Asian Americans scramble customary dichotomous schemas. Sociologist Eduardo Bonilla-Silva predicts a burgeoning Latin Americanization of the North American spectrum due to a number of factors: (1) changing demographics (population projects predict a minority-majority United States by 2050); (2) the advent of a "kinder and gentler" white supremacy; (3) the emergence of a Latin American–style "color-blind racism"; (4) the absorption of darker "others" by global capitalism; (5) the increase in interracial marriage, slight in black-white terms but massive in terms of Latinos, Asians, and Native Americans, only 33 percent of whom marry other Native Americans.[21]

The Bourdieu/Wacquant charge of a "brutal intrusion" into a Brazilian society without racism flies in the face of most of the serious research on Brazil, most authored by Brazilians, over the past half century or more. A gendered language positions Bourdieu/Wacquant as the protectors of a feminized Brazil violated by a brutal intruder, in this case a black male American scholar. The essay's reductionist notions of intercultural exchange break with the more complex drift of Bourdieu's own concept of "cultural fields." While Bourdieu's work in general discerns the interaction of structure and agency, these essays see only active U.S.-white domination and passive Third World victimization. In quasi-conspiratorial fashion, the authors speak of the "symbolic dominion and influence exercised by the United States over every kind of scholarly and, especially, semischolarly production, notably through the power of consecration they possess and through the material and symbolic profits that researchers in the dominated countries reap from a more or less assumed or ashamed adherence to the model derived from the United States."[22] These one-way formulations recall unproblematized Frankfurt School "hypodermic needle" cultural theories, whereby the culture industry "injects" passive consumers, as well as "media imperialism" theses that have imperialism "penetrating" Third World psyches, theses that have been revised even by their erstwhile proponents such as Ariel Dorfmann and Armand Mattelart. Bourdieu/Wacquant portray "researchers in the dominated countries" as either naive dupes enthralled by imperialist cultural products or as cynical opportunists lusting after "material and symbolic profits."[23] The denial of agency could not be more totalizing, a point reinforced by the fact that the bibliography of the "Cunning" essay includes *no* Brazilian scholars. At the same time, ironically, the bibliography cites favorably five American experts on Brazil (Charles Wagley, Anthony Marx, George Reid Andrews, Edward Telles, and Howard Winant), precisely those whom the theory would normally denounce as imposing their ethnocentric vision on Brazil!

Although stemming from an anti-imperial logic, the anxiety about African American "ethnic intrusions" finds an ironic precedent in the wariness of the Brazilian military dictatorship (1964–1985) toward any collaborations between black Brazilian and black American activists, seen by the regime as a menace to "national security." An official questionnaire exhorted censors to be vigilant about any direct or veiled allusions to the "Black Power movement." The junta's censors even forbade journalists to use the word "black" in a racial sense.[24] All-black musical groups such as Abolição were ordered to integrate. The "National Security" state banned as subversive any discussion of racial discrimination, including in the form of race-related census statistics. According to historian Thomas Skidmore, the forced exile of scholars such as Abdias do Nascimento, Florestan Fernandes, Fernando Henrique Cardoso, and Octávio Ianni was largely due to their questioning the nationalist consensus on Brazil as a racial democracy.[25]

We will not try here to undo all the folded misrepresentations in the second Bourdieu/Wacquant essay. Indeed, Brazilianist John French, in an essay titled "The Missteps of Anti-imperialist Reason," has already written a carefully calibrated but devastating critique.[26] After summarizing their argument fairly,

French points to the innumerable errors of evaluation in their text: the broad and undifferentiated caricature of American and Brazilian intellectual trends, the clueless misstatements about the current state of scholarship on race in Brazil, the misrepresentations of the positions of specific scholars, the agenda-driven idealization of the Brazilian racial situation, and the concomitantly schematic oversimplification of the U.S. situation. The authors, French argues, "clearly hold to a double standard when they compare the U.S. versus Brazil. They offer an excessively harsh and negative depiction of the racial situation in the U.S. and are intolerant of its national mythology; by contrast, they offer an excessively tolerant and positive depiction of the racial situation in Brazil while embracing its national mythology without criticism."[27] French then speculates as to why the two French sociologists would be so "unforgiving of U.S. illusions yet so accommodating of Brazilian ones."[28] He finds a clue in a footnote about what the authors call a "scientifically scandalous" book: Wieviorka's *Racist France.* "How long will it be," Bourdieu/Wacquant ask in a tone of ridicule, "before we get a book entitled *Racist Brazil* patterned after the scientifically scandalous *Racist France* of a French sociologist more attentive to the expectations of the field of journalism than to the complexities of social reality?"[29]

Apart from the fact that Bourdieu/Wacquant misrepresent Wieviorka's rich and varied work much as they caricature Hanchard's work, one is bewildered by such an apoplectic reaction to the idea of a French book about French racism or a Brazilian book about Brazilian racism. The authors' reaction reflects a surprising amnesia concerning French and Francophone intellectual history. Césaire did not require a "brutal ethnocentric intrusion" to find France racist when he wrote *Discourse on Colonialism*, nor did Fanon when he wrote *Black Skin, White Masks*, nor did Memmi when he wrote *Portrait of the Colonized* and *Dominated Man*. In fact, all of these authors found both France and the United States racist. John French speculates that the two authors might be making "opportunistic use of Brazil" in order to "attack intellectuals . . . who might undermine their cherished sense of Frenchness." If racism is by definition something that only North Americans do, French adds, "then neither France nor Brazil can be called racist."[30]

A white narcissism of national distinction thus leads some analysts to defend specific Black Atlantic societies as somehow exempt from racism, despite a shared history of conquest, colonialism, and slavery. A covertly national pathos, in this case, compromises the authors' methodology and lures them away from their own theoretical axioms. The view purveyed in French's essay and throughout our own text, in contrast, is of a historical and social continuum of racist ideologies and practices extending around the postcolonial Atlantic. In this context, books critical of "Racist America," "Racist France," and "Racist Brazil" hardly seem scandalous; rather, they seem inevitable, even salutary; the scandal would be if such books did *not* exist. The rendering innocent of France and Brazil only occurs, revealingly, in the context of cross-national comparisons. The comparative framework itself seems to trigger what might be called a "family protection" or "dirty laundry" syndrome, analogous to the ways that quarreling families suddenly unite in the face of outside criticism.

The facile dismissal of the possibility of a book about "Racist Brazil," furthermore, bespeaks a lack of engagement with the history of scholarship in Brazil. As we have seen with Ali Kamel, the authors write as if criticisms of Brazilian racism come exclusively from North Americans. Yet countless Brazilian books bear titles that, if they do not say precisely "racist Brazil," carry a similar charge. A quick look through our bookshelves garners the following titles (translated from Portuguese): *Racism and Anti-racism in Brazil* (1999), *Racism in Brazil* (2002), *The Genocide of Brazilian Blacks* (1978), and *Racism Explained to My Children* (2007). The title of a 2007 Brazilian book—*Racism: The Truth Hurts. Face It*— might be addressed to the racism deniers—of Brazil (and of the world generally). Even the mainstream newspaper *Folha de São Paulo* recognized a generalized Brazilian racism in a 1995 special investigative report entitled "Cordial Racism," in a verbal play on historian Sérgio Buarque de Holanda's celebrated description of the Brazilian as "cordial man." In any case, the dialogue between black Brazilians and African Americans and the critique of racism in Brazil did not begin with Hanchard. Whatever legitimate criticisms might be made of Hanchard's book— and some Brazilians have criticized it for privileging the African American Civil Rights model of activism as norm and for a certain smugness in its implication that Brazilian blacks are victims of false consciousness—the view of Hanchard as a race-obsessed imperialist bringing "ethnocentric poison" into a paradisal Brazil is clearly off the mark.

Bourdieu/Wacquant's tacitly idyllic portrait of Brazil is out of step with decades of critical scholarship. As we have seen, benign Freyrean myths of "racial democracy" had been deconstructed by Abdias do Nascimento and Guerreiro Ramos already in the 1940s and by the São Paulo school (Florestan Fernandes, Octávio Ianni, Fernando Henrique Cardoso) in the 1950s.[31] Bourdieu/Wacquant reverse the historical movement of scholarship; rather than cite the later critical work to discredit the earlier celebratory work, they draw on the idealizing fictions of the earlier work to discredit the more disenchanted conclusions of the later generations. The two authors belatedly enter a vast intertextual field whose contours they only dimly discern. While we have stressed the linked yet differentiated analogies between all the variegated racisms of the Atlantic, Bourdieu/ Wacquant draw a line of absolute difference between Brazil and the United States and between France and the United States, denying similarities, parallelisms, continuities, and relationalities.

On one level, Bourdieu/Wacquant are not completely wrong to note that racial relations are less "tense and hostile" in Brazil, a trait noted by countless observers. A number of features of Brazilian social life do indeed lend a more humane face to what is in structural terms a racially and economically hierarchical society. Many factors play a role in this relative lack of tension: a history that has favored conciliation over confrontation, a miscegenation that undercuts racial binarism, and the elaborately choreographed pas de deux between a top-down populism that plays down tensions and a bottom-up civility that slyly and ambivalently collaborates.[32] Many elements in Brazilian popular culture—the role playing of Carnival and the open-ended identifications of Candomblé—favor an extraordinary suppleness of code-switching and *jogo de cintura* (social adaptability). James Holston speaks of "ideologies of inclusion that . . . give personal relations of gender, racial, and economic difference a gloss of complicit accommodation, a sense of intimacy that obscures but maintains fundamental inequalities . . . [produced through] the (untranslatable) artifices of *jeitinho, malicia, malandragem, jinga, jogo de cintura,* and *mineirice*."[33] Despite the diminished racial tension, the material inequalities between the white elite and racialized subalterns have historically been greater than in the United States. Yet the "which is worse?" question is still the wrong question. More precisely, it is not wrong to point to better or worse situations; it is wrong to use a worse situation elsewhere to deny injustice at home. The two societies offer distinct modalities of white- and Euro-domination, one rooted in segregationist racism in a very rich country, the other in assimilationist paternalism in a relatively poor country, but with regional variations and many mixed forms in both sites. At this point in history, the various "racial formations" around the Black Atlantic conjoin social segregation, assimilation, and economic disempowerment. Ultimately, the point is to discern the relative coefficient of each element in the general mix and, more important, to discern what activists/ scholars can learn from one another in terms of analyses and solutions.

Bourdieu/Wacquant purvey the impression that the United States is essentially racist, while Brazil is only conjuncturally oppressive, constrained by imperialism and corrupted by American influence. Notice the following formulation: "Carried out by Americans and Brazilians trained in the United States, most of the recent research on racial inequality in Brazil strives to prove that, contrary to the image that Brazilians have of their own nation, the country of the 'three sad races' . . . is no less racist than others."[34] This passage raises a number of questions. First, why would critical intellectuals normally skeptical about nationalist doxa be so respectful of "the image that a nation has of itself"? Second, the locational determinism of the phrase "Americans and Brazilians trained in the United States" falsely conveys the image of a monolithic group of researchers advancing a single political position. Third, the authors speak as if Brazilians have a single image of their own nation, when in fact Brazil shelters a lively debate about competing images of the various *Brasis* (Brazils, in the plural). Fourth, the authors speak as if Brazil's self-image were static and transhistorical, when in fact it is in perpetual mutation. In sum, the formulation embeds a simplistic dichotomy between the vast totality of normal "Brazilians" holding a positive image of their country, on the one hand, and two outlier microfactions, on the other, that is, American scholars and Brazilians trained in the United States. All potential critics of the Brazilian racial formation are exiled, as it were, to join the American side.

In trying to discredit Hanchard, Bourdieu/Wacquant resuscitate myths long dismantled by critical Brazilian scholars, even if these myths retain some residual purchase in the hegemonic discourse. In defending Brazil, and implicitly France, against potential charges of racism, Bourdieu/Wacquant inadvertently revisit the old interimperial rivalries and the Anglo/Latin dichotomy. And while it would be simplistic to say that "all societies are racist" or even that any single society is simply and essentially and only racist, we can affirm, more prudently, that all those countries that participated, whether actively or passively, in colonialism and slavery are likely to exhibit not only the institutional traces of these systems of oppression but also the ongoing struggles against them.[35]

Some of the hostility to race-based scholarship derives, it would seem, from a historically problematic assumption that such work is allied to hegemonic power in the United States itself. It is in this context that Bourdieu/Wacquant criticize the role of U.S.-based foundations in supporting race-related research in Brazil:

> One would obviously need to invoke here also the driving role played by the major American philanthropic and research foundations in the diffusion of the U.S. racial doxa within the Brazilian academic field at the level of both representations and practices. Thus, the Rockefeller Foundation and similar organizations fund a programme on "Race and Ethnicity" at the Federal University of Rio de Janeiro as well as the Centre for Afro-Asiatic Studies of the Candido Mendes University (and its journal *Estudos Afro-Asiáticos*) so as to encourage exchanges of researchers and students. But the intellectual current flows in one direction only. And, as a condition for its aid, the Rockefeller Foundation requires that research teams meet U.S. criteria of *"affirmative action,"* which poses insuperable problems since, as we have seen, the application of the white/black dichotomy in Brazilian society is, to say the least, hazardous.[36]

While right to critique the unidirectionality of exchange, Bourdieu/Wacquant also seem to project their own assumptions about a state-dependent and centralized French cultural field onto very different contexts. In France, a highly centralized system is seen as incarnating the "general will," and both left and right have tried to harness the power and prestige of culture for political ends. In the United

States, in contrast, foundations step into the vacuum left by a neoliberal system that minimizes government support for the arts and for education.

In political terms, American foundations have had a long and often shady history. In the realm of economics, the Ford Foundation played a very pernicious role in funding the University of Chicago's economics program, a hotbed of neoliberal thinking led by Milton Friedman. Ford came to be associated with the shock-doctrine agenda of the neoliberal "Chicago Boys" in Chile and the "Berkeley Mafia" in Indonesia. In the mid-1970s, however, Ford did an about-face and became a leading funder of human rights activism. After severing its links to the Ford Motor Corporation in 1974, the Ford Foundation helped persuade the U.S. Congress to cut off military support to Argentina and Chile. As Naomi Klein points out, it was as if Ford were doing penance for its earlier sins: "After the left in those countries had been obliterated by regimes that Ford had helped shape, it was none other than Ford that funded a new generation of crusading lawyers dedicated to freeing the hundreds of thousands of political prisoners being held by those same regimes."[37]

Foundations play a highly contested role both in the United States itself and in the Global South, at times spreading neoliberal doctrine and at times compensating for the depredations of transnational capitalism. Although the Ford Foundation developed initiatives to promote social justice and to combat racism though legal, mediatic, judicial, and research activities,[38] it would nonetheless be difficult to discern any theoretical or political uniformity in the foundation-supported research on race, much less any orthodoxy imposed by U.S. institutions and scholars. Nor is it clear (1) that Affirmative Action is premised on the white/black dichotomy or (2) that foundations are dedicated to spreading U.S. racial doxa. In the end, the point is not to unequivocally defend or defame foundation-sponsored work but only to highlight the contradictions for leftist academics working in diverse locations who try to produce adversary scholarship partially funded by foundations or, for that matter, governments. A truly democratic society would not depend on the whims of philanthropic foundations to provide private Band-Aid solutions for deeply rooted public social problems. The challenge is to avoid reductionism: to recognize the weight, inertia, and shaping power of governmentality and to acknowledge the ways that myriad institutions and interests work over social projects, but without falling into a "vulgar institutionalism," whereby individuals, artists, and academics are seen as completely determined and ideologically reducible to their institutional locations and affiliations.

In the Bourdieu/Wacquant view, ideology spreads like the pods in *Invasion of the Body Snatchers*. Hanchard passively absorbs U.S.-style dichotomous thinking on race (even though, as an African American, he is himself its victim) and then passes it on to equally passive Brazilian intellectuals whose weak immune systems leave them prey to the contagion. Brazilians studying in the United States, equally powerless to resist, catch the virus and bring it back to Brazil. Rather than an "out-of-place" idea, race-inflected analysis is envisioned as an "out-of-place" ideological virus. Within the viral view, entire countries such as Great Britain—in an echo of perennial Anglo-Saxon/Latin quarrels—become *passeurs* for imperialism. Thus, a footnote to the essay posits England as "structurally predisposed to act as the Trojan horse by which notions of American scholarly common sense penetrate the European intellectual field."[39] This reductionist view, expressed again in a masculinist language of "penetration," forms the cultural correlative to the geopolitical analysis that sees Britain as facilitating the infiltration of neoliberal Anglo-American ideology into the European Union. Our problem is not with the critique of neoliberal ideology or even with the role of specific nation-states but rather with the conflation between critical intellectuals and their governments. To put it crudely, although Tony Blair may have been Bush's poodle, Stuart Hall was not. Nor was Edward Said the servant of the U.S. State Department, nor is Michael Hanchard the academic equivalent of Colin Powell. Bourdieu/Wacquant's self-narration as the saviors of a feminized Brazil is a little too reminiscent of a neocolonial rescue narrative, especially since the essay does not engage with Brazilian intellectuals at all. Progressive Brazilian intellectuals deserve allies and interlocutors, not "saviors," of any nationality.

Cultural Studies and Critical Utopias

In the same "Cunning of Imperial Reason" essay, Bourdieu/Wacquant also express disdain for "cultural studies":

> Thus it is that decisions of pure book marketing orient research and university teaching in the direction of homogenization and submission to fashions coming from America, when they do not fabricate wholesale "disciplines" such as Cultural Studies, this mongrel domain, born in England in the 1970s, which owes its international dissemination (which is the whole of its existence) to a successful publishing policy.[40]

Despite this acerbic dismissal of a complex field, it is precisely cultural studies—and more broadly multicultural, postcolonial, and transnational studies—that is methodologically equipped to deal with contemporary cultural syncretism in the Red, Black, and White Atlantic. While Bourdieu, in books such as *Distinction*, performed incisive critiques of social, educational, and cultural privilege, the coauthored polemical essays undermine possible cross-border alliances with those elsewhere who challenge elitist/racist conceptualizations of culture. In condemning cultural studies en bloc, the two authors, to pick up on Wacquant's formulation in another context, "judge [cultural studies] through the very categories of thought that [those fields] aim at transcending."[41] Their mockery of a "mongrel" domain, for example, forgets the colonialist tint of the "mongrel" trope in racist thinkers such as Gobineau, for whom hybridity and miscegenation signaled "degeneracy." The metaphor forms part of a set of binary pairs—mongrel versus pedigree, pure versus impure—historically deployed to reinforce elitist hierarchies. By reinstating the high/low hierarchy that "cultural studies" aims to transcend, the metaphor undercuts Bourdieu's own critique of the elitism of "the heirs" in education.

Bourdieu/Wacquant's casual dismissal of a multifaceted project called "cultural studies" exemplifies vulgar institutionalism at its most egregious. All the work of the Birmingham School and its innumerable heirs is portrayed as "nothing but" the effect of a marketing gimmick. Bourdieu's own work on sport, museumgoing, and the media, in a further ironic wrinkle, might elsewhere qualify as "cultural studies." Indeed, Bourdieu is an oft-cited figure within cultural studies, the transdisciplinary formation that mingled, as Bourdieu's own work did, the methods of the social sciences and the humanities. Even though the authors deride "French cultural studies," some of that field's practitioners, such as Marie-Pierre Le Hir, speak of the "longstanding historical ties between the Birmingham Center and the Bourdieu group" and posit Bourdieu's "reflexive sociology" as a methodological model.[42]

Bourdieu/Wacquant mockingly predict the kind of work that European cultural studies is already doing: "And one may forecast that, by virtue of the principle of ethnicoeditorial parthenogenesis in fashion today, we shall soon find in bookstores a handbook of *French-Arab Cultural Studies* to match its cross-channel cousin, *Black British Cultural Studies*, which appeared in 1997 (but bets remain open as to whether Routledge will dare *German-Turkish Cultural Studies*)."[43] One is struck at the tone of derision toward even the hypothesis of scholarship addressing racialized minorities in Europe. The underlying assumption, perhaps, is that "minorities" are by definition particular and not universal and, moreover, might be an American invention alien to Europe, and especially to France. But why not endorse, rather than ridicule, the prospect of "French-Arab cultural studies" and " German-Turkish cultural studies"? Given ethnic tensions in present-day France, it would seem that French-Arab cultural studies are exactly what the doctor ordered. And given recurrent waves of Islamophobia in Germany, what could be more vital than German-Turkish studies? Nor are European minority scholars merely "mimic men" imitating American doxa; they are intellectuals trying to formulate their own ambiguous social status within a situation of racialized minoritization.

French intellectuals such as Bourdieu/Wacquant have not yet "assimilated" the relevance of (multi)cultural and postcolonial studies to an irreversibly pluralized European culture. As François Cusset put it (prior to the recent efflores-cence of postcolonial studies in France),

> Among the major American intellectual currents of the last quarter century, virtu-ally none have been received to any significant degree in France, neither analytic philosophy, nor the convergences of pragmatism and Continental philosophy, nor radical multiculturalism, nor deconstructionist readings of literature, nor postcolonial theory and subaltern studies, nor even the new theories of gender identity—despite a timid, recent emergence, "slowly but surely," of the queer ques-tion. Indeed, France changes only slowly, or under duress.[44]

Brazilian anthropologist Eduardo Viveiros de Castro makes a cognate point about the reluctance of French intellectuals to pick up on the more radical implications of poststructuralism, underlining the paradox that the "Anglophone academy has been more open to Continental philosophy than French anthropology itself." The principal source of the rapprochement between philosophy and anthropology, he adds, "has taken place in English-speaking countries (not without provoking vio-lent reactions on the part of the local [French] academic cardinals)."[45]

The lack of engagement with these transnational currents has resulted in a gap between academic scholarship and the irrevocably hybrid cultural life of con-temporary France. Little of the cultural syncretisms typical not only of Parisian streets but also of popular French culture makes its way into the theorizations by French *maîtres à penser*. In Bourdieu's case, this oversight was perhaps correlated with the assumption that the "hard" social sciences need not deal with "soft" pop-ular culture or perhaps linked to the Frankfurt School equation of mass culture with false consciousness. In many countries, "cultural studies" names the attempt to close the gap between popular culture and academic theory, as well as between the social sciences and the humanities. The failure of cultural studies to take hold in the French academy is especially ironic in that French thinkers such as Henri Lefebvre, Roland Barthes, and Michel de Certeau, along with Césaire, Fanon, and even Sartre and Beauvoir, were all precursors of "cultural studies." Here again we find the same paradox we encountered earlier with postcolonial studies, where a movement that is partially the intellectual "offspring" of French thought has been shunned, at least until recently, by the metropolitan "parents."[46]

Bourdieu/Wacquant's curt dismissal of "British cultural studies" and "Ameri-can multiculturalism"—two complex projects falsely equated with single national origins—reveals a kind of specular repulsion. The two authors seem to be lashing out at alter egos, at cultural theorists who, apart from their national location, in some ways "look like them." They denounce British cultural studies, even though Stuart Hall's role and stature in Britain as an incisive critic of dominant media and elitist institutions parallels that of Bourdieu in France. Anglo-American radical pedagogy aims to undermine entrenched privilege in the school system, much as Bourdieu's work purports to do in France. It is this flailing out at phantasmatic doubles that raises warning flags about a hidden national and perhaps disciplinary narcissism at work.

As a post-Marxist field, cultural studies has questioned the base/superstructure model and detected resistance in sites previously dismissed as the loci of alienation and false consciousness. Although cultural studies has at times inflated, in a kind of Madonna syndrome, the quantum of resistance in mass culture, it has also detected utopian moments that go beyond prescriptive blueprints for social change. It has shown us that contemporary political struggle necessarily passes through popular culture. An encounter between Bourdieu and German writer Günter Grass, filmed by the television channel Arte (December 5, 1999), around the time of Bourdieu/Wacquant's two polemical essays, is very revealing in terms of contrasting conceptualizations of culture. Grass praises Bourdieu's project in *La Misère du Monde* as a critique of social oppression but notes a missing element: humor. Bourdieu responds that suffering is not a laughing matter, to which Grass responds that works such as Voltaire's *Candide* show that satire and parody can expose frightful social conditions. Intellectuals, he adds, must describe suffering but also insist on the capacity of people to resist, including through humor. Bourdieu responds, "Globalization does not inspire laughter; our era is not amusing." Grass responds that he is not saying that globalization is funny but only that the "infernal laughter" triggered by art can also be an indispensable arm in social struggle.

We agree with Grass that unamusing eras, especially, need the subversive tonic of laughter. For Brecht, a sense of humor was indispensable in comprehending dialectical materialism, and in this sense, Bourdieu's dismissal of humor as a form of social agency is undialectical. It reflects what literary critics would call a "genre mistake" or a "mimetic fallacy" in that it suggests that suffering-laden eras—and what era has *not* been suffering-laden?—cannot be treated in comic or satirical genres. Only science, in the austerely superegoish Bourdieu conception, can accurately register, analyze, and combat social oppression. French media sociologist Éric Maigret sees in the Grass-Bourdieu exchange an opposition between two visions: one (Bourdieu's) associates the mass of people with suffering, symbolic passivity, and dispossession while positing the intellectual as the designated spokesperson for the inexpressive masses; the other (Grass's) discerns both suffering and popular resistance.[47] Although Bourdieu gives lip service to "agency," he ultimately portrays common people (and Brazilian intellectuals) as "cultural dupes" beset by symbolic privation. His project, in this sense, could benefit from a more dialogical and nonfinalizing vision of culture and agency.

Bourdieu's work, through all its various moments—from the anthropological work in Algeria, through the Marx-, Weber-, and Durkheim-inflected sociology of education, to the work on symbolic violence in art and consumption, on to the polemical writings on television—conveys a thoroughgoing skepticism about popular culture. Bourdieu argues in *On Television* that television hinders serious thought since it is produced under the sign of simultaneity and velocity of direct transmission.[48] Such a view fails to explain why totalitarian regimes invariably try to *eliminate* live television and direct transmission. (One wonders what Bourdieu would have made of the role of social media in the "Twitter revolutions" in the Middle East, where "simultaneity and velocity" were crucial to revolutionary activism.) Within what Arlindo Machado calls Bourdieu's "Platonic and aristocratic" conception, the mass media signify the end of free thought and intelligence thanks to the reign of spectacularization and mercantilization.[49] The only real solution, for Bourdieu, lies in the "distinction" of the scientific expert.

Thus, although Bourdieu tries to mark off his difference from the elitist determinism of the Frankfurt School, he ends up by reaffirming the Adornonian equation of popular alienation and the dominant cultural industries. As Maigret puts it,

> Reading Bourdieu's writings can at first have a liberatory effect, engender a feeling of revolt, because they unveil the unknown corridors of privilege, the daily fabrication of power. But then they provoke a comedown when they reveal a metaphysical conception of closure within the social game, justified or rationalized through the Spinozist philosophy: awareness of determinism helps one become free. For most people, however, who lack access to this form of knowledge, there is no solution to the problem of symbolic violence since those who experience it fail to make sense out of their world and those who perpetrate it are also its victims.[50]

Thus, within Bourdieu-style analysis, everyone is trapped within a cruel and unequal social game, except those enjoying access to the truths of social science, who escape the shipwreck of capitalist modernity to tell the story of the disaster. Bourdieu displays no faith in what Maigret calls "the individual negotiation of meaning, or the collective management of social stakeholding."[51] For Bourdieu, people are doubly dominated, first by social and economic domination itself and then by their own naive belief in the legitimacy of this domination. But without a theory of popular agency, the dominated possess neither a valid culture nor a capacity to react. Bourdieu thus falls back into what Maigret calls an "astonishingly conservative discourse" inherent in the "old bourgeois rhetoric of culture."[52]

For conservatives, social life is a competition for status and power, wherein capitalism is perfectly matched to the actually existing human beings whose "nature" makes them winners or losers in that combat. Like the conservatives, Bourdieu's work also figures social life, including academic life, as a perpetual struggle for status, distinction, and autonomy via the accumulation of economic, academic, social, and symbolic power, even if his goal—and this difference is crucial—was to rearrange that system to end social oppression. In *Demand the Impossible: Science Fiction and the Utopian Imagination*, Tom Moylan distinguishes between scientistic "blueprint utopias," which form part of a totalizing metanarrative of progress, and "critical utopias," which seek "seditious expression of social change" carried on in a "permanently open process of envisioning what is not yet."[53] Critical utopias, in this view, are generated by the concrete dissatisfactions of everyday life under capitalism and aim at reimagining the possible, while retaining awareness of the structural obstacles that make utopias difficult to realize. It is hard to find in Bourdieu a "critical utopia" consonant with that found not only in Moylan but also in Marx ("the sigh of the oppressed creature") and in such writers as Bakhtin, Ernst Bloch, Herbert Marcuse, Fredric Jameson, Paul Gilroy, and many others. In the Bourdieuvian dialectic of structure and agency, the second term is downplayed, with little but science and a redemptive "reflexivity" as consolation.

Although Bourdieu expresses a quasi-Bakhtinian enthusiasm, in *Distinction*, for the satires and carnivalesque parodies that "satisfy the taste for and sense of revelry, the plain speaking and hearty laughter which liberate by setting the social world head over heels, overturning conventions and priorities,"[54] he ultimately flattens Bakhtin's carnival by suggesting in the "Postscript" that for Bakhtin the "popular imagination can only *invert* the relationship which is the basis of the aesthetic sociodicy" (emphasis ours).[55] If Bakhtin errs on the side of euphoric utopianism, Bourdieu errs on the side of bleak dystopianism. The left needs both what Ernst Bloch calls Marxism's "cold current"—the disabused analysis of economic stratification and social alienation—and its "warm current" (the intoxicating glimpses of collective freedom).[56] Which is why the left needs the warm current of Bakhtin and Bloch—not to replace Bourdieu but to complement the cold current of his thought.

Triangular Readings

After the publication of two special issues of the journal *Theory and Culture* and one special issue of *Black Renaissance Noire*, the two Bourdieu/Wacquant essays are by now among the most thoroughly dissected and "rebutted" essays in recent intellectual history, including within Brazil, where a special issue of *Estudos Afro-Asiáticos* (January–April 2000) was dedicated to the Michael Hanchard polemic.[57] Our spiraling focus here is on Brazilian intellectuals reading back to French intellectuals reading an African American reading Brazil.

The best-received aspect of the "Cunning of Imperial Reason" essay in Brazil was its denunciation of imperialism; Brazilian intellectuals were happy to see prestigious French intellectuals validate a longstanding Brazilian anti-imperial critique. But the Brazilian participants in the *Estudos Afro-Asiáticos* issue express surprise at seeing themselves portrayed as sheeplike followers of U.S. intellectual fashions, without acknowledgment of the long line of Brazilian historians, anthropologists, sociologists, activists, and cultural critics who have addressed race in Brazil. The French sociologists, for these Brazilian scholars, were inattentive both to the variety of the actual work and to the complexity of U.S.-Brazilian scholarly relations. For Bourdieu/Wacquant, American scholars of Brazil impose an alien bipolar American prism on their Brazilian "followers," yet ironically they only cite scholarship by North Americans, exactly those who according to their theory would favor an "American bipolar point of view." But we would argue that there is no single American (or Brazilian or French) point of view on race but only an unending battle over rival analyses of race, which explains why some U.S. analysts prefer Brazilian approaches to race and why some black Brazilians admire the African American model of activism.

Like other contributors, Jocélio Teles dos Santos scolds Bourdieu/Wacquant for speaking as if Brazilian intellectuals exercise no agency in the debate, while boomeranging Bourdieu's own terminology against his argument: "[Brazilian intellectuals] are not mere tabula rasa victims of the cunning of imperial reason and its hegemonic racial model. A serious in-depth reading of the existing bibliography—something one expects from serious intellectuals—would reveal all the resignifications one finds in the struggle over this 'field' of power."[58] Santos's usage of "resignification" conjures up a paradigmatic strategy whereby Brazilian intellectuals have indigenized and transformed ideas from elsewhere. Brazilian intellectual life, as Osmundo de Araújo Pinho and Ângela Figueiredo argue, has always been impacted by "foreign" models, especially French and North American ones. [59] While censuring one (North American) strand of influence, the Bourdieu/Wacquant account normalizes (while rendering invisible) the multicentury European, and especially French, influence in Brazil. The price of internal colonization, for Pinho and Figueiredo, was the "permanent malaise of the thinking and administrative stratum facing a nation composed of what to them were aliens, virtual foreigners in the country," resulting in elitist admonitions against "African barbarism" or the "illiteracy of the masses."[60] Entire disciplines, such as sociology, were imported whole cloth from abroad. Sociologist Alberto Guerreiro Ramos had spoken of the "canned" character of the social sciences in Brazil, where forms of anthropology were "literally transplanted from European countries or from the United States," constituting little more than "a rationalization or a distraction from colonial exploitation."[61] It was not Hanchard, therefore, who "first introduced alien ideas into the national intellectual panorama." Bourdieu/Wacquant seem seduced, as Pinho and Figueiredo put it, "by a vision of Brazil and its racial relations that for many of us seems completely unacceptable."[62]

Michael Hanchard, responding to his critics, stresses the transnational character of Afro-diasporic movements as drawing inspiration from a wide variety of Black Atlantic sources: the Haitian Revolution, Palmares and the *quilombos*, the Frente Negra, the Harlem Renaissance, the Francophone *Négritude* poets, African decolonization, and the U.S. Civil Rights and Black Power movements. A nationalist-essentialist approach, for Hanchard, blinds us to the diasporic conditions that complicate superficial distinctions between imperialist and non-imperialist nation-states. The Bourdieu/Wacquant analysis leaves little room for ideological or political divisions within countries or points of convergence across national borders. The authors do not imagine the possibility of internal antistate movements, as exemplified by the black American activists who resisted both state-mandated social apartheid within the country and the imperialism carried out beyond its borders. Both Martin Luther King, Jr., and Malcolm X condemned racism at home and imperialism abroad; indeed, they insisted on the intimate connection between the two phenomena. Bourdieu/Wacquant simplistically equate black American transnationalism with the foreign policy of the United States, apparently viewing multinational corporations, the U.S. government, liberal foundations, and the country's dominated populations as virtually interchangeable. Their formulations, for Hanchard, assume stable and internally coherent self-contained national units, presided over by a state whose policies determine the national ideological disposition of all citizens. American intellectuals and activists simply encode the dominant imperial DNA of the United States, a view as absurd, Hanchard suggests, as claiming that Gobineau, Georges Bataille, Julia Kristeva, Jacques Chirac, and Henri Lefebvre all instantiate a "French" mode of thinking. If nation-state affiliations determine ideology, Hanchard wonders, how did Bourdieu and Wacquant themselves escape from the prison-house of ideological domination?

Sociologist Sérgio Costa, meanwhile, questions the pertinence of "imperialism" to describe relations between intellectuals from the Global North and the Global South, since all societies feature a "postnational" aspect that "imperialism," with its connotation of unilateral domination, fails to capture. The debate, Costa points out, has at times degenerated into a fight between the supposed defenders of "racial democracy" and those who call attention to racialized oppression. This discursive reduction, Costa writes, "transforms the academic debate into a (false) moral quarrel around the monopoly on the protection of the victims of social oppression, whether it is a matter of Brazilian racism or of American imperialism, and is useless in terms of buttressing the theoretical reflection about existing social problems and the political means for solving them."[63] Costa thus points to the tensions within and between the competing national vanities of white elites, when the goal, in his view, should not be to exalt any single country as model but rather to forge the analytical tools, and the political and institutional mechanisms, needed to fashion societies where epidermic appearances no longer wield the same horrific power that they have historically exercised.

In sum, the reception of the Bourdieu/Wacquant essay in Brazil points to a general problem in narrating intellectual exchange according to a unilateral cultural imperialism thesis. Historically, Brazilian intellectuals have not only exercised agency in these transnational exchanges; they have also been in the vanguard of those theorizing the asymmetries of cultural production and dissemination. The appropriation of French ideas by the Brazilian modernists, for example, was selective rather than servile. Some French ideas were tasted and then spit out, while others were chewed, transformed, and digested so as to nourish Brazilian multiculture. More than a provocative trope, "anthropophagy" was a theory of cultural exchange. Brazilian literary theory and literary history have developed innovative theories of dependency, translation, and transtextuality as seen within the context of postcolonial domination. For literary critic Antônio Cândido, a kind of obligatory cosmopolitanism makes Brazilian literary analysts fundamentally comparatist, aware of the congenital connection of Brazilian literature to other literary traditions such as the Portuguese, the French, and the Anglo-American, existing always *in relation* to cultural currents from outside that shaped a literature at once dependent on and distinct from the dominant outside literary currents.[64]

Bourdieu/Wacquant rightly foreground the asymmetries in the global distribution of intellectual labor but fail to historicize them, seeing the process only in its latest American imperialist incarnation. Within the "crossings" of literary production and ideas, Brazil, for example, has operated at a severe disadvantage. Within the colonial imaginary, Europe represented culture, and Brazil agriculture; Europe "refinement," and Brazil sugar cane. In the international division of intellectual labor, Brazil was seen as a consumer, not a producer, of ideas, just as Brazil was a consumer of economic goods manufactured elsewhere. Brazil's relatively disadvantaged geopolitical position, and in the colonial period the concrete lack of academic institutions and publishing houses, moreover, led not only to scant academic production but also to diminished power to disseminate existing production. But these imposed limitations did not mean that Brazil did not produce *culture*. Brazil was from the beginning staggeringly creative in generating new forms of popular and erudite culture, ranging from Africanized cuisine and Islamicized architecture to urbane literature and richly syncretic music. For centuries, the slaveholding elite's aversion to work meant that most of the artisans, artists, and musicians in Brazil—for example, the baroque composers and sculptors in 18th-century Minas Gerais—were black or mestizo. Yet the dominant discourses stigmatized the black population—the only population that actually *worked*—as the cause of Brazil's "backwardness."

Modernist writer Mário de Andrade reflected on the processes of cultural discrimination that devalued the work of Brazilian artists, a question that came to the fore later in the 1960s and 1970s in the form of the "cultural dependency" debate. While "very optimistic about the creativity of our literature and other contemporary arts," Andrade suggested that Brazilian texts would never win the applause they deserved due to factors having nothing to do with artistic merit. Some countries, he wrote, "weigh in with great force in the universal scale; their currency is valuable or pretends to be valuable, and their armies have the power to decide in the wars of the future. . . . The permanence of the arts of any given country in terms of the world's attention exist in direct proportion to the political and economic power of the country in question."[65] Just as the prices of Brazil's raw materials were once set in Europe or North America, whether in Lisbon, Amsterdam, London, or New York, so the value of Brazil's cultural goods tended to be calibrated outside of Brazil, again in those very same world capitals.

The Bourdieu/Wacquant formulations about intellectual relations between France, Brazil, and the United States fail to take into account the fact that French and American intellectuals are jointly privileged vis-à-vis intellectuals in the Global South. Latin American academics in the humanities are likely to be familiar with both French and American scholarship, while French and American academics are much less likely to know the work of the Latin Americans. Brazilian intellectuals tend to read both the French (Deleuze, Rancière) and the Anglo-Americans (Jameson, Hall), while neither the Americans nor the French—with the exception of American and French "Brazilianists"—are likely to read Brazilians such as Antônio Cândido, Walnice Galvão, Heloisa Buarque de Holanda, Roberto Schwarz, Ismail Xavier, Sérgio Costa, and so forth. Bourdieu/Wacquant thus ignore the relatively empowered institutional status of French intellectuals vis-à-vis "the South." The French language, while having lost its earlier powerful position, still enjoys a global prestige rooted in a network that supports the dissemination of French ideas. Our point is not that São Paulo or Buenos Aires should become the new capitals of the Republic of Letters. Rather than replace one metropolitan capital with another, the point is to decenter the production and dissemination of artistic/intellectual work, generating more egalitarian flows of cultural work including currents moving South-South and South-North.

Theorizing Cross-Border Interlocution

Nation-state-based analyses, in sum, are inadequate to the multidirectional traffic of ideas. Loïc Wacquant's essay concerning the reception of Bourdieu's work in the United States, in this sense, can serve as a trampoline for our discussion of transnational intellectual interlocution.[66] For Wacquant, the reception of any "foreign" oeuvre is mediated "by the structures of the national intellectual field," resulting in "interferences" and "disjunctures" between the objective position of "the imported work in its native intellectual space" and the position of its international "consumers in the receiving academic space." Wacquant speaks of "sending" and "receiving" intellectual universes and of the "schemata" and "prisms" that shape the reception of foreign intellectual products. Bourdieu's theories, he laments, have been "judged through the very categories of thought that his theories aim at transcending." The hegemonic status of American social sciences, he further argues, makes them less attentive and open to foreign intellectual currents than foreigners are to American ones. Ethnocentric U.S. social theorists, in sum, have gotten Bourdieu wrong due to ethnocentric "misinterpretations," "misconstruals," and "uncontrolled projections," "splintered" and "fragmented" readings that miss the "main thrust" of Bourdieu's endeavor.

Wacquant may be correct to point out that many U.S. social scientists have gotten Bourdieu wrong, and he is undoubtedly right to score the reactionary drift of dominant social theory in the United States. (Ever since C. Wright Mills, American leftists have criticized the exceptionalist "sociology of celebration.") But if one looks at the broader academic spectrum of the humanities and the social sciences, the picture alters. There, American scholars are more likely to be reading the French writers than the reverse. The humanities, especially, form a bastion of Francophilia. American Ph.D. dissertations in the humanities proliferate in quasi-ritualistic homages to Foucault, Derrida, Lacan, Deleuze, Irigaray, and more recently Badiou and Rancière, or to French-inflected U.S.-located thinkers such as Spivak, Butler, and Bhabha, whereas the converse is hardly true in the humanities as taught in France. Laments about French victimization in this area therefore seem rather overstated.

Many of Wacquant's claims about the misapprehension of Bourdieu in the United States boomerang so as to apply with equal force to his own projections about the decolonizing projects we have been addressing. Like Bourdieu's "misinterpreters," Bourdieu/Wacquant themselves judge those projects, to paraphrase Wacquant, through the very categories of thought these projects aim at transcending. Our purpose here, in any case, is to question Wacquant's methodological choice of idiom and metaphors for treating the movement of ideas. Wacquant's language of "senders" and "receivers" not only evokes archaic, precybernetic forms of technology but also the psychologistic premises of a Saussurean linguistics dismantled by Bakhtin already in the late 1920s and by Derrida in the mid-1960s. A Bakhtinian/Voloshinovian "translinguistic" approach would see such transnational intellectual encounters as historically shaped and socially situated forms of interlocution. In a back-and-forth process, both speaker and listener shape, and are shaped by, partially shared and partially differentiated fields of discourse, while being constrained by the "social tact" (Bakhtin) of power relations. The national utterance, to paraphrase Bakhtin, takes place on transnational territory. The process is also to some extent reciprocal, especially in situations of relative equality—for example, that obtaining between French and American intellectuals—in which both speaker and listener impact each other. (The process in relation to the mass media, in contrast, is extremely unequal, whence the calls for the French "cultural exception.")

Wacquant's dichotomous terms—sender/receiver, export/import, native/foreign, producer/ consumer—draw overly bold lines between points of origin and points of reception within strongly demarcated national spaces. Yet it has been the implicit argument of this book that the globalized era of asymmetrical interdependencies requires a heightened sense of the (partially regulated) flow of ideas, of crisscrossing messages and multidirectional but still power-inflected channels of exchange, where nations and states are not necessarily coterminous. Wacquant's economistic "import-export" language implies a trade with national winners and losers, and negative or positive "balances of trade." But in the trade of ideas, one can "win" by "losing," as when an "imported" theory turns out to be useful for the "importing" nation. Brazilian modernism did not lose by borrowing (and resignifying) the European avant-garde, just as United States and Brazilian academics do not "lose" by "importing" the various "post-" thinkers or, for that matter, by importing Bourdieu. In short, the flow of ideas, despite a material, even commercial, dimension, is not reducible to the logic of the ledger book.

Wacquant's veristic and originary language, furthermore, sees only misinterpretations, mistranslations, and misconstruals rather than translinguistic reaccentuations and misprisions. Although translations can be accurate or inaccurate, they can also be seen as productive or unproductive, fecund or sterile. Wacquant writes as if the structuralist and poststructuralist move from verism and origin to intertextuality had never taken place. In his analysis, ideas are simply good or bad at their point of origin and then preserved or damaged during their transatlantic passage; they are never changed for the better during the journey. Reception in the United States, for him, is a veritable festival of misapprehensions; ideas sent from European ports are destined to a sad itinerary of degradation. French intellectuals "ship" off top-notch ideas at their point of departure, but this fragile cargo is mishandled when it arrives on American docks. Like ill-refrigerated cheeses, perfectly good French ideas "spoil" in other national climes. Europe alone, it seems, generates ideas; intellectuals in the Americas simply transcribe those ideas badly, in crooked lines. American intellectuals, in contrast, do not generate good ideas that then "go bad" on arrival in France. Rather, their ideas are already bad at their point of departure and therefore can only be barred at the border through intellectual protectionism. What Bourdieu/Wacquant implicitly call for, therefore, is not engagement with those ideas but rather a protective quarantine.

Within the Wacquant narrative, intellectuals such as Bourdieu "produce" knowledge, while Americans and Brazilians passively "consume" it. Ironically, Brazilian intellectuals and artists have been in the forefront of those dismantling this passive conception by demonstrating, in theory as well as practice, that dominated cultures can indigenize, transform, expropriate, cannibalize, and resignify "out-of-place ideas." Within the processes of indigenization, even misapprehensions can be fecund, as is suggested by Oswald de Andrade's ode to the "millionaire contribution of mistakes" or by Silviano Santiago's praise of "fecund errors" and Caetano Veloso's call for an "aesthetic of mistakes."

An economic dependency model, in this sense, fails to grasp the complexity of the cultural field. In "On Anthropophagic Reason: Dialogue and Difference in Brazilian Culture," poet/critic Haroldo de Campos envisions modernist anthropophagy as a brilliant strategic move for thinking the national within a dialogical relation to the universal. Picking up on Oswald's anthropophagic cues, Campos affirms the values of "appropriation, expropriation, dehierarchization, and deconstruction."[67] Brazilian culture, for Campos, adapts art to local times and places through a provocative transvalorization. Metropolitan ideas become "spiritual food" for renovation. Devoured, chewed, and digested, the texts from the center become a sustenance for what Eneida Maria de Souza calls a "multicultural feast" on the periphery.[68] Roberto Schwarz remind us in his essay "The National by Subtraction" that in an era when virtually everyone claims to be marginal, the Derridean recuperation of the copy offers narcissistic satisfaction, since it makes the periphery not only equal but even superior in that it has always recognized itself *as* peripheral. Unlike the First World, the more modest Third World easily accepts the rejection of origins and is therefore better prepared for modernity and postmodernity. But while a salve for the anxieties of Third World intellectuals, this recuperation of the copy, for Schwarz, is not a sufficient defense for national culture.[69]

In an example of what Althusserian Marxists called "uneven development," Bourdieu/Wacquant, who are incisive critics of neoliberal globalization, remain epistemologically Eurocentric in that they fail to make connections between Enlightenment philosophy and colonial practices in an earlier period and between coloniality and globalization in a later. In *Acts of Resistance*, Bourdieu argues eloquently for the preservation of welfare-state social entitlements, the results of "several centuries of intellectual and political battles for the dignity of workers." Bourdieu then slides into a revealing analogy. Rightly mocking the neoliberals who call the protection of social entitlements "conservative," he asks rhetorically, "Would anyone condemn as conservative the defense of the cultural achievements of humanity [such as] Kant or Hegel?"[70] In fact, many critical intellectuals would indeed find Hegel and Kant conservative and even colonialist and racist. Oblivious to the more unseemly aspects of European philosophical traditions, Bourdieu does not take into account how Hegel might be perceived from the vantage point of the native peoples whose "expiration" Hegel celebrated as a triumph of "Spirit." Denouncing false universalism while lauding one of its philosophical progenitors, Bourdieu scores the false universalism of globalizing doxa. (Bourdieu/Wacquant give as an example the "End of History" thesis of Fukuyama yet fail to note Fukuyama's self-declared Hegelianism.)

While Kant's and Hegel's work does indeed represent a brilliant cultural achievement of humanity, there is little "humanity" in their portrayal of non-European peoples. Bourdieu slides easily, then, from defending hard-won social "entitlements" within Europe to endorsing philosophers who felt "entitled" to condemn most of humanity to irrelevance in the name of a self-evident European superiority. We are not of course suggesting that the work of such philosophers is *reducible* to racism or that there are no progressive dimensions to their work. Yet the less savory aspects of their work should not be cleaned up in the usual whitewashing operation. A more "relational" method, to adopt a word favored by both Bourdieu and ourselves, would see a connection between "entitlements" within Europe and the lack of such "entitlements" in the colonies and neocolonies of the West. A relational method would discern not only an intimate connection between the wealth of Europe (*lato sensu*) and the poverty of the colonized world but also that linking (1) the philosophers' sense of "entitlement" to belittle non-European civilizations, (2) the historical entitlement of colonizers who appropriated non-European communal land in colonial times, and (3) the entitlement of the transnational corporations who patent indigenous knowledge under the pretext that the indigenous inhabitants hold no "title" to the land or its products.

Bourdieu's critique of social privilege within the French educational system is clearly pertinent to other similarly stratified educational systems. For Bourdieu, cultural capital is the accumulation of prestige through education, class standing, family status, and ritualized initiations into the privileged standing by which value is socially produced. Disadvantaged through his social origins in the rural south of France; Bourdieu suffered the French version of what Richard Sennett has called the "hidden injuries of class."[71] In *Sketch for a Self-Analysis*, Bourdieu speaks movingly of the ways that his "undistinguished" social background led to a "flagrant empathy for the [Algerian] natives."[72] Deploying analogy as a cognitive-affective instrument helped Bourdieu understand oppressive situations elsewhere. He perceives an analogy between his memories of the prestigious high school "leaders"—a kind of provincial micronobility—and the historical memory of the French nobility itself. Bourdieu evokes a variant of what we have called the "epistemological advantages" of those who observe the social scene from the "bottom": "Perhaps in this case the fact of coming from 'classes' which some like to call 'modest' offers virtues which are not taught in manuals of methodology: a lack of any scorn for empirical minutia, the attention paid to humble objects, the refusal of thunderous ruptures and spectacular breaks."[73] If the social wounds of Bourdieu's rural origins prodded him to see the hidden injuries of class, could not this same analogical capacity help expose the hidden (and not so hidden) injuries of race and gender? On a global scale, colonialist racism has produced a situation in which cultural and symbolic capital has unfairly accrued to one group and been unfairly subtracted from another group. Colonialism, slavery, racism, and neocolonialism, and their discursive corollary Eurocentrism, have deeply impacted the contemporary production and dissemination of knowledge. While addressing many different forms of capital—economic, social, cultural, and so forth—Bourdieu ignores the white "racial capital" inherited and passed on from generation to generation over the past centuries. A group of people has inherited advantages simply by, to paraphrase Beaumarchais, taking the trouble to be born—in this case to be born white.

Translational Relationalities

In *Race in Translation*, we have conceptualized the circulation of the race/colonial debates in term of multiple chromatic Atlantics. We have tried to forge mutually haunting connections between three divergent yet historically linked colonial/national zones, in order to demonstrate the potentialities of cross-border illumination. At the same time, our tale reveals a partly phantasmatic encounter buffeted by various nationalisms, narcissisms, and exceptionalisms. The aversion to multicultural/critical race/postcolonial studies, we have argued, is sometimes premised on national paradigms, so that the rejection is triggered more by projective anxieties than by any in-depth engagement with the decolonizing corpus. What is forgotten is that ethno-national identity, as a partly imaginary construct, forms a case of shifting identifications rather than an ontological essence or fixed list of traits (the ontologi-nation); France is not eternally Cartesian, Brazil is not perpetually carnivalesque, and the United States is not unfailingly puritanical. Although nation-states exercise unequal political and economic power, intellectual work is still not reducible to a single ethos or to state-dictated ideology. A passport does not stamp a determinate national character on a person, a text, or a discourse. Nor do culture and knowledge production conform to tidy political boundaries or obey the mandates even of the most authoritarian regimes.

Monolithic conceptualizations of nationhood muffle the intellectual heteroglossia of cultural zones characterized by a multiplicity of social dialects, jargons, and ideologies. Since nation-states are defined not by single political models but rather by endless internal struggles over rival models, the intellectual arena is necessarily dissensual and internally differentiated. Nation-states are polyperspectival and multichronotopic, forming dissonant polyphonies of partially discordant voices. Instead of a "Clash of Civilizations," we find, in Arjun Appadurai's inversion, a "Civilization of Clashes."[74] Our argument with some leftist intellectuals has ultimately revolved not around anti-imperialist geopolitics, on which we are in agreement, but rather around the reductionist representation of complex intellectual fields.

Attempting to move beyond national-exceptionalist accounts and binary comparisons, our book has registered certain historical and discursive convergences. Much as comparatists have discerned a convergence between racial dynamics in the United States and Brazil, Tyler Stovall now speaks of a "convergence" between black life in France and in the United States.[75] In the wake of the 2005 rebellions, it has become more difficult to deny the parallels and linkages between the racialized tensions in the diverse sites across the postcolonial Atlantic. Indeed, French, American, and Brazilian cities all display social fractures shaped by interwoven histories of coloniality and race. Fanon's colonial "two cities" have morphed into the postcolonial divide between banlieue and city center in France, between ghetto and white suburb in the United States, and between favela and *bairro nobre* (elegant neighborhoods) in Brazil. Thus, the three zones, and the discourses about them, have increasingly come to echo each other in ways not reducible to "globalization" and "Americanization." It is not a question of merely juxtaposing colonial/national histories within an additive approach, then, but rather of exploring their connectivities within a global system of intercolonial hegemonies and struggles. We have thus addressed national locations, but only in order to perform an analytical dislocation by constructing and deconstructing, threading and unraveling, the tangled webs of ideas and practices that constitute coimplicated national and regional formations.

We have proceeded from the assumption that all nations are, on one level, transnations, existing in a translational relationality of uneven interlocution. Rather than discuss intellectual works in terms of clear nation-state boundaries, we have highlighted the transnational interconnectedness of ideas. As intellectual work proliferates in borrowings, indigenizations, and adaptations, the coimplication of histories and geographies blurs the lines between "inside" and "outside." A translinguistic view of "translation," in this sense, challenges any idiom of "fidelity" and "betrayal" that would assume a one-to-one correspondence between an ethno-national culture and an intellectual field. Rather than conceive of adequate or inadequate copies of "original ideas," translinguistics stresses dialogism, interlocution, reinvoicing, and mediation. At the same time, these mediations do not escape the gravitational pull of history; they are produced and reshaped within specific geographies and political contexts. Each act of translation is situated, inevitably shadowed by the architectonics of inequality.

The movement of ideas, as we have seen, is multidirectional, with diverse points of entry and exit. As a plurilogue across multiple locations, the diverse critical race/coloniality projects have drawn on a range of discourses not reducible to a national origin, especially given the postcolonial dislocations of many of the intellectuals themselves. We have tried to track ideas in transit, pointing to their reaccentuation as they circulate through various zones in a back-and-forth that transcends an idiom of origin/copy, native/foreign, and export/import, within a narrative that foreground the in-between of languages and discourses.

Notes

All translations in the book are our own unless otherwise indicated.

NOTES TO THE PREFACE

1. While the term "Black Atlantic" has been in a wide circulation, the terms "Red Atlantic" and "White Atlantic" have appeared only sporadically. After writing our section on the "Red Atlantic," we discovered that a number of writers have referred in passing to the "Red Atlantic." Most of these authors use the expression either in the sense of "radical left" or in a historical-ethnographic sense of movements of peoples. We assume that core sense but overlay it with a more conceptual sense of the movement of ideas. The radical "red" remains as an overtone in our writing since we stress the link between indigenous social norms and Western radicalism. Jace Weaver stresses the "hermeneutical possibilities of the Red Atlantic" in an essay in *American Indian Quarterly* 35, no. 3 (Summer 2011), while Tim Fulford has spoken of a "Red Atlantic" in terms of the crucial role of the figure of the Indian within Romanticism. See his *Romantic Indians: Native Americans, British Literature, and Transatlantic Culture* (Oxford: Oxford University Press, 2006). Historians have occasionally spoken of a "White Atlantic" but have not linked it, as we do, to the concept of "critical whiteness studies."

2. On the theory of comparison, see not only R. Radhakrishnan's essay "Why Compare?" but also the entire *New Literary History* 40, no. 3 (Summer 2009) issue on the subject, with essays by Rita Felski and Susan Stanford Friedman, Ania Loomba, Bruce Robbins, Gayatri Spivak, Ella Shohat, Robert Stam, and others.

3. See Jack D. Forbes, *The American Discovery of Europe* (Urbana: University of Illinois Press, 2007), chapter 2.

NOTES TO CHAPTER 1

1. Frantz Fanon, *Toward the African Revolution* (New York: Monthly Review Press, 1967), 447.

2. David Roediger, *How Race Survived U.S. History* (London: Verso, 2008), 20.

3. Eugene Jolas, quoted in Emily Apter, *The Translation Zone: A New Comparative Literature* (Princeton: Princeton University Press, 2006), 113.

4. Gilles Deleuze and Claire Parnet, *Dialogues*, trans. Hugh Tomlinson and Barbara Habberjam (New York: Columbia University Press, 1987), 58.

5. Robert J. Miller, *Native America, Discovered and Conquered: Thomas Jefferson, Lewis and Clark, and Manifest Destiny* (Lincoln: University of Nebraska Press, 2008), 1.

6. Quoted in Matthew Restall, *Sete Mitos da Conquista Espanhola* (Rio de Janeiro: Civilização Brasileira, 2006), 158–159.

7. See Walter D. Mignolo, *The Idea of Latin America* (Oxford, UK: Blackwell, 2005), 22.

8. The occasional proposals to make Tupi the official language of Brazil are comically extrapolated in Lima Barretto's novel *O Triste Fim de Policarpo Quaresma* (1915).

9. Larry Rohter, "A Colonial Language Resurfaces," *New York Times* (August 28, 2005).

10. See Donald Grinde, Jr., and Bruce Johansen, *Exemplar of Liberty: Native America and the Evolution of Democracy* (Berkeley: University of California Press, 1991).

11. See John F. Kennedy, Introduction to William Brandon, *The American Heritage Book of Indians* (New York: Dell, 1961).

12. Felix Cohen, "Americanizing the White Man," *American Scholar* 21:2 (1952): 181.

13. Vandana Shiva quotes from Djelal Kadir, *Columbus and the Ends of the Earth* (Berkeley: University of California Press, 1992), 66, in her essay "Biodiversidade, Direitos de Propriedade Intelectual e Globalização," in Boaventura de Sousa Santos, ed., *Semear Outras Soluções: Os Caminhos da Biodiversidade e dos Conhecimentos Rivais* (Rio de Janeiro: Civilização Brasileira, 2005), 321.

14. Ibid. The 2010 film *Even the Rain* compares the colonialism of Columbus's time with contemporary globalization. Set in Cochachamba, Bolivia—the site of struggles regarding the privatization of water—this reflexive film stages the story of a film director who has chosen Cochabamba as a cheap location for a film about Columbus. The rebellion of a Taino leader against Columbus in the film comes to resonate with contemporary struggles against transnational corporations.

15. Ibid., 324.

16. More recently, indigenous activists from the Amazon region, identifying with the Navi people of *Avatar*, have teamed up with James Cameron in opposition to the same hydroelectric dam.

17. Davi Kopenawa Yanomami, "Discovering White People," in *Povos Indigenas 996/2000* (Brasilia: Instituto Socioambiantal, 2000).

18. Ailton Krenak, "The Eternal Return of the Encounter," in *Povos Indigenas*, 48.

19. Sandy Grande, *Red Pedagogy: Native American Social and Political Thought* (Lanham, MD: Rowman and Littlefield, 2004).

20. Eduardo Viveiros de Castro, *Métaphysiques Cannibales* (Paris: PUF, 2009), 5.

21. Charles W. Ephraim, *The Pathology of Eurocentrism: The Burden and Responsibilities of Being Black* (Trenton, NJ: Africa World, 2003), 3–4.

22. For more on recent archeological research into Palmares, see Ricardo Bonalume Neto, "O Pequeno Brasil de Palmares: Escavações Arquelogical Sugerem que o Quilombo de Zumbi era Multietnico como um Pequeno Brasil," *Folha de São Paulo* (June 4, 1995), 5–16. Palmares has great contemporary resonance in Brazil, as black nationalists invoke *quilombismo* and celebrate "Black Consciousness Day" on the anniversary of the death of the Palmarino leader Zumbi. Indeed, black farmers still cultivate the land that their ancestors settled, and a "quilombo clause" could give land titles to five hundred thousand descendants of the free black communities. Musical groups from Bahia, specifically Olodum and Ilê Aiyê, have organized support for the present-day descendants of the quilombos, composing lyrics such as "Quilombo, here we are / My only debt is to the quilombo / My only debt is to Zumbi." See James Brooke, "Brazil Seeks to Return Ancestral Lands to Descendants of Runaway Slaves," *New York Times* (August 15, 1993), 3.

23. R. K. Kent, "Palmares: An African State in Brazil," *Journal of African History* 6, no. 2 (1965): 167–169.

24. Palmares has been celebrated in two Brazilian films by Carlos Diegues, *Ganga Zumba* (1963) and *Quilombo* (1983).

25. See José Jorge de Carvalho, *Inclusão Étnica e Racial no Brasil: A Questão das Cotas no Ensino Superior* (São Paulo: Attar, 2005), 141.

26. See Germán Arciniegas, *America in Europe: A History of the New World in Reverse* (New York: Harcourt Brace Jovanovich, 1986), 120.

27. Indeed, Henry Louis Gates, Jr., in *Figures in Black*, points to Jean Toomer's concerns as as anticipatory of the postmodern and the poststructural. See Henry Louis Gates, Jr., *Figures in Black: Words, Signs, and the "Racial" Self* (New York: Oxford University Press, 1987), 210.

28. See Charles W. Mills, *Blackness Visible: Essays on Philosophy and Race* (Ithaca: Cornell University Press, 1998), 5.

29. Quoted in Mia Bay, *The White Image in the Black Mind: African-American Ideas about White People, 1839–1925* (Oxford: Oxford University Press, 200), 13.

30. Ibid., 25.

31. Quoted in ibid., 17.

32. Quoted in ibid., 16

33. Quoted in ibid., 62.

34. Joseph J. Ellis, *Founding Brothers: The Revolutionary Generation* (New York: Vintage, 2002), 102.

35. For an in-depth discussion of how these issues are reflected in the behavior and decisions of U.S. presidents, see Kenneth O'Reilly, *Nixon's Piano: Presidents and Racial Politics from Washington to Clinton* (New York: Free Press, 1995).

36. Mills, *Blackness Visible*, 87.

37. On the concept of "analogical structures of feeling," see Shohat/Stam, *Unthinking Eurocentrism: Multiculturalism and the Media* (New York: Routledge, 1994), 351.

38. Quoted in Bay, *The White Image in the Black Mind*, 16.

39. Quoted in Howard Zinn, *Passionate Declarations: Essays on War and Justice* (New York: HarperCollins, 2003), 231.

40. Michel Foucault, "What Is Enlightenment?," in Paul Rabinow, ed., *The Foucault Reader* (New York: Pantheon, 1984), 45.

41. See Louis Sala-Molins, *Le Code Noir, ou Le Calvaire de Canaan* (Paris: Presses Universitaires de France, 1987).

42. Ibid.

43. Montesquieu, "Chapter VII: Another Origin of the Right of Slavery," in *The Spirit of the Laws* (1748).

44. Sala-Molins, *Le Code Noir*.

45. Laurent Dubois, *Avengers of the New World: The Story of the Haitian Revolution* (Cambridge: Harvard University Press, 2004), 13.

46. Aimé Césaire, *Toussaint L'Ouverture: La Révolution Française et le Problème Coloniale* (Paris: Présence Africaine, 1981), 23.

47. Michel-Rolph Trouillot, *Silencing the Past: Power and the Production of History* (Boston: Beacon, 1995), 68.

48. Ibid., 70–107.

49. Quoted in Dubois, *Avengers of the New World*, 290–291.

50. Ept. 27, 1803 letter, in Germaine de Staël, *Correspondance Generale 1* (Paris: Hachette, 1982), quoted in Gilles Manceron, *Marianne et les Colonies* (Paris: La Découverte, 2005), 68.

51. From Victor Schoelcher's *Vie de Toussaint Louverture*, cited in Manceron, *Marianne et les Colonies*, 68.

52. Ibid., 142.

53. See Daniel Rasmussen, *American Uprising: The Untold Story of America's Largest Slave Revolt* (New York: Harper, 2011), 48.

54. Quoted in David. R. Roediger, *How Race Survived U.S. History* (London: Verso, 2008), 60.

55. Dubois, *Avengers of the New World*, 304.

56. Ibid., 305.

57. Quoted in ibid., 173.

58. Quoted in ibid., 242.

59. Ibid., 105.

60. William Wells Brown, *St. Domingo, Its Revolutions and Its Patriots* (Boston: B. Marsh, 1855), quoted in J. Michael Dash, *Haiti and the United States: National Stereotypes and the Literary Imagination* (London: Macmillan, 1988), 11.

61. Quoted in Dubois, *Avengers of the New World*, 305.

62. The Vastey citation is from his *Reflections*, quoted in J. Michael Dash, *The Other America: Caribbean Literature in a New World Context* (Charlottesville: University of Virginia Press, 1998), 44.

63. Quoted in Gary Wills, *"Negro Prresident": Jefferson and the Slave Power* (New York: Houghton Mifflin, 2003), 44.

64. For an early discussion of the anticolonialism of Diderot and other Enlightenment figures, see our *Unthinking Eurocentrism*, chapter 2 ("Formations of Colonialist Discourse"). Two key works which unearthed Diderot's often hidden contributions to these debates were Yves Bénot, *Diderot: De l'Athéisme à l'Anti-colonialisme* (Paris: Maspero, 1970), and Michèle Duchet, *Diderot et l' Histories des Deux Indes, ou L'écriture Fragmentaire* (Paris: A. G. Nizet, 1978).

65. Denis Diderot, *Supplément au Voyage de Bougainville*, quoted in William B. Cohen, *Français et Africains: Les Noirs dans le Regard des Blancs* (Paris: Gallimard, 1982), 251.

66. Sankar Muthu, *Enlightenment against Empire* (Princeton: Princeton University Press, 2003), 52.

67. Quoted in Bénot, *Diderot*, 209.

68. Jean-Paul Sartre, preface to Frantz Fanon, *Les Damnés de la Terre* (Paris: François Maspero, 1961).

69. See Yves Bénot, *La Révolution Française et la Fin des Colonies* (Paris: La Découverte, 1987), 26.

70. Sankar Muthu, "La Globalisation au Temps des Lumières: Diderot Observateur du Commerce Global et du Pouvoir Impérial," in Patrick Weil and Stephane Dufoix, eds., *L'Esclavage: La Colonisation, et Après . . .* (Paris: Presses Universitaires de France, 2005).

71. Diderot, *L'Histoire des Deux Indes*, IV, 33, quoted in Muthu, *Enlightenment against Empire*, 87.

72. Ibid., III, 41, quoted in Muthu, *Enlightenment against Empire*, 101.

73. Ibid., XVIII, 52, quoted in Muthu, *Enlightenment against Empire*, 102.

NOTES TO CHAPTER 2

1. Liv Sovik makes a brief reference to the concept of the "White Atlantic" in her essay "We Are Family: Whiteness in the Brazilian Media," *Journal of Latin American Cultural Studies* 13, no. 3 (December 2004): 315–325.

2. David T. Goldberg has argued that racialization has been constitutive of modern state formation, in that racialized distinctions instituted by the state have produced homogeneity out of heterogeneous populations. Thus, race is "integral to the emergence, development, and transformations (conceptually, philosophically, materially) of the modern nation-state." David T. Goldberg, *The Racial State* (Malden, MA: Blackwell, 2002), 4.

3. See Will Kymlicka, *Multicultural Citizenship* (Oxford: Oxford University Press, 1995).

4. See James Holston, *Insurgent Citizenship: Disjunctions of Democracy and Modernity in Brazil* (Princeton: Princeton University Press, 2008), 27.

5. Ibid., 41.

6. See Achille Mbembe, "Figures of Multiplicity: Can France Reinvent Its Identity?," trans. Jane Marie Todd, in Charles Tshimanga, Didier Gondola, and Peter J. Bloom, eds., *Frenchness and the African Diaspora: Identity and Uprising in Contemporary France* (Bloomington: Indiana University Press, 2009).

7. Azouz Begag, *Ethnicity and Equality: France in the Balance*, trans. Alec G. Hargreaves (Lincoln, NE: Bison Books, 2007), xxvi.

8. For a discussion of these issues, see Daniel Gordon, "Democracy and the Deferral of Justice in France and the United States," in Ralph Sarkonak, ed., *France/USA: The Cultural Wars*, Yale French Studies 100 (New Haven: Yale University Press, 2001).

9. Mike Davis, *Planet of Slums* (London: Verso, 2006).

10. Paulo Arantes quoted in Giuseppe Cocco, *MundoBRaz* (Rio de Janeiro: Record, 2009), 34.

11. Quoted in Mary del Priore, "Dans le Apaguer des Lumieres: Francophilia e Lusofobia na Capital do Brasil Oitocentista," in Carlos Lessa, ed., *Enciclopédia da Brasilidade: Auto-Estima em Verde e Amarelo* (Rio de Janeiro: Casa da Palavra, 2005), 158.

12. Pierre Rivas, *Diálogos Interculturais* (São Paulo: Hucitec, 2004), 34–35. Although Rivas is addressing Latin America in general, his comments apply very well to Brazil.

13. Victor Hugo "Le Vaste Brésil aux Arbres Semés d'Or," quoted in Mario Carelli, Hervé Théry, and Alain Zantman, eds., *France-Brésil: Bilan pour une Relance* (Paris: Entente, 1987), 142 (translation ours).

14. Quoted in George Raeders, *O Conde de Gobineau no Brasil* (São Paulo: Paz e Terra, 1997).

15. Paulo Emílio Salles Gomes, *Cinema: Trajetória no Subdesenvolvimento* (São Paulo: Paz e Terra, 1997), 90.

16. Gobineau quoted in Raeders, *O Conde de Gobineau no Brasil*, 134

17. Gobineau quoted in ibid., 137.

18. See Thomas Skidmore, *Black into White* (New York: Oxford, 1974).

19. See Oswald de Andrade, *Do Pau-Brasil à Antropofagia e às Utopias* (Rio de Janeiro: Civilização Brasileira, 1972).

20. See Patrick Petitjean, "As Missões Universitárias Francesas na Criação da Universidade de São Paulo (1934–1940)," in Amélia I. Hamburger, Maria Amélia M. Dantes, Michel Paty, and Patrick Petitjean, eds., *A Ciência nas Relações Brasil–França (1850–1950)* (São Paulo: USP, 1996).

21. Claude Lévi-Strauss and Didier Eribon, *Conversations with Claude Lévi-Strauss* (Chicago: University of Chicago Press, 1991), 38.

22. See John Murray Cuddihy, *The Ordeal of Civility: Freud, Marx, Lévi-Strauss, and the Jewish Struggle with Modernity* (Boston: Beacon, 1974).

23. Roger Bastide, *Estudos Afro-Brasileiros* (São Paulo: Perspectiva, 1973), 183.

24. For more on the critique of Eurocentric approaches to Afro-diasporic trance religions, see Robert Stam, *Tropical Multiculturalism: A Comparative History of Race in Brazilian Cinema and Culture* (Durham: Duke University Press, 1997), especially chapter 8.

25. Henri Troyat, "Brésil," *Les Oeuvres Libres*, quoted in Régis Tettamanzi, *Les Écrivains Français et le Brésil* (Paris: Harmattan, 2004), 186.

26. Roger Bastide, *O Candomblé da Bahia* (São Paulo: Companhia Editora Nacional, 1978), 10–11.

27. Bastide, *Estudos Afro-Brasileiros*, x–xi.

28. Roger Bastide, "Macunaíma em Paris," *O Estado de São Paulo* (February 3, 1946), quoted in Fernanda Áreas Peixoto, *Diálogos Brasileiros: Uma Análise da Obra de Roger Bastide* (São Paulo: USP, 2000), 16.

29. On Rouch, see Steven Feld, ed., *Cine-Ethnography: Jean Rouch* (Minneapolis: University of Minnesota Press, 2003).

30. See Jean Rouch, *Les Hommes et les Dieux du Fleuve* (Paris: Artcom, 1997).

31. For an excellent study of Rouch, Rocha, and their creative deployment of possession religions, see Mateus Araújo Silva, "Jean Rouch e Glauber Rocha, de um Transe a Outro," *Devires* 6, no. 1 (January–June 2009).

32. Bastide quoted in Peixoto, *Diálogos Brasileiros*, 117.

33. Bastide, *O Candomblé da Bahia*, 226.

34. See Leyla Perrone-Moisés, "Gallophilie et Gallophobie dans la Culture Brésilienne (XIXe et XXe Siècles)," in Katia Queirós Mattoso, Idelette Muzart-Fonseca dos Santos, and Denis Rolland, eds., *Modèles Politiques et Culturels au Brésil: Emprunts, Adaptations, Rejets XIXe et XXe Siècles*, 23–54 (Paris: Presses de l'Université de Paris-Sorbonne, 2003), 23.

35. Mario Carelli, *Culturas Cruzadas* (São Paulo: Papirus, 1994), 254.

36. Henry M. Brackenridge, *Voyage to South America, Performed by Order of the American Government in the Years 1817 and 1818, in the Frigate Congress*, 2 vols. (London: John Miller, 1820), 1:128–129, quoted in Denis Rolland, ed., *Le Brésil et le Monde* (Paris: Harmattan, 1998), 25–26.

37. Ibid.

38. See Thomas E. Skidmore, *O Brasil Visto de Fora* (São Paulo: Paz e Terra, 1994), 34.

39. See Stanley M. Elkins, *Slavery: A Problem in American Institutional Life* (Chicago: University of Chicago Press, 1959); and Marvin Harris, *Patterns of Race in the Americas* (Westport, CT: Greenwood, 1980).

40. Isabel Lustosa, "Nos, os Americanos e América," in Lessa, *Enciclopédia da Brasilidade*, 170.

41. Patricia de Santana Pinho, *Mama Africa: Reinventing Blackness in Bahia* (Durham: Duke University Press, 2010), 18.

42. A. Oliveira, "Aos Nossos Leitores," *O Alfinete* (September 3, 1918), quoted in Micol Seigel, "The Point of Comparison: Transnational Racial Construction: Brazil and the United States, 1918–1933" (Ph.D. dissertation, New York University, Graduate School of Arts and Science, 2001), 162.

43. José Correia Leite, "O Grande Problema Nacional," *Evolução* (May 13, 1933), quoted in Seigel, "The Point of Comparison," 171.

44. David J. Hellwig, *African-American Reflections on Brazil's Racial Paradise* (Philadelphia: Temple University Press, 1992).

45. Quoted in ibid., 49.

46. Quoted in ibid., 95.

47. Quoted in ibid., 96.

48. Ibid., 95.

49. France Winndance Twine, *Racism in Racial Democracy: The Maintenance of White Supremacy in Brazil* (New Brunswick: Rutgers University Press, 1998), 140.

50. Using a different methodology, anthropologist Robin E. Sheriff comes to similar conclusions in her *Dreaming Equality: Color, Race, and Racism in Urban Brazil* (New Brunswick: Rutgers University Press, 2001).

51. Kia Lilly Caldwell, *Negras in Brazil: Re-envisioning Black Women, Citizenship, and the Politics of Identity* (New Brunswick: Rutgers University Press, 2006), xviii.

52. Ibid., xxii.

53. Ibid., xix.

54. Ibid., 9.

55. Ibid.

56. See Pinho, *Mama Africa*, 20. Strangely, the argument seems to be about whether black Brazilians are misrecognizing their own oppression (the Twine view) or whether African Americans are misrecognizing black Brazilians as being oppressed.

57. See ibid.

58. Interview in *Revista Rap Internacional* (2001), quoted in Patricia de Santana Pinho, *Reinvenções da África na Bahia* (São Paulo: Annablume, 2004), 48.

59. Frederick Douglass, "Letter from Paris," in Adam Gopnik, ed., *Americans in Paris: A Literary Anthology* (New York: Library of America, 2004), 166.

60. Tyler Stovall, *Paris Noir: African Americans in the City of Light* (New York: Houghton Mifflin, 1996), xii.

61. James Weldon Johnson, "Along This Way," in Gopnik, *Americans in Paris*, 199.

62. Stovall, *Paris Noir*, 132.

63. Pascale Casanova, *La République Mondiale des Lettres* (Paris: Seuil, 1999), 49.

64. Frantz Fanon, *Black Skin, White Masks* (1967; repr., New York: Grove, 1994), 112.

65. Ibid., 116.

66. Stovall, *Paris Noir*, 48. Already in 1923, some white American tourists had persuaded the owner of a Montmartre cabaret to throw the Dahomean Kojo Tavalou out of the club, leading to protests in the French Parliament and government sanctions against any cabaret owners who did "not accept people of color alongside whites."

67. David Macey, *Frantz Fanon: A Life* (London: Granta, 2000), 93.

68. Stovall, *Paris Noir*, 297.

69. Brent Hayes Edwards, *The Practice of Diaspora: Literature, Translation, and the Rise of Black Internationalism* (Cambridge: Harvard University Press, 2003), 243.

70. Léopold Senghor, "To New York," in *The Collected Poetry* (Charlottesville: University of Virginia Press, 1991), quoted and analyzed in Emmanuel Chukwudi Eze, *Achieving Our Humanity: The Idea of the Postracial Future* (New York: Routledge, 2001), 125–127.

71. Stovall, *Paris Noir*, 90.

72. Much of this work has already been done, but this is not the place for a comprehensive bibliography. See, for example, Christopher L. Miller's *The French Atlantic Triangle: Literature and Culture of the Slave Trade* (Durham: Duke University Press, 2008), a dense exploration of the French Atlantic slave trade as represented in literature and film.

73. Barack Obama, *Dreams from My Father* (New York: Canongate, 2007), 123.

74. Fernando Jorge, *Se Não Fosse Brasil, Jamais Barack Obama Teria Nascido* (Rio de Janeiro: Novo Seculo, 2009).

75. Jean-Paul Sartre, "Orphée Noir" (1948), preface to Léopold Sédar Senghor, *Anthologie de la Nouvelle Poésie Nègre et Malgache de Langue Française* (Paris: Presses Universitaires de France, 1977).

76. Abdias do Nascimento and Elisa Larkin Nascimento, *Africans in Brazil: A Pan-African Perspective* (Trenton, NJ: Africa World, 1992), 46.

77. On Welles, Frank, and Vinicius de Moraes, see Stam, "The Power of Blackness," in *Tropical Multiculturalism*.

78. Obama, *Dreams from My Father*, 124.

79. In what might be called an international competition over race, Jorge also points out that Brazil had a black president before the United States did, in the person of the mulatto Nilo Peçanha—son, like Obama, of a black father and a white mother—who took office on June 14, 1909. Yet it is noteworthy that it took the election of Obama for Brazilians to take notice of its own "first black president."

80. Hallam cited in Theodore W. Allen, *The Invention of the White Race* (London: Verso, 1954), 29.

81. See Walter D. Mignolo, *The Idea of Latin America* (Oxford, UK: Blackwell, 2005).

82. See Roberto Fernández Retamar, *Caliban and Other Essays* (Minneapolis: University of Minnesota Press, 1989).

83. Darcy Ribeiro, *O Povo Brasileiro: A Formação e o Sentido do Brasil* (São Paulo: Companhia das Letras, 1995), 239.

84. It is also sometimes forgotten that the North/South division also inhabits the Euro-Latin countries themselves. Spain, Italy, and even France all have a south that is a little darker, poorer, more Arabized, and more Africanized than their respective norths. South of the Equator, the situation, like the climate, is reversed: Brazil's north, unlike the rich, white south, is poorer and darker.

85. Josiah Strong, *Our Country: Its Possible Future and Its Present Crisis* (New York: Baker & Taylor, 1885), 160–177.

86. William Allen White, editorial, *Emporia Gazette* (March 20, 1898).

87. Mignolo, *The Idea of Latin America*, 58–59.

88. Emmanuel Todd, for example, attributes U.S. imperialist tendencies to the Anglo-Saxon family structure, while claiming that "the United States has a major problem with race. France does not." Emmanuel Todd, *Le Destin des Immigrés* (Paris: Seuil, 1994).

89. Mignolo, *The Idea of Latin America*, 63.

90. Richard Morse, *El Espejo de Próspero: Un Estudio de la Dialéctica del Nuevo Mundo* (Mexico: Siglo Veintiuno Editores, 1982).

91. See Jeffrey Rosen, "Radical Constitutionalism," *New York Times Magazine* (November 28, 2010).

92. Mike Davis, *Magical Urbanism: Latinos Reinvent the U.S. City* (London: Verso, 2001). Census reports show that more Americans claim African than strictly English origin.

93. See Jorge G. Castañeda, *ExMex: From Migrants to Immigrants* (New York: New Press, 2007), xiii.

94. Gloria Anzaldúa, *Borderlands: La Frontera*, 2nd ed. (San Fransciso: Aunt Lute Books, 1999), 25.

95. Edwards, *The Practice of Diaspora*, 52.

96. Gerald Vizenor, *Manifest Manners: Postindian Warriors of Survivance* (Middletown, CT: Wesleyan University Press, 1993).

97. Senghor quoted in Edwards, *The Practice of Diaspora*, 32.

98. See Antonio Risério, *A Utopia Brasileira e os Movimentos Negros* (São Paulo: Editora 34, 2007), 34.

99. See Gerard Noiriel, *The French Melting Pot* (Minneapolis: University of Minnesota Press, 1996).

100. For Apter's richly textured discussion of translational/transnational issues, see *The Translation Zone: A New Comparative Literature* (Princeton: Princeton University Press, 2006), 6. See also Mona Baker's *Translation and Conflict: A Narrative Account* (New York: Routledge, 2006).

101. See Shohat/Stam, *Unthinking Eurocentrism: Multiculturalism and the Media* (New York: Routledge, 1994).

102. Édouard Glissant, "Le Divers du Monde Est Imprévisible," quoted in Walter Mignolo, *Local Histories/Global Designs: Coloniality, Subaltern Knowledges, and Border Thinking* (Princeton: Princeton University Press, 2000), 41.

103. See Édouard Glissant, *Poétique de la Relation* (Paris: Gallimard, 1990).

NOTES TO CHAPTER 3

1. Anibal Quijano, "Coloniality of Power, Eurocentrism, and Latin America," *Nepantla*

1, no. 3 (2000): 533–580; Mary Louise Pratt, *Imperial Eyes: Travel Writing and Transculturation* (New York: Routledge, 1992). See also Ella Shohat and Robert Stam, *Unthinking Eurocentrism: Multiculturalism and the Media* (New York: Routledge, 1994).

2. G. W. F. Hegel, *Lectures on the Philosophy of History*, trans. Leo Rauch (Indianapolis: Hackett, 1988), 92.

3. Vandana Shiva, *Monocultures of the Mind: Perspectives on Biodiversity and Biotechnology* (London: Zed Books, 1993).

4. See J. Michael Dash, *Haiti and the United States: National Stereotypes and the Literary Imagination* (London: Macmillan, 1988).

5. Hegel, *Lectures on the Philosophy of History*, 81.

6. Hegel, *Sämtliche Werke*, ed. J. Hoffmeister (Hamburg: F. Meiner, 1955), appendix 2, 243, quoted in Enrique Dussel, *The Invention of the Americas* (New York: Continuum, 1995), 24.

7. Quoted in Dussel, *The Invention of the Americas*, 199.

8. Hegel, *Lectures on the Philosophy of History*, 93.

9. Ibid., 96.

10. Francis Fukuyama, *The End of History and the Last Man* (New York: Free Press, 1992).

11. Charles W. Mills, *The Racial Contract* (Ithaca: Cornell University Press, 1997), 11.

12. Ibid., 1.

13. Paul Gilroy, *The Black Atlantic: Modernity and Double Consciousness* (London: Verso, 1993), 27; Charles W. Mills, *Blackness Visible: Essays on Philosophy and Race* (Ithaca: Cornell University Press, 1998), 113.

14. Marx to Pavel Annenkov, 1846, quoted in Kevin B. Anderson, *Marx at the Margins* (Chicago: University of Chicago Press, 2010), 83.

15. Quoted in ibid., 187.

16. Jack Goody, *The Theft of History* (Cambridge: Cambridge University Press, 2006), 54.

17. Mandela quoted in Amartya Sen, "Democracy and Its Global Roots," *New Republic* (October 6, 2003), 30.

18. Ibid., 31.

19. Edmund Husserl, *Phenomenology and the Crisis of Philosophy*, trans. Quentin Lauer (New York: Harper, 1965), 157.

20. Emmanuel Chukwudi Eze, *Achieving Our Humanity: The Idea of the Postracial Future* (New York: Routledge, 2001), 187.

21. Goody, *The Theft of History*, 14.

22. Max Weber, "Politics as a Vocation," in *Essays in Sociology*, ed. H. H. Garth and C. Wright Mills (New York: Macmillian, 1946), 26–45.

23. Simone Weil, *Simone Weil on Colonialism: An Ethic of the Other*, ed. and trans. J. P. Little (Lanham, MD: Rowman and Littlefield, 2003), 124.

24. Jean-Paul Sartre, *Black Orpheus*, trans. S. W. Allen (Paris: Présence Africaine, 1963), 7.

25. Jean-François Lyotard, "The Social Content of the Algerian Struggle" (1959), quoted in Phyllis Taoua's marvelous *Forms of Protest* (Portsmouth, NH: Heinemann, 2002), 189.

26. Elisabeth Young-Bruehl, *The Anatomy of Prejudices* (Cambridge: Harvard University Press, 1996).

27. Simone de Beauvoir, *The Second Sex* (New York: Penguin, 1972), xxvii.

28. Aimé Césaire, *Discours sur le Colonialisme* (Paris: Réclame, 1950).

29. We have in mind, to cite a tiny part of the scholarship, the work of Homi Bhabha, Diana Fuss, Henry Louis Gates, Jr., Louis Gordon, Neil Lazarus, David Macey, Anne McClintock, Christopher Miller, Benita Parry, Kristin Ross, Edward Said, Françoise Vergès, and Robert Young.

30. Jacques Derrida, "Structure, Sign, and Play in the Discourse of the Human Sciences," in Richard Macksey and Eugenio Donato, eds., *The Languages of Criticism and the Sciences of Man: The Structuralist Controversy*, 245–267 (Baltimore: John Hopkins University Press, 1970).

31. Frantz Fanon, *The Wretched of the Earth* (1963; repr., New York: Grove, 2004).

32. Octave Mannoni, *Prospero and Caliban: The Psychology of Colonization* (Ann Arbor: University of Michigan Press, 1991). See David Macey, *Frantz Fanon: A Biography* (New York: Picador, 2000), 323.

33. Fanon, *The Wretched of the Earth*.

34. Johannes Fabian, *Time and the Other: How Anthropology Makes Its Object* (New York: Columbia Univeristy Press, 1983).

35. Frantz Fanon, *Toward the African Revolution* (1964; repr., New York: Grove, 1988), 17.

36. Frantz Fanon, *Black Skin, White Masks* (1967; repr., New York: Grove, 1994), 110.

37. Ibid., 211.

38. Ibid., 202.

39. Ibid., 18.

40. Ibid. 19.

41. Jean Genet, *Les Nègres* (1959), preface, in *Théâtre Complet de Jean Genet* (Paris: Gallimard, 2002).

42. Fanon, *The Wretched of the Earth*, 102.

43. Ibid., 37.

44. See Antonio Sérgio Alfredo Guimarães, "Recepção de Fanon no Brasil e a Identidade Negra," *Novos Estudos* 81 (July 2008).

45. Karl Marx, *Capital*, vol. 1, ed. Friedrich Engels (New York: International, 1967), 751.

46. See Fernando Henrique Cardoso, "The Consumption of Dependency Theory in the United States," *Latin American Research Review* 3, no. 12 (1977): 7–24.

47. See, for example, Immanuel Wallerstein, *The Modern World System: Capitalist Agriculture and the Origins of the European World Economy in the Sixteenth Century* (New York: Academic, 1974).

48. Richard Drinnon, *Facing West: The Metaphysics of Indian-Hating and Empire-Building* (New York: Schocken Books, 1980).

49. Richard Slotkin, *Gunfighter Nation: The Myth of the Frontier in Twentieth-Century America* (New York: Atheneum, 1992), 110.

50. See the collection of interviews in *Eduardo Viveiros de Castro*, org. Renato Sztutman (Rio de Janeiro: Azougue, 2008), for quotation see p. 79.

51. See Manning Marable, *Dispatches from the Ebony Tower: Intellectuals Confront the African American Experience* (New York: Columbia University Press, 2000), 243–264.

52. Noliwe M. Rooks, *Black Money/White Power* (Boston: Beacon, 2006), 16.

53. Ibid., 22.

54. Warren Dean quoted in José Carlos Sebe Bom Meihy, *A Colônia Brasilianista: História Oral de Vida Acadêmica* (São Paulo: Nova Stella, 1990).

55. Levine quoted in Rubens Barbosa, *O Brasil dos Brasilianistas* (São Paulo: Paz e Terra, 2002), 62.

56. James N. Green, *We Cannot Remain Silent: Opposition to the Brazilian Military Dictatorship in the United States* (Durham: Duke University Press, 2010).

57. Barbara Weinstein, "Buddy, Can You Spare a Paradigm?," *Americas* 4, no. 57 (2001): 453–466.

58. We examine this topic in Shohat/Stam, *Flagging Patriotism: Crises of Narcissism and Anti-Americanism* (New York: Routledge, 2007).

59. A very partial list of the names associated with this constellation of fields would include Norma Alarcón, M. Jacqui Alexander, Paula Gunn Allen, Sonia Alvarez, Gloria Anzaldúa, Joel Zito Araújo, Talal Assad, Pat Aufderheide, Houston Baker, Derrick Bell, Sophie Bessis, Homi Bhabha, J. M. Blaut, Julianne Burton, Dipesh Chakravarty, Ward Churchill, James Clifford, Kimberlé Crenshaw, Carol Boyce Davies, Angela Davis, Richard Delgado, Vine Deloria, Manthia Diawara, Arif Dirlik, Anne Donadey, Ariel Dorfman, Richard Drinnon, Lisa Duggan, Enrique Dussel, Michael Eric Dyson, Arturo Escobar, Emmanuel Chukwudi Eze, Ruth Fankenberg, Robert Fisher, Shelley Fishkin, Juan Flores, Rosa Linda Fregoso, Coco Fusco, Diana Fuss, Teshome Gabriel, Paul Gilroy, Faye Ginsburg, Henry Giroux, Louis Gordon, Herman Gray, Inderpal Grewal, Donald Grinde, Ed Guerrero, Lani Guinier, Michael Hanchard, Donna Haraway, Sandra Harding, Paget Henry, bell hooks, Noel Ignatiev, Annette Jaimes, Francis Jennings, Caren Kaplan, Robin Kelley, Elaine Kim, Agostin Laó, Arturo Lindsay, Françoise Lionnet, George Lipschitz, James Loewen, Tommy Lott, Wahneema Lubiano, Oren Lyons, Peter Maclaren, George

Marcus, Armand Mattelart, Walter Mignolo, Toby Miller, Trin T. Minh Ha, Nick Mirzoeff, Chandra Mohanty, Cherríe Moraga, Toni Morrison, Fred Motin, José Muñoz, Abdias do Nascimento, Elisa Larkin Nascimento, Vidal-Naquet, Lucius Outlaw, Charles Payne, Gary Peller, Gyan Prakash, Mary Louise Pratt, Laura Pulido, Vincent Raphael, Cedric Robinson, David Roediger, Renato Rosaldo, Andrew Ross, Joef Rufino, Vicki Ruiz, Edward Said, Jenny Sharpe, Edward Soja, Hortense Spillers, Gayatri Spivak, Benjamin Stora, Herbert Schiller, Richard Slotkin, Doris Sommers, Eric Sundquist, Clyde Taylor, Kendal Thomas, Robert Farris Thompson, Alice Walker, Cornel West, Patricia Williams, Sylvia Winter, Robert Young, George Yúdice, and Howard Zinn.

60. See Cynthia A. Young, *Soul Power: Culture, Radicalism, and the Making of a U.S. Third World Left* (Durham: Duke University Press, 2006).

61. Fredric Jameson, *The Political Unconscious: Narrative as a Socially Symbolic Act* (Ithaca: Cornell University Press, 1981).

62. Raymond Williams, *Keywords: A Vocabulary of Culture and Society* (New York: Oxford University Press, 1976).

63. For a thorough overview of the changing meanings of "multiculturalism," especially in the Anglophone world, see Sneja Gunew, "Postcolonialism and Multiculturalism: Between Race and Ethnicity," *Yearbook of English Studies* 27 (1997): 22–39.

64. See United Nations Development Program, *Cultural Liberty in Today's Diverse World*, Human Development Report 2004.

65. We cite the report only to call attention to antecedent critiques that painted multiculturalism in opposite ways. Our own reservations about the UN report are that it is (1) overly marked by liberal "recognition" and "cultural rights" discourse; (2) idealist in its neglect of material history (especially in terms of the role of colonialism and imperialism in creating longlasting (yet morphing) structures of inequality and political economy (the sheer inertia of a racialized division of labor and profit within and

between countries, even in the "postcolonial" period); and (3) apolitical in that it proposes ideal solutions that are institutional and psychological—both of which are important but not sufficient—without examining deeper historically sedimented structural relations of power, for example, the role of corporate globalization and the U.S. military-industrial-infotainment complex in rendering progressive change exceedingly hard to achieve.

66. Brett Christophers, "Ships in the Night: Journeys in Cultural Imperialism and Post-colonialism," *International Journal of Cultural Studies* 10, no. 3 (September 2007): 285.

67. Edward Said, *Orientalism* (New York: Vintage, 1979).

68. The coloniality/modernity project is in some ways similar to the one we outlined in *Unthinking Eurocentrism: Multiculturalism and the Media* (New York: Routledge, 1994).

69. See Ramón Grosfoguel, preface to "From Postcolonial Studies to Decolonial Studies: Decolonizing Postcolonial Studies," special issue of *Review* 29, no. 2 (2006): 141–143.

70. Eduardo Batalha Viveiros de Castro, "Exchanging Perspectives: The Transformation of Objects into Subjects in Amerindian Ontologies," *Common Knowledge* 10, no. 3 (Fall 2004): 463–484.

71. Jack D. Forbes argues that native people from the Americas might have traveled to Europe before Columbus. See Jack D. Forbes, *The American Discovery of Europe* (Urbana: University of Illinois Press, 2007).

72. See Silviano Santiago, "O Entre-Lugar Cal Cultura Latino-América," in *Uma Literatura nos Trópicos* (São Paulo: Perspectiva, 1978), 11–28; Homi Bhabha, *The Location of Culture* (New York: Routledge, 1994).

73. Walter Mignolo, *Local Histories/Global Designs: Coloniality, Subaltern Knowledges, and Border Thinking* (Princeton: Princeton University Press, 2000), 11.

74. Arturo Escobar, "World and Knowledges Otherwise: The Latin American Modernity/Coloniality Research Program," *Cuadernos del CEDLA* 16 (2004): 31–67.

75. Quoted in Bernard Cassen, *Tout a Commencé à Porto Alegre . . .* (Paris: Mille et Une Nuits, 2004).

76. See Boaventura de Sousa Santos, ed., *Semear Outras Soluções: Os Caminhos da Biodiversidades e dos Conhecimentos Rivais* (Rio de Janeiro: Civilização Brasileira, 2005).

77. Andrea A. Lunsford, "Toward a Mestiza Rhetoric: Gloria Anzaldúa on Composition, Postcoloniality, and Spirituality" (1996), in A. A. Lunsford and L. Ouzgane, eds., *Crossing Borderlands*, 33–66 (Pittsburgh: University of Pittsburgh Press, 2004), 54.

78. See Encarnación Gutiérrez Rodríguez, Manuela Boatcă, and Sérgio Costa, eds., *Decolonizing European Sociology: Transdisciplinary Approaches* (Burlington, VT: Ashgate, 2010), 15.

NOTES TO CHAPTER 4

1. Richard Bernstein, *Dictatorship of Virtue: How the Battle over Multiculturalism Is Reshaping Our Schools, Our Country, and Our Lives* (New York: Vintage, 1995).

2. Arthur M. Schlesinger, Jr., *The Disuniting of America: Reflections on a Multicultural Society* (Knoxville, TN: Whittle Direct Books, 1991), 35.

3. William Phillips, "Comment," *Partisan Review* 59, no. 1 (1992): 12.

4. See Charles Krauthammer, "An Insidious Rejuvenation of the Old Left," *Los Angeles Times* (December 24, 1990), B5.

5. O'Rourke quoted in the Brazilian newsmagazine *Isto É* (February 1, 1995), 61.

6. This portrayal served as a decoy to distract attention from the deep substratal strains of moralistic puritanism within the right itself, evidenced in its obsession with controlling women's bodies and adults' sexual preferences. It was the right, after all, that narrativized HIV/AIDS as divine vengeance against homosexuals, that objected to the orifice-stuffing performance art of Karen Finley, and that censured the homoerotic photographs of Robert Mapplethorpe and the films of Marlon Riggs. Subsequent to the 1990s and the sexualized prosecutions of Bill Clinton, the hypocrisy of the right became more than evident, as many of the figures who berated Clinton were subsequently caught in their own sexual shenanigans.

7. Susan Moller Okin with respondents, *Is Multiculturalism Bad for Women?*, ed. Joshua Cohen, Matthew Howard, and Martha C. Nussbaum (Princeton: Princeton University Press, 1999).

8. On Al Jazeera, Žižek actually associated the phrase "clash of civilizations" with the multiculturalists, exactly those who have most combated Huntington's ideas. Žižek patronizingly told the Al Jazeera audience what they already know—that "Egypt deserves democracy just like everyone else." One would think that the relevance of multiculturalism to Egypt would be to point to that country's fantastic multiculturality, to argue for an interfaith Egypt featuring equality between Muslims and Copts, for example, and to teach Egyptian history in Western schools. Žižek also spoke of his discovery in a Qatar museum of a "wonderful plate" inscribed with a phrase from an Iranian philosopher to the effect that "only the foolish man invokes Fate as an excuse," for Žižek evidence that "even" the Islamic world can be enlightened. We are reminded of the ironic response of a Tunisian friend (Moncef Cheikhrouhou) to a European interlocutor's "reassuring" assertion that she believed "Arabs are human beings": "*Merci!*"

9. Lisa Lowe and David Lloyd, *The Politics of Culture in the Shadow of Capital*, (Durham: Duke University Press, 199

10. It is symptomatic, however, that the Declaration of the Rights of Indigenous Peoples was signed by most of the world but not by the United States, Canada, New Zealand, and Australia (which recently changed its mind), i.e., by the Anglo-dominant settler societies. President Obama did endorse statements about Native Americans' right to the land, however, which brought denunciations from the right about "giving the land back to the Indians."

11. Todd Gitlin, *The Twilight of Common Dreams: Why America Is Wracked by Culture Wars* (New York: Holt, 1995).

12. Gayatri Spivak, *In Other Worlds: Essays in Cultural Politics* (London: Taylor and Francis, 1987).

13. See, for example, Linda Martin Alcoff, *Visible Identities: Race, Gender, and the Self* (New York: Oxford University Press, 2006).

14. George Lipsitz, *The Possessive Investment in Whiteness: How White People Benefit from Identity Politics* (Philadelphia: Temple University Press, 1998), vii.

15. Walter Benn Michaels, *The Trouble with Diversity* (New York: Holt, 2006).

16. Ibid., 7.

17. Ibid., 3.

18. Ibid., 12.

19. Ibid., 17.

20. Ibid., 89.

21. Survey cited in Tim J. Wise, *Speaking Treason Fluently: Anti-racist Reflections from an Angry White Male* (Berkeley, CA: Soft Skull, 2008), 71.

22. Michaels, *The Trouble with Diversity*, 72.

23. Meizhu Lui, Bárbara J. Robles, Betsy Leondar-Wright, Rose M. Brewer, and Rebecca Adamson, *The Color of Wealth: The Story behind the U.S. Racial Wealth Divide* (New York: New Press, 2006), 1.

24. Mel King quoted in ibid., 268.

25. David Roediger, *Towards the Abolition of Whiteness* (London: Verso, 1994), ix.

26. David Roediger, "The Retreat from Race and Class," *Monthly Review* 58, no. 3 (2006), 51.

27. W. E. B. Du Bois, *Black Reconstruction in America, 1860–1880* (1935; repr., New York: Free Press, 1995), 700–701. ("It must be remembered that the white group of laborers, while they received a low wage, were compensated in part by a sort of public and psychological wage. They were given public deference and titles of courtesy because they were white. They were admitted freely with all classes of white people to public functions, public parks, and the best schools.")

28. Martin Luther King, Jr., "All Labor Has Dignity" (1968), in *"All Labor Has Dignity,"* ed. Michael Honey (Boston: Beacon, 2011).

29. Taylor quoted in Charles W. Mills, *Blackness Visible: Essays on Philosophy and Race* (Ithaca: Cornell University Press, 1998), 135.

30. Ibid., 39.

31. Michaels, *The Trouble with Diversity*, 82.

32. The problem of "racing Islam" has been addressed by critics such as Rabab Abdulhadi, Evelyn Alsutany, Moustafa Bayoumi, Nadine Naber, and Sherene Razack.

33. Michaels, *The Trouble with Diversity*, 74.

34. Michaels, *The Trouble with Diversity*, 60.

35. Ibid., 143.

36. Ibid., 65.

37. Arturo Escobar, "Latin America at a Crossroads: Between Alternative Modernizations, Postliberalism, and Postdevelopment," lecture at the Center for Latin American and Caribbean Studies, New York University, October 29, 2009.

38. During the course of history, culture and economics have gone hand in hand in the United States as well, for example, in the case of conflicts between the U.S. government and Native Americans. The ethos of private property and the imposition of individual "allotments" on Indian tribes, through the Dawes Act, meant nothing less than the social death of indigenous culture as a living mode of praxis.

39. Robert Blauner, *Racial Oppression in America* (New York: Harper & Row, 1972), 5.

40. Pierre Bourdieu and Loïc Wacquant, "La Nouvelle Vulgate Planétaire," *Le Monde Diplomatique* (May 2000): 6–7. Subsequent quotations in the text are from this version of the essay.

41. If the multicultural left certainly contributed to the widely noted decline of racism among young Americans and thus to the election of Barack Obama, the multicultural left, and the left generally, have so far been unsuccessful in pushing Obama to the left in terms of the wars in Iraq and Afghanistan, Guantánamo, single-payer health care, and corporate domination of the political system.

42. François Cusset, *French Theory: How Foucault, Derrida, Deleuze, & Co. Transformed the Intellectual Life of the United States*, trans. Jeff Fort (Minneapolis: University of Minnesota Press, 2008), 38–39.

43. On these debates, see Gary B. Nash, Charlotte Crabtree, and Ross E. Dunn, *History on Trial: Culture Wars and the Teaching of the Past* (New York: Knopf, 1997).

44. Weyrich quoted in Jodi Dean, introduction to Dean, ed., *Cultural Studies and Political Theory* (Ithaca: Cornell University Press, 2000), 7.

45. Even some of the "New Democrats" such as Joseph Lieberman (as in the manifesto "Why Our Universities Are Failing and What We Can Do about It") attempted to censure and stigmatize the "tenured radicals" of the critical university.

46. Quoted in Dean, introduction to *Cultural Studies and Political Theory*, 7.

47. Frank Ellis, "Multiculturalism and Marxism: An Englishman Looks at the Soviet Origins of Political Correctness," *American Renaissance* 10, no. 11 (November 1999).

48. Pierre Bourdieu, *Sketch for a Self-Analysis* (Cambridge, UK: Polity, 2007).

49. Gloria Anzaldúa., *Borderlands: La Frontera*, 2nd ed. (San Fransciso: Aunt Lute Books, 1999), 60.

50. On the other hand, critical race formulations about U.S. law, as we have seen, are often relevant to the constitutions and legal systems of the other colonial-settler states of the Americas, such as Brazil.

51. Pierre Bourdieu, *Acts of Resistance: Against the Tyranny of the Market* (New York: New Press, 1999), 19.

52. Will Kymlicka, *Multicultural Odysseys* (Oxford: Oxford University Press, 2007), 258–259.

53. We are thinking here of such figures as Howard Zinn, Cedric Robinson, Angela Davis, Kimberlé Crenshaw, Howard Winant, Ruth Gilmore, Herman Grey, Wahneema Lubiano, Manning Marable, Robin D. G. Kelly, Lisa Lowe, David Lloyd, Ramón Salvídar, Ramón Grosfoguel, David Roediger, George Lipsitz, Juan Flores, Avery Gordon, and countless others.

54. See Michel Wieviorka, ed., *Une Société Fragmentée? Le Multiculturalisme en Débat* (Paris: La Découverte, 1996).

55. George Yúdice, "A Globalização e a Difusão da Teoria Pós-Colonial," in *Cânones e Contextos: 50 Congresso ABRALIC–Anais* (Rio de Janeiro: Abralic, 1997).

56. See Benedict Anderson, *Imagined Communities: Reflections on the Origin and Spread of Nationalism* (London: Verso, 1991); and Eric Hobsbawm and Terence Ranger, *The Invention of Tradition* (Cambridge: Cambridge University Press, 1983).

57. Cusset, *French Theory*, 83.

58. Jodi Dean, *Žižek's Politics* (London: Routledge, 2006), xii.

59. Slavoj Žižek, "Multiculturalism, or, The Cultural Logic of Multinational Capitalism," *New Left Review* 225 (1997): 42.

60. Matt Taibbi, *Griftopia* (New York: Spiegel and Grau, 2010), 209.

61. Žižek, "Multiculturalism," 44.

62. Ibid., 44.

63. Mary Louise Pratt, *Imperial Eyes: Travel Writing and Transculturation* (New York: Routledge, 1992), 197.

64. See also our discussion of the whiteness of the musical's utopia. Ella Shohat and Robert Stam, *Unthinking Eurocentrism* (New York: Routledge, 1994).

65. We ourselves have examined the "imperial gaze" and the normative regard toward the Third World as it operates in TV network news, in Hollywood westerns, and in First World films set in the Third World. See our *Unthinking Eurocentrism*.

66. Žižek, "Multiculturalism," 47.

67. Slavoj Žižek and Glyn Daly, *Conversations with Žižek* (Malden, MA: Polity), 134.

68. Ibid.

69. Ibid., 144.

70. See J. Ayerza, "Hidden Prohibitions and the Pleasure Principle" (interview with Žižek, 1992), quoted in Ian Parker, *Slavoj Žižek: A Critical Introduction* (London: Pluto, 2004).

71. William David Hart, "Slavoj Žižek and the Imperial/Colonial Model of Religion,"

Nepantla 3, no. 3 (2002): 568.

72. Hugh Trevor-Roper, *The Rise of Christian Europe* (New York: Harcourt Brace Jovanovich, 1965), 9–11.

73. Homi Bhabha, "Of Mimicry and Man: The Ambivalence of Colonial Discourse," in *The Location of Culture* (London and New York: Routledge, 1994), 85–92.

74. Chinua Achebe, *The Education of a British-Protected Child* (New York: Knopf, 2009), 120.

75. Ho Chi Minh quoted in Phyllis Taoua, *Forms of Protest* (Portsmouth, NH: Heinemann, 2002), 51.

76. See Slavoj Žižek, *The Fragile Absolute, or, Why Is the Christian Legacy Worth Fighting For?* (London: Verso, 2000).

77. Slavoj Žižek, "A Leftist Plea for 'Eurocentrism,'" *Critical Inquiry* 24, no. 4 (Summer 1998): 988.

78 .Ibid., 1008, 1001.

79. Adrienne Rich, *On Lies, Secrets, and Silence* (New York: Norton, 1979), 306.

80. Žižek, "A Leftist Plea for 'Eurocentrism,'" 1006.

81. Ibid., 989.

82. Žižek and Daly, *Conversations with Žižek*, 147.

83. We refer here to Erich Auerbach's famous comparison of Racine and Shakespeare in *Mimesis: The Representation of Reality in Western Literature* (Princeton: Princeton University Press, 2003).

84. Slavoj Žižek, *First as Tragedy, Then as Farce* (New York: Verso, 2009), 33.

85. Arjun Appadurai, *Fear of Small Numbers: An Essay on the Geography of Anger* (Durham: Duke University Press, 2006).

86. Slavoj Žižek, *First as Tragedy, Then as Farce*, 97.

87. Ibid., 102.

88. For work on "the commons," see Peter Linebaugh, *The Magna Carta Manifesto* (Berkeley: University of California Press, 2009), 6.

89. Žižek, *First as Tragedy*, 111.

90. Susan Buck-Morss, "Hegel and Haiti,"

Critical Inquiry 26, no. 4 (Summer 2000): 821–865.

91. Žižek, *First as Tragedy*, 113.

92. Ibid., 114.

93. Ibid., 115.

94. Allan Bloom, *The Closing of the American Mind* (New York: Simon and Schuster, 1987), 36.

NOTES TO CHAPTER 5

1. See Thomas Brisson, *Les Intellectuels Arabes en France* (Paris: La Dispute, 2008).

2. Anouar Abdel-Malek, "Orientalism in Crisis," in Alexander Lyon Macfie, ed., *Orientalism: A Reader* (New York: NYU Press, 2001), 51.

3. See Abdallah Laroui, *La Crise des Intellectuels Arabes: Traditionalisme ou Historicisme?* (Paris: François Maspero, 1974).

4. Genet quoted in Edmund White, *Jean Genet: A Biography* (New York: Vintage, 1994), 522.

5. See Richard Wolin, *The Wind from the East* (Princeton: Princeton University Press, 2010), 321.

6. See Kristin Ross, *May '68 and Its Afterlives* (Chicago: University of Chicago Press, 2002), 158–169.

7. In the United States, intellectuals spoke of the lap-dissolve, expressed in an inversion of letters, from the demonizations of the CP (the Communist Party, i.e., lefties) to the demonization of PC (political correctness).

8. Pascal Bruckner, *Le Sanglot de L'Homme Blanc: Tiers-Monde, Culpabilité, Haine de Soi* (Paris: Seuil, 1983).

9. Ibid., 156.

10. Michael Rothberg calls Papon the "material embodiment of the links between the Holocaust and the violence of colonialism." Rothberg, *Multidirectional Memory: Remembering the Holocaust in the Age of Decolonization* (Stanford: Stanford University Press, 2009), 235.

11. The issue of *Les Temps Modernes* containing Sartre's essay on this "pogrom" was seized by Papon.

12. Bruckner, *Le Sanglot de L'Homme Blanc*, 12.

13. Ibid., 156. It is not clear how Bruckner could make such sweeping claims about how vast cultural complexes have "seen" each other. Such claims presume not only the essential transhistorical stability of cultures but also an omniscient European capacity to enter into other cultures, then manage to see them through their collective eyes, and then return to one's own set of collective eyes, only to conclude that one's own group alone is capable of "seeing themselves through others' eyes."

14. Ross, *May '68 and Its Afterlives*, 163.

15. A good example of European "good cop" domination is the EU policy (which is similar to U.S. policies) called CAP, or Common Agricultural Policy, whereby subsidies and tariffs richly reward European farmers (i.e., agribusiness) while depressing world food prices and undercutting African exports, thus impoverishing Africa.

16. Azouz Begag, *Ethnicity and Equality: France in the Balance*, trans. Alec G. Hargreaves (Lincoln, NE: Bison Books, 2007), 88.

17. Slavoj Žižek and Glyn Daly, *Conversations with Žižek* (Malden, MA: Polity), 129.

18. David Blatt, "Immigrant Politics in a Republican Nation," in Alec G. Hargreaves and Mark McKinney, eds., *Post-colonial Cultures in France* (London: Routledge, 1997), 40.

19. Ibid.

20. Begag, *Ethnicity and Equality*, 17.

21. Jim Cohen, "Postcolonial Colonialism?," *Situations: Project of the Radical Imagination* 2, no. 1 (2007).

22. Herman Lebovics, *Bringing the Empire Back Home* (Durham: Duke University Press, 2004), 132.

23. Following up on his earlier argument that African Americans had reintroduced "barbarism" into the midst of Western civilization, D'Souza has recently argued that Obama "channels" the anticolonialism of his Kenyan father so that "the U.S. is being ruled according to the dreams of a Luo tribesman of the 1950s." See Dinesh D'Souza, "Obama's Problems with Business," *Forbes* (September 27, 2010): 94. Reflective of the right's capacity to place the preternaturally calm Obama within the "angry black man" paradigm, D'Souza titled his forthcoming book *The Roots of Obama's Rage*.

24. The American right-wing spoof on PC, *The Official Politically Correct Dictionary and Handbook*, was translated into French in 1992, apparently taken by some French readers not as cynical parody but as a work of Zolaesque naturalism.

25. Tzvetan Todorov, "Du Culte de la Différence à la Sacralisation de la Victime," *Esprit* 212 (1995): 98.

26. Todorov cited in Bashir Ebrahim-Khan, "Is Islamophobia in Europe Leading to Another Holocaust?," *Muslim News* 201 (January 27, 2006), http://www.muslimnews.co.uk/paper/index.php?article=2274.

27. See Todorov, "Du Culte de la Différence à la Sacralisation de la Victime."

28. The word "hysteria," as feminists have long pointed out, traces back etymologically to "womb" in Greek and thus blames women themselves for their medical problem.

29. Françoise Giroud, *Le Nouvel Observateur* (March 1999).

30. Joan Wallach Scott, *Parité! Sexual Equality and the Crisis of French Universalism* (Chicago: University of Chicago Press, 2005), 71.

31. Michel Wieviorka, introduction to Wieviorka, ed., *Une Société Fragmentée? Le Multiculturalisme en Débat* (Paris: La Découverte, 1996), 5–6.

32. Clarisse Fabre and Éric Fassin, *Liberté, Égalité, Sexualités: Actualité Politique des Questions Sexuelles* (Paris: Belfond, 2004).

33. See Jean-Philippe Mathy, *Extrême-Occident: French Intellectuals and America* (Chicago: University of Chicago Press, 1993), 7.

34. Ibid.

35. Herman Lebovics, *True France: The Wars over Cultural Identity, 1900–1945* (Ithaca: Cornell University Press, 1992), xiii.

36. Jim Cohen, "Postcolonial Colonialism?"

37. David Blatt, "Immigrant Politics in

a Republican Nation," in Hargreaves and McKinney, *Post-colonial Cultures in France*, 40.

38. Herrick Chapman and Laura Frader sum up the historical-ideological logics that explain the present-day elision of race: (1) the strength of the founding myth of the republic as unitary and inclusive, with little room for group differences; (2) the tradition of Jacobin hostility to the church as an authority in the public sphere and the consequent relegation of matters of faith to the private sphere; (3) the Dreyfussard legacy of combating anti-Semitism through race-blind and religion-blind universalism. See Herrick Chapman and Laura L. Frader, introduction to Chapman and Frader, eds., *Race in France: Interdisciplinary Perspectives on the Politics of Difference* (New York: Berghahn Books, 2004), 4.

39. Ibid.

40. Jean-Philippe Mathy, *French Resistance: The French-American Culture Wars* (Minneapolis: University of Minnesota Press, 2000), 15.

41. Ibid., 14.

42. Merzak Allouache's film *Salut Cousin!* offers a striking example of this awkward fit when the aspiring rapper Mok, in a case of misfired syncretism, raps a song based on La Fontaine's fables—ironically the one ("The Country Mouse and the City Mouse") that reflects his own relation to his country cousin—until he is finally booed off the stage with shouts of "*on n'est pas à l'école!*" (we're not in grammar school!).

43. Mehdi Belhaj Kacem, *La Psychose Française* (Paris: Gallimard, 2006), 15.

44. See Elsa Vigoureux, "Enfants du Hip-Hop et de Derrida: Les Intellos du Rap," *Le Nouvel Observateur* (May 18, 2006).

45. Mikhail Bakhtin, "The Prehistory of Novelistic Discourse" (1940), in *The Dialogic Imagination: Four Essays*, ed. Michael Holquist, trans. Caryl Emerson and Michael Holquist (Austin: University of Texas Press, 1981).

46. We are indebted here to Veronique Helenon's excellent overview of the French rap scene in her "Africa on Their Mind:

Rap, Blackness, and Citizenship in France," in Dipannita Basu and Sidney J. Lemelle, eds., *The Vinyl Ain't Final: Hip-Hop and the Globalization of Black Popular Culture*, 151–166 (London: Pluto, 2006).

47. On French rap, see Charles Tshimanga, "Let the Music Play," in Charles Tshimanga, Didier Gondola, and Peter J. Bloom, eds., *Frenchness and the African Diaspora: Identity and Uprising in Contemporary France* (Bloomington: Indiana University Press, 2009).

48. Begag, *Ethnicity and Equality*, 44.

49. See Azouz Begag, "*C'est Quand il y en a Beaucoup . . .*" (Paris: Belin, 2011).

50. Ann Coulter, "This Is War: We Should Invade Their Countries," *National Review Online* (September 13, 2001), http://old.nationalreview.com/coulter/coulter.shtml.

51. Cited in Jean Michel Blier and Solemn de Royer, *Discriminations Raciales, pour en Finir* (Paris: Jacob-Duvernet, 2001), 19.

52. Ibid., 82–83.

53. Anti-immigrant and racist sentiments are clearly registered in French polls. A study by the National Human Rights Commission dated March 15, 2000, revealed that 70 percent of French people consider themselves racist. Polls also reveal the extent to which a larger public has absorbed the anti-immigrant discourses of the right. While many French whites might be hostile to Le Pen, 48 percent of them agree with the proposition that "because of immigrants, one no longer feels at home in France," while 63 percent find that "there are too many immigrants in France." TNS-Sofres Institute research carried out by *Le Monde* and RTL, cited in Durpaire, *France Blanche, Colère Noire*, 23.

54. Durpaire, *France Blanche, Colère Noire*, 184.

55. See Isabelle Rigoni, ed., *Qui a Peur de la Télévision en Couleurs?* (Paris: Aux Lieux d'Être, 2007).

56. Yazid Sabeg and Yacine Sabeg, *Discrimination Positive: Pourquoi la France Ne Peut Y Échapper* (Paris: Calmann-Levy, 2004), 110.

57. Begag, *Ethnicity and Equality*, 110.

58. A Michael Moore television sketch showed the "magic" by which an object seen as innocent in white hands (a wallet, a beeper, a cell phone) becomes something threatening in the hands of blacks, at least within the warped vision of police. Michael Moore, "Don't Shoot, It's Only a Wallet!," *The Awful Truth*, season 2, episode 2, Bravo (May 24, 2000).

59. Alain Badiou, *Polemics* (London: Verso, 2006), 112–113.

60. Ibid.

61. Jonathan Schorsch traces Jews' ambiguous relation to whiteness all the way back to the 17th century. See *Jews and Blacks in the Early Modern World* (Cambridge: Cambridge University Press, 2004), 166.

62. James Baldwin, "Negroes Are Anti-Semitic Because They're Anti-White," in Paul Berman, ed., *Blacks and Jews: Alliances and Arguments* (New York: Delacorte, 1967), 41.

63. Hannah Arendt, "Reflections on Little Rock," *Dissent* 6, no. 1 (1959).

64. Jews have a very long history in Africa. Apart from Ethiopian Jews and the Jews of North Africa, in the early 1990s geneticists discovered that 9 percent of the men from the Lemba people of South Africa carry a DNA signature characteristic of the *cohanim*, the hereditary caste descended from the biblical Aaron. See Richard Hull, *Jews and Judaism in African History* (Princeton, NJ: Marcus Weiner, 2009), 173.

65. See Jan Carew, *Fulcrums of Change* (Trenton, NJ: Africa World, 1988).

66. Barbara Fuchs, *Mimesis and Empire: The New World, Islam, and European Identities* (Cambridge: Cambridge University Press, 2001).

67. Anouar Majid, *We Are All Moors* (Minneapolis: University of Minnesota Press, 2009), 10. For an illuminating discussion of the same issue of Andalusia and Moorishness in the Americas, see Hishaam Aidi, "The Interface of al-Andalous: Spain, Islam, and the West," *Social Text 87*, vol. 24, no. 2 (summer 2006).

68. See Gilberto Freyre, "Orient and Occident," chap. 9 in *The Mansions and the Shanties* (New York: Knopf, 1963).

69. Freyre, *The Mansions and the Shanties*, 297.

70. Ibid.

71. José Martí, "España en Melilla," in *Cuba: Letras*, vol. 2 (Havana: Edicion Tropico, 1938); Carlos Fuentes, *The Buried Mirror* (New York: First Mariner Books, 1999).

72. See Freyre, *The Masters and the Slaves*, especially the chapter "The Portuguese Colonizer."

73. See ibid., chap. 9. For more on the notion of the Moorish/Sepahrdic Atlantic and the question of Orientalism, see Ella Shohat, "The Moorish Atlantic," in Evelyn Alsultany and Ella Shohat, eds., *The Cultural Politics of the Middle East in the Americas* (Ann Arbor: University of Michigan Press, 2012).

74. On the hyphen in the "Judeo-Muslim" and the "Arab-Jew," see Ella Shohat, "Rethinking Jews and Muslims" *MERIP* 178 (1992): 25–29; and Ella Shohat, "Taboo Memories, Diasporic Visions: Columbus, Palestine and Arab-Jews," in May Joseph and Jennifer Fink, eds., *Performing Hybridity*, 131–156 (Minneapolis: University of Minnesota Press, 1999).

75. See, for example, Allan Harris Cutler and Helen Elmquist Cutler, *The Jew as Ally of the Muslim* (Notre Dame: University of Notre Dame Press, 1986); Ammiel Alcalay, *After Jews and Arabs* (Minneapolis: University of Minnesota Press, 1993); and Majid, *We Are All Moors*.

76. Gil Anidjar, "Postface: Reflexions sur la Question," in Esther Benbassa and Jean-Christophe Attias, *Juifs et Musulmans: Une Histoire Partagée, un Dialogue à Construire* (Paris: La Découverte, 2006), 130.

77. On the splitting of the Jew and the Arab, see Edward Said's *Orientalism* (New York: Vintage, 1979); and on the place of the Arab-Jew as part of the splitting, see Ella Shohat's *Israeli Cinema: East/West and the Politics of Representation* (Austin: University of Texas Press, 1989); and Ella Shohat, "Columbus, Palestine, and Arab Jews: Toward a Relational Approach to Community Identity," in Keith Ansell-Pearson, Benita Parry, and Judith Squires, eds., *Cultural Readings of Imperialism* (London: Lawrence & Wishart in association with New Formations, 1997).

78. See Domenico Losurdo, *A Linguagem*

do Império, trans. Jaime A. Clasen (São Paulo: Boitempo, 2010).

79. See Aimé Césaire, *Discourse on Colonialism* (New York: Monthly Review Press, 1972), 14–15.

80. Hannah Arendt, *The Origins of Totalitarianism* (1951; repr., New York: Harcourt, 1973).

81. Quoted in Jean-Luc Einaudi, *La Bataille de Paris, 17 Octobre 1961* (Paris: Seuil, 1991), 225.

82. Fanon, *Black Skin, White Masks*, 122.

83. Ibid.

84. Jean-Paul Sartre, *Anti-Semite and Jew: An Exploration of the Etiology of Hate* (1948; repr., New York: Schocken Books, 1995), 108.

85. Fanon, *Black Skin, White Masks*, 10.

86. Ibid., 93.

87. Ibid., 165.

88. Ibid., 157.

89. For a complex and subtle mapping of the similarities and differences between various racisms, sexisms, and homophobias, see Elisabeth Young-Bruehl, *The Anatomy of Prejudices* (Cambridge: Harvard University Press, 1996).

90. Fanon, *Black Skin, White Masks*, 162–163.

91. Michael Rothberg argues strongly against this zero-sum approach, favoring instead what he calls "multidirectional memory," whereby the oppressive experiences of diverse groups are interarticulated within a "malleable discursive space" where positions "come into being through their interactions with others." Rothberg, *Multidirectional Memory*, 5.

92. Fanon, *Black Skin, White Masks*, 201.

93. See Peter Geismar, *Frantz Fanon* (New York: Dial, 1971), 139–140.

94. David Macey, *Frantz Fanon: A Biography* (New York: Picador, 2000), 467–468.

95. Simone de Beauvoir, *La Force des Choses*, vol. 2 (Paris: Livre de Poche, 1971), 243.

96. Macey, *Frantz Fanon*, 467–468.

97. See Yair Auron, *Les Juifs d'Extrême Gauche en Mai 68* (Paris: Albin Miche, 1998).

98. See Albert Memmi, *Decolonization and the Decolonized* (Minneapolis: University of Minnesota Press, 2006).

99. Bruckner, *Les Sanglots de L'Homme Blanc*, 219.

100. David Frum and Richard Perle, *An End to Evil* (New York: Random House, 2003), 9.

101. Pascal Bruckner, *La Tentation de L'Innocence* (Paris: Grasset, 1995).

102. In domestic electoral terms, American Jews have remained overwhelmingly liberal, including in their support for Obama. See "2010 Annual Survey of American Jewish Opinion," commissioned by American Jewish Committee, Consumer Opinion Panel, "Obama Administration" (April 2010).

103. Finkielkraut interviewed by Dror Mishani and Aurélia Samothraiz, "They Are Not Miserable, They Are Muslims," *Haaretz* (November 15, 2005). All translations from this interview in Hebrew are ours

104. Ibid.

105. Ibid.

106. Complete transcript available at http://lesogres.org.

107. Alain Finkielkraut and Peter Sloterdijk, *Les Battements du Monde* (Paris: Pauvert, 2003), 38.

108. For further elaboration, see the following works by Ella Shohat: *Le Sionisme du Point de Vue de ses Victimes Juives: Les Juifs Orientaux en Israël* (Paris: La Fabrique Editions, 2006) and also the original essay, Ella Shohat, "Sephardim in Israel: Zionism from the Standpoint of Its Jewish Victims," *Social Text* 19–20 (Fall 1988); *Israeli Cinema* (1989), and the new edition (London: I. B. Tauris, 2010); "Taboo Memories, Diasporic Visions: Columbus, Palestine and Arab-Jews" (1997) and "Rupture and Return: Zionist Discourse and the Study of Arab-Jews" (2001), both reprinted in *Taboo Memories, Diasporic Voices* (Durham: Duke University Press, 2006).

109. Finkielkraut and Sloterdijk, *Les Battements du Monde*, 47.

110. Jean Daniel, *La Prison Juive* (Paris: Odile Jacob, 2003).

111. Jean Birnbaum, *Les Maoccidents: Un Néoconservatisme à la Française* (Paris: Stock, 2009).

112. Ivan Segré, *La Réaction Philosémite, ou, La Trahison des Clercs* (Paris: Lignes, 2009).

113. See Guillaume Weill-Raynal, *Une Haine Imaginaire: Contre-Enquête sur le Nouvel Antisémitisme* (Paris: Colin, 2005).

114. See Guillaume Weill-Raynal, *Les Nouveaux Désinformateurs* (Paris: Colin, 2007).

115. Kacem, *La Psychose Française*, 52.

116. Christopher Wise, *Derrida, Africa, and the Middle East* (New York: Palgrave, 2009).

117. Joëlle Marelli, "Usages et Maléfices du Thème de l'Anti-Sémitisme . . .," in Nacira Guénif-Souilamas, ed., *La République Mise à Nu par son Immigration* (Paris: La Fabrique, 2006), 136.

118. As we learn Leila Shahid's *The Slums, the Near East, and Us* [*Les Banlieues, le Proche-Orient et Nous*] (Paris: Éditions de L'Atelier, 2006), Shahid, former spokesperson for the Palestinian Authority in France, Michael Warschawski, French Israeli founder of the Alternative Information Center (Jerusalem), and Dominique Vidal, editor of *Le Monde Diplomatique*, visited the banlieues in order to advance mutual understanding between Arabs and Jews.

119. Daniel Lindenberg, *Destins Marranes: L'identité Juive en Question* (Paris: Hachette, 2004).

120. Daniel Lindenberg, *Figures d'Israël: L'identité Juive entre Marranisme et Sionisme (1648–1998)* (Paris: Hachette, 1997).

121. Esther Benbassa and Jean-Christophe Attias, *The Jew and the Other* (Ithaca: Cornell University Press, 2004).

122. Melanie Kaye/Kantrowitz, *The Colors of Jews: Racial Politics and Radical Diasporism* (Bloomington: Indiana University Press, 2007), 199.

123. Tony Kushner and Alisa Solomon, eds., *Wrestling with Zion* (New York: Grove, 2003); Adam Shatz, ed., *Prophets Outcast: A Century of Dissident Jewish Writing about Zionism and Israel* (New York: Nation Books, 2004); and Kaye/Kantrowitz, *The Colors of Jews*.

124. Kacem, *La Psychose Française*, 52.

125. Fred Constant, *Le Multiculturalisme* (Paris: Flammarion, 2000), 35.

126. Ibid., 37.

127. Paul Thibaut, "Exception Française!," *Géopolitique* (January–March 2005).

128. Ibid.

NOTES TO CHAPTER 6

1. Antonio Sérgio Alfredo Guimarães, "The Race Issue in Brazilian Politics (the Last Fifteen Years)," paper presented at the conference "Fifteen Years of Democracy in Brazil," University of London, Institute of Latin American Studies, London, February 15–16, 2001.

2. Quoted in Ricardo Gaspar Müller, "O Teatro Experimental do Negro," in Müller, ed., *Dionysos* 28 (1988) (special issue on the Black Experimental Theatre).

3. Abdias do Nascimento, preface to *Sortilegio II* (Rio de Janeiro: Paz e Terra, 1979), 28.

4. Abdias do Nascimento, editorial, *Quilombo* (December 1948).

5. Ibid.

6. The overture editorial, and all the essays mentioned here, are assembled in the facsimile edition by Antonio Sérgio Alfredo Guimarães. See *Quilombo: Vida, Problemas, e Aspirações do Negro* (São Paulo: Editora 34, 2003).

7. Abdias do Nascimento and Elisa Larkin Nascimento, "Reflections on the Black Movement in Brazil, 1938–1997," in Antonio Sérgio Alfredo Guimarães and Lynn Huntley, eds., *Tirando a Máscara: Ensaios sobre o Racismo no Brasil* (São Paulo: Paz e Terra, 2000), 221–222.

8. Ibid., 228–229.

9. Peter Fry, preface to Yvonne Maggie and Claudia Barcellos Rezende, eds., *Raça como Retórica: A Construção da Diferença* [Race as Rhetoric: The Construction of Difference] (Rio de Janeiro: Civilização Brasileira, 2002).

10. Howard Winant, citing the research of Maria Ercilia do Nascimento, lists the groups in *The World Is a Ghetto: Race and Democracy since World War II* (New York: Basic Books, 2001), 233.

11. On the *afoxé* groups, see Christopher Dunn, "Afro-Bahian Carnival: A Stage for

Protest," *Afro-Hispanic Review* 11, nos. 1–3 (1992).

12. Freyre quoted in Michael Hanchard, *Orpheus and Power* (Princeton: Princeton University Press, 1994), 115.

13. Ibid., 142

14. Ibid.

15. S. M. C. Lima, "Multiculturalismo," in José Teixeira Coelho Netto, ed., *Dicionário Crítico de Política Cultural* (São Paulo: Iluminuras, 1997), 263–265.

16. The authors' e-mail correspondence with Italo Moriconi.

17. Leyla Perrone-Moisés, *Atlas Literaturas: Escolha e Valor na Obra Crítica de Escritores Modernos* (São Paulo: Cia das Letras 1998).

18. In *To Wake the Nations: Race and the Making of American Literature* (Cambridge: Belknap Press of Harvard University Press, 1993), Sundquist points out the ways that Melville can be usefully seen as a "black writer."

19. Perrone-Moisés, *Atlas Literaturas*.

20. The authors' e-mail correspondence with Italo Moriconi.

21. Caetano Veloso, *Verdade Tropical* (São Paulo: Companhia das Letras, 1997), 270; Albert Murray, *The Omni-Americans: New Perspectives on Black Experiences and American Culture* (New York: Vintage, 1970), 22.

22. G. W. F. Hegel, *The Philosophy of History*, trans. J. Sibree (New York: Dover, 1956).

23. Jessé Souza, "O Casamento Secreto entre Identidade Nacional e 'Teoria Emocional da Ação' ou por que é Tão Difícil o Debate Aberto e Crítico entre Nós," in Jessé Souza, ed., *A Invisibilidade da Desigualdade Brasileira* (Belo Horizonte, Brazil: UFMG, 2006), 100.

24. For a sophisticated critique of comparison as a method and of ethnocentrism in comparative Brazil-U.S. studies, see Micol Siegel, *Uneven Encounters: Making Race and Nation in Brazil and the United States* (Durham: Duke University Press, 2009).

25. João Capistrano de Abreu, epigraph in Paulo Prado's *Retrato do Brasil* (1928; repr., São Paulo: IBDC, 1981).

26. José Guilherme Merquior, *Saudades do Carnaval* (Rio de Janeiro: Forense, 1972), 117.

27. For a comprehensive comparative analysis of racial formation in the two countries, see G. Reginald Daniel's *Race and Multiraciality in Brazil and the United States: Converging Paths?* (University Park: Pennsylvania State University Press, 2006).

28. Ibid., 115.

29. Ibid., 87.

30. Ibid.

31. See Eugene Robinson, *Disintegration* (New York: Doubleday, 2010), 10.

32. James Holston, *Insurgent Citizenship: Disjunctions of Democracy and Modernity in Brazil* (Princeton: Princeton University Press, 2008), 281.

33. Nei Lopes, *O Racismo: Explicado aos Meus Filhos* (Rio de Janeiro: Agir, 2007), 151.

34. Holston, *Insurgent Citizenship*, 277.

35. See Alexei Barrionnuevo, "Group Questions Killings by Brazilian Police," *New York Times* (December 9, 2009): A12.

36. Edward Telles, in *Race in Another America*, uses the spatial metaphor of "vertical" and "horizontal" social relations to clarify some of these contradictions. In terms of vertical power relations, Brazil is one of the most unequal countries in the world, with nonwhites at the bottom of a grossly distorted economic pyramid, making the "vertical exclusion of mulattos and, especially, blacks . . . greater than vertical exclusion for blacks in the United States." For Telles, three factors— hyperinequality, a discriminatory glass ceiling, and a racist culture—are responsible for this vertical inequality. Edward Ellis Telles, *Race in Another America: The Significance of Skin Color in Brazil* (Princeton: Princeton University Press, 2006), 220–224.

37. Antonio Guimarães, quoting Sérgio Costa, "A Construção Sociológica da Raça no Brasil" (*Estudos Afro-Asiáticos* 1 [2002]), in Guimarães and Huntley, *Tirando a Máscara*, 28.

38. Antonio Risério, *A Utopia Brasileira e*

os *Movimentos Negros* (São Paulo: Editora 34, 2007), 15.

39. Ibid., 381.

40. African American discourse, meanwhile, might be said to be Asante-centric, given the key role of Ghana in pan-Africanism.

41. Risério, *A Utopia Brasileira*, 148.

42. On "cultural capital," see Pierre Bourdieu, "Cultural Reproduction and Social Reproduction," in R. Brown, ed., *Knowledge, Education, and Social Change: Papers in the Sociology of Education*, 71–112 (London: Tavistock, 1973).

43. Risério, *A Utopia Brasileira*, 212.

44. Hermano Vianna, "Mestiçagem Fora de Lugar," *Folha de São Paulo* (June 27, 2004).

45. Ibid.

46. Ibid.

47. Sérgio Costa, *Dois Atlânticos: Teoria Social, Anti-racismo, Cosmopolitanismo* (Belo Horizonte, Brazil: UFMG, 2006), 216.

48. Brazilian musicians and musicologists have commented on this shared feature of the two traditions. Composer and literary scholar Zé Miguel Wisnik notes that European intellectuals are sometimes surprised that "popular music in Brazil can dialogue with erudite traditions and thus produce something new." See Santuza Cambraia Naves, Frederico Oliveira Coelho, and Tatiana Bacal, eds., *A MPB em Discussão: Entrevistas* (Belo Horizonte, Brazil: UFMG, 2006). Even Chico Buarque, an anti-American in political terms, recognizes this commonality with the United States: "[Whereas in Europe] popular music is relegated, with few exceptions, to an artistic subworld, considered as basically an industrial and commercial product and nothing more, . . . in Brazil there is more malleability. . . . In this sense [the Americans] are closer to us." Ibid., 166–167.

49. See Rita Amaral and Vagner Gonçalves da Silva, "Foi Conta para Todo Canto: As Religiões Afro-Brasileiras nas Letras do Repertório Musical Popular Brasileiro," *Afro-Ásia* 34 (2006): 189–235. See also Zeca Ligeiro's NYU Ph.D. dissertation in performance studies: "Carmen Miranda: An Afro-Brazilian Paradox."

50. Five hundred years of coexistence among indigenous peoples, Africans, Europeans, and Asians in the Americas have also generated an infinite variety of forms of cultural syncretism and transformation. This mixedness character-izes both hemispheres and has found manifold expressions in art, whether in European/indi-gene romances such as that of Diogo Álvares and Paraguaçu in 16th-century Brazil or Cortés and Malinche in 16th-century Mexico, or Pocahantas and John Smith (later John Rolfe) in 17th-century North America. Brazilian films such as *Caramuru: The Invention of Brazil* or *How Tasty Was My Little Frenchman*, Venezu-elan films such as *Jericó*, and American films such as *Little Big Man* and *A Man Called Horse* tell stories of "white Indians" who assimilated to native ways. The narrative arts of the Americas proliferate in "mutational fictions" that point to the instability of racial identity and identifica-tion. In such fictions, characters undergo racial metamorphoses, "exceeding" the rigidities of racial classification. The chameleonic characters of films such as *Macunaima* in Brazil or *Zelig* in the United States literally change color and culture. Such racial metamorphoses render vis-ible and palpable a process that usually remains invisible—the process of synchresis when ethnicities brush up against and "rub off" on one another in the context of centuries of asym-metrical cultural contact between Europeans, Native Americans, and Africans. The theme of racial transformation comes up in manifold ways in U.S. popular culture, most obvious, perhaps, in the theme of "passing," whether in such classical race melodramas as *Imitation of Life* or in contemporary novels such as Philip Roth's *The Human Stain*, the story of a *New Yorker* writer (Anatole Broyard) who passed as white. In *Palindromes*, performers of different colors play the same character, while in *I'm Not There*, various performers, including a black teenager and a woman, incarnate the role of Bob Dylan. In *Soul Man*, a white student black-

ens up to take advantage of Affirmative Action. Patrick Swayze inhabits Whoopi Goldberg's body in *Ghost*. In the cable-television show *Quantum Leap*, white protagonists leap into other people's bodies. In *Coming Down to Earth*, Chris Rock dies and comes back in the form of an old white man. The African American performance artist Anna Deveare Smith incarnates a wide gallery of ethnicities in her one-woman performances such as *Fires in the Mirror* and *Twilight*. The humorous aspect of these various ethnic encounters is the basis of much of the sketch comedy of Richard Pryor, Whoopi Goldberg, Chris Rock, Wanda Sykes, and Dave Chappelle.

51. George Yúdice, *The Expediency of Culture* (Durham: Duke University Press, 2003), 154.

52. Over recent decades, the Tropicalists gained more public notoriety not only through their music but also because of Gil's appointment as minister of culture in the Lula government, the publication in English of Caetano's memoir *Tropical Truth*, and various Grammys and film appearances. Gil became embroiled in the debates about digital copyright law and the fight, through Creative Commons, against laws that privatize creativity through notions of "intellectual property rights." Just as Gil had earlier said in a song that he wrote music "to be heard on the radio," in "Pela Internet" (On the Internet), Gil "multiculturalizes" the discussion of the Net by linking it to the Afro-Brazilian culture of oriki and orixas, which were also concerned with "media" and communication.

53. Caetano Veloso, *Verdade Tropical* (São Paulo: Companhia das Letras, 1997), 105.

54. Ned Sublette, "Principles of Postmamboism," *BoingBoing* (blog), December 15, 2009, http://boingboing.net/2009/12/15/principles-of-postma.html.

55. Liv Sovik develops the *lied* association in *Aqui Ninguém é Branco* (Rio de Janeiro: Aeroplano, 2010), along with a probing analysis of the cultural politics of Brazilian popular music.

56. Stuart Hall, Chas Critcher, Tony Jefferson, John N. Clarke, and Brian Roberts,

Policing the Crisis: Mugging, the State, and Law and Order (London: Macmillan, 1978), 394.

57. In Brazil, blackface was not common, but in one instance the black community did protest the casting of a white actor in blackface in a Brazilian television version of *Uncle Tom's Cabin*. See Joel Zito Araújo's film *A Negação do Brasil* (2000).

58. Caetano Veloso, *Tropial Truth: A Story of Music and Revolution in Brazil* (New York: Random House, 2002), 7. For an illuminating analysis of Caetano's work, including of "Um Índio," see Guilherme Wisnik, *Caetano Veloso* (São Paulo: PubliFolha, 2005).

59. Fry, preface to *Raça como Retórica*, 8.

60. Olívia Maria Gomes da Cunha, "Bonde do Mal: Notas sobre Territórios, Cor, Violência, e Juventude numa Favela do Subúrbio Carioca," in Maggie and Rezende, *Raça como Retórica*, 86.

61. Ibid.

62. Ibid.

NOTES TO CHAPTER 7

1. See Raymond A. Winbush, introduction to Winbush, ed., *Should America Pay? Slavery and the Raging Debate on Reparations* (New York: HarperCollins, 2003), xii.

2. Nabuco quoted in Liv Sovik, *Aqui Ninguém é Branco* (Rio de Janeiro: Aeroplano, 2010), 146.

3. Kimberlé Williams Crenshaw, "Race, Reform, and Retrenchment: Transformation and Legitimation in Antidiscrimination Law," *Harvard Law Review* 101 (May 1988): 1331.

4. For a comparative study of remedial measures, consult Charles V. Hamilton, Lynn Huntley, Neville Alexander, Antonio Sérgio Alfredo Guimarães, and Wilmot James, eds., *Beyond Racism: Race and Inequality in Brazil, South Africa, and the United States* (Boulder, CO: Lynne Rienner, 2001)

5. Dinesh D'Souza, *The End of Racism: Principles for a Multiracial Society* (New York: Free Press, 1995), 537.

6. Frantz Fanon, "Racism and Culture," *Présence Africaine* 8–10 (1956).

7. Gary Peller, "Race against Integration,"

Tikkun 6, no. 1 (January–February 1991): 54–66.

8. See U. S. Mehta, "Liberal Strategies of Exclusion," *Politics and Society* 18, no. 4 (1990): 429–430.

9. De Tocqueville quoted in William B. Cohen, *Français et Africains: Les Noirs dans le Regard des Blancs* (Paris: Gallimard, 1982), 273.

10. This skewed approach harmed not only black individuals but also black nations. Newly independent Haiti in 1804 was forced to pay crippling indemnities for the "crime" of defeating the French and creating a republic modeled, ironically, on the French republic itself. It was these indemnities, and subsequent hostile actions by the United States, that left Haiti in its present shell-shocked and famished state. (In 2003, President Jean-Bertrand Aristide asked France to reimburse Haiti to the tune of $21 billion, for the "Independence Debt.")

11. See Ira Katznelson, *When Affirmative Action Was White: An Untold History of Racial Inequality in Twentieth-Century America* (New York: Norton, 2005).

12. William Julius Wilson, *More Than Just Race: Being Black and Poor in the Inner City* (New York: Norton, 2009), 28–29.

13. See Rosana Heringer, "Mapeamento das Ações e Discursos de Combate às Desigualdades Raciais no Brasil," *Estudos Afro-Asiáticos* 23, no. 2 (2001): 1–43.

14. See Joaquim B. Barbosa Gomes, "Ações Afirmativas, Aspectos Jurídicos," in Giralda Seyferth et al., *Racismo no Brasil* (São Paulo: Editora Fundação Petrópolis, 2000), 140.

15. José Jorge de Carvalho, *Inclusão Étnica e Racial no Brasil: A Questão das Cotas no Ensino Superior* (São Paulo: Attar, 2005), 60.

16. Ibid., 61.

17. Kimberlé Crenshaw, National Public Radio's Intelligence Squared U.S. Debate, "It's Time to End Affirmative Action," moderated by John Donovan, presented by Rosenkranz Foundation, November 13, 2007.

18. James Holston, *Insurgent Citizenship: Disjunctions of Democracy and Modernity in Brazil* (Princeton: Princeton University Press, 2008), 286.

19. This situation is shown in the 2007 PBS documentary *Brazil in Black and White.*

20. See Denise Ferreira da Silva, *Toward a Global Idea of Race* (Minneapolis: University of Minnesota Press, 2007).

21. Ali Kamel, *Não Somos Racistas: Uma Reação aos que Querem nos Transformar numa Nação Bicolor* (Rio de Janeiro: Nova Fronteira, 2006).

22. See Peter Fry, "Politics, Nationality, and the Meaning of 'Race' in Brazil," *Daedalus* 129, no. 2 (2000): 91.

23. Nei Lopes, *O Racismo Explicado aos Meus Filhos* (Rio de Janeiro: Agir, 2007).

24. See Peter Fry, *A Persistência da Raça: Ensaios Antropológicos sobre o Brasil e a África Austral* (Rio de Janeiro: Civilização Brasileira, 2005).

25. See João Feres, Jr., "Ação Afirmativa no Brasil," *Economica* 6, no. 2 (December 2004): 291–312.

26. Antonio Negri and Giuseppe Cocco, *GlobAL: Bipoder e Luta em Uma América Latina Globalizada* (Rio de Janeiro: Record, 2005), 149.

27. Carvalho, *Inclusão Étnica e Racial no Brasil*, 96.

28. Ibid., 61.

29. Carvalho, perhaps in an attempt to distance the Brazilian model from the negative image of the U.S. Civil Rights model, argues that Affirmative Action in the United States is co-optive and individualist, rooted in a competitive ethos of winners and losers, while the Brazilian model is rooted in a societal choice for change, an equality of results rather than equal opportunity per se. At the same time, he makes untenable generalizations such as the claim that "racial and ethnic minorities— blacks, Indians, Hispanics, Asians—never created a politicized common front based on solidarity." Ibid., 125.

30. Ribeiro quoted in Larry Rohter, *Brazil on the Rise: The Story of a Country Transformed* (New York: Palgrave, 2010), 76.

31. Carvalho, *Inclusão Étnica e Racial no Brasil*, 68.

32. Kamel, *Não Somos Racistas*.

33. Ibid., 18.

34. Ibid.

35. Ibid.

36. See George M. Fredrickson, "Race and Racism in Historical Perspective," in Hamilton et al., *Beyond Racism*, 14.

37. In metaphorical terms, one might suggest that white U.S. racism is like that of a snake that hisses and kills with bites and venom, while Brazilian racism is like that of an anaconda that slowly strangles with its suffocating embrace.

38. Ania Loomba points out that this American foil and a kind of Indian exceptionalism was even invoked by intellectuals from India when the Dalit, a group of roughly 180 million people who are debarred by the caste system from eating or studying with upper-caste individuals, from marrying outside their caste, from dressing above their station, and from drawing water from the wrong well and who regularly meet with hostility and even lynching, went to the Durban Conference on Racism and Xenophobia to protest racism in India. To discuss caste as race, some left intellectuals argued, was to follow an American imperialist agenda. In terms reminiscent of the Bourdieu argument against Michael Hanchard (discussed in chapter 8), it was argued that "race, then, as a central category for the struggle, may be self-evident in the US context, but not as useful in other settings." Vijay Prashad, "Cataracts of Silence," quoted in Ania Loomba, "Race and the Possibilities of Comparative Critique," *New Literary History* 40, no. 3 (Summer 2009): 510.

39. Kamel, *Não Somos Racistas*, 20.

40. Ibid., 101.

41. Ibid. On the idea of "neo-Freyrean," see Christopher Dunn's "A Retomada Freyreana," in Joshua Lund and Malcolm McNee, eds., *Gilberto Freyre e os Estudos Latino-americanos* (Pittsburgh: Instituto de Literatura Iberoamer-

icana, 2006).

42. See Negri and Cocco, *GlobAL*, 76.

43. While the United States would indeed do well to abandon all vestiges of the bicolor model in favor of a nonassimilationist spectrum model, Kamel's warnings about a new apartheid seem to imply that the mere introduction of some Affirmative Action measures will put Brazil on a reverse historical path toward legal segregation, even though these measures were meant to *combat* segregation. The reasoning here seems rather opaque.

44. David R. Roediger, introduction to Roediger, ed., *Black on White: Black Writers on What It Means to Be White* (New York: Schocken Books, 1998), 3.

45. Charles Mills, *The Racial Contract* (Ithaca: Cornell University Press, 1997), 109.

46. W. E. B. Du Bois, "The Souls of White Folk," originally published as an article in *Independent* (August 18, 1910) and republished in Du Bois, *Darkwater: Voices from within the Veil* (1920; repr., New York: Dover, 1999), 17.

47. Du Bois, *Darkwater*, 18.

48. Ibid.

49. Frazier quoted in Stephen Steinberg, *Race Relations: A Critique* (Stanford: Stanford University Press, 2007), 64.

50. Ibid., 64.

51. James W. Loewen, *Lies My Teacher Told Me* (New York: Simon and Schuster, 1995), 171–177.

52. Victor Hugo quoted in ibid., 179

53. David S. Reynolds, *John Brown, Abolitionist* (New York: Knopf, 2005), 106.

54. Douglass quoted in ibid., 104.

55. Malcolm X quoted in ibid., 498.

56. Lerone Bennett, Jr., quoted in ibid., 504.

57. See David Roediger, *The Wages of Whiteness: Race and the Making of the American Working Class* (London: Verso, 1991) and *Towards the Abolition of Whiteness* (London: Verso, 1994).

58. Don Jordan and Michael Walsh, *White Cargo: The Forgotten History of Britain's White*

Slaves in America (New York: NYU Press, 2007), 12.

59. Theodore W. Allen, The Invention of the White Race: The Origin of Racial Oppression in Anglo-America (New York: Verso, 1994); Noel Ignatiev, How the Irish Became White (New York: Routledge, 1995).

60. Caren Kaplan, "'Beyond the Pale': Rearticulating U.S. Jewish Whiteness," in Ella Shohat, ed., Talking Visions: Multicultural Feminism in a Transnational Age, 451–458 (Cambridge: MIT Press, 1998).

61. Ruth Frankenberg, White Women, Race Matters: The Social Construction of Whiteness (Minneapolis: University of Minnesota Press, 1993).

62. George Lipsitz, The Possessive Investment in Whiteness: How White People Benefit from Identity Politics (Philadelphia: Temple University Press, 1998), vii.

63. Ibid.

64. In "What Is This 'Black' in Black Popular Culture?,'" Stuart Hall speaks of the "end of the innocence of the black subject, or the end of the innocent notion of an essential black subject." Stuart Hall, "What Is This 'Black' in Black Popular Culture?," Social Justice 20, nos. 1–2 (Spring–Summer 1993): 112.

65. See Jeffrey D. Needell, "History, Race, and the State in the Thought of Oliveira Vianna," Hispanic American Historical Review 75, no. 1 (1995): 15.

66. Alberto Guerreiro Ramos, Introdução Crítica à Sociologia Brasileira (Rio de Janeiro: UFRJ, 1995), 220.

67. Ramos quoted in Iray Carone and Maria Aparecida Silva Bento, introduction to Carone and Bento, eds., Psicologia Social do Racism: Estudos sobre Branquitude e Branqueamento no Brasil [The Social Psychology of Racism: Studies on Whiteness and Whitening in Brazil] (Petrópolis, Brazil: Vozes, 2003), 47.

68. See Carvalho, Inclusão Étnica e Racial no Brasil, 91–93.

69. Carone and Bento, introduction to Psicologia Social do Racism.

70. Edith Piza, "Branco no Brasil? Ninguém Sabe, Ninguém Viu," in Antonio Sérgio Alfredo Guimarães and Lynn Huntley, eds., Tirando a Máscara: Ensaios sobre o Racismo no Brasil, 97–126 (São Paulo: Paz e Terra, 2000).

71. Rita Segato, "The Color-Blind Subject of Myth, or, Where to Find Africa in the Nation," Annual Review of Anthropology 27 (1998): 147.

72. Marco Frenette, Preto e Branco: A Importância da Cor da Pele (São Paolo: Editora Brasil, 2001), 21.

73. Ibid., 22.

74. Ibid., 29.

75. Ibid., 31.

76. Ibid., 54.

77. Ibid., 65–66.

78. Carvalho, Inclusão Étnica e Racial no Brasil, 102.

79. Ibid.

80. John M. Novell, "Uncomfortable Whiteness of the Brazilian Middle Class," in Yvonne Maggie and Claudia Barcellos Rezende, eds., Raça como Retórica: A Construção da Diferença [Race as Rhetoric: The Construction of Difference] (Rio de Janeiro: Civilização Brasileira, 2002).

81. See Angela Gilliam, "Women's Equality and National Liberation," in Chandra Talpade Mohanty, Ann Russo, and Lourdes Torres, eds., Third World Women and the Politics of Feminism (Bloomington: Indiana University Press, 1991), 60.

82. Novell, "Uncomfortable Whiteness."

83. Darcy Ribeiro, O Povo Brasileiro: A Formação e o Sentido do Brasil (São Paulo: Companhia das Letras, 1995), 239.

84. Novell, "Uncomfortable Whiteness," 257.

85. Elisa Larkin Nascimento, O Sortilégio da Cor: Identidade, Raça e Gênero no Brasil (São Paulo: Summus, 2003).

86. Sovik, Aqui Ninguém é Branco.

87. Patricia Pinho, meanwhile, points to the process by which many Brazilian immigrants to the United States become "unwhitened." Patricia de Santana Pinho, Reinvenções da

África na Bahia (São Paulo: Annablume, 2004), 219.

88. Kia Lilly Caldwell, *Negras in Brazil: Re-envisioning Black Women, Citizenship, and the Politics of Identity* (New Brunswick: Rutgers University Press, 2006).

89. Sovik, *Aqui Ninguém é Branco*, 69.

90. Caetano Veloso quoted in ibid., 71.

91. Caetano Veloso, *Verdade Tropical* (São Paulo: Companhia das Letras, 1997), 505.

92. Sovik, *Aqui Ninguém é Branco*, 147.

93. Alexandra Poli, "Faire Face au Racisme en France et au Brésil: De la Condamnation Morale à l'Aide aux Victimes," *Cultures and Conflicts* 59 (2005): 15.

94. Azouz Begag, *Ethnicity and Equality: France in the Balance*, trans. Alec G. Hargreaves (Lincoln, NE: Bison Books, 2007), 116.

95. See Robert C. Lieberman, "A Tale of Two Countries: The Politics of Color-Blindness in France and the United States," in Herrick Chapman and Laura L. Frader, eds., *Race in France: Interdisciplinary Perspectives on the Politics of Difference*, 189–216 (New York: Berghahn Books, 2004).

96. Erik Bleich, "Anti-racism without Races: Politics and Policy in a 'Color-Blind' State," in Chapman and Frader, *Race in France*, 166.

97. Gwénaële Calvès, "Color-Blindness at a Crossroads in Contemporary France," in Chapman and Frader, *Race in France*, 221.

98. Yazid Sabeg and Yacine Sabeg, *Discrimination Positive: Pourquoi la France Ne Peut Y Échapper* (Paris: Calmann-Levy, 2004).

99. See Léon-François Hoffman, *Le Nègre Romantique: Personnage Littéraire et Obsession Collective* (Paris: Payot, 1973), 47.

100. Ibid.

101. De Gaulle quoted in Pascal Blanchard, Éric Deroo, and Gilles Manceron, *Le Paris Noir* (Paris: Hazan, 2001), 154.

102. Ibid.

103. De Gaulle quoted in Jean-Baptiste Onana, *Sois Nègre et Tais-Toi!* (Paris: Éditions du Temps, 2007), 61.

104. See Didier Gondola, "Transient Citizens: The Othering and Indigenization of Blacks and Beurs within the French Republic," in Charles Tshimanga, Didier Gondola, and Peter J. Bloom, eds., *Frenchness and the African Diaspora: Identity and Uprising in Contemporary France* (Bloomington: Indiana University Press, 2009), 162.

105. Ibid., 160.

106. Frantz Fanon, *Black Skin, White Masks* (1967; repr., New York: Grove, 1994), 29.

107. Onana, *Sois Nègre et Tais-Toi!*.

108. Pap Ndiaye, *La Condition Noire: Essai sur une Minorité Française* (Paris: Calmann-Lévy, 2008), 89.

109. Ibid., 107

110. Pierre Tévanian, *La Mécanique Raciste* (Paris: Dilecta, 2008), 8.

111. Ibid., 74.

112. François Durpaire, *France Blanche, Colère Noire* (Paris: Odile Jacob, 2006), 13.

113. Ibid., 43.

114. Quoted in ibid., 26.

115. Ibid.

116. Ibid., 33.

117. Durpaire, *France Blanche, Colère Noire*, 85.

118. Ibid.

119. Françoise Vergès, *La Mémoire Enchaînée: Questions sur l'Esclavage* (Paris: Albin Michel, 2006), 48.

120. Frédérique Mouzer and Charles Onana, *Un Racisme Français* (Nantes: Duboiris, 2007).

NOTES TO CHAPTER 8

1. One can distinguish between "post-colonial" as chronological marker and "postcolonial," sans hyphen, as referring to the theory.

2. See Georges Balandier, *Sociologie Actuelle de l'Afrique Noire: Dynamique Sociale en Afrique Centrale* (Paris: PUF, 1971).

3. Dino Costantini, *Mission Civilisatrice: Le Rôle de l'Histoire Coloniale dans la Construction de l'Identité Politique Française* (Paris: La Découverte, 2008), 13.

4. In the case of Achille Mbembe's *De la Postcolonie*, for example, the book was first

written and published in French yet had more impact through its English translation.

5. For a brilliant and comprehensive analysis of these exchanges, see François Cusset's *French Theory: How Foucault, Derrida, Deleuze, & Co. Transformed the Intellectual Life of the United States*, trans. Jeff Fort (Minneapolis: University of Minnesota Press, 2008).

6. Nicolas Sarkozy, address at the University of Cheikh Anta Diop, Senegal (July 26, 2007).

7. Makhily Gassama, ed., *L'Afrique Répond à Sarkozy: Contre le Discours de Dakar* (Paris: Philippe Rey, 2008); Adame Ba Konaré, ed., *Petit Précis de Remise à Niveau sur L'Histoire Africaine à l'Usage du Président Sarkozy* (Paris: Le Découverte, 2008).

8. Nicolas Sarkozy, address to Union for a Popular Movement, Paris (April 22, 2006).

9. See Alain Badiou, *De Quoi Sarkozy Est-il le Nom?* (Paris: Lignes, 2007).

10. Seloua Luste Boulbina, "Ce Que Postcolonie Veut Dire: Une Pensée de la Dissidence," *Rue Descartes* 58 (2006): 13.

11. Daniel Lefeuvre, *Pour en Finir avec la Repentance Coloniale* [To Put an End to Colonial Repentance] (Paris: Flammarion, 2008), 13, 229.

12. Finkielkraut quoted in Costantini, *Mission Civilisatrice*, 15. Such comments, originally made in an interview with *Haaretz* and subsequently reproduced in *Le Monde* (November 24, 2005), provoked an enormous polemic in France. In the United States, meanwhile, Newt Gingrich, whose 1971 Ph.D. thesis was a "white man's burden"–style defense of Belgian colonial policy in the Congo, now "accuses" Barack Obama of being a Kenyan anticolonialist, a strange accusation from a supporter of the Tea Party, since the original Tea Party in Boston Harbor was nothing if not anticolonialist.

13. Sarkozy quoted in Catherine Coquio, introduction to Coquio, ed., *Retours du Colonial? Disculpation et Réhabilitation de l'Histoire Coloniale Française* (Paris: L'Atalante, 2008), 14–15.

14. Jacqueline Bardolph, *Études Postcolonia-*

les *et Littérature* (Paris: Honoré Champion, 2002), 17–18.

15. Friedrich Nietzsche, "On the Uses and Disadvantages of History for Life" [Vom Nutzen und Nachteil der Historie für das Leben] (1874), 187.

16. Anne Berger, "Traversées de Frontières: Postcolonialité et Études de Genre en Amérique," *Labyrinthe* 24 (2006): 11–37.

17. Rada Iveković, "Langue Coloniale, Langue Globale, Langue Locale," *Rue Descartes* 58 (2007): 28–29.

18. "Aimé Césaire Refuse de Recevoir Nicolas Sarkozy," *Le Monde* (December 7, 2005).

19. For the full text of the appeal, see Mouvement des Indigènes de la République, "L'Appel des Indigènes de la République," June 12, 2006, http://www.indigenes-republique.org/spip.php?article1.

20. Jean Daniel, "Les Damnés de la Républiques," *Nouvel Observateur* (March 9, 2005).

21. See Forence Bernault, "Colonial Syndrome," in Charles Tshimanga, Didier Gondola, and Peter J. Bloom, eds., *Frenchness and the African Diaspora: Identity and Uprising in Contemporary France* (Bloomington: Indiana University Press, 2009).

22. Pascal Blanchard, Nicolas Bancel, and Sandrine Lemaire, introduction to Blanchard, Bancel, and Lemaire, eds., *La Fracture Coloniale: La Société Française au Prisme de l'Héritage Colonial* (Paris: La Découverte, 2005), 11–12.

23. On this last point, see Alexis Spire, *Étrangers à la Carte: L'administration de l'Immigration en France (1945–1975)* (Paris: Grasset, 2005), 268–272.

24. Didier Lapeyronnie, "La Banlieue comme Théâtre Colonial, ou la Fracture Coloniale dans les Quartiers," in Blanchard, Bancel, and Lemaire, *La Fracture Coloniale*, 214.

25. Pap Ndiaye, *La Condition Noire: Essai sur une Minorité Française* (Paris: Calmann-Lévy, 2008), 346–347.

26. Marie-Claude Smouts, ed., *La Situation Postcoloniale: Les Postcolonial Studies dans le Débat Français* (Paris: Sciences Po, 2008), 24–25.

27. Iveković, "Langue Coloniale, Langue Globale, Langue Locale."

28. It is also important to note the continuing capacity for mass mobilization of the French left, whether in the 2005 resistance to the referendum on the European Constitution, the 2006 student mobilization against the CPE attack on employee rights, or the 2010 mass mobilization against the conservative changes to social security laws.

29. Many French writers have explored the neocolonial underside of contemporary French policy in Africa, for example. In *La Françafrique: Le Plus Long Scandale de la République*, François-Xavier Verschave explores the mechanisms of French neocolonialism in Africa, where the French political elite, both from the right and from the left, has entertained very close links with a series of African kleptocrats and dictators, whose interests it favors.

30. See, for example, Bernard Mouralis, *Littérature et Développement* (Paris: Silex, 1999) or Jean-Marie Grassin, *Littératures Émergentes* (Bern: Peter Lang, 1996).

31. Nacira Guénif-Souilamas, introduction to Guénif-Souilamas, ed., *La République Mise à Nu par Son Immigration* [The Republic Exposed by Its Immigration] (Paris: La Fabrique, 2006).

32. Ibid., 24–26.

33. Ibid.

34. Ibid., 8.

35. Ibid., 17.

36. Guénif-Souilamas spoke of "patriarchal feminists" in a talk given at La Maison Française, New York University, in November 2009. In the United States, meanwhile, the term has often been used in the context of critiquing white or Eurocentric feminist discourse of white women rescuing brown women from brown men (Shohat). See Ella Shohat, ed., *Talking Visions: Multicultural Feminism in a Transnational Age* (Cambridge: MIT Press, 1998). The formulation "white men are saving brown women from brown men" is from Gayatri Spivak's "Can the Subaltern Speak?," in Cary Nelson and Lawrence Grossberg,

eds., *Marxism and the Interpretation of Culture* (London: Macmillan, 1988).

37. Public statement to the French National Assembly, www.assemblee-nationale.fr, quoted in Achille Mbembe, "Provincializing France?," *Public Culture* 23, no. 1 (Winter 2011): 94–95.

38. Pascale Casanova, *La République Mondiale des Lettres* (Paris: Seuil, 1999), 218.

39. L'Institut du Tout-Monde, created at the initiative of Édouard Glissant, was founded as an attempt to "advance the understanding of the processes of creolization and to disseminate the extraordinary diversity of the imaginaries of peoples, expressed in a multiplicity of languages and in a plurality of artistic expressions and in unexpected modes of life." The goal is to construct an "international network of studies and research, a space of invention and formation, a place of encounters and memories." The ultimate goal of the institute is to "live the world differently." Fondation Euro-Méditerranéene Anna Lindh pour le Dialogue entre les Cultures, "Institut du Tout-Monde," http://www.euromedalex.org/node/5966.

40. Tyler Stovall and Georges Van Den Abbeele, introduction to Stovall and Van Den Abbeele, eds., *French Civilization and Its Discontents: Nationalism, Colonialism, Race*, 1–16 (Lanham, MD: Lexington Books, 2003), 3.

41. Ibid., 10.

42. One collateral effect of this influx of African academics on U.S. campuses has been occasional tensions with African American academics in black studies, who complain that African and Afro-Caribbean academics are being favored, along with tensions around the proper emphasis between those who emphasize specifically African American questions and those who emphasize diasporic questions. For an example of an African American evaluation, see Cecil Brown, *Dude, Where's My Black Studies Department? The Disappearance of Black Americans from Our Universities* (Berkeley, CA: North Atlantic Books, 2007).

43. Reported conversation with an African scholar, in Jean-Philippe Dedieu, "Des États-Unis Sortent des Voix Africaines, et Fidélité

Francophone," *Black Renaissance Noire* 5, no. 2 (Summer 2003).

44. Recent trends show that it is impossible to isolate French-speaking from English-speaking spaces in terms of the dissemination of scholarship around questions of race and coloniality. Indeed, African scholars such as the late Emmanuel Chukwudi Eze (Bucknell), Kwame Gyeke (University of Ghana, Temple University, and University of Pennsylvania), Jean-Marie Makang (University of Maryland), D. A. Masoli (Antioch College and University of Nairobi), Ngugi wa Thing'o (University of California, Irvine), Tsenay Serequberhan (Simmons College, Boston), Valentin Mudimbe (Duke University), and Kwasi Wiredu (University of South Florida) have been key figures in the critique of the Eurocentrism and racism of some major figures from the European Enlightenment, notably Hobbes, Hume, Locke, Kant, and Hegel.

45. Alec G. Hargreaves, "Chemins de Traverse," *Mouvements des Idées et des Lutte* 51 (September–October 2007): 24–31.

46. Our thanks to Jim Cohen for pointing this out.

47. Guiart quoted in Benoît de L'Estoile, *Le Goût des Autres: De L'Exposition Coloniale aux Arts Premiers* (Paris: Flammarion, 2007), 198.

48. Berger, "Traversées de Frontières."

49. See, for example, Balibar's essay "Y-a-t-il un Neo-racisme?" in the coauthored (with Immanuel Wallerstein) *Race, Nation, Classe: Les Identités Ambiguës* (Paris: La Découverte, 1988); and "Racism as Universalism," in *Masses, Classes, Ideas* (New York: Routledge, 1994).

50. See Ann Laura Stoller, "Colonial Aphasia: Race and Disabled Histories in France," *Public Culture* 23, no. 1 (Winter 2011): 121–156.

51. Ibid., 141.

52. Ibid., 131.

53. Paul A. Silverstein and Jane E. Goodman, introduction to Goodman and Silverstein, eds., *Bourdieu in Algeria* (Lincoln: University of Nebraska Press, 2009), 1–2.

54. See Phyllis Taoua, *Forms of Protest* (Portsmouth, NH: Heinemann, 2002), 257–258.

55. Originally published as "Les Études Postcoloniales: Une Invention Politique de la Tradition?," in *Sociétés Politiques Comparées: Revue Européenne d'Analyse des Sociétés Politiques* 14 (April 2009); published in English as "Postcolonial Studies: A Political Invention of Tradition?," *Public Culture* 23, no. 1 (Winter 2011): 55–84.

56. Bayart, "Postcolonial Studies," 59.

57. Ibid., 60.

58. Frantz Fanon, *A Dying Colonialism* (New York: Grove, 1965), 175.

59. Bayart, "Postcolonial Studies," 63.

60. Ibid., 65.

61. Bayart, "La Novlangue d'un Archipel Universitaire," in Smouts, *La Situation Postcoloniale*.

62. Jim Cohen, "Postcolonial Immigrants in France and Their Descendants: The Meanings of France's 'Postcolonial Moment'" (unpublished manuscript, provided to us by the author), based on a presentation in Amsterdam in 2009: "Postcolonial Immigration and Identity Formation in Europe since 1945: Towards a Comparative Perspective," IISG/KITLV Amsterdam.

63. See Alec G. Hargreaves, "Half-Measures: Anti-discrimination Policy in France," in Herrick Chapman and Laura L. Frader, eds., *Race in France: Interdisciplinary Perspectives on the Politics of Difference*, 227–245 (New York: Berghahn Books, 2004).

64. Ndiaye gives credit to American historian William Cohen, who published his book *The French Encounter with Africans* in 1980, subsequently translated into French as *Français et Africains: Les Noirs dans le Regard des Blancs* (Paris: Gallimard, 1982), for opening up the field of black history in France. The book was denounced at the time by Emmanuel Todd as propagating an illegitimate subject and a case of "flagrant historical delirium." See Ndiaye, *La Condition Noire*, 111.

65. Ibid., 360.

66. Ibid., 362.

67. Ibid., 353.

68. Didier Fassin and Éric Fassin, "Éloge de la Complexité," in Fassin and Fassin, eds., *De la Question Sociale à la Question Raciale? Représenter la Société Française* (Paris: La Découverte, 2006), 253.

69. Ibid., 130.

70. "Who Is Afraid of the Postcolonial?," special issue of *Mouvements: Des Idées et des Luttes* 51 (September–October 2007): 12.

NOTES TO CHAPTER 9

1. See Edward A. Riedinger, "Comparative Development of the Study of Brazil in the United States and France," in Marshall C. Eakin and Paulo Roberto de Almeida, eds., *Envisioning Brazil: A Guide to Brazilian Studies in the United States,* 375–395 (Madison: University of Wisconsin Press, 2005).

2. We found one trilateral study in our sense of exploring the relationalities of France, Brazil, and the United States: Georgette Medleg Rodrigues's 1998 study "French Attitudes toward US Influence in Brazil (1944–1960)," which explores, on the basis of diplomatic archives and published writing and memoirs, the official French efforts to exert its influence in the face of U.S. competition in a situation in which France itself was also feeling the pressure of American influence, challenged to present itself to Brazil as modern like the United States and as the incarnation of a traditional universality.

3. See Sergio Miceli, *A Desilusão Americana: Relações Acadêmicas entre Brasil e os Estados Unidos* (São Paulo: Sumaré, 1973), 40.

4. See Piers Armstrong, "Evolução de uma Dinâmica Relacional: A Hermêutica do Pensar a Cultura Brasileira a Partir dos EUA," in Cristina Stevens, ed., *Quando o Tio Sam Pegar no Tamborim: Uma Perspectiva Transcultural do Brasil* (Brasilia: Plano, 2000), 57.

5. Although the term "Brazilianist" came in the wake of similar expressions such as "Latinist" or "Germanist," it also has behind it an implied cultural hierarchy, internalized by many Brazilians. For historical reasons, many Brazilians find it surprising that non-Brazilians should choose to study Brazil. "Brazilianists" are invariably asked by journalists (and sometimes by academics), "How did you become interested in Brazil?" Those Americans and Brazilians who write about France, or French and Brazilians who write about the United States, in contrast, are rarely asked the same question. The assumption is that these "major" cultures are inherently interesting, while only some special experience or epiphany—a trip to Brazil, a love affair, a surprise fellowship, a stint in the Peace Corps—could possibly explain one's becoming "interested in Brazil."

6. A more transnational and less Francocentric narrative of the genealogy of "cultural studies," we argue, would include not only the French figures noted by Perrone-Moisés but also the Francophone writers such as Fanon and Césaire, along with C. L. R James from the Caribbean, James Baldwin and Leslie Fiedler from the United States, alongside the Italian Marxist Antonio Gramsci, British Marxists such as E. P. Thompson and Raymond Williams, and post-Marxist Stuart Hall.

7. Leyla Perrone-Moisés, "Pós-estruturalismo e Desconstrução nas Américas," in Perrone-Moisés, ed., *Do Positivismo à Desconstrução: Idéias Francesas na América,* 213–237 (São Paulo: USP, 2003).

8. Herman Melville, *Redburn* (1849; repr., New York: Penguin Books, 1986), 239.

9. Perrone-Moisés, "Pós-estruturalismo e Desconstrução nas Américas," 226.

10. Ibid., 230.

11. Ibid., 232.

12. François Cusset, *French Theory: How Foucault, Derrida, Deleuze, & Co. Transformed the Intellectual Life of the United States,* trans. Jeff Fort (Minneapolis: University of Minnesota Press, 2008), 2.

13. Ibid., xviii.

14. Ibid., 10.

15. Ibid., 8.

16. Ibid., 10

17. Ibid., 99.

18. Michael George Hanchard, *Orpheus and Power: The "Movimento Negro" of Rio de Janeiro and São Paulo, Brazil, 1945–1988* (Princeton: Princeton University Press, 1994).

19. Pierre Bourdieu and Loïc Wacquant, "On the Cunning of Imperial Reason," *Theory, Culture, and Society* 16, no. 1 (1999): 51

20. Ibid., 48.

21. See Eduardo Bonilla-Silva, *Racism without Racists: Color-Blind Racism and the Persistence of Racial Inequality in the United States* (Lanham, MD: Rowman and Littlefield, 2010), 183–185.

22. Bourdieu and Wacquant, "On the Cunning of Imperial Reason," 45–46.

23. Ibid., 46.

24. Robert Stam in conversation with Brazilian journalist Sérgio Augusto in September 1995.

25. See Thomas E. Skidmore, "Race and Class in Brazil: Historical Perspectives," in Pierre-Michel Fontain, ed., *Race, Class, and Power in Brazil* (Los Angeles: UCLA Center for Afro-American Studies, 1985).

26. John French, "The Missteps of Anti-imperialist Reason." The essay was published first as a Duke University Working Paper (no. 27) and was subsequently published in *Theory, Culture and Society* 17, no. 1 (2000): 121, a special issue devoted to responses to the Bourdieu/Wacquant essay.

27. Ibid., 122.

28. Ibid.

29. Bourdieu and Wacquant, "On the Cunning of Imperialist Reason," 44, 53, quoted in French, "The Missteps of Anti-imperialist Reason," 122.

30. French, "The Missteps of Anti-imperialist Reason," 122.

31. For Freyre's boldest statement affirming Luso-Tropical exceptionalism, see Gilberto Freyre, *O Luso e o Trópico* (Lisbon: Comissão Executiva do Quinto Centenário da Morte do Infante D. Henrique, 1961).

32. The experience of Brazilian Carnival, for example, involves a transracial gregariousness that is not available in the same way in the United States (or France). Both black and white Americans visiting Brazil frequently express a sense of relief at the lack of the racial tension that often pervades and poisons social life in the United States.

33. James Holston, *Insurgent Citizenship: Disjunctions of Democracy and Modernity in Brazil* (Princeton: Princeton University Press, 2008), 284.

34. Bourdieu and Wacquant, "On the Cunning of Imperial Reason," 44.

35. Immanuel Wallerstein argues that racism is disseminated throughout the world system, so that no part of the planet, in terms of local, national, and international policy, is free of it. See Immanuel Wallerstein, *O Declínio do Poder Americano* (Rio de Janeiro: Contraponto, 2004), 267.

36. Bourdieu and Wacquant, "On the Cunning of Imperial Reason," 46. Bourdieu/Wacquant seem to imply, absurdly, that some American foundations demand that Brazilian research teams conform to the rules of Affirmative Action, which, if true, would mean that they would have to engage Native Americans, Latinos, Asian Americans, and Pacific Islanders.

37. Naomi Klein, *The Shock Doctrine* (New York: Holt, 2007), 123.

38. See Sérgio Costa, *Dois Atlânticos: Teoria Social, Anti-racismo, Cosmopolitanismo* (Belo Horizonte, Brazil: UFMG, 2006), 198.

39. Bourdieu and Wacquant, "On the Cunning of Imperial Reason," 54.

40. Ibid., 47.

41. Loïc Wacquant, "Bourdieu in America: Notes on the Transatlantic Importation of Social Theory," in Craig Calhoun, Edward LiPuma, and Moishe Postone, eds., *Bourdieu: Critical Perspectives* (Chicago: University of Chicago Press, 1993), 241.

42. See Marie-Pierre Le Hir, "The Popular in Cultural Studies," in Marie-Pierre Le Hir and Dana Strand, eds., *French Cultural Studies: Criticism at the Crossroads* (Albany: SUNY Press, 2000).

43. Bourdieu and Wacquant, "On the Cun-

ning of Imperial Reason," 47.

44. Cusset, *French Theory*, 232.

45. Eduardo Viveiros de Castro, *Métaphysiques Cannibales* (Paris: Presses Universitaires de France, 2009), 66–67.

46. Despite the hostility of intellectuals such as Bourdieu/Wacquant, some academics, many of them French or French-speaking academics in the United States or in the United Kingdom, have begun to do cultural studies–style work on French popular culture itself, generating studies of the portrayals of French colonialism in the films of Brigitte Roüan and Claire Denis, for example, or the representation of diasporic minorities on French television or the role of hip-hop culture in the banlieue or "*métissage* in postcolonial comics." Catherine Liu sees MC Solaar's rap lyrics as the hybrid heir of both Public Enemy and Baudelaire and as the contemporary equivalent of Walter Benjamin's "ragpicker." French postcolonial studies has focused on exoticism in mainstream French writing, on Francophone theories of language and identity, and on the relevance of Anglo-Indian postcolonial theory to French culture. And some cinema studies scholars have detected a submerged colonial and racial presence in the French New Wave: the black man excluded from the fascist student party in Chabrol's *Les Cousins* (*The Cousins*), the anticolonialist Africans in Rouch's *Chronique d'un Été* and Marker's *Le Joli Mai*, the Black Panthers in Godard's *Weekend*, the allusions to colonial carnage in Chabrol's *Le Boucher*, and the coded references to the war in Algeria in Varda's *Cléo de 5 à 7*, Rozier's *Adieu Philippine*, and Demy's *Les Parapluies de Cherbourg*. See, for example, Dina Sherzer, ed., *Cinema, Colonialism, Postcolonialism: Perspectives from the French and Francophone World* (Austin: University of Texas Press, 1996). See also Kristin Ross, *Fast Cars, Clean Bodies: Decolonization and the Reordering of French Culture* (Cambridge: MIT Press, 1995).

47. See Éric Maigret, "Pierre Bourdieu, la Culture Populaire et le Long Remords de la Sociologie de la Distinction Culturelle," *Esprit* (March–April 2002): 170–178.

48. Pierre Bourdieu, *On Television* (New York: New Press, 1999).

49. See Arlindo Machado, *A Televisão Levada a Sério* (São Paulo: SENAC, 2000), 127.

50. Maigret, "Pierre Bourdieu," 175.

51. Ibid.

52. Ibid.

53. Tom Moylan, *Demand the Impossible: Science Fiction and the Utopian Imagination* (New York: Methuen, 1986), 213.

54. Pierre Bourdieu, *Distinction: A Social Critique of the Judgement of Taste*, trans. Richard Nice (Cambridge: Harvard University Press, 1984), 34.

55. Ibid., 491.

56. Ernst Bloch, *Atheism in Christianity* (New York: Herder and Herder, 1971).

57. Special issue on "On the Cunning of Imperial Reason" essay, *Estudos Afro-Asiáticos* (January–April 2002). Bourdieu/Wacquant mention the journal, not in terms of the work published there but only as an example of foundation funding for race-related research in Brazil. Wacquant himself, we would add, has also received research funding from American foundations.

58. Jocélio Teles dos Santos, "De Armadilhas, Convicções e Dissensões: As Relações Raciais como *Efeito Orloff*," *Estudos Afro-Asiáticos* 24, no. 1 (2002): 183.

59. Osmundo de Araújo Pinho and Ângela Figueiredo, "Idéias Fora do Lugar e o Lugar do Negro nas Ciências Sociais Brasileiras," *Estudos Afro-Asiáticos* 24, no. 1 (2002): 189–210.

60. Ibid.

61. Alberto Guerreiro Ramos, *Introdução Crítica à Sociologia Brasileira* (Rio de Janeiro: UFRJ, 1995), 165.

62. Pinho and Figueiredo, "Idéias Fora do Lugar," 193.

63. Costa, *Dois Atlânticos*, 54.

64. Antônio Cândido, *A Formação da Literatura Brasileira: Momentos Decisivos* (São Paulo: Martins, 1959).

65. Mário de Andrade, *Poesias Completas*

(São Paulo: Martins, 1972), 32–33.

66. Wacquant, "Bourdieu in America."

67. Haroldo de Campos, "Da Razão Antropofágica: A Europa sob o Signo da Devoração," *Revista Colóquio: Letras* 62 (July 1981): 10–25.

68. Eneida Maria de Souza, *Crítica Cult* (Belo Horizonte, Brazil: UFMG, 2002), 101.

69. Roberto Schwarz, *Misplaced Ideas* (London: Verso, 1997), 219.

70. Pierre Bourdieu, *Acts of Resistance: Against the Tyranny of the Market* (New York: New Press, 1998), 61.

71. Richard Sennett and Jonathan Cobb, *The Hidden Injuries of Class* (New York: Knopf, 1972).

72. Pierre Bourdieu, *Esquisse pour une Auto-Analyse* (Paris: Raisons d'Agir, 2004), 13.

73. Ibid., 126.

74. Arjun Appadurai, *Fear of Small Numbers: An Essay on the Geography of Anger* (Durham: Duke University Press, 2006), 18.

75. See Tyler Stovall, "'No Green Pastures': The African Americanization of France," in Elisabeth Mudimbe-Boyi, ed., *Empire Lost: France and Its Other Worlds* (New York: Lexington Books, 2009).

Index

Abdel-Malek, Anouar, 133, 245, 246
abolitionism, 18, 28, 29. *See also* antiracism
ABRALIC, 206
Abreu, João Capistrano de, 184
Abu-l Iasira, Sidi, 157
Académie Française, 146
Achebe, Chinua, 123
actors of color, 152
Acts of Resistance (Bourdieu), 114, 296–297
Adams, Henry, 21, 44
Adams, Paul, 52
Adorno, Theodor, 275
Affirmative Action, 209–239; attacks on, 101;
   backlash against, 215–216, 218–219; bicolor
   model/system, 223; black conservatives, 277;
   Brazil, 187, 211–212, 216–222, 323n29,
   324n43; Carvalho on, José Jorge de, 323n29;
   Civil Rights Act (1964), 211; Civil Rights
   Movement, 211; contrasts between Brazil
   and United States, 222–223; diversity, 211;
   Enlightenment, 209, 216; "fairness" issue,
   215; France, 211–212, 239; gradualism, 216;
   initiatives, 212–213; "racial democracy," 219;
   as racial discrimination, 219; racism, 214;
   remediation measures, 209, 213–214, 215;
   reparations, 98, 209; tax policy, 213; United
   States, 209–215, 323n29; white/black
   dichotomy, 283; whiteness studies, 209; for
   whites, 215–216; Žižek, Slavoj, 128
Affirmative Action (Sabeg and Sabeg), 239
"Affirmative Action in Brazil" (Feres), 220
Africa: black Brazilians, 44; Brazilian scholars of,
   271; cultural presence, xiii; Eurocentric view
   of, 216; Hegel's interpretation of, 247; Jews
   and, 317n64; traditions of public reason and
   pluralism, 65; trance religions, 36–37
African aesthetics, 48–49
African American rappers, 148
African Americans: black Brazilians, 278, 280;
   Bourdieu/Wacquant, 291; Brazil, 42, 44;
   Candomblé, 44; conservatives among, 152,
   277; France, 42, 44–49; miscegenation, 186;
   multiculturalism, 84–85; Native Americans,
   4; neoliberalism, 277; political power, 187;
   Republican Party, 152; transnationalism,
   291; voice in the academy, 122

*African-American Reflections on Brazil's Racial
   Paradise* (Hellwig), 42
Afro-Brazilian culture, 223, 271
Afro-Brazilian intellectuals, 177
Afrocentrism, 180
Afro-cosmopolitanism, 177
Agamben, Giorgio, 170
Age of Revolutions, The (Hobsbawm), 19
agency, 6, 11–12, 278, 287, 289
Ageron, Charles Robert, 263
Alcoff, Linda Martin, 100
Alencar, José de, 32
Alencastro, Luiz Felipe de, 271
Alexander, Jacqui, 80
Algeria, 29–30, 42, 254
Algerian independence, 61, 71, 159
Algerians: in France, 29, 130; massacre of in
   Paris, 135, 159, 251
Ali, Muhammed, 205
Alito, Samuel, 126–127
Alleg, Henri, 70, 159, 171, 246
Allen, Theodor, 232
Allen, Woody, 122
Almanac (Benjamin Banneker's), 15–16
Althusser, Louis, 128, 245, 246, 272
Amazon River, 10–11, 40
Ambedkar, Bhimrao Ramji, 211
"America" (the term), 58, 143
America in Europe (Arciniegas), 14–15
"American" (the term), 117
American differentialism, 138
American Enterprise Institute, 109
American ideas, 295–296
American intellectuals: French intellectuals, 286,
   294; Latin American intellectuals, knowledge
   of, 293; scholars of Brazil, 290; Wacquant,
   Loïc, 296
American Revolution, 1, 8, 27, 44
"American Scholar" (Emerson), 40
American studies, 80
Amin, Samir, 74, 76
Amkpa, Awam, 259
An End to Evil (Bruckner), 164
Anchieta, José de, 6
Ancient Society (Morgan), 9
Andean movement, 105–106

health care, 129; justice, 111; race, 102–103; "relationality," 111

classism, racism and, 227

Clastres, Pierre, 7, 12, 31, 33, 38

Clifford, James, 37

Clinton, Bill, 311n6

Closing of the American Mind (Bloom), 131

Cocco, Giuseppe, 13, 130, 220–221, 227

"Code Indigene," 29

Code Noir, 18, 29, 266

Coelho, Teixeira, 180

Cohen, Felix, 9

Cohen, Jim, 138, 144, 265

Cohn-Bendit, Daniel, 159, 170

Cold War, 95

Coleyn, Jean-Paul, 271

Collectif Égalité, 152

Colo, Gabriel, 271

Colonial Fracture, The (Bancel and Blanchard), 253–254

colonial genocides, 158

Colonial Massacres (Bénot), 23

"colonial multiculturality," 27

colonial novels, thematic analysis of, 246

Colonial Republicanism, 15

colonial studies, 244

colonialism, 249–254; Anglo-Saxon colonialisms, 250; Brazil, 98; capitalism, 91, 128; "dependency complex," 73; Enlightenment, xv, 78; Eurocentrism, 66; France, 53, 132–133, 247–248, 249, 252–254, 265–266; globalization, 91; Haiti, 18–19; Holocaust (Shoah), 157; indigenous critiques, 12; intercolonial rivalry, xiv; "Latin" colonialisms, 250; Marx, Karl, 64; Nazis, 157; neocolonialism, 91; nostalgia for, 249; police brutality, 153; race, xix; resistance to, xiv; settler colonialism, 250, 274; trickle-down colonialism, 24; United States, xix; Žižek, Slavoj, 120

"coloniality," 61

Colonizer and the Colonized, The (Memmi), 162

Color Witchcraft (Nascimento), 236

"color-blind" ideology, 42, 45, 144, 214–215, 241–242

"color-blind racism," 277

Colors of the Jews, The (Kaye/Kantrowitz), 172

Columbus, Christopher, 5, 10

commons, 130

communitarianism: Anglo-Saxon, 55; Brazil, xiv; France, xiv, 138, 141, 142; French republicanism, 243; United States, xiv

Comte, Auguste, 32

Condé, Maryse, 256, 258–259

Congo, Simon, 39

Congress of Negro Artists and Writers, 48

Congress Party (India), 123

Conquest, the: as "best school" for indigenous peoples, 124; conflicts initiated by, 11–12; enrichment of Europe, xv; frontier conquest, model of, 77; linguistic dimension, 5–6; Native American deaths, 104; police brutality, 153; Red Atlantic, 3

Conquest and Discovery Doctrine, 5

conscientização, 78

Constant, Fred, 173

Constantini, Dino, 245

constructivism, social, 12, 100

Cooper, David, 72

Cooper, Frederick, 264

Copeland, Aaron, 194

copyrights, 10

Coronil, Fernando, 87

cosmopolitanism, 292

Costa, Sérgio, 92, 193–194, 275, 291, 293

Coulter, Ann, 102, 151

"counter-Enlightenment," 78

CP (Communist Party), 95, 99, 154

Crenshaw, Kimberlé, 78, 212, 217

Creole consciousness, 54

"creolity," 60

creolization, 258

Crèvecoeur, J. Hector St. John de, 31

Critical Dictionary of Cultural Politics (Coelho), 180

critical law, 75, 78

critical pedagogy, 75

"critical race" (the term), 86

"critical race theory" (the term), 86

critical race theory: anticolonial movements, 86; aversion to, xvi, 298; Bourdieu/Wacquant, 114; decolonization of knowledge, 78; "decolonizing corpus," 82; Diderot, Denis, 23; Fanon, Frantz, 73; French intellectuals, 244; leftist arguments against, xvi; liberalism, 103; Marxism, 103; racism, 225; U. S. Constitution, 114, 115; Žižek, Slavoj, 120

critical utopias, 289

critical whiteness studies, 23, 24

cross-border interlocution, 293–298

cross-national comparisons, xviii, 184–185

Cruz, Manoel de Almeida, 179

Cuba, 119

Cuddihy, John Murray, 34

"Cult of Difference and the Sacralization of the Victim" (Todorov), 140

cultural capital, 297–298

cultural complexes, 315n13

cultural difference, 94–95

Cultural Revolution, 134
cultural studies, 284–287; Bourdieu, Pierre, 285; Bourdieu/Wacquant, 284–287; in Brazil, 206; Fanon, Frantz, 73, 286; French intellectuals, 132, 244, 286; of French popular culture, 332n46; genealogy of, 330n6; poststructuralism, 272; precursors, 286; transdisciplinary trends, 285
cultural syncretism, 284, 321n50
culture: in Bolivia, 104; capitalism, 97; economy, 111; indigenous peoples, 106
culture wars: Enlightenment, 1–2; France, 173; sobbing for the white man, 134–136; the term, usage of, xiii–xiv; United States, 70, 249–250; Žižek, Slavoj, 129
Cunha, Olívia Maria Gomes da, 208
Cunhambebe, 124
Cusset, François, 107, 109, 117, 275–276, 286
Cuvier, Georges, 240

"Daily Humiliation" (Badiou), 153
Dalit, 98, 324n38
DaMatta, Roberto, 183
d'Angola, Paulo, 39
Daniel, Jean, 168
Dash, J. Michael, 22
Dash, Michael, 62
Davis, Angela, 64, 77, 128
Davis, Mike, 31, 56
Davis, Miles, 45, 50
Daye, Hamed, 148
de Gaulle, Charles: Brazil, dismissal of, 38; independence path between US and USSR, 132; post-WWII activism, 71; Sartre, Jean-Paul, 110; Third World, France as defender of, 260; white normativity, 240
De la Littérature des Nègres (Grégoire), 22
"dead white males," 94
Dean, Warren, 81
Debray, Régis, 138
Debussy, Claude, 50
Declaration of Haitian Independence, 20
Declaration of Independence, 2, 16, 17, 70, 220
Declaration of the Rights of Indigenous Peoples, 311n10
Declaration of the Rights of Man and the Citizen, 28
Decolonization and Decolonized (Memmi), 162
decolonization of knowledge, 61–94, 248–255; American studies, 80; anthropology, 78–79; anticolonial movements, 68; area studies, 80–81; black studies, 79–80; dependency theory, 76; ethnic studies, 79–80; Eurocentrism, 61–68; France, 70–71; French Theory,

261; globalization, 90–91; historiography, 77; independence movements worldwide, 61; la République, decolonizing of, 248–255; Latin American studies, 81; law, 78; literature, canon debate in, 80; minority liberation movements, 68; modernity/coloniality research, 89–90; multiculturalism, 82–85; pedagogy, 78, 93; philosophy, 78; postcolonial studies/theory, 85–92; power structures and epistemologies, xiii; psychic fallout, 69; racial hierarchies, dismantling of, 70; radicalization of the disciplines, 75–82; revisionist history, 75, 77, 93–94, 109–110; "seismic shift" in, 61, 68–74, 79, 82, 178–179, 246; standpoint theory, 78; terminological panaceas, search for, 91–92; transdisciplinary trends, 79–80; United States, 70; Žižek, Slavoj, 123
"decolonizing corpus," 82, 115–116
deconstruction, 232, 273–274
Dedieu, Jean-Philippe, 259
Defert, Daniel, 133
Degler, Carl, 41
Delany, Martin, 21–22
Deleuze, Gilles, 60, 245, 272, 293, 294
Delgado, Richard, 78
"delinking," 76
Deltombe, Thomas, 254
Demand the Impossible (Moylan), 289
democracy, 12, 15, 64–65, 134–135. See also "racial democracy"
Democracy in America (Tocqueville), 31
Democratic Party, 99
Denis, Ferdinand, 32
"dependency complex," 73
dependency theory: Brazilian intellectuals, 71, 175; decolonization of knowledge, 76; in economics, 272; Fanon, Frantz, 74; Latin America, 89; Marxism, 76
Deren, Maya, 37
Deroo, Eric, 266
Derrida, Africa, and the Middle East (Wise), 171
Derrida, Jacques: American PhD. dissertations, 294; deconstruction, 273–274; dislocation of European culture, 72; French Theory, 245; intellectual exchange, 276; logocentrism, critique of, 272; Messianic Jew, 171; postcolonial studies/theory, 261; Spivak, Gayatri, 245, 275
"Des Cannibales" (Montaigne), 2, 7–8
Dessalines, Jean-Jacques, 20, 21
Destins Marranes (Lindenberg), 172
Diagne, Souleymane Bachir, 258–259
"dialogical anthropology," 79
diasporic longings, 42–49

Franklin, Benjamin, 7
Franklin, John Hope, 77
Frazier, E. Franklin, 41, 43, 230
freedom, Hegel on, 63–64
Freedom's Journal (newspaper), 15
Freire, Eduardo, 184
Freire, Paulo, 74, 78, 272
Freitas, Décio, 179
Freitas, Osmar, Jr., 179–180
French, John, 278–279
French Academy (Académie Francaise), 146, 251
French anthropology, 286
French antidifferentialism, 143–144
"French Attitudes toward US Influence in Brazil"
     (Rodrigues), 330n2
French canon, 145
French Civilization and Its Discontents (Stovall
     and Van Den Abbeele), 258
French critical theory. *See* French Theory
French Enlightenment, 1, 8, 32, 44
French ethnology, 260
French ideas, 295
French intellectuals, 244–269; 1990s, 244;
     achievements, 172–173; American intel-
     lectuals, 286, 294; Bourdieu/Wacquant,
     293; Brazil, influence on, 34; colonial novels,
     thematic analysis of, 246; critical race studies,
     244; critical race theory, 244; cultural studies,
     132, 244, 286; Jewish, 171; Latin American
     intellectuals, knowledge of, 293; leftists,
     161–162; multiculturalism, 145, 146, 182,
     244; negationism, 247; postcolonial studies/
     theory, 132, 244–246, 254, 255–261; post-
     structuralism, 272, 286; pro-American, 107;
     racism, 33; transnational currents, lack of
     engagement with, 286; Wacquant, Loïc, 296;
     Zionism, 169–170
French language, 57–58
French Oriental studies, 132–133
French poststructuralism, 272
French rappers, 147–149
French Republicanism, 142, 144, 243, 265
French Revolution, 1, 21, 28, 93
French Theory, 272–276; decolonization of
     knowledge, 261; influence abroad, 275–276;
     nouveaux philosophes, 275; postcolonial stud-
     ies/theory, 245–246; United States, 275
French Theory (Cusset), 109, 275–276
French universalism, 144
Frenette, Marco, 234–235
Freud, Sigmund, 54, 72
Freyre, Gilberto: Anglo/Latin dichotomy, 220;
     Brazilian identity, 156; conservatism, 175,
     178; indigenous peoples, 7; *Masters and

Slaves, 235; *Quilombo* (journal), 176; "racial
     democracy," 280; *Slave and Citizen* (with Tan-
     nenbaum), 41; Tannenbaum, Frank, 41; in
     United States, 40–41
Friedan, Betty, 193
Friedman, Milton, 283
Friedman, Susan Stanford, 301n2
"From Bob Dylan to Bob Marley" (Gil), 202–203
Frum, David, 164
Fry, Peter, 177, 207–208, 219–220
Fuentes, Carlos, 156
Fukuyama, Francis, 62, 63, 297
Fulford, Tim, 301n1
Furtado, Celso, 76
FWA (flying while Arab), 218

Gabriel's Rebellion, 21
Galeano, Eduardo, 76
Galvão, Walnice Nogueira, 40–41, 293
Gama Lima, Lana Lage da, 179
Gandhi, Mohatma, 205
Garrison, William Lloyd, 17
Garvey, Marcus, 210
Gates, Henry Louis, Jr., 186
gay rights, 212
Geismer, Alain, 159
generalizations, xix
Genet, Jean: Bayart, Jean-Françoise, 263; *Blacks,
     The (Les Nègres)*, 49, 74, 202; Palestinian
     cause, 161; United States tour, 133
Genovese, Eugene, 41
Géopplitique (journal), 174
Germany, 84
Gershwin, George, 194
Getz, Stan, 41
Gil, Gilberto: anticolonial coinages, 196; "From
     Bob Dylan to Bob Marley," 202–203; hybrid-
     ity, 202; indigeneity, xvii; "Mão de Limpeza,"
     201–203; race, xvii; samba, 194; S.O.B.'s in
     New York City, 39; Tropicália movement,
     197–198, 205, 206, 322n52
Gillespie, Dizzy, 45
Gilliam, Angela, 42, 78, 236
Gilroy, Paul, xx, 64, 206, 289
Gingrich, Newt, 2, 327n12
Ginsburg, Faye, 78–79
Giroud, Françoise, 141
Giroux, Henry, 78
Gitlin, Todd, 98–100, 131, 158
Glissant, Édouard: anti-imperialism, 256; "creol-
     ity," 60; at CUNY, 259; L'Institut du Tout-
     Monde, 328n39; *Memories of Empire*, 266;
     relational theories, 258; Third Worldism, 60;
     "transversalities," xx

tional corporations, 10–11, 105, 130; United States, 4, 5, 27, 28; Žižek, Slavoj, 129–130
indigenous rights, 4–6, 9
indigenous sovereignty, 4
indigenous thinkers, 13, 88
inequality, social, 107
inequality in Brazil, 220, 229
Inheritors, The (Bourdieu and Passeron), 107
Inquisition, 66
Institute for Afro-Brazilian Research, 177
Institute for Research on Black Culture, 178
intellectual labor, global distribution of, 292
intellectual property rights, 9, 90–91
intercoloniality, ii, 3, 42, 75, 78, 333
"interculturality," 91, 106, 140
"intersectionality," 111
"intertextuality," xviii
Iran, 65
Iraq War, 165, 260
Irigaray, Luce, 245, 294
Iroquois, 8–9
Iroquois and the Founding of the American Nation, The (Grinde), 9
Iroquois League, 9
Islam, 174
Islamic dress, 150
"Islamo-fascism," 164
Islamophobia, 149–151; France, 145, 149–150; history over the longue durée, 154–155; Judeophobia, 157; neoconservatism, 151; Orientalism, 150; racial profiling, 103; Republican Party, 151; the right, 151; Sarkozy, Nicolas, 149; sexist faith, accusation of, 257; Tea Party, 224; United States, 150; wedge-issues tactics, 150; Zionism, 169
Israel, 162, 163–164, 169
Israel, Menasse Ben, 172
Israeli Westernism, 167–168
Israeli-Palestinian conflict, 154, 157, 165, 169, 171
Isto É (magazine), 179
It's All True (film), 50
Ivekovic0107, Rada, 251, 255

Jackson, Michael, 203–204
Jaimes Guerrero, Annette, 115
James, C. L. R., 19, 21, 64, 130, 177
James, E. R., 42
Jameson, Fredric, 62, 81, 275, 289, 293
Japan, 65
Jeanson, Francis, 70, 246, 256
Jefferson, Thomas, 7, 8–9, 15–16, 39, 44–45
Jeffries, Leonard, 154
Jennings, Francis, 77, 115

Jew and the Other, The (Benbassa and Attias), 172
Jewish-Muslim relations, 154–157
Jewishness, 172
Jewish-over-black hierarchies, 166
Jews, 154–161; Africa and, 317n64; American Jews, 318n102; black anticolonialist thinkers, 159; black-Jewish relationship, 154, 161, 162; Fanon, Frantz, 159–161, 163; Finkielkraut, Alain, 170; France, 29, 159, 168; Jewish-black and Jewish-Muslim collaboration in France, 171; the left, 158–159, 171–172; liberalism, 318n102; miscegenation, 167; Muslim-Jewish relations, 154–155; Orientalism, 156; "relationality" of, 232; U. S. Census, 154; the West, 171
Jews for Racial and Economic Justice (JFREJ), 171–172
Jobim, Antonio Carlos, 194
Johansen, Bruce, 9
John M. Olin Foundation, 109
John the Baptist, 62
Johnson, Chalmers, 25
Johnson, James Weldon, 45
Johnson v. M'Intosh, 5
Jolas, Eugene, 4
Jones, Leroi (Amiri Baraka), 177
Jordan, Don, 232
Jorge, Fernando, 49, 307n79
Jospin, Lionel, 143
Journal of Race Development, 53
Joyce (singer), 195
Judeophobia, 157, 169
Jules-Rosette, Benetta, 47
Julien, Charles André, 263
July, Serge, 159
justice, 111

Kacem, Mehdi Belhaj, 147, 170, 173
Kadir, Djelal, 10
Kamel, Ali, 218–219, 223–228, 280, 324n43
Kane, Hamidou, 256
Kant, Immanuel, 78, 123, 297
Kapayo (documentary film), 11
Kaplan, Caren, 80, 121, 232
Kaufman, Deborah, 172
Kaye/Kantrowitz, Melanie, 158, 172
Kechiche, Abdellatif, 266
Keita, Salif, 146
Kelley, Robin, 64, 77
Kennedy, John F., 9
Kennedy, Randall, 78
Keywords (Williams), 83–84
Kgositsile, Keorapetse, 177

MAS (Movement for Socialism), 104
Maspero, François, 70, 246
Master Race Democracy, 15
Masters and Slaves (Freyre), 235
Mathieu, Martine, 246
Mathy, Jean-Phillipe, 143, 146
Mattelart, Armand, 278
Maximilian, emperor of Mexico, 54
Maxwell, Kenneth, 39
Mbembe, Achille, 29, 254
Mein Kampf (Hitler), 157–158
Meir, Golda, 167
Mello, Breno, 49
Melville, Herman, 7, 19, 80, 181, 273
Memmi, Albert: "colonized people," 254; *The Colonizer and the Colonized,* 162; *Decolonization and Decolonized,* 162; decolonization of knowledge, 70, 132; *Dominated Man,* 279; Islamic immigration in Europe, 162–163; *Portrait of the Colonized (Portrait da Colonisé),* 159, 279; postcolonial studies/theory, 245, 246, 262; turn to the right, 162–163
Memorial Zumbi, 177
Menasse Ben Israel, 172
Mendès France, Pierre, 165
Merkel, Angela, 96
Merquior, José Guilherme, 184
mestiçagem, 59, 237
mestizaje, 84
"mestizo essentialism," 237
mestizos, 58–59, 229
Metheney, Pat, 41
métissage, 59
Mexico, 54, 57, 84
Michaels, Walter Benn, 97, 101–105, 109, 119
Michaux, Henri, 263
Mignolo, Walter, 54, 87, 89
Miller, Robert, 4
Mills, C. Wright, 294
Mills, Charles: "antipodal" position of blacks, 230; critique of Western philosophy, 78; on Marxism, 103; "racial contract," 15, 63–64, 224; resistance to racial disrespect, 16; white supremacy, 64
Milner, Jean-Claude, 107, 169
minorities, identitarianism and, 137–142
minority liberation movements, 68
Miranda, Carmen, 41, 194
miscegenation: African Americans, 186; Brazil, 186–187, 188, 193, 227, 235–236; Gobineau, Arthur, Comte de, 285; "Great-Sperm-Theory-of-National-Formation," 236; Jews, 167; Kamel on, Ali, 223; *moreno* norm, 236; racism, 220–221; United States, 44, 59, 186–187

miscigenação, 59
mission civilisatrice, 14, 145, 249, 250, 257
"Missteps of Anti-imperialist Reason" (French), 278–279
Mitterand, François, 137
MLA (Modern Language Association), 80
MNU (Unified Negro Movement), 178
Moallem, Minoo, 80
"model minority" discourse, 166
modernism, modernity, 37, 66–67, 296
modernity/coloniality research, 89–90, 91
Mohanty, Chandra T., 78, 80, 100
Mohanty, Satya P., 100
Mohawk, John, 115
Mohawks, 6
Moisés, Massaud, 40–41
Monénembo, Tierno, 263
Monk, Thelonious, 45
Monroe Doctrine, 39, 40, 77
Monsieur R., 148
Montaigne, Michel de, 2, 7–8, 33, 124
Montesquieu, Charles de Secondat, baron de, 8, 18
Moog, Vianna, 183
Moore, Michael, 233
Moors, 170–171
Moraes, Vinicus de, 50, 194, 228
Moraga, Cherríe, 57
Morales, Evo, 104–105, 130
moralism, 116
More, Thomas, 1
Moreira, Moraes, 195
Morgan, Lewis Henry, 9
Moriconi, Italo, 181, 182
Morin, Edgar: decolonization of knowledge, 70; Jews and the West, 171; lawsuits against, 247; May 1968 movement, 159; negationism, 169; postcolonial studies/theory, 246
Moroccans, 130
Morrison, Toni, 121
Morse, Richard, 54–55
Mosse, George, 158
Motta, Ed, 195
Moura, Clóvis, 74, 179, 234
Moura, Jean-Marc, 266
Mouralis, Bernard, 265
Mouzer, Frédérique, 243, 268
Moylan, Tom, 289
Mudimbe, Valentin, 89, 259
"multicultural coloniality," 27
multicultural identity politics. *See* identity politics
multicultural left, 12, 98
"multiculturalism" (the term), 86, 92, 96–97

race (*continued*)
"one-drop rule," 186–187; passing, 321n50; U. S. Constitution, 30; Veloso, Caetano, xvii. *See also* critical race theory
Race as Rhetoric (Maggie and Rezende), 207–208
Race in Another America (Telle), 320n36
"Race Traitor" manifestoes, 241
"race treason," 232, 241
race/coloniality discourse, 131
"racial contract," 15, 63, 224
"racial democracy": Affirmative Action, 219; Brazil, 175–179, 185, 189, 193; Freyre, Gilberto, 280; multiculturalism, 181; myth of, 280
"Racial Equality Law," 222
racial metamorphoses/transformations, 321n50
Racial Oppression in America (Blauner), 107
racial profiling: Brazil, 218; France, 151, 218, 239, 252; hip hop, 148–149; Islamophobia, 103; social identities, 100; United States, 218
racism, 223–227, 234–236; Affirmative Action, 214; Anglo-Saxonists, 56; anticommunitarianism, 242; anti-Semitism, 162, 171; anti-Third Worldism, 162; Brazil, 33, 43, 185, 188–189, 193–194, 223–224, 225–226, 234–236, 277–278, 280, 324n37; Carvalho on, José Jorge de, 235; class war, 129; classism, 227; "color-blind racism," 277; critical race theory, 225; Enlightenment, 78; exterminationist racism, 157–158; Fanon on, Frantz, 214; France, 29–30, 44–45, 145, 151, 316n53; French intellectuals, 33; globalization, 91; Hegel, G. W. F., 78; imperialism, 291; Kant, Immanuel, 78; the left, 103; neoliberalism, 90; as "opinion," 214; outlawing of, 101; populist outrage, 129; "reverse racism," 140; Sarkozy, Nicolas, 247–248; social advantage, 102; socialism, 119; sociological theory, 107; United States, 77, 116, 185, 188–189, 190, 223–224, 225–226, 281, 324n37; Wallerstein on, Immanuel, 331n35; Žižek, Slavoj, 129. *See also* antiracism
Racism in Racial Democracy (Twine), 43
Racist France (Wieviorka), 279
Radhkrishnan, R., xviii
"radical pedagogy," 78, 110, 249–250
radical philosophy, 75
radicalism, worldwide retreat from, 114
Raffik, 146
Rainbow Atlantic, 3–4
Ramos, Lázaro, 227
Rancière, Jacques, 293, 294
Raoni (Kayapo Chief), 11
Rappa, 196
rappers. *See* hip hop

Rasmussen, Daniel, 20
Ravel, Maurice, 50
Raynal, Abbé, 23
Reagan, Ronald, 174
Red Atlantic, 2–8; Brazil, 26; connotations, 3; conquest, 3; cultural syncretism, 284; Discovery Doctrine, 4–5; France, 26; "Indian" as inspiration for social critique, 7–8; interchange between European and indigenous thought, 12; nation-states, 6; relations with Black, White Atlantics, 3; the term, usage of, xv; Tropicália songs, 205; "Um Índio" (Veloso), 204; United States, 26
Red Pedagogy (Grande), 12
"reflexive anthropology," 36, 37, 75, 79
Reis, Joáo José, 179
"relationality": class, 111; complexification of, 4; Diderot, Denis, 24; geopolitics of, 24; of intra- and extra-European, 157; of Jews, 232; nations as transnations, 299; postcoloniality, 86; resentful transferences, 161; revisionist disciplines, 92
religious syncretism, 35
Removing the Mask (Guimarães and Huntley), 207
reparations, 209–211; Affirmative Action, 98, 209; Brazil, 210; Enlightenment, 209; Native Americans, 210; phases in reparations discussion, 210; premise underlying, 210–211; Risério, Antonio, 190; segregation, 211; slavery, 210; *Walker's Appeal* (Walker), 209
Reproduction (Bourdieu), 107
Republican Party: black conservatives, 152; identity politics, 93; Islamophobia, 151; Tea Party, 224; wedge-issues tactics, 16, 99. *See also* Tea Party
Republicanism: Atlantic, xv; Blacks, 14–15; Colonial, 15; Enlightenment, xv, 1, 20, 28; French, 142, 144, 243, 265; indigenous peoples, 14–15; Reds, 14–15
Requerimiento document, 5
Restall, Matthew, 301n6
Retamar, Roberto Fernández, 94
Retrato do Brasil (Prada), 184
"returning the gaze," 121
Revere, Paul, 8
"reverse anthropology," 79
"reverse racism," 140
revisionist history, 75, 77, 93–94, 109–110, 114
Rezende, Claudia Barcellos, 207–208
Ribeiro, Darcy, 7, 53, 177, 236
Ribeiro, João Ubaldo, 219
Ribeiro, Matilde, 222
Rice, Condoleezza, 103

About the Authors

ROBERT STAM is University Professor at New York University. Among his many publications are *François Truffaut and Friends: Modernism, Sexuality, and Film Adaptation* (2006); *Literature through Film: Realism, Magic, and the Art of Adaptation* (2005); *Literature and Film: A Guide to the Theory and Practice of Adaptation* (2005); *Companion to Literature and Film* (2004); *Film Theory: An Introduction* (2000); *Tropical Multiculturalism: A Comparative History of Race in Brazilian Cinema and Culture* (1997); and with Ella Shohat, *Unthinking Eurocentrism: Multiculturalism and the Media* (1994), *Multiculturalism, Postcoloniality, and Transnational Media* (2000), and *Flagging Patriotism: Crises of Narcissism and Anti-Americanism* (2007). He has received Fulbright, Guggenheim, and Rockefeller Grants, and fellowships at Bellagio and at the Davis Center for Historical Studies at Princeton. He has taught in France, Tunisia, Brazil, and Abu Dhabi. His work has been translated into French, Italian, Greek, Farsi, Japanese, Chinese, Korean, Portuguese, Spanish, Swedish, Norwegian, German, Hebrew, Arabic, Ukranian, Estonian, and Serbo-Croation.

ELLA SHOHAT is Professor of Cultural Studies at New York University. Among her many publications are *Taboo Memories, Diasporic Voices* (2006); *Israeli Cinema: East/West and the Politics of Representation* (1989, 2010); *Le sionisme du point de vue de ses victimes juives: les juifs orientaux en Israel*, 1988; 2006); *Talking Visions: Multicultural Feminism in a Transnational Age* (1998); *Dangerous Liaisons: Gender, Nation, and Postcolonial Perspectives* (coedited, 1997); and with Robert Stam, *Unthinking Eurocentrism: Multiculturalism and the Media* (1994), *Multiculturalism, Postcoloniality, and Transnational Media* (2003), and *Flagging Patriotism: Crises of Narcissism and Anti-Americanism* (2007). She has also co-edited a number of special issues for the journal *Social Text*, including "Edward Said: A Memorial Issue," "Palestine in a Transnational Context," and "911—A Public Emergency?" Her work has been translated into numerous languages, including: French, Portuguese, Spanish, Arabic, Hebrew, Turkish, German, Polish, Japanese, Dutch, and Italian. Shohat has also served on the editorial board of several journals, including: *Social Text*, *Critique*, *Meridians*, and *Interventions*. She is a recipient of such fellowships as Rockefeller and the Society for Humanities at Cornell University, where she also taught at the School of Criticism and Theory. In 2010, she was awarded a Fulbright research/lectureship at the University of São Paulo.

Lightning Source UK Ltd.
Milton Keynes UK
UKHW010031200320
360651UK00001B/560